New World Disorder

Lessons from Brexit, The Trump factor, Populism, Wars, Terrorism, '1984' and The Matrix, Economic Bubbles and Crashes, Concentrations of Wealth and Income, Massive Debt and Austerity:

The Case for Economic Democracy, Reformed Political Democracy and A Coming Together of All People

David Egan

About the Author

David Egan is from Ireland and lives in Ireland. He graduated from Oxford University in England and from NUI Galway in Ireland where he got undergraduate and postgraduate degrees and qualifications in Computer Science, Management, Systems Analysis, Data Analytics and Information Technology. He works in the Information Technology sector and the Voluntary sector. His interests include Economics, particularly the history of economic crashes, Politics, Philosophy, Literature, The Arts, History, Information Technology and Current Affairs.

Dedication

The basic freedoms, democratic rights, national and sovereign rights, and human rights we have today did not come about by accident or good luck, or by idle talk, complaining, wishful thinking, praying or chanting nor have they always existed as assumed by the young and naive. They are the end result of a long struggle, great effort, sacrifice, work and determination over many decades and centuries by brave people against great opposition, terrible injustices, oppression, dispossession, tyrants and their state apparatus, hypocrites and Pharisees, violence, death, and adversity. In many cases they had to overcome the subservience of the sheep - the naysayers, the idle talkers, the bystanders, the onlookers whose subservience and complacency kept people oppressed and in bondage for many centuries. This book is dedicated to Thomas Jefferson, George Washington, Thomas Paine, James Madison, Abraham Lincoln, Wilberforce, Wolfe Tone, James Stephens, Pearse, Connolly, Clarke, Barry, Lafayette, Sieyes, Marat, Brissot, Voltaire, Simon Bolivar, Bernardo Higgins, Pankhurst, Luther King, Gandhi, Kenyatta, Mandela, and the many other similar people in the USA, Ireland, France, Italy, South America, Asia, and other countries who fought for these democratic freedoms and rights, such as the US Declaration of Independence, the US Bill of Rights, Rights of Man (Paine), the French Declaration of the Rights of Man, the South American Declarations of Independence, the US Emancipation laws after the Civil War, the ending of slavery, the Vote for Women, the legalisation of trade unions and worker's rights, the Irish Proclamation of Independence, Polish Declaration of Independence, the UN Declaration of Human Rights, the defeat of Hitler and Fascist dictatorship, the fall of Communist dictatorship, the overthrow of imperialism and colonialism, the overthrow of dictatorships around the world, the US Civil Rights Laws and other such laws and proclamations worldwide. Today, these freedoms, civil rights and human rights, Constitutional rights, National Sovereignty and Democracy are under serious attack and threat in most countries around the world. There is an urgent need to defend these hard won freedoms and democratic rights, through reforming political democracy and spreading economic democracy to make the market defend these vital democratic and human rights through serving all of society and all people in all nations. An economic democracy which enhances, defends and strengthens political democracy and freedom.

Table of Contents

Introduction

Today's world has become dominated by Brexit, the Trump factor, the rise of Populism worldwide, the distrust of elites and their policies which mostly serve themselves, federalism and the desire to centralise power and take it away from nations and peoples, massive bail outs of banks, bondholders, speculators and fraudsters by taxpayers and enforced by government austerity policies. This has created economic uncertainty mixed with deflation and recessions, this uncertainty is being worsened by globalisation and it's race to the bottom, automation and new technologies replacing humans, high levels of unemployment, the build up of excessive debt, the growing concentrations of wealth and income, the speculative bubbles and crashes, and the fears and rumours of wars and 'regime changes' and indeed whole industries which profit from war, terrorism and destruction. The world in the first decades of the 21st century faces many unique, unprecedented and quite daunting challenges.

This book analyses and examines these problems and their root causes, and proposes deep and profound changes to economics, banking, politics, government, laws, business, international relations, the press and media, and societies. These changes and solutions address causality, the root causes of problems. In this book you will see that a very different and better world is possible.

Firstly, there is the continuing financial booms and busts which have imposed and will continue to impose great financial costs, suffering, massive new debt and national bankruptcies on countries, accompanied by the enforcement of bail outs and harsh austerity policies and recessions. It is ordinary people, taxpayers, the poor, the elderly disabled who are paying for this massive bail out of banking, speculators and gamblers debt, and which is actually legalised robbery from ordinary people. Its also the same people who pay through loss of their jobs , livelihoods, careers, homes, families, lives, etc. during the recessions and depressions caused by these crashes. This economic construct is an appalling fraud committed against ordinary people as you will see in this book. These bubbles and crashes and bail outs or mass theft from ordinary people are likely to continue into the future as the same policies are being pursued ; nothing has really changed since 2008. Indeed, Quantitative Easing has added further funds to this bail out while devaluing money, and stimulating more speculation and bubbles, and creating the ideal conditions for future crashes.

This bail out of the banks, big corporates and the rich is really 'Socialism For The Rich' amounting to several trillion dollars globally and this was paid for by vicious and ruthless 'Capitalism For The Working and Middle Class, Disabled and Poor' in the form of austerity policies, tax increases, wage cuts, work benefit cuts, cutbacks in public services, cuts to social welfare, deflation, recessions / depressions, globalisation, higher unemployment, home evictions, the build up of massive private debt, home evictions, negative equity, and the ruthless exploitation of these economic difficulties by vulture funds and corporate raiders / asset strippers. There was no bail out of the ordinary people, the workers, the taxpayers, the debtors.

Secondly, many nations are drowning in a sea of debt which is multiples of their GNP and their tax revenues. And structures are in place to worsen this over time. Yet, all of this debt whether government debt, business debt, private debt, family debt results from money created out of nothing by private banks and central banks. Most people (including some economists) are completely ignorant of the root cause of the problems in banking, economics and politics. Money is created out of nothing when a loan is made or a mortgage is made by the bank. This is in the form of electronic credits. This new money creation is a form of fraud, as its created out of thin air, and this also means the bank brings no (financial) consideration to the loan / mortgage contract, making it null and void in law. As you will see in this book, in legal terms, nobody owes anything to the bank as it fraudulently created the money out of nothing when making a loan and lodged it into the borrowers account. This fraud is clearly exposed later in the book. And the compounded interest associated with this alleged "debt" is not even created with the new money and must be extracted from the existing money supply, creating severe economic turbulence, crashes, and instability over time. This is worsened by the fact that most of this fraudulently created money has been used for speculation in assets, property and derivatives bidding up prices to unsustainable levels and creating massive speculative debt in the process, creating speculative manias, bubbles, crashes and recessions / depressions over time. This then destroys jobs, livelihoods, businesses and nations. This money creation fraud acts to enslave people, families, businesses, governments and whole nations with massive debt and an unstable economic system. This debt enslavement is modern day slavery and puts many people in danger of losing homes, incomes, jobs, livelihoods, businesses, etc. (You won't learn this in schools, Universities, and in the press and media)

Yet despite all of the crashes, bail outs, austerity policies and recession costing trillions of dollars, there is continuing banking and money creation frauds, speculation frauds and new bubbles, which are now being magnified by zero interest rates or negative real interest rates and Quantitative Easing by Central

Banks to the value of $15 trillion (2017). Worryingly, there is free money, zero interest money, for speculation now estimated to be over $1,200 trillion globally, over 20 times the world economy. Quantitative Easing is based on the 'Greater Fool Theory' where some fool or sucker becomes the final buyer of worthless assets or funder of bankrupt banks and businesses, and in this case the fool or sucker is the Central Bank and taxpayers. And these fools (taxpayers and central bank) are being burdened with government austerity policies and public service cutbacks to fund continuous bail outs of banks, speculators and fraudsters. The long period of Quantitative Easing and manipulated negative real interest rates has been an admission by central banks and governments that markets are broken and have failed and that the system is broken. The medicine is not curing the ill patient but worsening the patient and giving him new illnesses.

Thirdly, the type of economics dominating most societies today and for the last 40 years is called Neo Liberal economics or Neo Classical economics and it has failed many times, most notably in the crash of 2008, where governments and central banks panicked and had to intervene to save the financial system and whole economies from total collapse. But 2008 was not the only crash, the facts and evidence show that were many others, according to the IMF we have had 425 systemic crashes between 1970 and 2010. This consisted of 145 banking crashes, 204 monetary collapses, and 76 sovereign debt crises. And prior to 1970 there were many other crashes in the 20th century, the 19th century, the 18th century and 17th century. And this is likely to continue. Neo Liberal economics has been the cause of all of these crashes. These failed economics policies are supported and enforced by slick, smug, and deceitful politicians who act like spin doctors, smooth talking the taxpayers, and always claiming that everything is alright, stable and that the fundamentals are sound, just prior to crashes and even in the middle of recessions / depressions. Spin and lies have come to dominate politics and political discourse. Unfortunately, most politicians have been brainwashed by Neo Liberal economists and Monetarists and neo con war promoters and they (politicians) behave like parrots. Politicians repeat and repeat, but they never think, they never analyse, they never challenge and never expose the flaws and defects in these failed economic ideologies. These discredited economic ideologies claim that crashes cannot occur, that markets always clear and are self correcting, that markets reflect real values not speculative values, that speculative bubbles reflect real value and rational expectations and should not be interfered with, that equilibrium exists, that debt does not matter, that Debt to GDP (or GNI) and Debt to Earnings is irrelevant during bubbles, that Price of asset to cost of building the asset is irrelevant in bubbles, that regulation is not necessary that fiat money created out of nothing by banks and compounded with interest which is mostly pumped into speculation and bubbles is always good for economies, that government deficits must be cut in the middle of economic crashes, recession and depressions, that the globalisation and it's race to the bottom will benefit everybody, that recessions and depressions can be ignored as "supply will always create its own demand" (even during a financial system collapse). These fairy tales and nonsense are still believed by the gullible, the naive, the ignorant and the superficial.

The option is always open to politicians and governments to stop behaving like parrots and to learn the facts and the evidence. In addition to these bubbles, crashes, bail outs and large scale theft from ordinary people and taxpayers, Neo Liberal economics imposes many other additional burdens on peoples and nations, for example there is the growing threat of environmental disasters (many of them caused by humans) which are continuing to impose massive financial costs and human losses worldwide. These environmental disasters are growing in intensity and becoming more common and more destructive. And then there is continuing terrorism which is spreading worldwide, accompanied by manipulated wars and 'regime changes' for profit, resources and childish geo-political dominance which foment more injustices and more terrorism and there are concerns that this will escalate to nuclear, biological and chemical warfare.

And also unsurprisingly, there is the corruption of legal systems and political systems and the dominance of the 'pay to play' system of bribery. New vehicles, forms, structures and processes are used to hide corrupt payments and deceive the people. Globally, these arrangements affect the distribution of trillions of dollars every year, negatively impacting the lives of ordinary everywhere. Then there is the repression of human rights and Constitutional rights in many developed western nations which has created an Orwellian '1984' world dominated by Big Brother (and it's regime changes, wars, extreme neo-liberalism and bank bailouts). The presence of this Big Brother is now felt in all areas of democratic societies as the over intrusive Deep State and 'Shadow Government' creates 'totalitarian creep' which is directly undermining hard won democratic rights and freedoms. Today, this Big Brother or the Deep State ('Shadow Government') is out of control, unaccountable, and not subject to proper checks and balances. And to worsen matters there is a compliant and subservient press and media, which has been caught lying, deceiving and misleading the people and generally acts to always support this Big Brother and '1984' world, imparting new meaning to the word 'doublespeak'.

These political maladies have been accompanied by large scale corporate and government pollution and poisoning of water, air, land, and food for many years, and more illnesses, genetic damage, and diseases are emerging from this. Disgustingly, this is being accompanied by unaffordable and rising health insurance and healthcare costs caused by the rip offs and monopoly power of big corporates and banks, and a refusal by the state sector and private sector to invest in adequate healthcare systems. Poisoned peoples denied even basic health rights by the very people and organisations profiteering from poisoning. While banks, bankers, corporate executives and Deep State ('Shadow Government') personnel can break many laws and commit serious crimes and escape arrest, prosecution and jail, and get away with crime, the ordinary people are punished very harshly for minor offences and wrongful allegations of such offences. Legal and justice systems have completely broken down and have been brought into disrepute in many developed countries.

To add further to our woes, there is the high costs of living imposed by:

i) cartels, protected monopolies, oligopolies, property interests, and restrictive practises which overcharge and rip off ordinary people and enforce high charges for the basic necessities of life. Studies show that this costs 5 billion euros per year in the case of Ireland (Competition Authority, Ireland) and tens of billions of euros per year in bigger countries such as Britain, France, USA, etc.. These are massive costs imposed on economies and these costs undermine competitiveness and living standards.

ii) compounded interest rates which imposes additional costs on producing, storing, transporting, accounting for, marketing, selling and buying of goods and service

iii) high taxes, too many taxes, government levies, rates, and charges to support over bloated government programmes, which include bail outs for banks and big corporates, corporate welfare and subsidies, loan repayments to banks (which created loans out of nothing), massively over-priced government contracts which are not audited, and 'pork barrel' politics.

iv) excessive speculation in the prices of houses, land, and assets fuelled by banks (creating money out of nothing in the form of loans), making homes unaffordable for many people

v) the high social costs and welfare costs of Globalisation and automation which are added to products and services and also deducted from your wages.

This is imposing an excessive cost base on countries leading to overly high prices and a losses in competitiveness, businesses and jobs. All of these high costs and rip offs benefit the elites, the very rich, the powerful, and the well connected. And while the costs of living are high and keep rising, the real wages for ordinary people have fallen or remained stagnant for many years in western developed countries due to globalisation with its vicious 'race to the bottom' combined with increasing levels of automation destroying jobs, careers, factories, livelihoods and communities worldwide. All of this is fuelling higher concentrations of wealth and income and imposing artificial restrictions on resources, money, access to credit, consumption and socio-economic development, and access to jobs and local investment. And this is inciting more social injustices, more racism, deeper class divisions, more ghettos, industrial wastelands, and tribalistic hatreds, accompanied by high crime rates, mental illness rates, suicides, and social disorder, more police brutality and denial of rights, and sadly the rise of extreme ideologies and movements of the far right and the far left. There is an unrelenting war against the ordinary people and their families by corrupt elements of the state and corrupt corporate and banking interests. And this is creating a very negative and destructive dynamic in most societies.

For too long, the issues above have been and are still being ignored by politicians, governments and economists. Among most ordinary people in countries worldwide, there is a very high level of dissatisfaction, anger, disillusionment and disgust with politics, politicians, policy makers and elites and the constant news of corruption, waste, self serving misbehaviour, cover ups, and lies by those in power which has worsened the factors mentioned above. Those in power have proven themselves to be too smug, self contented and self interested and they are far too insulated from the terrible consequences of their actions. In recent years, there has been a strong backlash against corrupt political elites in Britain, the USA, France, Ireland, Greece, Spain, Austria, Hungary, Czech Republic and other EU countries and in Central and South America. The election of Donald Trump as US President, Brexit and the resignation of pro-Brexit government figures, the referendum in Italy and resignation of Renzi, are evidence of new and far reaching changes worldwide. This populist movement of the right and of the left is growing globally. The current obsession with Trump, Populism, Brexit and the rise of the right is merely a symptom of much deeper problems which continue to be neglected, ignored and fobbed off. It's important to look at the causative factors behind the disorders mentioned above and behind the rise of new movements, politics, and policies which have risen in reaction, and the wide ranging effects emerging from this.

What this Book is About

This book approaches the current turmoil in politics and economics from four angles :

a) What are the lessons to be learnt from this disorder and chaos in the world ?

b) What constitutes causality and what are the factors involved ? How do we deconstruct causality, the causal factors behind this disorder and chaos ? what are the dynamics, the driving factors, the hidden forces, the relationships, the inter-relationships and interconnections ?

c) What are the solutions based on causality ? what constitutes freedom and its responsibilities ? what are the responsibilities attached to freedom and rights ? and how are they intrinsically linked to the great disorder and controversial issues confronting countries and the world ? how do we apply responsibilities and the lessons of causality to change, create, re-create, transform, and restructure systems, ideologies, socio-economic structures, political structures, technologies and innovations, methodologies, transfers of wealth and income, laws, Constitutions, new bodies, banks, credit, principles, regulations to tie freedom to its responsibilities, to reform political democracy, to create economic democracy as a bulwark for political democracy and freedom, and resolve the great disorder and chaos in the world today.

d) How do we use these new innovative solutions to overcome the artificial divisions of social class, race, religion, gender, age, disability, ethnic identity, colour ? how do we end these hateful divisions which have poisoned societies and the world for too long ? how do we come together as one human race and work together for the benefit, the progress and the upliftment of all ? how do we transcend the artificial political divisions of right and left, liberal and conservative, democrat and republican, labour and tory, capitalist and marxist, etc. to find common ground, to stand for universal principles of fairness, humane values, human rights, social justice, individual sovereignty, national sovereignty, wider ownership of property and wealth, Constitutional protections and democratic protections, and the right to be treated with respect, equality and dignity ? how do we restore power and democracy back to the people ?

Section 1 Problems and Causality

Chapter 1   What is Freedom ? What kind of society do you want for yourself and for your family, friends and country ? Comparative Views of Freedom

"I see in the near future a crisis approaching that unnerves me and causes me to tremble for the safety of my country. . .. . corporations have been enthroned and an era of corruption in high places will follow, and the money power of the country will endeavour to prolong its reign by working upon the prejudices of the people until all wealth is aggregated in a few hands and the Republic is destroyed. I feel at this moment more anxiety for the safety of my country than ever before, even in the midst of war."
President Abraham Lincoln, *Nov. 21, 1864*

(letter to Col. William F. Elkins)

Source: <u>The Lincoln Encyclopedia: The Spoken and Written Words of A. Lincoln</u>
<u>Arranged for Ready Reference</u>, Archer H. Shaw (NY, NY: Macmillan, 1950)

'We hold these truths to be self-evident: that all men are created equal; that they are endowed by their Creator with certain unalienable rights; that among these are life, liberty, and the pursuit of happiness'
US Declaration of Independence, 1776

Ideas matter, political ideas and related economic ideas matter as evidenced by the wars, revolutions, coups, cold war, genocides, concentration camps, gulags, new political systems and turmoil which defined the 20th century. And perceptions of freedom matter for similar reasons<u>. It is very important for the reader and for the general public to acknowledge the great power of ideas and of perceptions of freedom and of how they shape ordinary people's lives and major events.</u> The sentiments, hopes, and fears of Presidents Abraham Lincoln and Thomas Jefferson have a particular relevance to our world today. In the USA, Europe, and many other countries worldwide there is a strong and growing sense of dissatisfaction, anger and disillusionment with the political system and economic system. The most visible expression of this is the rise in populism of the left wing and the right wing and the rejection of the politics, policies, actions and structures created by 'elites' and the so called 'centre'. Other aspects involve deep seated cultural wars over religion, race, identity, natural resources, social class, gender and what constitutes human dignity. Is this anger, dissatisfaction and rebellion justified ? and why has it emerged ? has it been brewing for years or decades ? is it another example of the Hegelian Dialectic which has radically transformed politics, economics and societies over time ? If so, then what are the dynamics of this Hegelian Dialectic, this transformation, this disorder, backlash, turmoil, ferment? Perceptions of freedom underlie political ideologies, economics and economic ideologies, sociology, laws, rights, personal beliefs, social structures, business structures, community structures, inter cultural relations and international relations, and life for most people in the world today. Freedom is worthy of discussion, deep analysis and deconstruction in books about politics, economics, sociology, and law. But this is rarely done. Ironically most problems in the world today emerge from these very perceptions of freedom or more accurately misperceptions of freedom, including an inability to distinguish freedom from licence, freedom from excessive control, freedom from coercion, manipulation and political correctness, freedom from old prejudices, conditioning, discrimination and social exclusion, and distinguish freedom from ideologies which excessively repress, limit, control, restrict and oppress people often in the (false) name of freedom. There is also the incapacity to realise that freedom comes with responsibilities attached. One sees strong contradictions in left wing ideologies, right wing ideologies, centrist ideologies, libertarian ideologies, populist ideologies and religious - political ideologies which severely limit, restrict or destroy freedoms. Freedom has been the most misunderstood subject in human history and ironically this has worked against the attainment of freedom, and still does today. Looking at the real world and the real lives of real ordinary people, and the many events which characterise the world instead of the world of theories, abstractions, misperceptions, skewed facts, misinformation, and the prejudices of academics and economists, there are some great burning questions which need to be answered.

Are the people who claim to be free really free ? does freedom really exist ? are people truly free ? are people free to think for themselves, to reason for themselves, to make up their own minds, to express themselves, and to act and to live as free individuals ? are people free to question and even reject old outdated views, theories, prejudices, discrimination, stigma, theologies and ideologies ? can enslaved people misperceive themselves to be free ? what does it mean to be free ? what is freedom ?

Is it Freedom and Democracy ? or is it Slavery ? Looking at the Facts

The facts, the evidence, the proofs, and the experiences of most ordinary people's lives show that misperceptions and misunderstandings about freedom are common, and that those who believe themselves to be free are in fact enslaved, oppressed, controlled, deceived, manipulated and overly restricted in so many, many ways, and this has made them unfree. This unfreedom or slavery is maintained mostly through ignorance and fear, and it runs very deep in societies. This is (brutally) enforced through social structures, skewed laws and rules, skewed regulations, corruption, very narrow government policies, police and military actions, fake news and censorship of the press and media, cover ups by the state and by powerful corporates, Globalism and Federalism, repressive religious conditioning, repressive social conditioning, prejudices, hatreds, and social exclusion, fraudulent debt creation and debt enslavement, and highly distorted forms of income and wealth distribution all of which combine together to create slavery and desperation for the vast majority of people. This exists in supposedly "free" and "democratic" countries. Repression itself expresses itself in many forms, but always uses control through fear and desperation. At the centre of this enforced desperation, repression and control is historically high levels of debt (debt slavery) and very high wealth and income inequality and the excessive limitations which this imposes on the freedom of most people, and the accompanying excessive stresses which severely restrict or destroy personal opportunities, personal potential, personal growth, personal choices and options, work and social inclusion, the acquisition of knowledge, facts and wisdom, civil and human rights, liberty and the 'pursuit of happiness'. This scenario where powerful and wealthy elites impose economic desperation and accompanying political and social domination on the masses is not new, it has existed for many centuries and millennia in different forms - from slavery in the ancient world and the Americas, to serfs in medieval times in Europe and Czarist Russia to workers paid subsistence slave wages in Victorian times to impoverished tenant farmers in Famine era Ireland and later, to the slave labour of Communist societies and Fascist societies to bonded labour in Asia to the globalised world of today where slave labour is exploited in developing and third world countries and this is used to impose low paid subsistence jobs, loss of rights, and higher levels of unemployment on western developed nations. These changes have intensified divisions, prejudices and discrimination between peoples and this has been worsened by "regime changes" and wars for resources to further extend the control and domination of the elites. This is Globalism, the so called 'New World Order' proposed by several politicians, governments and 'intellectuals' but it is in reality a disgraceful 'New World Disorder' which is exactly like the old world order with it's serfdom, slavery, empires, etc. The dynamics and structures are the same throughout all history. Today, the evidence shows that Federalism and Globalism are the 'New Imperialism', and share the same characteristics. Trump, Brexit, populism of the left wing and populism of the right wing, strikes, riots, yellow vests protests, social disorder, political fragmentation in countries, etc. etc. are all a reaction against this Globalism and Federalism, or the New Imperialism.

Let us look briefly at the facts and the evidence today. Research by Dr. Richard Wilkinson and others clearly shows that high rates of inequality can be very destructive to societies and to freedom and democracy. It adversely affects health, life expectancy, crime rates, murders, rapes, divorce rates, infant mortality, mental illness, child pregnancies, trust, obesity, education, social mobility etc. etc.. These studies and charts measure fundamental aspects of freedom. They measure freedom.

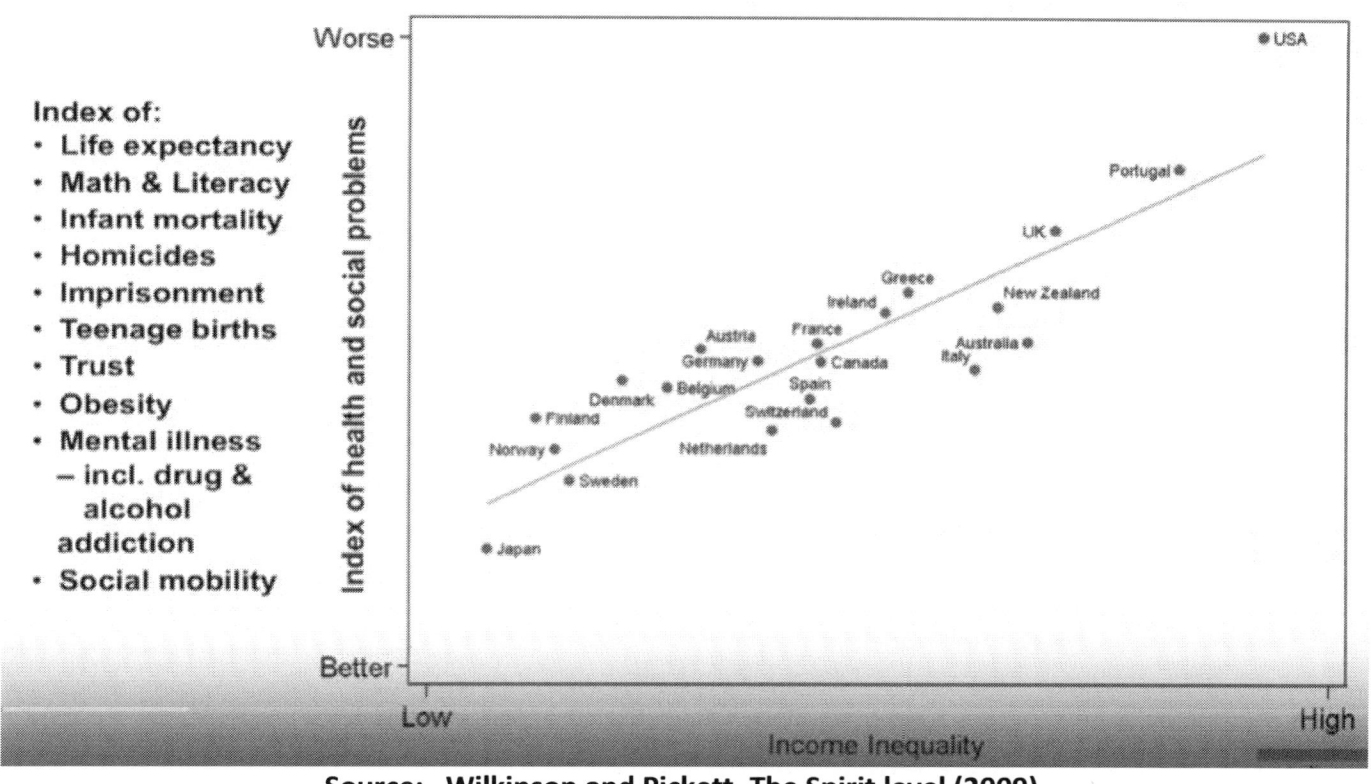

Source: Wilkinson and Pickett, The Spirit level (2009)

There is a correlation between these negative social factors and high levels of inequality but no correlation between these negative social factors and the growth in GNP or the size of GNP. It's not the growth of GNP which matters but how that GNP (or wealth and income) is distributed which matters. The economic argument of growing "a bigger pie for all" is irrelevant if the growing pie mainly benefits the richest 1% - 5%. The economic growth argument is completely false, its the economic growth and wealth and income distribution which matters. Wilkinson also measures UNICEF indicators for child health and development against inequality for several countries. This shows that inequality damages and hurts children, adversely affecting their health, growth, development, educational opportunities, and career prospects.

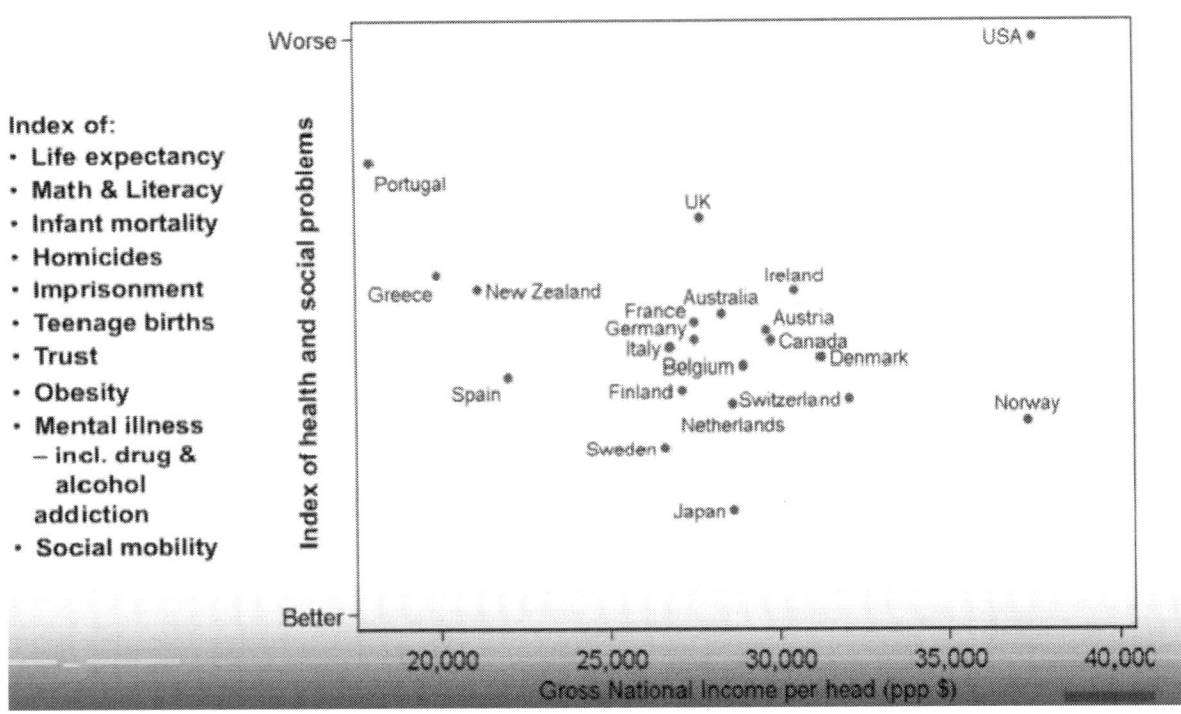

Source: Wilkinson and Pickett, The Spirit level (2009)

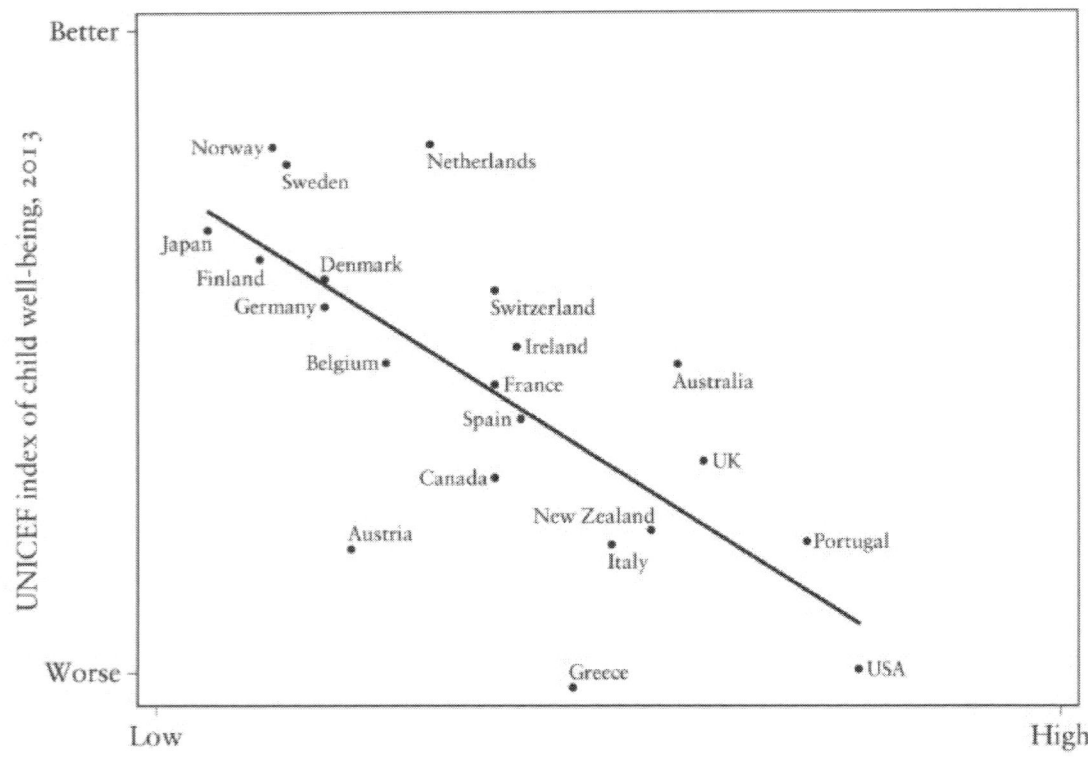

Source: Richard Wilkinson, The Inner level (2018)

Dr. Richard Wilkinson provides further charts in his new book 'The Inner Level: How More Equal Societies Reduce Stress, Restore Sanity and Improve Everyone's Well-being' (Penguin, 2018) and uses many variables to measure the destructive effects of inequality, including the UNICEF Index of Child Well Being, Stress and Anxiety levels, Mental illnesses, Civic Participation, Support for Populist leaders, Child Bullying, Crime levels, Imprisonment rates, Bullying in the workplace, Anti Social Behaviour, Homelessness, Life Expectancy, Gambling, Drug Abuse, Educational Performance, and Social Mobility. Inequality worsens all of these factors, and the most unequal countries suffer the most. Other research bodies and studies have confirmed this in the past and continue to do so.

The following social indicators confirm this.

- Oxfam Humankind Index
- Genuine Progress Indicator
- OECD Better Life Index

- The Social Progress Index
- Unicef Index of Child Well Being
- Index of Health and Social Problems (Wilkinson, 2009)

These factors directly and indirectly affect one's freedom, one's opportunities, and one's rights, and can act to restrict, limit, undermine even destroy freedoms. In effect, they destroy freedom. They also have a direct bearing on politics and political and social changes. These factors also affect economic performance at the individual level and collective levels and national levels and have major impacts on demand and supply, on innovation and growth, on wages, cost of living, and economic drivers, and are of great importance to economists and politicians, who ironically ignore these factors in their studies, papers, research and national policies.

I am not proposing socialism, communism or fascism here, but a new type of capitalism, a democratic capitalism or economic democracy. This is proposed and detailed in the second section of this book. Economics, business, political and legal courses in schools and Universities have refused to teach and examine these issues. Throughout this book, we will look at these factors and their wide ranging effects, and look at the many political and economic ideologies and political systems and analyse how they address these factors. Research findings, charts, statistics and facts are provided in Chapter 5. You will see that an Iron Curtain has descended over many countries. Democracies are being turned into oligarchies and plutocracies which are destroying basic freedoms, Constitutional rights, civil and human rights, democracy, justice, national sovereignty, dignity respect, trust, communities and family.

Let us briefly look at the forces which are attacking and crushing Freedom, Democracy, Civil and Human Rights, Constitutional rights, Families, Communities and Societies :

1. **Crisis in Societies**

   What crisis dominates your society ? the hospitals crisis, the healthcare crisis, the housing crisis, the homeless crisis, the evictions crisis, long traffic jams and lack of infrastructure investment, the pensions crisis, the insurance crisis, farming crisis, military pay crisis, the national debt crisis, budget deficit crisis, currency crisis, inflation or deflation crisis, war / conflict crisis, the policing crisis, the corrupt courts crisis, the crime and drugs crisis, etc. ? all of these crisis emerge from 2 or 3 common factors which are rarely taught in schools and Universities and are very rarely mentioned in the press and media and by politicians. We will discuss and analyse these 2 or 3 factors in this book. Ask yourself what freedom really is ? are people meant to live their lives over indebted, over taxed, over charged, robbed, over burdened, over priced, over stressed, over worked, over anxious, over coerced, over worried, over policed, over insecure, over regulated, over restricted, while underpaid, under appreciated, undervalued, abused, under represented or not represented ? is this really freedom ? why is life structured in such a perverse, stressful and oppressive manner ? the points below will further examine this unfreedom.

2. **The decline in real wages over 30 years and the need to have 2, 3 or 4 jobs and massive debt to survive**

   Why do two parents in western countries have to work 2, 3 or 4 jobs just to exist and survive when over 30 years ago, one working parent working in one job could support a big family, a mortgage, a car, health insurance and children's education, and a decent standard of living ? Several research studies show that your real wages, that is the real wages for workers (the bottom 90%) have stagnated or slightly declined for over 30 years while prices have kept rising for products, services, homes, education, childcare, medical bills. As we shall see below, these high prices are maintained by cartels, monopolies and oligopolies which are legally and politically allowed to rip off people and rig markets (and worsen competitiveness). At the same time the wages, health entitlements, pension, holiday and other work benefits of workers have been cut, reduced, slashed or eliminated to supposedly "improve competitiveness" under Globalisation. And these workers are being replaced by workers from third world countries who will work for 10% or less of the minimum wages in western countries, and this is being driven by Globalisation. While labour replacing technologies are automating many jobs and further reducing the need for human workers. The end result is that real wages have stagnated or fallen for most North Americans and most Europeans. And this is getting worse as globalisation increases the financial pressures on ordinary people and families. Globalisation and it's "globalised race to the sewer" is destroying many jobs, careers, people, families and communities. Is this really freedom ?

3. **Debt Slavery based on Fraudulent Debt**

The decline in real wages over the last 30 years in the USA and Europe led to a rise in debt and indebtedness as ordinary people used debt to fund and maintain their living standards in developed countries and pay for the high costs of living there. This has been well documented in several studies. Indeed most families have a net worth close to zero once debt is subtracted from their holdings. Many developed countries have total debt which is several multiples of their GNP / GNI. This high cost of living is the result of substantial power of cartels, monopolies and oligopolies and price fixing and excessive speculation in the prices of land, property and assets fuelled by banks. This has contributed to "debt slavery" which is imposing massive limitations on the freedom and security of ordinary people. Debt slavery is the opposite of freedom, as we shall see in this book.

Most people (including some economists) are completely ignorant of how money is created and what debt really is, and how it is the root cause of the problems in banking and economics. Private banks do not lend out their deposits as claimed by many economists and in schools and Universities. 97% of all money is created of nothing when banks give out loans and mortgages. When a bank gives a loan or mortgage to a borrower it

(a) creates money out of nothing and

(b) creates a signed promissory note of the value of this newly created money. This promissory note is owned by the borrower and it's value is lodged into the borrower's account, and appears as newly created money lodged into the borrowers account. It now belongs to the borrower, and this also means the bank now owes the borrower this sum of money. Lodgements or deposits are legally seen as loans by a customer to a bank. Legally, the bank now owes the borrower this sum of newly created money (created out of nothing). This new money exists as electronic credits in the bank. The bank creates a liability in its accounts showing that it owes this money to the borrower and then it creates another entry to claim that the bank repays the money to the borrower, by falsely alleging it buys the promissory note off the borrower and provides him/her with "money", falsely called a "loan". In reality, the bank merely gives the borrower's newly created money back to the borrower in this transaction, and fraudulently calls it a "loan". These accounting entries in the bank now show that no money is owed to the bank and no money is owed to the borrower. The bank misrepresents this to the borrower by falsely claiming that the borrower owes this newly created money to the bank. Legally nobody has loaned any money, neither the borrower owes money to the bank or the bank owes money to the borrower, as the money has been created out of nothing and has been put into the borrower's account by the bank, creating a new deposit, and this was "repaid" back to the borrower by the bank. Nothing is owed. This new money creation is a form of fraud, as the money is created out of nothing, which is a fraud under law, and this also means the bank brings no (financial) consideration to the loan / mortgage contract, making it null and void. Furthermore the bank misrepresents the situation and does not disclose all relevant facts about the contract in dealings with the borrower, which is another breach of contract. The end result is that the customer owes nothing to the bank and the bank owes nothing to the customer. This can be proven through examining the accounting records of the banks. The legal and Constitutional issues around this are examined later in this book.

Compound interest multiplies this debt by 3 or 4 times over 30 - 40 years. And this interest is not created when the money is created by the bank, and this money has to be extracted from the existing money supply creating severe economic instability and turbulence over time. This has created debt slavery and accompanying fear and misery for many millions of people, over 90% of the people in developed and developing countries.

4. **Control of the Money Supply and The Allocation of Resources and Newly Created (Credit) in an Economy**

Today, private banks control 97% of the money supply and they alone decide how much new money is created and where it is allocated. In reality they control how resources are allocated in an economy through their loans (new money creation) and political influence. Studies show that most newly created money, between 70 - 80%, is used for speculation in assets, property, and derivatives. The maximisation of bank profits decides where this new money is allocated in an economy, and speculation is the top profit maximiser for banks. This involves trillions of dollars every year, globally. This focus on speculation and casino economics has created massive financial crashes in the past and will do so into the future, posing serious risks to nations, democracies, workers, families and communities. It is the single most important factor in Economics yet this is not taught in schools and Universities.

This new money **is not** used for investment in hospitals, schools and Universities, apprenticeships, production of products, innovation, infrastructure, policing and justice, social housing, affordable private housing, sports and amenities for communities, sustainable energy, green energy, public services, etc.. The research and books of Professor Richard Werner of De Montfort University and Southampton University in Britain confirms the above. The Internet documentary '97% owned' and the work by Positive Money https://positivemoney.org have done much to expose this scandal.

5. **Unaffordable House prices which are Unaffordable for Young People and Couples and lead to Massive Debt. Inflated Rental prices which are also Unaffordable for People.**

The massive increase in house prices since 1972 is directly linked to the large scale increase in the money supply created by private banks. There is a direct correlation. The collapse of the Bretton Woods system and the Gold standard in 1971 gave private banks and central banks the power to create unlimited amounts of new money. Most of this newly created money was created by private banks and pumped into loans for speculation in assets, shares, property and derivatives. This greatly inflated the price of houses and put them beyond the reach of many people, especially young people and couples It also put many people into massive debt and left them vulnerable to changes in the economy such as financial crashes, recessions and depressions and accompanying evictions. And this corrupt debt system has bankrupted governments and reduced their ability to invest in public housing, affordable housing and the provision of serviced lands for housing / mobile homes ; this is explained in points below.

6. **Unstable Economic Systems Designed to Crash and Destroy Jobs, Livelihoods, Innocent Families and Communities. Evictions and Fear of Evictions in this Highly Unstable Economic System**

Financial crashes, recessions and depressions are directly caused by this defective money creation system which creates excessive debt and speculation and vast misallocations of resources. Have we had enough of bubbles and crashes ? according to the IMF we have had 425 systemic crashes between 1970 and 2010. This consisted of 145 banking crashes, 204 monetary collapses, and 76 sovereign debt crises. These have destroyed hundreds of millions of jobs, livelihoods, families, communities around the world. And governments, businesses and banks are continuing with the same policies which caused these crashes in the past, and this will cause crashes in the future. Do we want more crashes and more bail outs and austerity costing taxpayers trillions of dollars / euros in the future ? should many millions of people and families be put at the mercy of a financial system designed to crash and destroy their jobs, careers, dignity and lives ?

This type of bank controlled Economics puts most families at risk of eviction. Are families meant to be evicted from their homes based on fraudulent debt and fraudulent money creation and speculative asset price rigging and a casino economics (enforced by governments) which create outrageous prices and accompanying debts and equally outrageous bubbles and crashes which imperil and destroy people's jobs, livelihoods, careers, and homes ? should children be forced into homelessness as a result of this ?

7. **Economic Costs of Fraudulent Banking, Debt and Fraudulent Economics**

   The cost to the American economy of the financial crash and accompanying deep recession in terms of lost output, gdp, productivity, bail outs, higher unemployment, lost revenues and earnings has been estimated at $24 trillion (Dr. William K. Black), a truly massive loss. The financial crash of 2008 also led to the loss of 9 million jobs and 6 million evictions from family homes in the USA. There were similar massive losses of trillions of euros for Europe including Ireland, Britain, Spain, Cyprus, Greece, Portugal, Italy, etc.. Globally 34 million people lost their jobs and $26 trillion was wiped off the value of shares. Are these massive losses evidence of a system which is broken, a failed system with failed economic ideologies and policies ? if so, then why has it not been changed ? why are more financial bubbles being inflated ?

8. **Governments have been turned into Beggars. National Debt Enslavement and the Over Taxation of Peoples.**

   Governments have lost their traditional right to create money or print money. In the past, Constitutions gave them this power but this has been usurped, undermined, denied, and lost. This power has been given to private banks and to central banks and they create money out of nothing and lend it to governments, and charge them interest. A debt and interest created out of nothing by banks – a fraudulent debt. In the eurozone, the ECB has taken away this right from national central banks and from governments, and has over centralised real power in Europe. This reduction of governments to beggar status has over many decades led to the accumulation of massive national debts which are crippling countries and pose high risks for these countries. For example, many countries balance high debt levels with new speculative bubbles and the risk of more speculative crashes, a rise in interest rates (on the debt) and severe financial crisis. For example, Ireland is a small country with a population of 4.7 million people, in 2019 Ireland was 213 billion euros in debt (CSO Ireland and statista.com). The Irish national debt is over 252 % of government income (a figure used by investors and banks). Ireland had a 38 billion euro national debt in 2007 (NTMA and Finfacts). This massive increase in the Irish national debt occurred as a result of the crash in 2008 and the bank and speculator bail outs forced on the Irish government (by EU, ECB and IMF) and the accompanying austerity policies, higher unemployment, lower tax revenues, and recession which cost the economy over 100 billion euros (Patrick Honohan: Cost of banking crisis 'more than €100bn', Irish Times, March 11th, 2015). The interest on the national debt amounted to 5 - 7 billion euros per year, and over 60 billion euros was paid in interest from 2009 - 2019. This national debt in 2019 amounts to 44,000 euros for every man, woman and child in Ireland. Ireland has the highest national debt per capita in the EU and one of the highest in the world (figures in Chapter 7). Ireland was forced to pay 42% of the total cost of the whole European banking crisis. The debt to GNI ratio was 111% in 2017, 116% in 2015 (CSO). This is unsustainable & causing considerable economic, social and political problems.

Some countries in Europe and in North America, South America and Japan have similar high debt levels and high debt per capita ratios and many were also forced to bail out banks and speculators after crashes. This is National Debt Enslavement for taxpayers, also called "debt slavery". This enslaves you, your family, your children, your grandchildren and great grandchildren. In reality it is mass theft and robbery from taxpayers.

This results in higher taxes, new taxes and levies, over-taxation, and cuts to vital public services, such as cuts to hospitals, cuts to education, cuts to policing, cuts to infrastructure, cuts to social housing and affordable housing, cuts to community development, cuts to pensions, etc. etc.. One can see the results of this in the hospitals crisis, the healthcare crisis, the housing crisis, the homeless crisis, the evictions crisis, the long traffic jams and lack of infrastructure investment, the pensions crisis, insurance crisis, farming crisis, the budget deficit crisis, the policing crisis, the courts crisis, the prisons crisis, the crime and drugs crisis, etc. all of which emerge from this excessive build up of fraudulent debt. This greatly restricts the freedom and opportunities of most people in societies.

9. **Total Debt**

Other debts such as private debt, mortgage debt, business debt, bank debt add further to this debt problem and in combination with national debt forms Total Debt. Today many developed nations have Total Debt to GNI / GNP ratios ranging from 120% - 600%, this is not sustainable. Iceland had a Total Debt to GNP ratio of 850% prior to the crash in 2008. This high total debt leaves many countries vulnerable to severe recession or depression if another crash occurs. This is analysed further in Chapter 7.

10. **Measuring Debt and National Income**

Some governments like to conceal the level of debt in a country while inflating national income figures beyond their real value. Other factors act to distort national income. When measuring debt whether it is national debt or business debt or mortgage debt it is important to use some accurate and effective indicators such as national debt to GNI / per capita, business debt to GNI / GNP, total private debt to GNI / GNP, mortgage debt to GNI / GNP, etc. The use of GDP is inaccurate, ineffective and outdated, as multinational firms can move the proceeds of sales and profits / interest income / debt and interest payments / commissions / grants / high salaries and bonuses / capital gains / dividend income / corrupt payments / crime proceeds / capital allowances / Intellectual Property income and royalties in many countries through one country for tax reasons yet that country may not benefit from these funds and the taxation of them, but this is wrongly classified as GDP (national income) eg. Irish GDP in 2015. These are BEPS activities, and include other forms such as capital allowances for firms operating out of tax havens, Section 110 SPV funds, Dutch Double Dipping, QIAIF and L-QIAIF funds. They have allowed businesses and banks making tens or hundreds of billions of euros per year to pay no tax or less than 1% tax in some cases for decades. Research and studies show that this can greatly distort national income figures, and can lead to GDP being from 105% - 162% of GNI for a country. In 2018, the GDP to GNI ratio was 162% for Ireland but it was 100% for the other EU countries (CSO). This is a massive distortion of national income and makes accurate measurement impossible and EU rules regarding credit and monetary stability unattainable. This massive tax evasion by big corporations, private equity firms, vulture funds, individuals, hedge funds and banks over the last 20 years occurred at a time when many western countries went deeper into debt and face a crisis from this high debt level.

11. **Socialism for the Rich**

The government bail outs of banks, big corporations and the rich, amounted to over $15 trillion globally after 2008 and in addition to this there was the continuing corporate welfare and corporate subsidies amounting to hundreds of billions of dollars per year. Quantitative easing hand outs alone are estimated at $15 trillion globally - a massive (debt) burden and currency depreciation to put on the backs of ordinary people and taxpayers. This was a massive bail out of the rich – "Socialism for the Rich". A case where "moral hazard" and the "free market" were completely ignored.

At the same time, the working class, ordinary taxpayers, the poor, the elderly, sick and disabled were given pay cuts, benefits cuts, income cuts, higher taxes, new taxes, new levies and charges, employee lay offs and job losses, cutbacks in public services, vicious austerity policies, high mortgage repayments, business closures, evictions from homes, etc. to pay for the bail outs of banks, speculators, and gamblers or 'socialism for the rich'. These were called "austerity policies" by governments, and they created great hardship and suffering for millions of working class and middle class people in Europe and North America after 2008. Many ordinary people and families became victims of Vulture Funds which evicted and raped whole economies. Are underpaid and over indebted people and their families meant to be robbed through government austerity policies to bail out corrupt banks, speculators, bondholders and fraudsters, who are some of the richest people in the world ? should nations, homes and businesses have been asset stripped to fund these bail outs and appease the Vulture Funds ?

This raises an important question - Why was there was no bail out of the ordinary people, the workers, families, the taxpayers, the mortgage holders ? Is this freedom, is this democracy ?

12. **Tax Evasion and Lack of Government Funding for hospitals, housing, schools, pensions, training programmes, back to work programmes, community programmes, family stability, police, military, law and order, roads and infrastructure, rural investment, farming, etc.**

Tax evasion and tax havens were briefly discussed above. The total cost of tax evasion has been estimated at $3.1 trillion per year globally. This is a large financial loss to government and taxpayers and public services (Tax Justice network report, James Henry, November 2011, http://www.tackletaxhavens.com/Cost_of_Tax_Abuse_TJN%20Research_23rd_Nov_2011.pdf)

Total untaxed monies lodged in offshore tax havens is estimated to be $32 trillion (Tax Justice Network, James Henry, 2012, http://www.taxjustice.net/cms/upload/pdf/Price_of_Offshore_Revisited_120722.pdf)

This deprives small countries of tens of billions of euros per year and big countries of hundreds of billions of euros per year for essential public services such as hospitals, housing, schools, pensions, training programmes, back to work programmes, community programmes, family stability, police, military, law and order, roads and infrastructure, rural investment, farming, etc.. And this tax evasion increases the national debt burden on ordinary taxpayers and on their children and grandchildren.

13. **Law and Order**

You will see in Chapter 10 that most western democratic countries suffer from widespread corruption ; their societies are defined by vast corruption such as corrupt police, corrupt judges and courts, corrupted laws, corrupt politicians and governments, corrupt state agencies, corrupt civil servants, corrupt lawyers, corrupt bankers, corrupt healthcare, etc. and this is destroying these countries. Why are these same criminals not arrested, prosecuted and jailed while ordinary people are prosecuted and jailed for very minor offences or accusations of such ?

14. **High Costs Of Living and The Role of Cartels and Price Fixing. Trickle Upwards Economics.**

Why are you paying too much money for homes, health insurance, cars, fuel, healthcare, education, loans / mortgages, energy, food, childcare, etc. ? there is the high costs of basic products and services and the high cost of living imposed by:

i) cartels, protected monopolies, oligopolies, property interests, and restrictive practises which overcharge and rip off ordinary people and enforce high charges for the basic necessities of life. Many are owned by elites, the richest 1 -5 %. Studies show that this costs 5 billion euros per year in the case of Ireland (Competition Authority, Ireland) and tens of billions of euros per year in bigger countries such as Britain, France, Netherlands, USA, etc.. These are massive costs imposed on economies and these costs undermine competitiveness and living standards.

ii) compounded interest rates which imposes additional costs on producing, storing, transporting, accounting for, marketing, selling and buying of goods and service

iii) high taxes, too many taxes, government levies, rates, and charges to support over bloated government programmes, which include bail outs for banks and big corporates, corporate welfare and subsidies, loan repayments to banks (which created loans out of nothing), massively over-priced government contracts which are not audited, and 'pork barrel' politics.

iv) excessive speculation in the prices of houses, land, and assets fuelled by banks (creating money out of nothing in the form of loans), making homes unaffordable for many people

v) the high social costs and welfare costs of Globalisation and automation which are added to products and services and also deducted from your wages.

15. **Basics of Life and Trickle Upwards Economics**

Are pensioners and people who worked all their lives to be robbed of their pensions by a financial system based on over speculation, fraud, criminality and corruption which transfers funds upwards to the richest 1% ? a trickle upwards economics.

Should the basics of life and existence such as social security, private pension plans, state pension plans, life savings in banks and other financial institutions, food stamps, basic welfare, medical care plans for the elderly, disabled and unemployed, and government healthcare systems be cut, reduced, replaced, eliminated or wiped out to support the following:

- o over speculation and related frauds and crashes involving speculation in trillions of dollars and losses of trillions of dollars globally
- o derivatives which are speculation based and worth over $1,200 trillion
- o bank and speculator bail outs by government and taxpayers involving trillions of dollars
- o manipulated wars and regime changes which cost trillions of dollars per year and mostly benefit large banks, the military industrial complex, and the Deep State
- o corporate welfare and subsidies, and tax evasion schemes, costing tens / hundreds of billions of dollars each year in many countries.
- o a Deep State and Shadow Government (in big countries) which commands hundreds of billions of dollars per year and where trillions of dollars have gone missing, been misappropriated, and are unaccounted for. In 2001, Donald Rumsfled the defence minister of the USA claimed that over $2 trillion was missing and unaccounted for. In 2018, the US government has stated that 21 trillion is missing and unaccounted for. The CAFR scandal is just one example of this.
- o the robbing of natural resources such as oil, gas, minerals and depriving governments and taxpayers of many billions of euros / dollars per year

16. **High Concentrations of Wealth and Corrupt Politics and Corrupt Laws**

The money and interest creation system and speculation system mentioned above and the accompanying government bail outs, Globalisation and the cartels, monopolies and rigged pricing system transfer vast amounts of wealth from the 99% to the richest 1%. Are people meant to live in societies where there are high concentrations of wealth and income and where the richest 1% own a large disproportionate share of wealth and income ? In Chapter 10, you will see that in the USA, the richest 1% own 40% of the wealth, which is more than the bottom 90% combined and the richest 1% get 24% of national income. This is comparable to inequality in the 19th century or Victorian Age. Research studies show that the interests of the richest 1% are served and protected by politicians and governments, and laws and regulations are created to serve their interests. This is done via 'pay to play' politics based on lobbying, bribery, corruption, funding, revolving door, and insider networks; politicians are bought and paid for. The writings of Professor Lawrence Lessig of Harvard University and other researchers and whistleblowers confirm this [29]. The "swamp" in many capitals is getting bigger. <u>Democracies have been turned into corrupt oligarchies.</u>

17. **The Failure of EU Federalism**

EU Federalism has destroyed the sovereignty of nations, has imposed a democratic deficit upon Europe where many nations are ruled an unelected elite in the EU Commission, EU bureaucracy, and Lobbyists, a monetary union which ruined several EU nations while enriching Germany, the funding of massive speculative bubbles in several European countries by big German and other European banks and the ECB, the imposing of massive debt upon Ireland, Greece, Portugal, Spain to bail out European and global bankers and speculators after the crash, a debt which bankrupted these countries and is robbing the taxpayers of these countries, no borders control and mass migration, the ruination of national fish industries, support for globalisation and the ruination of family farms and native industries, undermining of law and order through ineffective EU laws and courts, vast corruption in the EU institutions and no system of oversight and accountability, a new EU army to enrich the military-industrial complex and banks which profit from more wars and regime changes, etc.. The New Imperialism. This is discussed and analysed more in Chapter 2

18. **World Population and the Distribution of Wealth and Resources**

Are half the world's population meant to be condemned to absolute poverty and misery, while the richest 1% of the world increased their wealth from 30% to 50% in the period from 2000 to 2010 ? Oxfam's research has shown that over the last 25 years, globally, the top 1% have gained more income than the bottom 50% put together [12]. Since 2015, the richest 1% has owned more wealth than the rest of the planet. By 2016, 8 wealthy men had as much wealth as half of the world's population, that is 3.5 billion people, according to Oxfam [12]. This is the end result of globalisation combined with the current system of money and debt creation (out of nothing) by private banks which imposed massive debt on countries in order to extract, exploit and rob their resources, and the accompanying Neo Liberal policies enforced by the IMF, World Bank and USA on developing and third world countries. I would encourage readers to read 'AN ECONOMY FOR THE 99%' by Oxfam in 2017 and available at https://www-cdn.oxfam.org/s3fs-public/file_attachments/bp-economy-for-99-percent-160117-en.pdf

19. **Environmental Pollution and Related Diseases and Illnesses and the Healthcare Crisis**

Today, there is a high rate of Cancers, neurological illnesses, heart diseases, autoimmune and other immune system illnesses, gastric diseases, glandular diseases, lung diseases and kidney and liver diseases resulting from toxins and pollutants in food, water, air, drinks, land, vaccines, and products. But, politicians and big businesses and banks oppose Environmental Protection and Regulations. Are people, including children, meant to consume pollutants and toxins and suffer the consequences in terms of diseases, chronic illnesses, cancers and poor health ? and be denied affordable medical care and hospital care ? and be denied affordable medical insurance ? and overcharged for medical care and medicines ? and suffer underfunded and overcrowded hospitals and clinics ? the poisoning of water in Flint, Michigan (USA) recently is just one of many examples of contamination of water, food, air, land, products and services. Is this really freedom ? or is it slavery and misery ?

The Environmentalists and green lobby fail to understand that the present system of banking and debt creation favours pollution, deregulation and environmental destruction. The profits from this are privatised and the damage and personal and family losses are socialised.

20. **Healthcare**

Are ordinary people in modern developed countries to be bankrupted to receive basic medical treatment or bankrupted to pay expensive medical insurance so as to get protection from the corporate poisoning of food, water, air, land and the environment mentioned above ?

21. **Fake News and Unfree Press and Media**

Ownership of the press and media has become highly concentrated in most countries. This has led to the development of "fake news" consisting of lies, deception, distortions, half truths, cover ups, censorship and manipulations, which promotes certain political agendas. Should they be entitled to censor the news, the truth and the facts ? should fake news be used to manipulate the masses ? are honest journalists and whistleblowers meant to be hounded out of their jobs by corrupt executives ? what did the founders of democracy say about a free press and media & its relationship to voters and democratic processes ?

22. **Oppression of Honesty and Integrity**

Are state whistleblowers and corporate whistleblowers who report corruption, frauds, and crimes to the general public to be harassed, fired from jobs, framed or falsely accused of crimes, jailed or even killed ?

23. **The Promotion of Hatred, Discrimination and Prejudices within Families, Communities, Societies**

Are people meant to be divided against each other through manipulated hateful divisions based on race, class, religion, gender, disability, age and ethnic group ? who are the real dividers of people ? who are the people profiteering from these tribalistic divisions and hatreds ? are people meant to grow up and to live in economically created environments of acrimony, suspicion, distrust, selfishness, greed, prejudice, sneering, stigma, and hate which pits people against each other and destroys families, family values, community values, human values, and social values ?

24. **Crime**

Crime, drugs, human trafficking, and gangs, are out of control in developed counties. Are ordinary people meant to suffer the consequences of liberal policies which worsen crime and gangs ? why are governments not taking the problem of crime seriously ? why are there so many mass shootings ? why do governments falsely claim there are no funds for community development and community integration, family supports, youth facilities, sports facilities, psychiatric, psychological and holistic treatments, youth diversion programmes, employment initiatives, apprenticeships, etc. and crime prevention when they waste billions of euros / dollars on bail outs of the rich, corporate subsidies, tax breaks for the rich, paying off fraudulent debts, and more arms spending?

25. **Education**

Education systems have failed to properly educate people and provide with critical thinking skills, logic and basic reasoning, deep research skills, analytical skills, and the forensic skills to uncover lies and deception by governments, corporates and large organisations. Can dumbed down, poorly educated, ignorant people in developed countries consider themselves to be free, when they are enslaved in so many ways (by lies, deceptions, fraud, inequality and massive debt) ?

26. **Political and Legal System Corruption which denying people their Constitutional Rights, Civil Rights and Human Rights**

In Chapter 10, you will read how corruption of political systems, legal systems, the police, medicine and healthcare, and government agencies has led to massive human rights abuses and cover ups in democracies worldwide. It is truly shocking. Are people meant to be victims of corrupted legal systems which deliver injustices, denial of rights, no due process, evidence tampering, cover ups, the framing of innocent people, perjuries and manipulations, racism, sexism, and corrupt verdicts, and which destroy many innocent people and families ?

27. **Warehousing of People**

Many western countries including the USA have large prison populations, the US has 2.3 million people in jail (2017), one of the highest in the world. There are more coloured people in jail than in college / universities in the USA. This is the government response to the economic effects of Globalisation and Automation and High Concentrations of Wealth and Income in many countries. Societies have also warehoused large numbers of the working class, the unemployed, disabled, the elderly, and vulnerable poor families with criminals, drug addicts and terrorists in large apartment complexes and ghettos with no social services, no recreational facilities and no community supports. These have become crime ridden, anti social, violent, no go areas which denigrate and destroy human dignity. All of the above represents a warehousing of people, of significant percentages of the populations of countries. Is this really freedom? Are these countries really free and democratic ?

28. **Born Enslaved not Born Free. Reduced to Human Chattel.**

Are people born and reared to be debt slaves, to pay massive debts back to banks which created this money and interest out of nothing ? and are they also tax slaves who have to pay for the bail out of the banks and rich speculators after a financial crash and pay for the tax evasion schemes of global corporations, banks and vulture funds ? and have their lives and families threatened or destroyed by unjust and highly unstable economic system?

Are people mere chattel to be used, lied to, and discarded by a failed and mostly corrupted economic system and political system, a vicious system which treats ordinary people as dirt, as disposable, worthless items ?

29. **Terrorism**

Are innocent ordinary people and their families meant to be victims of mindless terrorism which emerges from manufactured conflicts and 'regime changes' which serve the interests and aims of the rich elite in some developed countries, their Globalism which is the New Imperialism ? The same rich elite which supports wars, regime changes and terrorism also supports mass migration into western democracies.

30. **Big Brother, 1984 and The Destruction of Privacy. And The Attack on Free Speech**

in the USA there are the Patriot Acts, the NDAA, the secret courts, the TSA which monitors movement of people, the NSA which monitors everybody, and there is large scale illegal surveillance, and many other laws and surveillance policies which severely restrict freedom and rights and undermine the US Constitution. Other developed countries have similar policies in place. Are people meant to suffer oppressive laws which are unconstitutional, anti democratic, and anti human rights and which have produced a Big Brother society, and a '1984' world ? is this freedom ? In addition to this, the rich elites and their political puppets in developed countries are imposing new forms of political correctness which is severely restricting freedom of speech and undermining old Constitutional rights.

31. **Surveillance ?**

Why is there no surveillance, arrests, convictions and jailings of corporate criminals, banking criminals, corrupt politicians, corrupt deep state employees, corrupt judges, prosecutors, police ?

32. **Microchipping**

There are calls to microchip people so they can pay for goods and services faster and more efficiently. There is a high probability that this would be used to control people and to further limit and destroy their freedoms, and extend the existing Big Brother surveillance and oppression. We have seen a lot of evidence of this desire to control and manipulate people by elites, by big government and big corporations in recent decades and in the present, and this trend is likely to continue. The microchipping of people would lead to more control over people, to substantial loss of freedoms, loss of rights and human dignity, and to fascist tyranny.

33. **Wars**

Are your children meant to be conscripted and coerced to be military cannon fodder for unnecessary, artificially created, manipulated wars and conflicts which benefit the rich elite and their interests ? wars are highly profitable. Wars which murder hundreds of thousands / millions of working class people and bankrupt nations [30]. Wars in the name of the New Imperialism. I would advise readers to read Chapter 12 of this book as it explains the causes of many modern wars and "regime changes".

34. **Moral Cowardice**

Religions and religious leaders preach about justice, fairness, honesty, integrity, truth, morality, respect for persons, human dignity, and responsibilities yet they ignore the points mentioned above and do not preach about them. These religions and religious leaders who preach a lot in religious buildings should mention the great social injustices, hateful divisions, crimes, evils, and corruption detailed above and tell people NOT to be docile, subservient, accepting, tolerant and obedient to these evils mentioned above.

These are pointed questions which reveal much about our modern world. They point to the very forces which crush freedom, democracy, rights, and human dignity. Are people just rats on a treadmill in a globalised 'race to the bottom' while their societies fall apart ? **Are they really free ? is this really freedom ?** The facts and evidence show that this is not freedom, this is tyranny, corrupt oligarchy, oppression, despotism, the very antithesis of freedom. Politicians may tell you that this is freedom and democracy, but it is not. It is the opposite of freedom and democracy. It is modern day slavery, it is oligarchy, a return to feudalism. It is grinding oppression overseen by oligarchy, even in so called 'democracies' in 'developed' and western countries. It is a betrayal of Washington, Jefferson, Madison, Wilberforce, Lincoln, Voltaire, Lafayette, Paine, Bolivar, Pearse, Connolly, and the many millions of men and women who sacrificed their lives for freedom and democracy. It is clearly a return to the feudalism and serfdom of the Middle ages.

Yet these questions above are the really important questions of our time. These are the existential questions of our era, which need answering. Answers may appear to be presented or offered by the dominant economic, political and social opinion makers at a given point in time in human history, but this is mere opinion, subject to prejudices, mental conditioning, and lack of insight, and these opinions have been proven wrong many times. As we shall see in this book most accepted political opinion and economist opinion is wrong, erroneous, contradictory, and misguided.

This book 'New World Disorder' addresses these issues and is aimed at a global audience and has relevance for all countries and all peoples. The main thrust of this book will be to deconstruct and expose the failures of the present economic system and its accompanying political and social systems, and their outdated philosophies or theologies. And delve deeply into how they are destroying freedom, democracy, individual choices, free will, families, homes, social capital, social cohesion, communities, and nations. It will also examine so called alternative 'solutions' and ideologies which ironically have similar defects, flaws and outcomes. These 'solutions' have ignored structures of causation, causality and it's intricate and interlinked nature and the special relationship of freedom to its responsibilities. This book proposes a new system, novel solutions, which address structures of causation and root causes, and proceeds from the point of cause, while closely integrating freedom to its accompanying responsibilities. This is a delicate balance, which needs to be finely tuned over time. It is based on previous and continuing refinements of economic democracy ideas first used and supported by Enlightenment philosophers and activists and by Washington, Jefferson, Adams, Hamilton, Madison,

Jackson, and Lincoln in the early decades of the American Republic and further enhanced over time by other writers and politicians. Many of the problems and solutions are interlinked in a complex causality, and there has been some repetition in this book in order to address this and support arguments in separate sections of the book.

In the present world, we must deal with capitalism, it is ubiquitous and cannot be ignored or dismissed. There are many types of capitalism, not just one as commonly assumed. And these different types of capitalism can vary widely with different forms, structures, priorities and processes. Capitalism is capable of many permutations and combinations, many possibilities and matrix combinations and distinct matrices, many types of outcomes, there is no one type of capitalism and no one capitalist size fits all countries and peoples. The so called 'Washington Consensus' or Neo Liberal economics imposed on the world by the IMF, World Bank, GATT, the WTO and by military and intelligence interventions, and by governments and institutions for many decades has many defects and flaws and has proven itself to be a failure and subject to crashes and collapses. While no one ideology fits all countries or even most countries, there are different economic matrices possible encompassing various economic and social constructs.

These include combinations and mixes of freedom and accompanying responsibilities, degrees of regulation and deregulation, varying resource allocations and misallocations (including highly skewed allocations), varying wealth and income concentrations, multiple wealth generative mechanisms, taxes to reduce speculation or increase it, taxes to increase actual productive investment and research or decrease it, state investment versus privatisation or private investment, pro debt or anti debt money creation policies, policies which increase or reduce constrained, unrealised, unmet demand and supply, false or manipulated scarcity or abundance, currencies which reflect actual economic conditions and trading conditions or manipulated currencies designed to destroy other countries, sustainable high tech energy systems or costly fossil fuels which are limited and have economic externalities, anti discrimination and social justice combinations measured against doing nothing and letting things worsen, trade and employment combinations, pro fraud and corruption and anti fraud and corruption policies, and a myriad of incentives and disincentives which push economies in many directions. There are multiple levels and degrees of trade offs in these matrices.

The Hegelian Dialectic has played a major role in resolving this and will continue to do so, producing opposing opinions and positions, conflict, new solutions, new synergies and forms over time, which dominate for a period and then are challenged and change again in an ever changing flux. This Hegelian Dialectic with its constant friction of opposing viewpoints produces sharp differences of opinion, heated debates, polarisation, political protests, turbulence and turmoil, conflicts, wars, revolutions, new ideologies, new political movements, new types of government, social upheavals, political reforms, innovations and economic reforms which ultimately lead to resolutions, many temporary, others more lasting, and some permanent. Yet, the central question of what constitutes freedom and responsibility keeps re-emerging in different forms.

The present dominant form of economics is Neo Liberal Economics also called 'Neo Classical Economics' and this has dominated the world since the mid 1980's, first gaining prominence under Margaret Thatcher and President Reagan. The many flaws and defects in Neo Liberal Economics or 'Free Market' Economics are listed and discussed in sections below and also in Chapter 4. The effects of their flaws, defects and errors on freedom, responsibility and democracy will also be examined. Other forms of capitalism and forms of socialism, communism, social democracy and liberalism and other ideologies will also be analysed and discussed. Alternative types of economics and the many combinations and permutations of capitalism possible will also be presented in the book. New options, new combinations, new matrixes, new possibilities, new economics will be explored, while others can be derived and formulated from what is presented.

Failed economic ideologies have over time proven to be highly destructive of freedoms, responsibilities, social order, social capital, politics and democracy. They act like Cancer on a body. Nothing happens without cause and effect, and many of the effects or symptoms found in economic system failures arise from causes which are too inconvenient and politically difficult to face and tackle. Over time, that is decades and centuries, one sees the same causes and effects repeating themselves in a pattern ; this calls into question the underlying mentalities and theories which formulate causes. Does repeating the same mistakes over and over again for decades and centuries indicate intelligence and progress or does it indicate stupidity, error and regress ? do awards and prizes including Nobel prizes applaud great new insights or a continuation of the same old failed orthodoxies and theories ? do they reward failure and promote failure ? Analysing causes, and why the same pattern keeps repeating and repeating, it is clear that causes are derived from the fact that the majority of economists and economic and political commentators live in a bubble or ivory tower detached from reality and the real world, and thus are content to persist in regurgitating failed economic models, and enforcing failed economic orthodoxies over and over again, while ignoring their failures and devastating consequences, which they are shielded from. In fact economists act collectively to censor all opposing views and stop all efforts to reform failed economic systems. Most economists live in a echo chamber of their own failed ideologies and delusions.

Like some failed mantra which keeps repeating endlessly economics has become entrapped in a cult of self deception, delusion, childish naivety and failure, and unable and possibly incapable of introspection, self reflection and self correction. Their arrogance masks their inability to understand Popper's Theory of Falsification. According to Popper all theories including economic theories are subject to falsification including the present economic system, and this in light of consistent crashes and failures certainly needs to be acknowledged by more of our most acclaimed economists who presume to know everything and to offer advice and policies to governments, banks and businesses. Popper's falsification theory and reality has been very apparent to the world since the crash of 1929, and in the recent crash of 2008, but nothing has been learnt. Indeed economists have refused to learn.

The answer lies in deconstructing the points of economic failure, ideological failure and the roots of economic problems and related political problems, their workings and internal dynamics, in the domain of cause and effect, and deriving solutions which emerge at the level of cause. Proceeding from cause, we present new options, new possibilities, new matrices, new causes to resolve these complex problems.

Freedom is not Insignificant

Freedom is not insignificant, despite the efforts of many to render it meaningless and irrelevant, and to undermine and subvert it in such a way that it becomes the very opposite of freedom. The long process of human evolution shows a clear striving and movement towards freedom over the course of history, with some progression forward and some regression backward over time. Freedom and democracy is an evolving form, capable of progressing forward or regressing backwards depending on the forces aligned against it. By freedom, I mean freedom in all spheres, economic, political, legal, cultural, social, religious and spiritual. The freedom of all persons to grow, to develop, to think and act for themselves, to realise their true potential, and thrive economically, politically, culturally, socially and spiritually in democratic and free environments. Succinctly portrayed in the immortal phrase, the right to "life, liberty and the pursuit of happiness" in the Declaration of Independence. And further delineated in Constitutions and Bills of Rights worldwide to encompass freedom of expression, freedom of the press, freedom to protest, freedom to vote, freedom to chose governments and to recall or impeach them, freedom from discrimination and prejudice, freedom from coercion, the enforcement of human rights, freedom of association, freedom of religion, freedom of thought, etc.. These were and will continue to be radical but necessary ideas and rights. However, there are powerful forces in society, even democratic societies who strongly oppose these freedoms and have undermined and subverted these freedoms. Democratic rights, freedom, may be inherent or even divinely given, but ultimately they must be defended, and this defence requires the exercise of responsibilities by all persons. It is extremely important for all persons to realise that freedom has to be defended, must be defended, and this has and will continue to be the most important responsibility in relation to freedom.

Freedom itself relies on the responsibilities attached to freedom in order to survive and exist. Without responsibilities there can be no freedom. This is a well known fact which has been greatly neglected by supporters of freedom and democracy for too long, and this will be discussed throughout this book. Responsibilities are the most overlooked aspect of freedom, and all progressions forward and regressions backward in respect of freedom must be judged in light of how well freedom is matched to its accompanying responsibilities. As we shall see in this book, all criticisms of freedom and democracy and strong reactions against it arise from deficiencies in or neglect of the responsibilities attached to freedom.

The issue of the responsibilities attached to freedom has been subject to the Hegelian Dialectic over the course of history. One sees a constant battle between opposing views, primarily between those which support traditional and inherited viewpoints and those with counter-viewpoints based on remedying the flaws, defects, errors and injustices inherent in the opposing (traditional) viewpoints. Resolution often involves some form of synthesis and further resolutions, though in some cases it involves outright rejection and the formation of new systems. Synthesis comes in many forms. The responsibilities which are attached to freedom were first widely elucidated by Hobbes in his book 'Leviathan' where he proposed that the state take on some powers to protect the basic rights (natural rights) of individuals who would otherwise have suffered a 'poor, nasty, brutish and short' and unfree life. A state which would establish certain rules and regulations which would prevent 'a war of all against all'. Certainly the libertarian, neo liberal and neo classical economics' support for the 'law of the jungle' was found to be ineffective and dangerous then, as it is now today. Locke further refined this particular concept of freedom in the context of expanding individual rights and the state's obligation to protect these rights under law, while limiting the powers of the state to prevent tyranny. This was a very delicate balance or social contract between the individual and the state, implying responsibilities on both sides. Locke also recommended rebellions or revolutions to overturn corrupt tyrannical governments and foreign occupation of countries, which where despotic conditions where the social contract was being undermined or destroyed. Locke's intervention represented a very new and necessary improvement or upgrading, a further refinement of the responsibilities attached to freedom. Rousseau further refined Locke's theories in his works on the 'social contract'.

The French philosophers, American philosophers such as Thomas Paine, Jefferson and Madison and the German Immanuel Kant built upon Locke's assertions and added to them, and stated the importance of national sovereignty, the vote and democratic representation via parliaments, written social contracts between the state and the individual in the form of Constitutions, Bills of Rights and Declarations of the Rights of Man, the separation of powers, equality for all, the separation of church and state, fraternity between citizens, justice for all under law, the importance of checks and balances, the need to tax economic rents and remove the privileges of the landed aristocracy and royalty, and the need for oversight of government and state institutions, etc. Thus the social contract between the state and the individual and between individuals themselves greatly expanded, as humanity developed a greater consciousness of the responsibilities attached to freedom. This marked the 'Age of Enlightenment' in the mid 18th century and into the first two decades of the 19th century. Its also been called the 'Age of Reason' and it saw a parallel growth in scientific discovery and progress. This expansion of consciousness at the time was the key factor, and as we shall see in Chapter 12`, the expansion of consciousness is the means by which real change occurs, and is an ongoing process. Prior to the Enlightenment, humanity was enslaved, robbed, murdered, tortured, and oppressed by corrupt, tyrannical and perverted monarchs, aristocrats and religious leaders, and this was believed to be normal, even ordained by God.

For the next 200 years after the Enlightenment, this social contract and consciousnesses of rights and freedoms was deepened, added to, and expanded, and we saw the domino effects of this via the Abolitionists, the Chartists, the critical analysis of American democracy by De Tocqueville where he called for responsibilities to balance rights, nationalists demanding national freedom in many countries and openly challenging empires, the liberation of South American countries, the 1848 revolutionaries and revolts, the writings of John Stuart Mill, the cooperatives movement, the trade union movement, the labour movement, the giving of the vote to working class people, the suffragettes, the nationalist uprisings in the 20th century, the New Deal of the 1930's, the social safety nets after world war 2, the GI bill, the ending of colonialism and empires in Africa and Asia in the latter half of the 20th century, the disability rights movement, the civil rights movement in many countries, etc. and a continuous upgrading of this social contract, some involving revolts, some involving wars, some involving protests, some involving changes to education, others involving changes to political structures and socio-economic structures and others involving deep changes to laws. Some others involved new political parties and new organisations engaged in persistent agitation for change, which has been continuous over time.

All immersed in a great striving and struggle to attain freedom and to match freedom to its accompanying responsibilities in new and challenging economic and social environments, with some successes and some failures. This struggle for freedom has always been opposed, often viciously by supporters of the status quo. It has been opposed in the past and in the present. In all cases, freedom and its responsibilities were opposed by conservatives, conservative parties, traditionalists, and defenders of the status quo, oppressive laws, imprisonment, hangings, forced transportation, police brutality, police and judge corruption, sabre charges by cavalry, illegal spying and surveillance by the police and secret services, perversions of justice, human rights abuses, religious sectarianism, imperialism, use of the press to censor and to condemn reforms, social exclusion, and the use of stigma and discrimination. This is explored in some detail in Howard Zinn's books, especially the book 'A Peoples History of the United States' [20]. In this book he describes the traditional forces of conservatism, toryism and imperialism which imposed tyranny and oppression for centuries on most countries while opposing all reforms and all changes and all forms of progress. This book provides one of the best expositions of the dark forces which oppose freedom, democracy and the ordinary people. Zinn and others also mention right wing reactionary forces and left wing reactionary forces which imposed similar forms of tyranny and oppression, in the form of different variants of communism and fascism. There are always forces at work wishing to centralise power, to grab and take power, to expropriate power from the people and to impose one narrow ideology on everybody, and to use various forms of oppression to enforce this.

These examples provided practical examples of Hegel's' Dialectic, a constant uncovering and exposure of the inner contradictions and injustices in a system, which create conditions for conflict, followed by the perpetual struggle between polarities or opposing forces providing new and emergent forms which dominate for a while before undergoing new challenges and contradictions, and a repetition of this process of conflict between polarities again and again. At a deeper level the same forces, the same dynamics and the same struggles keep re-emerging over time in different guises ; there is continuity amidst much change. This has continued into the modern age and taken on new more sinister forms. And today this old continuing struggle is at the forefront of politics, current affairs, news, economics, resource allocations, laws and legal processes, and sociology, dominating much public discourse and public apprehension.

This correlation or relationship between freedom and its responsibilities has exercised the great minds of the past and continues to do so to this day. The great philosopher, psychiatrist and writer Viktor Frankl stated in his book 'Man's Search for Meaning' that freedom is only possible through the implementation and use of responsibilities. He wrote 'I recommend that the Statue of Liberty on the east coast be supplemented by a statue of Responsibility on the west coast'. This is a very important point, not just for America but for all countries. Frankl's book provides deep philosophical insights into why this is necessary. He mentioned his experiences in the concentration camps in World War 2 and how the war and these camps provided a stark example to the world of what happens to politics, economics and countries when there are no responsibilities attached to freedom, and no responsibilities attached to economics, in particular social responsibilities. He provides moral reasons, logical and rational reasons, and spiritual reasons for working for these responsibilities, and in this he delves much deeper into issues of purpose, meaning and existence. As we shall see in this book all of these are inter-related. And they are very relevant in today's world. This emphasis on social responsibilities echoes the insights of the great John Stuart Mill in his works On Liberty (1859) and Representative Government (1861) which outlined the conditions necessary for freedom, including overcoming the tyranny of majorities, preventing excessive state interference, and the exercise of individual responsibilities, collective responsibilities, social responsibilities, and government responsibilities all working together, in unison and in alignment, requiring vigilance and active participation by citizens in this regard. The purpose being to prevent tyranny, oligarchies, dictators and structures of injustices, and build the social cohesion necessary for freedom and democracy to thrive and evolve. Even Adam Smith, the great father of free markets supported these principles, and stated that economics and profits should be used to create just societies which would provide for the needs of all people in his book 'Theory of Moral Sentiments'.

The harsh repetitive lessons of history show that the answer does not lie in Communism, Socialism, Fascism, Religious dictatorship, Monarchism or any other forms of dictatorship or federalism. These have failed miserably throughout history and created vast misallocations and mismatches of resources, destroyed democratic rights and human rights, and inflicted great suffering and injustices on humanity. Communism is estimated to have murdered over 70 million people in the 20th century, Fascism including Nazism and military dictatorships in Europe, Asia, Africa and Central and South America murdered 60 million people in the 20th century, Monarchism and Imperialism murdered hundreds of millions of people throughout history, and Religious controlled governments and extremism also murdered hundreds of millions of people throughout history.

For many centuries and even today, fools have claimed that these regimes were ordained by God, and this was used to justify their existence, but it is very clear that demons and devils ordained these regimes. We have seen their rotten fruits and their results, and we know them. All of these failed ideologies relied on a centralisation of power in the form of an over powerful state or private oligarchy, the serfdom or enslavement of the masses, and the destruction of individual freedom and rights. This was often enforced by violence and criminality, such as brute military force, executions, imperialism, invasions, corrupt laws and courts, concentrations of wealth and income, corrupt federalist structures, all of which empower those at the centre of the empire. In this we see the real enemy of freedom, the real evil, and this has been a recurring theme throughout history. And it remains the greatest nemesis of freedom today and into the future.

The Relationship of Freedom to Order and Chaos

The Enlightenment and the progressive movements which emerged from it represented an increasing desire to impose order on the chaos which was inherited from past or more primitive centuries. Yet each freer system contained elements of order and chaos. Freedom itself remains vulnerable to the permutations of order and chaos. Both of the latter can promote different levels of freedom and unfreedom, while people remain oblivious to this. It is important to point out that there are two opposing polarities within economics, politics, sociology, law and philosophy — Order and Chaos. It is vital to understand this when discussing economics, politics, sociology, law and philosophy. Many different ideologies or "isms" are analysed below in relation to the amount of order and chaos they cause and perpetuate and the level of freedom and unfreedom which results from this. They claim to promote freedom but in most cases promote the exact opposite. These many "isms" are recent constructs and provide superficial, ineffective and temporary solutions to highly complex and multifaceted problems. The chaos inherent in them ultimately leads to their failures. The human experience throughout history up to the present day clearly shows that many ideologies which allegedly support order actually promote chaos at many levels. From the economic instability and crashes to the wars and regime changes and accompanying refugee disasters to the promotion of ghettos of crime, addiction and abuses to the racism, class warfare and prejudices which distort and destroy human relations to the high rates of divorces and family breakdowns and child abuse cases to the swamps of corruption in capital cities to the bail outs of the rich and powerful which bankrupted nations and (vital) public services. One sees chaos almost everywhere. Indeed chaos seems to be the default of human societies. The great philosopher Nietzsche predicted this in his writings in the late 19th century and he was correct. He further surmised that humanity would need supermen to overcome the great challenges posed by this growing chaos and disorder which he attributed to the loss of faith in God, morality, ethics, and the "order" imposed in previous ages. While he was correct and right about the order promoted by these principles and codes of behaviour, he failed to see that these "ordered" systems of the past had many contradictions and flaws which rendered them inadequate and self-destructive. They contained within them the chaos and the perpetuating factors of chaos. They were immersed in chaos and indeed perpetuated further chaos and new forms of chaos for centuries and millennia. The Hegelian Dialectic brutally exposed these flaws over many centuries and the resulting chaos and turmoil enforced difficult changes in an evolutionary context. Yet each new ideology, synthesis or system which emerged also contained and promoted chaos and disorder, providing the means for their own future self destruction. The inability to differentiate order from chaos and to see how political, economic, social systems which appear "ordered", "natural", justified, normal contain significant chaos and disorder and inner contradictions which ultimately undermine them remains the greatest challenge to academics, politicians, governments, journalists, historians, media commentators, and members of the general public. Unfortunately, many "intellectuals" and key decision makers fail to see this and many have become trapped in echo chambers which promote and entrench chaos.

None of the existing political and economic ideologies and sociological and psychological constructs and philosophical ideas can overcome the chaos inherent within them and the chaos they can cause and have caused. Central to this understanding is the delicate balance between rights and responsibilities, as one intrinsically depends on the other. It is the inability to understand one's responsibilities and discharge or implement one's responsibilities which ultimately undermines the rights and freedoms of individuals, groups, families, communities, and nations and which sows the seeds of chaos. We are as humans interlinked to each other in many ways, a myriad of ways, and the seeds of disorder, of chaos once sown resonates throughout the human race in a domino effect. However the seeds of order, including responsibility, cooperation, justice, democracy, respect can also be sown and positively affect the human race in ever growing domino effects. This book address this point.

If one wishes to understand politics then one must understand the economics, the economic ideologies and structures, and accompanying social beliefs and social structures which underlie politics. Also the laws which emanate from politics need to be understood in this same context. We will examine some of the ideologies purporting to represent freedom and human progress, and how well they match freedom to its responsibilities and how much order and chaos they sow. As we shall see, there are many false views and notions about freedom which fail to pass the necessary test of aligning freedom to its responsibilities. We examine these ideologies and belief systems below.

Liberalism

There has in recent years (circa 2017) been an unprecedented backlash against Liberalism and the centre and what they stand for. This backlash has taken the form of populism of the right wing and the left wing, and growing nationalism. This affords us an opportunity to analyse why this is happening and what has gone wrong with Liberalism. Liberalism presumes to support freedom, democracy and human rights, yet it actually works against them ; liberalism tolerates and supports the following:

(a) crime and criminals and anti-social behaviour facilitated by corruption of laws, of politicians, of legal systems and their employees, and of sentencing for several decades. A liberal system which is too soft and lenient on crime, refuses to jail criminals and in many cases refuses to investigate and prosecute serious crimes, especially white collar crimes. A liberal system which aids and abets crime, and has led to high crime rates globally. This includes violent crime, burglaries, harassment, paedophile rings and child trafficking, white collar crime and fraud, and political corruption which has destroyed millions of lives and cost individual nations billions of dollars.

(b) liberals ignore the victims of crime and do nothing to support victims or rehabilitate them and support them. This has also resulted in high costs to society and vast economic losses.

(c) creating excessive dependency on social welfare and the creation of communities and ghettos overly dependent on social welfare which can lead to alcohol abuse, drug abuse, anti social behaviour and crime. The alienation of the individual from wider society, and the destruction of individual initiative, motivation, respect and dignity and the blocking of constructive and positive engagement with society.

(d) failing to properly fund third level education and apprenticeships and accompanying work placement programmes as a means to reduce welfare dependency, addictions and crime.

(e) tolerating, accepting and tacitly supporting disrespect, irresponsibility, dishonesty, corruption and unaccountability at all levels of society. And the accompanying breakdown in families, relationships, communities and in individuals.

(f) regime changes and wars instigated by liberals and by neo-cons. Liberal leaders in developed countries arming, funding and supporting 'regime changes' in other countries which in many cases involved arming extremists and terrorists and this led to the forced migration of large numbers of people out of these countries. These regime changes tend to create vacuums of power often filled by religious extremists, dictators and autocrats, creating more problems into the future. Liberals (and no cons) ignored the problems they themselves created.

(g) unlimited mass immigration, resulting from the regime changes and wars of liberals and neo cons, which is beyond the capacity of some countries to absorb. Inadequate public services, funding, and public infrastructure for immigrants, the disabled and the unemployed which has been decimated by recurring financial crashes, bailouts of bankers and fraudsters, austerity policies and recession, which have been caused and enforced by liberals.

(h) liberals letting religious extremists and terrorism into western countries and creating 'no go' areas in them and making these societies more vulnerable to terrorism

(i) liberals have provided generous social welfare payments, free housing, free medical care, free education and other handouts to religious extremists and terrorists in western developed countries who are plotting to commit acts of terror and criminality and destroy democracy and freedom. And attacks have occurred and will continue to occur. All paid for by liberals.

(j) too much tolerance of political extremism and hate speech and incitements to hatred, violence, and terrorism under the false guise of protecting "freedom of speech", "freedom of expression" and "religious freedom", tolerance and pluralism

(k) corruption and 'pay to play' politics which has reduced some liberals and conservatives and politics in general down to the level of prostitution

(l) deregulation of banks, derivatives, shares, hedge funds, and commodities which led to the crash in 2008 and previous crashes and the loss of millions of jobs and homes in Europe, Asia and North America and trillions of dollars lost in GDP, economic growth, productivity and employment

(m) corruption of legal systems, policing and legal processes. Most liberals ignore this and fob off the many victims of this.

(n) the passing of new oppressive laws which are anti Constitutional and anti human rights and anti privacy in order to fight a terrorism which is being created by failed government policies, regime changes, an out of control military industrial complex and excessive interference in other countries, and an international agenda which is anti human rights and anti justice.

(o) monopolies, oligopolies and restrictive practises which cause vast misallocations of economic resources, excessive prices and costs and misuse of political power

(p) throwing vast amounts of government money at symptoms of problems instead of addressing and resolving the root causes. An willingness to analyse and resolve root causes.

(q) globalisation and automation and their 'race to the bottom' and the accompanying denigration of workers, industrial wastelands and ghetto-isation of societies while enriching the businesses which make donations and other payments to liberals during elections

These are the issues which liberalism tolerates, supports, aids, abets and facilitates and these are the issues which are undermining and destroying liberalism, freedom and democracy, worldwide. Through destroying responsibilities and their related and dependent freedoms, Liberalism is in effect destroying itself. Liberalism with its plurality and excessive tolerance promises a utopia of harmony, tolerance and peace but Liberalism is weak and excessively tolerant and surrenders to religious extremist forces, to criminality and to political and legal corruption and great social injustices, which are destroying freedom, and whose intent is to destroy freedom. These forces (a) – (p) represent a very considerable challenge and threat to Liberalism and to democracy today and into the future.

Liberalism, in its naivety, forgets that the purpose of extremism, in its many forms, is very clear and unambiguous, it is to attack and destroy freedom and liberalism itself, overthrow democratic freedoms and impose forms of oligarchy, dictatorship and subservience. These extremist forms vary from the imposed dictatorship of religious fanatics and fundamentalists to that imposed by criminal gangs to the one imposed by corrupt politicians, bankers, judges, police, and business cartels. Liberalism protects, nurtures and tacitly supports these social ills. This is the Achilles heel of liberalism. Most liberals are ignorant of this fact.

Liberalism's utopia has become a hellish dystopia. This liberal surrender is enforced on whole societies and ,on non liberals by 'Political Correctness' which stifles, (viciously) opposes and attacks free speech, free expression, freedom of belief, all opposing viewpoints to liberalism, law enforcement, law and order, Constitutional rights and protections, tolerance of diversity by all groups, personal responsibilities, group responsibilities, and collective responsibilities and the many freedoms which are dependent on these responsibilities. This political correctness has infected society at many levels - the political system, the legal system, the educational system, the business system, the sociological system imposing a new form of dictatorship which is devoid of rationality, logic, responsibilities, and foresight

This has become further complicated by mass immigration into western countries which is beyond the ability of many countries to absorb. This has placed new social and economic stresses on countries, especially in those countries bankrupted by financial crashes, recession, austerity and bail outs of corporate and banking criminals. These bail outs have led to severe cuts to public services and public infrastructure which has diminished the ability of countries to cater for immigrants, the unemployed, disabled and other vulnerable people within these countries. Liberals dismiss and ignore these stresses and concerns, yet these same liberals hypocritically supported (a) the policies which created and still create bubbles, crashes and bailouts and accompanying harsh austerity policies (b) the regime changes and wars which forced many immigrants to leave their homes in the Middle East, Asia and some parts of Africa. Ironically, these wars instigated by liberals and their neo-con allies have intensified religious extremism and hatred for western countries, and this feeds in to extremism within western countries which threatens liberalism itself. These facts are conveniently forgotten or dismissed by liberals. One sees a Jekyll and Hyde personality among liberals, where their own mistakes, errors and evils are ignored, denied, dismissed while the presumed evils of the critics of liberalism are viciously attacked. The foreign policies, regime changes, and the Neo Liberal policies of liberals have led to the most outrageous human rights abuses, yet these same smug and self contented liberals presume to support a highly diluted version of human rights and fairness dressed up as 'Political Correctness' which respects neither rights or responsibilities. There is a contradiction and hypocrisy here which liberals refuse to acknowledge, and in some cases lack the intellectual capacity to understand.

Expanding on this, liberalism has over several decades become far too tolerant of abusers of the system and of the irresponsible, the criminal, the anti social and degenerates, and of dishonesty, corruption, disrespect, vulgarity and nastiness, of the massive banking and bondholder burdens, the high costs, the fear, the disorder, the chaos, the coercion and oppression that they impose upon societies. It has encouraged and facilitated the very worst, vilest, and basest forms of human behaviour. One sees the results in the form of increased breakdown of families, relationships, friendships, communities, and within individuals, and the increasing prevalence of security everywhere to protect people from the ever rising consequences of social breakdown. These social costs are enormous and growing every year and contributing to the financial bankruptcy and ethical and moral bankruptcy of countries. This extends into many areas of life, and to all classes of society, undermining, damaging and poisoning all it touches. All of it has emerged from lack of responsibility and the presence of mass irresponsibility, and failure to recognise that freedom comes with responsibilities attached. Responsibilities are neglected, ignored, despised and hated by liberals, who wrongly believe that responsibilities represent a loss of freedom or a regression backwards. While opposing responsibilities for certain social groups and for liberals, liberalism imposes severe limitations and draconian restrictions in the form of political correctness on all forms of dissent and opposition, and it misuses laws, police, courts and politicians to ruthlessly impose this political correctness on people. At the same time, this political correctness gives the forces of extremism, of crime and of corruption plenty of rights, latitude and liberties to do as they please. Political correctness directly attacks and undermines responsibilities.

This is now the case in Nordic countries, Germany, France, and other European countries, and to an increasing degree in North America. The attacks in Paris in 2015 and 2017, in Nice in 2016, in Belgium in 2016, in Germany in the New Year period of 2015-2016, and Christmas period of 2016, the attacks in the USA since 2001, the attack in Madrid in 2004, the attacks in Britain in May 2017 and 2005, and many aborted attacks in Britain since 2005, the attacks in Sweden in 2016 and 2017. The results are very apparent, one sees acts of terrorism, riots, high and rising crime rates, stabbings, cover ups of crimes (by certain groups), the gagging and censoring of police, rapes and increasing sexual crimes against women, increasing hate crimes, corruption and cover ups of these despicable crimes, no go areas in many towns and cities, ghetto-isation and worsening tribalistic divisions, racist chants during marches and other forms of expression, intolerance and hatred of democracies and their freedoms, and political cowardice, all encouraged by this liberalism and political correctness.

Legal systems have been brought into disrepute in all developed countries, especially liberal countries. While the root causes of crime are ignored and dismissed. This undermines and destroys justice, and represents a considerable threat to freedom, rights and democracy in our modern world. This has led to higher crime rates in several countries and states dominated by liberals and liberalism. One sees a liberal hell, which ironically is becoming too hellish even for smug liberals in their cosy, exclusive estates.

Liberalism seeks to resolve problems by ignoring them and ignoring causality, and by building false solutions based on superficial analysis, false and weak willed concessions, compromises borne of childish naivety and a need to be liked, and surrender-focussed consensus which do nothing to address and resolve underlying causes, and destroys both responsibilities and freedom. Liberals ignore causality, ignore root causes, as they believe them to be too inconvenient, too difficult, too complex, too divisive, and too time consuming to use and apply. Liberal (and centrist) presidents, prime ministers, ministers, and leaders have been stifled by trying to achieve false consensus and false concessions and these have created economic and social disasters, which are becoming more and more difficult to untangle and resolve over time. Furthermore, liberals have an inability to think, plan and act strategically and holistically, particularly at the strategic systems level, and they tend to prefer unrepresentative subsets, parts, subsections which are not representative of the whole. To worsen these errors and defects, Liberalism then throws money at problems without trying to understand them and analysing the deficiencies of liberalism itself, and without remedying underlying causes and structures of causation, and without addressing the core issue of responsibilities. Vast amounts of money, resources, time, and skills are wasted while the problems remain and worsen over time.

Liberals, despite their many defects and failings, tend to be self righteous and condescending and fail to self reflect, they do not condemn and stop the political corruption and bribery, social injustices, economic dislocations, 'regime changes' and wars that liberals engage in, but use lies, deception, disinformation, political correctness, and threats to stifle and silence opposing voices and those demanding truth. They fob off, ignore, disregard, mock, belittle, disrespect and pay no heed to important issues and criticisms and the concerns of ordinary people and communities. Liberals are often seen as 'elites' or part of an 'elite establishment' which dismisses, ignores, neglects and denigrates the ordinary people. The errors and flaws of liberalism are denied and covered up. This has created great anger and frustration with liberals worldwide and is a major factor behind the rise in populism of the right and the left.

Globalism and Globalists

This established itself in the early 1980's with the advent of Globalisation, and is commonly called 'Liberal Globalism' and their supporters termed 'Liberal Globalists', though it has the support of conservatives, neo cons, centrists, liberals and some leftists, and these have implemented it to varying degrees in their respective countries. Some of the strongest and most vocal supporters of Globalism are conservatives, the most vicious being the neo cons with their dystopian visions of the world and of the future. Indeed, Globalism shares many characteristics with liberalism, the neo cons and neo liberal economics. Globalism is a naive and infantile belief that globalisation will solve all the world's problems and that one can ignore and dismiss problems at national level, get rid of national sovereignty, ignore and dismiss national culture and traditions, open up one's borders and societies to all ideologies including religious extremists, terrorists and their terror networks, create wars and regime changes around the world, create international speculative bubbles and crashes and expect ordinary taxpayers and people to bail out the banks and speculators. And also pursue a globalised 'race to the bottom', and totally ignore the defects and errors in the economic and political ideologies which underpin globalism. These are the core values of globalism, and as we shall see, they have proven to be disastrous.

Globalists have globalised the problems and defects of liberalism, the neo cons and the extreme variants of Neo Liberal economics, and this has supported and encouraged the following :

➢ the very worst aspects of globalisation's and automation's 'race to the bottom' which destroyed many jobs, and the livelihoods of millions of ordinary people, families and communities in developed countries. This trend is projected to worsen as globalisation and it's constant cost cutting and outsourcing, automation and AI combine together to keep reducing the need for workers while increasing the (tax free) returns to capital and to big banks, Wall street and London.

➢ the so called 'regime changes' and wars created or instigated by globalists, including liberals and neo cons in the early part of the 21ˢᵗ century and the accompanying refugee crisis which led to the immigration crisis and the incapacity of many countries to absorb this sudden high level of migration. This capacity was further reduced by the financial crash, recessions, debt and austerity also imposed by liberals, no cons and centrists. A globalisation of regime changes, wars, emigration and refugee crises primarily benefitting liberal globalists while destroying the lives of millions of innocent people.

➢ the mass migration issues and terrorism and criminality supported by liberals above

➢ globalists (liberals and right wing extremists) also deregulated banks, shares, derivatives, hedge funds and commodities, and created and propped up globalised speculative bubbles, crashes, bailouts and austerity. In particular, the enforcement of Neo Liberal economic policies, including the repeal of important legislation such as the Glass Steagal act and Futures and Commodities regulations under President Clinton and his "advisors and maintained under President Bush which exposed the USA to dangerous levels of speculation. The globalisation of Neo Liberalism and it's defects and flaws including banking crashes.

➢ socially destructive speculative bubbles and crashes, followed by bail outs of banks, bondholders and the rich and the enforcement of harsh austerity policies on ordinary people and families and essential public services which were fully supported by liberals, centrists, and conservatives. A globalisation of financial and banking fraud, and accompanying speculative bubbles and crashes.

➢ the disgraceful cover ups of financial crimes and non punishment of these criminals on a national scale and international scale. A globalisation of cover ups of financial crimes and white collar crime.

➢ the cover ups of serious crimes by government employees, police, prosecutors, powerful business people and religious institutions. The state's ability to cover up crimes is considerable, and pits the individual against the corrupt state. A globalisation of corruption destroying democratic freedoms and rights.

➢ an unacceptably high level of violent crime and theft, and the failure to prevent recurring crime and resolve the root causes of crime. The overcrowded prisons, hospitals and court schedules and the globalisation of crime. Liberal judges, prosecutors, police, academics and politicians have played a major role in the worsening of this. On a global level this liberalism has poisoned many nations and created unacceptable levels of disorder.

➢ the mass tax evasion and use of offshore tax havens which is destroying developed countries and states, and enforcing newer levels of austerity, poverty and hardship, and cutbacks and under-investment in public services. A globalisation of tax evasion and criminality.

➢ the 'pay to play' system of corruption and lobbying where lobbyists pay money to politicians or their foundations or their offshore tax evasion accounts in order to get government contracts and other favours. This has corrupted governments, politicians, law making and legal systems, enriched many liberals, and in effect globalised political corruption

➢ excessive federalisation of powers at an international level at the expense of national sovereignty. The diminishing of national sovereignty, the power of the people, the people as sovereign, national constitutions, and national culture and identity.

➢ the failed healthcare systems and the continuing power of monopolies and oligopolies to manipulate and control healthcare prices, rip off customers, and severely limit or deny access to basic healthcare. And the accompanying worsening of the health of peoples through bad diets, too little exercise, and the poisoning of food, water and air for profit and the unwillingness to invest strategically in healthy living, illness prevention and advanced hospitals, diagnostics and healthcare systems by individuals, organisations and the government. Responsibility for this exists on many levels.

➤ the intensification of the factors which led to high concentrations of wealth and income and to ghetto-isation, social prejudices, racial tensions, and great social injustices. A globalisation of poverty, misery and social injustices.

This is what globalists support, this is their agenda, this is the result of their policies. This is what has hijacked liberalism in recent years. Globalism at its heart is all about enriching the politicians, their cronies and the already rich, while their own peoples and nations are ignored, dismissed and left to suffer. It's about self enrichment, self serving and self importance while sacrificing the public interest. This is the real legacy of many ex leaders of governments in North America and Europe over the last 25 years. Their 'New Word Disorder'. Yet, they have tried to deny what was already obvious to many people. Globalists in this politically correct mode undermine and destroy their own traditional values, demolishing justice, freedom, rights, dignity, responsibility and transparency on many levels, and yet many of them are oblivious to these facts. The destructive effects are felt at the national level, the local level, the community level, and concentrated among the underclass, the working class and the abandoned middle class. This has created a serious ongoing conflict between globalists and nationalists, between liberals and populists, and between federalists and sovereignty supporters, and at a deeper level between honesty, integrity, trust, justice, stability and freedom on one side and corruption, selfishness, greed, oligarchy, instability, injustices, smugness and indifference on the other side. From the rise of President Trump in the USA to the increasing rise of nationalist movements and left wing and right wing populism in Europe and Asia, we are seeing a rejection of liberal globalism and centrism in many countries. This trend is projected to continue.

Libertarianism

Ironically, some libertarians live in a childish fantasy where responsibilities are presumed not to exist, and this provides the mechanism for the failure of libertarianism. All Libertarians should read two books 'Leviathan' by Hobbes and 'A Peoples History of the United States' by Howard Zinn to understand why humans need order, honest and accountable government, laws, regulations, morality, ethics and principles. For example, the natural outcome of variants of libertarianism would be excessive concentrations of wealth and income, vicious oligarchies (often mistaken as democracies), a 'law of the jungle' where skewed markets, globalisation, the 'race to the bottom', mass de-industrialisation in combination with labour replacing automation would worsen existing inequalities and benefit the rich and powerful, creating a regression backwards to Hobbesian savagery and Victorian times of the 19th century with great social inequalities and social injustices. It would according to Hobbes be a "a war of all against all". There would be widespread bigotry, racism and discrimination (in the name of 'freedom'), an equilibrium of misery, poverty and limitation with suppressed / depressed aggregate demand, and unregulated markets producing speculative manias and crashes, which would not represent freedom, and would require brutal private repression, military repression or some form of state repression in order to exist. Thus real freedom would be destroyed in the name of a type of 'freedom' which is not freedom, and is neither free or responsible. There can be no freedom without responsibility. The 'Dark ages' were the high point or pinnacle of libertarian ideology when excessive greed, selfishness, social injustices and savagery ruled Europe and much of the world. The defects, flaws and failures of supposedly "free" markets, Neo Liberal and Neo Classical economics are discussed in depth in Chapter 4 of this book.

Monetarism

Monetarism is closely allied to libertarianism and Neo Liberal economics and Neo Classical Economics. Indeed the same criticisms of Libertarianism also apply to Monetarism and Neo Liberalism. Monetarism has many defects, errors and weaknesses. Economics itself does not exist in a vacuum or black box, and the money supply does not move on its own, as it requires direction and use. The direction and uses of the money supply can take many forms pushing money growth in many possible directions, including wrong ones such as the creation of market failures, intensification of dynamic disequilibrium (see Chapter 4), huge speculative booms with massive accumulations of debt (money printed out of nothing) and crashes and accompanying deflation, large scale unsustainable debt, recessions and austerity, and to various types of inflation or deflation. Milton Friedman and his disciples have ignored this important point. Let us look briefly at inflation and deflation. Both inflation and deflation can cause severe political and social instability, and one has only to look at the rise of extreme political ideologies in the 1930' to see the consequences of this. The monetarist view of inflation is quite simplistic and of no real value in policy formation. There is a build up of inflation over time as the total accumulation of inflation over many years which imposes a continuing and permanent higher cost of living. Over time these high price levels become engrained and disconnected from productivity levels, real competitive prices and real conditions in markets, and it is monopoly capital, big businesses and banks themselves which play a major part in imposing these high costs and prices. Consider the following:

(i) increasing the money supply does not always lead to inflation as narrowly understood by monetarists. The best example of this was the Quantitative Easing which created $15 trillion in new money after the crash of 2008 (up to 2017), yet inflation remained very low and in many cases there was deflation. This fact contradicts and discredits monetarist and their monetarist theories. Though there was inflation in financial assets, bonds, property, and derivatives caused by over speculation but this type of inflation and its disastrous economic consequences is always ignored by monetarists. The velocity of money either stagnated or went down as banks and speculators engaged in speculation in assets and did not diffuse this money to the wider economy for consumption and related investment. Monetarism ignores money creation and associated asset price inflation and the high economic costs, business costs and social costs of this.

(ii) Monetarists fail to differentiate between money supply growth and credit which goes to the speculative sector and that which goes to the productive sector. This is a major failing of monetarism. The work, research and empirical findings on these aspects of money supply growth and credit by Dr. Richard Werner of Southampton University should be read by Monetarists, Neo Liberals and other right wing economists.

(iii) while too much debt based on new money creation (out of nothing) chasing a very limited supply of goods, services, financial assets, derivatives can lead to inflation, this in the case of actual physical goods and services is also dependent on the rate of production, capacity utilisation and expansion, investment in production and capacity expansion, supply and productivity. The key question is - is this new money and debt being used to speculate in financial assets, property and derivatives **OR** to invest in production, innovation, productivity and increasing supply ? The former draws vast amounts of money away from production and supply creating deficiencies in production, productivity and capacity. If combined with rising demand this deficiency in production supply can lead to significant inflation. Yet, Monetarism favours, encourages and supports speculation and its dynamic disequilibrium, and presumes it to be self-resolving, but unfortunately it causes a reduction in productive investment and productivity, and causes asset price inflation, economic bubbles and crashes, severe recessions and long depressions. Monetarism through its defective understandings actually promotes economic failure.

(iv) reinforcing the point above further, monetarists fail to differentiate between new money debt which is created for consumption, for long term productive investment, for production focussed productivity, for fiscal expansion and recovery during recessions / depressions (1933-1936 in the USA is a good example), for human capital and productivity on one side AND that which is created for pure speculation in asset prices. They lump all debt together, everything together into broad monetary aggregates. They see graphs, charts and aggregates but fail to deconstruct and differentiate.

(v) interest rates which impose additional costs on producers, factories, extractors, farmers, distributors, storage costs, sellers, and consumers of products and services. This causes significant inflation and inflationary pressures over time. High levels of debt also impose additional costs and increase inflationary pressures. Monetarists consider these factors to be unimportant and ignore them. I would advise all Monetarists to read Michael Montagne's analysis at http://www.perfecteconomy.com

(vi) money is created out of nothing by banks and interest is charged on it, yet the money to pay off the interest is not created thus putting additional pressure on the system to pay it off or print more money. This puts pressure on the system to print more money and create more and more debt. Compound interest and excessive (speculative and economic rent caused) debt tends to increase costs and inflationary pressures while also sucking money out of the economy creating much economic instability. This fact is ignored by monetarists. I would advise all Monetarists to read Michael Montagne's analysis at http://www.perfecteconomy.com

(vii) fractional reserve of 1-10% for checking accounts or current accounts. In the case of savings accounts, time deposit accounts, CD's, mutual funds, money markets, and shadow banking a fractional reserve of zero. Several big developed countries have no reserve requirements. The continuous parasitic costs of fractional reserve lending and the parasitic profits in the region of 40% and the debasement of the currency are ignored by monetarists. Indeed some monetarists and neo liberals support this in the name of "freedom".

(viii) inbuilt factors in the economy which keep prices high and maintain upward pressure on prices – monopolies, oligopolies, cartels, restrictive practises, land owners, economic renters, patent holders, political patronage of industries, state protected private companies, etc. Monetarists ignore this.

(ix) monetarists do not realise that supposedly free markets are not free and are actually skewed markets and are subject to Dynamic Disequilibrium. Monetarists do not understand Dynamic Disequilibrium. See Chapter 4.

(x) the godfather of Monetarism, Milton Friedman famously claimed that there are no "free lunches" in economics. Speculation provides 'free lunches' in the form of price rigging, fraud, insider trading, massive debt and leverage, financial crimes and capital gains to the rich. And banks printing money out of nothing and charging interest on it is the ultimate "free lunch". Milton Friedman was wrong, the rich elites and banks get plenty of free lunches. This is discussed in Chapters 4, 5 and 7.

(xi) this same man, Milton Friedman won prizes for research into movements in monetary aggregates but failed to expose that this money and accompanying interest was created out of nothing and was termed "debt" and could be used for productive, speculative, consumption or bailout purposes and this use determined the course of economic activity and related indicators. The fact that speculative use has dominated was ignored by him and his disciples.

(xii) monetarists condemn and oppose regulation of the banks and financial industry, yet they forget the financial crashes and depressions which have resulted from deregulation and 'soft touch' regulation or no regulation. Monetarists are in many cases personally insulated from the effects of these crises.

(xiii) rising energy or commodity prices resulting from actual scarcity or price rigging / false scarcity or speculation. Ironically, monetarism and neo liberalism strongly support these activities and their destructive effects on economies, naively and childishly believing them to be "free market".

(xiv) price rises and cost of living pressures on wages. These can cause wages to rise. Monetarists ignore these price rises and cost of living pressures, while they condemn the worker's plea for wage rises.

(xv) fiscal policies and monetary policies which can worsen inflation or impose severe recession and deflation, as a result of failing to address the underlying factors, mentioned here.

(xvi) sharp divisions between Capital and Labour which encourage industrial strife, where Capital tries to extract more from Labour in the form of higher prices, higher debt, higher rents and lower wages, and Labour tries to extract from Capital in the form of higher wages and lower prices. In inflationary periods, this stimulates higher prices and higher wages, and a wage-price inflationary spiral, often resulting in stagflation. In deflationary periods it feeds higher unemployment, lost sales and business closures. In effect, a lose-lose situation for everybody.

Since new money is created out of nothing in the debt creation process, both money and debt are intimately tied together ; this is the debt-money creation cycle. The direction of the debt-money creation is very important, for example is it fuelling speculation in assets and derivatives, government spending, monopoly / oligopoly price rises, restrictive practise price rises, salary and wage rises, excess consumer credit, etc ? Is the direction increasing inflationary pressure or reducing them or moderating them ? Indeed debt and money creation for speculation and consumption at the expense of more productive investment, productivity growth, cost control, competitive competition and innovation which could improve supply and capacity can only lead to inflation of assets, commodities, derivatives, goods, services, and/or wages, depending on what the debt and speculation is used for or directed at. This creates significant disequilibrium, a dynamic disequilibrium which will be discussed later. Friedman's narrow view of mere increases in the money supply completely ignored the factors above, and did not explain the structure and direction which is imposed upon the money supply.

Commodity, currency and energy price shocks worsen the inflationary debt-money cycle mentioned above. The inability to dynamically adapt to this disequilibrium is the key factor. Losses in production, productivity, competitiveness, falling demand and falling sales revenues for businesses, higher unemployment, rising prices feeds into itself and produces the type of stagflation witnessed in the 1970's. Monetarism failed to resolve this through producing deflation, depression, increased businesses bankruptcies and closures, deindustrialisation, outsourcing, and higher unemployment, and high levels of enforced poverty. Keynesianism also failed to cope with this.

The monetarist's preference for deflation, austerity policies, debt deflation and liquidations, depression and high unemployment shows that the Monetarist version of equilibrium is an equilibrium of limitation, misery, and poverty with suppressed / depressed aggregate demand. A perverse equilibrium more suited to Victorian conditions in the 19th century. Monetarists have also forgotten the fact that economics depends on stable political structures, stable social structures based on the exercise of social responsibilities which rely on low concentrations of wealth and income, sustainable debt, high levels of employment or full employment, regulation of banking, money creation and financial trading to curb excessive speculation and fraud, and the maintenance of trust and cooperation between individuals in order to exist. To the extent that monetarism or disordered economics destroys these factors of order and stability, it encourages instability, chaos and disorder, and thus it undermines its own effectiveness, practical application and its validity and credibility. Only a fool would presume to attain optimal outcomes from a narrow erroneous type of economics which promises optimisation while creating and perpetuating the very economic and social disorders and market failures which makes optimisation impossible. Certainly, Friedman and his disciples should have studied the inner causes and dynamics of market failures and dynamic disequilibrium, and how their ideology has promoted speculative booms and crashes and accompanying austerity, depression, poverty, injustices, etc. These defects and flaws in monetarism and its version of 'free markets' are detailed in Chapter 4 of this book. Importantly, monetarism and its defects has paved the path to tyranny, fascism, communism, war, concentration camps and gulags, all of which flow naturally from their own uncontrolled and unstable economics which they believed and still believe to be "free" or "freedom". Monetarists fail to comprehend the basic concepts first expressed in Hobbes' 'Leviathan' of a false freedom consisting of a 'war of all against all' which is pure monetarism and neo liberalism, and further critiqued by Locke, the French and American philosophers in the context of the need for protection of rights and freedoms through the enforcement of social responsibilities.

The facts of history, including failures in Europe, North America and South America, show that Monetarist economics produced the opposite of freedom and encouraged all manner of tyranny, dictatorships, injustices, slavery and instability under the false guise of "freedom". To further illustrate this point and the subject of freedom and democracy, I would strongly advise all monetarists and neo liberals to read Viktor Frankl's 'Man's Search for Meaning' and the works of the economist John Perkins [10]. Frankl's book relates his experiences in the concentration camps in World War 2 and how the war and these camps provided a stark example to the world of what happens to politics, economics and countries when there are no responsibilities attached to freedom, and no responsibilities attached to economics, including social responsibilities. Monetarist and neo liberal economists may be free to delude themselves in failed theories which fail spectacularly, but should they be free to enslave others ?

Neo Liberal Economics and Neo Classical Economics and Hayek's Ideas

Firstly let us examine the failures and defects of Neo Liberal economics, Neo Classical economics and Free Market Economics. Many of the defects in Monetarism also apply to Neo Liberal economics. We will begin by looking at the facts and the evidence :

• Neo Liberal economics dominates economics and the western world today but it is not new. It was very dominant in the 19th century, the Victorian age, especially during the Irish Famine of 1845 – 1849, where 2 million Irish people starved to death and died of related diseases due to Neo Liberal economic ideas which deprived them of the means to buy food and then shipped millions of tonnes of food out of Ireland to other countries. The British government did nothing as they felt it might interfere with the free market. Reports from the time showed that some right wing British politicians, advisors, and intellectuals were pleased with the high death rate and emigration rate. This has been interpreted by many people as genocide. Neo Liberal economics has led to the same outcomes in other countries in the developing world and third world. Neo Liberalism if it is pursued vigorously can lead to genocide.

• Neo Liberal economics led to massive bubbles and crashes, and very costly taxpayer and consumer bailouts, costing trillions of dollars. The financial crash of 2008 led to the direct loss of $5 trillion in the

USA, the loss of 9 million jobs and 6 million evictions from family homes. There were similar massive losses in other countries worldwide, including Ireland, Britain, Spain, Cyprus, Greece, etc.. Globally 34 million lost their jobs and $26 trillion was wiped off the value of shares. The global cost of bailing out the banks and financial institutions between 2007 and 2014 was $13 trillion (Andrew Haldane, Bank of England estimate) and $15 trillion by 2017.

• Between 1970 and 2010 there has been 145 banking crashes, 204 monetary collapses and 76 sovereign debt crises, totalling 425 systemic crises in that period according to the IMF. This includes the severe financial crash and crisis in Thailand in 1997, Russia in 1998, Brazil in 1999, the dot com crash in the USA and Europe in 2000, Argentina in 1998-2002, and Mexico in 1994. The 2008 banking crash is one of many such crashes, which will continue to occur as reforms have not been implemented. At present, the speculative derivatives market is worth $1,200 trillion (World Gold Council, December 2013) more than 20 times the world economy and shares in the USA are highly over priced relative to earnings in early 2017. This is primed to crash again and again, and when the shares, bonds and derivatives markets crash it will be systemic and devastating due to the globalisation of speculation and accompanying debt.

• the cost to the American economy of the financial crash in 2008 and accompanying deep recession in terms of lost output, gdp, productivity, bail outs, higher unemployment, lost revenues and earnings has been estimated at $24 trillion (Dr. William K. Black). Are these massive losses evidence of a system which is broken, a failed system with failed economic ideologies and policies based on Neo Liberal and Neo Classical economics ?

• build ups of large unsustainable government debt from (i) bailing out bankers, speculators and fraudsters after the last crash in 2008 (ii) banking and monetary fraud which causes excessive debt (iii) many regressive government policies to fuel previous booms and then fuel bailouts of bankers, speculators and fraudsters every time ; this leads to significant debt accumulation over time (iv) 'pork barrel politics' which provides subsidies, grants, (over priced) contracts, (under priced) state and natural assets, and government funds to special interests, big banks, speculators and corporations. And the large, unsustainable private sector debts in the form of bank debt, financial speculation debt, mortgage debt and debt accumulated through political corruption. This in turn is leading to government / national bankruptcies, inability to raise money on the bond markets, government austerity policies, vulture funds enforcing home evictions, high personal bankruptcies and business bankruptcies. A system which is financially bankrupt and morally bankrupt, and will remain so.

- destructive government austerity policies to bail out bankers, fraudsters and speculators led to higher national debts and enforced debt repayments or deficit reduction imposed by extra taxes, extra levies and charges, pay cuts, deep cutbacks in essential public services costing trillions of dollars in bailout monies and lost economic growth, GDP, and productivity. The cost of financial system crashes similar to that in 2008 in terms of bailout costs, austerity, recession, lost output and lost GNP is estimated to be hundreds of billions of dollars for large countries like the USA, Britain, France, Spain, Italy, etc. and tens of billions of dollars for small countries such as Ireland, Belgium, Portugal, Latvia, etc. This adds up to trillions of dollars over several years and decades, massive losses to economies. For example, it is estimated that Britain lost £5 trillion in lost output and GNP from the 2008 crash and other developed countries suffered similar proportionate losses in output and GNP (Reinhart and Rogoff 2010, 2014, Will Hutton 2010, Summers and Fatas 2015, Ball 2014, Blanchard, Cerutti, and Summers 2015)

- government bail outs of bankers, speculators and fraudsters is based on the 'Greater Fool Theory' where the sucker or fool is left holding worthless assets or funding bankrupt businesses. After 2008, this fool was the central banks and taxpayers. These bail outs cost $15 trillion globally, and included Quantitative Easing and other forms of liquidity injections into banks and big corporates. This emerged from the failures of markets, and Neo Liberal and Neo Classical economics.

- banking fraud and money fraud, investment fraud, interest rate rigging and currency rigging, insider trading, fraudulent investment offerings, false investment ratings, Ponzi schemes and financial system crimes costing trillions of dollars. A system which robbed, defrauded and destroyed the lives of many millions of pensioners, investors, employees and ordinary people worldwide, Yet guilty bankers, speculators and fraudsters have not been prosecuted and jailed for these serious crimes. Many of these criminals have corrupt political protection.

- a corrupted banking system which prioritises speculative investments in assets, property and derivatives and boom-bust cycles, while underfunding, ignoring and neglecting productive capital investment, long term productive investment, entrepreneurs and public infrastructure investment. And corrupts the political system to achieve this.

- continued de-industrialisation and outsourcing of millions of jobs to cheap developing and third world countries. And the importation of cheaper migrants to replace native workers and graduates. In the USA, 70,000 businesses have moved abroad or closed since 2001 as a direct result of globalisation. In 2016, some 90 million Americans are unemployed or under-employed, scraping a bare existence with part time jobs, minimum wages and zero hour contracts. While American ghettos were suffering over 50% unemployment during this time. This globalisation has been combined with new automation and labour replacing technologies, and this is leading to growing levels of unemployment, underemployment and reductions in real wages in developed countries. Vast areas of cities and industrial & rural regions in developed countries have become ghettos and industrial wastelands mired in poverty, crime, desolation and hopelessness.

- in the USA, oligarchy has enabled the richest 1% of the population to accumulate 40% of the wealth [15], the richest 1% own more wealth than the bottom 90% [16]. The wealth of 1/2 of 1% of the United States population roughly equals that of the lower 90%. The bottom 80% has 7% of the wealth [17]. 75% of US wealth is owned by 10% of the US population according to studies by Dr. Jospeh Blasi. The richest 1% take 25% of national income [15]. More details of this wealth concentration is provided below and in Chapter 5.

- oligarchy mixed with political corruption in developed countries and developing countries, including the 'pay to play' system where large amounts of money are paid directly and indirectly to politicians for access to them and use of them. This has imposed massive debt and other costs on nations which has impoverished and enslaved whole peoples. Globally, this system of corruption has produced mass poverty and starvation, high levels of unemployment and under-employment in a world of plenty, affecting approximately 3 billion people [11] and destroyed freedoms and democratic rights and disempowered the people of many nations, and facilitated many types of crimes and conflicts [10]. The works of the famous economist John Perkins have provided deep insights into this [10]

- large scale tax evasion through the use of offshore tax havens and tax loopholes in laws, costing trillions of dollars per year and over $32 trillion in total (studies listed in later chapters) accompanied by cutbacks in essential public services, crumbling public infrastructure, underfunded schools and Universities, under resourced police forces, underfunded and overcrowded hospitals, larger and larger ghettos, and high levels of crime, social divisions and racism. Sadly, it has enforced savage cutbacks in health systems forcing millions of people to wait overly long periods in trolleys in corridors in hospitals and wait long periods for basic medical treatment or no treatment in many cases.

- has made many millions of people homeless worldwide after the 2008 crash and after previous crashes. Continues to make housing a basic need, over priced and out of reach for many people and families. Forced many people into extremely high, unsustainable debt to buy basic housing, leaving them vulnerable to eviction, especially after speculative crashes.

- high levels of corruption in all areas of life, including political corruption, legal system corruption, corruption of courts, police corruption, public service corruption, banking corruption, sports corruption and religious corruption, and no proper checks and balances and no oversight to prevent this and safeguard the public. This leads to denial of freedoms and excessive coercion of the people. A corrupt oligarchy bordering on fascism.

- Continuing environmental destruction and the poisoning of water, food, air and land by businesses and organisations. And the rise in many diseases and chronic illnesses from this increased toxicity accompanied by the over burdened health systems and rising cost of healthcare in most countries.

- degeneration of culture, entertainment, sports and the arts. In many ways art reflects the human condition at a point in time and its social outlook, its aspirations and hopes, its politics, economics, current affairs, spiritualities, theologies, philosophies and social relations. Modern art has become crass, meaningless, and vulgar, and neither inspires or uplifts. And we have over glorified role models in society who are vile, vulgar, brainless, superficial and shallow and have a poisoning effect on the youth. This has become dominant, widespread and pervasive, a dictatorship of poor mediocrity.

- the net effects of monopoly capital, monopolistic and oligopolistic prices, cartel prices, unfair trade, speculative prices, and high concentrations of wealth and income which impose false scarcity, high prices and high costs of living, and high levels of constrained, unrealised, unmet demand or deficiencies of effective demand on countries and peoples. Reducing consumption, demand, growth and employment and limiting opportunities and freedoms.

- Neo Liberal Economics based wars for resources and strategic economic advantages and military advantages, similar to the wars of Empires in past centuries. The vast military industrial complexes have become over reliant on the continuing incitement of hatreds, conflicts, race riots, terrorism and wars, and this has become highly profitable for them. There is a strong incentive to continue and intensify these conflicts. These conflicts have widened out to encompass western countries, and produced terrorism, extremism, new fears and hatreds. And this has been accompanied by western government attacks on democratic rights and Constitutional rights, the coercion of many innocent people, and the emergence of Big Brother and police states, surveillance states and various hybrids of concentration camps, even in developed western (supposedly civilised) countries.

- The many defects in Neo Liberal and Neo Classical economics are analysed in depth in Chapter 4

Some call this freedom, this is not freedom, and it is certainly not democracy. It is the opposite of freedom. It is oligarchy, dictatorship by elites, and feudalism, and it is legitimised theft, fraud and criminality, and in many cases tyranny. These are very real failures in our modern world, and these failures impact all of us in one way or another. They extract monies and private property from us, the ordinary people, they restrict and destroy our freedoms and our liberties, they coerce us, they greatly restrict public (state) resources and the distribution of such, they kill our children in wars, they deprive us of rights and due process under law, they corrupt our political and legal processes and inflict great damage on the masses, and diminish the quality of life factors and social capital which makes life worthwhile. The failures of this neo liberal economics and it's subservient politics will be discussed in some depth throughout this book.

Hayeks' ideology suffers the same defects and flaws as those of Neo Liberal and Neo Classical economics, mentioned above. And there is considerable overflow between these ideologies and Hayek's ideology. Though Neo Liberals and Neo Classical economists have generally supported corporate welfare and subsidies and the massive funding of the Deep State and Shadow Government programmes in big countries amounting to trillions of dollars per year, while at the same time pretending to be supporters of 'small government'. Hayekians are divided over this hypocrisy. Hayek in his book 'Road to Serfdom' condemned the centralisation of power and economic resources in communist societies and socialist societies, and their inefficiencies, but his own economic theories has achieved similar economic and political outcomes, including a high concentration of wealth and income and an oligarchy with centralized government where politicians and governments are controlled and manipulated by a centralized power structure - powerful corporate and banking interests. And vast state resources and private resources used to enrich the rich and maintain the oligarchies, and their absolute control over the people.

Hayek's system of oligarchy has in practice and would consist of corporate command economies, where workers are alienated, treated like slaves with no input, no benefits, no ownership, no rights, no respect, no dignity, and reduced down to the level of serfs. Hayek's ideal world is a 'law of the jungle' where skewed markets, globalisation, the 'race to the bottom', mass de-industrialisation in combination with labour replacing automation would worsen existing inequalities and benefit the rich and powerful, creating a regression backwards to Hobbesian savagery and Victorian times of the 19th century with great social inequalities and social injustices. Ironically, Hayek's world would share many similarities with the communist world with political power and wealth highly centralized, and most of the people reduced down to serfdom.

A world where corporates are free to poison rivers, the land, the air, the food for more profit, and charge exorbitant interest rates, and create all kinds of fraudulent investment products to cheat, rob, and rip off people. And of course, ignore the health effects of such poisoning of people, ignore the illnesses and diseases emerging from it, while and making hospitals and health insurance too expensive for everyone so that profits can be maximized for monopolies, oligopolies, restrictive practices and cartels. This is the true morality, ethics and 'freedom' of such right wing ideologies. Hayek presumed to write about freedom and liberty, yet there are many contradictions and inconsistencies in his arguments. Hayek and his modern day followers could learn much about how Hayekian-style economic imperialism destroys the sovereignty of nations, enforces oligarchy, coercion and tyranny, and undermines the democratic rights and freedoms of peoples by reading the works of Perkins [10]. The very people involved in destroying democracy and freedom in these countries were strong followers of Hayek and his right wing ideologies, and most were fascists. And they enforced centralised power structures, oligarchy and feudalism in their countries.

Essentially, Hayek could not comprehend that freedom requires responsibilities, including social responsibilities in order for the many parts of freedom and society to work together and for political democracy to exist. There is a need for social capital, cooperation, trust and a cohesion of responsibilities to preserve freedom and make it palatable to all. Like monetarists and libertarians, Hayekian believers fail to comprehend the basic concepts first expressed in Hobbes' 'Leviathan' of a false freedom consisting of a 'war of all against all' which may appear to be free but is not. Hayek's' version of 'spontaneous order' was well described by Hobbes as being 'nasty, brutish and short'. Hobbes' book was further refined by Locke, the French and American philosophers and Kant in the context of protection of rights through enforcement of responsibilities, and the need for institutions, customs, laws, oversight bodies, regulations and social capital to do this. These contributions were opposed by Hayek. Hayek and his followers should read the works of De Tocqueville where he provided a critical analysis of American democracy in the early 19th century, exposing the social and political problems caused by excessive greed, selfishness, materialism, social irresponsibility, high inequalities, intolerance, racism and the crimes, losses, coercion, and social disorders which resulted. For example, the free market in slaves led to civil war in the USA.

Certainly, Hayek and his disciples should have studied the inner causes and dynamics of market failures and dynamic disequilibrium, and how their ideology has promoted speculative booms and crashes and accompanying austerity, depression, poverty and market failures. And how in many cases throughout history these failures paved the path to tyranny, fascism, communism, war, concentration camps and gulags, all of which flowed naturally from a vicious, uncontrolled and unstable economics which they believed and still believe to be "free" or "freedom". These failures are outlined in Chapter 4 of this book.

Fundamentally, Hayek was ignorant about serfdom despite writing about it and importantly he was ignorant about oligarchy from which serfdom originated and continues to originate from. Oligarchy as supported by Hayek has existed for many centuries from the feudal Dark Ages to the harsh Victorian age of the 19th century, and imposed its own skewed markets (not free markets), dynamic disequilibrium, slavery, misery, and destruction of inherent freedom and democratic rights. The same 'equilibrium of misery, poverty and limitation with suppressed / depressed aggregate demand mentioned in sections above. This is more closely analysed in Chapter 4 and Chapter 5.

Keynesianism

Keynesianism is often cited as protective of freedoms and of economic and political stability, and has been used by mostly liberal, social democratic, and left leaning governments and in some cases conservative governments since the end of World War 2. Keynesianism offers many benefits and many innate protections of democracy and freedom, and facilitates the use and exercise of responsibilities for this purpose. Keynes was correct in his analysis concerning the 19th century and the Depression of the 1930's, as so called 'economic equilibrium' was likely to settle far below equilibrium conditions or optimal conditions in societies where the allocation of resources were skewed by high concentrations of wealth and income, oligarchy, high levels of constrained, unrealised, unmet demand and supply, and also by large accumulations of debt which led to debt deflation. The narrow view which 19th century economics had of labour as a commodity neglected the fact that labour is a consumer who spends money on goods, services and commodities and this consumption creates economic growth, sales, profits, capital returns, labour returns, and the growth of capital, and by imposing artificial limitations and restrictions on labour it imposes severe negative effects on demand, economic growth and economic potential or 'equilibrium'.

These perverse Victorian economic conditions had their own very narrow and limiting laws of supply and demand and types of dynamic disequilibrium from which misery, poverty and limitation were self reinforcing. One could term it an 'equilibrium of misery, poverty and limitation with suppressed / depressed aggregate demand, from which Walras and others could derive mathematical models of dubious justification. This perversity tended to reinforce itself over time leading to overly long depressionary times and after slow 'recovery' led to a grim repetition of the same below equilibrium conditions and misallocation of resources distorted by high inequalities etc. and the same economic limitation, reduced demand, instability and tendency towards crashes again and again.

Keynesianism was useful and effective during the 1930's and for a few decades after world war 2 when reconstruction and economic stimulus were necessary. It rebuilt countries and whole continents through its stimulation of aggregate demand and aggregate supply, greatly increasing the capital stock and productive capacity of developed countries, and also building up human capital in the form of higher education, skills, new technologies, research and development and productivity enhancement, creating new middle classes who were vital to sustained economic growth and to democracy. It greatly reduced both constrained, unrealised, unmet demand (or effective demand) and constrained, unrealised, unmet supply within nations. It also stabilised currency fluctuations, exchange rates, and encouraged international trade which were vital to economic growth. Yet over time, serious defects and weaknesses emerged in Keynesian economics including

- Excessive leakages out of developed countries in Europe and North America which have de-industrialised as a result of Globalisation. Deindustrialisation has destroyed the industrial and productive base and the regenerative power of Keynesian spending. These leakages come in the form of increased imports, stagnant or falling real wages in the developed world and increased real wages of workers in developing and third world countries, increased exports of jobs and factories to cheaper developing countries, higher national debt and interest payments and worsening balance of payment deficits and capital account deficits in the country implementing Keynesian policies.
- The excessive build up of debt over many years from increased government borrowing and expenditure. The means to reduce this debt over time becomes impaired as a result of stagnant or falling real incomes and increased leakages out of the economy from Globalisation. The sheer weight of high national debt and servicing costs can enforce government cutbacks and fiscal contraction even during a recession / depression when a fiscal stimulus is desperately needed. This is worsened by government adding private banking debt to the national debt, and this was certainly proven true in the period 2008-2015. Some countries are so over-burdened with both national debt and private (family and businesses) debt that they just cannot engage in Keynesian policies. The writings of Richard Koo [4] and others provide deep insights into this.
- As pointed out by Krugman [19] developing countries and third world countries are prevented from engaging in stimulatory Keynesian policies after crashes and during recessions / depressions by the IMF, World Bank, and Washington as they fear frightening off foreign investors and capital, and these same

financial bodies are brainwashed by failed Neo Liberal thinking. Yet the austerity, fiscal and monetary contraction, deepening recession and continuing (speculative) debt overhang which is imposed by the IMF, World bank and others does even more damage to these economies and their reputations, depresses economic growth and future growth trajectories, and provides a worse proposition to international investors. Ironically, under the watchful gaze of austerity hawks, the same mistakes were made inside the EU after the crash of 2008

• Inbuilt inflationary pressures. There is a build up of inflation over time as the total accumulation of inflation over many years and accompanying increase in general price levels and cost of living. Over time these become engrained and also disconnected from productivity levels, real competitive prices and real conditions in markets. These inflationary pressures are discussed in sections above.

Since new money is created out of nothing in the debt creation process, both money and debt are intimately tied together ; this is the debt-money creation cycle. The direction of the debt-money creation is very important, for example is it fuelling speculation in assets and derivatives, government spending, monopoly / oligopoly price rises, restrictive practise price rises, salary and wage rises, excess consumer credit, etc. ? Is the direction increasing inflationary pressure or reducing them or moderating them ? Indeed debt and money creation for speculation and consumption at the expense of more productive investment, productivity growth, cost control, competitive competition and innovation which could improve supply and capacity can lead to inflation of assets, commodities, derivatives, goods, services, and/or wages, depending on what the debt and speculation is used for or directed at. This creates significant disequilibrium, a dynamic disequilibrium which will be discussed later.

Commodity, currency and energy price shocks worsened the inflationary debt-money cycle mentioned above. Monopoly and oligopoly capital, restrictive practises and economic rents will increase the upward pressure on prices. The inability to dynamically adapt to this disequilibrium is the key factor. Losses in production, productivity, competitiveness, falling demand and falling sales revenues for businesses, higher unemployment, rising prices feeds into itself and produces the type of stagflation witnessed in the 1970's. Keynesianism failed to cope with this. Monetarism also failed through producing deflation, depression, increased businesses bankruptcies and closures and higher unemployment, and high levels of enforced poverty.

• During recessions / depressions Keynesian economics cannot resolve the continued persistence of bad debts or toxic assets and deflated assets from the previous crash. Borrowers are unlikely to borrow money to purchase toxic assets or assets which are likely to decrease in value due to deflation. Deleveraging of individual, family, business and government debt also feeds this deflation or recession. This slows down the debt creation process and money creation process, producing a longer recession /

depression, or slower recovery. The writings of Richard Koo [4] and others provide deep insights into this problem. Bankers will be reluctant to lend money for the purposes of acquiring toxic assets or lend money to businesses / individuals which are already highly indebted or have defaulted on some debts or suffered a decrease in their credit ratings. Though there are exceptions to this, such as where governments bail out toxic assets and put them on sale to vulture funds. Banks will lend to such vulture funds.

• Keynesian bailouts may not be as stimulatory as presumed as some banks have a tendency to hold on to central bank loans and / or government bailout money and use it to write off some toxic assets and bad debts or use the money to improve their balance sheets through acquisitions of other businesses which have been weakened by the recession. They don't pass on the loans to businesses and individuals. This happened in Japan in the 1990's when the central banks pumped money into banks for the purpose of increasing liquidity and loans to businesses. See Richard Koo[4]

• Keynesians neglect the dynamic disequilibrium caused by banks creating new money and interest out of nothing to fuel both speculative manias and consumption and related productive investment. The interest money is not created when the loan is created and thus it has to be sucked out of an unstable economic system and this creates inherent deflationary effects and further instability.

• Excessive government involvement in the economy which creates inefficiencies and high costs. These in turn increase the costs for businesses and consumers. It can also crowd out more productive and efficient private investment. Many of the criticisms of Liberalism above apply here.

• Widespread beliefs about the state of the economy and its future prospects. If this is negative, or austerity driven, then consumers will hoard extra cash, investors will shift investment into safe instruments such as gold, silver and rare commodities and / or into savings in secure banks. In a globalised world economy this cannot be remedied by a national government.

The above factors were all worsened by the new type of Globalisation, speculation, automation and mass tax evasion which emerged in the mid 1980's and is still with us. Increased leakages out of a national economy in a globalised world combined with high costs and massive national debt levels and deficits ultimately reduced the effectiveness of Keynesian fiscal and monetary stimulus, and the stimulant effect of each dollar / euro spent by government. Interestingly, the new economics being enforced on nations by Globalisation today is bringing us all back to pre Keynesian times, and this is most visible in the debt deflation and depression and accompanying austerity policies which occurred after the financial crash of 2008.

Socialism & Marxism

Alternative solutions on the left fail on the same grounds, and again this relates to the excessive centralisation of power and wealth and the denial of this to most of the population, the ordinary people. Socialism and its diluted variants in western democracies fails for the same reasons as Liberalism mentioned above. Observe the Marxists and Communists dreaming of their socialist utopias and loudly spouting maxims and doctrines in public, while doing nothing to relieve the grinding injustices, crimes, homelessness, poverty and suffering all around them in the present. Day dreaming and wishing for socialist utopias in the future while ignoring the very real suffering, crimes, and injustices in the present day means a continuation of this indefinitely. This day dreaming and endless talking of distant utopias is one of the chief failures of Marxism. Despite these failings, one still sees great arrogance and naivety among some Marxists. Does Marxism exercise responsibility ? Does Marxism match freedom to its responsibilities ? Marxism as practised in the old USSR, China, North Korea and other places, and defined by Lenin as the 'dictatorship of the proletariat' presumes to offer freedom while giving all rights and privileges to the state and it's centralised bureaucracy, and depriving the people of their rights and freedoms. Marxism undermines, blocks and destroys freedom, let us examine the facts and evidence.

- the human rights abuses, the false imprisonments, the gulags, the torture of prisoners, the summary executions, the killing of prisoners for their organs which are then trafficked, the mass killings during the reign of terror and the purges in the Soviet Union where millions of people were murdered. It is estimated that Communism murdered 100 million people in the 20th century.
- censorship of the press and media. No freedom of the press
- no freedom of speech and freedom of assembly
- a police state which was Orwell's '1984' world with Big Brother.
- no checks and balances to state power, and no due process. The dictator and his cronies had the right to harass, to frame, to imprison and murder anyone they did not like. And make it appear legal and justified.
- no freedom of religion and spirituality. Religious and spiritual persecution. False imprisonments
- no incentives for individual initiative, motivation and drive to improve oneself and to achieve in life
- the covering up of state crimes and corruption of legal systems and politics
- It tolerated racism and pogroms against certain races. Some races were put into gulags.
- the corruption of Communist / Socialist leaders, commissars, generals, KGB heads, and members of the nomenklatura who live lavish lifestyles. A type of 'state capitalism' where the profits or surplus

value is enjoyed by top state officials and their cronies while the ordinary people have little or nothing.

- the use of the same money and banking system as capitalists where money and interest is created out of nothing by state banks and most people are reduced down to debt slavery

It was a nightmare world of Big Brother and '1984' where peoples, rights, freedoms and dignity were crushed by an oppressive state. This is certainly not freedom. The book 'Gulag Archipelago' and other works by Aleksandr Solzhenitsyn give one an idea of the failures of Communism and State Socialism. These works should be compulsory reading in all schools and Universities in all countries.

There was a lot of evidence provided by a Dr. Anthony Sutton in the USA that powerful American banking and corporate interests funded, supplied and invested in Communism in the USSR, Korea, Vietnam and other places. This was used as a means to profit from funding their industrial development and war machines, and also to fund the war machines of communism, fascism, and capitalism during wars and during the cold war. His three books 'Western Technology and Soviet Economic Development' provide evidence of this profiteering by some big corporate and banks, and his other books and writings corroborate this [30]

The chief failure and weakness of Marxism and it's hybrids and variants is the excessive centralisation of power, a type of federalism where the centre dominates and rules, and the complete absence of checks and balances and of oversight. The importance of checks and balances and multiple forms of oversight and accountability arises because all power corrupts to a degree, while absolute power corrupts absolutely. The greatest guarantee of democratic freedom and rights lies in the ability of political, economic and legal systems to use multiple checks and balances, to oversee, to monitor, to audit, to be self critical, to be made accountable, to take actions and remove the corrupt, and to self correct over time without fear, favour or prejudice. Corruption whether in the Marxist form or the extreme right wing form will exist and thrive as these systems lack the necessary checks and balances and means for oversight and self correction.

Marx's theory of surplus value was never distributed to the workers who created the value, it was appropriated (or expropriated) by the state under false pretences and firstly given to the commissars, generals, government bureaucrats and their cronies to live comfortable, often extravagant lives. The workers lived a bare subsistence on what was left over. And again here we see the results of excessive centralisation of power. Human dignity and freedom are undermined, while the individual is reduced down to being a tool of the state, an abstract, disposable item. Marxism destroys individual initiative, motivation and desire for self improvement and advancement, and destroys personal innovation and technical innovation. Firms operating within Marxism may have the superficial appearance of being 'worker controlled firms' or have aspirations to being such, but one always finds the overwhelming power of the commissars, the party officials, the party and its agents, the Nomenklatura, and the state's interests in such firms. This makes economic democracy impossible, partly because it makes political democracy impossible. These firms are forced to live under political Marxism which severely restricts freedom in a political, social and economic sense. Lenin's dictum of one party rule and the 'dictatorship of the proletariat' is quite clear, it involves dictatorship in its political form and economic form. This is not freedom. The failure of Marxist economics and its hybrids and variants to accurately predict and calculate many diverse quantities and needs, many changing preferences and utilities, and constantly changing environmental conditions, and match demand to supply and match supply to demand, in addition to its inability to motivate and incentivise workers and managers led to large scale mismatches, with high numbers of consumers regularly forced to queue for long periods for basic necessities. And in many cases they went without their desired goods and services as significant levels of constrained, unrealised, unmet demand and constrained, unrealised, unmet supply predominated in the economy. This was exemplified by significant over capacity and under capacity in several sectors of the economy. Sufficient levels and optimal levels of supply and demand could not be attained. The end result was poorly performing economies operating well below capacity, chronic shortages, economic stagnation, national bankruptcy, and industrial stagnation accompanied by a lack of inventiveness, technological innovation and process innovation and the inability to adapt dynamically to dynamic disequilibrium in the real world. Centralised bureaucratic structures will always fail in a world where widespread decentralised local decision making combined with very limited (or restricted) centralised decision making is necessary to match diverse needs and quantities in a dynamically changing environment.

Many modern Marxists are excessively tolerant of religious extremism and of crime in democracies worldwide, and have become very similar to liberals. And again, there is this misguided belief in a far off socialist utopia, where all Marxists and all others will live in happiness and peace, though they forget that the religious extremists, political extremists and criminal gangs have the opposite aims and objectives to Marxists. This is misguided tolerance borne of excessive naivety by Marxists.

National Security State

Since 2001, we in the developed world and most of the developing world are now living in the Big Brother society described in the book '1984'. Wikileaks, Edward Snowden, Julian Assange, Chelsea Manning, and other whistleblowers have shown the world a significant portion of this Big Brother surveillance society. The passing of laws such as the Patriot Acts and the National Defence Authorisation Act in the USA and similar laws in other countries and the continuous erosion of judicial oversight and Habeas Corpus rights and human rights provides more proof of this. While continuous war in the form of hot wars, civil wars, 'regime changes' and terrorism have become a constant, just as in the book '1984'. Furthermore, the instigators of this continuous war are intimately tied to the military industrial complex and national security state, some refer to this as the 'Deep State' or 'Shadow Government'. One sees close parallels between the Big Brother controllers in '1984' and today's 'Shadow Government' and it's national security state. It is true to say that we now live in a Big Brother society, a '1984' world. This type of national security state is a relatively new introduction in western developed countries. It has been facilitated by new communications technologies, miniaturisation and imaging technologies and most importantly by a 'Deep State' and 'Shadow Government' which is continuous in nature and can command trillions of dollars in tax monies, much of it unaudited and unaccounted for. In today's world access to money, resources, funding is the key factor, the determining factor for any organisation or set of policies, and if this is unlimited and unaccountable, then one finds abuses of power, outrageous abuses in many cases.

While national security for nations and peoples is necessary and a social good, and is required in an uncertain and unstable world, it needs to be administered in a more careful, measured and holistic manner. The current form is Orwellian in nature and has a Big Brother which is at war with the people including law abiding people, not protecting them. There has been an over emphasis on security, surveillance both legal and illegal of all persons (innocent and guilty), and in restricting democratic rights, undermining Constitutional rights, which risk destroying freedom and democracy under the false premise of protecting freedom. False in the sense that the national security state does not look at the bigger picture and does not analyse the root causes of the threats and resolve them, including the social injustices, inequalities, imperialism, pillaging of resources, environmental destruction, deep divisions and festering hatreds, the corruption and 'pay to play' system in developed countries, the incitement of extremism, regime change, conflicts, mistrust which create the disharmony which ultimately leads to national security issues and threats. In many cases the promoters of the national security state are the very people promoting, funding and supporting the social injustices, inequalities, imperialism, pillaging of resources, extremism, regime changes, conflicts, etc. for their own profit, material advantage and power.

Central to this is corruption, bribery and the 'pay to play' system where politicians and governments can be corrupted by special interests which profit from war and terror, rogue states, terror supporters and criminals, and this has severely corrupted and undermined the major democracies. This creates a self perpetuating dynamic over time which controls presidents, prime ministers, parliaments, senates, and congresses, holding them in servitude to corrupt paymasters. President Eisenhower warned of the growth and power of vast military-industrial complexes and national security state and today they are all powerful and overly dependent on wars, conflicts and fossil fuels, and on perpetuating them for profit and gain, and this has created an environment which has become very insecure for many people worldwide. This has directly led to a world dominated by Big Brother and the environment of '1984' and this is likely to continue as the military industrial complex or national security state creates more and more conflict for profit while implementing greater restrictions on freedom and destroying Constitutional and human rights and democracy in the process. The manipulated continuous war state requires continuous national security, accompanied by continuous attack against basic rights and freedoms. Yet, the war mongers, the corrupted politicians, the people inciting injustices, regime changes, extremism, terrorism, conflicts, etc. for profit and power are never put under surveillance, arrested, prosecuted and jailed. Why is that ? By not addressing root causes and taking responsibility, the national security state chases shadows, and has become entrapped in shadows and effects, endlessly trying to find the wrong solutions in even more surveillance, more security and more destruction of democratic and Constitutional rights and freedoms. In doing so it destroys the freedoms and democracies it is allegedly trying to protect. This national security state is not subject to oversight, and to checks and balances, and has actively undermined any which previously existed.

State Capitalism

Forms of state capitalism where (i) the state owns and controls all firms (Marxism and its hybrids and variants) (ii) the state owns some firms in strategic economic sectors while controlling the number of private firms dominant in other sectors and controlling and using sovereign wealth funds to increase the state's profits and for strategic political gains (China in the 21st century, Singapore, Norway) (iii) vast military industrial complexes, national security complexes, and other industries which rely on state contracts. These all restrict freedom and democracy to varying degrees. They prevent the development of free enterprise and the accompanying development of independent thought, freedom of expression and pluralism. In many cases they involve a Big Brother and '1984' type environment to enforce compliance and silence opposition or a gradual march to this type of totalitarianism.

Fascism

This failed ideology emerged in the mid 1920's and was initially based on combining nationalism with dictatorship and right wing ideals to achieve nationalistic aims. It merged dictators with big industry and big banks to create a right wing totalitarian state which would force the people to serve their interests. Thus it appealed to those with nationalistic sentiments, racists, religious extremists, business owners and right wingers. It involved a very narrow, intolerant and misguided form of nationalism which appealed to naive, gullible and childish people who looked for 'father figures' , but ironically it became anti-nationalist once in power, as it attacked the people of the nation and their rights, it repressed the people, it turned the people of the nation against each other, and involved the nation in unnecessary wars and in all cases brought ruin to the nation. Fascism is the antithesis of freedom and democracy, and of all human virtues. Let us examine the facts and evidence:

- the human rights abuses, the false imprisonments, the concentration camps, the torture of prisoners, the summary executions, the mass killings of millions of civilians during the second world war and the mass killings of civilians by dictators in Latin America and Asia. It is estimated that Fascism lead to the murders of 60 million people in the 20th century.
- censorship of the press and media. No freedom of the press
- no freedom of speech and freedom of assembly
- a police state which was Orwell's '1984' world with Big Brother
- no checks and balances to state power, and no due process. The dictator and his cronies had the right to harass, to frame, to imprison and murder anyone they did not like. And make it appear legal and justified.
- limited freedom of religion and spirituality. Religious and spiritual leaders who spoke out against the dictator or fascism were imprisoned or executed
- perversion of incentives for individual initiative, motivation and drive to improve oneself and to achieve in life towards oppressing others, attacking others and limiting the basic freedoms of others
- the covering up of state crimes and corruption of legal systems and politics
- it promoted the worst forms of racism and in some cases genocides

- Hitler's Nazis and Tojo's Japan were an example of Fascism at it's worst
- the corruption of fascist leaders, generals, and members of the governing class who live lavish lifestyles. A type of 'state capitalism' where the profits or surplus value is enjoyed by top state officials and corporate business leaders, while the ordinary people have little or nothing.
- the use of the same money and banking system as capitalists where money and interest is created out of nothing by private banks and most people are reduced down to debt slavery

It was a nightmare world of Big Brother and '1984' where peoples, rights, freedoms and dignity were crushed by an oppressive state. Some variants of it emerged in South America, Asia and Africa in the latter half of the 20th century up to more recent times, and produced the same predictable results. This evil and failed political system had the support and backing of wealthy elites in developed democratic countries and of some religious leaders of the Christian churches.

There was a lot of evidence provided by a Dr. Anthony Sutton in the USA that powerful American banking and corporate interests funded, supplied and invested in Hitler and Fascism in nazi Germany and also funded Communism in the USSR, Korea, Vietnam and other places. This was used as a means to profit from funding their industrial development and war machines, and also to fund the war machines of communism, fascism, and capitalism during wars and during the cold war. His three books 'Western Technology and Soviet Economic Development' provide evidence of this profiteering by some big corporate and banks, and his other books and writings corroborate this [30]

Fascism ignores economic and social problems and causality and seeks to impose dictatorship and brutality to suppress these problems. Yet suppression does not solve the problem and does not solve causality. This suppression along with the defects and contradictions within fascism creates many more problems and contradictions, which ultimately challenges and overthrows fascism. Fascism remains a significant threat to freedom and democracy today, as one sees the ever increasing power of the state, particularly the national security state or Deep State and the negative economic and social effects of uncontrolled and disordered globalisation, which unfortunately veers towards fascism.

Religious Fundamentalism

For many centuries religious fundamentalists have promised peoples a utopia, a 'heaven on earth' if they submitted to their religious dictatorship. Religion, especially religious leadership and structures are like many ideologies and are subject to many human weaknesses, human naivety, frailty, gullibility, corruption, manipulation, self importance, hypocrisy, crimes, greed and ego. The end results have been a 'hell on earth' with oppression, tyrannical dictatorship, religious wars, the mass murder of hundreds of millions of people, torture, genocide, inquisitions, witch hunts, gulags, reigns of terror, the physical and sexual abuse of women and children, and human rights abuses. And in the modern day terrorism combined with war and genocides. The end result of religious fundamentalism in power throughout history and in modern times is and always will be a hell on earth. It can exist as (a) religious extremism and fundamentalism dominating a country and it's government or (b) exist within democratic countries as covert groups operating within democracies and subverting them. Its overt form is one of dictatorship, denial of human rights, state brutality, genocide, wars, and terrorism at home and abroad. It's covert form hides within democracies, and remains hidden and insidious and involves the use of stealth, corruption, the 'pay to play' system of bribery, secrecy, sleeper cells, misdirection, cover ups of crimes by religious institutions and leaders, strategic business and economic cooperation, and political manipulation and the cynical use of demographics and population growth to gain voter power, as a means to acquire political power within countries. It works within democracies to ultimately destroy democracy and impose religious laws and religious dictatorship. It's extremist leaders are protected and never condemned, excommunicated, boycotted or banned from churches and communities.

The primary targets of religious fundamentalists are women, children and the weak and vulnerable who can be easily targeted and subjected to abuses, injustices and terror. Yet, the larger aim is to take over countries and to control peoples. It is often aided and abetted and facilitated by liberals and lefties / socialists within democracies who foolishly and naively believe that religious extremists should be given their rights and the right to do as they please, including the right to challenge, plot against, overthrow and abolish democracies and democratic freedoms. These liberals and lefties are the modern day 'Quislings'. Unfortunately, some politicians, civil servants, police and prosecutors in western democracies are weak, egotistical, selfish and greedy and can be intimidated or bought. This is a very significant threat to democracy and freedom.

Technocracy

The domination of the Internet and cyber technologies in combination with major advances in Artificial Intelligence (AI) and microchip technologies may lead to new forms of tyranny and fascism which could destroy freedom and democracy globally. There is a strong push for microchipping people in order to speed up commercial transactions and provide secure authentication of such. This proposed system is a very great danger to democracy. It would lead to:

(i) excessive centralisation of power and control by big government and / or big corporates

(ii) serious restrictions of an individual's freedom. The chip could be used to economically exclude a person, socially exclude a person and possibly even kill a person. It is wide open to abuses.

(iii) data breaches and invasions of privacy

(iv) illegal surveillance and breaches of one's Constitutional rights and human rights

History is full of examples of rulers using technology to control, to manipulate and to oppress peoples and this is still true today and will be true into the future. Technocracy has the potential to include the worst aspects of Fascism, Communism and Religious Fundamentalism, and it needs to be handled with great care so that it does not undermine, corrupt, distort or overthrow democracy.

Monopolistic & Dictatorship Capitalism which serves the richest 1% - 5%   VS Democratic Capitalism which serves 100% of the people

Capitalism can take may shapes and forms, todays' world is dominated by Neo Liberal Economics also termed 'Monopolistic & Dictatorship Capitalism', which serves the richest 1% - 5%, and this is being imposed by the US and UK on the rest of the world, and it represents a very serious threat to democracy and freedom. This is discussed in more detail in Chapters 4, 5 and 6. This book proposes Democratic Capitalism which is the opposite of Monopolistic & Dictatorship Capitalism. Democratic Capitalism serves 100% of the people and is explained, detailed, analysed and proposed in Section 2 of this book.

The Migrant Crisis

This has presented serious challenges to several ideologies, including the left wing, right wing, libertarians, populists, liberals, globalists, etc.. it has also set ideologies against each other. Migration cuts across many ideologies. For example, Sweden a peaceful country, endured 257 bombings in 2019 and 167 bombings in 2018 and its gun crime rate has risen tenfold since 2009 and this has been linked to the policy of open borders. Research figures and statistics and news reports show that bombings, terrorist attacks, killings, rapes, drugs trafficking, paedophilia and child abuse, child trafficking and human trafficking and other crimes have risen substantially since 2005 in several EU countries and North America and provided ample evidence of this threat. The level of migration into a country is an issue best dealt with by individual countries in their own individual ways. Countries will naturally differ from each other in this. While accepting in refugees fleeing oppression and death is a basic humanitarian responsibility of a country, one has to weigh it against the threat posed by terrorists and criminals who can pose as false refugees. The evidence shows that law and order and national security must be the primary consideration in migration policies and border policies. Individual countries must take responsibility for their own borders and their own national security and not allow foreign federalist structures dictate to them.

Summation

In summation, Freedom and Democracy faces some very serious threats, some obvious and others less obvious which are actively trying to destroy them. In many cases, these threats are using freedom and democracy to destroy freedom and democracy, in a manner similar to the way Hitler used democracy to undermine and destroy it in the 1930's. And the way Lenin used perceptions of democracy and democratic control in the period 1919 to 1923 to create a centralised communistic dictatorship, which Stalin fully exploited later. Democracy is seen as a means to an end, the end being the demolition of democracy from within and the imposition of centralised control (or federalism), dictatorship, slavery and oppression.

One must remember that these threats to freedom and democracy are in many cases using democracy itself to achieve their extremist objectives. This is extremely important. It is very apparent here that the greatest weakness of democracy and freedom is the lack of responsibility existent in it, and the lack of responsibility within their supporters. For, ultimately freedom without responsibility cannot exist, as freedom must be defended, and this defending of freedom requires a strong commitment to responsibility and courage which means facing down, challenging, overturning, and defeating the threats to freedom and democracy. Central to this defence is eternal vigilance which includes checks and balances and oversight, the very essence of responsibility which is worth repeating again:

'The importance of checks and balances and multiple forms of oversight and accountability arises because all power corrupts to a degree, while absolute power corrupts absolutely. The greatest guarantee of democratic freedom and rights lies in the ability of political, economic and legal systems to use multiple checks and balances, to oversee, to monitor, to audit, to be self critical, to be made accountable, to take actions and remove the corrupt, and to self correct over time without fear, favour or prejudice.'

Common Fallacies

One of the greatest fallacies or delusions of the modern age is the promotion of a very narrow version of "self reliance" which totally ignores reality and the bigger picture. This will also be examined throughout this book. One cannot have "self reliance" in an economy controlled by:

- very high concentrations of wealth and income which severely limit opportunities and "self reliance" for most of the population of a country. Resources are limited and concentration limits them even more. And the wealthy have a higher propensity to save, to hoard and to hide vast monies in foreign tax havens, thus depriving home economies of higher levels of consumption, aggregate demand and related higher levels of investment, employment and income generation. One encounters the paradox of thrift and the liquidity trap.

- most people are at the mercy of monopoly, oligopoly and cartel capital and land owners and the high prices they impose on societies. There are highly skewed markets and accompanying dynamic disequilibrium which can weaken and bankrupt individuals, and small and medium sized businesses (See Chapter 4).

- banks have the power to create money out of nothing and to allocate this credit where they want. This gives the banks enormous power over businesses, entrepreneurs, individuals, consumers, politicians, and government. Studies show that banks prefer lending to large businesses and to big speculators. Small and medium sized businesses in the production sector find it difficult to access credit at affordable interest rates. Banks have the power to ruin businesses, jobs, careers, families, communities, etc. and one example is the aftermath of financial crashes.

- a world which is interdependent, individuals depend on other individuals and families to buy their products or services, supply them, sell products and services, provide jobs, provide education and skills, provide investment or funding, provide infrastructure, socialise with, provide family environments, etc.. Every person is reliant on others. No individual is an island.

- the world of business and economics has a lot of discrimination based on race, religion, gender, age, unemployment, disability, ethnic group and colour.

- there is no equality of opportunity as studies and research show that children born into poor families and working class families are far more likely to end up in poverty or low paid work due to reduced educational opportunities, family instability, community instability, alcohol and drug abuse by parents and peers, lack of encouragement and motivation during childhood, denigration and lack of self esteem issues, insufficient funding and resources for state schools, tuition and academic advancement, lack of business contacts and lack of political contacts and academic contacts, and class and racial based discrimination and prejudices.

- widespread money creation and debt fraud, and the build up of massive unsustainable debt based on the aforementioned fraud which skews markets and opportunities

- unregulated and uncontrolled speculation which enriches a few wealthy people while creating higher costs, misallocating vast resources (away from production), and posing systemic risks to an economy

- mass theft from taxpayers, home owners and small investors to bail out banks, speculators, and fraudsters who have strong political connections. Unjust property, debt and mortgage laws which are the result of lobbying by fraudsters designed to rob the people

- bail outs, austerity and deflationary economic policies by governments which destroy economic growth, sales, businesses, jobs, self reliance and the ability of people to meet loan obligations

- political corruption and legal corruption which undermines the validity of laws and the operation of laws, and the power of the individual. No respect for Constitutional rights and human rights
- the poisoning of air, land, food and water by very powerful corporate and banking interests which undermine the health of the people and the nation and their ability to engage in "self reliance".

Human Nature ? What are the responsibilities attached to freedom in today's world ?

'Human nature' is often used as an excuse to justify great social inequalities and social injustices, and hateful social divisions and conflicts, yet human nature is not 'cast in stone', it is not one narrow minded permanent construct, it is an evolving form, very flexible and capable of many possible directions, many combinations and permutations. It is a fact that human nature needs direction, guidance, structure, knowledge and a means to higher consciousnesses, and meaningful purpose. Human nature is based on consciousness, it proceeds from consciousness, it emanates from consciousness, and the lower the consciousness the worse the outcomes and the higher the consciousness the better the outcomes. This book proposes a mass movement to higher consciousness and part of this involves Economic Democracy and Industrial Democracy and Social Justice and the ending of corruption, in addition to other consciousness-driven initiatives and actions. These would enable the fuller development of all individuals, their minds, their hearts, their spirits, and the realisation of one's potential along with the fuller expansion of individual and group consciousness. The measures proposed in this book would greatly support and improve individual opportunities, initiative, ambition, responsibility, motivation, drive and determination, the desire for self improvement and advancement, and for personal innovation and technical innovation over time.

These are good, natural and desirable characteristics which have built successful economies and societies, but this new system would go much further. It would also build greater awareness of the interconnectedness of life, encouraging empathy, responsibility, trust, respect, cooperation, teamwork, moral courage, and tolerance and balance personal ambition with individual, family, community, collective and social responsibilities in order to preserve and protect freedom, social cohesion and democratic structures. It would return power back to the people through very new democratic structures involving all areas of human life, while at the same implementing checks and balances and forms of accountability to ensure that responsibilities match freedoms. The combination of increased economic and social opportunities with increased individual responsibility and collective responsibility would be vital, providing the foundation for extraordinary human progress. At the same time it would greatly diminish insatiable greed, selfishness and unlimited individualism, and excessive concentrations of wealth and income which have been found to be destructive to persons, families, communities, societies and whole economies. It would enable the individual to expand his or her consciousness and sense of being and relationship to others in the world, and to appreciate and to work with democratic collective structures such as teams (work, community, sporting and non sporting), families, friends, colleagues, relationships, communities, community organisations and centres, local government and civic bodies, companies, cooperatives, spiritual organisations, charities and voluntary bodies, and organisations involved in the defence of democracy and freedom, for the good and upliftment of all, and in doing so it would encourage a new social consciousness, social responsibility and a more humane social order on a global scale. It would be a new form of capitalism - Democratic Capitalism.

It would be a fuller and more comprehensive realisation of the Four Freedoms put forward by the great President Franklin Roosevelt in a famous speech in 1941:

> *"In the future days, which we seek to make secure, we look forward to a world founded upon four essential human freedoms.*
>
> *The first is freedom of speech and expression—everywhere in the world.*
>
> *The second is freedom of every person to worship God in his own way—everywhere in the world.*
>
> *The third is freedom from want—which, translated into world terms, means economic understandings which will secure to every nation a healthy peacetime life for its inhabitants—everywhere in the world.*
>
> *The fourth is freedom from fear—which, translated into world terms, means a world-wide reduction of armaments to such a point and in such a thorough fashion that no nation will be in a position to commit an act an act of physical aggression against any neighbour—anywhere in the world.*
>
> *That is no vision of a distant millennium. It is a definite basis for a kind of world attainable in our own time and generation. That kind of world is the very antithesis of the so-called new order of tyranny which the dictators seek to create with the crash of a bomb."*

OURS...to fight for

Freedom of Speech

Freedom of Worship

Freedom from Want

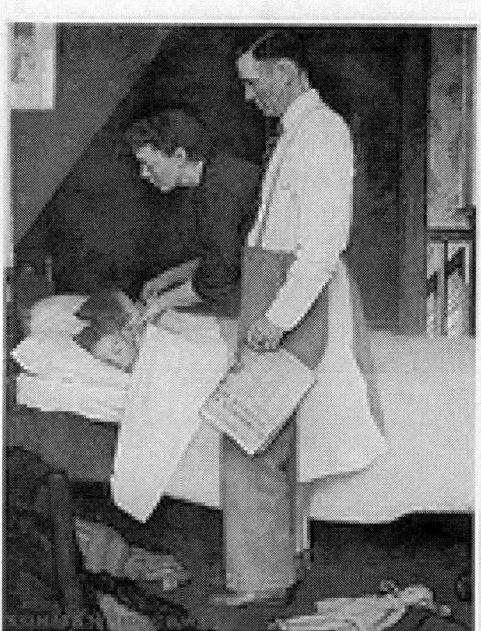

Freedom from Fear

Chapter 2   The Emergence of Brexit and Its Implications

'government of the people, by the people, for the people'

President Abraham Lincoln, The Gettysburg Address, 1863

No discussion of modern freedom, democracy and modern economics can ignore the importance of Brexit. The issue of Brexit and the European Union emerged in 2016 and exposed the very complex interplay between freedom and responsibility (or lack of it), between democracy and national sovereignty on one side and centralised federalist structures on the other side which are similar to imperialist (and also communist) structures in the past, between the corruption, cover ups and the privileges of elites or fairness, accountability and transparency for all persons, between the interests of wealthy countries at the centre of Europe and weaker countries on the periphery of Europe, between controlled immigration or mass immigration and 'open borders', between spending on essential public services and public infrastructure or bailing out bankers, speculators and fraudsters via austerity programmes and the imposition of massive debt on nations, between Quantitative Easing for banks or Quantitative Easing for the people, between globalism and globalisation on one side and the interests and needs of the nation state, between spending money on developing one's nation, businesses and infrastructure or sending that money to a foreign federalist structure for other uses, between the need to protect nations from terrorism or allow terrorism to spread through 'open borders' and 'freedom of movement', between economic stimulation of depressed regions or the continued neglect of such regions, between tax payment for essential public services or massive tax evasion and tax havens, and between peace, cooperation and stability or wars and 'regime changes' and arms spending for profit and the enrichment of elites. These and other forces compete and interplay at European level creating searing tensions which test European unity and cohesion. These are very big battles which will determine the destiny of nations and continents and will need to be examined more closely.

Brexit and related economic developments worldwide have given us all time for reflection, pause and introspection. Looking at Brexit in the cold light of day, it is not a surprising or unexpected development, it is clear that centralisation of power or excessive federalism and imperialism which dominates other countries, and actually takes rights, national sovereignty, monies, natural resources, national identity and culture, dignity and freedoms away from nations has been the cause of break-ups, conflicts and wars in the past. And this will continue to be so into the future. History provides us with many examples from the past, and some very clear guidance on this. Observe the centralisation of power and federalism in empires such as the Soviet Union, the short lived Nazi empire, the British empire, the French Empire, the Ottoman empire, the Austro-Hungarian empire, the Spanish empire etc., all of whom failed. They were all centralised federalist structures. This was old style federalism. These federalist empires were all seen as "normal" and "normality" in their day and they were backed by the state, legal systems, the police, the churches, religions, and the press and media. This federalism was mainly imposed by a combination of violence and fear of violence, and expanded through invasions. The purpose of their invasions and occupations were to acquire land, wealth and other resources and most importantly to exercise power and control over peoples, and to do this by centralising power, by federalising power. In the last Chapter we examined the failures of ideologies such as fascism, colonialism, communism, state capitalism, national security states, hayekism, monetarism, etc. and all of these ideologies shared one thing in common, they led to excessive centralisations of power, to federalism in various forms , to oligarchy, to high concentrations of wealth and accompanying power, to the suppression of human freedom, rights, and national sovereignty. This excessive concentration of power and wealth may be intended or unintended, it may even be accidental, but it is ultimately arrived at under the present human conditioning and mindsets.

Centralisation of power and accompanying imperialism have always provided centralised government structures, federalist structures, comprised of corrupt, unaccountable and power hungry bureaucracies to rule over several countries and peoples, and this has fuelled abuses of power, cronyism, arrogance and superiority, the exploitation and disempowering of peoples, the marginalisation of peoples, the neglect and fobbing off of weaker peoples, the crushing and grinding down of weaker peoples, and the creation of deep resentment, distrust, divisions, rebellion and in many cases wars in the past. It has always been federalist in nature. This system is a strong divider and breaker.

In European terms, for many centuries kings, emperors, and dictators, tried to conquer Europe and establish an empire, a federalised structure with control and power at the centre. This was opposed by nations and peoples and did not work. These empires fell, often by violent means. There is a natural suspicion and distrust in most European nations of federalist structures or centralised power structures based in other countries which have control, power and jurisdiction over many nations. The important point here is that it was not nationalism which caused most conflicts and wars, it was imperialism and colonialism which took powers away from peoples, cultures, and nations, and imposed federalist structures and centralised control which caused so many wars in the past. It was and still is a game for control, power and domination working against the human need for democracy, freedom, sovereignty, decentralisation, accountability, people power, culture and identity. It was and still is the imperialist presumption of superiority and the imperialist suppression of national identity, national culture and national sovereignty and national expression which created reactionary often drastic nationalist movements for freedom. This in turn created simmering tensions and conflicts at the international level and between power blocs and alliances. Today, the evidence shows that Federalism and Globalism are the new imperialism, and share the same characteristics.

Democratic Deficit

The European Union and its present federalist structure, which aims to centralise power and control, needs to be seen in a broader historical context. And there is today, an urgent requirement to examine and analyse the EU in the context of centralised power structures, federalism, imperialism and restrictions to sovereignty and freedom and the historical aspects of this. There is a well known **democratic deficit** in the European Union which is well acknowledged by nearly everybody, including eurocrats and non eurocrats. This democratic deficit is directly linked to the excessive federalisation and centralisation of control and power in Europe. This democratic deficit has been increasing in recent years under the 'European Union' as Europe becomes more federalised, and power shifts from the capitals of European countries to Brussels and Frankfurt. European nations are losing their national sovereignty, their national government, their local governments, their fiscal, monetary and currency rights and freedoms, their trading rights, their law making powers, their immigration powers, their fishing rights, their cultures and traditions, etc.. This is a very serious loss.

The EEC

The EEC was set up in 1958 and was originally a free trading area in Europe designed to regenerate a war torn Europe, improve trade, economic growth, agricultural and industrial productivity, socio-economic prosperity, preserve and enhance democracy and civil rights, and to be a force for constant peace in Europe especially between Germany and France, and act as a counterbalance against communism. The EEC was not a centralised federalist state or structure and did not centralise control and power. <u>This is a very important point.</u> Under the EEC, national sovereignty was preserved and there was little intrusion into national affairs by the EEC institutions for several decades. National freedom, rights and sovereignty flourished and this coincided with a period of great economic growth and expansion in Europe. This period from the late 1950's to the late 1990's proved that national sovereignty and national currencies were compatible with a common market, a customs union and strong economic growth and high levels of employment. By the late 1990's, all this had changed, the EEC had transformed into a more centralised or federalised structure, the European Union. This began with renaming the EEC and calling it the 'European Union' in 1993, under the Maastricht treaty, accompanied by gradual moves to create a common currency, the euro, and transfers of monetary, fiscal and currency powers to the EU centre, accompanied by transfers of law making powers, business regulations, foreign policy powers, presidential powers, territorial boundaries and other powers to the EU centre.

European Union

Federalisation really began in 2002 with the wider establishment of a new European currency, the euro and by 2015, 19 EU states were using this new currency. This new currency transferred many national powers to the ECB and the EU Commission, and together with other changes, including the Nice treaty and Lisbon treaty, an EU Constitution, the creation of an EU President and EU Foreign Minister marked an increasing federalisation and centralisation of EU power. One has to go back to the Roman empire to find a comparable centralised power structure in Europe. This was achieved at a cost of significant loss of national sovereignty and reduction in the economic, political and legal power of individual nations, which reduced national parliaments down to the status of a city council, rubber stamping laws and rules applied from above, namely from Brussels or Frankfurt. Yet this loss of national power was not enough as many eurocrats called and have continued calling for even more federalisation, a Federal Europe which would replace nation states. Many European peoples fought for and worked for national freedom for centuries, and this national freedom was achieved at great personal cost and financial cost by ordinary people, and this forms part of their national and cultural identity, but today they are being asked to reject this national freedom and sacrifice it, and replace it with foreign control – federalism. Yet, the experience of recent years shows clearly that this federalist structure does not serve the best interest of individual nations, particularly those on the periphery. This European Union represents a very significant and worrying departure from the old EEC and it's beliefs. This federalism and 'federalisation' requires much closer inspection and analysis.

EU Federalism and The Democratic Deficit

Federalism has become the new imperialism. Federalism empowers the EU centre by disempowering the periphery, the nation states, especially smaller states. By disempowering nation states it disempowers the ordinary people within these nations. The EU centre now has control of many vital areas which were once controlled by nations. Examples of this EU centre control of EU nations :

1. Control of the fiscal policy of nations by the EU centre. Limitations imposed upon government deficits and borrowing, even in the middle of crashes, economic crisis, the imposition of massive bank bailout costs on a country (by the EU and ECB), recessions and depressions. This includes the 3% deficit limit and 60% debt to GDP limit. After the banking crash of 2008, the ECB, IMF and European Council (the Troika) forced nations to bail out European bankers, speculators, and fraudsters and this increased the national debts of countries, including Ireland, where Debt to GDP went from 25% to 125% after the bail out enforced by this Troika. This pushed debt to unsustainable levels, well beyond the euro deficit and debt limits, and this caused national bankruptcies and sovereign debt crises. Ireland itself paid over 40% of the cost of bailing out European banks, which was very high when one considers how small Ireland is. Similar bail out programmes were enforced on Spain, Portugal and Greece after 2009. In the case of Greece, the country was further bankrupted by more debt than it could bear, which the EU centre and Troika knew was unpayable and unsustainable. The EU centre lent money for these banking, bondholder, speculator and fraudster bailouts to national governments and then enforced harsh austerity policies on nations to meet these debt repayments ; this included tax increases, new taxes, new charges and levies, new charges for use of natural resources and public resources, wage cuts, fiscal contraction, privatisation, asset stripping of individuals, families, businesses and governments, and severe cuts to public services and necessary state investments during a time of severe recession, and depression in some cases. This has had devastating effects on periphery countries, pushing unemployment to over 20% in Spain and Greece, and imposing deflationary and depressionary conditions similar to the 1930's depression, and all of this was carried out to save and protect private European and non European banks and speculators, and in many cases fraudsters and some of whom should have been jailed, but were not. This increased total debt to GDP / income ratios for countries, as more debt was added onto economies and the ability to generate economic growth and income was reduced due to austerity policies in the middle of downturns, recession /

depression. Governments borrowed more to make up for the shortfall in tax revenues, income and funds from austerity policies ; and this vicious cycle continued. Yet throughout this financial crisis the EU centre demanded that these bankrupted countries remain within the deficit limits and debt limits required for euro membership, and demanded more austerity, wage and benefits cuts, public service cuts and economic contraction to achieve this. Furthermore, the EU authorities and German government are allowed to receive and assess the budget proposals of other national governments prior to the budget being presented to a national parliament, and also the EU authorities and Germans have the power to reject these proposals or the entire budget. And punitive measures can be applied by the EU centre to ensure compliance. Democratic elections and referendums and representatives have been ignored by the EU centre, who were only interested in dictating terms to countries. Countries on the periphery were badly affected by this dictating of terms by the centre, in many cases by German politicians and their cronies in Brussels. Does this sound like dictatorship and imperialism ?

Had the Troika specified that the ECB bail out the banks, speculators and fraudsters then there would have been less national debts, no sovereign debt crisis and no austerity policies imposed upon taxpayers. But this was blocked by Germany and austerity hawks on the board of the ECB. In other countries such as the USA, the Federal Reserve bailed out the banks and speculators. The ECB did not follow the established central bank policies of other countries. The EU centre and ECB should have read and heeded the paper 'The Permanent Effects of Fiscal Consolidation' (Fatas et al. 2015) published in Economics journals in 2015 which is a particularly good analysis of the failures and permanent damage of austerity policies in Europe, North America and other countries [9] . The failures of this type of enforced austerity by a foreign federal EU structure are further detailed in Chapter 7 of this book. This idiotic austerity policy had the full support of austerity hawks in the EU centre, all of whom were too frightened, scared and timid to pursue and jail the banking and corporate criminals who created the crash and mess. This was a disgrace.

This vital point here is that enforcement of bail outs and additional national debt, and accompanying austerity policies and limits to deficit spending and debt levels on all Eurozone countries has taken place during a severe recession / depression or 'Balance Sheet Recession', when all EU countries, especially creditors, should be writing down debt, writing it off and restructuring it, the ECB acquiring most banking bad debt, and national governments borrowing, spending and investing more in order to stimulate the entire EU economy and bring about recovery. This is in turn would improve income, GDP, and debt to income ratios and the ability to pay off debt and facilitate the growth of new credit and more sustainable debt. Furthermore, countries and businesses were prevented from taking advantage of zero interest rates, after the crash, due to these artificial limitations imposed by the EU centre. This fixation on enforcing austerity policies while ignoring their negative recessionary and deflationary effects has largely benefitted the EU centre while destroying the EU periphery. This has greatly strained and undermined the relationship between the EU centre and the periphery and fragmented and polarised Europe.

2. The EU centre, particularly the EU Commission and EU parliament, are dominated by international banking interests and it will sacrifice countries on the periphery and EU laws, customs and principles to protect these banking interests. The bailout loans given to Ireland, Greece, Spain and Portugal costing hundreds of billions of euros have been used to bail out big German, French, Dutch, Swiss, American, British banks, bondholders, hedge funds, brokers, developers and speculators, some of the wealthiest people and families in the world. These wealthy speculators lost their bets or speculative investments and expected taxpayers to bail them out. This was a "socialism for the rich" administered by the EU centre. And the EU centre enforced this bail out. Requests by national governments and taxpayers to 'burn bondholders', and get debt write downs and write offs were ignored or dismissed by the EU centre, and in some cases threats and blackmail were used by the EU centre to enforce the bail out. This was exposed in a very enlightening documentary 'State Secrets and Bank Bailouts' in 2013, and is viewable on the Internet.

Why should the Irish, Spanish, Greek and Portuguese working class and poor bail out big French, Dutch, Swiss American, British banks, bondholders, hedge funds, brokers, developers and speculators who are some of the wealthiest people in the world ?

3. Control of the monetary policy and interest rates of nations by the EU centre. This includes monetary policies which worsen (i) the effects of speculative booms and (ii) the destructive effects of crashes and accompanying bailouts, recessions / depressions on individual countries. Periphery countries are worst affected by this. For example low interest rates and easy credit which benefits the EU centre may cause speculative bubbles and excessive borrowing in the periphery countries, while high interest rates which benefits the EU centre may cause excessive reductions in aggregate demand, incomes, increased business closures and high unemployment in periphery countries. The

interest rates set by the EU centre, the ECB in this case, does not reflect actual economic conditions and needs, trading conditions, and risk factors in periphery countries. The interest rates set by the ECB largely benefit Germany, but not all EU countries are Germany. It is impossible for a central bank such as the ECB to set interest rates which are accurate for individual EU countries, especially for periphery countries which vary greatly from EU centre countries.

Research by Dr. Mark Blyth of Brown University in the USA shows that interest rates diverge widely between eurozone countries yet they are forced to have one interest rate and one currency, thus proving that vast differences exist between countries. This enforcement of one artificial interest rate creates great tensions and divergence between the centre and the periphery.

4. Control of the currency and currency printing of nations by the EU centre, and the destruction of competitiveness of peripheral countries, particularly southern EU countries and Ireland. This currency printing is controlled by the ECB not by nation states. National currency is intimately tied to the actual economic conditions within a country, and reflects the real economic status of a country. Merging very different countries into one currency, such as the euro, causes periphery countries to lose their own currency and to lose an important tool for (i) measuring their own economic conditions, keeping sight of their own economic status, needs, and requirements (ii) managing their economies and relative competitiveness and adapting their currency to changes in the national economy and/or international economy. For example, in some periods the euro will be overvalued relative to the economy of the periphery country and in other times it will be undervalued relative to the economy of a periphery country, and in all cases the periphery country has no power to devalue or revalue the euro currency. During the severe recession of 2008 – 2012, the euro was overvalued for depressed periphery countries such as Greece, Italy, Ireland, Portugal, Spain, Estonia, Latvia. This power now rests in a foreign centre, the ECB, largely controlled by stronger countries, such as Germany, with no interest in the periphery countries.

In reality, the euro has enabled Germany to trade successfully with an undervalued currency relative to their economy and helped them build massive trade surpluses while periphery states, such as Greece, Spain, Italy and others, who are at a disadvantage with an overvalued euro relative to their economies. This has caused trade deficits, capital deficits, budget deficits, massive debt, austerity and economic stagnation in these peripheral countries. The euro subsidises German industry while punishing weaker periphery countries. Also, the euro is not resilient for national economies. Downturns in the international economy or national economy cannot be offset by national currency devaluations and revaluations. After crashes, downturns, or during recessions and depressions the euro forces periphery countries to undergo harsh austerity programmes, wage cuts, debt deflation, loss of essential public services, loss of tax revenues, loss of growth, loss of infrastructure investment in order to pay down debt and bank bailout costs and reduce down living standards to compete internationally using this overpriced euro. This creates a horrific form of debt slavery which burdens periphery countries. This creates a great disconnect between the centre and the periphery, making the EU centre an enforcer of austerity, liquidity traps, debt deflation and worsening of recession / depression on the periphery countries. In reality and in practise, periphery countries are reduced down to the level of vassal states, slave states, disempowered servants of the EU centre who are the 2 - 3 strong dominant countries.

5. The euro is deflationary for many EU countries during crisis periods such as downturns and worsens them, while the same euro is inflationary when Germany wishes to inflate its own economy with low interest rates, fuelling increased money creation by banks and easy credit and speculative manias in Germany and other EU countries (not already burdened by excessive debt). In the early 2000's prior to 2008 the EU centre and its euro currency encouraged and supported a massive European speculative bubble based on vast accumulations of debt, which sucked in Ireland, Spain, Portugal and other EU countries. It ended in disaster in 2008. The euro exacerbates divergences between the big EU Centre countries and the peripheral countries, intensifying negative economic aspects, which have the effect of destroying the economies of the peripheral countries.

6. This system is quite similar to the Gold Standard in the past which crucified countries and peoples on 'a cross of gold'. The Nobel Prize winning economist, Joseph Stiglitz has written a devastating critique of the euro in his new book 'The Euro : And its threat to the future of Europe'. He points out these same flaws and defects in the euro which have made it a failure for several EU countries and worsened their economies and growth rates, and he recommends the abandonment of the euro. These flaws in the euro were first predicted by Professor Martin Feldstein of Harvard University in papers he published in the 1990's, prior to the introduction of the euro. Feldstein has been proven right.

The euro is also similar to past policies in Latin American countries and Asian countries which pegged their currencies to the dollar while ignoring actual economic conditions and over speculation in their own economies ; the result was the severe Latin American crisis and Asian crisis of the 1990's.

7. Takes the power of Quantitative Easing away from national governments and gives it to the EU centre, which is the ECB which is largely controlled by Germany and German Interests. The latter are strongly opposed to Quantitative Easing for other countries outside Germany. In the past, many governments had the legal and Constitutional power to print money or create money via electronic credits, and to monetise debt, but this power has been taken away and given to the EU centre, the ECB. This meant that individual nations could not get their own central banks to carry out Quantitative Easing to bail out the European banks and speculators, write down debt for borrowers and provide money for government spending and investment. The ECB forced national governments and taxpayers to bail out these banks and speculators. This had the effect of adding bank debt onto the national debt during a recession / depression and bankrupting some countries. This a considerable loss of power for nations.

8. The euro acts against the economies of many nations and also against the local communities and regions within these nations. During recessions, depressions, economic shocks, outsourcing and globalisation and after crashes, these nations and their local communities and regions are deprived of vital purchasing power, investment, public services, employment, economic growth, and this was worsened when the EU centre enforced bailouts of banks and gamblers, austerity policies, tax increases, public service cutbacks, fiscal and monetary contraction, etc.. This sucked money and purchasing power out of local economies destroying local and regional economies and individual nations. The inflexiblity of the overpriced euro in combination with fiscal and monetary contraction devastated both national economies and local and regional economies durign the 2008 crash. While local currencies would have had the opposite effect and benefitted local communities and regions. One should compare and contrast the euro with the local currencies supported by Dr. Bernard Lietaer.

9. The lost economic growth in the EU after 2008 resulting from the euro and accompanying austerity policies and their deflationary effects and lack of currency flexibility, and fiscal and monetary flexibility is estimated to be trillions of euros. This has proven disastrous for Europe. The comparsion between the US recovery after 2008 and the Eurozone stagnation during this time shows the defects in the euro in this respect.

10. In Chapter 6 Debt Enslavement : Who was Responsible for the Irish, Greek, Spanish, Portuguese and EU wide Financial Crash and Crisis ? the defects in the federalist structure of the EU and its euro and the role of this in the financial crash of 2008 and post crash depression are detailed.

11. Under normal conditions Central Banks bail out bankrupt banks, as they are the lender of last resort and it's their historical duty to do so, but the ECB refused to do this after the 2008 crash. The ECB forced the Irish taxpayers to bail out Irish and European banks and speculators. Little Ireland was forced to pay 42% of the total cost of the whole European banking crisis, at a cost of close to €9,000 per person, according to Eurostat. The Germans and Finns opposed giving the ECB this traditional power, and they forced national governments or taxpayers to be the lenders of last resort to the European banks. This was an extraordinary error and deficiency in the set up of the ECB and euro. The ECB was not a properly constituted and functioning central bank, it behaved like a political bank expounding the failed theories of some German politicians obsessed with protecting banks, gamblers, speculators and fraudsters while blaming and punishing taxpayers. And ignoring inflation in asset prices, share prices, land and property prices and derivatives and related massive debt accumulation while getting into a panic about slight rises in the prices of consumer goods which they call "inflation". This incompetence and incoherence by the ECB encouraged bubbles and crashes, and greatly increased the national debt in Ireland, Spain, Portugal, Belgium, Italy, Cyprus and Greece where governments were forced into bailouts of national and mostly foreign banks, hedge funds, private equity firms, financial institutions and speculators. The ECB failed to fulfil the duties of a central bank and monitor systemic financial risks to the EU economy and national economies, and to bail out bankrupt banks which posed systemic risks to an economy. This was a major failing of the ECB and of the EU authorities, and was highly irresponsible. This was yet another example of domination of EU federalism by Germany. While the EU centre and EU bureaucrats were punishing and stagnating periphery countries with an overvalued euro currency, stringent borrowing and debt limits, and harsh austerity policies and massive new debt, they were also subjecting these periphery countries to the rigours of a globalisation 'race to the bottom' making it more and more attractive for European businesses to locate to China, India, Vietnam and other low cost Eastern countries and to import from these countries. This has proved devastating to periphery countries in Europe.

The euro when it was designed and implemented had no structure and mechanisms for closing down insolvent banks, particularly large banks, and preventing contagion and systemic risk in the

European banking system. There was no coherent structure for clearing insolvent and bankrupted banks out of the system and refunding depositors and overseeing and regulating.

12. There are no automatic transfers between the EU centre and periphery during times of economic crisis and severe recession or depression. In common currency countries such as the USA, the Federal government and Federal Reserve Bank (central bank) bail out banks after a financial crash. In addition, if a state in the USA has a systemic banking crisis or a severe debt or economic crisis, then the Federal government and other states transfer funds to that state to rescue it, bail it out, and help it recover. There are automatic transfers from the centre to the periphery. But, in the EU, the EU centre forces individual countries to bail out banks and to deal with economic crashes and national economic crisis, even when this forces a country into national bankruptcy and a sovereign debt crisis. The ECB refuses to bail out European banks. The EU centre imposes massive debt burdens and harsh austerity policies on a periphery country in the middle of an economic crisis or during severe recession or depression, which worsens it. This has bankrupted countries and greatly increased the national debt levels of countries in the Eurozone, pushing several over the debt and deficit limits for euro membership. By imposing massive debt and austerity in the periphery countries, they diminishes their ability to pay down debt, increase incomes, and recover. The EU centre is an imposer, a punisher, and a judger which refuses to accept the responsibilities attached to economic and monetary union.

13. Since 2014, Quantitative Easing by the ECB amounting to €60 billion to €80 billion per month has bailed out European governments and some banks and big corporates. This has been accompanied by very low interest rates or negative real interest rates during this time. However the newly created money did not diffuse into the wider economy within countries and a significant proportion was used for speculation in assets and derivatives, pumping up the stock markets, bond markets and other asset markets, and also to fund continuing government bail out programmes for banks and speculators and higher national debts. It created more speculative bubbles. It was not pumped into the productive sector and into consumption, and thus did not reach the ordinary people, the consumers, the productive businesses, and stimulate aggregate demand and did not stimulate supply to a level approximating with full employment, strong recovery and growth. Quantitative Easing has produced disappointing results and low growth or no growth and continuing high levels of unemployment in Europe and elsewhere. It failed to deal with the high levels of debt overhang and accompanying dent deflation, that is private debt, government debt, business debt, bank debt,

and household debt which has a negative effect on consumption, aggregate demand and associated levels of investment.

14. Eurocrats in Brussels and Frankfurt are obsessed with using debt to solve all the problems in the EU. They naively believe that piling more debt upon more debt is the solution to every problem. They have constructed the EFSF, EFSM, ESM, European Fiscal Compacts, Troikas, bond purchasing, short and long term repos, etc. to create more debt to solve problems. They cannot understand that debt slavery creates more and more problems, not solutions. In Chapter 7 we will propose alternatives to this debt slavery.

15. **Single Market**

    the Single European Act was signed in 1986 and was due to come into full effect in January 1993. There was meant to be a single European market for goods and services. By 2017, there is no single market for insurance, bank interest rates, automobiles, pharmaceuticals, loans and mortgages, medical services, legal services, accountancy services, and most services across the EU. After 24 years, there is still no single market. In the case of Ireland this adds 5 billion euros per year to the price of goods and services, and is undermining competitiveness and living standards (Competition Authority Ireland). It is also adding tens of billions of euros in extra costs to big EU nations and undermining living standards. This failure of the EU authorities to achieve the single market after 24 years is quite extraordinary.

16. Individual MEP's in the European Parliament cannot initiate or propose new legislation. The European Commission, an unelected body, has these powers only. Once a law is passed by the EU Parliament, only the European Commission can amend or repeal that law. This means MEP's have less power than members of parliament in individual countries. This is a serious democratic deficit.

17. Law making has been transferred from EU nations and national parliaments to the EU centre in Brussels. Over 60% of laws within European nations have emerged from the EU Commission and EU Parliament. The EU Commission is the most powerful, it can propose and draft legislation and vote on it, and it meets in secret and it's activities are secret. Lobbying and the influence of powerful banks and big corporates on the EU Commission and EU committees is kept secret. There is no effective independent oversight, no transparency and no accountability, and no checks and balances of the EU Commission, the secretive committees, the EU Parliament and other EU

authorities. This is the very antithesis of freedom and democracy. It is similar in many ways to Communist dictatorship or Fascist dictatorship.

18. EU laws can overrule national laws and Constitutions. Many of these conflict with national needs, national requirements, the national interest and with national culture and traditions. This is a major loss of national sovereignty.

19. Over 100,000 EU laws and regulations have been passed by 2019

20. Small nations such as Ireland have less than 2% of the vote in the EU Parliament and in EU law making. Other small EU nations have similar representation of less than 2%

21. Most nation states in the European Union do not have the right to a referendum to accept or reject EU treaties and EU laws. This deprives nations and their peoples of an important democratic right.

22. The French and Dutch rejected an EU Constitution treaty in referendums in 2004, so the EU centre created a new treaty called the Lisbon treaty which contained 99% of the EU Constitution treaty. This Lisbon treaty was rejected by the Irish in a referendum. After threats and intimidation, the Irish held another referendum and the Lisbon treaty was accepted. So the decision of the French and Dutch, and Irish voters, was undermined, subverted, rejected.

23. When the Irish people voted against the Nice treaty (2001) and the Lisbon treaty (2008), they were asked to vote again on these treaties. The Irish verdict was not accepted by the EU elite and they demanded a second vote, this was unprecedented in the EU or old EEC. In the second vote, the voters were subjected to threats and intimidation on both occasions. The second votes resulted in acceptance of these two treaties but calls for a third vote were rejected.

24. **Control of the EU by Big Corporates and Banks**

There are 30,000 lobbyists in Brussels influencing, directing and co-creating EU laws, regulations, policies and treaties. And billions of euros being spent per year on lobbying the EU Commission, EU Parliament, and EU institutions. This lobbying affects the creation of new EU laws, policies and regulations. Ordinary voters in nation states have no input into this. The people, the voters, have been disempowered. And there is no effective independent oversight of this lobbying.

The EU Commission is dominated by big industrial interests and banking interests and their lobbyists, while the EU Parliament is dominated by 2 large political party groups and by the same industrial and banking interests and their lobbyists. Research has shown that secretive commitees dominated by big banking and businesses interests working with the European Commission (an unelected body) have vast powers to propose, amend and repeal EU legislation, regulations, rules and policies. EU laws passed by these institutions can conflict with the political, economic and social interests of individual EU nations. This is anti democratic and actually resembles a dictatorship. The EU centre and it's laws and rulings support freedom of movement in goods, services, labour and capital. This was carried out without protecting labour rights, labour entitlements, union rights, collective bargaining rights, etc. in EU countries. In fact, the Viking, Laval, Rüffert and Luxemburg rulings indicate that the EU opposes these labour and union rights and favours freedom for corporates and banks. The EU Commission has recently opposed collective bargaining in Greece and other EU countries and it also favours privatisation measures which actively oppose labour rights. The EU also supports large scale immigration into EU countries which are experiencing unemployment which further drives down wages and undermines Labour rights. Many regions inside several EU countries have experienced a fall in real wages and a rise in poverty since the creation of the Single Market in the mid 1990's and mass immigration since 1999. This contributed to the Brexit vote result in the UK in 2016.

25. The EU Federalist structure does not have direct democracy and it opposes direct democracy. In fact, the EU centre and its power structure is the exact opposite of direct democracy. Sovereignty, people power, voters, the will of the people, and national constitutions within individual nations, especially periphery nations, are being ignored, dismissed and replaced by centralised bureaucratic power in Brussels dominated by unelected commissioners, unelected presidents, unelected eurocrats, big corporates and banks, all presided over by Fuhrer type Commissioner or President.

26. European nations have lost the power to control immigration from outside the EU into their countries. This power has been transferred to the EU centre in Brussels and Strasbourg. The migration crisis into Europe caused by 'regime changes' in the Middle East and throughout Africa put excessive pressures on EU countries, particularly countries on the periphery and those experiencing economic recession / depression and austerity policies. Many countries could not absorb the large influx of migrants fleeing wars in the Middle East and Africa. The EU centre and its Military-Industrial complex and big banks played a major role in supporting 'regime changes' and wars, and creating the refugee crisis. And then this same EU elite welcomed the large scale migration into Europe which put massive new pressures on the periphery and those suffering from economic crashes, austerity and economic crisis. This was particularly true in the case of Britain and

Brexit.

27. Foreign policy is controlled by an unelected EU Commissioner, and the EU Commission is influenced by the lobbyists of big banks and corporates, many of whom profiteer from wars, regime changes and regional conflicts. The wars and so called 'regime changes' in the Middle East and North Africa and resource wars in Africa and Asia instigated by liberals and mentally imbalanced neo cons in western nations have benefited lobbyists and big banking and corporate interests at EU level and the EU centre, and have complicated the role of the Commissioner. While these wars have enriched and been supported by elites in large EU countries, the EU centre, they did not have the full support of the periphery nations. The antagonising of Russia and other states by the EU centre is also against the long term interests of the EU and it's founding charter.

28. The ECB and European regulators have no reliable, accurate and accountable European system for investigating, measuring and quantifying banking risks and systemic risks. They have no effective indicators for quantifying excessive rises in the prices of assets and debt and the risks these pose at a systemic level. This proved disastrous in 2008 and 2009. The ECB is over focussed on consumer price inflation while it has ignored the more dangerous risks of asset price bubbles and crashes and the accompanying systemic risk to countries and the Eurozone. The ECB has proven itself incompetent and ineffective in this important financial area.

29. There is not the same level of worker mobility in Europe as in the USA. There are strong language and cultural barriers in Europe which prevent mobility of workers. This leads to a concentration of unemployment in weaker, peripheral countries and regions which cannot be resolved by fiscal, monetary and currency policies in periphery countries due to limitations and restrictions imposed by the EU centre. These imposed limitations are fiscal, monetary, currency, banking and political.

30. The ECB is tasked with maintaining low inflation in the EU and has no powers to interfere in national government policies, fiscal policies and government functions. Firstly the ECB failed in its inflationary target. The ECB allowed large inflationary rises in the prices of property, homes, shares, assets, and derivatives and the fuelling of this with easy credit from EU banks and low interest rates during the boom years prior to 2008. This asset inflation inflicted severe costs on workers and their families and loss of competitiveness on businesses. Yet, this was ignored by the ECB, the EU authorities and the Germans. Secondly, when the crash came in 2008, the ECB went beyond its powers when it enforced austerity fiscal policies on some national governments and taxpayers (

Ireland, Greece, Cyrus, Italy, Spain and Portugal) to bail out banks, bond holders, speculators and fraudsters. The ECB used threats and blackmail to enforce this, including bomb threats and the withdrawal of Emergency Liquidity Assistance (ELA). This interference in government policies, including the use of blackmail, was illegal and unethical under EU laws. The ECB failed in its own mission and its own responsibilities, it failed to control inflation of speculative assets, failed to regulate and oversee the EU banking system, failed to establish a monetary union, failed to provide an EU wide deposit insurance scheme similar to the FDIC in the USA, failed to act as a lender of last resort to banks, failed to promote growth, employment and stability as other central banks do, and lastly failed to maintain its independence from governments.

31. The ECB, the ESM and their allied financial bodies such as the BIS and IMF are not subject to audits and oversight and legal accountability. Yet these same institutions can threaten the governments of countries and enforce various types of bail outs and austerity policies on countries. This lack of accountability for financial institutions is unacceptable in these circumstances.

32. Fishing rights in and around national waters are controlled by the EU and not by nations. Poorer periphery countries and regions are placed at a disadvantage as they have weak industrial cases. Individual countries have lost tens of billions of euros over several years as large factory ships take fish out of national waters.

33. The EU has ignored serious political, legal and banking corruption within nation states and human rights abuses in these nations. Yet these states have signed up to EU and UN treaties regarding this.

34. The EU ignores high unemployment levels, deindustrialisation and growing poverty in nation states and regions of nation states as evidenced by support for TTIP and several WTO treaties. The EU has only been concerned with maintaining low inflation, the imposition of austerity programmes and debt repayments.

35. Every year there are new regulations and rules for products and services coming from EU institutions which further burden small businesses in nations. Most of these businesses cannot afford the lobbying power of large corporations, multinationals and banks.

36. EU institutions and lobbyists are not subject to independent oversight and accountability and legal sanctions, but many national governments are subject to this

37. Nations have to pay EU fees and other charges and payments to the EU, even if these nations are in recession / depression, over indebted and in austerity programmes. In many cases the money being sent to the EU is greater than the money being received by nation states.

38. The EU institutions are attempting at present to take control of taxes in nation states by implementing a 'common consolidated EU tax' for corporations and investment. This ignores the economic and social conditions within nation states which are being complicated by continuing booms and busts, and Globalisation and the 'race to the bottom'

39. International trade deals are made by the EU centre not by nation states. In some cases, such as WTO agreements, EU trade agreements, and TTIP, individual nation states may reject several provisions in a trade treaty or reject the treaty, but the EU centre can ignore this and enforce the trade treaty on all EU nations. The secretive private courts recommended by TTIP and CETA are a direct attack on national sovereignty and laws.

40. The EU centre ignores, dismisses and fobs off the serious concerns of periphery countries. In certain cases it despises them, disrespects them, and denigrates them. The worst example of this was the 'extend and pretend' policies of the EU centre in reaction to the financial crisis in Europe from 2008 – 2013, particularly the case of the Greek crisis. The roots of the problem were ignored and extended indefinitely, while they pretended that the problem was solved and rectified. Yet the problems kept re-emerging. The threats against Ireland by Trichet of the ECB including a threat to bomb Dublin and remove emergency lending was another example. The EU centre exists to serve the interests of the biggest and richest countries, mainly Germany, the powerful industrial and banking interests and their lobbyists, the elite or richest 1%, and the eurocrats and to ignore the periphery countries and the ordinary people. This is the essence of federalism, the basis of the conflict between the centre and the periphery in Europe and around the world.

This represents a very significant loss of national sovereignty by nation states, and of economic and legal sovereignty. It also involves a very significant loss of democratic freedoms and democratic rights of ordinary people, a loss of worker's rights and entitlements, a loss of national and cultural identity, a loss of fairness and accountability, a loss of the dignity and respect of ordinary people. While more and more power is being given to the EU centre, there is a lack of democracy and accountability in the EU centre itself, there is a 'democratic deficit'. It has the characteristics of a dictatorship. Should nations be deprived of their sovereignty and their freedoms and democracies for this ? national freedoms which were achieved at great human cost over decades and centuries. This is a very important question today.

Corruption and Democratic Deficits

The first point we need to address is corruption and waste which has been a problem in EU institutions for decades. Corruption when it involves vast resources and monies, hundreds of billions of euros, and the lives and destinies of many countries and peoples is not insignificant. From 1994 to 2006, the auditors of the EU institutions refused to sign off on the EU accounts, and stated that the accounts were not fair and accurate and contained several serious errors. From 2006 – 2015, these same accounts were found to have several serious errors. These amounts are the in the tens of billions of euros per year over a long period of time (https://fullfact.org/europe/did-auditors-sign-eu-budget/). Over time, this represents a considerable sum of money lost to errors, fraud, corruption and waste. However, there is no oversight and monitoring of bribery, corruption and conflicts of interest in the EU institutions, so these figures are an underestimate of the scale of corruption, fraud and waste. The resignation of the EU Commission in 1999 over allegations of corruption points to serious issues of corruption within EU institutions, and the cash for laws scandal involving Ernst Strasser and the Dalligate affair provide other similar examples. This corruption was first publicly exposed in the book 'The Rotten Heart of Europe' by an ex-Eurocrat Bernard Connolly in the 1990;s. His seminal book delves into the secretive world of EU bureaucracy and the power of lobbyists, how deals are made and laws and policies formed, how this is undermining democratic accountability, transparency, integrity, value for money and efficiency, fairness, freedom and democracy throughout Europe. It provides an interesting read, and deep insights into the abuses of power at the EU centre. Another great book about corruption and abuses in the EU centre 'The Great European Rip-off: How the Corrupt, Wasteful EU is Taking Control of Our Lives' by David Craig and Matthew Elliott confirms the findings of Bernard Connolly. It also exposes the serious democratic deficit in Europe and the totalitarian nature of the EU bureaucracy. A book by a former EU accountant and MEP, Marta Andreasen, 'Brussels Laid Bare' further exposes large scale waste and fraud in EU institutions. While Roger Bootle's important book 'The Trouble with Europe: Why the EU isn't Working, How it Can be Reformed, How Brexit Could Change Europe' corroborates the findings of the aforementioned books, concerning vast waste, corruption, inefficiencies and no accountability inside EU institutions. These books should be read by all eurocrats, all euro sceptics and those people interested in the European Union.

Today, there is still no EU oversight, no proper independent and transparent auditing of the EU grants, EU bureaucracy, EU Commissioners, EU Commission decisions, EU parliament politicians, EU institutions, EU lobbyists, EU law making processes, no means for uncovering conflicts of interest inside the EU institutions, and many treaties such TTIP are negotiated in secret. Lobbying is intense and widespread within the EU centre and according to the books above, the whistleblowers, researchers, and others, corruption is rife in the EU centre. Furthermore, eurocrats can break laws within Belgium and never suffer criminal prosecution. There is a smug sense of entitlement within the EU bureaucracy which facilitates corruption. Corruption and it's destructive effects increases in proportion to the level of excessive centralisation or federalisation of power, it is one of scale and magnitude, a fact often conveniently ignored by federalist exponents and supporters. Again we see the importance of checks and balances, and oversight and accountability, this time at the European centre.

Most EU law is created in secret in the European Commission, an unelected and unaccountable bureaucracy. It consists of political appointees from EU countries, they are not elected, and some of them lack the qualifications and experience to deal with very complex issues. Its affairs are conducted in secret, and it is regularly engaged by lobbyists for big business, big banks, arms businesses, big pharma, the oil industry, and representative bodies for big industry. The Commission's views and accompanying laws have always represented the financial interests of these rich and powerful lobbies, industries and banks. The EU parliament is also subjected to this lobbying, and their laws are also influenced, or one could say derived to serve these interests. This has been exposed in research, Transparency International, documentaries, books and by whistleblowers. This is termed 'regulatory capture' in economics and is one of the most important areas of modern economics, though it is often ignored by mainstream economists. In Brussels there are 30,000 lobbyists who are in almost constant contact with EU institutions and eurocrats. Many of these lobbyists are ex eurocrats and a revolving door exists between lobbyist firms and EU institutions. Expenditure on lobbying in the EU is difficult to assess due to its hidden and discreet nature, but some estimates put it at billions of euros per year (https://lobbyfacts.eu/)

For example in the USA, it was estimated in 2008, that successful congress men had to raise $978 million in total and senators had to raise $410 million in total and the presidential candidate $1.8 billion to be elected (Centre for Responsive Politics, 'Stats at a Glance', www.opensecrets.org). These campaign monies were paid by big businesses, banks, PAC's, very wealthy individuals and lobbyists, and they expect and often demand political favours in return. The European Union operates on a similar basis and one can see legions of lobbyists living and working in Brussels and travelling to and from this city / country every day. Recent research by Gilens and Page over many years shows a direct correlation between the preferences of the very wealthy and their lobbyists and the passing of legislation and use of certain policies by governments. This provides proof of the political power of wealthy corporations, banks, individuals and their lobbyists. This is one of the most important studies ever conducted in political science. This is the process of 'regulatory capture', one of the most important areas of modern economics. Lobbying is big business in Brussels, the centre of the European Union, as it is in other capitals such as Washington DC, London, Beijing, Ottawa, etc.. There is a correlation between the EU laws and policies created by the EU centre and the interests of big lobbyists representing big corporations, banks and wealthy individuals. This regulatory capture places small and medium sized businesses and entrepreneurs at a distinct disadvantage as they lack the financial resources and lobbyists to influence and leverage EU Commissioners and major European parliament leaders. And, furthermore, they suffer the costs of regulation and laws which favour large businesses and banks, while punishing them. In effect, a 'regulatory discrimination' is used which works against small and medium firms, workers, unions, taxpayers, and voters who do not possess the financial resources necessary for regulatory capture. Regulatory capture encompasses the many forms of corruption, both overt and covert, which insidiously works to undermine and destroy democracy and freedom from within, while giving the false appearance of 'democracy'.

It is important for all persons to realise that within this environment of regulatory capture and corruption, over 60% of new laws within nation states come from the EU centre — the EU Commission and Parliament. These laws are not voted on and cannot be amended or repealed by voters within nation states. They are imposed upon nations from above (the EU centre and their lobbyists) and they cannot be changed by the voters or people within these nations. This is a serious democratic deficiency or 'democratic deficit'. The original purpose of democracy was to have citizens within nations vote on laws or have their parliament vote on laws, and to have some forms of appeal in the form of new elections, voter recall, and judicial oversight to ensure that laws conform to a national Constitution. The EU centre has undermined this.

Austerity as a means of 'Punishment' of the Innocents and the EU Periphery

In most EU countries there have been severe cutbacks in public spending, welfare, education, policing health and social services since 2008 enforced by EU and ECB sponsored austerity programmes and policies and the fact national governments were forced by the EU to take on massive private debt accumulated from speculative bubbles fuelled by neo liberal economics. While the EU does have some adequate social programmes which provide sufficient social safety nets in some countries, these have been severely cut back by the aforementioned austerity factors, which emerged from the failures of neo liberal economics. It is interesting to note that the failure of neo liberal economics is the driving force behind booms and busts and also the austerity policies and the destruction of European social values, solidarity and ideals, and the EU project. Yet, ironically, the EU centre is supporting and promoting this neo liberal economics. Neo liberal economics is being further strengthened by the increasing centralisation or federalisation of economic and political power, of law making and of domestic and foreign policies in the EU, all of which ultimately serves the interests of the lobbyists, big banks and big businesses. The secret TTIP treaty negotiations provided one recent example of this. The EU centre has become a federalist state which is obsessed with power but lacks the responsibilities attached to it. Should it be encouraged to continue taking more power, law making, sovereignty, natural resources and economic freedom away from nation states, and away from the periphery ? As we have seen above, and shall see in the next few paragraphs this control and domination from the centre has many negative consequences for countries and for the European ideal of solidarity.

Let us look at the austerity programmes imposed by the EU centre on nation states to bail out banks, speculators and fraudsters after 2008. The EU centre and its 'troika', imposed some very harsh austerity measures on Ireland, Greece, Spain and Portugal to bail out criminals. For Ireland, they (i) prevented the Irish from giving bank bondholders a haircut (moderate losses on their bonds). The ECB president Mr. Trichet threatened to bomb Dublin to enforce this corrupt deal (ii) prevented the Irish from buying bank bonds and debt on the secondary market at cheap prices. This would have helped reduce the debt taken on by the Irish government by 50% or more (iii) imposed a 100% bail out of banks, bondholders, speculators and fraudsters on the Irish government and taxpayers. This bankrupted Ireland and forced the Irish government into an emergency loan programme and vicious austerity policies to pay off this debt. It enforced a similar debt and austerity programme on Spain and Portugal. Greece was bankrupted by too much debt fraudulently taken on by Greek politicians and foreign bankers, and was forced by the troika to enter a vicious austerity programme which involved shutting down many essential public services and hospitals, tax rises, pay cuts, closing banks, laying off hundreds of thousands of workers, and selling off state assets and natural resources. The Greeks were also prevented from buying their debt cheaply on the secondary debt market. And Greek tax evaders were allowed to continue hiding over a hundred billion euros in offshore tax havens. Greece was raped to bail out political and financial criminals. No corrupt Greek politicians and foreign bankers went to jail for some serious crimes, in direct contrast to Iceland where these criminals were prosecuted and jailed. These bail outs and enforced austerity programmes were outrageous abuses by the EU centre. Between 2009 and 2013, Ireland lost more than €18,000 per capita while Spain saw its average wealth shrink by €13,000 per person – as a result not only of their respective rescue programs but also the burst of their spectacular real estate bubbles. The Greeks, meanwhile, saw their national wealth contract by €17,000 per capita. By contrast, in the Netherlands, Belgium, and Germany, wealth grew during the same period by €33,000, €24,000, and €19,000 per capita respectively, due in large part to the massive influx of the ECB's flood of liquidity and of financial investments, mainly from the euro's loser nations. See graph below:

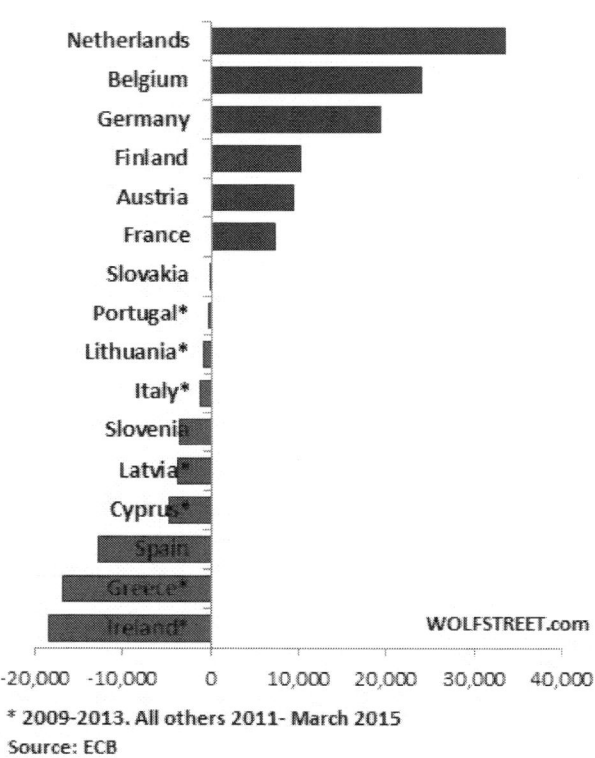

As its monetary policies spread over the Eurozone, the ECB is powerless to reduce these gaping disparities that its own policies helped create, it said. Its economic stimulus plan, if you can call it that, distributed funds among Eurozone nations based purely on their relative size, without taking into account the particular economic needs of each one.

Source http://wolfstreet.com/2015/10/21/ecb-sheds-doubt-on-its-power-euro-stuck-in-limbo/

On March 11th 2015, the Governor of the Irish Central Bank, Mr. Patrick Honohan, stated to an Irish Parliamentary committee investigating the banking crisis that the total cost of the bank bailout in Ireland was **over €100 billion** – Patrick Honohan: Cost of banking crisis 'more than €100bn', Irish Times, March 11th, 2015. http://www.irishtimes.com/news/politics/oireachtas/patrick-honohan-cost-of-banking-crisis-more-than-100bn-1.2134967. This total cost of €100 billion included **(a)** government borrowings from the troika and international lenders **(b)** use of higher taxes, new taxes, charges and levies to fund the banks and bondholders bailout **(c)** lost economic output, income, productivity and taxes from imposing austerity to bail out the banks and bondholders. In 2011, estimates of Ireland's total debt, including government, business and private debt was over 660% of GDP (see diagram below in chapter 7). Ireland's GNP in 2014 was 155 billion (CSO, Ireland). This means the cost of the banks and financial institutions bailout was 64% of GNP (100/155). This is the most costly bailout in the history of the world. Spain, Italy, Greece, UK, Belgium, France, Cyprus and Portugal have government debts which are over 100% of GNP and total debt (government, business, banking, household debts) which are a few times GNP (see charts below). In Ireland 50% of mortgage holders in arrears are in danger of losing the family home.

Source: Half of mortgage borrowers in arrears may lose properties, Irish Times newspaper, April 3rd 2015. http://www.irishtimes.com/business/economy/half-of-mortgage-borrowers-in-arrears-may-lose-properties-1.2162581

The EU centre or bureaucracy with its harsh and stringent austerity programmes and its budgetary and fiscal rules prevented Ireland, Greece, Spain, Italy, Portugal, Latvia and other countries on the periphery from spending money on essential public services during a deep recession, spending which could have stimulated economies and lifted them out of recession. Examples being social housing for the high number of homeless people, hospitals in need of repair and expansion, resolving severely depleted accident and emergency services in hospitals, long hospital waiting lists for medical attention, doctor's clinics, nursing and doctor services in poorer regions, debt relief for the large number of families in mortgage distress, education and schools, retraining of unemployed, tax relief for long term productive investment and innovation, etc.. But, the EU centre enforced a massive bail out of bankers, fraudsters and speculators on these national governments. This disordered and misguided set of priorities by the

EU centre, particularly the bailout has created massive national debt, austerity and recession, and crowded out productive investment in national economies, making adequate investment in essential public services and social services impossible. This has had devastating effects on these national economies, and was a disgraceful misuse and misallocation of economic resources and political power by the EU centre.

The EU centre has over the years become dominated and controlled by Germany and by German interests. This is the key factor. This shaped the EU response to the financial crash in Europe in 2008, and the vicious bail outs and austerity programmes imposed upon EU nations. As we shall see later in this book, Germany has forgot the bail outs of Germany after World War 2, specifically the Marshall plan aid, and the many forms of free money, grant aid and loans given to Germany and the write off of German debt under the London Debts agreement (1953). Germany needs to remember this, and extend the same generosity to other EU nation states.

The loss of control over fiscal policy and monetary policy represents a major loss of sovereignty for an EU country and loss of ability to respond to an economic crisis. This is a major weakness in a world which is being globalised and subjected to sudden and unexpected flows of capital, monies, trade and investment, grants, subsidies and tax incentives for international firms, and increasing automation and replacement of workers, within an unstable global economic system. This binds down individual governments and prevents them from playing a more active role in securing new private productive investment and state investment to build up their economies. The fact that large international companies can play off governments against each other through the use of tax incentives, grants and other forms of state assistance complicates this further, and creates great tensions and misunderstandings between individual European countries and between the European centre and the periphery in Europe. The central point is that this loss of control of fiscal and monetary within the EU disempowers countries and peoples in a global environment of ever more uncertainty and instability, and this in turn creates a greater need for even more generous tax concessions, grants and other subsidies to attract international firms to periphery countries.

Countries immersed in austerity, recession, depression, massive debt are desperate for international firms and capital and for injections of new credit and spending power. The unwillingness or inability of a centralised bureaucratic government in Brussels / Frankfurt to respond to recessions or depressions in individual countries or on the periphery of Europe and stimulate them is a major factor and serves to worsen this situation, especially when combined with it's over eagerness to impose extra debt, extra taxation, large public expenditure cuts, loss of economic output and revenues, privatisation of essential public resources, and imposition of harsh austerity policies in the middle of a recession (or depression / deflation). This points to a serious disconnect between the centre and the periphery in the European Union. It is a significant point, as it presents a very clear division between the centre and periphery, a conflict of interests, a clear divergence of interests, most notably represented in the appalling treatment of the Greek people during the financial crisis of 2008 – 2015. This has created much more than a democratic deficit in Europe, it has created a movement towards imperialist control which is against the original ideals of the EEC in the 1950's.

Expanding on this further, during recessions and depressions individual countries cannot adapt dynamically and implement stimulatory fiscal and monetary policies to promote recovery, growth and employment and during booms they cannot implement tight fiscal and monetary policies to curtail overheating and speculative bubbles in the economy. And to compound this error, there are no automatic transfers between the centre and periphery or countries during recession / depression, and there are no transfers in reverse to cool down over heating. In fact the opposite is the case in Europe, the EU centre imposes more debt, more taxation, more cuts, more austerity, and more transfers out of periphery countries in recession to the centre, this is commonly referred to "austerity policies" brutally imposed by the centre. Contrast this with the automatic transfers between the federal centre and the peripheral states in the USA, the Quantitative Easing to stimulate economic activity, and the willingness of the FDIC and Federal Reserve (not taxpayers) to bail out bankrupt banks and financial institutions throughout America there points to major differences between 'federalisation' in the USA and the European Union.

The euro currency was poorly designed from the start, the euro is not backed up by a lender of last resort to bail out banks, a European style FDIC style institution to protect depositors, an independent European regulatory and oversight system to regulate, audit and oversee banks, financial institutions, traders and derivatives, a European SEC to oversee trades which can pose systemic risks to the banking system and currency and no EU policies for curbing speculation in asset prices and accompanying vast accumulations of debt. There was and is no responsibility at EU level or at the centre of Europe. The euro currency does not reflect local conditions within EU countries, and often acts to undermine the economies of these nations. The euro currency is overvalued at times when it should be undervalued within these countries, and at other times its undervalued when it should be overvalued. Individual countries cannot devalue or revalue to suit conditions in their own countries and are thus stuck in an inflexible system similar to the Gold Standard in the past. The euro currency is incapable of adapting to or reflecting local economic conditions within individual nations, and this is a major disadvantage. It worsens speculative booms and crashes and debt accumulation, and then intensifies the accompanying austerity policies, pay cuts, employment cuts, debt liquidation depressions, and recessions. It works against the interests of many EU nations.

The setting of interest rates at Euro level also does not reflect conditions within individual countries and worsens the effects of speculative booms, crashes and accompanying austerity and recessions. The end result is that freedom and sovereignty to act locally in countries has been lost, and the massive risks and costs are borne by those countries and peoples on the periphery while those at the EU centre fail to take any responsibility, fail to oversee and provide stability. The EU centre just imposes the austerity, debt and other financial punishments on the periphery. Again, we see the centre acting as an enforcer. All of this has served to widen the divisions, resentments, distrust, and disconnect between the centre and the periphery.

The loss of a country's ability to print money and to set interest rates is no trivial matter as money creation and interest rates intimately linked to local economic conditions, needs and requirements in a given country. They are specific to that country and its needs at a given point in time. This should include the power for a national government to engage in Quantitative Easing regardless of EU centre interests or German interests. Giving this power to a central bank in a foreign country which genuinely does not give a damn about the country is a big mistake. Ireland learnt about this during the Trichet letter and phone bomb threat which enforced a bail out of banks and speculators and harsh austerity policies on the Irish people. The ECB is solely concerned with inflation and the imposition of austerity, and it is unconcerned about unemployment, investment, fiscal and monetary stimulus, growth, the high economic and social costs of austerity, regulation of banking, de-industrialisation, and the globalisation 'race to the bottom', particularly in countries in the periphery. This works to exacerbate the division between the centre and the periphery, and inflict greater economic and social pain on the periphery. No country or people should be reduced down to using a begging bowl to get its own currency and what it needs from a foreign and alien centralised power structure.

TTIP and Similar Treaties - Globalism on Steroids

To worsen this austerity, the centre in Europe has consistently supported a sinister Globalisation of TTIP, the de-industrialisations of regions in Europe, the imposition of massive bail outs and accompanying debt, open borders, the 'race to the bottom' and the bidding down of wages. TTIP which was negotiated in secret and its content deliberately kept secret and hidden away from the general public and the press and media, is a trade agreement which will have negative effective effects on industry, agriculture, trade, services and employment in the European Union. It is a managed trade agreement, not a free trade agreement. Managed trade agreements favour politically connected large businesses, banks, financial institutions, industrial farms, speculators, hedge funds, and their lobbyists. TTIP has the following characteristics:

- it will undermine agriculture and food safety requirements, and the health of consumers in the European Union in the interests of enriching large multinational corporations. This involves the controversial areas of GMO's, illegal growth hormones, over use of antibiotics, dangerous pesticides and herbicides in foods, additives, toxins and carcinogens, toxic in foods in water. The WTO has consistently ruled in favour of treaties and provisions which support this corruption of foods, drinks, water and animal care, and the resultant human health effects and diseases which have arisen from this.

- it will undermine environmental standards, destroying the environment, enabling large corporations to pollute rivers, lakes, ground water, land, air and foods in the interests of attaining higher profits. The costs of these economic externalities will be borne by the taxpayers, government health systems, and by those people who continue to get diseases, cancers and chronic illnesses from this environmental pollution. And again there is a precedent here, as WTO has consistently supported treaties and provisions which led to environmental damage and pollution.

- it will undermine and destroy workers wages, rights and unions, it will continue the trend of outsourcing jobs to cheap developing countries. This is forcing a global 'race to the bottom' or 'race to the sewer' with workers in high priced European countries competing against workers in developing and third world countries on subsistence wages which are 6 -20 times lower. These goods and services are then sold at high prices in developed countries for massive profits, enforcing continuing high costs of living in developed countries. And these profits are often funnelled through tax havens to avoid paying tax in developed countries. This will serve the interests of enriching large corporations, banks and speculators.

- it will give corporations the right to sue national governments for any loss of profits from government laws to protect the environment, food safety, the health of consumers and workers, and the protection of workers and pensioners rights in new special courts. This will directly undermine the sovereignty of nations and democracies, and impose extra costs on taxpayers and ordinary people.

- It will cause more damage to the climate and impose more climate damage costs on countries, and undermine efforts to stop climate change

- it will lead to continued de-industrialisation in the European Union as more firms are forced out of business or forced to move to China, India, Malaysia, Vietnam etc. to survive. And this will reduce the tax base, public services base, infrastructure base, and the pensions base in EU countries, and reduce the purchasing power required to sustain the economies of these countries.

- it will concentrate the wealth created from new labour replacing technologies and new innovations in fewer and fewer hands, leading to further concentrations of wealth and income and to worsening social divisions

- it will undermine and destroy Fairtrade in developing countries by giving preference to large industrial farms in developing countries run by large corporations or big landowners. This will worsen poverty and exploitation in developing countries

- It will cause dumping on world markets, where state subsidised products are dumped onto other weaker countries (with no state subsidies), destroying farms, local businesses and livelihoods in these weaker countries. This has been the experience with NAFTA and other similar trade agreements.

- It will deprive weaker and poorer countries of valuable medicines and drugs due to long extensions to patents and intellectual property and artificial restrictions in the supply of medicines. This has been the experience of the TRIPS agreements enforced by the WTO.

- It will increase the power of monopolies, oligopolies,regulatory capture, and economic renter activity in developed countries and impose high costs of living.

- It will force reductions or eliminate in many cases the resources available for state spending on community development programmes and social programmes to improve employment, housing and social cohesion

- it will facilitate and intensify international unlimited speculation in assets, stocks and derivatives, and create bigger financial bubbles and crashes which have had devastating effects on economies and peoples. It will enable speculators to avoid paying the social costs or externality costs of their activities, while imposing these costs on taxpayers, consumers, workers and small and medium sized businesses in

Europe in the form of higher prices for goods, assets +and services and high bail out costs after crashes. This breaches many economic principles and legal principles / laws.

- it will facilitate continuing large scale tax evasion, enabling large corporations to use tax loopholes in several EU countries and tax havens abroad to reduce their tax bill to zero or less than 3% in many cases. Yet these corporations will use the infrastructure, education systems, Universities, electricity, courts, police, health systems, and other services paid for by taxpayers. These services, which are vital to industry and trade, are paid for by taxes and taxpayers, not by tax evasion. TTIP's support of tax evasion will undermine the tax revenues and tax base of many countries.

- it will worsen inequalities between the EU centre and peripheral countries. The EU centre has no plans or strategies for reducing these inequalities, the only plan they have is more austerity, more (failed) neo liberal economics and more debt for countries on the periphery and more federalisation to enforce this.

This has been confirmed by Wikileaks, whistleblowers, some MEP's and human rights organisations. TTIP is managed trade, not free trade. It is carefully managed to benefit large international corporations at the expense of workers who are consumers, taxpayers, farmers, the environment, the health of peoples, the healthcare systems of countries, Fairtrade producers, local communities, and small and medium sized businesses in Europe. TTIP and other similar agreements are mass theft or larceny from workers, taxpayers, governments, farmers, health systems, small and medium sized firms in developed countries.

Serious Challenges and Threats

These policies pursued by the EU centre, notably Germany and its allies at an EU level after 2008 had the effect of strengthening the centre while significantly weakening and draining the periphery and weaker regions within the periphery of Europe. The control and domination of fiscal and monetary policy, of national budgets, of money creation, of regulations, of debt accumulation and enforcement and accompanying austerity upon peoples, of natural resources, of laws, of treaties, by an EU centre has had several unforeseen consequences, all negative. This will continue to worsen relations between the EU centre and the periphery. As mentioned above, different nations have different conditions, different challenges to meet and diverse needs in a dynamic and changing world and these differ substantially from nation to nation, and this cannot be controlled by a foreign politburo or centre imposing its will on all nations ; the failure of Communism in the Soviet Union provided evidence of this. All nations are subject to dynamic disequilibrium, which regularly imposes adverse economic conditions on them, often suddenly and unexpectedly.

An IMF Report in 2016 and a Report of Societe Generale bank in 2016 and an assessment by some top economists including Dr. Joseph Stiglitz the Nobel Prize winner [9] support these claims, all agree that the EU is in serious trouble with high unemployment, low productive investment levels, very high government debt levels, low economic growth, a fragile and unstable banking system, a poorly designed and functioning euro currency, continuing austerity policies which were destroying growth, and an increasing divisions between the rich countries at the centre of the EU and the poorer countries on the periphery of the EU. They mentioned the high risk of the EU fracturing, with some countries leaving the euro currency and / or leaving the EU to pursue their own policies and resolve their own economic issues and other issues.

Foreign policies and responsibilities tend to favour the big lobbyists at the centre, and the centre itself is subject to high degrees of control via regulatory capture. For example, the EU centre and big EU countries supported 'regime change' in the Ukraine, which involved the overthrow of a democratically elected government there, and the continued encirclement of Russia, and the antagonising of Russia. This was an unusual change in EU policy, and one which goes against 70 years of EU strategy. These destabilisation policies have worked against peace, cooperation and trust between Europe and Russia and against the best interests of EU member states. Though it is important to realise they do benefit the big lobbyists, the large arms companies, banks and other industries with a financial interest in inciting and preparing for wars. The EU centre has lost track of its own origins and original aims back in the 1950's, and is reversing over 70 years of peace in Europe, and undermining the great work of previous EU leaders in protecting and preserving peace, order and stability in Europe.

This change in EU policy began in 2003 when the EU centre supported so called 'regime change' in the Middle East and joined forces with the American neo cons and their allies in Europe, including big lobbyists, the large arms companies, the banks, big oil, telecommunications, the journalist and news channel cheerleaders, and others with a financial interest in war. They have integrated support for 'regime change' into the foreign policy of the EU, despite the divergence of views between EU member states on this topic. Some big EU countries at the centre and their allies have strongly supported 'regime change' in the Middle East, providing funding, press and media support, arms, goods, services, military assistance and intelligence to rebels and religious extremists in their efforts to overthrow governments in the Middle East. These wars have created large increase in sales and profits for war related industries, oil related industries and big banks in Europe and North America. While big industrialists, bankers, oil men, lobbyists, eurocrats, neo cons and politicians became enriched and empowered from the profits of these wars, the ordinary people of the middle east went through hell with millions forced to flee their own homes. Many drowning in small overcrowded boats and dinghies, or starving and freezing in wastelands. Others forced to live in impoverished unsanitary conditions in refugee camps and holding areas. These idiotic profit-driven 'regime changes', and wars have intensified religious extremism and racism across the Middle East, North Africa and in Europe, and this has borne bitter fruit for Europe and North America.

The forced migration of peoples resulting from these western backed wars in the Middle East and Africa and the loss of control over migration by individual EU countries during a period of deep recession (or depression), austerity, growing poverty, homelessness, and large scale public cutbacks caused a great increase in religious and racial tensions and divisions in Europe, and exposed a centralised European government which is out of touch with reality, and prepared to ignore and neglect problems it itself was partially to blame for. Their policies failed to address the root causes of the crisis , namely the misguided 'regime changes' in the Middle East and North Africa, the lack of proper peace building programmes and UN competence, and the large deficiencies in EU economic policy, public spending and infrastructure to cope with this type of refugee crisis in the middle of an economic crisis. What we see is a clueless EU bureaucracy, which had complete lack of understanding and self awareness, and possessed no strategic direction, no plans, no decisive actions, and no coherence in policy both domestic and foreign. EU policy failures and incompetence had the net effect of fomenting more racism, religious extremism and terrorism within Europe.

Important questions need to be asked : Does support for foreign 'regime changes' and wars give the EU centre and its allies the right to arm and fund religious extremist rebels, overthrow stable governments, bomb cities, towns and innocent civilians , destroy freedoms, and create instability and chaos ? Does the EU centre and its allies have the right to launch racist and genocidal wars in the form of 'regime changes' in the Middle East ? Does freedom of movement give the EU centre the right to undermine the national security of nations, and indirectly spread religious extremism and terror throughout Europe ? Should there be any safeguards ? Does democracy, sovereignty and freedom matter and should they be defended ? should the EU centre be enforcing massive cutbacks in essential public services at a time when these are desperately needed to cope with genuine refugees of their foreign wars and higher numbers of unemployed people ? The facts and evidence strongly suggest that the centre or centralised power structure does not really care about such issues, and sees itself as an enforcer, an imposer, a dictator, an extractor of wealth, a dismissive and disinterested bureaucracy. We see here many aspects from past empires and their imperial or centralised power structures.

A New Type of Europe, which is Not Federalist, Protects National Sovereignty and Democratic Freedoms and is United via a Customs Union and Single Market and a Commitment to Global Peace

In past centuries, kings, emperors, generals, fascist dictators and communist dictators tried to conquer, control and dominate Europe, and centralise their power via federalism and federalist structures. And destroy the national sovereignty and culture of nations. They failed. We have seen the democratic deficit and many other flaws and defects in the European Union and its federalised structure. The serious democratic deficits in the European Union arising from excessive federalism, which is imperialistic in nature, structure and function is not working, is ineffective, is failing and not serving the people of Europe. It is becoming the antithesis of democracy, freedom and national sovereignty. Alternatives are possible. These alternatives could inform the ongoing Brexit debate and possible solutions. A new type of non federalised, freer Europe is possible and would encompass the following:

- A Europe where individual sovereign nations make agreements between each other to reject, reverse, and overturn federalism and centralised control of Europe by Brussels and Frankfurt. This may have to be done on a country by country basis. The objective being a new Europe which disbands and reverses federalism and all structures of federalism, and restores sovereignty, national freedom, and dignity to all nations within Europe. If this cannot be done within the European Union then it will have to be done outside the European Union.

- The formation of a non federalised Europe of free, democratic, sovereign and independent nations, in control of their own fiscal and monetary policies, their own national currencies and money creation policies, their own laws, has their own Constitution, their own migration policies which prioritise skills, qualifications, economic needs and requirements and balances this with national security priorities.

- This non federalised Europe could form a single market and customs union between these countries similar to the EC of the 1980's, where all European nations are free to trade with each other and invest in each other to encourage trade, investment, full employment and prosperity within Europe. An end to the cartels, monopolies and restrictive practises which exist today. The present single market is a failure as most EU countries have cartels, monopolies and substantial price fixing.

Migration policies would prioritise skills, qualifications, economic needs and requirements and balances this with national security priorities between these nations. There would be no open borders and mass migration.

- A Europe which goes back to the old ideals, policies and structures of the EEC which allowed for national sovereignty and national control over most economic matters and legal matters and also for 'Community Preference' where producers were required to locate their production facilities in Europe not in the Far East and North Africa.

- A Europe of direct democracy where individual nations restore political power and sovereignty back to their own peoples. This would be the opposite of federalism which dominates Europe at present. Proposals for direct democracy are presented in this book.

- A Europe where individual countries properly regulate their banking system and financial system through an agreed international system. Some economic indicators and checks and balances are recommended in this book. As European banks are interlinked and interdependent, a European Regulator could be installed to oversee the European banking system and protect the interests and rights of European investors, depositors and customers and prevent systemic collapses of the banking sector in individual nations and collections of nations.

- A Europe where a national central bank bails out the banks, speculators and bondholders during a financial crash, similar to 2008 and national governments are free to write off or write down these debts. Taxpayers and government should not be forced to bail these out. This is detailed in Chapter 7.

- A Europe which uses Quantitative Easing for the People not just for banks, bondholders and speculators. This is detailed in Chapter 7.

- A Europe which is responsible, and takes its responsibilities seriously, in particular those responsibilities which are attached to freedom and democracy. This includes European cooperation in the defence of freedom and human rights from all forms of attack including religious extremism, terrorism, political corruption, theft and fraud by bureaucrats in European and national bodies, legal system corruption, the crimes and frauds of banks (including systemic banks), criminality including elite paedophile rings, child trafficking and drug trafficking, the abuses of the Deep State, (or 'Shadow Government') the 'regime changes' and the illegal interference in and manipulations of other nations, and the undermining of human rights and Constitutional rights to further the hidden agenda of elites.
A Europe where individual nations decide their own immigration policies based on these factors above and the need to protect national security.

- A Europe which abolishes the euro and restores national currencies to all nations. The introduction of a national Bancor as a unit of account for each country for international trade, first proposed by the economist John Maynard Keynes in 1945. This would be accompanied by an International Clearing

Union to process this. Each nation would have their own National Bancor, and this country Bancor rate determined by their economic status, their trading status, their balance of payments, their current and capital account. National Bancors would differ between countries. This would allow country Bancors to depreciate or appreciate according to how much Bancor they receive or pay out for international goods, services and capital and their balance of payments while safeguards would be put in place to discourage speculation in Bancors such as introducing an international tax rate of 50% or more for speculation in these currencies. This is detailed in a later chapter.

- The new Bancor Protocol introduced in 2017, enables diverse crypto currencies, electronic currencies, national currencies, local currencies, regional currencies, and some commodity currencies such as gold and silver to be automatically converted into another currency and to be both highly liquid and a store of value. It provides an entirely new paradigm for low cost international trade. The Bancor Protocol, crypto currencies and Blockchain technologies will produce currency solutions far superior to the euro currency and other currencies.

- A Europe which implements the economic democracy measures proposed in this book. And distributes wealth, income and power to all the peoples of Europe and gives them a greater stake in the economic system, the capitalist system, the social system and the political system.

- A Europe which de-globalises and focuses on production, full employment and growth within Europe. This would help individual nations reach full employment targets. This was originally a policy in the EEC, and called 'Community Preference' but was abolished in the new European Union which has enforced globalisation.

- A Europe where national governments are transparent and accountable to their peoples and where there are proper checks and balances to ensure this. There are some recommendations in Chapter 10.

- A Europe with a common human rights Constitution where the human rights of all persons are recognised and enforced. A European Court of Human Rights as part of the UN which vindicates and defends human rights. It's important that human rights supersede national sovereignty as one cannot always trust corrupt politicians to protect the rights of people or groups that they dislike. Human rights are a fundamental aspect of life itself, and are common values shared by all humanity.

- A Europe which protects celebrates and respects national cultures, traditions, literature, music and people's identity within European nations. Instead of attacking them, undermining them and trying to suppress them.

- A Europe which refuses to antagonise Russia, China and other big powers and seeks to build peaceful, respectful and cooperative relations with these countries. A Europe which works for lasting peace and justice in the Middle East. And work with them to improve human rights and democratic freedoms which are fundamental human values in all nations and societies. A Europe which strategises for global peace not for war. A Europe which refuses to be controlled by powerful military industrial interests which promote 'regime changes', paranoia, and wars, and profit from them.

- A Europe which works with the USA, Russia, China to stop the rape of Africa's natural resources and compensate Africans for the massive theft of its natural resources since the early 1970's and ensure ordinary Africans benefit from the extraction and trade in such resources in the present and future. And provides similar protections and supports to weak Asian countries and South American countries. This new policy based on respect and cooperation would do much to build peace and greater prosperity around the world.

- European countries which cooperate with each other in terms of collective security, while working together to build peace, compromise, consensus and respect between all nations in Europe itself and in other parts of the world.

This new Europe is possible, it is practical and feasible and would serve the best interests of European nations and Europe as a whole. It could become an example for other trading regions such as the proposed US - Canada free trading area. These would be free nations which would respect human rights as laid down by the UN and EU, while requiring and demanding human responsibilities to match these rights, not liberal free for alls which have encouraged and supported extremism, fraud and criminality. This in effect would outlaw, imprison, and remove if necessary all forms of religious extremism, political extremism, terrorism, corruption and bribery, bigotry and prejudice which have poisoned human relations in the Europe and elsewhere. Misguided tolerance, irresponsibility and liberalism should not be used to promote and facilitate criminality, fraud, and terrorism. In these free nations, the rights of voters in nation states would not be over ruled by an EU centre or unelected EU bureaucracy. And nation states would not be forced by an EU centre to be robbed and asset stripped to bail out corrupt bankers, fraudsters and speculators. This new Europe would prioritise the building of peace, trust and cooperation between the EU, Russia, China and North America, and achieve this, while working together to increase global economic output, GNP, and prosperity for all peoples and nations. A new type of Europe which is prosperous, free, democratic, united, just, fair, and at peace with itself and the rest of the world.

Chapter 3 The Dangers posed by 'Fake News', Deception and a Censored Press and a Self Interested and Self Serving Elite

" Let me tell you why you're here. You're here because you know something. What you know you can't explain, but you feel it. You've felt it your entire life, that there's something wrong with the world. You don't know what it is, but it's there, like a splinter in your mind, driving you mad. It is this feeling that has brought you to me. Do you know what I'm talking about?... This is your last chance. After this, there is no turning back. You take the blue pill - the story ends, you wake up in your bed and believe whatever you want to believe. You take the red pill - you stay in Wonderland and I show you how deep the rabbit-hole goes."

The Matrix movie

He who controls the past controls the future. He who controls the present controls the past.

Orthodoxy means not thinking — not needing to think. Orthodoxy is unconsciousness.

Don't you see that the whole aim of Newspeak is to narrow the range of thought?

1984 by George Orwell

And no official of my Administration, whether his rank is high or low, civilian or military, should interpret my words here tonight as an excuse to censor the news, to stifle dissent, to cover up our mistakes or to withhold from the press and the public the facts they deserve to know............................. And that is why our press was protected by the First Amendment-- the only business in America specifically protected by the Constitution- -not primarily to amuse and entertain, not to emphasize the trivial and the sentimental, not to simply "give the public what it wants"--but to inform, to arouse, to reflect, to state our dangers and our opportunities, to indicate our crises and our choices, to lead, mold, educate and sometimes even anger public opinion

President John F. Kennedy, Speech, April 1961

The right to a free, independent and informed opinion based on facts, evidence, corroboration, verification, statistics, figures, and proofs is a prerequisite for democracy, democratic participation and democratic societies. It has Constitutional protections in many countries and these protections need to be implemented and protected more vigorously. One's perception is all important here, as it leads to opinions, mindsets, actions, voting, activities and deeds, and how this perception is formed is of vital importance to understanding freedom, democracy and the world. Indeed the manipulation of perception is the most powerful tool for good or evil in the world today and in the past also. The press and media play a vital role here as does the radio wave spectrum and the Internet including alternative media, social media, Wikileaks and other such web sites and books, literature, whistleblowers and Scientific Journals. They can be used to promote, protect, maintain and improve freedom, democracy and human rights through the medium of truth, honesty, accountability and integrity, or they can be used undermine, erode, deny and destroy these freedoms and rights through the use of lies, deception, misdirection, manipulations, slanders, bigotry, and mockery. Unfortunately the latter has gained the upperhand. And freedom, democracy and human rights and accountability are under attack.

Brexit and other similar events may be regarded as drastic events, but they are mere symptoms of a far deeper malaise, and deep rooted problems in developed nations. This was briefly mentioned in the problems above which manifest over time and remain pent up and bottled up, until they unleash. Drastic events usually flow from a build up of pent up forces, which are refused or denied expression over time, until they finally and suddenly explode. There are precedents from the past, such as the years 1517, 1642, 1688, 1776, 1789, 1798, 1808 - 1833, 1848, 1861, 1867, 1911, 1916 - 1921, 1917, 1949, 1950's, 1960's, 1989 where uprisings and revolutions lead to freedom and to deep and lasting changes in many countries. History tells us again and again that these pent up forces are often ignored, dismissed, suppressed and even mocked by the mainstream press, academics , politicians and commentators at these points in history, because they are blinded by self interest and self contentment. And by the fact that their primary work is to serve themselves and serve the interests of self contented elites who are detached from reality and genuinely do not care about people or society or indeed the world. Thus the elite and their servants become detached, locked away from the real world, and trapped in their own circle, endlessly circulating their own narrow views, delusions, lies, deceptions, and partial truths among themselves, in an echo chamber, and indoctrinating the rest of society through their press and media, economists, journals, "intellectuals" and academics, while ignoring the wider effects, which are often destructive in the extreme at the personal level, the family level and community and national levels.

Many of the elite and their intellectuals and academics live in an 'Echo Chamber' of lies, half truths, and self reinforcing delusions. The rich, the self interested and self contented are happy with the status quo of worsening economies, massive debt, crashes followed by austerity and recession / depression, political corruption, manipulated wars and worsening terrorism, legal system failures and corruption, environmental destruction and the poisoning of water, land, food and air, collapsing healthcare systems, higher concentrations of wealth and income accompanied by great social injustices, pain and suffering, more social instability and conflict ; like Nero they are content to play the harp, drink and socialise while Rome burns. The important factor here is that the self interested and self contented elites can hide away from the rest of society, protected in exclusive and expensive communities, often gated and patrolled by strong security, personally protected by bodyguards which are backed up by police, military and intelligence services. The self interested and self contented are insulated from the destructive results or consequences of their actions. One is reminded here of the monarchies and aristocracies of the past and their system of feudalism. The mainstream press and media and Deep State have acted to reinforce this and maintain it, while blocking and censoring all voices which may question or upset this feudal order.

Concentrations of Power and Press Censorship & The Manipulation of People's Minds

The sudden emergence of Wikileaks and the revelations of Edward Snowden, Julian Assange, Daniel Elleberg and many other whistleblowers in governments, state bodies, big newspapers, the media, the police, the military, Universities, think tanks, intelligence services, the legal profession, the tax service in the first two decades of the 21st century proves that:

(a) governments and politicians have hidden agendas and regularly lie to their peoples, and engage in covert criminal acts, and the mainstream press and media and commentators are used to cover this up. This is outlined in more detail in Chapter 10. Some of this has been exposed in recent documentary films CitizenFour, Killswitch and The Most Dangerous Man in America, and the research and writings of Professor Lawrence Lessig of Harvard University [29]

(b) the mainstream press and media regularly lie to the people and often conceal important facts and evidence and news stories

(c) serious crimes by wealthy and powerful people and by certain religious institutions are often covered up by the press and media

(d) the press and media is not free in the sense that it is in many cases manipulated, controlled and coerced by state forces and / or powerful corporate forces.

(e) the promotion of one form of economics in the press and media and in Universities, termed 'Neo Liberal economics' or 'Junk Economics' by Dr. Michael Hudson. This type of economics has misrepresented the ideas of Adam Smith, and promoted the monopolies, oligopolies and cartels and extraction of economic rents which Adam Smith strongly opposed. [28]

(f) the press and media tend to distract people and dumb them down with petty, superficial trivial and sensational nonsense about sports, celebrities, sex gossip, fashion and shopping

(g) there is an appalling lack of ethics and courage in the press and media and among some journalists. And a lack of commitment to truth, evidence and facts

(h) scientific research has been undermined by fraud, deception, lies and cover ups since the 1980's and scientific journals have published and even supported this fraudulent research. This has undermined the credibility of science worldwide. Dr. John Ioannidis and others have written much about this in recent years, exposing fraudulent research and the corruption of many scientists and doctors.

(i) Dr. Steve Keen and Michael Hudson have exposed censorship in top Economics Journals. This is stifling debate in the field of Economics and leading to poorer understanding of Economics, continuing failed economic policies and a 'dumbing down' in the teaching of Economics.

The real reasons for wars, conflicts, regime changes, bank crashes, bank bail outs, austerity policies, the state of the economy, the level of debt, the unemployment stats, the illegal state surveillance, false flag attacks, the activities of the Deep State or 'Shadow Government', political corruption, crimes by politicians, dubious political policies and laws, and many other political moves have been exposed in Wikileaks and by other types of whistleblowers and in some alternative press and media. This has shocked many people worldwide, many of whom childishly believed the lies and deceptions provided to them by politicians, by state agencies, and the mainstream press and media and by academia. In some countries misguided (often corrupted) governments and prosecutors are bringing false and trumped up charges against Wikileaks personnel and other whistleblowers, when they should be giving them legal immunity and awards for bravery and services to freedom and democracy. Throughout history, freedom and democracy has often been defended by those people who exposed the enemies within the state.

Let us examine how this came about. In 1983, 50 corporations controlled most of the press and media in the USA. In 1992, this number was reduced down to 30. And by 2005, this was reduced to 6 corporations. This means that 6 corporations control the press and media in the USA, and what

Americans accept as 'facts' or 'reality'. The control of their perceptions. This is an extraordinary concentration of power. Since the mid 1990's, there has been massive consolidation in the press and media industry, with many big acquisitions, mergers, and takeovers, and many independents driven out of business. The industry today may be even more concentrated and controlled when one considers that cross share holdings are quite common in the press and media industry and other industries. Today, the press and media are owned by a handful of very rich individuals and their associates in most countries. The entire press and media, the mainstream media, in most developed countries have come under the increasing financial control of :

(i) a few owners and their political biases or hidden agendas

(ii) a few big advertisers who can and do influence content and news stories

(iii) the national security state or 'shadow government'

All three act have the power to cover up news stories exposing the real underlying reasons for wars, regime changes, political corruption, legal system corruption, social injustices, paedophile rings, child trafficking, environmental destruction, food and water safety issues, pollution, serious crimes by powerful people, abuse of worker's rights, social injustices, exploitation of children and women, support for foreign dictators, genocides, etc. Notable examples including the press and media supporting the illegal invasion of Iraq in 2003 and not revealing the truth about it, covering up the secretive undermining and overthrow of governments in Libya Egypt, Tunisia, Ukraine and Syria in the period 2008 - 2016, and Iran in 1953 and many countries in South America and Asia, the failure to expose banking corruption and financial crimes during the bubble period prior to 2008, the real state of economies and the failures of Neo Liberal economics, the robbery of taxpayers to pay for bank bail outs, the high concentrations of wealth and income and their negative effects on societies, the arrest of many wealthy paedophiles in 2017, concealing the poverty, unemployment and serious social injustices enforced by globalisation and by austerity after 2008, not reporting child trafficking and elite paedophile rings, hiding political support for states which are funding and arming Isis and other terrorists, the 'pay to play' system and bribery of politicians and their foundations by foreign governments, organisations, and by terrorist supporting states, covering up the immigration crisis and the fact that many countries could not absorb sudden mass influxes of people, covering up the spread of terrorism into Europe and North America in the period after 2002, the legal system corruption, the false flag attacks, providing misleading and false polls prior to a US election and a British referendum, overt manipulation of public opinion during elections, and concealing the political use of the military or intelligence services to unnecessarily bully and intimidate major world powers. These are highly important news stories which never get reported and properly analysed and discussed in the mainstream press and media.

There is an increasing tendency for them to distract and misdirect people and provide superficial, petty and sensational news stories to distract and entertain the masses, and immerse them in sports, fashion, sex gossip, celebrity lifestyles and shopping. Their sports heroes take on the role of gods to be worshipped and adored. All of this is human garbage to dumb down their minds. This dumbing down of the masses diminishes their critical thinking skills, their ability to question events and authorities, and keeps most people focussed on trivia and nonsense. This makes people easier to control and manipulate.

Mainstream media is becoming dominated by false news, lies, distortions, manipulation, cover ups, censorship, and an willingness to report on controversial issues and supply facts and evidence, and also by superficial nonsense to sidetrack people. Many examples of this abound in several developed countries. In addition to this, important news stories of vital public interest are often concealed in insignificant sections of newspapers or news broadcasts, barely mentioned, or omitted. Those journalists and news broadcasters determined to expose the truth in the public interest are often threatened with suspension, dismissal or violence or worse, and then blacklisted. This concentration of power and ability to censor provides the means to do this and is a very grave threat to freedom of the press and freedom of opinion in all democracies.

Today, public opinion is largely contained and policed through a compliant or subservient press and media, journalists, economists, academics and intellectuals which continuously feed the masses manipulated news and so called 'facts' which are in some cases lies, half truths or distortions. It is very similar to the activities of the 'Ministry of Truth' in the book 1984. It is actually the 'Thought Policing' of 1984, as it takes control of minds and perceptions and also causes ordinary people to become Thought Police themselves, unknowingly and unwittingly enforcing conformity on everybody else. This has created rigid systems and greatly narrowed and restricted human freedoms, human potential and human diversity. It even affects ordinary communications between people where they feel that they must repeat the lies, deceptions and half truths as if they were truths and facts, similar to the 'newspeak' in 1984. The conformists have integrated this 'newspeak' into their vocabulary, their minds, their way of thinking and acting. Many have lost the ability to question, to research, to analyse and deconstruct, to think for themselves, to disprove, to debate, to dispute this 'newspeak'. This is all eerily similar to that in the book '1984' by Orwell. The combination of this thought policing via the press and via individuals thought policing each other, and the high levels of surveillance after 9-11 and accompanying wars and terrorism, means that we are actually living in a '1984' type world.

It also has the flavour of the film 'The Matrix', where the controlling and manipulation of people's thoughts, mindsets, thought patterns, actions, free will and consciousness in a mass surveillance environment creates an oppressive and unfree world which is widely misperceived to be 'normal' and 'free'. And this thought policing today is reinforced through an ever more powerful police, military, intelligence and national security state, which is becoming more militarised and more intrusive. Even religions and religious leaders play a part in this thought policing by encouraging people to be compliant, to obey, to bow and crawl to Big Brother and the dictatorship of a '1984' society. Even when this contradicts and goes against religious and spiritual teachings. Marx's 'opium of the masses' has been replaced by spineless, moral cowardice and hypocrisy which is widespread.

Observe the great difference between the news released by Wikileaks, whistleblowers, investigative journalists, and alternative news media on one hand and the sanitised and largely manipulated news of many of the mainstream press and media. There are vast differences here. The controlled press and media enforces a form of cognitive dissonance which is becoming engrained in the mindsets of elites and the minds of the working classes and under classes maintaining subservience, obedience, and slavery in this game. This increasing concentration of press and media ownership, and of manipulation, control and censorship is remarkably very similar to that used in Nazi Germany and Stalin's Soviet Union.

We often hear about new communications technologies acting as liberating forces, but even in today's modern communications age with its advanced technologies, where mobile mediums of communication are ubiquitous and everywhere with most people in a near continuous state of communication, large sections of society are fed lies and deceptions, and kept in total ignorance and denied important truths and facts. Important events affecting peoples, countries and sections of society can be ignored, dismissed, denigrated, damned, belittled, excluded, etc. by a press and media which is largely controlled. This in turn adversely affects public opinion and government policies which are derived from public opinion, leading to the wrong policies, the wrong actions and the wrong direction, which ultimately inflicts unnecessary pain, suffering, loss and anguish on the people. Worryingly, it both engrains and intensifies injustices, corruptions and threats to freedom and democracy, and aggressively defends this corruption against all forms of dissent.

While there is ongoing censorship in mainstream communication mediums and channels which is undemocratic and anti Constitutional, ultimately the bitterness and frustration finds expression in new, emerging and alternative communications mediums and this leads to a backlash, which nearly always catches the mainstream of the self interested and self contented by surprise. At the heart of this today is the conflict between the censored (or controlled) mainstream press and media on one side and the new alternative media or uncensored digital media and the leaks from whistleblowers on the other, with the latter emerging to challenge the mainstream. It is the new technologies and new mediums of communication which are informing the masses of people of the injustices, the corruption, the denial of freedoms, the neglect, and the socio-economic exclusion inflicted upon them mostly by elites and feeding the frustration and the ongoing backlash worldwide. Looking at Brexit, populism and other similar events internationally, one sees the deeper context and meaning of these changes. There is a very deep desire within peoples for justice, for fairness, for human dignity, to be heard and acknowledged, to be shown respect, for self determination, for freedom, for sovereignty, and for matching freedom to its responsibilities. In many ways, the Internet and Digital Age is similar to the invention of the Printing Press and its effects on the Reformation and the Age of Enlightenment. A meeting or merging of new, radical, innovative political and economic ideas with new technologies and distribution mechanisms pushing humanity forward into new uncharted territory.

We may today be in a New Age of Enlightenment, the Digital Age Enlightenment, where the old failed orthodoxies and ways of thinking and doing things are being openly challenged and being dismantled and overthrown. This enlightenment is being driven by digital media, information systems and channels and new ideas, and also by an intense hunger for truth and justice, and by popular discontent. This is not trivial as information is power, and it is information and actions resulting from information which have traditionally driven social progress for centuries and millennia and will continue to drive social progress or social regress worldwide, ultimately providing populations with a choice between slavery on one side or freedom with responsibilities on the other side. The great lesson of history is that centralisation of power whether in the form of federalisation, monarchy, imperialism, foreign occupation, fascist or communist dictators, theocracies, corrupt unaccountable bureaucracy, the Deep State, control of the press and media, control of corrupt politicians, governments and judges by corrupt elites, high concentrations of wealth and income ultimately leads to slavery, to servitude, to feudalism, to hateful divisions, to grinding social injustices, to economic collapse, to human failure, to destruction, to conflicts and wars. This is as true today as it was hundreds of years ago.

Ultimately hard choices must be made. And risks must be taken. A free press and media requires the following features in order to function effectively and protect hard won freedoms and democratic rights

- A total commitment to truth and exposure of the truth. And backing this up with facts, evidence, proofs and corroboration from independent parties and sources. This should be the code of ethics, the legal oath and basic legal requirement for all journalists. Enforceable through the courts and regulators.

- A total commitment to transparency and accountability in the press and media and in government and government activities. The government exists to serve the people, to expose corruption, crimes and wrong doing, they are not there to oppress, manipulate, deceive, mislead and spy on the people.

- Better oversight, sanctions, and enforcement of standards to ensure a total commitment to truth in the press and media and in the scientific literature and medical literature.

- New laws should limit the amount of control one person or one company or holding company or corporate conglomerate has to a maximum of 10% of all press and media in a country. This would include all direct and indirect ownership, including the use of different front companies, straw men, use of majority and minority shareholdings, cross share holdings, and offshore investment vehicles. And furthermore, 12 independently owned companies must not own more than 50% of the press and media in a country. And these 12 must represent opposing and diverse views. And again, this would include all direct and indirect ownership, including the use of majority and minority shareholdings, front companies, cross share holdings, and offshore investment vehicles. Break up concentrations of press and media power to ensure a broad diversity of opinion, and a commitment to truth, facts, evidence, honesty and integrity, even it means offending the powerful and the wealthy.

- Public exposure of conflicts of interest, including the involvement of banks, corporates, wealthy individuals, the Deep State or Shadow Government in suppressing news stories

- Net neutrality should be preserved and also expanded to every country globally.

- A person's data must be made their personal and legal property. Those companies wishing to acquire and use this data must (i) inform the person and get their permission to do so (ii) pay for this data (iii) offer them an opt out (iv) provide details of how this data was used and how much has been paid and is owed for the data (v) provide evidence of compliance with data protection laws

- State monopolies in radio, television and the press and media should be broken up. Private monopolies should also be broken up. Alternative media and small and medium sized media companies should be allowed to transmit over the infrastructure used by these broken monopolies.

- Criminal penalties for falsifying the news and providing fake news stories. Covering up news stories dealing with the crimes committed by wealthy or powerful people. RICO criminal charges for conspiracy to do this.

- Legal and Constitutional protection of an Independent press and media free of manipulation, interference and control by private interests and state interests

- The national security state or Deep State should be prevented from interfering with the press and media. If there are national security issues in relation to press and media stories this should be clearly stated in advertisements or in news stories in the press and media. And relevant details of great importance to national security omitted from news stories under court order. The public being informed of such measures.

- The legal and Constitutional protection of alternative press and media, and more extensive use of Internet technologies and new communications technologies to expose the truth and provide truthful news. More web sites like Wikileaks should be encouraged to be set up.

- Ensuring that freedoms are matched to responsibilities and that hate speech and incitements to hatred and violence are made subject to legal processes and adjudication and appropriate legal punishments.

- Greater freedom in the book and paper publishing field. Amazon and some other companies have established publishing companies which enable people to self publish and have their books sold online and in retail shops. Paper based versions of books are printed on demand after a purchase online, while e-book versions can be downloaded to computers within minutes.

- Freedom to publish papers on Economics. Both Dr. Steve Keen and Michael Hudson have exposed censorship in top Economics Journals. Expose the defects in Neo Liberal economics or 'Junk Economics' as termed by Dr. Michael Hudson in the press and media and in Economics Journals and other academic literature [28].

- Scientific research which is undertaken by independent, accountable and transparent research bodies with no conflicts of interest. A total commitment to scientific truth.

- Scientific Journals which are independent, accountable and transparent and have a total commitment to truth, and are subject to rigorous scrutiny by the general public, scientists, regulators and government. Enforceable through courts and regulators.

- Freer use of the radio spectrum and analogue and digital broadcast spectrum for alternative press and media

- A press and media which constantly engages with the general public to inform and to educate, to present truths, to challenge, to analyse and debate the evidence and facts, to deconstruct events and facts, to be vigilant in the protection of freedoms and rights, and stimulate vigorous debate, critical thinking, logic and higher level reasoning.

Chapter 4   The Causes and Nature of Economic Crashes: The Fatal Flaw in Neo Liberal and Neo Classical Economics and 'Free market' Economics

'In a time of universal deceit, telling the truth is a revolutionary act'
Anonymous

'I am in a state of shocked disbelief.......... I found a flaw in the model that defines how the world works,.............Absolutely, precisely, you know that's precisely the reason I was shocked, because I have been going for 40 years or more with very considerable evidence that it was working exceptionally well'
Alan Greenspan, former Federal Reserve chairman, testifying before US Congress in October 2008 that there were serious flaws and defects in Neo Liberal and Neo Classical economics which were exposed in the 2008 crash

People of the same trade seldom meet together, even for merriment and diversion, but the conversation ends in a conspiracy against the public, or in some contrivance to raise prices.
Adam Smith, The Wealth of Nations, 1776

'If you want a picture of the future, imagine a boot stamping on a human face - forever.'
George Orwell, 1984

There is one anomaly or great contradiction in Economics, which has never been rectified. It relates to the central tenet or principle of free markets - the pricing and the pricing mechanisms and the allocation of "scarce resources" including money creation and credit (created out of nothing or 'thin air'). The current dominant economic theories have been proven to be wrong. This fatal flaw in economics and in accompanying political ideologies and policies should be taught in all schools and Universities, but it is not being taught at present (2017). Books on politics and economics have also neglected or ignored this important factor.

Let us begin with the dominant economic theory, often termed neo-classical economics or neo liberal economics or free markets theory which is promoted by most academic economists and bank economists which states that markets can reach an 'equilibrium state' and that prices and price adjustments reflect accurate present and future conditions and will serve to clear (surplus or scarce) quantities and provide an "efficient allocation of resources". They have used many types of marginal analysis to justify this. In the real world, price adjustments are driven by more powerful forces which inefficiently allocate resources and create dynamic disequilibrium, excessive speculative prices and excessive debt based on these prices, speculative crashes, mass bankruptcies, deflation and debt deflation, and self reinforcing cycles of recession and depression, and vast misallocations of capital and resources and marginal disutility. The famous Federal Chairman, Alan Greenspan discovered that his Neo Liberal and Neo Classical economics contained serious flaws and defects in 2008 and he stated this to the US Congress : he discovered dynamic disequilibrium which has existed for a long time.

Dynamic Disequilibrium

There is no free market, and there is no equilibrium, and markets do not automatically clear and self correct back to optimum conditions, but there is a skewed market which is not free and which is shaped by the forces of dynamic disequilibrium. And there are different degrees of dynamic disequilibrium. As we shall see in this chapter, this dynamic disequilibrium affects demand side factors and supply side factors and market status factors. The facts and evidence of history support and indeed prove Dynamic Disequilibrium, between 1970 and 2010 there has been 145 banking crashes, 204 monetary collapses and 76 sovereign debt crises, totalling 425 systemic crises in that period according to the IMF. This averages about 10 per year. This includes the severe financial crash and crisis in Thailand in 1997, Russia in 1998, Brazil in 1999, the dot com crash in the USA and Europe in 2000, Argentina in 1998-2002, and Mexico in 1994. There have been many, many crashes prior to 1970 throughout history and they all share the same characteristics and dynamics, and have dynamic disequilibrium at the heart of them.

The financial crash of 2008 led to the direct loss of $5 trillion in the USA, the loss of 8 million jobs and 6 million evictions from family homes. The cost to the American economy in terms of lost output, GDP, productivity, bail outs, higher unemployment, lost revenues and earnings has been estimated at $24 trillion (Dr. William K. Black). There were similar massive losses in other countries worldwide, including Ireland, Britain, Spain, Cyprus, Greece, etc.. Globally 34 million people lost their jobs and $26 trillion was wiped off the value of shares. The global cost of bailing out the banks and financial institutions between 2007 and 2014 was $13 trillion (Andrew Haldane, Bank of England estimate), though newer estimates for 2017 out it at $15 trillion.

At present, the speculative derivatives market is worth $1,200 trillion, and when combined with other speculative assets the total is $1,500 trillion, more than 25 times the world economy (World Gold Council, December 2013). The 2008 banking crash is not unique, it follows a well established pattern, one of many crashes throughout history, which will continue to occur as reforms have not been implemented.

Why are economic systems so unstable and why are they so vulnerable to Dynamic Disequilibrium ?

Let us begin by addressing causality, the cause and effect relationship behind Dynamic Disequilibrium. 97% of all money is created out of nothing when banks give out loans and mortgages. When a bank gives a loan or mortgage to a customer it

(a) creates money out of nothing and

(b) creates a signed promissory note of the value of this newly created money.

This promissory note is owned by the borrower and it's value is lodged into the borrower's account, and appears as newly created money lodged into the borrowers account. It now belongs to the borrower, and this also means the bank now owes the borrower this sum of money. Lodgements or deposits are legally seen as loans by a customer to a bank. Legally, the bank now owes the borrower this sum of newly created money (created out of nothing). This new money exists as electronic credits in the bank. The bank creates a liability in its accounts showing that it owes this money to the borrower and then it creates another entry to claim that the bank repays the money to the borrower, by falsely alleging it buys the promissory note off the borrower and provides him/her with "money", falsely called a "loan". In reality, the bank merely gives the borrower's newly created money back to the borrower in this transaction, and fraudulently calls it a "loan". These accounting entries in the bank now show that no money is owed to the bank and no money is owed to the borrower. The bank misrepresents this to the borrower by falsely claiming that the borrower owes this newly created money to the bank. Legally nobody has loaned any money, neither the borrower owes money to the bank or the bank owes money to the borrower, as the money has been created out of nothing and has been put into the borrower's account by the bank, creating a new deposit, and this was "repaid" back to the borrower by the bank. Nothing is owed. This new money creation is a form of fraud, as the money is created out of nothing, which is a fraud under law, and this also means the bank brings no (financial) consideration to the loan / mortgage contract, making it null and void. Furthermore the bank misrepresents the situation and does not disclose all relevant facts about the contract in dealings with the borrower, which is another breach of contract.

And the compounded interest associated with this alleged "debt" is not even created with the money and must be extracted from the existing money supply, creating severe economic turbulence, crashes, and instability over time. This is really important, private banks do not create interest money when creating new money out of nothing and lending it out, and this means there can never be enough money in the system to pay off the debt. This creates a classic debt and interest trap, which is quite fatal to economies when one considers that interest compounds over time so that the borrower often pays back 150% - 250% of the original loan. This leads to interest creating more debt, and multiplying debt many times across the economy. This compounding of interest, through its effects on consumption and investment negatively affects the business cycle intensifying and deepening it depending on debt levels. Interest grows exponentially, and this is in contrast to economies and businesses which grow naturally or linearly. This creates a conflict between interest and economies. This compound interest acts as a parasite, it sucks money out of the real economy affecting consumption levels, aggregate demand and accompanying investment levels, imposing costs on extraction, production, storage, distribution, selling and purchasing. The compound interest rate system is unsustainable. It imposes significant constrained, unrealised, unmet supply and constrained, unrealised, unmet demand or deficiencies in effective demand. It is a strong dynamic disequilibrium factor. An excellent analysis of the effects of interest is provided by Margrit Kennedy in her book 'Interest and Inflation Free Money' (1995) [23] and by Michael Montagne at http://www.perfecteconomy.com

This is worsened by the fact that most of this fraudulently created money (loans) 70-80% has been and continues to be used for speculation in assets, property and derivatives bidding up prices to unsustainable levels and creating massive speculative debt in the process, creating speculative manias, bubbles, crashes and recessions / depressions over time. This involves trillions of euros / dollars / pounds per year. These factors above create vast instabilities in an economic system and are the creator of Dynamic Disequilibrium. It determines the allocation of resources in an entire economy. And this massive allocation of resources is strongly skewed towards Dynamic Disequilibrium. Yet this is not taught in schools and Universities and very rarely mentioned in the press and media.

This money creation fraud acts to enslave people, families, businesses, governments and whole nations with massive debt and an unstable economic system. This debt enslavement is modern day slavery and puts many people in danger of losing homes, incomes, jobs, livelihoods, businesses, etc. This inbuilt economic instability adversely affects demand and consumption and investment levels. It imposes significant constrained, unrealised, unmet supply and constrained, unrealised, unmet demand or deficiencies in effective demand, making 'equilibrium' impossible. It is a strong dynamic disequilibrium factor. Yet the law of demand ignores this or dismisses it.

The work of Professor Richard Werner in Britain and Mike Montagne in USA is important here as their research over 30 years conclusively proves that money is created when new debt is created, and the present money system and its circulation is based on the excessive build up of debt and interest. Compound interest leads to a multiplication of existing debt, and also new debt and interest has to be acquired once existing debt and interest is partially paid down in order to keep the circulation flowing and economies growing, and this leads to a further multiplication of debt. Thus, we are caught in a debt trap. This multiplication of debt and the continuous extraction of money out of the system via higher interest payments (debt servicing charges) on massive accumulations of debt creates great imbalances and instabilities, undermines the viability of both speculative investments and productive investments, and this leads to crashes. I would advise all persons to read Michael Montagne's analysis of excessive debt and debt limits at http://www.perfecteconomy.com.

Speculation, private debt and credit growth are not irrelevant and not insignificant. In fact they have major effects on consumption and demand. There is a correlation between the growth in credit and growth in employment (reduction in unemployment) and between the growth in private debt and employment. Recent research by Dr. Steve Keen has confirmed this link, which has existed for over 100 years [1]. Figures show that rises in debt creation or a rise in credit leads to lower unemployment during the boom phase, prior to a crash and the reverse is true after a crash [1]. This fuels higher consumption, aggregate demand and related investment during the boom phase. However, after a crash, when prices fall and bankruptcies increase, the high levels of private debt and other debt remain diminishing consumption and demand. This connection between falling or collapsed prices for assets and the fact that the debt is continuous and keeps rising (via interest) for these assets is the key to understanding why economies crash and remain in recession or depression.

The important point here is that in all countries, debt overhang after crashes has acted to reduce or reverse credit growth, and deflate aggregate demand and consumer purchasing power. And this fall off in demand adversely affected investment and aggregate supply especially productive businesses and small and medium sized businesses dependent on local trade, regional trade and national trade. This typically produces slow growth, prolonging recessions and depressions. This has been confirmed in research by Dr. Steve Keen. Japan and its 'Lost 20 years' being a notable example. Debt and credit and their relationships to unemployment and other economic indicators are ignored by Neo Liberal and Neo Classical economists, and are presumed to be irrelevant and unimportant, and are omitted from their models.

In 2015-16, Japan had a total debt of 400% of GDP, Portugal had a total debt of 358% of GDP, Greece had a total debt of 317% of GDP (despite debt write downs and write offs of tens of billions of euros), Ireland had a total debt of 390% of GDP and a private debt to GDP of 293% (Irish Central Bank Quarterly Financial Accounts Ireland 2016) and Spain had a total debt of 313% of GDP (McKinsey & Company [7]). The USA with its government debt of $20 trillion has a debt of 111% of GDP while the total debt (household, federal and state governments, corporate, banking) is $67 trillion which is 372% of GDP. Total US unfunded liabilities (social security, veterans, medicare and other government debt) are $106 trillion which is 588% of GDP. (US Debt clock web site). This creates great limitations and restrictions on aggregate demand, consumption, and credit growth creating vast levels of unmet, unrealised demand and consumption.

The **Cantillon Effect** is also a factor here. As newly created money or credit, especially Quantitiative easing remains concentrated among the richest 1 – 5% who tend to speculate or save this money. This traps the money among the richest section of society and it circulates there. The velocity of money among the richest 1 -5 % may be high while at the same time the velocity of money among the bottom 90% of a population can be very low. This can skew markets and national economies and cause them to operate well below optimum levels. We saw this in the period 2008 – 2016. This sucks vast amounts of money out of the circular flow of income in a country and this adversely affects consumption, aggregate demand and the investment which is dependent on this demand.

This dynamic disequilibrium arises from a combination of factors which interconnect and influence each other creating various negative synergies over time. These are detailed in sections below relating to the demand curve and the supply curve. These individual factors and their connectedness or synergies can determine the level of skew, disequilibrium and disorder in a skewed market, and in most cases they serve to intensify and worsen dynamic disequilibrium. Essentially, dynamic disequilibrium within individual parts of an economic system which is interconnected creates increased disequilibrium within the individual parts themselves, and in their relationships with each other, and within clusters of related parts which can extend further to other parts and clusters, accelerated by loss of confidence, which can in certain, recurring circumstances lead to a freezing of credit and capital markets and contagion, and become fully systemic. Yet dynamic disequilibrium continues to dominate parts, clusters, relationships and the system and the resultant forms and outcomes. Ultimately, the parts of the system are dynamically connected to each other and to the whole system and vice versa and the feedback mechanisms are many, overlying and complex.

There are levels or degrees of dynamic disequilibrium relating to how dysfunctional, inefficient and unstable the allocation of resources actually are. Economies and markets are complex adaptive systems with characteristic of emergence and systems theory, and this can only be understood by deciphering the agents of turbulence and flux and their complex actions, relationships, interactions and results. There is no short term or long term equilibrium in markets as markets are fundamentally dynamic disequilibrium systems, and are constantly changing, unstable and in flux, with many agents interacting in myriad ways to produce new and unexpected forms of emergence. While some economies may be in a mild form of economic turbulence or dynamic disequilibrium often mistaken for 'growth', 'recovery', 'progress', it is the trajectory of the economy and dynamic disequilibrium which is most important. Only at the point of a crash do politicians, economists and commentators suddenly realize that dynamic disequilibrium exists and is the driving force at all times.

It is important to emphasise and re-emphasie that markets and economies are not static and do not consist of a few variables and "all other factors being equal" as proposed by the economic models used by most economists today. Following from this, in most cases it is impossible to produce exact predictions or predictable results. Most economic predictions are based on extrapolations of past events, superficial analysis of some variables but no understanding of their constituent parts and their relationships, no understanding of dynamic disequilibrium, and looking at charts but not the fundamental factors underlying them, ignoring human frauds based on greed, refusing to factor in historical precedents, using very limited models and "educated" guesses. Their ineffective predictions provide ranges of figures not exact figures. But these ranges tell us nothing, mislead economists and policy makers, and in many cases are wrong.

Dynamic disequilibrium creates vast misallocations of resources, unrealistic prices which do not reflect returns, utility or intrinsic value, provide inadequate quantities, false scarcity amidst great abundance and considerable economic and social instability and financial losses ; this will be discussed throughout this book. Fleeting appearances of equilibrium may be perceived to exist briefly in this disequilibrium environment but the dominant forces of disequilibrium will push and pull against this, and enforce the dominant state of dynamic disequilibrium. Let us examine demand and supply curves in this new context.

Defects in Law of Demand and Market Demand Curve under Conditions of Dynamic Disequilibrium

- The law of demand is based on one consumer and one product or many identical consumers, clones, with identical tastes and preferences, marginal utility, income, propensity to consume and purchasing activities and a few products. In the real world, what is true for one consumer is not true for all consumers. All consumers are not identical, they have widely different tastes and preferences, different marginal utility, utility maximising, incomes, propensity to consume, and purchasing activities. And there are many products and services, and millions of combinations and permutations which make optimum choices and utility maximisation impossible. And these consumer preferences and purchasing decisions and utilities change as income changes. There are differences, divergences and contradictions between consumers and aggregates and classes of consumers. During speculative booms the demand curve points upwards as price increases and expected future price increases creates more demand. There are many different types of individual demand curves and social class demand curves, and these cannot be aggregated accurately to give the market demand curve. The market demand curve is an inaccurate representation of reality.

- All consumers do not accept more goods at lower prices, there are significant differences within aggregates of consumers or social classes of consumers. Price falls (and price rises) can emerge from many factors, some of them may caused by conditions which lead certain classes of consumers to reduce their demand. For example workers may have to take wage cuts or suffer lay offs and unemployment or capital flight to cheaper country, so that prices for products are reduced ; but these workers may not be able to afford them or reduce their demand for them. As explained above some classes of consumers increase their consumption when prices rise, while others remain stable, while others may decrease consumption. Some defer consumption until prices fall further, some hoard their money, some cannot consume due to high private debt levels, and some cannot consume due to the deluded austerity policies of austerity hawks.

- Income rises or falls can radically change consumer preferences, marginal utility, utility maximising and purchases and their individual demand curves and classes demand curves. There are significant differences between individuals and between aggregates. This is complicated further by the fact that this is changing and in constant flux, providing inconsistencies and dynamic disequilibrium. The dynamic disequilibrium caused by globalisation and automation, particularly their race to the bottom creates significant discontinuities, divergences, inconsistencies, and contradictions.

- Price rises or falls can change consumer preferences, marginal utility, utility maximising and purchases and their individual demand curves and classes demand curves. And this also is in constant flux, providing inconsistencies and dynamic disequilibrium.

- Price discrimination for identical products and services in different markets. This is pure manipulation, and bears no relationship to costs, marginal efficiency, marginal utility factors, etc. and is cynically used to rip off consumers in developed countries. For example, medical drugs involve price discrimination between countries and price differentials of 100% - 5,000%. This indirectly enforces high costs of living in developed countries while exploiting low wage markets in developing and third world countries providing significant disequilibrium.

- Skewed markets and anti-competitive practises as outlined in sections below destroy marginal utility and reduce consumers down to levels of marginal disutility dependent on the level of skewing or anti competitive behaviour by suppliers / producers and bankers. This skewing of the market creates extra costs, great imbalances in the market and in the allocation of scarce resources. This distortion is a significant dynamic disequilibrium factor adversely affecting both demand side and supply side factors.

- In respect of demand for investment products and services, this is mostly governed by speculation, the herd mentality, and short term gains in terms of days, a month or quarterly returns. This herd mentality is mutually reinforcing between traders and firms. In most cases, it is not based on business fundamentals and accurate analysis and predictions. This speculative, short term driven system provides imperfect information, and this itself is driven by generous financial incentives. This imperfect information comes in the form of false and fraudulent investment ratings, false accounting, legalized Ponzi schemes, price rigging, insider trading, front running and price manipulations in real time (as described by investor Michael Lewis), laddering of stocks and spinning of stocks, wrong or fraudulent information about financial assets, properties, derivatives and their future returns, interest rate rigging, currency rigging, packaging and selling defective or loss making investment products while secretly betting against them. And this false information and fraud was greatly assisted by hysteria and hype in the financial press and media and among most economists, investment advisors and managers. All of these cause irrational expectations and make utility maximization impossible. And the refusal of ministers and government officials to prosecute these fraudsters and white collar criminals in the USA and other developed countries provides strong incentives to continue committing frauds and financial crimes. All of this serves to provide disutility or disutility maximization to investors and create irrational expectations and irrational agents in the form of losses. The boom and bust of 2008 provided a classic case of this. This is the key to understanding dynamic disequilibrium.

- The cost of financial system crashes similar to that in 2008 in terms of bailout costs, austerity, recession, lost output and lost GDP is estimated to be trillions of dollars for large countries like USA, Britain, France, Spain, Italy, etc. and hundreds of billions of dollars or more for small countries such as Ireland, Belgium, Portugal, Latvia, etc. . The cost to the American economy of the financial crash in 2008 and accompanying deep recession in terms of lost output, gdp, productivity, bail outs, higher unemployment, lost revenues and earnings has been estimated at $24 trillion (Dr. William K. Black). It is estimated that Britain lost £5 trillion in lost output and GNP from the 2008 crash and that other developed countries also lost billions / trillions of dollars in lost output and GDP (Reinhart and Rogoff 2010, 2014, Will Hutton 2010, Summers and Fatas 2015, Ball 2014, Blanchard, Cerutti, and Summers 2015). This adds up to trillions of dollars of losses over several years or decades. This also imposes losses on aggregate demand and aggregate supply which affect consumers and their capacity to buy, and their demand curves. This dynamic disequilibrium regularly creates vast economic losses, in addition to destroying funding for consumption, aggregate demand, profits and returns to capital, physical capital and human capital formation, innovation and sustainable economic growth. We see here practical examples of economies governed by dynamic disequilibrium.

- Consumption and demand curves (both actual and potential) have been largely affected by the failures of austerity policies which are identical to the Depression of the 1930's. There are austerity hawks today similar to Mellon (in the 1930's) enforcing a liquidation of labour, stocks, debt, capital, businesses, real estate, farmers, etc. in the name of austerity and 'balanced budgets', deficit reduction, and fiscal and monetary contraction in the middle of severe economic recession and depression. Accompanied by massive private debt overhang from previous speculative manias and wars, and a new deflationary gold standard in the form of the euro. This creates new weaknesses in demand, and serious ongoing defects in demand and economic growth which has a short term and long term negative effect on demand. It has the effect of producing Balance Sheet Recessions and repeats of the 'lost 15 years' in Japan as described by Dr. Richard Koo, and a worsening of existing recessions / depressions, according to leading economists such as Krugman, Stiglitz, Shiller, Hudson, etc.. In many respects it is a repeat of the mistakes of the 1930's.

- **Rentiers and the Structure of Economies**

The economist Adam Smith claimed that free markets were markets which were free of the economic rent and monopolistic activities of landlords, inherited wealth, monopolists, oligopolists, cartels and banks [28]. He criticised and condemned them for extracting economic rents and undermining free competition, yet today they are dominating the market, distorting it and skewing it [28]. These rentiers or economic rent seekers and enforcers have the full support of free marketers who misinterpret Adam Smith and wrongly use Adam Smith to underpin their beliefs.

The research and works of Dr. Michael Hudson shows that the rentiers or FIRE sector (Finance, Insurance, Real Estate) now dominate many developed economies and account for most of the credit created and most of the debt and most of the money used in transactions[28]. They rely on speculation, debt and abuse of monopoly position or cartel position to extract interest, dividends, high fees, excessive charges and capital gains from abusing their monopoly position or cartel position. It was this speculative sector which crashed economies in 2008 and in 2000 and gave the world 425 systemic crashes between 1970 and 2010 (IMF report). Government austerity policies were enforced in many countries to bail out these rentiers or FIRE class at taxpayer's expense. Banks could be compared to big aristocratic landlords in past centuries in the sense that the creation of credit (out of nothing) could be compared to land, and interest and repayments could be compared to land rent. Dr. Hudson goes on to explain how Neo Liberal economics supports this rentier or speculator class and this is leading to speculative bubbles and crashes, a globalisation 'race to the bottom', excessive concentrations of wealth and income, debt deflation and asset stripping (foreclosures, evictions, seizures of assets) and to a new Debt Dependent class (bottom 95%) and Debt Beneficiary class (top 5%). The rentiers make up most of this Debt Beneficiary class, the top 5%. There is an entirely new structure for economies and societies where Debt and Rentier dominance are the major economic issues and the Debt Beneficiary class act as a parasite on the Debt Dependent class [28]. It is a return to feudalism and serfdom. This new economic structure affects aggregate demand, consumption, supply, output, investment decisions, credit allocation, credit availability, debt composition, debt vulnerabilities and economic growth. And it also affects the equation $MV=PT$ when one integrates the massive value of money and credit created to speculate and inflate assets and the high numbers of transactions during a bubble phase or bull market, and accompanying inflationary rises which affect the rest of the economy.

- The scale of speculation today needs to factored into demand curves and theories and presumptions of 'equilibrium'. In 2008 prior to the crash, the derivatives market was worth $800 trillion which is 12 times the world economy. Today it is estimated to be $1,200 trillion, about 20 times the world economy (World Gold Council, December 2013). Much of these derivative trades and profits are redirected through offshore tax havens. This is a massive siphoning of resources away from productive capital investment by businesses and away from consumption by ordinary working people, thus affecting the circular flow of income within countries, demand and consumption curves and theories, providing discontinuities, outflows, and further dynamic disequilibrium.

- Quantitative Easing valued at $15 trillion to bail out banks, big corporate and some governments has mostly been pumped into speculation in shares in stock markets, derivatives, government bonds and other forms of assets, creating new bubbles. From 2008 to 2015, the value of the global stock of investable assets increased substantially by about 40 percent, from $350 trillion to over $500 trillion. The figure of $500 trillion is over 9 times the global economy and presents a new level of systemic risk to economies. Quantitative Easing did not reach the productive sector, the consumption sector (bottom 60%) and the wider economy and stimulate consumption, aggregate demand, and related supply and economic growth to desired levels ; it proved to be ineffective and disappointing. This policy distorts and skews markets, inflating speculative bubbles, while adversely affecting consumption, aggregate demand and associated productive investment levels.

- Skewing of Markets and National Economies
Markets can be skewed to great extremes by very high concentrations of wealth and income and the many distribution effects of this. Consumer Demand, including actual demand and potential demand (and related investment including national and regional businesses) is greatly affected by the

siphoning of vast amounts of monies away from labour to capital (the very wealthy) through :

(a) outsourcing jobs and production to cheap developing and third world countries under a certain type of 'Globalization' with managed trade and skewed markets. A globalised 'race to the bottom'. These goods and services are then sold at inflated prices in developed countries. This system enforces a reduction in real wages for workers and the shrinking middle class in developed countries and the enforcement of high prices and costs of living in these same countries. Some notable examples in our time are the 'rust belt' and the ghettos and industrial wastelands in the USA and Europe, and use of the 'China price' and 'wages of India in the American workplace' to intimidate suppliers, producers and workers.

(b) increased automation and labour replacing technologies and accompanying higher productivity rates which mostly enrich capital and wealth owners. These high productivity rates have overtaken wage rates to labour for decades. In the USA, the productivity rate has been higher than the wage rate for over 25 years, and this gap has been growing wider. This is due to worsen as seen by advancements in artificial intelligence, expert systems for professional services, automation of offices, factories, warehouses, and homes, wireless networking, robotics, drones, and driverless cars and trucks. These will continue to replace workers.

(c) the great market and political power of monopoly / oligopoly capital, cartels, patents, restrictive practices, land and property owners, or FIRE sector (Finance Insurance and Real Estate) and their ability to extract large economic rents and supernormal profits and impose high costs of living on workers and labour [28]. Increasing prices and imposing higher costs of living on societies, these monopolies / cartels / FIRE sector have also reduced the real wages of workers and the middle classes and the purchasing power of wages. This has been enforced via globalization, banning unions and collective bargaining, increased automation in the workplace, outsourcing, political influence and new laws, etc.. This has greatly increased profits, capital gains and incomes for the wealthiest 5%. Indeed, the high rate of productivity growth in North America and Europe from the 1980's to 2000's from new technologies and innovations increased the incomes, profits and capital gains of monopolies, oligopolies, patents holders and cartels while wages stagnated for most of the working class and middle class during this time period.

The research and works of Dr. Michael Hudson shows that the rentiers or FIRE sector (Finance, Insurance, Real Estate) now dominate many developed economies and account for most of the credit created and most of the debt and most of the money used in transactions[28]. There is an entirely new structure for economies and societies where Debt and Rentier dominance are the major economic issues and the Debt Beneficiary class (top 5%) act as a parasite on the Debt Dependent class (bottom 95%) [28]. It is a return to feudalism and serfdom.

New technologies and forms of e-commerce have enabled takeovers, mergers, and consolidations of industries on a global level and led to the creation of new international monopolies and oligopolies. This has concentrated the returns to capital at an international level. One example being the FANG shares on stock markets and the increasing dominance of high tech firms which have penetrated new industries. And the increasing dominance of just a few big firms in the Big Pharma sector, banking sector, insurance sector, military industrial sector, and real estate sector. This has led to rounds of business closures, price pressures on suppliers, the bankruptcy of some suppliers, wage reductions, etc.. This enriches and consolidates the economic and political power of the rentier class or FIRE sector while simultaneously impoverishing the working and middle class and disempowering them.

(d) speculation in assets and derivatives leads to very high returns to capital, to speculators and to banks, and the income from this in terms of profits, dividends, interest and capital gains goes to the richest 1%-5%. One has seen massive increases in the income and wealth of capital owners, top executives of banks and big corporates and speculators in the last 2 decades. This includes the massive increases in executive pay which range from 50 to 400 times the wages of ordinary workers in a business. Company buybacks, involving trillions of dollars over the last decade, has fuelled this as executives and speculator shareholders artificially prop up share prices and loot companies. This is one of the main driving forces behind the high concentrations of wealth and income in several countries. <u>Speculation to rephrase a monetarist term provides 'free lunches' in the form of price rigging, fraud, insider trading, massive debt and leverage, financial crimes and capital gains to the rich. And banks printing money and interest out of nothing is the ultimate "free lunch".</u>

Massive financial gains from speculation and fraud during booms drains the productive sector of the economy and deprives it of affordable funds for investment and profits via consumption. Large banks and medium banks have consistently favoured funding for speculation over funding for the productive sector. Bank loans for speculation are often 3 – 7 times higher than loans for the productive sector. In some countries where a few large banks dominate the banking market, this can lead to massive loans for speculation while the productive sector is starved of funds for investment. This deprives the economy of long term productive investment, and reduces or eliminates the traditional income, wages, benefits, and productivity returns to labour. It leads to stagnation in real wages or reductions of such for workers, which has been found in many studies. Real wages in the USA for ordinary workers and the middle class have stagnated for the last 30 years and the real minimum wage is lower today than it was 60 years ago. Furthermore speculation in assets and derivatives is based on the enforcement of low wages and loss of benefits and bad working conditions on workers through globalization, automation, and neo liberal policies which lead to higher share prices and more gains from speculation. It imposes new economic structures where the grinding down of workers and their families for less and less resources is related to speculation in shares, assets and derivatives ; one feeds off the other.

These payments to capital owners, to executives, banks and speculators are much higher than their productivity and are not justifiable in an economic and business sense. And most workers are deprived of participation in capital ownership, in employee share ownership. The theory of 'solely maximizing shareholder value in the short term' to maximize financial gains for executives and large speculative shareholders has worsened speculation, creating a casino economy which further concentrates wealth. This is occurring in many developed countries. The research and works of Joseph Stiglitz, Paul Krugman, Thomas Piketty, Hudson, and many others confirm this [8].

(e) wages have been squeezed and reduced in developed countries so as to increase profit margins and 'shareholder value' over the last 25 years. This has a political dimension and legal dimension in addition to an economic dimension. As we have seen above real wages for working class and middle income Americans stagnated for 30 years, while profits, dividends, capital gains and executive salaries rose by large amounts during this time. One very important consequence of the stagnation in real wages is that workers got into more debt in order to buy over priced homes and over priced products and services and maintain high living standards and expectations in developed countries. This large rise in private debt levels has created significant financial system and economic instability in many countries, which flared up in 2008. There is a correlation between the stagnation (or fall) in real wages and the rise in private debt levels in developed countries [1]. This correlation has been significant since the early 1980's when Neo Liberal policies and globalization began under Thatcher and Reagan. The high debt repayments and compounded interest act to siphon even more wealth away from workers and the poor to the already rich. Studies by Margaret Kennedy and other economists show that interest is a form of 'trickle up' economics where the wealth and income trickles up to the wealthiest in society, largely benefitting the richest 5% [23]

(f) government austerity policies to bail out rich bankers, speculators and fraudsters, and enrich vulture funds and protect their assets and the assets of the very rich, which was achieved by imposing new taxes, levies and charges on the working and middle classes and vicious cutbacks in pensions, social security, state healthcare, social programmes, hospitals, welfare and education. In reality, governments and troikas loaded private banking debt and speculator debt onto whole nations and taxpayers which bankrupted them and then enforced 'deficit reduction' measures and austerity on them ; this has been mass theft and robbery of the taxpayers, unemployed, disabled, elderly, and ordinary people, seizing their private property and income, and may be unconstitutional. At the same time taxes were reduced or eliminated for the FIRE sector and Rentiers and for economic rent. And Quantitative Easing was used to maintain and improve asset prices and protect the wealth of the richest 5% and the vulture funds, while debasing the currency and eroding real wages. During austerity, vulture funds suck large amounts of money out of economies and redirect them through tax loopholes and offshore tax havens. All of these policies directly transfer wealth and income from the bottom 95% to the richest 5%.

(g) the nature of government policies and budgets which have the effect of reducing or eliminating taxes on the FIRE sector and on speculators, rentiers and economic rents while increasing or maintaining high taxes on the working class and middle class and the productive sector. And imposing cutbacks in pensions, social security, state healthcare, social programmes, hospitals, welfare and education. This involves large redistributions of wealth and income to the richest 5%.

(h) the nature of debt enslaved societies, this is discussed further in Chapter 7. The massive government debt burden (to bail out banks) and private debt burdens (to compensate for lower real wages) and interest payments imposed upon taxpayers, consumers, workers / labour. Most debt and compound interest repayment is concentrated in the bottom 98% of wealth and income owners and this debt enslavement represents a transfer of wealth from the bottom 98% to the richest 2%. Compound interest itself can increase the debt from 150% - 400%.

(i) in the USA and some other countries the high costs of University or college education and the excessive burden of massive student loans ranging from $50,000 - $100,000 on graduation after 4 years means many Americans cannot afford third level education. This deprives many of the high tech skills, business skills and scientific skills to succeed in the world and reduces their productivity or keeps them in a low state of productivity. The rich or richest 5% can afford these high costs and most of them send their children to Universities and colleges, and they graduate debt free, and this creates a continuous productivity gap between the rich and everybody else which reinforces concentrations of wealth and income over time. Piketty and others have found this in recent and ongoing research.

(j) politics and political institutions have become corrupted by 'pay to play' politics in several developed nations, including the USA. The government serves the interests of the richest 1% and mostly neglects the rest. The government refuses to invest in third level education, in the high tech skills, business skills and scientific skills necessary for personal and national productivity gains and innovation in the 21st century. And refuses to invest in the infrastructure to support new high tech economies. Governments and politicians say that there is no money to do this. Yet these same governments have and continue to spend trillions of dollars on the Deep State, the Shadow Government, wars and regime changes, bail outs of banks and big corporates, and corporate welfare and subsidies. This is a major failing of certain governments.

This is a major failing of certain governments. They prefer to bankrupt individuals and families with massive debt while refusing to invest long term in the people, the infrastructure, new innovations and the nation.

(k) the continuing concentration of wealth and income via inheritance and the use of tax loopholes, tax havens and tax evasion schemes. Inheritance has become a major factor as wealth is siphoned off at an international level.

(l) the redirection of sales, profits, revenues, fees through offshore tax havens and tax evasion schemes. Conservative estimates put the monies in tax havens at $32 trillion but the real figure may be in the region of $70 trillion (Tax Justice Network, James Henry, 2012, http://www.taxjustice.net/cms/upload/pdf/Price_of_Offshore_Revisited_120722.pdf). The total cost of tax evasion has been estimated at $3.1 trillion per year (Tax Justice network report, James Henry, November 2011, http://www.tackletaxhavens.com/Cost_of_Tax_Abuse_TJN%20Research_23rd_Nov_2011.pdf)

These factors **(a)** to **(l)** all combined together to increase the returns to capital (the very wealthy) and hide this massive wealth through tax havens. This national and international structure also imposes the economic costs of hoarding on labour and governments, keeping levels of aggregate demand, output and employment well below optimum levels (or "equilibrium" levels). This hoarding effect was briefly mentioned by Keynes in the 1930's. These monies in tax havens are often recycled back into economies again and again to speculate in asset prices, property prices and derivatives, and the profits returned to tax havens. So they serve as a suction of wealth from developed and developing countries. Ironically during financial crashes, vast amounts of taxpayers' money were used to bail out these wealthy speculators and their failed investment products. The end result of this is ever increasing concentrations of wealth and income, and greater inequalities, which worsens and reinforces itself over time. The fact that these tax havens hide wealth makes it very difficult for governments and economists to estimate the wealth or GNP of their peoples and nations and official statistics figures. This system misallocates resources on a massive scale, trillions of dollars per year, and contributed to the speculative booms and crashes which have had and will continue to have disastrous consequences for countries. This massive siphoning and misallocation of resources affects the whole economies of countries, it reduces aggregate demand and potential demand (in productive sector) and aggregate supply, while increasing both constrained, unrealised, unmet demand and constrained, unrealised, unmet supply, thus producing significant dynamic disequilibrium in the system. The international scale of this imposes dynamic disequilibrium on all countries, and must be factored into all economic analysis.

- **Velocity of Money**

High concentrations of wealth and income increase hoarding, savings, monies in offshore tax havens, while reducing consumption and aggregate demand among most (90%) of a population, and this in combination with debt overhang (and high repayments) can create a paradox of thrift, and this reduces investment profitability and potential, which in turn can lead to a liquidity trap, further distorting markets. The richest 1 - 5% who have most of the wealth and income in a country have a higher propensity to speculate and save and a reduced propensity to consume and spend, while the bottom 90% and particularly bottom 60% have a high propensity to spend and consume. But the latter are deprived of these resources for consumption through high concentrations of wealth and income, loss of jobs from an economic downturn, debt overhang and repayments, and an inability to increase credit. This can cause a lack of consumption and aggregate demand causing or prolonging economic downturns, recessions and depressions. This can lead to a fall in velocity of money. This occurred notably in the USA in 2018 - 2019.

The Cantillon effect is also a factor here. As newly created money or credit, especially Quantitiative easing remains concentrated among the richest 1 – 5% who tend to speculate or save this money. This traps the money among the richest section of society and it circulates there. The velocity of money among the richest 1 -5 % may be high while at the same time the velocity of money among the bottom 90% of a population can be very low. This can skew markets and national economies and cause them to operate well below optimum levels. We saw this in the period 2008 – 2016. This sucks vast amounts of money out of the circular flow of income in a country and this adversely affects consumption, aggregate demand and the investment which is dependent on this demand. In addition to this, the continuous withdrawal of interest money, which was not created during the loan and money creation process, causes 'trickle upwards' to the richest and further suction out of the economy and losses in consumption, demand and investment, creating a 'Balance Sheet Recession'. These are major Dynamic Disequilibrium forces. Here are some supporting facts below [7]

U.S. savings rose during the 2007–2009 recession, both residential and non-residential investment fell significantly, approximately $560 billion between Q1 2008 and Q4 2009. (FRED Database-Residential and Non-Residential Investment-Retrieved July 2014)

Private sector financial balance (gross private savings minus gross private domestic investment) rose from an approximately $200 billion deficit in Q4 2007 to a surplus of $1.4 trillion by Q3 2009. This surplus remained at $720 billion in Q1 2014. An enormous amount of savings was tied up in the banking system, rather than being invested. (FRED Database-Private Sector Financial Surplus-Retrieved July 2014)

A Literature Summary on Balance Sheet Recession Research -
http://www.nextnewdeal.net/rortybomb/new-report-literature-summary-new-balance-sheet-recession-research

Private Sector Financial Surplus

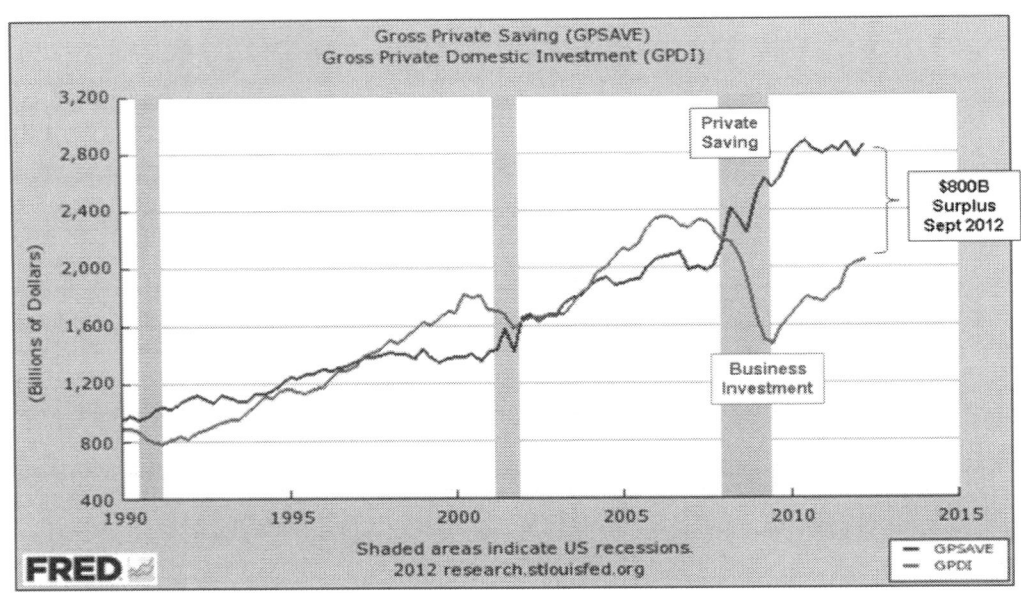

- Real wages have been stagnant for 30 years in the USA, mostly due to globalisation, downsizing, outsourcing and automation. Americans have maintained their standard of living by going into massive debt and by two parents working. By 2008 and again in 2016 private household debt in the USA was very high by historical standards. During inflationary periods or speculative booms, the high rate of debt accumulation fuels unsustainable rises in prices which creates significant disequilibrium resulting in a big financial crash or in some cases stagflation. Also during times of recession, depression, and uncertainty, high personal debt levels and business debt levels will adversely affect consumption and aggregate demand while high government debt levels will adversely affect consumer spending through higher taxes, levies and charges. This combined government debt burden, business debt burden and personal debt burden can lead to a debt deflationary cycle and liquidity traps such as that witnessed during the period 2008 – 2015 and Japan's lost 15 years and the Great Depression of the 1930's. And again, we see more disequilibrium or dynamic disequilibrium. This has been described by Richard Koo and others [4].

- Say's law needs to be amended - Deficient Supply and Deficient Demand creates its own disequilibrium of inadequate demand and inadequate supply which can become self reinforcing. Chapter 4 of this book outlines these many deficiencies and the role of Dynamic Disequilibrium in this. This includes a discussion of how the sticky prices of powerful monopolies, oligopolies and cartels keep prices artificially high and from falling. Demand and the factors related to demand are vitally important to investment and supply, as evidenced by the failures of Quantitative Easing and low real interest rates which largely benefitted speculators in asset prices. Neo liberal, Neo Classical, Hayekian, globalist, free market (actually skewed market) and monetarist policies have the effect of worsening Dynamic Disequilibrium and tend to deflate demand, restrain and reduce demand, and worsen demand deficiencies and this feeds into creating more supply deficiencies. This creates a synergy of deficient demand and deficient supply.

- Vast differences in income and wealth distribution and continuing debt overhang which negatively affects:

    o propensity to consume and propensity to save at a collective level

    o propensity to consume is adversely affected by debt overhang after crashes and during recessions which reduces disposable incomes and propensity to consume, and the related propensity to invest

    o consumer preferences

    o consumer credit creation, credit worthiness and access to credit

    o consumer purchasing potential

    o marginal utility

    o utility maximising

    o purchases and their individual demand curves [8]

    o savings rates and investment rates, and this is heavily impacted by the widespread use of tax havens holding over $32 trillion.

    o debt rates

    o consumption rates, aggregate demand

    o constrained, unrealised, unmet demand or what is known as 'deficiencies in effective demand'.

The best example of this is the 19th century when massive inequalities in wealth and income combined with a gold standard restricted money supply created great limitations on consumer potential and supplier and investor potential and forced a situation where consumption was well below equilibrium or optimum and supply and investment was well below equilibrium or optimum. It was a century marked by great poverty and inequalities with some limited industrial progress.

- Unmet, unrealized demand and highly constrained demand or deficiencies in effective demand due to the factors mentioned above can create large scale misallocations of resources, spare capacity, redundant capacity, high unemployment and under employment of people and resources, ghettos, derelict sites and buildings in the middle of a housing crisis, and the existence of great scarcity in the middle of great abundance. All of which adversely affect demand and demand curves.

- Discrimination and prejudice and stigma affect many people's ability to get employment and get higher education or high level skills and training. This is controversial yet still exists in the human condition (despite the many promises of politicians). This in turn affects consumer demand, the supply of labour, the supply of working hours, productivity, and increases constrained, unrealised, unmet demand in an economy.

- Defects in Keynesianism are discussed in Chapter 1.

- The use of racial groups and discrimination to manipulate supply. This is controversial yet part of the human condition, and creates contradictions between groups of investors and consumers creating imperfect information, restrictions to competition, manipulation of quantities or expectations, and faulty pricing with knock on effects on demand.

- The markets for products and services may enter a brief period of stability but the forces of disequilibrium will be dominant, with many falling victim to discontinuities in the form unforeseen disruptive and destabilising forces which affect consumption, supply and investment returns in a country, this includes the disruptive factors mentioned above. This impacts both supply and demand, pricing and debt accumulation and payback capability, and consumer potential, creating discontinuities, dislocations, in effect disequilibrium.

- Neoclassical economists presume all things are equal but the markets, economy, prices, quantities, firms, and incomes and preferences are dynamic and constantly changing, and creating levels of volatility and dynamic disequilibrium. The only theories which can model this are chaos theory, emergence theory, complexity theory and quantum theory, but none of these are used by mainstream economists.

Defects in Law of Supply under Conditions of Dynamic Disequilibrium

- Many markets are dominated by private monopolies, oligopolies and cartels which extract economic rents and impose 'sticky prices' and restrictions on price and supply. There are also the state protected sectors, the government subsidized private firms, and government protected restrictive practices (the professions) and their 'sticky prices' for products and services, professional fees, and (professional and executive) salaries and bonuses. The prices charged are far higher than marginal revenue and marginal costs. These 'sticky prices' impose and enforce high costs of living, especially in developed countries. Ordinary working people and their families are largely powerless in the face of the excessive high prices charged by these forces. For example, certain big businesses, the professions and landowners listed below can extract economic rents or monopolistic prices for their services, and impose high costs or inflexible costs on businesses, workers, governments and society:

I. lawyers, barristers, accountants. Many cases exist of over charging, often by extravagant amounts.

II. doctors, hospital consultants and dentists

III. pharmacies and chemists

IV. pharmaceutical drugs. The very high prices for drugs charged by pharmaceutical companies, through government manipulation or monopolistic practises or price collusion by cartels. Price differentials between countries range from 100% - 5,000%

V. FIRE sector firms (Finance Insurance and Real Estate), most of whom extract economic rents

VI. health insurance being excessively expensive due to monopolistic / oligopolistic / cartel prices charged by insurance firms, pharmaceutical companies and other healthcare suppliers

VII. the small number of insurance companies in a country or state which often leads to price collusion. And an inability of customers to access insurance from other countries or states.

VIII. big banks and collusion between big banks to keep interest rates, charges and fees high, restrict the number of banks participating in clearing houses, manipulate and limit the allocation of credit, fund speculation at the expense of productive investment, and restrict the entry of new banks and financial institutions. This can severely limit the growth and employment of small and medium sized firms in an economy. Research by Dr. Richard Werner of the University of Southampton has published and lectured extensively on this subject. In the case of LIBOR the banks illegally rigged the rates costing many businesses and organisations a lot of money.

IX.   state contracts where private firms overcharge government for products and services.

X.   selling of state assets, including natural resources, at very low cost or below cost to (politically connected) private firms. This usually includes natural resources, infrastructure, tv, radio, mobile phone and telecommunications bandwidths, state lands and properties. They abuse their power to over charge and to extract economic rents.

XI.   private property owners, land owners and landlords who have a monopoly and financially benefit from the provision of free public services and infrastructure near to their property or lands. The lack of a land value tax.

XII. The concentration of land ownership in a country. 10% of landowners own 53 - 90% of land in many countries.

XIII. car dealerships and their cosy relationships with government, which include VRT taxes and sole dealership deals.

XIV. undertakers

XV.   commercial property landlords, and their upwards only rent. This can include excessive prices for rents of commercial property and residential property. And this directly feeds into higher costs for businesses, workers and consumers.

XVI. cosy relationships between some businesses and professional services firms and local government and central government which has led to very high costs

XVII. the pricing by semi-state bodies

XVIII. Building materials

XIX. big pharmaceutical companies using patents and trademarks to restrict supply and competition and enforce higher prices

XX.   subsidised big farmers and industrial farms

XXI. oil companies, gas companies and electricity companies, and other energy and resource companies with a monopoly or oligopoly or engaged in restrictive practises

XXII. firms using monopolistic control of one business area to assist or compliment market dominance in another related business area

XXIII. manufacturers of operating systems who can actively discriminate against software vendors and use this discrimination to market and sell their own software so as to dominate a market

XXIV. Telecommunications companies and cable companies with a monopoly or oligopoly or engaged in restrictive practises

These restrict supply and competition and lead to higher prices, higher costs in the form of economic rents. They also redistribute wealth from the working classes, the unemployed and the poor to the wealthy and upper incomes. And they also stifle innovation and technological progress.

- **Single Market**

    the Single European Act was signed in 1986 and was due to come into full effect in January 1993. There was meant to be a single European market for goods and services. There was meant to be a single European market for goods and services. By 2017, there is no single market for insurance, bank interest rates, automobiles, pharmaceuticals, loans and mortgages, medical services, legal services, accountancy services, and most services across the EU. After 24 years, there is still no single market. In the case of Ireland this adds 5 billion euros per year to the price of goods and services, and is undermining competitiveness and living standards (Competition Authority Ireland). It is also adding tens of billions of euros in extra costs to big EU nations and undermining living standards. This is causing significant distortion of markets and market forces, and large economic dislocations. This failure of the EU authorities to achieve the single market after 24 years is quite extraordinary.

- The law of supply is based on one firm and one product and many identical customers, clones, with identical tastes and preferences, marginal utility, income, propensity to consume and purchasing activities and a few products. In the real world, what is true for one supplier is not true for all suppliers and what is true for one consumer is not true for all consumers. All suppliers (and consumers) are not identical, they have widely different preferences, profit maximising strategies, different marginal costs, earnings, market competitors, skewing of the market (see sections below), propensities to produce, and selling activities.

- In respect of supply of investment products and services, this is mostly governed by speculation, the herd mentality, and short term gains in terms of days, a month or quarterly returns. This herd mentality is mutually reinforcing between traders and firms. In most cases, it is not based on business fundamentals and accurate analysis and predictions. This speculative, short term driven system provides imperfect information, and this itself is driven by generous financial incentives. This imperfect information comes in the form of false and fraudulent investment ratings, false accounting, legalized Ponzi schemes, price rigging, insider trading, front running and price manipulations in real time (as described by investor Michael Lewis), laddering of stocks and spinning of stocks, wrong or fraudulent information about financial assets, properties, derivatives and their future returns, interest rate rigging, currency rigging, packaging and selling defective or loss making investment products while secretly betting against them. And this false information and fraud was greatly assisted by hysteria and hype in the financial press and media and among most economists, investment advisors and managers. All of these cause irrational expectations and make utility maximization impossible. And the refusal of ministers and government officials to prosecute these fraudsters and white collar criminals in the USA and other developed countries provides strong incentives to continue committing frauds and financial crimes. All of this serves to provide disutility or disutility maximization to investors and create irrational agents and irrational expectations in the form of losses. The boom and bust of 2008 provided a classic case of this. This is the key to understanding dynamic disequilibrium, the very core of dynamic disequilibrium.

- Deregulation of banking beginning in the 1980's which removed important safeguards in banking, such as capital requirements, debt to capital requirements, reserve requirements, separation of commercial banking from investment banking, adequate risk management, full disclosure, lending provisions etc. which created high risk banking and increased financing for speculation while reducing it for purely productive purposes. As banks and show banking has become more interconnected in deregulated and more globalised world, the risks multiplied, meaning the collapse of one big bank would threaten many others in a contagion effect. This led to vast economic losses during 2008 and other financial crashes.

The cost of financial system crashes similar to that in 2008 in terms of bailout costs, austerity, recession, lost output and lost GNP is estimated to be trillions of dollars for large countries like USA, Britain, France, Spain, Italy, etc. and hundreds of billions of dollars for small countries such Ireland, Belgium, Portugal, Latvia, etc. (Reinhart and Rogoff 2010, 2014, Will Hutton 2010, Summers and Fatas 2015, Ball 2014, Blanchard, Cerutti, and Summers 2015). This adds up to trillions of dollars of losses over several years or decades. This also imposes losses on aggregate demand and aggregate supply which affect businesses and their supply curves.

This dynamic disequilibrium regularly creates vast economic losses, in addition to destroying funding for productive capital formation, human capital formation, innovation and sustainable economic growth and supply side factors in an economy. We see here practical examples of economic systems governed by dynamic disequilibrium

- **Rentiers and the Structure of Economies**

The economist Adam Smith claimed that free markets were markets which were free of the economic rent and monopolistic activities of landlords, inherited wealth, monopolists, oligopolists, cartels and banks [28]. He criticised and condemned them for extracting economic rents and undermining free competition, yet today they are dominating the market, distorting it and skewing it [28]. These rentiers or economic rent seekers and enforcers have the full support of free marketers who misinterpret Adam Smith and wrongly use Adam Smith to underpin their beliefs.

The research and works of Dr. Michael Hudson shows that the rentiers or FIRE sector (Finance, Insurance, Real Estate) now dominate many developed economies and account for most of the credit created and most of the debt and most of the money used in transactions[28]. They rely on speculation, debt and abuse of monopoly position or cartel position to extract interest, dividends, high fees, excessive charges and capital gains from abusing their monopoly position or cartel position. It was this speculative sector which crashed economies in 2008 and in 2000 and gave the world 425 systemic crashes between 1970 and 2010 (IMF report). Government austerity policies were enforced in many countries to bail out these rentiers or FIRE class at taxpayer's expense. Banks could be compared to big aristocratic landlords in past centuries in the sense that the creation of credit (out of nothing) could be compared to land, and interest and repayments could be compared to land rent. Dr. Hudson goes on to explain how Neo Liberal economics supports this rentier or speculator class and this is leading to speculative bubbles and crashes, a globalisation 'race to the bottom', excessive concentrations of wealth and income, debt deflation and asset stripping (foreclosures, evictions, seizures of assets) and to a new Debt Dependent class (bottom 95%) and Debt Beneficiary class (top 5%). The rentiers make up most of this Debt Beneficiary class, the top 5%. There is an entirely new structure for economies and societies where Debt and Rentier dominance are the major economic issues and the Debt Beneficiary class act as a parasite on the Debt Dependent class [28]. It is a return to feudalism and serfdom. This new economic structure affects aggregate demand, consumption, supply, output, investment decisions, credit allocation, credit availability, debt composition, debt vulnerabilities and economic growth. And it also affects the equation MV=PT when one integrates the massive value of money and credit created to speculate and inflate assets and the high numbers of transactions during a bubble phase or bull market, and accompanying inflationary rises which affect the rest of the economy.

- The crowding out of productive investment by excessive speculative investments, which have a tendency to crash. This includes access to funding from banks, private equity funds, pension funds, mutual funds and insurance funds. Productive businesses are crowded out of the funding market by speculators. This severely reduces aggregate supply and potential supply in the productive sector and the long term sustainable incomes, wages and aggregate demand which arises from productive investments.

- 97% of all money is created out of nothing by Commercial banks when making loans / mortgages. See section above in Defects in Law of Demand section to understand the supply and demand aspects of this and the dynamic disequilibrium it causes.

- Banks do not create interest money when creating new money and lending it out, and this means there can never be enough money in the system to pay off the debt. See section above in Defects in Law of Demand section to understand supply and demand aspects of this and the dynamic disequilibrium it causes.

- Quantitative Easing valued at $15 trillion to bail out banks, big corporate and some governments has mostly been pumped into speculation in shares in stock markets, company buybacks, derivatives, government bonds and other forms of assets, creating new bubbles. From 2008 to 2015, the value of the global stock of investable assets increased substantially by about 40 percent, from $350 trillion to over $500 trillion. The figure of $500 trillion is over 9 times the global economy and presents a new level of systemic risk to economies. Quantitative Easing did not reach the productive sector, the consumption sector (bottom 60%) and the wider economy and stimulate consumption, aggregate demand, and related supply and economic growth to desired levels ; it proved to be ineffective and disappointing. This policy distorts and skews markets, inflating speculative bubbles, while adversely affecting consumption, aggregate demand and associated productive investment levels..

- In the real world, 'regulatory capture' of governments, government bodies and central banks by big corporations, banks and wealthy individuals plays a major role in the skewed market, not the assumed 'free market'. This often involves corruption and lobbying, which are often the same thing. For example in the USA, it was estimated in 2008, that successful congress men had to raise $978 million in total and senators had to raise $410 million in total and the presidential candidate $1.8 billion to be elected (Centre for Responsive Politics, 'Stats at a Glance', www.opensecrets.org).

Expenditure on lobbying in the EU, specifically Brussels, is difficult to assess due to its hidden and discreet nature, but some estimates put it at billions of euros per year (https://lobbyfacts.eu/). These campaign monies were paid by big businesses, banks, PAC's, very wealthy individuals and lobbyists, and they expect and often demand political favours in return. Recent research by Gilens and Page over many years shows a direct correlation between the preferences of the very wealthy and their lobbyists and the passing of legislation and use of certain policies by governments. This provides proof of the political power of wealthy corporations, banks, individuals and their lobbyists. This is one of the most important studies ever conducted in political science. The recent supreme court decision regarding the case of Citizens United has served to worsen this and provides further proof of both the political power and judicial power of lobbyists and their backers. This is the process of 'regulatory capture', one of the most important areas of modern economics. This involves the creation of laws, deregulations, subsidies and risk transfers which enable banks, corporations and professionals to gain economic rents or super-normal profits, examples include:

(i) agricultural subsidies in developed countries and the profits which result from this within developed countries and the 'permission' to dump these goods on to developing and third world countries

 (ii) subsidies and tax breaks to big companies and banks

(iii) state contracts where politically connected private firms overcharge government for products and services The role of the Deep State and Shadow Government in this.

(iv) the selling of state assets at very low cost or below cost to (politically connected) private firms, and this includes natural resources, tv, radio, mobile phone and telecommunications bandwidths, state lands and properties

(v) the free use of or low cost use of expensive state assets / infrastructure by private firms with political connections, while other firms and consumers have to pay high costs for these

(vi) state grants, aid, and special tax concessions for international firms which are not as generous or available for other national firms

(vii) state protection of patents, trademarks and copyright, often for excessively long periods and extensions of these periods which give some firms monopoly power

(viii) the state enabling pharmaceutical companies to engage in monopolistic practises and cartels involved in price collusion

(ix) protection from criminal prosecutions and judicial decisions which favour lobbying, corruption and other aspects of regulatory capture

(x) deregulation of banking and the government bailout of certain banks and financial institutions and not others. The privatisation of banking gains and the socialisation of banking losses - 'socialism for the rich'

(xi) state protection of those firms or professionals involved in restrictive practises, monopolies and oligopolies

It gives 'economic rents' to these corporations, banks and professionals which influences the market structure, the number of competitors, prices, incomes, quantities, and the behaviour of the market.

- **False Scarcity**

  The imposing of false scarcity by firms with monopoly power, oligopoly power, or cartel power. The artificial oil crisis and price hikes in 2008 was one example. The electricity crisis in California some years ago was a good example of false scarcity. The food crisis in 2007-08 and many other commodity and resource crisis's in history provide other examples. The deprivation of land to farmers in developing countries to grow food for local and national markets, and the resulting food shortages and high prices for food. The famous economist and Nobel Prize winner Amartya Sen has written extensively about false scarcity, and how starvation is mostly the result of lack of money or other resources to provide the means of exchange for survival. This includes lack of money, access to jobs, access to capital, access to land, access to wealth, access to surplus wealth and assets, and access to credit. And this lack is the result of decisions by governments, economists, international organisations and human prejudices. Another example is the existence of land banks hoarded by property developers, speculators and banks during periods of housing shortages. Hoarding of wealth combined with excessive concentrations of wealth and the imposition of massive national debts provide further avenues for creating false scarcity in a world of abundance. In reality, we live in a world of great abundance, it is overflowing with abundance and with willing and skilled labour, yet the monopoly power and oligopoly power of certain big firms and property owners has created false scarcity and high levels of constrained, unrealised, unmet demand in several sectors and many countries, in the interests of extracting economic rents and supernormal profits. This is a major factor in dynamic disequilibrium.

- There are high costs of entry, and significant barriers to entry, including brand name loyalty and domination within a market, high technology costs, fixed asset costs, the power and networks of existing businesses in the market including their ability to use their position to dominate suppliers, developers, customers, competitors, politicians and laws, the increased returns to scale of large firms, below cost selling to bankrupt competitors, high marketing costs to establish a new business, market penetration costs, proprietary technologies, patents and trademark costs, continuous innovation and research costs, and the high costs imposed by those companies and professions in the protected sector of an economy.

- **Shareholder Value**

  The notion that a firm's main objective or sole objective is to "increase shareholder value" has been totally discredited by the rigging of share prices by top executives, speculators, investment banks and by massive share buybacks where executives use a firm's profits, reserves, revenues or debt to buy large numbers of the firm's shares so as to increase the value of the shares and the financial benefits to the executives. This has been well researched by Dr. William Lazonick, emeritus professor of economics at the University of Massachusetts Lowell in the USA.

- High concentrations of wealth and income increase hoarding, savings, monies in offshore tax havens, while reducing consumption and aggregate demand, and this in combination with debt overhang (and high repayments) can create a paradox of thrift, and this reduces investment profitability and potential, which in turn can lead to a liquidity trap, further distorting markets. The richest 1 - 10% who have most of the wealth and income in a country have a reduced propensity to consume and spend, while the bottom 80% and particularly bottom 60% have a high propensity to spend and consume. But the latter are deprived of these resources for consumption through high concentrations of wealth and income, loss of jobs from an economic downturn and debt overhang and an inability to increase credit. This can cause a lack of consumption and aggregate demand causing or prolonging economic downturns, recessions and depressions. This can skew markets and national economies and cause them to operate well below optimum levels. We saw this in the period 2008 – 2015. This sucks vast amount of money out of the circular flow of income in a country and this adversely affects consumption, aggregate demand and the investment which is dependent on this demand. In addition to this, the continuous withdrawal of interest money, which was not created during the loan and money creation process, causes 'trickle upwards' to the richest and further suction out of the economy and losses in consumption, demand and investment. These are major Dynamic Disequilibrium forces.

Also view the point above in the Defects in the Laws of Demand section titled 'Skewing of Markets and National Economies'

- Say's law needs to be amended - Deficient Supply and Deficient Demand creates its own disequilibrium of inadequate demand and inadequate supply which can become self reinforcing. Chapter 4 of this book outlines these many deficiencies and the role of Dynamic Disequilibrium in this. This includes a discussion of how the sticky prices of powerful monopolies, oligopolies and cartels keep prices artificially high and from falling. Demand and the factors related to demand are vitally important to investment and supply, as evidenced by the failures of Quantitative Easing and low real interest rates which largely benefitted speculators in asset prices. Neo Liberal, Neo Classical, Hayekian, globalist, free market (actually skewed market) and monetarist policies have the effect of worsening Dynamic Disequilibrium and tend to deflate demand, restrain and reduce demand, and worsen demand deficiencies and this feeds into creating more supply deficiencies. This creates a synergy of deficient demand and deficient supply.

- From a productive investment point of view, the scale of speculation needs to factored into it. In 2008 prior to the crash, the derivatives market was worth $800 trillion which is 12 times the world economy. Today it is estimated to be $1,200 trillion, about 20 times the world economy. Much of these derivative trades and profits are redirected through offshore tax havens. This is a massive siphoning of resources away from productive capital investment and away from consumption by ordinary working people. Derivatives are in most cases pure speculation and pose very serious risks to economies, and represent a very significant driver of dynamic disequilibrium.

- The interlocking nature of many fraudulent speculative investments and the fact that many such investments are related to each other, are part of each other and in some cases are bets on each other. When a few of these investments fail, they trigger a domino effect which affect other similar investments, and these then affect less risky investments (ABB or higher), and so on and on to crash investment products, investment markets, industries and banks. The MBS and CDO scandals in the USA in 2008 -2012 revealed the extent of this domino effect. This had a large impact on the actual and potential supply of capital for productive purposes and on profit and demand side factors such as employment and consumption.

- Vast differences in income and wealth distribution and continuing debt overhang which negatively affects:

  o savings rates and investment rates, and this is heavily impacted by the widespread use of tax havens holding over $32 trillion.

  o propensity to invest is adversely affected by debt overhang after crashes and during recessions which reduces disposable incomes and propensity to consume.

  o propensity to consume and propensity to save at the collective level

  o consumer preferences which ultimately affect investment returns and supply potential

  o consumer credit creation, credit worthiness and access to credit

  o consumer purchasing potential

  o consumer marginal utility

  o consumer utility maximising

  o the marginal efficiency of capital and investment (supply) decisions

  o debt rates

  o investment rates, aggregate supply

  o constrained, unrealised, unmet supply or deficiencies in effective supply

These modern day wealth and income inequalities are discussed in detail above in the Defects in the Law of Demand section. The best example of such high inequalities is the 19th century when massive inequalities in wealth and income combined with a gold standard restricted money supply created great limitations on consumer potential and supplier and investor potential and forced a situation where consumption was well below equilibrium or optimum and supply and investment was well below equilibrium or optimum. It was a century marked by great poverty and inequalities with some industrial progress.

- Unmet, unrealized demand and highly constrained demand or deficiencies in effective demand due to the factors mentioned above can create large scale misallocations of resources, spare capacity, redundant capacity, high unemployment and under employment of people and resources, derelict sites and buildings in the middle of a housing crisis, and the existence of great scarcity in the middle of great abundance. All of which adversely affect supply and supply curves and related demand and demand curves.

- The false 'Crowding Out' Argument

  Some right wing economists claim that government involvement in the economy causes a 'crowding out' of private investment and is always bad. Let's look at the facts. In the USA government bodies such as DARPA, RAND, the National Science Foundation, the NIH, and other government research organizations many of them tied to Universities created the most important inventions of the Digital Age and Modern Age, including the Internet, computers (in cooperation with the British government), microchips, computer networks, computer programmes and software, Google, GPS systems, computer screens, encryption, touch screens for computers, mobile phones and smartphones, the Bar Code, the accelerometer (used in Wii), satellite communications, supercomputers, optical digital recording, funding for Universities and research centres, seismic imaging, RSA cipher, infant formula, fire resistant clothing, goodyear tyres, vaccines, civilian aviation, wind turbines, cleaning bacteria, the Human Genome project, led lighting, fluorescent lights, modern water purification techniques, memory foam, anti corrosion coating, cochlear implants, insulin pump, charge coupled device, water filters, MRI imaging, research funding for new treatments for Cancer, advanced prosthetics, and Doppler radar. In Britain government sponsored research led to the deciphering of DNA, invention of jet engines, computers, enigma and cipher technologies, carbon fibre, DNA profiling, the atomic clock, iris recognition, graphene. Many inventions came about inside government funded Universities. These inventions changed the world. This is often forgotten by Neo Liberal and Neo Classical economists, Monetarists, Hayekians, and Libertarians. Indeed, depriving governments of funding for research and innovation and focusing solely on increasing share holder value and speculative gains every quarter as advised by these economists tends to reduce the amount spent on research and development, innovation and long term growth.

- Neo Liberals and free market supporters claim that free markets can cure 'homelessness' when the facts and evidence show that free markets are actually rigged markets which act to expropriate the maximum rents and maximum prices from housing shortages and do very little or nothing to alleviate housing shortages and homelessness. In fact, these rigged markets create, intensify, exploit and profiteer from shortages and scarcities and have no interest in the plight of homeless people and families. Many governments have realized this and have invested substantial monies in social housing and in grants and tax incentives for first time house buyers.

- Assuming the market demand curve is in general or most cases downward sloping, an increase in total market output will mean a fall in market price. The supply curve for a firm must then be downward sloping not horizontal or upwards [1] The increased competitive pressures implied by more products in the market in addition to efficiencies of scale will put downward pressures on prices. At some point it will level out and may slope upwardly if monopolistic or oligopolistic dominance can be established.

  Though there are exceptions here where speculation and price rigging can keep pushing up prices of products and new products, until a crash occurs.

- Empirical evidence and research shows that a firm's marginal cost is constant or declining over long output ranges. Diminishing returns is not a factor. Though this changes once full capacity is reached. However the creation of new capacity (new factories, outsourcing production, etc.) returns one to the original condition above. This conflicts with neo classical economic theory about supply. This has recently been the subject of research and discussion by Dr. Steve Keen

- For competitive profit maximizing firms, price does not always equal marginal cost and marginal revenue due to the downward sloping market demand curve [1]

- I refer readers to the analysis of TTIP in Chapter 2 of this book. It itemises many of the defects and flaws in TTIP and in current and previous WTO treaties in terms of economic externalities, consumer disutility and supplier disutility

- In the markets of the real world, competitive firms are affected by the pricing policies and marketing policies of other firms and react to them. Prices are not static as suggested in some models.

- The scandals in relation to currency rigging and interest rate rigging (labor scandal) provide further examples of disequilibrium which affects investments, discounted investment decisions, investment projects, loan repayments and the marginal efficiency of capital.

- Discrimination and prejudice and stigma affect many people's ability to get employment and get higher education or high level skills and training. This is controversial yet still exists in the human condition (despite the many promises of politicians). This in turn affects consumer demand, the supply of labour, the supply of working hours, the supply of capital, productivity, and increases constrained, unrealised, unmet demand and constrained, unrealised, unmet supply in an economy. Also termed deficiencies in effective demand and effective supply.

- Not all firms have the same access to public funding, bank credit and interest rates. These will differ due to firm size, market dominance, economies of scale, perceptions of growth potential, innovation advantages / disadvantages, political power, and banking connections, and the nature of banking in a given region or country which create great differences between competitive firms. In investment terms, this also affects profitability and the marginal efficiency of capital. These variables are impossible to model in industrial terms and globalisation terms.

- Schumpeter's creative destruction now on a global scale with Globalisation makes it difficult for firms to plan for the future and determine the marginal efficiency of capital, the cumulative effects of dynamic disequilibrium on demand and supply, and stay solvent. This creates a global level of dynamic disequilibrium which can felt at the local level.

- **Economic Indicators**

  The wrong Economic indicators for measuring risk, and in many cases no indicators for measuring risk and no provisions made to reduce it. This is a major failure of neo liberal economics and neo classical economics. Many banks and financial institutions and businesses failed to measure and realise the added risk inherent in Globalisation and mass speculation based on high debt levels, and the level of dynamic disequilibrium. The crash of 2008 provided an example of the consequences of this. This inability or unwillingness to measure risk and mitigate against it creates great instability and significant dynamic disequilibrium. It also produces false and misleading economic forecasts. The following indictors were missing, ignored or neglected:

  1. Total private debt to GNP / GNI and it's growth per year for the last 10 - 20 years. In Ireland and some other countries where GDP figures are unreliable and distorted by large flows of BEPS funds and tax avoidance / evasion funds into a country, the Gross National Income (GNI) and debt per capita figures are more accurate and reliable. Is private debt to GNP (or GNI) at or greater than 130% and is the growth of private debt to GNP at or greater than 10% per year for 1 year or more ? Is this debt based on speculation in rising asset prices ? Sudden slow downs in such high debt growth would suggest a crash may be imminent. This is based on the latest research findings of Dr. Steve Keen and Richard Vague [1]. Richard Vague has shown that financial

crashes since the 1850's have involved private debt to GNP / GDP of 150% or more and an increase in that ratio of 17% or more over 5 years [21]

2. For Banks: total bank debt to capital / income / assets / reserve levels / share price ratio. This must include all off balance sheet vehicles and instruments. And exposure of this debt to speculative bubbles and the FIRE economy (Dr. Michael Hudson). This would measure the sustainability and viability of the debt. Stress tests involving simulated losses should be made public to all investors and members of the public.

3. For Shadow Banking: total debt to capital / income / assets / reserve levels / share price ratio. This must include all off balance sheet vehicles and instruments. And exposure of this debt to speculative bubbles and the FIRE economy (Dr. Michael Hudson). This would measure the sustainability and viability of the debt. Stress tests involving simulated losses should be made public to all investors and members of the public.

4. Price-Earnings ratios, Price-Sales ratios, Debt to Capital ratios, Debt to Earnings ratios for assets, stocks, bonds, property, derivatives, companies, groups of companies, industries, sectors, and indexes. Including CAPE as proposed by Robert Shiller. And comparison to historical Price-Earnings ratios and the other ratios with particular emphasis on previous booms and busts. And total stock market valuation to GDP. High ratios have been linked to bubbles and excessive risk.

5. Growth in Private Debt, Household Debt and Bank Debt by themselves and in relation to Growth in Speculative Asset Prices. Sudden slow downs in this high credit growth would suggest a crash may be imminent [1]. This needs to done for speculative asset categories, such as property, shares, derivatives, commodities, bonds and other assets prone to speculation.

6. Inter bank lending volumes. Repo rates, Repo volume. Sudden declines indicate a crisis is about to begin or has already occurred. This may require central bank and government action.

7. Inverted yield curves. Fall in the velocity of money or very low number.

8. Broad Bank Credit Growth to Nominal GDP / GNI growth, Productive sector credit growth to Nominal GDP /GNI growth and Speculation sector credit growth to Nominal GDP / GNI growth and other indicators proposed by Dr. Richard Werner of Southampton University.

9. Level of Speculation and level of Crowding Out of Productive Investment

- Speculative Credit and Debt which rises faster than income, earnings, and profits for the whole economy, the banking sector, and other sectors. Credit for speculation rising faster than Nominal GDP / GNI.

- Total Debt for speculative FIRE economy (Financial, Insurance and Real Estate firms) and debt for non speculative economy. Rate of credit growth for both.

- The growth of (i) non speculative GDP and GNI and (ii) speculative GDP and GNI, including the FIRE economy (Finance Insurance and Real Estate) as used by the economist Dr. Michael Hudson.

- The amount of economic output, GDP and GNI due to monopolies, oligopolies, restrictive practises, and cartels and speculative increases in land values and capital gains. And ratio of this to output, GDP, and GNI created by competitive productive firms.

- Growth in Quantitative Easing measured against growth in Speculative Asset prices. This would facilitate closer analysis of Quantitative Easing.

- Quantitative Easing for speculation in FIRE economy measured against Quantitative Easing for non FIRE economy and production. In absolute terms and in GDP and GNI terms.

  This could be on year by year basis and a quarterly basis. This would compare and contrast the real economy against the speculative economy.

10. Total debt — government, bank, business, private, and household debt as a percentage of GDP / GNI. How fast debt is growing for government, bank, business, private sectors relative to GDP and Tax Revenues.

11. Total National debt as a percentage of Government revenues. National debt per capita.

12. The exact or precise composition of all derivatives, CDO's, MBS's and other types of packaged securities and packaged assets including all tranches and subdivisions of the product. And verification of the income and earnings integrity, feasibility, capacity and potential for each product and sub product. This will require forensic and independent analysis of these types of products and what they contain and the credit worthiness and payment details of the constituent parts of the investment product / derivative.

13. New indicators for measuring increases in land values from the provision of public infrastructure and services nearby and proximity to towns and cities and measuring capital gains from financial assets. This would serve as a means of taxing these economic rents and measuring the extent of speculation.

14. House Prices

  House prices need to be compared against historical prices adjusted for inflation and adjusted for average industrial earnings. In general throughout history house prices have been stable, and have been 4 – 7 times average industrial earnings. Though in speculative bubbles they can rise much higher, reaching 10 – 20 times average industrial earnings. These new indictors and measurements would identify housing bubbles and help end them or prevent them.

15. Measuring National Overhead Costs

    New GDP and GNI measures to separate overhead costs from national output. Dr. Michael Hudson in his works advised that it is necessary to calculate the overhead costs imposed by the interest, capital gains, land value gains, and the economic rents of the Financial, Insurance and Real Estate sector (FIRE sector)[36] And subtract these overhead costs from national output in order to get accurate GDP and GNP figures. These firms are not involved in producing goods and services, but they impose significant overhead costs on producers. This would provide net national output, or net GDP / GNI.

16. Indicators derived from some of William Black's works

    - Level of coercion and pressure applied to appraisers to keep pushing up the prices of assets beyond their true worth or intrinsic worth and inflate a bubble
    - Level of liar's loans, ninja loans and subprime loans for assets and level of packaging of these into other investment products and sale of them to investors, eg. CDO's, MBS's prior to 2008.
    - Level of regulator failure or refusal to regulate assets and derivatives posing contagion risks and systemic risks to an economy

17. Corruption and Fraud Indicators

    Special software will need to be developed to identify patterns in financial trading which would indicate price rigging, insider trading, rigging of IPO prices, laddering of stocks and spinning of stocks, ponzi schemes, frauds, sec filings, debt and bond transactions, financial flows between main players and all intermediaries, growth of private credit and debt, offshore flows of funds, false ratings, rigging property, derivatives or other assets. Information from whistleblowers and police and regulators could also be fed into this system. It would have a heuristics system, dynamic adaption and artificial intelligence system to provide precise tracking.

18. Measures or weights for assessing Contagion risk and Systemic risk in the FIRE sector. This would be based on the interconnections and inter-relationships between firms in FIRE sector and also between firms in the FIRE Sector and non FIRE sector.

19. Inter Sectoral transfers of funds outlining surpluses and deficits which may pose instability and crash risks as devised by Wynne Godley

20. Revised GNP and GNI measures. We need the following:

GNP and GNI Diffusion figures

The level of diffusion of wealth and income to the general population needs to be measured.

- Concentration of wealth and income. See table in Chapter 5.

- Employee share ownership, Cooperative ownership and Community share ownership expressed in GNI terms and GNP terms and Population terms. How much of the GNP and GNI goes to them.

- The rate of diffusion of capital and wealth to the general population via Employee share ownership and Community share ownership measured in deciles of the population.

- The Capital income (dividends, profits, interest capital gains) going to deciles of the Population.

- The Wage income going to deciles of the Population.

GNP and GNI and Social Indicators

- Measuring Child Well Being, Stress and Anxiety levels, Mental illnesses, Civic Participation, Support for Populist leaders, Child Bullying, Teen pregnancies, Crime levels, Imprisonment rates, Bullying in the workplace, Anti Social Behaviour, Homelessness, Life Expectancy, Gambling, Drug Abuse, Educational Performance, and Social Mobility against GNP and GNI diffusion figures

GNP and GNI Renewable Energy and Resources figures

- Per capita and GNP and GNI level of Renewable Energy and Resources figures. These indicate the level of economic resilience and energy independence of a country.

21. Daily / Weekly and Monthly Liquidity ratio and Cashflow ratio. How dependent is a bank / firm on outside liquidity to remain in business and how vulnerable is a business.

22. Inclusion of home prices and mortgage payments and rental payments in the Consumer Price Index and all measures of inflation

23. Indexes of dividends paid by a business or range of businesses or composite of businesses in a given year and historically. And contrasting this with the rise in prices of these investments. This

would show the exact correlation between dividends and share prices. This would help identify speculation.

- Neo classical economists assume in their models and theories that all firms produce, price and sell at profit maximizing levels, but this is not the case in the real world. Many firms operate at below profit maximizing levels for several reasons. In the real world private firms are information seekers and information maximizers, not profit maximizers. Their level of output begins with trial and error and approximate calculations, based on available information, and these output levels are adjusted to improve profitability as information improves. Profit maximizing is mostly not attained but it is aspired to, and a firm may achieve close approximations. It is information which is maximized in the prevailing conditions, which determines the optimum output, though not necessarily the profit maximizing level of output.

- Supply is skewed and manipulated by various forms of state capitalism where (i) the state owns and controls all firms (Marxism and its hybrids and variants) (ii) the state owns some firms in strategic economic sectors while controlling the number of private firms dominant in other sectors and controlling and using sovereign wealth funds to increase the state's profits and for strategic political gains (China in the 21st century, Singapore, Norway) (iii) vast military industrial complexes, national security complexes, and other industries which rely on state contracts. This adversely affects quantities, prices, expectations, and the market, producing some disequilibrium.

- Neo Classical and Neo Liberal economists ignore and omit banks, debt and money from their models of the economy. They presume that they are not important. This is a major error and failing in these economic ideologies and models. This is dangerous to economies as governments, many banks and corporates rely on these failed models, and there have been hundreds of crashes / crises over the last 60 years which are the result of these defective economic ideologies.

- Neo Classical and Neo Liberal economists in their models and theories presume that there are no externalities, a condition where one firm(s) activities imposes illegal or unethical costs and losses on other firms and society (taxpayers) and does not have to pay for it, eg. pollution, fraud, corruption.

- Neo Classical and Neo Liberal economists assume in their models and theories that output is largely constant regardless of the number of firms, in reality total output fluctuates up and down as the number of firms changes in the industry.

- Unsustainable speculation driven credit creation and the buildup of massive debt which acts to reinforce the factors of instability mentioned here and undermine supply

- The use of racial groups and discrimination to manipulate supply. This is controversial yet is part of the human condition, and creates contradictions between groups of investors creating imperfect information, restrictions to competition, manipulation of quantities or expectations, and faulty pricing.

- Neoclassical economists presume all things are equal but the markets, economy, prices and incomes and preferences are dynamic and constantly changing.

- Firms cannot sell as much as they like or produce at a given price. Consumer tastes and preferences and incomes change over time providing fluctuations in the demand for a firm's products. There is no permanent linear relationship. Dynamic disequilibrium provides volatility, a firm will experience increases and decreases, surpluses and shortages, and in recessionary or deflationary conditions reduced aggregate demand and possible bankruptcy.

- Many of the factors above which affect demand also affect supply and reduce the potential of supply, often far below optimum levels, profit maximization levels, or market / equilibrium levels. Thus is impossible to reach equilibrium in a system which is fundamentally in a state of dynamic disequilibrium.

- Vulture fund capitalism which relies on economic crashes followed by government bail outs and austerity policies and Quantitative Easing to stabilise and improve the prices of distressed assets and stablise speculative markets, so vulture funds can acquire these assets cheaply at 20 - 40 cents or less on the dollar and sell them at 100 cents or more on the dollar. For example, vulture funds acquired hundreds / thousands of mortgages at 20 - 40% of their value, held them for a short period, charged higher interest or higher rents or higher repayments and increased them in many cases, and then sold them at 100% or more of their value. The sales and profits were engineered to pass through foreign tax havens so as to avoid paying tax. The owners of these individual mortgages (for homes and properties) were prevented from bidding for their own mortgages at 20 – 40% of their value by laws and government policies. It was a system designed for the benefit of vulture funds. This imposed large unnecessary costs on ordinary people and societies while depriving governments of important tax revenues. This distorts capital markets, returns, supply and pricing mechanisms. The same applies to government debt for countries in distress (Ireland and other EU countries after the 2008 crash and Latin American, Asian and African countries in the past) where debt can be bought cheap for 20 – 40 cents on the dollar and then sold for 100 cents or more on the dollar once the government enforces bail outs and austerity on the taxpayers and people of a nation to maintain the value of the debt.

In 2009 -2011, vulture funds, hedge funds, speculators and private equity firms made a double win from Ireland or the Irish government, they profiteered from (a) buying Irish debt cheap in secondary markets and then selling it at 100 cents or more on the dollar after the Troika bail out (b) buying distressed Irish properties cheap and then selling them at 100 cents or more on the dollar and charging excessive rents. Governments and Troikas now provide the floor for asset prices and the means for them to increase which enables vulture capitalism to thrive and make massive profits. Profits for vulture capitalism are typically in the millions or billions of dollars worldwide. See diagram below:

Distortions and Defects in the Supply of Capital under Conditions of Dynamic Disequilibrium

Tax payers and the government

Governments intervened in markets to bail out banks, bondholders, speculators, assets, and financial institutions. Bailouts were mostly funded by taxpayers and in some cases by the printing of money, Quantitative Easing. This involved the transferring of massive banking and private debt onto government balance sheets, and the enforcement of austerity, recession and tax increases and additional taxes, levies and charges on taxpayers.

It was the taxpayers and the state which paid the cost of bailing out these assets and preserving their prices over time, while the vulture capital Funds and large equity funds and wealthy investors made the profits from this. This was not equitable and fair to the taxpayers and government which bailed out the assets and financial institutions.

For example: the taxpayer pays 100% of the original cost of bailing out the asset or its added to the national debt. The vulture capital fund buys the asset at 25% of its original value and sells at a profit for 100% or more of its original value. The profit would be millions of euros / dollars per deal. The taxpayer or government made a massive loss and had an increase in its national debt while the vulture capital fund made a massive profit.

Prices of distressed assets. Profits to be made from Enforcement of Bailouts and Austerity

This bailout and austerity had the effect of protecting the prices of assets at prices ranging from 30 – 90% below the original cost. It provided a 'floor price' for this capital. Vulture capital Funds and large equity funds and wealthy investors were able to buy these assets at prices ranging from 20% - 50% of their original value. The continuing bailout and austerity enforced on taxpayers protected the prices of these assets, and the gradual improvement in the economy, in addition to Quantitative Easing which enabled speculators to enter and bid up prices again in the market, led to price increases for these assets.

The vulture funds profit from higher interest, rent, and repayments and from selling the asset(s) at 100% more of the value. And engineering the sale and profits through tax havens to avoid paying tax. Individual deals would have involved profits ranging from tens of millions of euros to hundreds of millions of euros for individual investors. Yet, it was the taxpayers and the state which paid the cost of bailing out these assets and preserving their prices over time, while the vulture capital funds and large equity funds made the profits from this. The net result was the taxpayer or government made a massive loss and had an increase in its national debt while the vulture capital fund made a massive profit. This was not equitable and fair to the taxpayers and government which bailed out the assets and financial institutions. This gross distortion of capital supply markets represents a new paradigm in economics termed 'socialism for the rich'.

Market Volatility and Failure under Conditions of Dynamic Disequilibrium

- The dynamic disequilibrium which affects both demand and supply produces volatile markets which fail to produce optimal outcomes, create misallocations of scarce resources, and reach a point of failure such as a crash / recession / depression regularly. The business cycle, booms and busts, inflationary and deflationary conditions, great poverty in the midst of abundance, etc. are the natural outcomes of dynamic disequilibrium.

- The 25 elements of market failure mentioned later in this Chapter show the effects of dynamic disequilibrium in financial markets and asset price speculation markets.

- Economic agents are not well defined, the incentives, their effects and the utility functions are not well defined, the economic environment is not well defined, and economies are constantly changing and in flux. This produces a state of dynamic disequilibrium.

- The markets for products and services may enter a very brief period of stability but the forces of dynamic disequilibrium will be dominant, with many falling victim to discontinuities in the form unforeseen disruptive and destabilising forces which affect consumption, supply and investment returns in a country, this includes business relocations to cheaper developing and third world countries, new competition which is cheaper, better quality, better (politically) connected, or faster, increased automation and downsizing which replaces workers (consumers), energy price shocks, commodity price shocks, migration and demographic changes, financial flows to and from tax havens, economic recessions / dislocations in regions of a country, wide capital, current account and balance of trade fluctuations, etc. This impacts both supply and demand, pricing and debt accumulation and payback capability, creating discontinuities, dislocations, in effect disequilibrium.

A system of dynamic disequilibrium produces disequilibrium prices, quantities, expectations, and disequilibrium allocations of resources, and skewed markets not free markets. This dynamic disequilibrium and it's misallocation of resources can include high levels of unemployment and under used resources, high levels of constrained, unrealised, unmet demand and supply, speculative booms and busts, debt overhang, debt deflation and deflationary periods including recessions and depressions, stagflation, mass poverty, and vast misallocations of resources over time. The works of Dr. Steve Keen [1], Dr. Hyman Minsky [2] Robert Shiller [2] Charles Kindleberger [2],

Irving Fisher [3] Galbraith [2] Richard Koo [4] William Black, Bob Haugen [5] and Mian and Sufi [6] and Joseph Stiglitz [8] and Fama and French (2004) largely disprove the efficient markets theory, and provide some strong evidence of dynamic disequilibrium over long periods of time. The award winning documentary film 'Inside Job' provides some great insights into the widespread frauds and criminality in the financial industry and in politics, all of which facilitate an intensification and worsening of dynamic disequilibrium factors.

The Productivity of Capital under Conditions of Dynamic Disequilibrium

While it may be possible to link wages to productivity over time in a given country, this can be completely undermined by factors such as globalization, the 'race to the bottom', the 'China price' and labour replacing technologies and automation. In fact, wages can be priced less than the rate of productivity for long periods of time, resulting in significant increases in the returns to capital. The surplus going to capital then pumped into speculation in assets and luxurious hedonistic lifestyles. This has certainly been the case in the USA where real wages have stagnated for 30 years and the real minimum wage is less than it was 60 years ago, while productivity increased by large amounts. It is far more difficult to link executive salaries and other benefits to productivity, particularly in the financial services industry and in cases where executive pay is many millions of dollars per year and 50 to 450 times greater than the pay of ordinary workers in a business. This exorbitant pay is dominated by irrational expectations, hype, speculation, skewed markets and the herd mentality, and social prejudices not by productivity. Owners of capital also saw large increases in earnings and profits during this time. Similarly it has become very difficult to measure the productivity of capital in an era dominated by fraud, deception, price rigging, insider trading, false accounting, speculation and hype.

Firstly we will examine the Price-Earnings ratio. Price-Earnings ratios are used by many investors to assess investments. Asset price speculation pushes price-earnings ratios to unsustainable and unrealistic levels, and well beyond the underlying earnings / returns one could expect in the medium to long-term. In fact, there is a relationship between low prices and high returns (low price-earnings ratios), which undermines the efficient markets theory . The graph below developed by Dr. Robert Shiller presents these facts over a hundred year period. It uses 20 year annualized returns as the key measure.

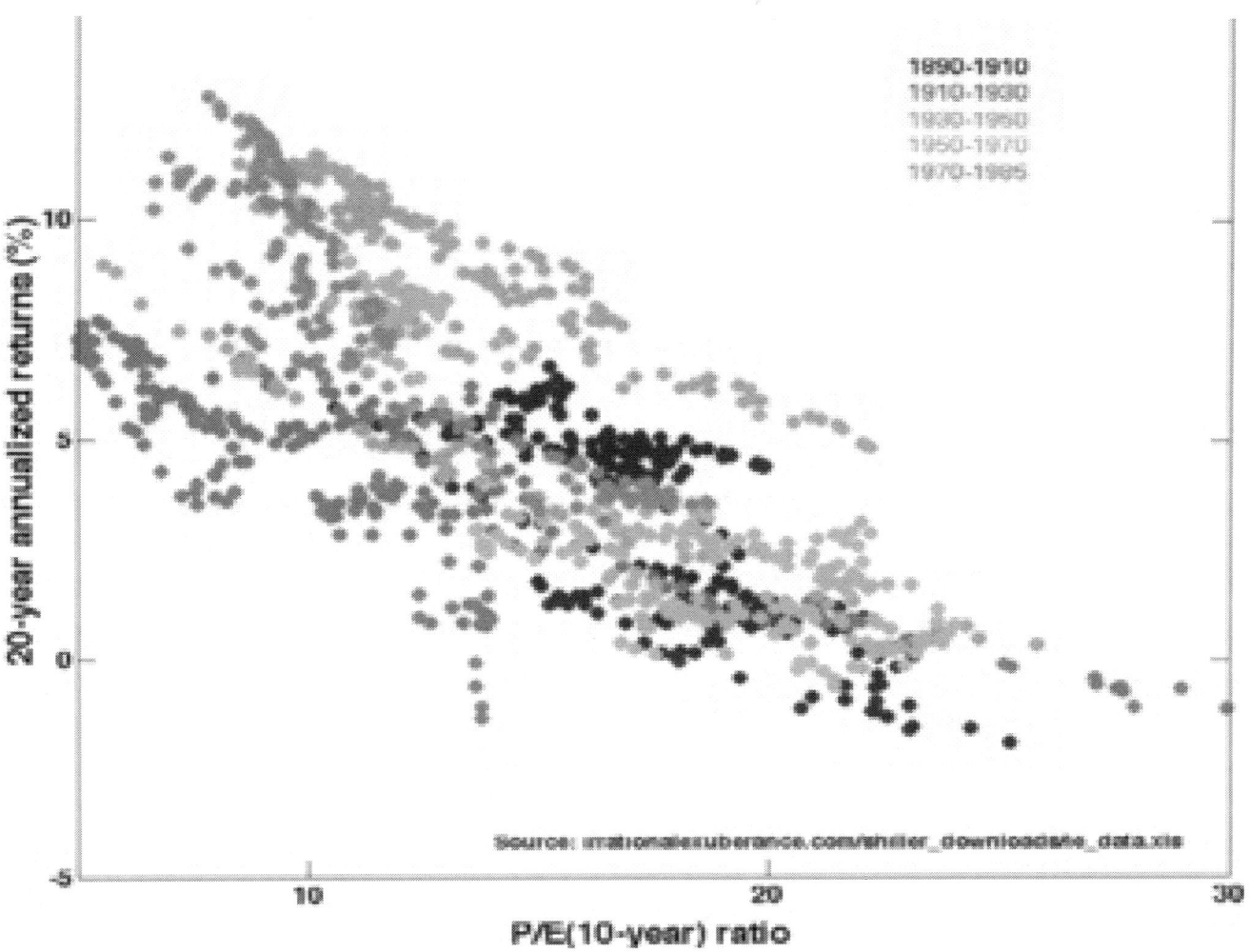

Source: Professor Robert Shiller, Yale University Professor of Economics at Yale University.

In the chart above, we can see a correlation between stocks with low price-earnings ratios and higher returns over 20 years. There is a clustering of stocks of price-earnings ratios of 5-17, delivering mid level returns to high returns. The vast majority of high returns have P-E ratios ranging from 6 to 15. Those with lower price-earnings ratios tend to have higher returns. Those with high Price-Earnings ratios, especially those with 18 or greater provide little or no returns. While 20 or greater provides very small returns or losses, and studies show that ratios greater than 28 are likely to crash. The range 6 - 15 seems to be a good price earnings ratio in relation to a measure of capital returns, capital security, and accurate investment potential. One sees many stocks and assets with very high P-E ratios during speculative booms, and at the beginning of tech bubbles. Asset prices and expectations of these prices

175

far exceed their earnings and earning capacity during all speculative bubbles. This disconnect between asset prices and the earnings of these assets is the key to understanding speculative bubbles and market failures. In recent years, Shiller has developed Cyclically Adjusted Price-Earnings (an average of prior 10 years earnings), called CAPE, to establish a more accurate Price-Earnings ratio. Again high P-E ratios of 28 or more usually signal that prices are too high and likely to crash in the near future. Most neo-classical and neo liberal economists and those who support rational expectations theory and efficient free markets theory claim that these high P-E ratios accurately reflect existing and future returns and the real, intrinsic value of investments. The evidence contradicts this and strongly suggests that the high price-earnings ratios during booms are merely speculation and that they do not reflect real intrinsic value, real value, real prices and long-term returns on investment.

The evidence suggests that an investor should invest in stocks which have a strong business history and long term strategic competitive advantages, and whose stock prices are low or P-E ratios are low, within the 6 – 15 range, as this minimises the negative effects of dynamic disequilibrium. Though investment returns are not guaranteed within this P-E ratio. Under conditions of dynamic disequilibrium, shrewd investors must play a game of probabilities combined with partial certainties to minimise losses and realise gains. Despite the most careful risk management strategy, the risks of dynamic disequilibrium and a system in constant flux and in many cases riddled with fraud and corruption can undermine even the most experienced and shrewd investors. Indeed, speculative manias and crashes, and the herd mentality, cause a reduction in the value of good investments which are not speculative. We all know of older high profile investors who followed very wise and successful investment strategies for decades, yet even they suffered some losses during the financial crash of 2008 -2010. This low P-E ratio investing and investing in fundamentals and long term value is the complete opposite of speculation in assets, property and derivatives advised and promoted by most economists and investment managers and advisors and commentators in the financial press and media. This clearly shows that there are two separate spheres in the investment world which contradict and conflict with each other:

(i) productive investment which is based on actual production of goods and services which produces returns over the medium to long–term, and long-term investment analysis and planning based on this. This typically involves low P-E ratios, a focus on yearly returns, and buying into long-term strategic competitive advantages, long term innovations value, brand dominance, and in depth analysis of accounts, financial statements, financial ratios, marketing plans and results, etc.

(ii) asset price speculation, property speculation, commodity speculation and derivatives speculation. This is based on false, defective, misleading and often manipulated pricing and pricing mechanisms and short term returns fuelled by larger and larger amounts of debt, followed by a financial crash. This typically involves high P-E ratios, a focus monthly or quarterly returns, short term gains, bonuses and commissions to keep pushing up the price of assets, property, commodities, derivatives beyond their intrinsic worth, and various types of fraud and insider trading.

Most economists fail to differentiate between these two types of investment, and lump them together under the term 'investment' and confuse matters further by including this 'investment' term in their efficient markets hypothesis, rational expectations theory and free market theories.

The Price to Sales ratio is also a useful measure and follows the same logic as that for the Price to Earnings ratio. Though some economists and analysts reckon the Price to Sales ratio is more accurate as sales cannot be fraudulently adjusted or manipulated due to stringent corporate laws and IRS (Tax authority) rules and guidelines. According to the efficient markets theory, rational expectations theory, and the neo-classical school of economics, higher Price-Earnings ratios and higher Price-Sales ratios are always accurate and reflect real value, higher current and future returns and profitability, but they didn't and don't. This graph above disproves the efficient markets theory and rational expectations theory that prices always efficiently reflect the expected returns and underlying value of investments. During a speculative boom most prices reflect the speculative price not the (productive) investment price or long term value of an investment. Prices in speculative booms are driven by irrational expectations, irrational prejudices (including those of economists), irrational projections, hysteria in the press and media, share or asset price rigging, wrongful and manipulated facts, frauds, Ponzi schemes, greed or fear, restrictive practices and manipulation, and credit and debt build up which reinforces these factors. This pushes prices towards a crash.

Shareholder Value Fallacy

The notion that a firm's main objective or sole objective is to "increase shareholder value" has been totally discredited by the rigging of share prices by top executives, speculators, investment banks and by massive share buybacks where executives use a firm's profits, reserves, revenues or debt to buy large numbers of the firm's shares so as to increase the value of the shares and the financial benefits to the executives. This has been well researched by Dr. William Lazonick, emeritus professor of economics at the University of Massachusetts Lowell in the USA.

Why Bubbles and Crashes Occur

The works of Dr. Steve Keen[1], Dr. Hyman Minsky [2] Charles Kindleberger [2] , John Kenneth Galbraith [2] , Robert Shiller [2] , Irving Fisher [3] and Richard Koo [4] , William Black, Bob Haugen [5] and Mian and Sufi [6] have confirmed the above and provided deep insights into the fallacy of the efficient markets hypothesis, rational expectations theory, and the defective pricing and pricing mechanisms of the market and the dynamic disequilibrium of markets. This was most apparent during the speculative booms and busts over the last 350 years, where these facts have been proved many times. In particular, Nobel Prize winner Robert Shiller has in his book 'Irrational Exuberance' (3 editions) [2] provided deep insights into the reasons why bubbles occur and why they crash, much of it based on behavioral economics, the disconnect between prices and real earnings (Price-Earnings ratios), and the role of credit or leverage in fuelling pure speculation in prices which have no relationship to earnings and real value. Shiller provides Price-Earnings graphs for the stock market, bond market and property market going back to 1871 to prove his point. In this he echoes the sentiments of Minsky, Kindleberger, Galbraith, Fisher, Keynes, and others in the past. There is a potent combination of factors which when working together can intensify dynamic disequilibrium providing bubbles and crashes and severe economic consequences.

The above authors and their works and the facts of history confirm that there are fatal flaws in free market economics and neo classical economic theories which can be deconstructed and classified into **25 elements which combine together:**

1. Imperfect, imprecise, inaccurate, corrupted, fraudulent and dysfunctional information, pricing and pricing processes, and a herd mentality and irrational expectations which reinforces this. And excessively high Price-Earnings ratios and Price-Sales ratios which reflect this.

2. The False and Naive belief in a new era, a new paradigm, a new world resulting from new discoveries or new technologies and innovations which can insulate economies from crashes

3. Regulator failure, perverse incentives, and moral hazard

4. False and fraudulent financial ratings by Ratings Agencies

5. Deregulation which enabled, encouraged and legalised fraud, theft and excessive risks and speculative bubbles

6. The Strategic use of Credit Default Insurance and Swaps to facilitate fraud

7. Government Subsidy to 'Too big to fail' banks and those involved in fraud and crime

8. Money Creation and Loans by private banks which fuels and increases Speculative Asset Prices

9. Credit and Debt which rises faster than income, earnings, and profits. Credit for speculation rising faster than Nominal GDP. Growing Mismatch between Speculative Debt and the Capacity to repay it.

10. The Derivatives Effect and The Scale Effects — New and Emerging Threats

11. High Concentrations of Wealth and Income which increase the propensity to save and to speculate and also increase private debt

12. Land Values and Speculation

13. The recent introduction of Quantitative Easing to promote Company Buybacks and prop up asset prices and bubbles

14. Balance Sheet Weaknesses

15. Risks of Contagion and Systemic Collapse & The Degree of Interconnection and Interlinkage

16. The Crowding Out Principle. Werner's Division of Credit and Money Supply into that used for Speculation and that used for Productive investment.

17. Debt Limits

18. The Rise in Input Prices and the cumulative effects of dynamic disequilibrium forces

19. 'Sticky' Monopolistic, Oligopolistic, Cartel Prices and Economic Rents which prevent 'clearing of the market'

20. Use of the wrong Economic indicators, wrong tools and wrong reasoning to measure economic growth, systemic risks and dynamic disequilibrium

21. The Minsky Financial Instability Hypothesis and The Minsky Moment

22. The Financial Capture of Economists

23. Regulatory Capture

24. Government Interference and Irresponsibility

25. How the above factors create Fluctuating Yield Curves and Short Run and Long Run Debt Cycles

1. Imperfect, imprecise, inaccurate, corrupted, fraudulent and dysfunctional information, pricing and pricing processes, and a herd mentality and irrational expectations which reinforces this. And excessively high Price-Earnings ratios and Price-Sales ratios which reflect this.

This is briefly discussed in the section above titled 'Productivity of Capital'. Behavioural economics plays a major role in markets, and asset prices are easily stimulated by wrong, imperfect, imprecise information and the hype, rumours and sensation which promotes it. Most importantly there is an asymmetry of information between the seller and the buyer, and between insiders and outsiders which affects behaviour. One side possesses inside knowledge, hidden information, secret deals, and the means to manipulate and other types of hidden advantages while the other side does not possess this, and relies on trust, hunches, 'gut feelings', hype and other aspects of the herd mentality. This asymmetry of information is the key to understanding fraudulent pricing, bubbles, crashes and market failure, and dynamic disequilibrium. This is greatly facilitated by the fact that most investors presume themselves to be well informed, aware, knowledgeable but in reality are uneducated, inexperienced (in the operations of asymmetry and skewed markets), ill informed, act on gossip, rumour and hearsay, and hype and sensation in the press and media. They are the main drivers of this herd mentality, pushing up prices to unrealistic levels. This confirms the findings of the Nobel Prize winner Daniel Kahneman concerning the differences between people who act automatically on hunches without thinking and analysis and those others who carefully analyse, calculate and gather facts and evidence, often for nefarious ends. His book 'Thinking Fast, Slow' provides an excellent analysis of this. The end result is a market with wrong information and wrong signals, which makes prices unrealistic, artificial and unsustainable, and creates significant dynamic disequilibrium. Prices typically rise far above historical Price-Earnings ratios, and approach levels seen in previous crashes in history.

The Nobel Prize winner Robert Shiller has in his book 'Irrational Exuberance' (3 editions) [2] and other books provided deep insights into the reasons why bubbles occur and why they crash, much of it based on behavioral economics and how it creates the disconnect between prices and the real earnings and earnings potential (which prices are based on). Certain types of human behavior work with the expansion of credit or leverage to fuel unsustainable price rises, hysteria and bubbles. Some of this behavior, much of it criminal, unethical and fraudulent is itemized below. The works of Dr. Steve Keen [1], Dr. Hyman Minsky [2] Charles Kindleberger [2], Robert Shiller [2], Galbraith [2] Irving Fisher [3] and Richard Koo [4] William Black, Bob Haugen [5] and Mian and Sufi [6] have also confirmed this and also provided deep insights into the defective pricing and pricing mechanisms of the market and the dynamic disequilibrium of markets. They have consistently exposed the fallacy of the efficient markets hypothesis and rational expectations theory. This was most apparent during the speculative booms and busts over the last 350 years, where these facts have been proved many times. At the core of this is human behavior and the role of Behavioral Economics.

This behaviour typically involves speculation in property, shares, derivatives, bonds, commodities, property, currencies and other assets which leads to a situation where price rises cause demand increases, and expectations of price rises causes further increases in demand. This is fuelled by greed and the herd mentality, where the expectation of future price rises leads to increased demand and buying and to further expectations and so on ; a herd mentality based on irrational expectations not rational expectations as presumed by many economists. The herd mentality is mindless, unthinking, unquestioning, illogical and irrational, and easily manipulated and controlled by special interests. It can be fed a multitude of lies, deceptions and frauds from "trusted", "respectable" and "reliable" sources which act against the best interests of the herd. In this paradigm there is the herd on one side and the controllers, manipulators or 'insiders' who lie, deceive, defraud, rob, cheat and manipulate the herd on the other side. These two sides are in a classics parasite-host relationship.

For example, the herd has been (and may still be) fed false and fraudulent investment ratings by ratings agencies. While corrupted regulators who refuse to regulate assure the herd that prices are trustworthy and that bubbles will never crash. The demand curve (for the herd) in economic charts is reversed, the direction of this type of demand curve being manipulated through greed and fear, and exploitation of these emotions. This is the exact opposite of what is taught in schools, colleges and Universities. The supply curve and demand curve and their elasticities and prices are manipulated through a combination of restrictive practises in relation to the supply of assets, restricted information, wrong information, asymmetry of information, fraudulent information, frauds and financial crimes, and the mass speculation and the herd mentality which feeds off this imperfect information and contributes to the generation of even more imperfect information.

Central to this theme of 'imperfect information' was deregulation and lack of regulation and oversight. Since the mid 1980's deregulation has been praised, strongly supported, and implemented by Neo Liberal and Neo Classical economists and political conservatives and it assisted the mass speculation, fraud and other financial crimes in the period between 1998 and 2008. This issue of imperfect information and in many cases manipulated and fraudulent information added to the disequilibrium of markets in a most dynamic manner and included the following:

- Control Frauds : Fraud by those in high executive positions and oversight positions

Dr. William Black a well known and highly respected economist, University Professor and US Regulator in the USA wrote a book about this called 'The Best Way to Rob a Bank is to Own One: How Corporate Executives and Politicians Looted the S&L Industry' [24] He is vastly experienced in discovering financial frauds and one of the main regulators responsible for jailing corrupt bankers, mortgage providers, speculators and politicians in the early 1990's. He identified 5 ways which banks, mortgage companies and financial institutions commit fraud and bankrupt themselves, and these 5 rules still apply today [24]

1) Grow like crazy (very fast). This is done via crappy loans and false appraisals and other forms of fraud involving asset price rigging, insider trading, selling of fraudulent products, etc. many of them mentioned in sections below.

2) Make crappy loans at a premium interest rate. This includes

(b) create liars loans, ninja loans and subprime loans, and then package them and securitise them and create CDO's and MBS for banks and hedge funds in Wall street, London, Frankfurt, Beijing, and other financial centres.

(a) appraisal frauds which bid up the prices of properties / assets well beyond their true worth. This also includes real estate agents getting potential buyers to bid against themselves and against false bidders. Appraisers who refused to do this were fired and blacklisted. There was coercion and blackmail in many cases. These rigged property prices or other asset prices provide the means to provide massive loans for overpriced properties and assets

3) Employ extreme leverage (high levels of borrowing). This enables banks to fund speculation (by others) and also to participate in speculation in assets and derivatives and make profits from capital gains

4) Provide trivial loss reserves (for future losses). And also conceal loses from shareholders and regulators

5) Regulators which refuse to regulate and legal systems which refuse to investigate and prosecute fraud and financial crimes and jail the guilty parties. This creates moral hazard and provides incentives to keep committing frauds and crimes.

This certainly explained the reasons for the Irish financial crash in 2008. These frauds and thefts were facilitated by no prosecutions and jailings of guilty parties after the 2008 crash. This was in contrast to the Savings and Loan crash of 1990-91 in the USA where over one thousand bank executives and speculators were convicted and jailed or fined. All were given criminal records in the 1990's. But after the 2008 crash nobody was prosecuted, jailed and given criminal records. The evidence points to cover ups, perversions of justice, and refusals to enforce the law.

- false and fraudulent information about investment products and false investment products being created by banks, mortgage companies, investment banks and financial businesses, and marketing of these fraudulent products in the press and media. The mass creation of liar's loans, ninja type mortgages and subprime loans throughout America and the packaging and securitising of hundreds of thousands of these loans into bad quality investment products such as CDO's and mortgage backed securities (MBS), and false and manipulated risk ratings for these products by ratings agencies. These were sold at inflated prices for inflated profits. They also charged (and still charge) hidden fees which further boost their profits on these fraudulent investment products. These same Banks and brokers secretly bet against these 'investment' products through credit default swaps when selling them at high prices to investors. The fraudsters made double the profits for their crimes, firstly by selling defective and fraudulent products and secondly by claiming on credit default insurance payouts from insurance companies. And the employees and executives of these investment banks, commercial banks, brokerages and hedge funds made large bonuses from these activities. These 'free market' frauds (or practises) contributed to the financial crash of 2008.

- the involvement of some government subsidised firms in promoting bad mortgages and loans and selling fraudulent investment products. In the USA, Fannie Mae and Freddy Mac, which were subsidised and guaranteed by the US government facilitated the granting of subprime mortgages or ninja mortgages to people and the packaging of these mortgages into MBS's and CDO's and the purchase and sale of these to national and foreign investors. The investors were not told about the true status of these investment products and the mortgages within them. This fraud amounted to hundreds of billions of dollars prior to 2008 and was international in scope.

- brokers using clients money to bid up asset prices while secretly using their own money to make easy capital gains from these deals, conflicts of interest in financial contracts and trades, fraudulent misrepresentation of facts in investment contracts, and the payment of large bonuses and share options to bankers / brokers from these activities. Many large well known investment banks, brokerages, commercial banks, hedge funds and insurance companies were involved in these frauds totalling hundreds of billions of dollars prior to 2008. However, these frauds are old and date back over a century.

- incentives and bonuses to keep selling assets at higher and higher prices regardless of their real value and integrity of the investment, and current and future returns, and the use of hype, hysteria, rumours, and the press and media and herd instinct to achieve this. And facilitation of this by banks which create money (credit) out of nothing.

- widespread insider trading, rigging of IPO prices and bribing of executives, laddering of stocks and spinning of stocks, price rigging of financial products, lying to regulators and regulatory bodies, creating false reductions in supply for products and services in order to artificially inflate prices, 'gazumping' or illegal and unethical price manipulation of assets, legalised Ponzi schemes, commercial banks creating billions of euros / dollars / sterling out of nothing for speculation in shares, property, assets and derivatives.

- lenders (banks and mortgage firms) and real estate firms pressurising appraisers to keep inflating the prices of property beyond their real worth. New debt and money creation by lenders facilitated this price rigging upwards and fraud, drawing in many desperate people looking for homes and property. These parties made commissions, extra fees, higher mortgage loan profits, and higher profits from speculation from pumping up the prices of properties. Ordinary people and families were forced to buy over priced houses and take out massive mortgages, which were far greater than the real price and worth of properties. This amounted to theft and robbery from ordinary people and families.

- similar price rigging and manipulation of commodities, currencies, derivatives, property and other assets which keep pushing prices up, far beyond their real worth or intrinsic value. And well beyond their income / dividend generating capacity. In real estate this was known as 'gazumping' of prices where bidders bid against themselves or against false bidders. By the time prices have reached their peak the big players or fraudsters have already pulled out of the market, leaving investors, pensions funds, institutional investors, families and ordinary working people to suffer massive losses. This is the real game of big banks, many real estate firms, big brokerages and hedge funds.

- the 'Greater Fool Theory' much publicised by Galbraith and others in their works [2] where naive fools indoctrinated with free market theories believe that buying and re-buying over priced assets will lead to easy riches ultimately leads to one of these fools holding worthless assets once the market crashes. Yet it causes great anxiety throughout the boom as holders of assets are unsure if they will be the fools left holding deflated worthless assets. Milton Friedman's obsession with freedom to choose, does not integrate the necessity of choosing wisely based upon accurate, perfect information. He failed to comprehend the distortions caused by fraud, insider trading, price rigging, etc. which impaired choice and the perceptions and calculations behind choice. The 'Greater Fool Theory' may need to be expanded to integrate foolish economists.

- concealing losses on assets and investments in order to falsely boost profits, share prices, and bonuses for executives in banks, financial institutions and shadow banking entities. Investors and regulators were provided with fraudulent information.

- use of off-balance sheet vehicles and frauds, use of various fraudulent investment vehicles and derivatives, and use of repos to conceal losses or inflate earnings or assets, theft of funds from savings or deposit accounts to speculate on markets, bankrupt banks illegally manipulating balance sheets and earnings reports to fraudulently acquire investment funds or loans, bankrupt banks / firms loaning money to (often bankrupt) borrowers, banks involved in share rigging through giving loans to existing investors to support its own shares.

- the great importance of big or major speculators who can rig some markets to draw in as many 'suckers' as possible and make massive profits from price speculation, capital gains and fees. They quietly pull out of the market once it reaches a certain price level, creating conditions for a selling panic followed by a crash. A domino effect is created by this pull out of big speculative players, and this domino effect hastens the crash.

- a shadow banking system subject to no regulations and laws, and which gave out loans, traded in investment products and services, committed frauds, and engaged in many of the activities mentioned in this chapter, and had assets worth trillions of dollars prior to the 2008 crash. It posed systemic risk to the economy in 2008 and 2009, yet even today it is not subject to oversight, regulation, rules, or laws.

- the recent invention of front running and price manipulations in real time (as described by investor Michael Lewis) which uses high technology and high speed telecommunications in new ways to rip off investors and trades fractions of a second before a trade is made.

- corporate and banking executives selling shares and share options at inflated prices and making massive profits while concealing losses and weak balance sheets. These losses and weaknesses are usually exposed some time after the sales of shares are made. This causes massive share price losses and dividend losses for investors who are not given this information.

- breach of legal audit requirements by auditors, false accounting by banks, financial companies and businesses, the hiding of financial losses, conflicts of interest and deliberate failures by oversight bodies, and fraudulent acceptance of state money by regulators and oversight bodies which refused to carry out their duties. Lobbying, political corruption and corrupt laws and amendments to laws.

- company buybacks where company profits are used to buy shares in the company and to increase share prices. And increase the capital gains of executives and favoured share holders who own shares and options.

- Corporate raiders and junk bonds which artificially bid up speculative share prices and asset strip productive companies

- widespread tax evasion, use of offshore tax havens and investment vehicles to 'wash' tax evasion money and criminal laundered money in Europe and North America and to speculate and evade regulators, laws and taxes.

- large banks laundering money for criminals, terrorists, child traffickers, despotic dictators, and regimes seeking to build nuclear weapons. And using this money to speculate in shares, property and other types of assets.

- the LIBOR scandal and the illegal rigging of interest rates by banks, circumventing of capital controls, liquidity controls, fractional reserve guidelines, breaches of conflicts of interest rules by banks, the currency rigging scandals, using derivatives to hide losses, providing false collateral and false financial information to get loans, the theft of shareholder's funds to pay for excessively high executive salaries and bonuses, the breaches of company laws and corporate governance laws

A breeding ground (or cesspit) of fraud and criminality which was not punished by criminal prosecutions and jailings in courts in several countries. Legal systems unable to or unwilling to enforce laws. And markets being unable to function efficiently or effectively from the over-supply of imperfect information or wrong information. The award winning documentary film 'Inside Job' provided some important insights into the widespread frauds and criminality in the financial industry and in politics and government.

The differences between genuine investment, fraud, speculation and criminal activity have become more blurred over time, as vast amounts of criminal laundered money and tax evasion funds from foreign tax havens and 'front companies' also fuels this speculation in shares and assets, particularly property in big European cities and American cities, skewing and misdirecting statistics and posing other dangers to countries.

2. The False belief in a new era, a new paradigm, a new world resulting from new discoveries or new technologies and innovations which can insulate economies from crashes

All speculative booms throughout history have been preceded by new discoveries or new technologies and innovations. This at first improves businesses, productivity, and consumer choice and has many positive effects, however after some time it creates irrational exuberance and excitement which translates into speculation in the assets or products associated with these discoveries or new technologies. Credit and money which could be funnelled into productive investment, productivity and innovation is channelled into speculation and easy gains. And this is accompanied by the usual fraud, over pricing, manipulation, credit growth and debt for speculation, etc. well described in section 1 above. This is reinforced by the herd mentality and indeed it is policed by it. All dissenters and people who warned about the risk of a crash were ruthlessly ridiculed and condemned by those profiteering from the speculative mania and by their economists, financial experts, professors, bankers, politicians, and newspaper editors who were cynically used to silence opposition. Plenty of 'free market' nonsense was peddled by snake oil salesmen. Academic credentials and professional qualifications were used to prop up these shams, frauds, and ponzi schemes in the eyes of the naïve and gullible public. This is well described by John Kenneth Galbraith in his works on crashes [2]. A conformity is enforced on society to support the speculative mania, and the bubble gets higher and higher until it crashes.

3. Regulator Failure, Perverse Incentives, and Moral Hazard

A system where traders, bankers, brokers, investment managers and advisors have financial incentives to speculate, to buy and sell over priced assets, fraudulent assets, and to keep driving prices up by criminal means if necessary, to engage in illegal trading activities, and provide false and fraudulent information. These financial incentives are a significant driver of speculative booms and accompanying debt creation. Examples of these frauds and financial crimes are provided in section 1 above. Excessive greed and fraud is not rational and does not involve rational expectations, and does not care about crash risks, contagion risks and systemic risks. The incentives to provide imperfect, imprecise and fraudulent information, to manipulate the herd mentality, and to commit frauds and financial crimes were strengthened by :

(a) the refusal of regulators to regulate. This in some cases involved regulatory capture by banks, financial institutions and corporations, which politically blocked regulation and regulator activities. In many cases regulators deliberately ignored breaches of regulations and laws or actively cooperated with banks and financial institutions in breaching regulations and laws.

(b) the promotion of 'light touch regulation' by Bush, Gordon Brown, Brian Cowen and other politicians which encouraged fraud and excessive risk taking in the financial sector and asset price speculation sector.

(c) No regulation of the shadow banking system and the build up of excessive debt and risks in this sector totalling trillions of dollars prior to the 2008 crash.

(d) the refusal of police, prosecutors, regulators, judges, and ministers and government officials to prosecute financial crimes and jail the criminals in the USA, Europe, and many other developed countries prior to and after the 2008 crash. In many cases there was political interference in legal processes and the legal system. One of many examples include several US banks found guilty of fraud, embezzlement and criminal activity prior to the 2008 crash, and they were given small fines to pay and nobody was jailed. Another is the case of the HSBC bank in 2012, where there was evidence of breaches of banking laws and of money laundering for drug dealers and terrorist organisations, and the US Justice Department was prevented and blocked from prosecuting bank executives. There was illegal political interference in the case, certain politicians and civil servants actively assisted criminals in escaping prosecution and jail. This was the subject of a great film 'All the Plenary's Men" by John Titus in 2017.

(e) the bail out of these bankers, speculators and fraudsters by governments and taxpayers which created incentives to privatise gains and socialise losses. This created moral hazard.

This lack of regulation led to massive theft from investors and later from taxpayers to bail out fraudsters and criminals. There is evidence that these criminals are protected by corrupt politicians and their 'advisors' and compromised legal and judicial systems.

This promotes moral hazard, and provides strong incentives to continue committing frauds and crimes and put financial systems and economies at systemic risk in the present and future. These perverse incentives continue to exist today and are one of the strongest factors of dynamic disequilibrium.

4. False and Fraudulent Financial Ratings by Ratings Agencies

These fraudulent ratings were applied to investment products, derivatives, assets, services, firms, banks and financial institutions by the 3 leading agencies prior to the 2008 crash. The most infamous examples were mortgage backed securities and CDO's. This was coordinated by large investment banks, stock brokers and financial institutions paying off ratings agencies. Most investors and large pension funds and institutional investors relied on these rating agencies in order to assess investment products prior to investing. While ratings agencies increased their profits from fees by several multiples prior to 2008, they exposed large pension funds and other investors to massive losses in 2008 and afterwards.

5. Deregulation which enabled, encouraged and legalised fraud, theft and excessive risks and speculative bubbles

In the USA, the repeal of the Glass Steagal act by President Clinton, and the introduction of the Gramm–Leach–Bliley Act led to the deregulation of banks, insurance companies, securities companies and financial institutions. This removed important safeguards and oversight from these financial businesses which had existed since the 1930's. This was accompanied by the refusal of SEC to regulate and protect securities and trading and the refusal of the Federal Reserve to regulate and protect banking during the decade prior to the 2008 crash. The BASLE accords for banking were completely ignored by banks and regulators. Fraud, inside trading and other criminal activities were ignored by the SEC, the police, and the FBI. This deregulation in all of its forms led directly to increased financial fraud and crimes. Then there was the deregulation of commodities, derivatives, and futures by the Commodities Futures Trading Commission on the advice of Lawrence Summers, Robert Rubin and Alan Greenspan. These three gentlemen strongly opposed and undermined any attempts to regulate them. One of the derivatives which remained unregulated was Credit Default Swaps and these played a major role in the 2008 crash. Furthermore, it was these same men who helped repeal the Glass-Steagal act in 1999 which had kept investment banking separate from commercial banking and had other safeguards to protect banks. The same nonsense about 'free markets' and supposedly 'self correcting mechanisms' were peddled prior to 2008, but they were proved wrong, very wrong. The decision to repeal Glass Steagal, to deregulate derivatives and futures, and the refusal of some government bodies to properly regulate banks and financial institutions proved to be a disastrous mistake for the USA and led to the crash in 2008. A fact that Alan Greenspan admitted to after the crash. This was brilliantly exposed in a Public Broadcasting Service *Frontline* report, "The Warning" in the USA.

In Europe, there was similar regulatory capture and accompanying deregulation nonsense, some of if lobbied for and attained in Brussels and others in European capitals. Prior to the European crash of 2008-2011, there was no European Financial Regulator for massive cross border financial flows, no European SEC for cross border trading, no European lender of last resort, no EU investigatory authority to uncover frauds and financial crimes, no EU deposit insurance, false and defective stress testing of European banks which gave them all a safe and good rating prior to 2008, bought and bribed national politicians and (legalistic) cover ups of such, while the ECB, EU parliament and EU authorities and national governments engaged in various forms of deregulation and failed to properly regulate the banking system, the shares and assets markets, the credit markets, shadow banking, property markets, and derivatives market throughout Europe. This exposed whole countries in the Eurozone to financial collapse.

Reckless deregulation is predicated on the belief that massive financial gains can be privatised by an elite few, while financial losses paid for by taxpayers, governments and pension funds (through massive losses).

6. The Strategic Use of Credit Default Insurance and Swaps to Facilitate Fraud

It is a well known fact that many high profile banks and financial institutions took out credit default insurance and swaps on investment products they sold and which they knew to be defective and fraudulent prior to 2008. This type of insurance is relatively new and enabled these firms to make profits both from selling the defective investment products and from claiming an insurance payout when they failed. This was often done secretly. They knew they would fail, so the insurance payout was guaranteed. Yet this placed the buyer in a losing position, and they lost heavily, unfortunately most buyers wrongly trusted the reputation, prestige and high status of these banks. If the buyer took out credit default insurance, this would impose an extra cost on the buyer while the actual loss would impose heavy losses on the insurance company. Large insurance firms such as AIG and others were pushed to the point of bankruptcy by these type of insurance products. Ultimately, fraudulent investment products were going to impose heavy losses on firms and the economy. When this was revealed in Congressional hearings into the 2008 crash there was shock that banks and brokers would behave in such a manner. Yet nothing has been done, there were no laws against this and today this is still the case.

in 2008, American International Group (AIG) lost more than US$18 billion through a subsidiary over the preceding three quarters on credit default swaps (CDSs) The United States Federal Reserve Bank announced the creation of a secured credit facility of up to US$85 billion, to prevent the company's collapse by enabling AIG to meet its obligations to deliver additional collateral to its credit default swap trading partners.

7. Government Subsidy to 'Too big to fail' banks and those involved in fraud and crime

Some banks have become so big and so interconnected to the speculative economy and real economy that governments have declared them "too big to fail". This is a recent new development. This means that governments and taxpayers will bail out these banks if they make major losses or at risk of insolvency, bankruptcy or illiquidity. This subsidy takes the form of (i) direct government grants or loans to bail out banks and financial institutions (ii) Quantitative Easing by governments amounting to trillions of dollars / euros to provide funds, loans and liquidity to banks (iii) interventions by central banks in the Repo market to provide liquidity and loans to banks amounting to trillions of dollars / euros (iv) a few big firms which are non banks such as AIG also have this government guarantee or subsidy.

This form of government subsidy encourages these banks and firms to make very risky speculative investments which can produce large profits in the short term but also carry the risk of massive losses. These banks and firms cannot lose as the profits are privatised, while the losses are socialised. This enables banks to create more and more risky speculative investments and instruments and reap the profits off them, knowing that any financial crash will not affect them as the governments and taxpayers are there to bail them out. This destroys 'moral hazard' and free market principles. This has become in recent decades the biggest factor in global speculation and bubbles and one of the main drivers of dynamic disequilibrium. No other businesses are given these government subsidies.

This gives banks and financial institutions a massive competitive advantage in the market and in fund raising as the government and taxpayers have agreed to subsidise them. Other factors connected to this relate to big banks actively involved in laundering money for major criminals and terrorist organisations and brutal dictators which has come to light in recent years. This was exposed in several books and documentaries, one notable one being 'All the Plenary's men' by the lawyer and prosecutor John Titus. And this laundered money has also been used for speculation and frauds by banks and financial institutions. Would the noted economist Adam Smith have approved of all of this ?

8. Money Creation and Loans by private banks which fuels and increases Speculative Asset Prices

As stated earlier in the Chapter, 97% of all money is created out of nothing by banks when they make loans. This amounts to trillions of dollars per year. Most of these loans are used to fuel speculation in asset prices, property and derivatives. Whole economies can become subject to speculation or dominated by speculation due to the power of the banks to create money (out of nothing) and determine how and where it is allocated ! Control of the money supply has been given to private banks. This newly created money in the form of credit and debt are essential for the creation of speculative bubbles, they are it's fuel. Asset price accelerators and accompanying bubbles involves a combination of:

(a) Private banks which create money (credit) out of nothing with no state interference, and this money is pumped into loans to buy over priced, over hyped assets or derivatives and keep increasing these prices for easy capital gains and profits for speculators and banks. Massive profits come in the form of capital gains, dividends, high rents, professional fees and overcharging, compound interest, interest rates arbitrage, packaging and selling speculative assets and derivatives based on speculative assets, buying back properties or assets after a crash at a fraction of the original price, and various insurance scams derived from these activities. The important point is that money and interest created out of nothing by banks, in the form of new loans or credit fuels all of this speculative activity and creates massive levels of debt.

Richard Vague has shown that financial crashes since the 1850's have involved private debt to GDP of 150% or more and an increase in that ratio of 17% or more over 5 years [21] Dr. Steve Keen has also produced data which shows a strong causal link between private debt to GDP, credit growth, speculative prices, crashes and unemployment levels over long periods of time [1]. Some of his lectures showing charts and data are available on YouTube on the Internet.

(b) low interest rates or a sharp reduction in interest rates helps improve the prices of speculative assets, brings in more borrowers to the speculative market, and makes speculation more profitable

(c) Quantitative Easing by central banks, and giving it to banks and big corporates, who use a significant amount of this money for speculation. This is a new accelerator of speculative asset prices. And in recent times Central Banks have been investing in stock markets and pushing up stock prices, as part of their "diversification of risk".

(d) expansionary government fiscal policies and monetary policies

(e) reduction of capital gains taxes and other taxes on speculation and speculative assets to increase the incentives for speculation and the profits from such

(f) plenty of bidders for limited assets. In some cases, manipulated scarcity.

(g) the herd mentality and brokers or intermediaries which have the power to lie, deceive, and manipulate and keep pushing up asset prices. See Section 1 above

(h) very little or no government regulation. Most politicians confuse speculation with productive investment and cannot understand the difference between the two. Naive politicians supported 'light touch regulation' which provided a licence for speculative fraud and criminality. Regulators are easily undermined and compromised by corrupt or incompetent politicians.

These are the accelerators of asset prices. Credit is the fuel of asset price rises and bubbles but it works in combination with the other aforementioned accelerators to inflate massive bubbles. This becomes a self reinforcing cycle where more and more debt drives up speculative prices and these higher prices provide new incentives for banks to keep funding speculators and drive up prices further. As long as the prices keep going up profits are made by banks and speculators. This easy credit is complemented by lower interest rates and often reduced taxes on speculation which increase the incentives to borrow and speculate. A debt-speculative price spiral builds up. A mountain of debt builds up a mountain of fraudulent over-priced assets. This sets up the crash which inevitably follows.

The massive expansion in debt inflates the financial bubble and the contagion risks and overall risk to the banking system and whole economy. The fractional reserve of 5% or less for household deposits or only 10-20% of total deposits means banks have no reserve requirement for 80-90% of their deposits. This enables them to create as much money as they desire, and this fuels further disequilibrium. Government attempts to control the money supply failed in the 1980's (Thatcher government) due to the fact that money is mostly created (out of nothing) by commercial banks, not central banks or government banks ; it is endogenously determined not exogenously determined [1]. These facts were succinctly portrayed on Kunstler

Financialization is what happens when the people-in-charge "create" colossal sums of "money" out of nothing — by issuing loans, a.k.a. debt — and then cream off stupendous profits from the asset bubbles, interest rate arbitrages, and other opportunities for swindling that the artificial wealth presents. It was a kind of magic trick that produced monuments of concentrated personal wealth for a few and left the rest of the population drowning in obligations from a stolen future. The future is now upon us.

kunstler.com

9. Credit and Debt which rises faster than income, earnings, and profits. Credit for speculation rising faster than Nominal GDP (or GNI) . Growing Mismatch between Speculative Debt and the Capacity to repay it.

All debt is reliant on income streams and returns whether in the from of profits, dividends, rent, fees, etc. and capital gains to pay it off. The speculative boom undermines this at its later stages, as speculative prices and speculative debt builds up to unrealistic and unsustainable levels outpacing income and earnings and the means to pay it off. The mismatch between speculative debt and the funds to pay it off leads to a crash. Yet the herd mentality remains stuck in the mindset of profiteering from a rising market. Research by Dr. Richard Werner of Southampton University has found that credit rises faster than Nominal GDP (or GNI) [27]. This is important as GDP or GNI reflects the real underlying economy, and the means to pay off debt. Large differences between credit for speculation and Nominal GDP signify a bubble and a progression towards a crash.

As debt becomes more multiples of income or profitability, and multiples of price, this total debt (including compound interest) becomes unsustainable and the speculative prices become unsustainable. There is a large rise in all types of debt - speculator debt, bank debt, household debt, and business debt, and in many cases a rise in government debt during such booms, as stimulus is used to further inflate the bubble. These types of debt become linked to each other and in many cases dependent on each other, creating domino effects and contagion once the crash comes. This pushes bank debt to multiples of its income and share capital, and similarly for businesses, and on a larger scale pushes total private and public debt to multiples of GNP. The over leveraging of banks is a key factor as small percentage losses can leave them unable to meet loan repayment obligations. Prior to 2008, bank leverage ratios ranged from 18 – 40, which is high by historical standards, and much of this leverage was dependent on speculation in assets and derivatives. This vulnerability is a key factor in financial crashes.

Speculative asset prices and incomes may fluctuate up and down over time, but the debt associated with them remains fixed, this creates a disconnection and a contradiction between asset prices and income on one side and debt on the other side ; there is a large expansion of speculative debt far beyond the ability of income to repay it or increasing prices to repay it in the medium to long term, and it is this mismatch or disequilibrium which causes crashes and recessions / depressions, and poses systemic risk to banks, businesses and countries [1,2,3,4,5,6,7] .

During the boom phase, income can match price rises in the initial phase but it cannot match price rises and debt rises in the later phases, and one sees high debt & price to income ratios. This creates unsustainability which ultimately leads to a crash and a financial crisis. Though this fact is ignored by the press and media, by economists, financial commentators and governments. The present speculation and debt system is in reality a Ponzi scheme, a fraud which creates excessive debt & price to income ratios, and enriches a few people at the top before imploding and ruining and robbing millions of ordinary people of their incomes, savings and pension and robbing nations and taxpayers of their tax incomes and national assets.

10. The Derivatives Effect and The Scale Effects – New and Emerging Threats

The current value of the derivatives market at $1,200 trillion presents a very real and very serious risk to the global economy. They are based on bets, and bets on bets, on movements in indexes, on mathematical algorithms, on arbitrage, on swapping risks and swapping risky products, on innovations in insurance, and in most cases do not relate to actual goods and services. Derivatives have failed before in the past and caused massive financial losses:

- In 2008, American International Group (AIG) lost more than US$18 billion through a subsidiary over the preceding three quarters on credit default swaps (CDSs). The United States Federal Reserve Bank announced the creation of a secured credit facility of up to US$85 billion, to prevent the company's collapse by enabling AIG to meet its obligations to deliver additional collateral to its credit default swap trading partners.

- The loss of US$7.2 Billion by Société Générale in January 2008 through misuse of futures contracts.

- The loss of US$6.4 billion in the failed fund Amaranth Advisors, which was long natural gas in September 2006 when the price plummeted.

- The loss of US$4.6 billion in the failed fund Long-Term Capital Management in 1998.

- The loss of US$1.3 billion equivalent in oil derivatives in 1993 and 1994 by Metallgesellschaft AG.

- The loss of US$1.2 billion equivalent in equity derivatives in 1995 by Barings Bank.

- UBS AG, Switzerland's biggest bank, suffered a $2 billion loss through unauthorized trading in 2011

Debt creation scale and momentum are the key factors determining the extent of the speculative boom and the crash. For example a crash where hundreds of billions of dollars, even trillions of dollars, are invested in speculative Ponzi schemes will produce a much greater crash than one with millions of dollars invovled. In the present day, the scale is in the trillions of dollars / euros. In 2008, as the financial crisis erupted worldwide, Iceland had a private and public debt of 850% of GDP most of it based on speculation in shares, currencies, assets, property and derivatives. This led to the crash of the economy in Iceland and to a severe political crisis and economic crisis. In 1990, Japan had a private debt to GDP of 208% prior to its big crash. Ireland had private debt to GDP of 310% in the 2008 crash. The USA had a private debt which was 170% of GDP prior to the crash in 2008 which compares to one of 145% of GDP prior to the crash in 1929.

In 2015 -16, Japan had a total debt of 400% of GDP, Portugal had a total debt of 358% of GDP, Greece had a total debt of 317% of GDP (despite debt write downs and write offs of tens of billions of euros), Ireland had a total debt of 390% of GDP and a private debt to GDP of 293% (Irish Central Bank Quarterly Financial Accounts Ireland 2016) and Spain had a total debt of 313% of GDP (McKinsey & Company [7]). The USA with its government debt of $20 trillion has a debt of 111% of GDP while the total debt (household, federal and state governments, corporate, banking) is $67 trillion which is 372% of GDP. Total US unfunded liabilities (social security, veterans, medicare and other government debt) are $106 trillion which is 588% of GDP. The UK had a private debt of 200% of GDP prior to the crash, the highest in its history. From 1880 to 1980 private debt in the UK was below 72%. This explosion of private debt in the decade prior to the crash of 2008 was a major factor in causing the crash there. The fact that this massive private debt was linked to speculation to assets and derivatives in the aforementioned countries is the key factor. From 2008 to 2015, the value of the global stock of investable assets increased substantially by about 40 percent, from $350 trillion to over $500 trillion. This represents speculation in these asset prices, and Quantitative Easing played a major role in this. The figure of $500 trillion is over 9 times the global economy and presents a new level of systemic risk to economies.

In mid 2017, the ECB had acquired €4.2 trillion in distressed assets and government bonds, almost 40% of the GDP of the EU ; this is what happens when supposedly "free markets" are proven to be unfree, rigged and out of control. Today, the total debt worldwide is estimated at $195 trillion which is approximately 300% of world GDP, this too is unsustainable. Today trillions of dollars are tied up in speculative investments which are over-priced, while the high risk derivatives market alone is worth over $1,200 trillion (World Gold Council, December 2013). This scale is unprecedented in human history. Every day hundreds of billions of dollars are used to speculate in shares, assets, commodities and derivatives where the prices and pricing mechanisms are defective, inaccurate and in many cases fraudulent. Yet massive debt, in the trillions of dollars, is built upon these inaccurate or fraudulent prices. New technologies and means of printing electronic money credits by banks have increased the efficiency of money creation and the sheer scale of debt creation and the scale of speculation worldwide. This issue of excessive and unsustainable debt is further explored in Chapter 7 of this book. The following chart below gives an example of the scale of speculative debt, in international terms. There is enough speculative debt here to crash the world economy, and put all developed countries into bail outs and government austerity programmes for 30 years or more, worsening the existing enslavement of mankind.

•	**Review of World Financial Instability.**		
•			
•	**Summary: (World: US Dollars: Approx).**		
•	11.	Total Value of Derivatives (Notional):	1,200 Trillion (1.2 Quadrillion).
•	10.	Total Value of All Assets (Fin. /Real Estate):	318 Trillion (8. Plus 9.)
•	9.	Total Value of Financial Assets:	198 Trillion
•	8.	Total Value of Real Estate:	120 Trillion
•	7.	All Debt. (Owned by Banks):	257 Trillion (5. Plus 6.).
•	6.	Total Priv. Debt. (Owned by Banks):	193 Trillion (Priv./Corporate).
•	5.	Total Gov. Debt. (Owned by Banks):	64 Trillion
•	4.	World GDP:	60 Trillion
•	3.	Total Value of Derivatives (Cash Val.):	20 Trillion
•	2.	Total Value of Circulating Currency:	4 Trillion
•	1.	Total Value of Gold Reserves:	1.5 Trillion
•			
•	Ref: World Gold Council Dec. 2013.		

For home mortgage holders, the consequences of this are very serious, as they become entrapped in a fraudulent system which over-prices their property, provides over priced mortgage debts, and then crashes the system, leaving them with an under-priced property, an over-priced mortgage debt, increased taxes, levies and charges (for bank & business bailouts) and a higher probability of them losing their jobs and the means to pay back the mortgage debt. When money created out of nothing by banks to fuel speculation and fraudulent prices is taken into consideration, the present system is upon deeper analysis a criminally fraudulent system which defrauds and robs many hard working individuals and families of their incomes, homes, and livelihoods. For example, between 1994 and 2007 new house prices rose by 400% in Dublin and second hand house prices rose by 500%, while incomes rose between 60 – 70% in that time period. The United States witnessed a dramatic rise in household debt in the years before the Great Recession, the total amount of debt for American households doubled between 2000 and 2007 to $14 trillion. The crash and Great American Recession resulted in the loss of eight million jobs between 2007 and 2009, and more than four million homes were lost to foreclosures [6]. In 2015, 31,000 families in Ireland have been officially threatened with evictions by the banks and 120,000 families are in serious danger of being evicted. Over 50% of mortgage holders in arrears are in danger of losing of the family home. This speculation and debt system, and accompanying bailout system is a system of theft, a criminal fraud, a Ponzi scheme, which robs people of private income, personal property, and is unconstitutional and illegal.

The economic losses to individuals and families are considerable.

11. High Concentrations of Wealth and Income which increase the propensity to save and to speculate and also increase private debt

The rich have a higher propensity to save and to speculate than the middle class, working class and the poor. The statistics provided in this book show a correlation between high concentrations of wealth and income and speculation and the creation of speculative bubbles. The statistics also show a correlation between high concentrations of wealth and income and the massive build up of private debt by the middle class, working class and the poor as they attempted to maintain basic living standards in high priced western countries. This is in part influenced by the higher propensity to save by the rich which restricts consumption led growth and wage increases. There was also a correlation between high concentrations of wealth and income and the large build up of speculative debt to fund speculation during the economic growth phase prior to the crash. So an economy with high and growing concentrations of wealth and income faces 3 important systemic risks prior to a crash, and these play a significant part in worsening financial crashes:

(i) the massive build up of private debt by the middle class, working class and the poor as they attempted to maintain basic living standards in high priced western countries

(ii) large build up of speculative debt to fund speculation during the economic growth phase prior to the crash

(iii) speculation which is based on false and rigged prices and manipulation.

Debt itself has its own limitations and indeed debt imposes its limitations on an economy and this along with other factors in a economy create the ideal conditions for a crash.

12. Land Values and Speculation

Fred Harrison found a direct correlation between speculation in land values and the build up of massive debt and crashes, most notably the 2008 crash [22]. Several countries had a land and speculation bubble prior to 2008, though this was complicated by accompanying frauds (CDO's, MBS's, derivatives) which fed off this land and property speculation and magnified the bubble and collapse. Land is in limited supply and cannot be produced and is required for housing, for offices and infrastructure and thus is an easy target for speculation. In fact land values tend to rise faster and higher than most other speculative assets, and far higher than wages and GDP. His research shows that the rise in land values also plays a role in increasing the costs of goods and services produced in the economy. Yet many western governments refuse to adequately tax land values and introduce controls on land speculation, and this has resulted in large scale tax losses for governments in many countries. This neglect by governments has contributed substantially to inflating speculation in land values and the creation of other assets including derivatives related to this, creating massive speculative bubbles and debt bubbles. The works of Fred Harrison have made an important contribution to public understandings of this issue [22].

13. The recent introduction of Quantitative Easing to promote Company Buybacks and prop up asset prices and bubbles

This has became a very significant new factor in the period after the 2008 crash, particularly in Europe and the USA. In the period, 2008 to 2017, central banks and governments engaged in Quantitative Easing valued at $15 trillion to bail out banks, insurance firms, some big businesses and government bonds and took distressed (or over speculated) assets off their balance sheets. Much of this newly created money was then pumped into speculation in shares in stock markets, derivatives, and especially company buybacks to increase share prices and share options for top executives. This was illegal for decades but has been legalised in recent years and has enabled top executives and their cronies to make vast sums of money from speculation in the company's stock while loading the company with massive debt. Speculation in government bonds and other forms of assets have created other bubbles from this 'free money' or Quantitative Easing. Some central banks have gone further and bought shares in stock markets pumping up the prices of these shares, in order to "diversify risk" in their portfolios. From 2008 to 2015, the value of the global stock of investable assets increased substantially by about 40 percent, from $350 trillion to over $500 trillion. This represents speculation in these asset prices, and Quantitative Easing played a major role in this. The figure of $500 trillion is over 9 times the global economy and presents a new level of systemic risk to economies. It was not diffused into the productive sector, the consumption sector (bottom 60%) and the wider economy to stimulate consumption by consumers and investment by firms in the productive sector and small and medium sized firms.

Quantitative Easing assisted the speculation in government bonds by keeping interest rates artificially low supposedly to stimulate productive investment and consumption. It had the opposite effect and stimulated over speculation in financial assets and bonds and derivatives. Central banks have in recent times joined with private banks to participate in inflating speculative bubbles. The direct involvement of central banks in this is very significant when one considers that they can pump many billions and trillions of dollars into speculation and debt accumulation. This has had the net effect of being an asset price stimulator as described in Section 4 above and also worked to increase total debt levels related to speculation, thus posing serious systemic risks to many already over indebted economies. And a repeat of the same mistakes made prior to the 2008 crash. This endless repetition of disaster arises from the ignorance, incompetence, stupidity and hubris of politicians, governments, their so called "advisors" and top economists, who apparently never learn the lessons of the past.

14. Balance Sheet Weaknesses

Prior to 2008 and even today, some banks and firms chose to include their assets and liabilities on balance sheets, while others chose to hide them offshore via 'structured investment vehicles' or engage in asset, liability and transaction frauds under the cover of these vehicles. This enabled one to circumvent regulations, guidelines, laws, the concerns of investors and shareholders. In Europe, some banks even secretly borrowed money to improve the appearance of their balance sheets and profits at the end of the financial year or to engage in secret share price rigging, so as to deceive investors and share holders. Deception came in many guises. The balance sheets of banks, shadow banking institutions and other financial institutions, pension funds and other types of investors contained massive amounts of over-priced speculative assets and also assets which were fraudulent and defective and had no real value. This ranged from billions of dollars to trillions of dollars. Worthless assets such as CDO' s and mortgage backed securities and derivatives had false AAA or AAB ratings, and this caused major balance sheet problems once their true value was established. Yet the market panic led to a collapse in the price of such products, beyond what was reasonable or logical. Markets have always been governed by irrational expectations. The scale of asset fraud placed these financial institutions at risk of insolvency, liquidity problems, and collapse and through contagion placed the financial system at risk of systemic collapse if a crash occurs or prices fall and (asset) earning capacity falls. This threat of systemic collapse emerges from the effects of interlinking and contagion discussed in the next section. In the event of central banks bailing them out, this places even the central banks at risk if they already have too many distressed assets on their balance sheets from continuously having to bail out an unstable financial system. Scale is important here, and we are dealing with failed speculative assets worth trillions of dollars on the balance sheets of central banks and governments. Selling distressed speculative (over priced) assets into economies burdened by austerity policies, recession / depression and deflation depresses their prices further and worsens balance sheets. Selling conditions inevitably become very difficult and this can lead to severe losses for banks, financial institutions and even central banks and taxpayers. These are the end results of speculation and credit which gets out of control and intensifies dynamic disequilibrium.

15. Risks of Contagion and Systemic Collapse & The Degree of Interconnection and Interlinkage

This can apply to classes of investment products and other related products, to sectors of an economy and related sectors, to banks and related banks and financial institutions, and to countries and collections of countries. This is dependent on the degree of inter-relatedness and interconnections and interlocking relationships between investments, between banks, between economic sectors, and between countries. In Behavioural economics contagion is triggered by the 'Minsky moment' or the transition from excessive greed to excessive fear and the level of contagion determined by the inter-relationships and inter-dependencies.

(i) large investments banks, insurance companies, retail banks, hedge funds, stock brokers and financial institutions, money markets, shadow banks, mortgage companies, and big property developers which had become linked to each other, and dependent on each other for loans, liquidity, daily Repos, many types of investment products, securitized debt, credit default insurance and swaps, medium term and long term loans, deposits, bonds, shadow banking instruments, corporate paper and bonds, cross investments, derivatives, etc.. These interconnections and interlinkages provided the means for contagion, once a key player or players failed. Globalisation has internationalized this risk. And this field had become increasingly consolidated through mergers, takeovers and acquisitions and concentrated nationally and internationally thus increasing the total network effect of a bubble and crash.

(ii) many fraudulent speculative investments and the fact that many such investments were related to each other, were linked to each other, were part of each other, were used as collateral for each other, and in some cases were bets on each other, and also related to other less speculative investments amounting to billions, even trillions of dollars.

(iii) Bank debt, corporate debt, household debt (including home equity) and personal debt, government debt, all become linked to each other and in many cases dependent on each other, creating domino effects and contagion once the crash comes

(iv) New technologies, the Internet, and the aforementioned greater consolidation of banks, financial institutions and industries provided fast, instantaneous communications and new globalised trading and communications opportunities online which globalised the interconnectedness and the level of risk a given bank or firm is exposed to. It globalised the individual risk, the network risk and systemic risk ; the systemic risk being the most serious yet most ignored. For example, today the global speculative derivatives market is worth $1,200 trillion, more than 20 times the global economy.

(v) the availability of inter bank credit, the Repo market, the Repo rate and the level of central bank intervention to provide liquidity to banks. There is a correlation between the Repo rate, liquidity between banks, crashes and recessions.

These were and still are the primary determinants of contagion. This created an interlinked, interlocking system where when a few big investments fail, through over speculation or the discovery of fraud, they create major losses and liquidity and solvency problems for a key bank(s) or financial institution(s), for example a Bear Stearns or Northern Rock, and this in turn frightens investors and depositors and causes bank runs, client withdrawals of funds, law suits, and share price collapses, and this panic freezes the credit markets and capital markets as other big banks refuse to loan out money to other banks out of fear of increasing their own exposure and risk, and this blocks trades, loans, transfers and liquidity. This bankruptcy of a bank / financial institution does not remain isolated, and it affects other banks and firms which are immediately interconnected and interlinked to them through their dealings in the past, and these are then forced to realise losses. More cases of fraudulent investment products and over priced speculative assets are uncovered in these other banks and firms and this creates more losses and more panic. This diffuses into their interconnections with other banks, big insurance firms and other firms to trigger a domino effect of more losses and further freezing of credit and capital markets, and more liquidity and insolvency problems, which affect other similar banks and firms and other types of speculative investments elsewhere and cause these to endure losses or go bankrupt and so on and on. This initiates a selling panic and deleveraging panic and bank runs and money market runs. Due to imperfect, wrong and imprecise information and the herd mentality as discussed in Point 1 above, everybody panics and tries to get out at the same time. In the case of insurance companies such as AIG which insured against losses on CDO's and MBS's the losses drove them to bankruptcy in 2008. If AIG and similar insurance giants had been allowed to fail then the big investment banks, commercial banks and shadow banks would have had to bear the losses and they too would have failed. The interlinking and interconnections diffuses the losses and the panic regionally, nationally and internationally.

The loss of investor confidence and the freezing of liquidity markets and capital markets resulting from panic has effects which extend far beyond a few banks and firms involved in speculation and bad investments, and negatively affects unconnected less risky investments and firms (ABB or higher) in the wider economy causing them to endure losses, lose value, lose access to credit and liquidity, or fail. This further enhances the existing selling panic, deleveraging panic and runs and progresses on to crash the prices of investment products, investment categories, leading indexes, crashing investment projects, investment markets, commercial banks, liquidity markets, insurance firms and industries in a domino effect to create a systemic crisis. When one considers that this fraudulent and speculative market is measured in trillions of dollars and many banks and firms are part of this and interlinked in it, and they themselves are linked to others in the wider non speculative economy, and that this affects the actual flow of money in an economy, then one understands the systemic risk it poses to nations. The Icelandic crash and the MBS and CDO scandals in the USA in 2008 -2011 revealed the extent of this domino effect. This was seen in the Latin American crashes and Asian crashes of the 1990's and the global crash of 2008. The timely intervention of governments and central banks in 2007 – 2009 prevented full contagion and systemic breakdown. The free market if left to itself would have led to a complete breakdown of the financial system and national economies, worse than the 1930's.

16. The Crowding Out Principle. Werner's Division of Credit and Money Supply into that used for Speculation and that used for Productive investment.

Dr. Richard Werner of the University of Southampton has produced important research in the area of monetary economics, including proposals for Quantitative Easing in the 1990's and after the 2008 crash and the new 'Quantity Theory of Credit' which provides important new insights into economics and shows that credit and money supply growth created by banks needs to be divided into that which is used for speculation and that which is not used for speculation [27]. And he proposes similar measures for measuring GDP and GNP. This division between money creation (by banks) for speculation at the expense of less money creation (by banks) for productive investments is important and is the basis of the 'crowding out principle' discussed below.

The fact is that incomes, earnings, revenues, rents, dividends and profits from productive investments are the lifeblood of an economy, not speculation which shifts paper and credits around. Indeed speculation often feeds off the strength of the productive economy, and a weakening productive base will affect the speculative economy regardless of how high speculative prices rise. Many studies confirm that banks provide 3, 4, 5, 6, 7 or more times more funding for speculative investments than productive investments during boom periods and bubbles. This is particularly true in the case of large banks and where a few large banks dominate the banking market, eg. Britain. During 'booms' and bubbles massive amounts of funds, credit, loans and capital are drawn away from the productive sector, from production of goods and services and productivity growth and wasted on speculation in asset prices and derivatives. For the last 20 years over 70% of new money creation and debt in developed countries has gone into speculation and speculative instruments. This is known as the 'crowding out' principle, where productive investment has been crowded out of the funding markets by speculation, and this leads to a weakening of sustainable growth and demand. This rations credit and increases its cost to productive businesses. This drain of funds and investment away from production has many unforeseen consequences, it undermines and destroys the fundamentals of the real economy upon which long term sustainable growth is based upon, and short to long term earnings, dividends, income, wages generation is based. This creates new stresses and strains on the economy and further dynamic disequilibrium, which affects economic growth, earnings and prices, including the sustainability of speculative prices.

Other disequilibrium factors including increased relocations of productive businesses to foreign countries, increased replacement of workers in developed countries with cheaper workers from developing / third world countries, increased labour replacing automation, regional economic decline, sharp fluctuations in the balance of trade and payments, fluctuations in employment levels, and energy price shocks also play a role. The resultant lack of strong or continued growth in the real non speculative economy reduces the real income growth necessary to sustain high speculative asset prices and continued rises. This in turn (i) reduces the earnings, revenues, rents, dividends, profits necessary to meet speculative debt repayments (ii) increases default risks (iii) increases the Price -Earnings ratios and Price-Sales ratios.

17. Debt Limits

There are practical limits to how much private debt and bank debt can be borne in an economic system, destabilised by over speculation, fraud, excessive debt and interest, and dynamic disequilibrium forces. Research by Richard Vague has shown that financial crashes since the 1850's have involved private debt to GDP of 150% or more and an increase in that ratio of 17% or more over 5 years [21]. This has been validated by recent research by Dr. Steve Keen which show that private debt to GDP ratios of 130% or more and credit growth of 10% or more for over 1 year, and the presence of a speculative bubble(s) indicate that a crash is imminent. Dr. Steve Keen has also produced data which shows a strong causal link between private debt to GDP, credit growth, speculative prices, crashes and unemployment levels [1]. Some of his lectures showing charts and data are available on YouTube on the Internet.

In 2008, as the financial crisis erupted worldwide, Iceland had a private and public debt of 850% of GDP most of it based on speculation in shares, currencies, assets, property and derivatives. This led to the crash of the economy in Iceland and to a severe political crisis and economic crisis. In 1990, Japan had a private debt to GDP of 208% prior to its big crash. Ireland had private debt to GDP of 310% in the 2008 crash. The USA had a private debt which was 170% of GDP prior to the crash in 2008 which compares to one of 145% of GDP prior to the crash in 1929.

Again, I must emphasise that the work of Mike Montagne is important here as his research over 30 years conclusively proves that money is created when new debt is created, and the present money system and its circulation is based on the excessive build up of debt and interest. Compound interest leads to a multiplication of debt, and also new debt and interest has to be acquired once existing debt and interest is partially paid down in order to keep the circulation flowing and economies growing, and this leads to a further multiplication of debt. Thus, we are caught in a debt trap. This multiplication of debt and the continuous extraction of money out of the system via higher interest payments (debt servicing charges) on massive accumulations of debt creates great imbalances and instabilities, undermines the viability of both speculative investments and productive investments, and this leads to crashes. I would advise all persons to read Michael Montagne's analysis of excessive debt and debt limits at http://www.perfecteconomy.com. He provides some useful simulated models, mathematical proofs and deep insights into this, which far surpass those of most economists and prize winners. Highly leveraged banks and firms and speculators can only sustain small losses before they have insolvency issues. For example a leverage of debt to capital of 30 : 1 will become unsustainable and cause insolvency if losses are 4% or more. And there are ample opportunities to incur such losses in an economy over heated by too much speculation and fraud and diminishing profitability in the productive economy. The most vulnerable debt is that used for over speculation in the prices of assets, especially in conditions which involve a weakening industrial base and stagnant or reduced real wages, and a general weakening of the income generation required to sustain the high prices of assets (and derivatives). Mathematically it is impossible for debt based on speculation in assets to continue indefinitely, though many mainstream economists believe it is possible, with many using the excuse of transfers of wealth from one party to another being always benign and harmless, to the soft landing scenarios or plateau scenarios to justify their ignorance. Once a certain debt limit based on speculation is reached, then its unsustainability becomes apparent, whether through excessive rises in input costs and interest costs and falls in profitability, excessive debt servicing burdens, interest rate rises, energy shocks or other external shocks, excessive debt to earnings ratios, debt to capital ratios, debt to gdp ratios, excessive price to earnings ratios, sudden discoveries of fraudulent assets and non existent returns, mini crashes or peripheral crashes, bad economic news, panic and increased short selling, the failure of a bank, a major crash which creates contagion and further crashes. Ultimately limits are reached, the strains become too much, and the 'Minsky moment' is arrived at.

18. The Rise in Input Prices and the cumulative effects of dynamic disequilibrium forces

The rise in Input prices such as commodities, wages, raw materials, transport, interest payments or debt servicing costs, excessive debt levels, and the economic rents of the FIRE sector (Rentiers) during a speculative boom reduces the profitability of investments and of future investing and this leads to lower earnings and lower expectations of future earnings. This in turn causes a fall off in investment in affected sectors and this progresses to affect speculative asset prices and markets. It also reduces the ability of banks, firms, investors, speculators and households to pay off their speculative debts, and as this worsens it creates increasing default risks and crash risks. As mentioned earlier debt repayment is dependent on earnings, incomes, profits, capital gains, etc. and once a large mismatch occurs between speculative debt and the income necessary to repay it, a crisis occurs. The scale of this crisis or adjustment depends on the herd mentality and other factors mentioned in this sector of the book, which may cause a panic and accompanying 'correction' or create the conditions for a major crash.

These are examples of dynamic disequilibrium forces in action, which are fundamentally disruptive and they work to inflame and over develop speculative booms, while creating the conditions for crashes and accompanying austerity / recessions. And they tend to be self-reinforcing worsening bubbles, crashes, and downturns.

19. 'Sticky' Monopolistic, Oligopolistic, Cartel Prices and Economic Rents which prevent 'clearing of the market'

In the Defects in Law of Supply section above we examined the Rentier economy, the effects of monopolies, oligopolies, restrictive practices and cartels. The failure of the 'sticky' prices of monopolies, oligopolies, cartels, state protected sectors, government subsidized (private firms), economic renters and restrictive practices, and professional fees, (professional and executive) salaries to adjust to changing market conditions and the strong disequilibrium forces mentioned in points 1 to 23 here and clear the market. The market does not clear, it remains stuck, and there is a skewing of prices and quantities in favour of the most dominant parties. This imposes significant additional costs on economies and have the effect of reducing the earnings, incomes, profits etc. necessary to repay speculative debt, during the latter stages of the bubble. This is discussed in Point 17 above in the context of the rise in input prices and dynamic disequilibrium during the bubble phase. Some naive and inexperienced economists think that it's possible for monopolistic, oligopolistic, restrictive practises and cartel prices, professional fees, executive salaries and bonuses to adjust dynamically and to miraculously 'clear the market' and create an illusory equilibrium out of disequilibrium. Their models and theories have been proved wrong many times [1,2,3,4,5,6] The markets don't clear, they get stuck in a self reinforcing negative dynamic, first they are fuelled by greed, the herd mentality, irrational expectations and hysteria in the bubble phase and then by fear, panic selling and panic deleveraging, liquidity crisis and credit freezing, and a descent into chaos in the crash phase, and later by debt overhang, austerity, debt deflation and depression.

20. Use of the wrong Economic indicators, wrong tools and wrong reasoning to measure economic growth, systemic risks and dynamic disequilibrium

The current tools for measuring economic growth and bubbles and crashes and risks produces false and misleading economic forecasts. I refer the reader to a list of **Economic Indicators** listed earlier in this Chapter and in Chapter 7 which provide an early warning system for economic bubbles and crashes and also measure the general health of an economy and it's productive forces. These tools should have been used to monitor and assess economic growth and systemic risks to the financial system and economy. These indicators should be made available to the general public and should contain red flag warnings based on previous crashes.

21. The Minsky Financial Instability Hypothesis and The Minsky Moment

Hyman Minsky, the great economist, correctly stated that powerful speculative forces and high debt levels build up in an economy over time and inevitably lead to a speculative bubble and a crash. The Minsky moment is the point in time when the boom turns into a crash. This can range from a few hours to a few days and involves significant levels of panic, when the herd mentality moves into panic mode. The sudden realisation that:

➢ prices are incorrect and unsustainable and that they do not reflect real value or may fall in the near future

➢ that income, profits, sales, earnings, revenues, returns cannot match the prices of assets and do not justify the high prices of assets. And there is inadequate and insufficient income, profits, revenues, returns to meet repayments of speculative debt and interest. The massive accumulation of debt and multiplication of this debt by compound interest as stated by Mike Montagne and others, increases debt servicing pressures across the economy, and adversely affects incomes, consumption, revenues and profitability, and the viability of many investments. Default risks increase and the number of defaults, contagion risk, and scale of speculative debt become key factors in determining the timing and severity of the crash. Again the natural dynamic disequilibrium forces create a disconnect between reality and speculative expectations, and this finds expression in many forms to create the conditions for a crash.

> that the assets are worthless and / or based on fraud, deception and false ratings, rigging and deliberate manipulation. And that contagion risks may be present causing a panic regarding exposures.

> a rise in interest rates can affect the margins and repayments of speculators causing defaults and panic

> the sudden withdrawal of credit by banks or imposition of new restrictions on credit (such as in 1929) and the fact that speculative prices are fuelled by this credit supply

> realisation that there is no 'greater fool' around to buy over priced speculative assets, as more and more people are trying to sell them

> high debts used to buy worthless assets or assets which are suddenly declining in price mean borrowers cannot meet their debt repayment obligations and are forced to sell to cut their losses

> the sudden collapse of one big player in the system from above factors, such as a bank, financial institution, hedge fund or brokerage which has links to many others. For example Bear Stearns and Northern Rock in 2008.

> panic and uncertainty leads to the freezing of liquidity markets and capital markets and blocking of trades, loans and transfers as banks and firms try to minimise losses and their exposure

leads to the Minsky moment and an avalanche of panic, fear, sell offs, debt deleveraging and contagion. The panic, sell offs and losses often start with the speculative investors, then move to ordinary investors and then to cautious investors, as found by Minsky. Sellers sell at a loss in order to avoid further losses by selling later in the day or tomorrow or the day after. Many sellers try to do this at once driving prices even lower. The herd mentality controls this process. This leads to hysteria and falls in the prices of financial assets, and a self reinforcing cycle of selling, price falls and credit defaults, fuelled by the herd mentality, which leads to a crash. This verifies that booms produce prices and pricing mechanisms which are defective, flawed and wrong and that bank credit both reinforces and drives up these false prices and creates unsustainable debt which remains fixed and burdensome. While the prices of the bought assets collapses, the debt remains fixed and this contradiction creates the momentum for a recession / depression and debt deflation after a crash.

22. The Financial Capture of Economists

Many professors and academic economists also did work for banks, financial services firms, hedge funds, insurance companies and other types of businesses where they praised and supported deregulation, speculation, derivatives, etc. and denied or ignored the risks including systemic risks which appeared prior to the crash in 2008. They received very large fees, donations and other financial rewards for doing this. Yet they were not required to declare any conflicts of interest. These same economists also misdirected and misled their own students in Universities with these false theories about economics. This has brought the field of economics into serious disrepute and contributed to the mindsets, thinking and perceptions which cause financial crashes.

23. Regulatory Capture

This specifically relates to regulatory capture of the state and its' bodies. This includes capture of incompetent, economically illiterate, corrupt and ineffective politicians, 'government advisors', senior civil servants, and government 'economists' and of regulators and a regulatory and oversight system which is defective, disinterested, has conflicts of interest and not fit for purpose. The term 'buffoon' is often to describe the type of persons typically in powerful government positions and regulatory positions who make the most outrageous mistakes and refuse to acknowledge them and correct them and then try to pretend that they don't matter. They are often blinded by their own arrogance and self importance, and they fail to see or understand the responsibilities attached to power. Power to these people is imbued with perks, bonuses, expense accounts, porcine appetites, financial gains, self-importance, self aggrandisement and the social status that comes with power. In one country, a certain prime minister responded to the financial crash and crisis by talking gibberish and nonsense in a drunken haze to the press and media. This shows the appalling lack of political, banking and economic expertise at government level in many countries. Such people are easy targets for regulatory capture.

Regulatory capture of politicians, government, government bodies and central banks by large corporations and banks is a key factor, perhaps the most important factor. Campaign contributions prior to and during elections have and continue to be a vital part of this capture. Then there is the childish admiration for speculators and fraudsters with their lavish attire and lifestyles. And of course, there is also the 'revolving door' where bankers become ministers or secretaries of the treasury / commerce or regulators or other similar positions and big corporate executives are given ministerial roles in government, and retired government ministers are given executive roles in banks or big corporates plays an important part in this regulatory capture and the corruption of government.

Regulatory capture results in fiscal policies, monetary policies, money printing and credit policies, regulatory policies, new laws, amendments and repeals, and deregulation policies which stimulates speculation and further inflates booms while imposing the costs of crashes and crisis on taxpayers, government, ordinary working people and pension funds. Deregulation in the form of repeal of existing laws, amendments of laws and new (hidden) subsidies for banks and politically connected private firms, and the deliberate undermining of regulators, have the effect of facilitating and intensifying speculation, and excess debt accumulation and systemic risks to the financial system.

Many economically illiterate politicians and governments do not understand economics and banking and do not know the difference between speculation on one side and productive investment on the other. And they confuse one with the other and wrongly believe that a bubble is good, a sign of a strong and growing economy. This ignorance is a key factor in the worsening of speculative bubbles and crashes.

24. Government Interference and Irresponsibility

Government or state interference in an economy which encourages and supports financial speculation and excessive credit, reckless deregulation and frauds and financial crimes, regulatory capture and the serving of special interests, has a political, economic and social cost. During the late 1990's and first decade of the 21st century, the mismatch between savings and investment and between savings and consumption in the USA became more severe, and were caused by a depletion of America's tax revenues at government level and new structural changes in the American and globalised economy causing a stagnation and fall in real wages and the propensity to save. In fact, these changes increased the propensity to borrow, and one sees a significant rise in private debt and government debt over this period, up to the present day. One further point on this relates to greater use of offshore tax havens from the 1980's onwards, aided and abetted by Globalisation. This has amounted to many trillions of dollars, and has significantly reduced tax revenues, and increased the borrowing requirement of government. The Reagan policy of tax cuts, corporate welfare and military over expenditure, and budget deficits left the USA with massive unsustainable debt. The debt went from $800 billion to $2.5 trillion under Ronald Reagan, who claimed to be a 'Fiscal Conservative'. This was a massive rise in debt by Reagan who originally campaigned to reduce spending, reduce the deficit and the national debt.

George Bush snr. another alleged 'Fiscal Conservative' increased the national debt from $2.5 trillion to $5 trillion. And again much of this went on military expenditure and corporate welfare and subsidies. The Clinton's era of budget cutbacks, new economy growth, and budget surpluses improved America's economic position, but corporate welfare and subsidy programmes and large tax cuts for big business, the wealthy and corporate executives (share options and bonuses), meant massive debt still remained. Clinton left a national debt of $5 trillion. The Clinton era was replaced by the Bush era of budget deficits, wars and military spending, corporate welfare and subsidies, a large expansion of the Deep State and Shadow Government, and massive debt accumulation, which further undermined the American economy. President George W Bush provided additional incentives for speculation and the inflation of the bubble in his cuts to capital gains tax, dividend tax and other taxes for the rich. George W Bush who was yet another 'Fiscal Conservative' managed to increase the national debt to $10 trillion. President Obama tried to bail out corrupt bankers, financial institutions, speculators and fraudsters and the many victims of the financial bust and de-industrialised economy, while also spending hundreds of billions of dollars on funding the military industries, Deep State and Shadow Government, and this increased the national debt up to $20 trillion.

At the individual level and family level, the continuing de-industrialisation and a move to a low paid service industry jobs economy combined with the fall in real wages, easy credit and low interest rates were the main factors in private debt accumulation. And this private debt was further accelerated by banks, financial institutions and speculators engaging in over speculation in stocks, assets, derivatives and real estate which added to the price and debt burden imposed on ordinary people, businesses and institutions, providing unsustainable debt which had devastating economic consequences in 2008 and thereafter. Today the USA has a massive unsustainable total debt burden estimated to be over 500% of GDP which is crippling America economically, socially and politically. During this time, from the late 1980's to 2012, long term productive investment in the private sector and state sector (schools, colleges, hospitals, retraining, research, infrastructure) declined, as it became 'crowded out' by over speculation in the financial and assets sector and by the massive level of debt accumulated. The US government like many other western governments undermined, neglected and destroyed its own productive base, in the hope of illusory returns from speculative investments, which failed and have now imposed a massive debt burden and economic on the American economy and people. This vast economic imbalance has had negative and largely unforeseen consequences on stocks, assets, banking and economic performance.

Fiscal Conservatives

All of these so called 'Fiscal Conservatives' in North America and Europe tend to increase government debt, private debt and bank debt and impose speculation costs on the economy and massive bail out costs on taxpayers and countries. One should ask these 'Fiscal Conservatives' why they support the robbing and bankrupting of social security plans, private pension plans, state pension plans, life savings in banks and other financial institutions, medical care plans for the elderly, disabled and unemployed, and government healthcare systems through the following:

- over speculation and related frauds and crashes involving speculation trillions of dollars and losses of trillions of dollars globally
- bank and speculator bail outs by government and taxpayers involving trillions of dollars
- manipulated wars and regime changes which cost trillions of dollars and mostly benefit large banks, big corporates and the Deep State
- corporate welfare and subsidies, and tax evasion schemes, costing tens / hundreds of billions of dollars each year in many countries.
- a Deep State and Shadow Government (in big countries) which commands hundreds of billions of dollars per year and where billions, even trillions of dollars have gone missing, been misappropriated, and are unaccounted for. The CAFR scandal being one of many examples.

Why do they support 'socialism for the rich' and 'vicious capitalism for the poor and working class'?

Political or government interference over time supported speculation in prices as politicians benefit from temporary increased tax revenues (from speculation), or expectations of increased tax revenues even if they never occur, increased political funding of their political parties and personal political campaigns from speculators and those businesses which benefit from speculation, and the financial bubble of increased credit creation and money supply. Regulatory capture was a key factor in the inflation of the bubble in Ireland, in Europe and in the USA, and aligned the interests of government with those of speculators, banks and developers. In Ireland this was manifested in many tax reductions and tax reliefs specifically for property speculation, and this inflated the property speculation bubble further. This inability to govern is often accompanied by reckless government spending, debt accumulation and loose monetary policies which live off the bubble and further inflate the bubble. This was further complicated and perhaps worsened in the Eurozone, by the fact that monetary and credit policies were set by Germany in Germany's interests, disconnecting it from other economies which may

213

be experiencing the exact opposite economic conditions to Germany. Thus Germany indirectly played a role in inflating the bubble in Ireland and other EU countries. In Ireland, reckless fiscal and monetary policies further fuelled asset price speculation and the scale of the bubble countries prior to 2008.

In Ireland and some other developed countries, there are no bodies such as the SEC in the USA, and financial crimes such as insider trading, price rigging, frauds, Ponzi schemes, laddering of stocks and spinning of stocks and other assets and other financial crimes are not investigated and prosecuted. In Ireland, there has only been two successful prosecutions of bankers, while several dozen bankers escaped prosecution and jail. Indeed one banker's case was thrown out of court because a state official allegedly destroyed important evidence in the investigation phase. It's amazing how bankers escape justice, one has to wonder what really lies behind all of this ? As we shall see in Chapter 10 of this book, corruption is widespread, corruption is the new norm, while honesty and integrity are rare exceptions. These are serious deficiencies. In many developed countries, regulators tend to be largely controlled by their political masters and their banker lobbyists, and there is significant 'regulatory capture' where banks and big corporations control or influence both government and the regulator, effectively controlling and amending the applicable regulatory laws and the regulator. A combination of lobbying by businesses, banks and financial institutions, political funding, granting of favours and other measures helped promote new deregulation laws, removal of controls and safeguards, and the undermining of banking regulations and regulators in the EU and North America in the period prior to 2008. During the boom, regulators were strongly encouraged to ignore excess speculation, breach of bank capital requirements, liquidity requirements, and reserve requirements, and bank debt to equity and debt to income guidelines, share rigging, and many other financial crimes, and the build up of excessive debt. Both the SEC and Federal Reserve bank failed to regulate the American banking system and stock market prior to the 2008 crash. The result was a defective regulatory and oversight system which promoted speculation and crashes. During the boom phase and early crash phase, many bankers, brokers and speculators will lie to or mislead regulators, realising that many of these regulators are former bankers like themselves and they can exploit 'cosy relationships'. The evidence suggests that regulators could not be bothered regulating and overseeing while the economy was growing in the boom or bubble years. Lastly, there were no serious criminal legal penalties for non compliance with laws, regulations and Accords. Nobody was jailed and the fines were very small when compared to the vast profits from fraud, financial crimes and speculation, these small fines can be paid out from the company's and shareholder's funds. Thus, there are many incentives to break the law and engage in criminal activity, and put the banking system, financial system and national economy in danger of a serious crash and collapse. Investigations by some leading Irish journalists, academics and intellectuals revealed a lot of corruption and cronyism capitalism in Ireland prior to the 2008 crash and its aftermath ; the books 'Wasters' by Shane Ross and Nick Webb (2010), and 'The Untouchables' by Shane Ross and Nick Webb (2012), http://www.shaneross.ie/books/ provide deep and interesting insights into this phenomenon.

25. How the above factors create Fluctuating Yield Curves and Short Run and Long Run Debt Cycles

The great contradiction in economics is that whole economies can crash and create mass business closures, unemployment, deflation, recession and depression yet the fundamentals of the economy, the productive economy, can be sound and quite strong. The speculative economy acts as a parasite on the real productive economy, draining it during a boom and bankrupting it during a crash and accompanying recession / depression. This parasitical speculative economy is fed by another parasitical entity – the banks which create out of nothing and lend it out to speculators, developers and dealers to fuel speculation in prices and these banks then extract monies from it in the form of debt repayments and interest. (After crashes the banks also extract through repossessions, evictions, foreclosure sales, insurance payments etc.) The banks and government policy create the conditions for speculative activity and the debt cycle and accompanying yield curves. Yield curves are mere reflections of this speculative activity and money creation and they provide early warning signs of a crash.

The debt cycle shows the rapid and prolonged expansion of credit and debt which at first fuels innovations and breakthrough technologies, production, higher productivity, infrastructure investment, new business start ups, and enhanced conditions for new investment and a new economic paradigm. This brings about more employment, more consumption, more aggregate demand and more investment and a rise in living standards for most people, and this creates even more investment opportunities through the multiplier effect. This starts the upswing in Economic Cycles. This in turn provides the basis for increased lending and credit (and money) creation and more debt and lower interest rates which remains sustainable as production and productivity grows.

Growth in incomes, sales and profits creates increased opportunities for both productive investment and for speculation in prices of land, property, assets, shares, and commodities. At some point this

215

progresses on to fuel large scale speculation in prices and an expansion in credit and money creation to keep fuelling this speculation. The speculative economy tends to outpace and outgrow the productive economy, as massive gains are made from price speculation in the mid cycle. The factors listed above from 1 – 24 come into play, and provide momentum for a speculative bubble. This typically occurs at the mid level of the upswing. The scale of the bubble is determined by debt and the rate of new money creation (new debt) pumped into speculation This intensifies the dynamic disequilibrium forces listed in 1 -24 above and in prior sections above leading to financial instability. There are practical limits to debt and to price speculation in the real world, but this is ignored by investors and the press and media. This instability grows and can exist un-noticed for several months and even be mistaken for "corrections to the market" but is followed by one unexpected crash which initiates panic selling, bank runs, loss of confidence, and as contagion spreads this is followed by further failures, bank runs, economic crisis, debt deleveraging, debt repayments, higher savings or hoarding, austerity policies, deflation, bankruptcies, and liquidations and recession / depression in the downswing. This causes a collapse in employment, investment, consumption and aggregate demand related investment creating a vicious cycle with it's own feedback loops, leading to gluts of many products and assets which reinforces debt deflation. The short run cycle corresponds to the well known business cycle and last for several years, typically 7-9 years. The long run cycle of debt corresponds to several business cycles combined together with a large accumulation of debt and high price rises over time. Modern innovations magnify and intensify the speculation and debt processes and cycle peaks and depths. The crash when it occurs in the long term cycle is spectacular and causes major financial crisis and accompanying deflation, recession and depression. The crashes of 1929, 1987, and 2008 correspond to this long run cycle. Yield curves have moved in line with these debt and speculation cycles.

This is followed by a bottoming out of the economy, as debt is paid down, written down, written off, and bankruptcies and liquidations reduce debt, and in modern times, central banks and governments come in to bail out banks, financial institutions and some businesses. This is followed by a gradual and slow recovery, depending on debt levels and the burden of debt and debt servicing, This can be stimulated via debt write off, write downs, liquidations and by governments stimulating their economies, and new efficiencies and technological innovations in business, which brings about credit recovery and the creation of new debt. Followed by gradual aggregate demand increases. This then progresses on to new growth and a new business and debt cycle and on to another round of speculation. The cycle repeats itself again and again. There is no exact time period for each cycle, as debt cycles have their own characteristics and peculiarities. Technological innovations and revolutions, in line with Man's evolution, happen to coincide with debt cycles, but are not defined by these. Debt cycles predate modern technological innovations. The creation of money out of nothing by banks and the accumulation of vast debt is a process which is centuries old, and it is the abuse and misuse of this privilege which creates the cycles we have witnessed for some time now. The accumulation of debt over time to fuel over speculation, fraud, and over consumption is constant, and ultimately proves unsustainable. Innovation in modern times has increased the speed of debt creation and speculation, the scale of this and the momentum of this, creating higher curves on this debt cycle. Compounded interest, particularly on debt which is based on speculation magnifies this.

Excess debt, or debt overhang after crashes must be removed from the system before we progress to the next upswing of the debt cycle, as new technological innovations and business innovations require fresh new capital, new debt creation, new lending, new confidence, new entrepreneurs, new consumption, new purchasing power (higher employment levels and credit availability). The options available include:

- deleveraging of private debt, business and bank debt, and later of government debt
- bankruptcies and liquidations
- deflation
- debt write offs & debt write downs
- debt forgiveness. In previous centuries debt forgiveness was known as a debt jubilee
- debt restructurings
- Quantitative Easing including bank bail outs, purchase of distressed assets from banks, purchase of commercial paper, debt and shares from big corporates, and direct loans to big corporates
- 'Quantitative Easing for the people'. See Chapter 7
- stimulatory fiscal policies, currency policies and monetary policies to stimulate economic growth to assist debt repayments

All economic cycles have followed this pattern for centuries.

These 25 elements or fatal flaws in free market economics are part of the overall picture of dynamic disequilibrium. They provide a glimpse into the dynamics and workings of dynamic disequilibrium, which is behaviourist in nature and thus subject to the flaws of human nature. Some cry out for government action but unfortunately this too is ruled by the consciousnesses controlling human nature. Not all government or state action is the same, and subject to blanket condemnation or praise. Government actions in this respect can act to lessen or reduce dynamic disequilibrium or to worsen and intensify it. Ignorance of dynamic disequilibrium always worsens its effects

The Consequences and Results of this flaw

The sudden realisation that prices and/or returns are incorrect and unsustainable and that they do not reflect real value or may fall in the near future, "the Minsky moment" , leads to sell offs as some nervous or shrewd investors get out early, these initial price falls fluctuate but continue and start a momentum, next follows the inability of pure speculators to meet loan repayment obligations, then panic or distress selling at reduced prices to cover debt repayments, the herd mentality begins to dominate, and is fed by a press and media based on hype and hysteria. This is accompanied by credit restrictions for buyers and speculators as banks seek to limit their exposure and losses, a liquidity crisis and credit freeze begins as banks refuse to lend to each other and to businesses and speculators. The disconnect between debt which is fixed and asset prices and incomes which fluctuate becomes apparent, and there is a mass sell off, devaluation and deflation in the prices of assets with high associated debts in order to minimise losses, reduce exposures, with domino effects on business balance sheets. This leads to contagion, to cashflow, liquidity and solvency problems for banks, businesses and speculators, increased insolvencies, increased bankruptcies which cause further bankruptcies, more price falls and volatility which encourage further price falls in a vicious cycle which fuels higher unemployment, reduced aggregate demand, falling sales and profits, a contraction of credit growth or zero credit growth, and further debt deflation and so on. The panic feeds itself and reinforces itself through negative feedback loops. And in certain cases government austerity policies which decrease the money supply and aggregate demand further, leading to consumers losing jobs or fearing such and restricting their spending, more hoarding of money, the collapse in consumption and sales based on this, businesses cutting back production, employment and investment, loss of business and investor confidence, and a downward spiral which feeds and reinforces itself and maintains a recession or depression. This was the idiocy of economic policy in many EU countries after the crash of 2008.

This collapse gathers a momentum of its own, and creates its own continuous disequilibrium state, with certain characteristics:

- pushing down the prices of assets below their intrinsic worth, causing deflation, impoverishing both lenders and borrowers

- maintenance of excessively high debt levels (from speculative boom years) and high repayment levels by households, businesses and banks which discourages new borrowing by businesses, investors and consumers and reduces aggregate demand and aggregate supply (investment) and money supply growth. Reductions in household spending arising from high debts, high debt repayments, negative equity or lower home equity, and fears concerning existing and future job / income.

- private savings (including debt repayments) becoming much greater than private investment and a 'balance sheet recession' occurs as described by Richard Koo [4]

- reductions or stagnation in the demand for money (loans) at all interest rates and the failure of low interest rates or zero rates to stimulate consumption and investment. Money demand is not totally reliant on the real interest rate, but on other factors, (which differ widely in the aggregate) such as total existing debt levels, existing repayments burden, wage/salary factors, future income / profit and employment expectations, and anticipated returns on investment which are dependent on aggregate demand levels, investor and consumer confidence and economic growth levels ; a liquidity trap with several determinants.

- Credit growth stagnates or collapses and this adversely affects consumption, investment and employment. See the works of Dr. Steve Keen [1]

- the stifling and suppression of wages/salaries and profit growth which stifles consumer confidence and spending and investor confidence. A vicious cycle.

- the persistent existence of deflation induced reductions in consumption and debt deflation all of which are described by Fisher, Minsky, Shiller, Kindleberger, Galbraith, Keen, Hudson, Black, Koo, Mian and Sufi [1,2,3,4,6,7]

- These factors when combined reduce the impact and effectiveness of Quantitative Easing and fiscal stimulus and monetary stimulus measures.

It is a self-reinforcing system, a new disequilibrium level, which destroys values, prices, assets, jobs, investor and consumer confidence, further reducing aggregate demand and the money supply, etc. and destroys the capability of the financial, business, banks, government and households system to grow, to make earnings, incomes, profits, tax revenues so as to pay off the massive debts it created (during speculation or the bubble phase). The graphs and statistics in the References section below provide further insights into this [7]. In addition to the liquidity trap there is also a debt trap where highly indebted governments cannot use fiscal and monetary stimulus as this would increase the high debt burden, frighten the financial markets, increase interest rates on debt and make future borrowing more difficult, and they cannot increase taxes or engage in intense cutbacks as this would increase existing deflationary pressures, reduce growth and the tax revenues from growth. This was the conundrum faced by 'Abenomics' in Japan in 2014 - 2015. There is also the lost productivity and lost productive output from the consequences of price speculation, bubbles, and the accumulation of massive speculative debt, crashes and debt deflation, deflation, and austerity. This loss of productivity affects competitiveness and income, and makes the high debt levels even more unsustainable. Some governments in the west and east are foolishly trying to re-inflate another property, shares, assets and derivatives bubble whilst the state sector and private sector is trapped in excessive debt, and this will expose these governments to further systemic risks and losses in the future, and will do nothing to rectify the serious flaws and defects in their economic systems.

This financial crash and deflationary spiral or paradigm above brutally exposes the defective pricing processes upon which the efficient markets hypothesis and the "free market" is based upon. The free market through this fatal flaw lacks both efficiency and effectiveness, and has lost credibility, and this has proved to be extremely costly - these costs are still being paid for today through lost GDP, lost economic growth, higher taxes, new taxes, higher living costs, cutbacks in essential public (state) services, lost jobs, home repossessions, lost investment, etc., punishing the taxpayers, businesses, consumers, governments, mortgage holders, the unemployed, the evicted families, etc. The facts and evidence clearly show that it is the wrong people, innocent people who are being punished with austerity, deflation, imposed recession and cutbacks. To rephrase and reshape terms often used by neo classical economists, there is significant marginal disutility and high aggregate levels of marginal disutility, demand inadequacy and supply inadequacy. In terms of marginal disutility, there is the desire to fulfil demand but inability to do so through unemployment, less disposable income, declining or no profits, and business bankruptcies, which delivers disequilibrium not equilibrium. In addition to this there are large losses in the marginal productivity in labour and capital, but this has been conveniently ignored by those who support neo classical economics and the efficient markets hypothesis. Over the period 2007 - 2014, the total cost of the bail out of banks and financial institutions was $13 trillion worldwide, a very considerable sum in global terms, and significant debt and taxpayer burden or disutility. (Andrew Haldane, Bank of England estimate).

Strangely, lessons have not been learned ; the 'lost 20 years' in Japan has been completely forgotten. There is a naive and immature belief that austerity will automatically lift economies out of recession and deflation. This false belief has been dominant in Germany from 2008 - 2015, yet Germany itself was the beneficiary of anti-austerity measures, free financial aid, and large debt write offs, write downs and restructurings after world war 2, in the form of the Marshall Plan aid, other aid programmes and the London Debt Agreement (1953). As we shall see in Chapter 7, austerity worsens recessions, depressions and deflation, by reducing public expenditure, consumer spending and associated business sales, profits and investment potential, reducing GNP and increasing debt to GNP ratios, increasing unemployment and emigration, reducing investor confidence, enforcing Balance Sheet Recessions, all of which reduce aggregate demand and (commercial bank) money supply growth and related aggregate supply (good and services). In the period 2010-2015, many developed countries were in recession, deflation or depression and it was not possible to successfully export into them, in order to reduce the effects of austerity at home. And austerity measures have totally ignored the deflationary effects of high household, business, government and banking debt levels, and the need for debt write downs, write offs and restructurings [1,2,3,4, 6,8]

Thee is also another naive belief that the current form of Quantitative Easing will solve all the economic problems in Europe, the USA, Japan and other parts of the world. Ben Bernanke the head of the Federal Reserve was disappointed with it, as were the Japanese and the British. Quantitative Easing is capable of being used in many different ways to achieve many types of results, but it must take into the account the effects of excessive household, business, banking and government debt, the preference of businesses to pay down debt instead of maximising sales and profits (Balance Sheet Recessions), and debt deflation, and act decisively to resolve this. Post crash, after 2008, money printing called 'Quantitative Easing' and taxpayer bailouts in the USA, UK and Japan have proved mostly ineffective and disappointing. Quantitative Easing is based on the 'Greater Fool Theory' where some fool or sucker becomes the final buyer of worthless assets or funder of bankrupt businesses, and in this case the fool or sucker is the Central Bank and taxpayers.

Misdirected and Ineffective Quantitative Easing has fuelled :

- speculation in shares, bonds, derivatives, property, and other asset prices

- high executive bonuses and salaries

- company buybacks, where companies buy their own shares and prop up their prices. This produces massive gains for company executives who have share options and shares and for corporate raiders. This activity has been valued at several trillion dollars over the last 15 years in the USA alone.

- highly indebted households using the money to repay debt and save instead of spending, and businesses using the money to pay down debts and save, instead of maximising sales, profits and investment expansion. This reduces borrowing by consumers and businesses and the lending levels of banks. The Balance Sheet Recession factor. Reducing M2, the commercial bank money supply [1,4]

- banks using the money to pay down their own debts and improve their balance sheets but not lending adequate amounts of new money to productive businesses and consumers to stimulate recovery / growth. Many indebted consumers and businesses unwilling or incapable of borrowing. The Balance Sheet Recession factor. Government austerity policies, high taxes, and public service cutbacks in the middle of a recession in Europe and other parts of the world reduced consumption and the profitability of productive businesses and thus their investment potential to businesses. Reducing M2, the commercial bank money supply and it's diffusion to businesses and consumers [1,4]

- socialism for rich and vicious and ruthless capitalism for the working and middle classes and for the elderly, the disabled and unemployed

The government tries to increase money supply through Quantitative Easing and increasing reserves in the banks, while cautious and fearful banks, and over-indebted and fearful businesses and consumers and the forces of debt deflation and disequilibrium described above in previous chapters act to reduce debt and save, and thus reduce the money supply or restrain it's growth as they did in the period of Ben Bernanke's leadership of the Federal Reserve [1]. This has exposed a very wide disparity between the financial and speculative economy on one side and the production and consumption economy on the other side. The results have been economic stagnation, deflation or very low inflation, very low growth or no growth, continued high unemployment, and disappointing economic results. The fatal defect has been ignored and overlooked in the past and present, and it is not being addressed and resolved by economists, regulators, politicians and governments in the present age.

Morality

Strangely, many neo liberal economists, neo classical economists, hayekians, monetarists and conservatives and their followers believe in morality, and subscribe to some religions and to religious versions of 'morality'. Many attend churches, synagogues and temples. Some even consider themselves 'holy' and 'good living' and 'decent'. These people are highly influential in the economies of nations and government of nations, and most economies are driven and influenced by 'values', 'ethics', morality, principles, and 'moral hazard'. The real core 'principles', 'values', 'morality', and 'ethics' here were large scale private enrichment at taxpayer expense, investor expense and home owner expense. This private enrichment was achieved via speculation and its massive debt (created out of nothing by banks), bribery of politicians, public officials and regulators, and the defrauding of investors, pension funds, insurance funds, social security funds, and ordinary workers of trillions of dollars which led to financial crashes, national bankruptcies and massive state (taxpayer) expense through bailouts and austerity policies. And the loss of millions of jobs, and businesses, and millions of family homes and the breaking up of many families and communities. And millions of pension funds and savings reduced down to a fraction of their worth for those who retire, condemning many elderly to poverty and destitution. This was mass theft and larceny from ordinary people both during the bubble phase and the post crash bailout phase. These are the real, perverted, corrupted 'values', ethics, principles, and morals of our societies and neo liberal economics. A morality based on greed, selfishness, self centeredness, fraud, lies, deception, religious hypocrisy, bribery, corruption, irresponsibility, theft and social injustices. This is the morality of the right wing and neo liberals.

This has also demolished the principle of 'moral hazard' which was supposed to be a vital part of free market principles. These 'morals' and morality depict an image of immoral, corrupted, selfish, greedy and fattened pigs slobbering and competing at the trough giving the false appearance of morality, righteousness, honesty and decency.

Economic Modelling

Modern economic models need to integrate the following:

- dynamic disequilibrium

- the 25 elements of market failure and bubbles and crashes

- the defects in the law of supply in this chapter

- the defects in and law of demand in this chapter

- the market volatility and failure in this chapter

- the short run and long run debt cycle and where exactly one is at a given point in time

- the excessive debt and interest in an economy as shown by Dr. Steve Keen, Richard Vague, Richard Werner and others.

- the negative economic effects of money and interest created out of nothing by Mike Montagne at www.perfecteconomy.com

- the productivity of capital factors in this chapter

- the role of momentum and scale in inflating speculative bubbles and risks including systemic risks mentioned in this chapter

- irrational expectations and actions, and behavioural economics and how they contribute to bubbles and crashes

- the effects of excessive government / banking / business / household debt to income / GNP ratios and the relationship to speculation and unsustainable asset prices

- crashes, recession, excessive debt, austerity and debt deflation and how this reinforces itself over time

These economic models should include these factors in the context of gradations, degrees, levels and phases of dynamic disequilibrium, while using the insights provided by chaos theory, evolutionary economics and emergence theory, complexity theory, behavioural economics and the herd mentality, and aspects of the new economic models being developed by Econophysics to provide more realistic economic models and representations of the real world. This more detailed analysis of facts, empirical evidence and statistics and the modelling of such would help better inform public policy makers.

Chapter 5   A New Iron Curtain in Today's World : The Necessity of Changing Course and Moving to Economic Democracy

'an iron curtain has descended across the Continent.'
Winston Churchill, 1946

'During my lifetime I have dedicated myself to this struggle of the African people. I have fought against white domination, and I have fought against black domination. I have cherished the ideal of a democratic and free society in which all persons live together in harmony and with equal opportunities. It is an ideal which I hope to live for and to achieve.'
Nelson Mandela, Speech from the Dock, 1964

Historically, the wider diffusion of wealth and income to the general population and accompanying reduction in inequalities has coincided with the spread of democracy and freedom worldwide. Wider political representation and participation of the working class, rural farmers, and the unemployed and disabled in politics, activism and legal changes has greatly assisted this diffusion of wealth. The ending of feudalism, oligarchy, imperialism and colonialism in Europe, the Americas, Africa and Asia from the mid 19th century to the latter decades of the 20th century provided evidence of this desire for change, radical change and for human dignity, respect, freedom and equality. This was proven by peoples struggle and victory for the vote, for representation, for national freedom and sovereignty, for a decent living wage, for equality before the law, for democratic rights, for human rights, for respect and dignity in all areas of life, for social justice, for social inclusion signifying a very new and increasing public consciousness. This was a truly radical new development in human societies and human consciousness. One has to measure this against the corrupted systems in place prior to the mid 19th century. These had lasted for thousands of years, reducing mankind down to tyranny and slavery. This has been well described by many authors, though Howard Zinn's book 'A Peoples History of the United States' [20] provides one of the best and most lucid accounts of this. Indeed this book goes further and shows how these same forces have not disappeared, but taken on new forms and have continued to oppose freedom, democracy, rights and the ordinary people up to the present day. This book should be required reading in all schools in all countries.

Many young people today do not understand that the freedoms they enjoy today are very new and did not always exist. They have no comprehension of the great struggles, the great sacrifices and suffering endured by generations of people to achieve these freedoms ; freedoms which young people have today and naively take for granted. This road to freedom has been a slow but steady progression, encompassing both political democracy and economic democracy, whose philosophical roots go back to Locke, Hume, Montesquieu, Voltaire, Rousseau, Jefferson, Madison and Paine. These people bravely challenged the status quo of the time and this upset most people, particularly the merchants, workers and peasants who had resigned themselves to and surrendered to tyranny, slavery, despotism and the worst aspects of human nature. Unfortunately most people at a given point in history are sheep easily controlled by political and religious nonsense. The slow gain in momentum in the 19th century came with the Chartists, the Abolitionists, the Rochdale Pioneers and Cooperatives movement, and the revolutionaries of 1848, and moving on to the labour union movement, the formation of labour parties and left wing parties, the anti-trust laws of the early 20th century, the suffragette movement, and on to nationalism and the desire for national sovereignty, and to universal suffrage, women's rights, and experiments with various types of socialism. From there it progressed on to the New Deal era of the 1930's and 1940's to cope with the collapse of free markets, and to wars and the defence of democracy and freedom and on to the Keynesian social democratic era in Europe and the Americas and the great economic boom from 1946 to 1980, and the civil rights movement in the USA and other countries and the ending of colonialism in Africa and Asia in the 1960's and of apartheid in Africa in the 1990's. It has been a long rocky ride against self contented and self interested elites, and also against sheep and their ignorance and indifference, but there has been a major improvement in democratic representation and living standards for ordinary people most countries. This has marked a democratisation of wealth and income, which is intimately tied to political democracy and the rights inherent in it.

This 'democratisation of wealth and income' or diffusion of wealth, income and power to the ordinary people from the mid 19th century to the present represents an unstructured somewhat chaotic form of incremental progress, encompassing elements of economic democracy and industrial democracy. An evolution in form which is ongoing. By empowering the ordinary people through the wider diffusion of wealth and income, and the accompanying power associated with it, it provides the required social stability and underlying foundation for people power, for achieving democracy, specifically a democracy with a 'government of the people, by the people and for the people'.

However, this changed radically in the early 1980's when new economic policies namely Neo liberal economic policies and Monetarism were enforced in western nations and developing nations. This was the era of Thatcher and Reagan. These economic and political policies involved the breaking of the unions, many bankruptcies and business closures through government austerity policies, globalisation, outsourcing and downsizing, mass layoffs of workers, de-industrialisation and loss of manufacturing jobs in western countries, the end of secure wages and benefits, significant reductions in real wages, high levels of unemployment, mass deleveraging, increased foreclosures and evictions, increased automation of the workplace, deregulation, cuts to automatic economic stabilisers (unemployment payments), cuts to pensions, a shift in the tax burden to the working and middle class, a severe reduction in credit growth initially, mass privatisations, a rise in the use of offshore tax havens, the introduction of new policies to support speculation in the financial sector, and a massive build up of private debt. It created a high level of fear and job insecurity among most workers, and it effectively broke and beat down the working class and middle class ; and this was it's intended purpose. This led to rising returns to capital at the expense of less and less returns to labour. Inequalities in wealth and income grew wider from 1980 onwards and this was matched by the high rise in stock market prices ; several graphs and studies confirm this. This was accompanied by the formation of excessive social divisions, tribalistic hatreds, prejudices and stigma, family and community breakdowns, higher crimes and more conflicts. In developing and third world nations these policies were enforced by ruthless dictators with the full support of Washington. These economic policies and ideologies undermined and continue to undermine democratic structures, freedoms, social contracts, labour rights, legal rights, human rights, legal processes and government legitimacy in several countries, which took generations to build. By 2017, it had succeeded in reversing the rights, equalities, freedoms, and socio-economic progress achieved in the period 1945 – 1980. Wealth and income inequalities had returned back to Victorian times of the 19th century in several big western nations.

A New Iron Curtain

There has been a massive redistribution of wealth in the USA and other developed countries since 1981. This redistribution of wealth has flowed from the poor and working class to the rich. In the USA, the top one percent of Americans gained $21 trillion in wealth since 1989 while the bottom 50 percent lost $900 billion (Matt Bruenig, founder of People's Policy Project) This was a massive redistribution of wealth. Matt Bruenig broke down the Federal Reserve's newly released "Distributive Financial Accounts" data series in 2017 and found that, overall, "the top one percent owns nearly $30 trillion of assets while the bottom half owns less than nothing, meaning they have more debts than they have assets." The graph below illustrates this.

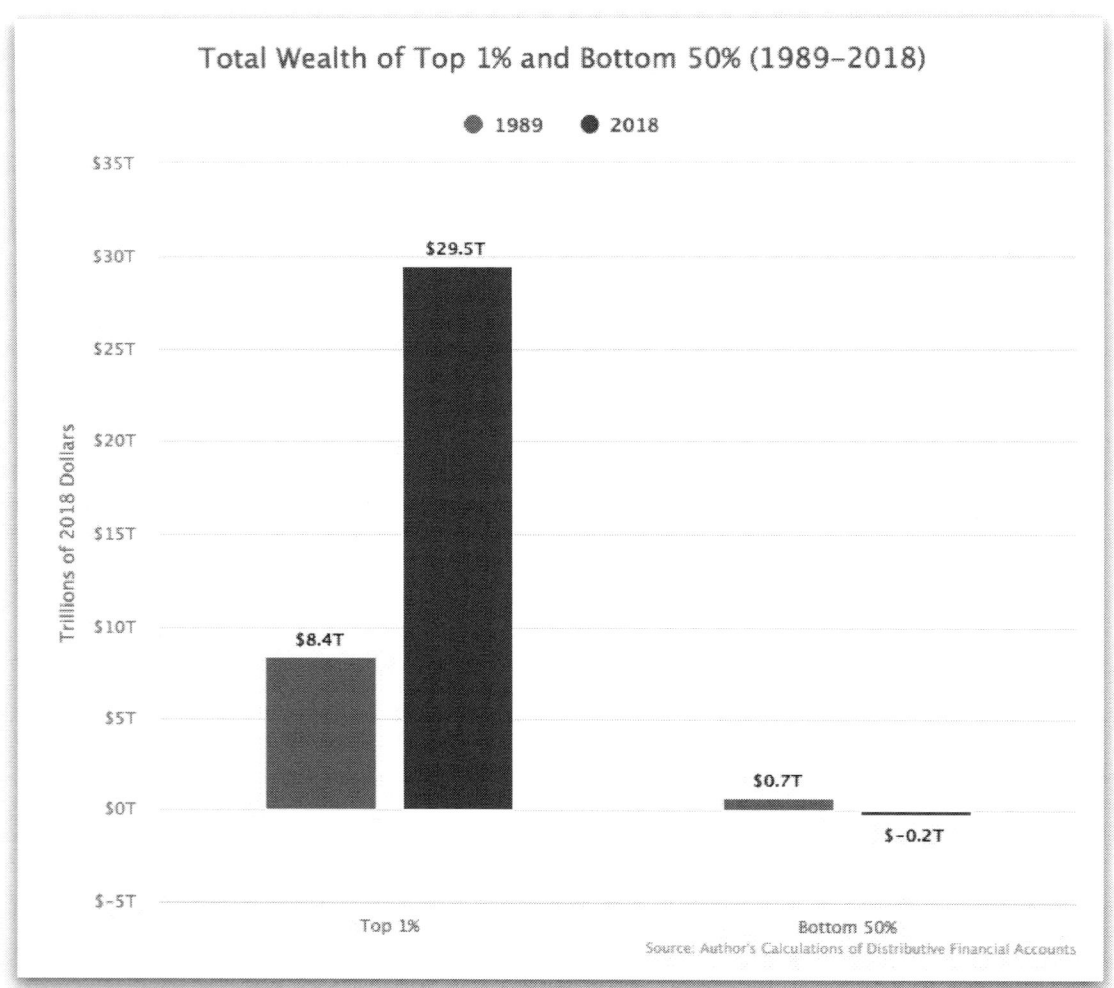

Piketty's work is the leading international authority on this subject. It is quite detailed and shows that over 90% of income gains have gone to the richest 1% in the last decade, and most other people (bottom 99%) have not experienced growth in their income and that this is a new development in the history of the USA and other developed countries [8]. The graphs on the following page from Piketty's work depict the extent of income concentration in the USA and how this has worsened on recent times.

Inequality Has Increased With Each Expansion in the Postwar Era

Percent share of income growth received by the top 10 percent and bottom 90 percent of earners during expansions

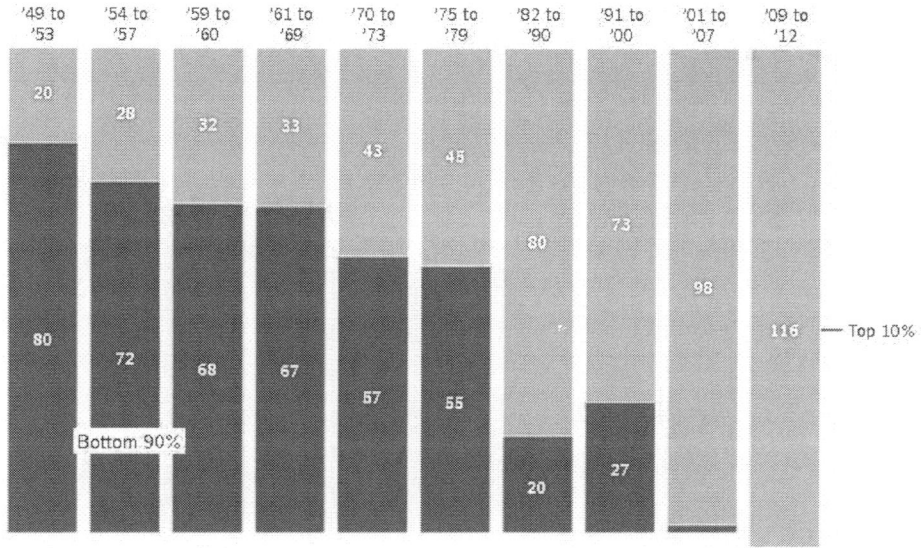

The bottom 90 percent experienced a decline in income from 2009 to 2012, meaning their share of income gains was negative.

Source: Pavlina R. Tcherneva calculations based on data from Thomas Piketty and Emmanuel Saez and N.B.E.R.

Most Income Gains in Recent Expansions Went to Top 1 Percent

Percentage share of income gains during economic expansions accruing the top 1 percent and bottom 99 percent of earners

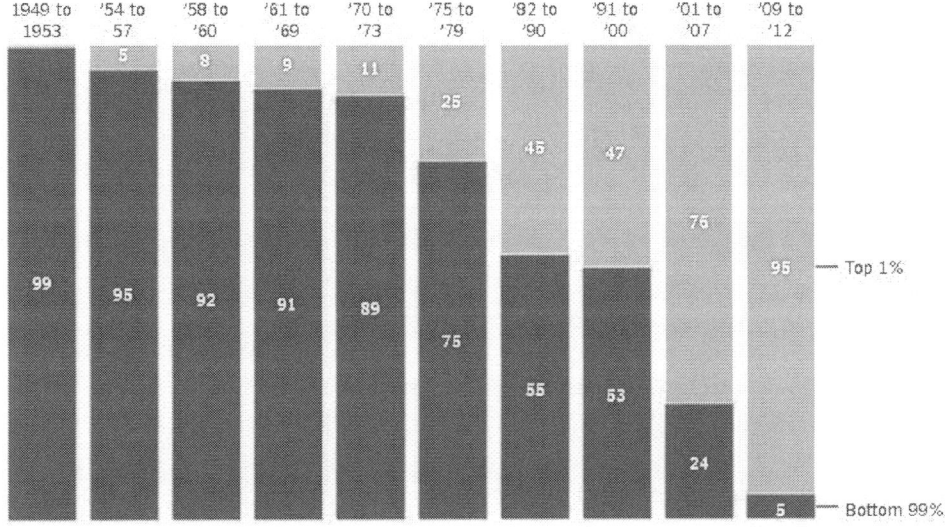

Source: Pavlina R. Tcherneva calculations based on data from Thomas Piketty and Emmanuel Saez and N.B.E.R.

Source: Capital in the Twenty First Century. Thomas Piketty (2014). Belknap Press.

http://www.amazon.com/Capital-Twenty-First-Century-Thomas-Piketty/dp/067443000X/ref=pd_bxgy_b_img_y

Yet Piketty's figures are an underestimate due to significant tax evasion and avoidance by the rich, and the use of capital gains and depreciation to conceal personal income and wealth. The concentration of wealth and income would be much higher if tax havens were included. Piketty found that the top 10% of earners commanded 50% of national income in 2007 just prior to the 2008 crash. The top 1% got 24% of national income in 2007, equivalent to levels seen in 1928 prior to the crash in 1929 [8]. This was confirmed by Saez in 2013, showing that the top 1% got 23.5% of national income (Striking it Richer: The Evolution of Top Incomes in the United States (Updated with 2012 preliminary estimates), 2013). This was very high by historical standards.

Income inequality is at very high levels historically in the USA and in other developed countries applying Neo Liberal economic policies as seen in the graphs below.

FIGURE I.I. Income inequality in the United States, 1910–2010

Source: Capital in the Twenty First Century. Thomas Piketty (2014). Belknap Press.

INCOME INEQUALITY IN ANGLO-SAXON COUNTRIES, 1910-2010

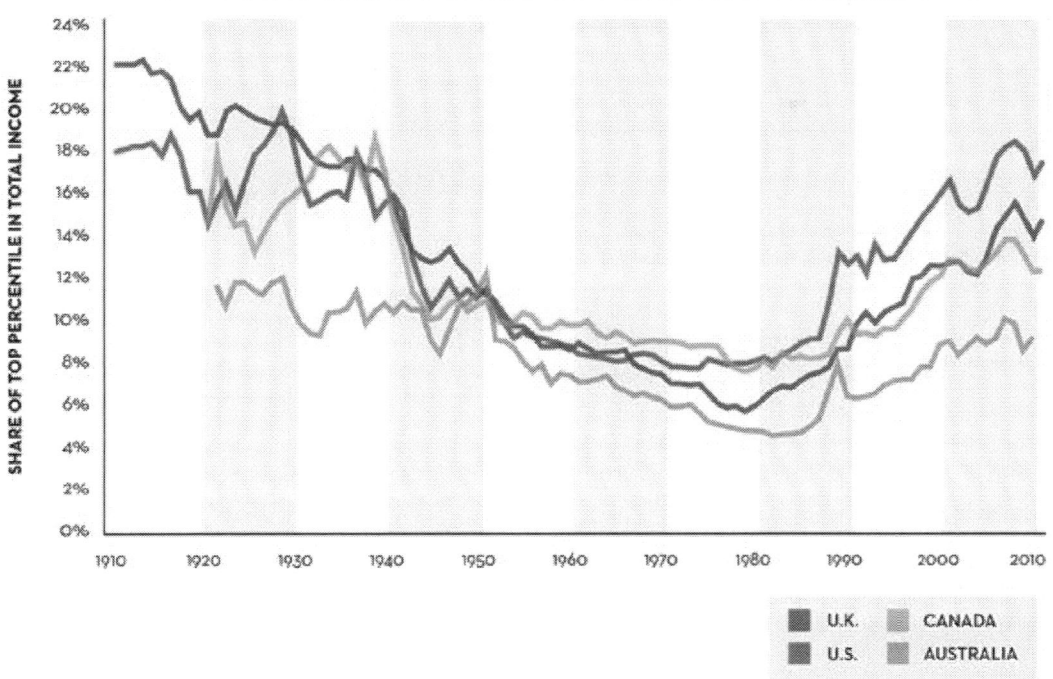

Source: Capital in the Twenty First Century. Thomas Piketty (2014). Belknap Press.

http://www.amazon.com/Capital-Twenty-First-Century-Thomas-Piketty/dp/067443000X/ref=pd_bxgy_b_img_y

In fact wealth and income inequality increased markedly after 1980 which corresponded to the introduction of Neo Liberal and Neo Classical economic policies, Monetarism and Globalization in many countries. The era of Thatcher and Reagan. The U shape points upwards in the graph from 1980 onwards.

As regards wealth concentration Piketty states that in America the richest 10% owned 71% of the wealth and the richest 1% owned 34% of the wealth in 2010. While in Britain the richest 10% owned 70% of the wealth and the richest 1% owned 28% of the wealth in 2010 [8] . The bottom 33% have no net wealth in these countries. Piketty's findings were mostly confirmed by Saez and Zucman in 2013 and 2014. Other studies show the richest 1% of the population accumulated 40% of the wealth [15], the richest 1% own more wealth than the bottom 90% [16] .

Some studies show that the wealth of 1/2 of 1% of the United States population roughly equals that of the lower 90%. The bottom 80% has only 7% of the wealth [17]. 75% of US wealth is owned by 10% of the US population according to studies by Dr. Jospeh Blasi and this corresponds to research by Piketty, Saez and Zucman below. Research by Saez and Zucman of the NBER in America show similar high concentrations of wealth, see chart below

WEALTH	0.01%	0.1%	1%	10%	BOTTOM 90%
1979	3%	8%	24%	67%	33%
2012	11%	22%	42%	77%	23%

CAP INCOME	0.01%	0.1%	1%	10%	BOTTOM 90%
1979	7%	16%	40%	86%	14%
2012	23%	42%	70%	97%	3%

Sources: WEALTH: Saez & Zucman, NBER, 2014

The richest 0.1% have as much wealth as the bottom 90%, and the richest 1% have almost twice the wealth of the bottom 90%. This is an extraordinary concentration of wealth and may be the highest concentration of wealth in history. Yet, these figures by Saez and Zucman may be an underestimate as the wealth and income directed through tax havens has not been included. The concentration of wealth and income would be much higher if tax havens were included.

The following study by a Professor at Harvard University corroborates this:

https://www.youtube.com/watch?v=QPKKQnijnsM&feature=youtu.be

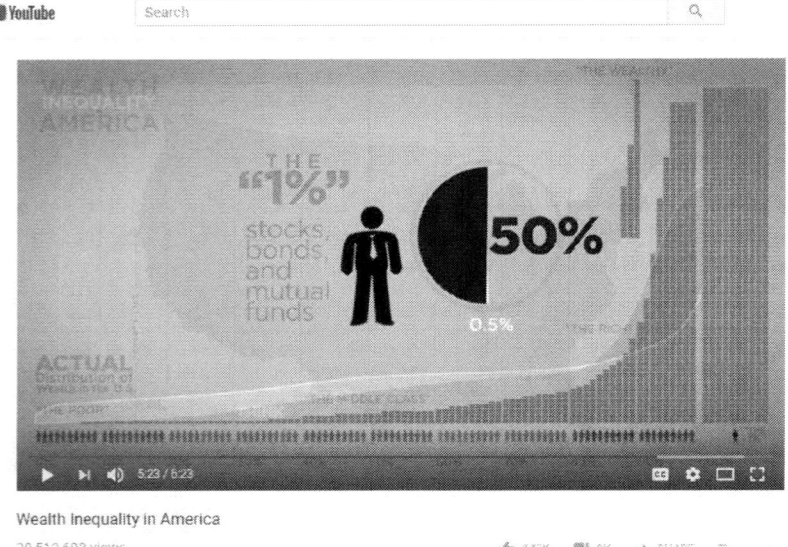

Wealth Inequality in America
20,512,692 views

This study states that the richest 1% own 40% of all wealth and own 50% of all stocks, bonds and mutual funds, and they get 24% of all income. While the bottom 80% own only 7% of wealth. The bottom 50% own only 0.5% of stocks, bonds and mutual funds. (Building a Better America—One Wealth Quintile at a Time, Norton et al. 2011, Perspectives on Psychological Science, http://www.people.hbs.edu/mnorton/norton%20ariely%20in%20press.pdf)

As regards the 'benefits' of economic growth, and so called 'trickle down economics', further research by Saez in 2013 confirms the top 1% captured 95% of the income gains in the first three years of the recovery between 2009 and 2012. (Striking it Richer: The Evolution of Top Incomes in the United States (Updated with 2012 preliminary estimates), 2013). Saez also found that the top 10% of earners commanded 50.4% of national income in 2012, the highest in 100 years. And some studies show the richest 1% also take 25% of national income [15]. In 2010 the richest 1% of Americans captured 93% of the nation's income growth (Bloomberg news, Emmanuel Saez, UC Berkeley, http://www.bloomberg.com/news/articles/2012-10-02/top-1-got-93-of-income-growth-as-rich-poor-gap-widened)) Robert Reich believes the figure is closer to 95% of income growth going to the top 1% during the recovery from 2009 onwards [26]. According to Joseph Stiglitz, the Nobel Prize winner, real incomes stagnated or fell for most Americans during the decade up to 2011, while they increased for the richest 1% ; US median household income in 2012 was at the same level as in 1989, it had stagnated ; the real minimum wage is lower today than it was 60 years ago in the USA. Brookings Institute has found that real median income for male workers was less in 2014 than it was in 1973 (US Census Bureau, https://www.census.gov/content/dam/Census/library/publications/2015/demo/p60-252.pdf) Real incomes have been reduced slightly or stagnated, while prices rose substantially. New findings by Piketty, Saez and Zucman show that while real income (inflation adjusted) for the bottom 50% of Americans stagnated between 1980 and 2014, it increased by 300% for the richest 1% of Americans during that time [25]. This certainly shows a trickle up economics not a trickle down economics.

In fact income and wealth gaps are opening up within the richest 1% bracket itself, most markedly between the richest 1% on one side and the richest 0.1%, 0.01%, 0.001% on the other, in terms of income and wealth. There are growing concentrations of wealth occurring within this 1% bracket, with greater and greater levels of wealth becoming even more concentrated. The growing divide between the 99% and the 1% is being mirrored by a growing divide between the 1% and the 0.1%, 0.01 and the 0.001%. This shows that vast amounts of America's wealth are concentrated within the 1% bracket. This depicts an economic system with excessive concentrations of wealth and income, which works for the 1% and against the majority of people, the 99%, depriving most of essential and basic resources, and severely economically and socially restricting people, and posing a danger to democracy itself.

This means most Americans actually own no wealth and have little real income, with many reduced down to debt slavery, spare change, squalor and poverty. And many are locked out of the economy and cannot reap the benefits of economic growth. This is leading to social upheaval and political upheaval and issues of racism, colour, social class, religion, gender, identity, alienation and mental illnesses accompanied by crimes and mass shootings, conservative and liberal tags, right and left tags which are all being used to worsen the situation while ignoring the deep rooted causes. People have become too busy blaming each other and attacking each other instead of addressing the causes and dynamics of excessive concentrations of wealth and income, and how to resolve this problem at the level of causality, and through positive political, legal, social and economic actions.

This has been the subject of some recent books, 'The Price of Inequality' and 'The Great Divide' by the Joseph Stiglitz are the best books on the economic and social impact of this change within many countries. He describes in some detail the reasons for and consequences of this new 'iron curtain' which has descended upon the USA and other developed countries. Also , 'Capital in the Twenty First Century' by Thomas Piketty, a leading French economist and Economic Democracy: The Political Struggle for the 21st century by JW Smith provide further insights into this [8] . Overall, some sobering facts about oligarchy have emerged and the incredible concentration of wealth.

Other countries have also seen a big increase in the wealth going to the richest 1% at the expense of the bottom 90% of the population.

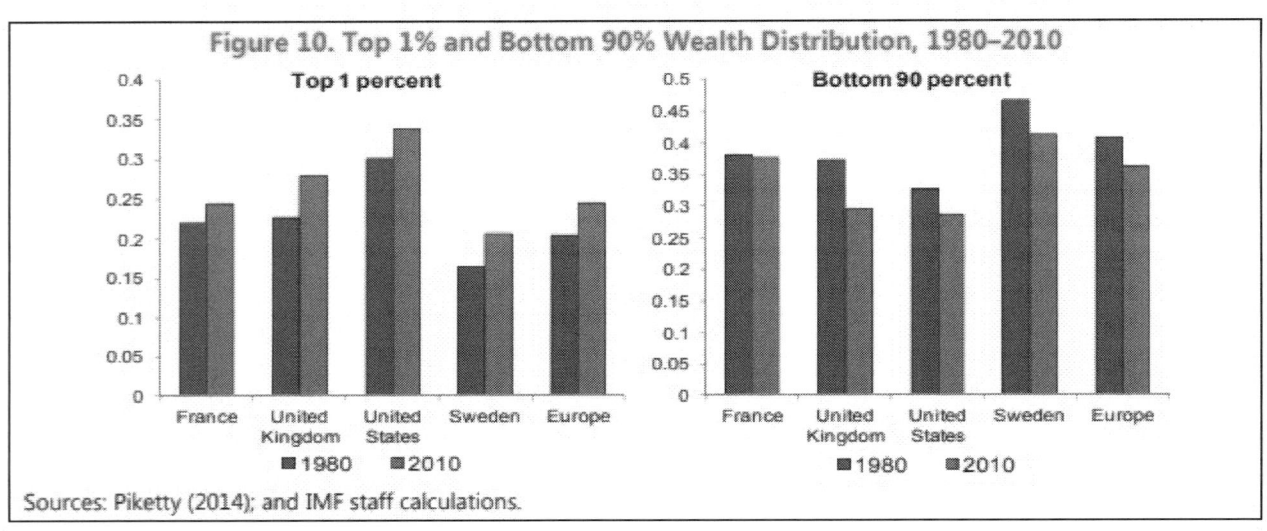

Figure 10. Top 1% and Bottom 90% Wealth Distribution, 1980–2010

Sources: Piketty (2014); and IMF staff calculations.

Recently Jason Hickel of the London School of Economics stated that the wealth ratio between the world's richest countries increased from 44:1 in 1973 to 80:1 in 2014 [13]. To put this in a global context, the richest 1% of the world increased their wealth from 30% to 50% in the period from 2000 to 2010. Oxfam's research has shown that over the last 25 years, globally, the top 1% have gained more income than the bottom 50% put together [12]. Since 2015, the richest 1% has owned more wealth than the rest of the planet. By 2016, 8 wealthy men had as much wealth as half of the world's population, that is 3.5 billion people, according to Oxfam [12]. This is an amazing example of the concentration of wealth globally, this is possibly the highest concentration of wealth in history. Globalisation in it's present format is not working.

Estimates suggest that almost half of the world's wealth is now owned by just 1 percent of the population, amounting to $110 trillion—65 times the total wealth of the bottom half of the world's population (Fuentes Nieva and Galasso 2014). I would encourage readers to read 'AN ECONOMY FOR THE 99%' by Oxfam in 2017 and available at https://www-cdn.oxfam.org/s3fs-public/file_attachments/bp-economy-for-99-percent-160117-en.pdf This Oxfam report is recommended reading for all economists, politicians, governments and those people with an interest in politics, economics and sociology, and also those people interested in philosophy, religion and spirituality. Another study in 2012 includes the effects of tax evasion and tax avoidance and tax havens in these concentrations of wealth calculations [14].

Consider the following global statistics regarding those who make $2 or less per day, an international measure of extreme poverty

- Africa - 650 million people make $2 or less per day
- India - 890 million people make $2 or less per day
- China - 480 million people make $2 or less per day
- Rest of Asia – 810 million people make $2 or less per day
- Latin America - 105 million people make $2 or less per day
- Globally, there are 3 billion people on $2 or less per day
- Mexico is a very poor country with high levels of extreme poverty. Yet, there are 5.6 billion people in other countries with average incomes less than Mexico.

Source: World Bank Reports and 'World Poverty, Immigration and Gumballs' by Roy Beck

These statistics are reflected in the following graph produced by the World Bank in 2012

Global income growth from 1988 to 2008

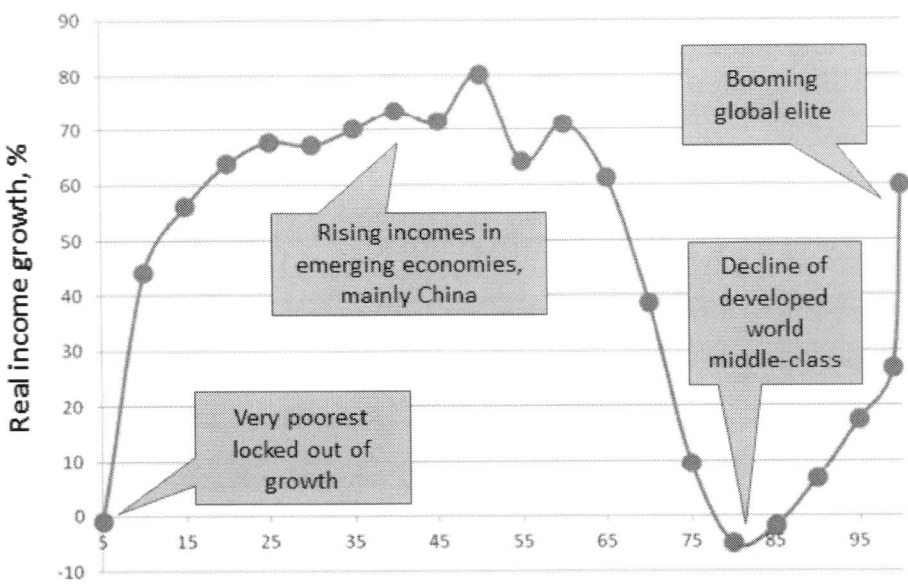

Poorest ← Percentile of global income distribution → **Richest**

This shows that globalisation largely benefitted wealthy elites and middle classes in emerging economies such as China Taiwan, Russia, India and Brazil and oil rich countries such as Saudi Arabia, UAE, Bahrain and a few others, and wealthy elites in the USA and Europe. While the middle class and working class in North America and Europe suffered a big loss in real earnings. The end result has been a massive redistribution of wealth from the poor and working class to the rich. It also stops social mobility and opportunities for advancement, as this Neo Liberal Globalisation does not invest in public infrastructure such as public schools, Universities, hospitals, roads, bridges, rail, airports, sea ports, etc. but it starves them of funds while it concentrates more and more wealth and income in private hands, often through the use of tax evasion and tax havens.

Neo Liberal economic policies which have consistently bankrupted and wrecked many countries have not resolved this problem for the last 30 years. In fact these policies have worsened the problem. This high and growing concentration of wealth and income has created a new 'Iron Curtain'. This Iron Curtain separates the 1% from the 99%, the haves from the have nots in most countries. This is an 'equilibrium of misery, poverty and limitation with suppressed / depressed aggregate demand, similar to conditions in Victorian times or the Feudal era of medieval times in the past. These are obvious examples of oligarchy in both developed countries and in developing and third world countries. This is oligarchy and a return to feudalism and serfdom, not democracy. The Gini Coefficient is good and informative, but not the most effective means of measuring inequality. It does not break down the wealth owned and income earned by the richest 0.1%, 1%, 2% up to 10% and comparing this to the bottom 99%, 98%, 97% down to 90%. It also does not include the wealth in tax havens and foundations. These new measures show how skewed the wealth really is. The Neo Liberal Economic system is specially constructed to deliver most of the economic gains to the richest 1-10%. The following tables should supplement the Gini Coefficient as it provides a better analysis and report of the level of skew in wealth and income distribution

Wealth Ownership and Increase in Wealth (Similar table for Income)

Socio-Economic group	Total Wealth including wealth in offshore tax havens	Percentage of Total National Wealth	Increase in Wealth over time period
Richest 1%, 0.5%, 0.1%, 0.01%, 0.001%			
Richest 2%			
Richest 3%			
Richest 4%			
Richest 5%			
Bottom 90%			
Bottom 50%, 20%, 10%			

Causative Factors

These massive wealth and income inequalities are being achieved and worsened via the following methods:

(a) outsourcing jobs and production to cheap developing and third world countries under a certain type of 'Globalization' with managed trade and skewed markets. A globalised 'race to the bottom'. These goods and services are then sold at inflated prices in developed countries. This system enforces a reduction in real wages for workers and the shrinking middle class in developed countries and the enforcement of high prices and costs of living in these same countries. Some notable examples in our time are the 'rust belt' and the ghettos and industrial wastelands in the USA and Europe, and use of the 'China price' and 'wages of India in the American workplace' to intimidate suppliers, producers and workers. Many studies confirm this, including a recent IMF study in 2015 titled 'Causes and Consequences of Income Inequality: A Global Perspective' (Norris et al. 2015).

(b) increased automation and labour replacing technologies and accompanying higher productivity rates which mostly enrich capital and wealth owners. These high productivity rates have overtaken wage rates to labour for decades. In the USA, the productivity rate has been higher than the wage rate for over 25 years, and this gap has been growing wider. This is due to worsen as seen by advancements in artificial intelligence, expert systems for professional services, automation of offices, factories and homes, wireless networking, robotics, drones, and driverless cars and trucks. These will continue to replace workers. Many studies confirm this, including a recent IMF study in 2015 titled 'Causes and Consequences of Income Inequality: A Global Perspective' (Norris et al. 2015).

(c) the great market and political power of monopoly / oligopoly capital, cartels, patents, restrictive practices, land and property owners, or FIRE sector (Finance Insurance and Real Estate) and their ability to extract large economic rents and supernormal profits and impose high costs of living on workers and labour [28]. Increasing prices and imposing higher costs of living on societies, these monopolies / cartels / FIRE sector have also reduced the real wages of workers and the middle classes and the purchasing power of wages. This has been enforced via globalization, banning unions and collective bargaining, increased automation in the workplace, outsourcing, political influence and new laws, etc.. This has greatly increased profits, capital gains and incomes for the wealthiest 5%. Indeed, the high rate of productivity growth in North America and Europe from the 1980's to 2000's from new technologies and innovations increased the incomes, profits and capital gains of monopolies, oligopolies, patents holders and cartels while wages stagnated for most of the working class and middle class during this time period.

The research and works of Dr. Michael Hudson shows that the rentiers or FIRE sector (Finance, Insurance, Real Estate) now dominate many developed economies and account for most of the credit created and most of the debt and most of the money used in transactions[28]. There is an entirely new structure for economies and societies where Debt and Rentier dominance are the major economic issues and the Debt Beneficiary class (top 5%) act as a parasite on the Debt Dependent class (955) [28]. It is a return to feudalism and serfdom.

New technologies and forms of e-commerce have enabled takeovers, mergers, and consolidations of industries on a global level and led to the creation of new international monopolies and oligopolies. This has concentrated the returns to capital at an international level. One example being the FANG shares on stock markets and the increasing dominance of high tech firms which have penetrated new industries. And the increasing dominance of just a few big firms in the Big Pharma sector, banking sector, insurance sector, military industrial sector, and real estate sector. This has led to rounds of business closures, price pressures on suppliers, the bankruptcy of some suppliers, wage reductions, etc.. This enriches and consolidates the economic and political power of the rentier class or FIRE sector while simultaneously impoverishing the working and middle class and disempowering them.

(d) speculation in assets and derivatives leads to very high returns to capital, to speculators and to banks, and the income from this in terms of profits, dividends, interest and capital gains goes to the richest 1%-5%. One has seen massive increases in the income and wealth of capital owners, top executives of banks and big corporates and speculators in the last 2 decades. This includes the massive increases in executive pay which range from 50 to 400 times the wages of ordinary workers in a business. Company buybacks, involving trillions of dollars over the last decade, has fuelled this as executives and speculator shareholders artificially prop up share prices and loot companies. This is one of the main driving forces behind the high concentrations of wealth and income in several countries. Speculation to rephrase a monetarist term provides 'free lunches' in the form of price rigging, fraud, insider trading, massive debt and leverage, financial crimes and capital gains to the rich.

Massive financial gains from speculation and fraud during booms drains the productive sector of the economy and deprives it of affordable funds for investment and profits via consumption. Large banks and medium banks have consistently favoured funding for speculation over funding for the productive sector. Bank loans for speculation are often 3 – 7 times higher than loans for the productive sector. In some countries where a few large banks dominate the banking market, this can lead to massive loans for speculation while the productive sector is starved of funds for investment. This deprives the economy of long term productive investment, and reduces or eliminates the traditional income, wages, benefits, and productivity returns to labour. It leads to stagnation in real wages or reductions of such for workers, which has been found in many studies. Real wages in the USA for ordinary workers and the middle class have stagnated for the last 30 years and the real minimum wage is lower today than it was 60 years ago. Furthermore speculation in assets and derivatives is based on the enforcement of low wages and loss of benefits and bad working conditions on workers through globalization, automation, and neo liberal policies which lead to higher share prices and more gains from speculation. It imposes new economic structures where the grinding down of workers and their families for less and less resources is related to speculation in shares, assets and derivatives ; one feeds off the other.

These payments to capital owners, to executives, banks and speculators are much higher than their productivity and are not justifiable in an economic and business sense. And most workers are deprived of participation in capital ownership, in employee share ownership. The theory of 'solely maximizing shareholder value in the short term' to maximize financial gains for executives and large speculative shareholders has worsened speculation, creating a casino economy which further concentrates wealth. This is occurring in many developed countries. The research and works of Joseph Stiglitz, Paul Krugman, Thomas Piketty, Hudson, and many others confirm this [8]. Many studies confirm this, including a recent IMF study in 2015 titled 'Causes and Consequences of Income Inequality: A Global Perspective' (Norris et al. 2015).

(e) wages have been squeezed and reduced in developed countries so as to increase profit margins and 'shareholder value' over the last 25 years. This has a political dimension and legal dimension in addition to an economic dimension. As we have seen above real wages for working class and middle income Americans stagnated for 30 years, while profits, dividends, capital gains and executive salaries rose by large amounts during this time. One very important consequence of the stagnation in real wages is that workers got into more debt in order to buy over priced homes and over priced products and services and maintain high living standards and expectations in developed countries. This large rise in private debt levels has created significant financial system and economic instability in many countries, which flared up in 2008. There is a correlation between the stagnation (or fall) in real wages and the rise in private debt levels in developed countries [1]. This correlation has been significant since the early 1980's when Neo Liberal policies and globalization began under Thatcher and Reagan. The high debt repayments and compounded interest act to siphon even more wealth away from workers and the poor to the already rich. Studies by Margaret Kennedy and other economists show that interest is a form of 'trickle up' economics where the wealth and income trickles up to the wealthiest in society, largely benefitting the richest 5% [23] Many studies confirm this, including a recent IMF study in 2015 titled 'Causes and Consequences of Income Inequality: A Global Perspective' (Norris et al. 2015).

(f) government austerity policies to bail out rich bankers, speculators and fraudsters, and enrich vulture funds and protect their assets and the assets of the very rich, which was achieved by imposing new taxes, levies and charges on the working and middle classes and vicious cutbacks in pensions, social security, state healthcare, social programmes, hospitals, welfare and education. In reality, governments and troikas loaded private banking debt and speculator debt onto whole nations and taxpayers which bankrupted them and then enforced 'deficit reduction' measures and austerity on them ; this has been mass theft and robbery of the taxpayers, unemployed, disabled, elderly, and ordinary people, seizing their private property and income, and may be unconstitutional. At the same time taxes were reduced or eliminated for the FIRE sector and Rentiers and for economic rent. And Quantitative Easing was used to maintain and improve asset prices and protect the wealth of the richest 5% and the vulture funds, while debasing the currency and eroding real wages. During austerity, vulture funds suck large amounts of money out of economies and redirect them through tax loopholes and offshore tax havens. All of these policies directly transfer wealth and income from the bottom 95% to the richest 5%.

(g) the nature of government policies and budgets which have the effect of reducing or eliminating taxes on the FIRE sector and on speculators, rentiers and economic rents while increasing or maintaining high taxes on the working class and middle class and the productive sector. And imposing cutbacks in pensions, social security, state healthcare, social programmes, hospitals, welfare and education. This involves large redistributions of wealth and income to the richest 5%.

(h) the nature of debt enslaved societies, this is discussed further in Chapter 7. The massive government debt burden (to bail out banks) and private debt burdens (to compensate for lower real wages) and interest payments imposed upon taxpayers, consumers, workers / labour. Most debt and compound interest repayment is concentrated in the bottom 98% of wealth and income owners and this debt enslavement represents a transfer of wealth from the bottom 98% to the richest 2%. Compound interest itself can increase the debt from 150% - 400%.

(i) in the USA and some other countries the high costs of University or college education and the excessive burden of massive student loans ranging from $50,000 - $100,000 on graduation after 4 years means many Americans cannot afford third level education. This deprives many of the high tech skills, business skills and scientific skills to succeed in the world and reduces their productivity or keeps them in a low state of productivity. The rich or richest 5% can afford these high costs and most of them send their children to Universities and colleges, and they graduate debt free, and this creates a continuous productivity gap between the rich and everybody else which reinforces concentrations of wealth and income over time. Piketty and others have found this in recent and ongoing research.

(j) politics and political institutions have become corrupted by 'pay to play' politics in several developed nations, including the USA. The government serves the interests of the richest 1% and mostly neglects the rest. The government refuses to invest in third level education, in the high tech skills, business skills and scientific skills necessary for personal and national productivity gains and innovation in the 21st century. And refuses to invest in the infrastructure to support new high tech economies. Governments and politicians say that there is no money to do this. Yet these same governments have and continue to spend trillions of dollars on the Deep State, the Shadow Government, wars and regime changes, bail outs of banks and big corporates, and corporate welfare and subsidies. This is a major failing of certain governments.

This is a major failing of certain governments. They prefer to bankrupt individuals and families with massive debt while refusing to invest long term in the people, the infrastructure, new innovations and the nation.

(k) the continuing concentration of wealth and income via inheritance and the use of tax loopholes, tax havens and tax evasion schemes. Inheritance has become a major factor as wealth is siphoned off at an international level.

(l) the redirection of sales, profits, revenues, fees through offshore tax havens and tax evasion schemes. Conservative estimates put the monies in tax havens at $32 trillion but the real figure may be in the region of $70 trillion (Tax Justice Network, James Henry, 2012, http://www.taxjustice.net/cms/upload/pdf/Price_of_Offshore_Revisited_120722.pdf). The total cost of tax evasion has been estimated at $3.1 trillion per year (Tax Justice network report, James Henry, November 2011, http://www.tackletaxhavens.com/Cost_of_Tax_Abuse_TJN%20Research_23rd_Nov_2011.pdf)

These factors **(a)** to **(l)** all combined together to increase the returns to capital (the very wealthy) and hide this massive wealth through tax havens.

Destructive Social Effects and Economic Effects

High concentrations of wealth and income increase hoarding, savings, monies in offshore tax havens, while reducing consumption and aggregate demand, and this in combination with debt overhang (and high repayments) can create a paradox of thrift, and this reduces investment profitability and potential, which in turn can lead to a liquidity trap, further distorting markets. The richest 1 - 10% who have most of the wealth and income in a country have a reduced propensity to consume and spend, while the bottom 80% and particularly bottom 60% have a high propensity to spend and consume. But the latter are deprived of these resources for consumption through high concentrations of wealth and income, loss of jobs from an economic downturn and debt overhang and an inability to increase credit. This can cause a lack of consumption and aggregate demand causing or prolonging economic downturns, recessions and depressions. This can skew markets and national economies and cause them to operate well below optimum levels. We saw this in the period 2008 – 2015. This sucks vast amount of money out of the circular flow of income in a country and this adversely affects consumption, aggregate demand and the investment which is dependent on this demand. In addition to this, the continuous withdrawal of interest money, which was not created during the loan and money creation process, causes 'trickle upwards' to the richest and further suction out of the economy and losses in consumption, demand and investment. These are major Dynamic Disequilibrium forces. This iron curtain presents serious challenges and threats to democracy, freedom and social stability. The many consequences are manifested in higher levels of unemployment and under employment, excessively low wages due to wages growing at less than the rate of productivity, zero hour contracts, temporary employment contracts with no rights and conditions, more families forced to work 2, 3 or 4 jobs and take on debt just to maintain living standards, the large pockets of de-industrialisation, empty businesses and industrial wastelands, the high number of business bankruptcies, the growing poverty levels, the vulture fund capitalism and the high level of home evictions and homelessness, the crumbling public infrastructure, the underfunded and overcrowded hospitals, the high and growing crime rates, racism, social conflicts, the high family breakdown rates etc.. Its a well known fact that high inequality drives up crime rates and many studies confirm this. For example, the US has the highest rate of people in jail in the developed world and is also the most unequal country in the developed world. If one examines the statistics since the early 1980's, one sees a high rise in inequality and a high rise in the rate of jailings.

These inequalities and social insecurities and injustices are brilliantly portrayed in the new book 'The Precariat : The New Dangerous Class' (2016) by Guy Standing. This book exposes the new iron curtain in its brutal form and the forces which are undermining democracy and freedom in most developed countries. A darker world being increasingly dominated by economic insecurity, stagnant or lower real wages for most people, and by great wealth, extravagance, waste and opulence for a very small minority. The reality is that a new iron curtain has descended on most countries worldwide. This iron curtain exists within developed nations and between nations. It divides the haves from the have nots within developed countries and divides those countries at the centre from those countries on the periphery in international terms. This iron curtain has entered into many areas of life dividing people against each other whether it be in communities, families, regions, states and nations. It touches into the deepest, most meaningful and most intimate parts of man, and poisons them.

This 'iron curtain' is rapidly changing the traditional relationships between workers, business, government, individuals, families and communities. A new feudalism or feudal order is arising in this fast paced globalised technological age. The few who are benefitting from this new system the "haves" are increasingly cutting themselves off from those who are not, the "have-nots" in the form of large walls, barriers, fenced communities, social exclusion, country clubs, golf clubs, laws, and new forms of discrimination and prejudice. These walls are not just physical, they are also social, mental, spiritual, emotional, psychological, financial, political, legal and economic they enter into all areas of human life and relationships. Yet these walls are eating away at the soul of mankind, corrupting, manipulating, twisting, perverting everything they come into contact with. Like previous walls and iron curtains this new iron curtain is destroying social cohesion, social capital, family values and cohesion, community values, social responsibilities, civic virtues, co-operation, trust, solidarity and human freedom. The new struggle for economic survival is fuelling a 'war of all against all' as meant by Hobbes.

As more and more of the earth's limited productive resources and limited monies are acquired, controlled, used up and concentrated in the hands of the 'haves' the wealthy property owning classes there is less left over for the 'have-nots', who are forced into the margins, into more debt, more uncertainty, more poverty, criminal activities and misery just to exist. The 'have-nots' include 4 billion people [15] who are unemployed, underemployed, on less than subsistence wages, those on less than 2 dollars a day, the 'working poor' on low, subsistence wages subjected to high taxes, artificially high mortgages and artificially high prices for basic products and services, many of them on temporary work contracts with no medical insurance, no rights and no benefits, the ill and the disabled, the elderly, the poor and the destitute in developing and third world countries. They are treated like social outcasts, like scum, they are isolated, discriminated against, they are identified by their clothes, their appearance, their accent, their job, their transport, their address, etc. and subjected to vile abuse by the feudal overlords and their servants. There is no freedom, no democracy, no dignity, no liberty here only a hard and continuous grinding down of people's lives, families, communities and regions. The world is entering a new feudalism as bad as Communism, Fascism, Militarism, Toryism, Monarchism and it's Imperialism in the past. The forces of tyranny mentioned by Howard Zinn in his works [20] have always been with us, have taken on new forms and have always been in opposition to freedom, to democracy, to rights and to the ordinary people.

On the other side of the iron curtain are the 'haves', the wealthy elite within developed Western nations and small wealthy elites within developing and third world nations. The rich on this side of the iron curtain live lives of luxury, ease and opulence in comparison to the those on the other side of the 'iron curtain'. They enjoy all the benefits of the economic system, such as control over most if not all of the earth's limited productive resources, they enjoy large incomes from their property and wealth, comprehensive medical insurance, perks and benefits, large salaries, large mansions and subsidised apartments, cars and gyms, generous share options and golden handshakes worth millions of dollars, the best private education for their children, zero or very low taxes, they siphon off millions of dollars from speculation in property, shares, stocks, bonds, derivatives, currencies etc. and when the crash comes it is the ordinary working class man / woman, the unemployed, the disabled and the poor who pay the price and bail out the banks and the rich. They write laws and trade treaties to protect their home industries or speculative frauds and avoid paying taxes and acquire even more wealth at the expense of others, they drain productive potential and limited resources of the earth away from the poor, the unemployed, the dispossessed and the starving masses towards themselves so that they can acquire even more wealth. Such is the perverted nature of the system. Indeed they claim it is uneconomic to build state medical clinics, hospitals, food development projects and clean water facilities, schools and Universities, and roads for people in developing and third world nations but somehow it is economic to sell them guns or build yachts, luxury goods and large mansions. The sheer global scale of this iron curtain means that it reaches into every person's life, ensuring that it is more widely felt, more oppressive and more parasitic than any iron curtain or empire which has existed before in human history.

In many countries the "haves" have succeeded in privatising government property, social property and community property so that they acquire even more control over resources, in many cases private monopolies have replaced public monopolies. The reality of this is that public wealth and investment which has been financed by taxpayers over several decades and built to serve the public interest has been transferred over at a large discount to wealthy investors, the "haves" who have only to serve their own private interests. This represents a massive transfer of wealth from the ordinary working taxpayer to wealthy investors and corrupt political interests. Studies in a number of countries have shown that the prices charged for products and services by private monopolies are much the same as those previously charged by public monopolies when adjusted for changes in inflation and the cost of living and in some cases standards of service and quality have deteriorated under private monopolies.

Research by Dr. Richard Wilkinson and others clearly shows that high rates of inequality can be very destructive to societies and to freedom and democracy. It adversely affects health, crime rates, murders, life expectancy, divorce rates, infant mortality, mental illness, child pregnancies, trust, obesity, education, social mobility etc. etc.. There is a correlation between these negative social factors and inequality but no correlation between these negative social factors and the growth in GNP. Its not the growth in GNP which matters but how that GNP (or wealth and income) is distributed which matters. The following charts by Dr. Richard Wilkinson show this.

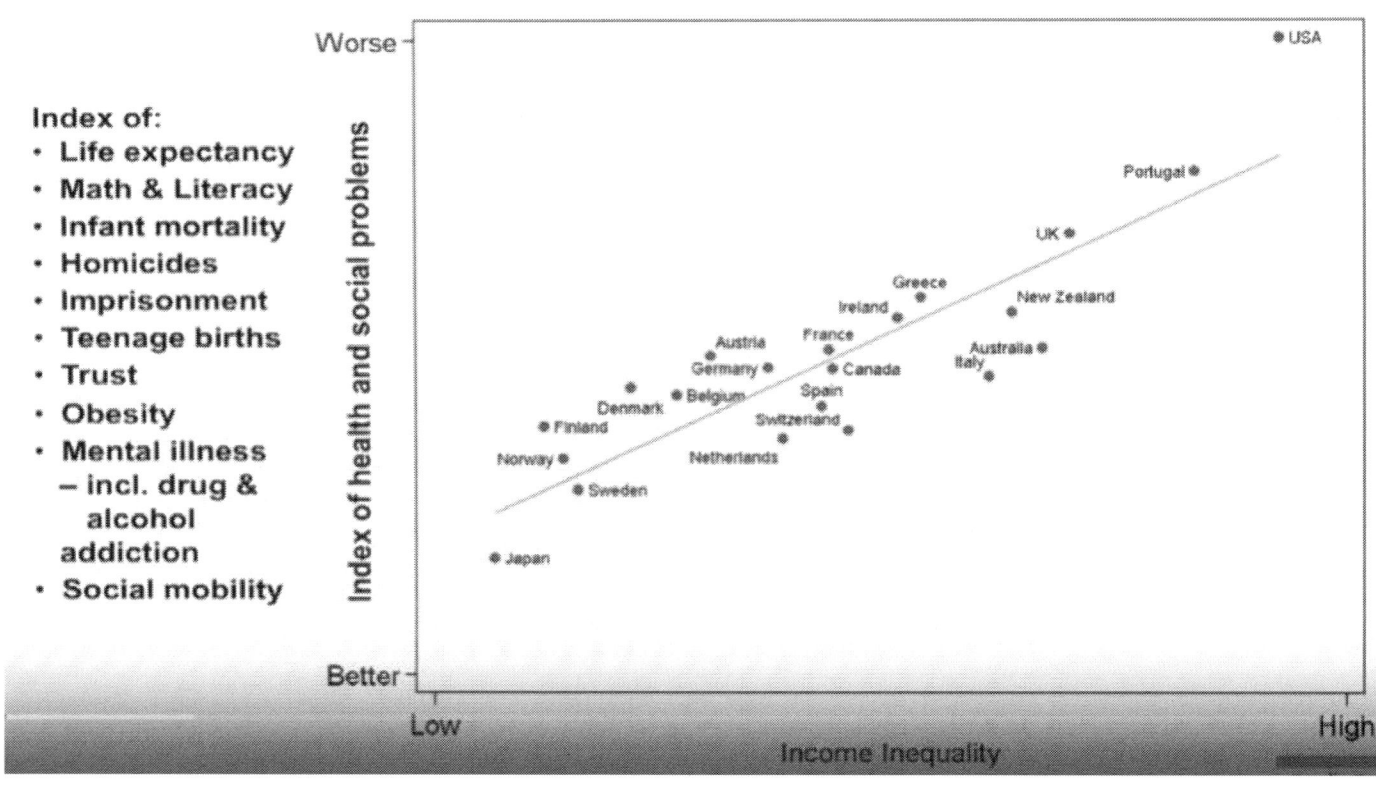

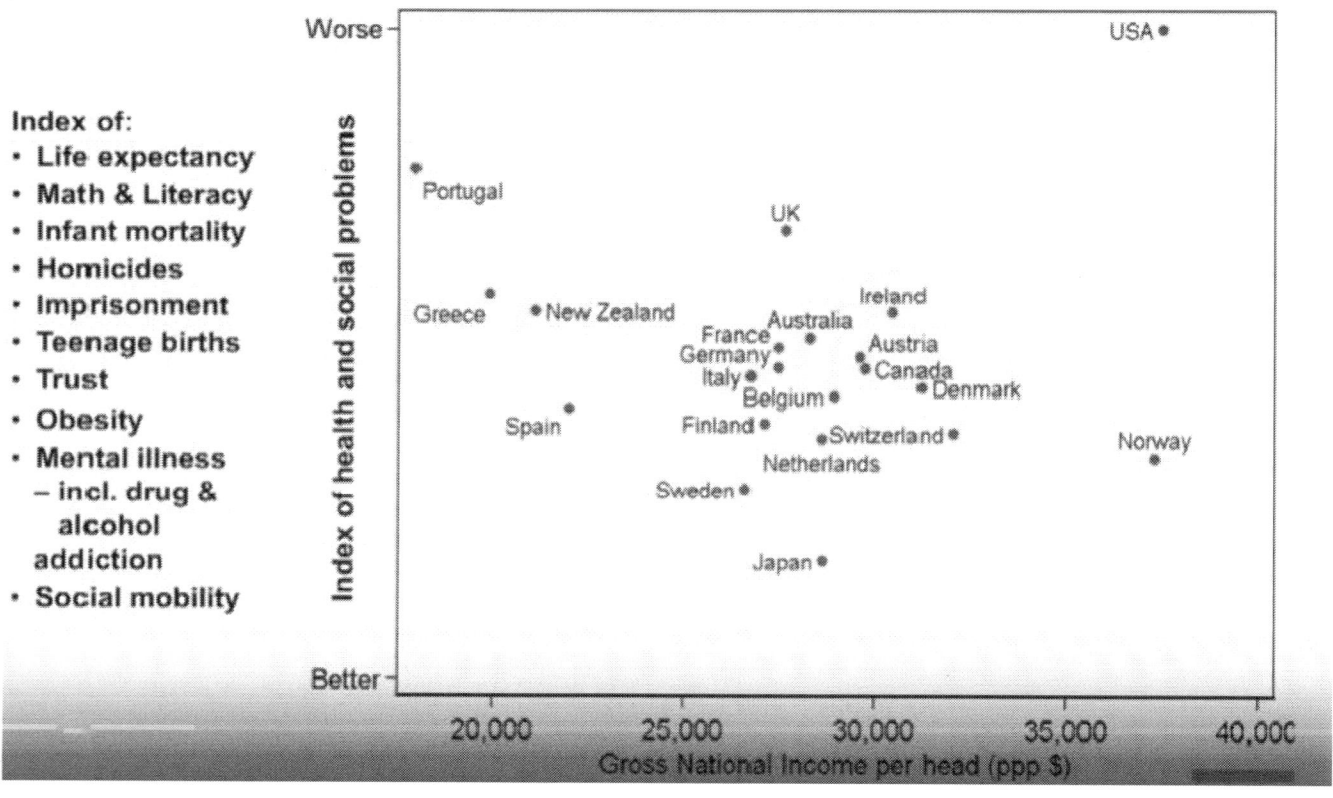

Source: Wilkinson and Pickett, The Spirit level (2009)

Dr. Richard Wilkinson provides further charts in his new book 'The Inner Level: How More Equal Societies Reduce Stress, Restore Sanity and Improve Everyone's Well-being' (Penguin, 2018) and uses many variables to measure the effects of inequality, including the UNICEF Index of Child Well Being, Stress and Anxiety levels, Mental illnesses, Civic Participation, Support for Populist leaders, Child Bullying, Crime levels, Imprisonment rates, Bullying in the workplace, Anti Social Behaviour, Life Expectancy, Gambling, Drug Abuse, Educational Performance, and Social Mobility. These factors also affect economic performance at the individual level and collective levels and national levels and have major impacts on demand and supply, and are of great importance to Economists, who ironically ignore these factors in their studies and research.

The following table outlines the main social outcomes of this Iron Curtain

The Iron Curtain

Privileged section - Richest 1 - 5 % of population in countries	General Public section - Bottom 95% of population in countries
• Attend excellent private schools, charging fees which are too expensive for working class and middle income families. Schools which are well resourced, funded and staffed and provide top quality, world class education. Act as feeder schools to top Universities.	• Attend state or public schools which are underfunded, under resourced and under staffed and subject to regular funding cuts and staff cuts as a result of state budget cuts and austerity and the massive amount of funds in offshore tax havens. Poor quality education. Many bright students fail to thrive.
• Can easily afford University fees and expenses. A debt free University education.	• Parents do not have enough resources and support networks for their children to enter or finish High school. Many cannot afford University and either have to go without it or go into student debt.
• Use of wealth and social status to get entry into top Universities by legal or illegal means.	• Massive student debt or parent debt to acquire a basic college or University education. Grants and state assistance subject to government cuts, under investment and austerity policies. Worsened by the trillions of dollars hidden away in offshore tax havens.
• Careers protected by exclusive social connections and networks, which protect and insulate them from globalisation and outsourcing	• Certain right wing politicians and political parties demanding more cuts to spending on schools and Universities, and this has the effect of further reducing educational opportunities for this class of people, and increasing the debt levels of those who do attend University.
• Great private hospitals which are use state of the art technologies and top doctors and consultants, and provide excellent, high quality medical care. No waiting lists.	• Student debt becomes unpayable due to the outsourcing of jobs to developing and third world countries and the importation of skilled migrant workers, increased automation in the workplace, government austerity policies and other factors mentioned in this book
• Gated communities, and exclusive expensive private neighbourhoods which are crime free and where neighbours are respectful, friendly and considerate to each other.	• State or public hospitals which are underfunded, dirty, dilapidated, use older technologies and have long waiting lists, and provide poor quality medical care. Patients forced to sleep on trolleys or chairs for days awaiting medical attention. Subject to cutbacks in the form of government
• Jobs and Careers which provide excellent health insurance and employment benefits.	
• Exclusive social connections which ensure access to high paying jobs, job promotions, and career advancement	

- Total income or salaries of executives and professionals range from 50 to 400 times bigger than the lowest paid worker

- Plenty of employment benefits such as excellent health insurance, pension plan, stock options, free lunches, free accommodation when travelling, gym membership, holiday pay, a car, bonuses at the end of the year.

- Job safe from automation and 'slave labour' in cheap developing countries

- No need to worry about "competitiveness" as job is secure and protected. Market models and structures and laws are designed to protect their income and interests.

- Given a stake in the capitalist system in the form of share holdings, share options, investment opportunities, and bonuses.

- Excellent health and high quality education about health and lifestyles. A high degree of protection from polluted foods, water, air and land. In fact, many of their businesses profiteer from this pollution.

- They are the Debt Beneficiary class. They make significant interest, profits, economic rent and dividends from the trillions of dollars of debt created annually.

- The main beneficiaries of compound interest which sucks wealth and income from the poorer sections of the population (bottom 90%). A trickle upwards economics.

- They benefit from speculation in assets and derivatives which involves trillions of dollars in transactions per year. They also get bailed out by taxpayers and government after

- cuts, under-investment and austerity policies. Higher death rates for patients and those on waiting lists. Worsened by the trillions of dollars used to bail out bankers and speculators, and for military-industrial spending, and the trillions of dollars hidden away in offshore tax havens.

- Many families forced into bankruptcy to pay medical bills

- Certain right wing politicians and political parties demanding more cuts to healthcare and hospitals and this has the effect of further reducing healthcare and medical care for this class of people, forcing many into bankruptcies, continued illnesses or early deaths.

- Neighbourhoods plagued by alcohol abuse, drug abuse, gambling, unemployment, crime, domestic violence, derelict buildings, social neglect, predatory lending and loan sharks, disrespect, bullying and anti social behaviour.

- Certain right wing politicians and political parties demanding more cuts to community centres and community development grants and this has the effect of worsening the crime and violence in these communities.

- Zero hour contracts and jobs and careers which provide no health insurance or low quality health insurance (private or state). Many employment benefits are cut or eradicated in order to 'improve competitiveness' or improve 'productivity' which really mean increasing the profits and tax free (offshore) income of the richest 5%.

- Long hours working for little pay and the eradication of overtime pay rates in order to improve "competitiveness".

- Jobs can be replaced by automation, downsizing and restructurings, and 'slave labour' in less developed countries. Also cheap labour can be transferred over to developed countries for job contracts.

- Suffer bad health and in many cases chronic illness from low cost lifestyles which impose limitations on what is consumed. Poor education crashes.

- The power to abuse monopoly or oligopoly power, cartels and restrictive practises to extract higher prices and economic rents, and build vast wealth at public expense

- Right wing politicians and governments provide this class with generous corporate welfare and subsidies amounting to hundreds of billions of dollars per year. In addition to bail outs of their banks, financial institutions and corporates worth trillions of dollars. Yet, they call for vicious government cutbacks to educational and health services, unemployment benefit, food stamps, and community development for the bottom 50%. This is a vicious attack on innocent people, human rights, Constitutional rights, and democracy.

- A vibrant and thriving private infrastructure which is privatised and exclusive, and excludes people.

- Can escape prosecution for crimes because of their social status and perceived importance

- Access to the best lawyers for court cases. They can actively use this to attack poorer and weaker sections of society in the courts.

- They can use offshore tax havens, transfer pricing and trusts to evade paying taxes.

- Respect and honour for the person in employment and in socialising circles, and during social events, and within communities and neighbourhoods. Don't suffer from racism or other prejudices and bigotry inflicted by society.

- Very low risk of being prosecuted and jailed.

about health and lifestyles. And the continued pollution of foods, air, water, and land which adversely affects health.

- They are the Debt Dependent class. High debt and compound interest suck wealth and income out of this class of people. A trickle upwards economics.

- They are the victims of over speculation in assets and are forced to pay higher prices for over pricd assets, eg. Homes

- They have to pay very high prices for the products and services produced by monopolies, oligopolies, restrictive practises and cartels.

- Wages are 50 to 400 times less than the salaries of top executives. Real wages have stagnated for over 25 years. Globalisation and 'race to the bottom, worsening this.

- Excluded from social connections which could provide access to good paying jobs and careers.

- Given no stake in the capitalist system. Treated as 'wage slave' in globalised 'race to the bottom'.

- Forced to pay high taxes on wages, on food, on clothes, on property, on services, on cars, and pay levies for water, garbage removal.

- Higher risk of being prosecuted, fined and / or jailed. The bottom 50% have a much higher probability of this. In some countries this is linked to race, ethnic group, religion and social class.

- Victims of racism, gender inequality, religious discrimination, age discrimination and all manner of prejudices and bigotry.

- Higher probability of being harassed and badly treated by the police. In some countries this is linked to race, ethnic group, religion and social class.

- A crumbling underfunded public infrastructure which is subject government cuts, under investment and austerity policies and to further cuts due to the massive amount of funds in offshore tax havens.

- Cannot access affordable legal representation in

- Can ignore the victims of racism, gender inequality, religious discrimination, age discrimination and all manner of prejudices and bigotry.

- Higher probability of no police harassment

- Substantial political power and lobbying power in capital cities which they use to serve themselves

- They make massive profits from wars, conflicts and regime changes. Their sons are able to escape military duty due to various deferments and legal and political manipulations.

- During times of austerity, they can buy up repossessed homes, business assets and farms at a discount, and hold them or sell them on at inflated prices and profits. Profit from asset stripping.

- The beneficiaries of the bail out of bankers and fraudsters after financial crashes through government austerity policies. They maintain their jobs, careers, and the value of their assets is protected by taxpayer bailouts.

- Free use of public infrastructure and public services. Yet, the wealthy use tax havens and tax evasion to avoid paying the taxes to pay for this.

- courts. Most are victims of abuses of state power, police power and corporate power and they cannot get justice through the courts.

- No monopoly or oligopoly power and restrictive practises power to extract higher prices and economic rents

- Disrespect, discrimination, prejudice and belittlement for the person in employment and when socialising, and during social events, and within communities and neighbourhoods. Treated like dirt, scum, second class citizens.

- Bottom 20% forced to live in ghettos and suffer social exclusion, prejudice and stigma and no options for material advancement. High risk of getting involved in crime.

- No political power and lobbying power in capital cities

- Suffer evictions from family homes during times of recession or after financial crashes

- Sons are conscripted to fight and often die in the wars, conflicts and regime changes which mainly benefit the rich, the big banks and corporate. Many return in body bags.

- Forced to bail out bankers and fraudsters after financial crashes through government austerity policies. This payment is in the form of higher taxes, new taxes and charges, wage cuts and job losses and cuts to public services.

- Use of public infrastructure and public services which they pay for through taxes and charges. They cannot use tax havens and tax evasion

Does Society Exist ?

One supporter of this new Iron Curtain was former British premier, Mrs. Margaret Thatcher who went so far as to suggest that "society does not exist" and that existence consisted of self-centred, greedy, selfish, self serving, materialistic individuals separated from each other by walls and barriers running around extracting as much as they can from the economic system while undermining and destroying others. What she was saying was that human beings do not matter they are just economic units, things, automatons, objects to be used and abused according to her narrow materialistic ideology. What a sad and pitiful mentality. Yet Mrs. Thatcher should have looked at her own life, her own circumstances before making such rash statements. Mrs Thatcher was raised in a family which loved and cared for her, there was sharing, and a sense of belonging and a communal sense of responsibility. And she lived in a community which supported her and supported her family's small business. She grew up in a community of people which felt a certain sense of love, belonging and shared responsibility which aided, assisted and supported each other. This sense of communal solidarity and responsibility was strengthened during and after the second world war. As a youngster she went to church on Sundays where there was a common search for God, spiritual teachings which emphasised love and caring for others, and an environment where there was a sense of fellowship, love, support and caring among people. She probably played team sports where there was team-work, mutual assistance and solidarity between team members. At different times of her life, she had some other people who genuinely cared for her as she grew up eg. parents, friends, relations, neighbours, teachers, doctors, nurses, pastors / priests, police, etc.. All of points to social relations and interdependence, and the existence of society. These are the characteristics of society which she claimed did not exist.

Mrs Thatcher also grew up in a stable economic, social and political climate which was the result of government intervention to protect and serve society eg. police, the military, courts, laws, regulations, schools, universities, hospitals, health services, roads, bridges, railways, social welfare and social safety nets, government assistance to industry, Keynesian economic policies, etc. and the government spending to build electricity networks and telephone networks throughout Britain, yet she condemned and rejected all of this. These state investments or society investments provided the basic security, basic services and infrastructure for children such as Margaret Thatcher to grow and develop. According to people of her mindset with her obsession with individualism, greed and selfishness all of these things were supposedly Socialist, Marxist or Communist. Yet without these people and services in her life and the positive qualities they contributed how would she have coped, how would she have survived ?. Every person is both individual and social in the sense that we each have the need for a relationship with other people in order to grow, develop and thrive. Interdependence is a fact of life. The growth of responsibility both for oneself and for other people runs parallel with the development of social life from the earliest periods of human history. At first people were drawn together for physical reasons such as the need for shelter, food, subsistence, procreation, protection and defence. This developed, evolved and deepened over time to encompass many social aspects, family values and community values, spiritual values, social capital and society values, which evolved into the construct we know as society. As a result of this a sense of duty emerged towards family members, community members, friends, work colleagues, ones guests, the old, the weak and strangers and society in general. The Judeo-

Christian tradition developed this further and outlined the spiritual significance of love of others and love of God. Other religious traditions such as Buddhism, Judaism, Islam, Hinduism, and Deism, also stress similar values and the importance of love of and consideration for ones fellow man in their spiritual teachings. Even Secular Humanism and Atheism and other secular ideologies recognise the great social and economic value of love, compassion, peace, cooperation and social justice. Certainly the high economic costs and social costs of hatred, social divisions, greed, selfishness, imperialism, tribalistic divisions have been felt in the turmoil of the 20th century.

Thatcher was wrong. Society does exist. And this society is governed by responsibilities, duties and obligations to each other in order to facilitate civilisation, order, democracy, freedom, business transactions, justice, human rights and human progress. We as humans are comprised of more than what is visible on the immediate surface, we are not selfish automatons, things, robots, abstractions, objects unconnected to each other in a narrow limited materialistic order condemned to reap the disorder and chaos of unlimited greed, selfishness, corruption, outrageous abuses, injustices, conflicts, prejudices, bigotry and human stupidity.

Thatcher and Saville: Two Icons of the 1980's and It's Dominant Ideology and Belief System

Chapter 6   Who was Responsible for the Irish, Greek, Spanish, Portuguese and EU wide Financial Crash and Crisis in 2008 ?

'Where there is darkness, let us sow light'

St. Francis of Assisi

Slavery has not been fully abolished in the modern world. In this chapter and the next chapter we will examine this in some detail in the context of debt slavery and modern day feudalism. In the current world of economics, 'responsibility' is a word and activity which is much under-used, misunderstood and misinterpreted. Many events are wrongly presumed to exist naturally or be part of some 'natural order' or part of some childish economic equilibrium, but they are far from natural and in many cases emerge from errors, flaws, mistakes, un-admitted failures, irresponsibility, lack of (economic) education, unintended consequences in accepted, tolerated "norms" or perceptions of normality. And in worst cases emerge from corruption, misdirection, lies and deceit which pervert "normality" and perceptions of such. Yet responsibility must rely on analysis of facts and evidence and the deconstruction and unravelling of complex causes including the irresponsibility and defects in economics and the erroneous opinions, prejudices and viewpoints of economists. This in turn facilitates the fuller understanding of responsibility, and the taking of responsibility, and responsible actions and remedies.

For example, the following must bear responsibility for the speculative boom and crash which destroyed Europe in 2008 :

(i) the European Central Bank which created money out of nothing and gave billions of euros at very low interest rates to Irish, Spanish, Portuguese, Belgian, Greek banks and other European banks for speculation in property, shares, assets and derivatives, and also allowed billions of euros in banking, bondholder and institutional funds to cross national borders and never carried out due diligence and proper regulation, monitoring and checks of the EU banking system. It facilitated, supported and indeed oversaw a massive speculative and credit bubble for several years and did nothing about it. It has consistently failed to deal effectively with over-speculation and the development of financial bubbles which pose systemic risks to economies. Either the ECB and EU institutions were ignorant of the effects of speculation or they knew about it and let it inflate and collapse. In either case they showed a total lack of responsibility.

(ii) German, French, Irish, British, Danish, Finnish, Swiss, American and Dutch banks created billions of euros out of nothing when making loans to gamblers and speculators in EU countries. Money created out of nothing was used to fuel rising property prices, asset prices, shares, commodities and currencies and risky derivatives where a crash in prices was guaranteed and a massive debt crisis and financial crisis also guaranteed. A massive Ponzi scheme was created which was ignored by regulators, governments, economists and oversight bodies. And this irresponsible activity was unregulated at national level and European level. This exposed depositors, shareholders, bondholders, and also the banking system and nation to excessive risks and was totally reckless and irresponsible. The blame ultimately lies with the European Commission and Parliament, the ECB and to a lesser degree with national politicians most of whom were totally ignorant about banking and economics, and integrity and ethics.

Shadow banking firms encompassing hedge funds, financial institutions and investment vehicles also pumped billions of euros into speculation in other EU countries. They did not carry out due diligence and proper investigations and checks. These European banks and investment firms made a business investment and lost, yet expect to be refunded 100% of their investments. After the crash, much of this bank debt was sold in the secondary debt markets at 30 – 50% of face value and bought by "investors" or vulture capitalists, and now the Irish taxpayers are being forced to pay 100% of this debt. Irish taxpayers have been forced to refund speculators and gamblers 100% of their speculative investments ; this is unfair and unjust. The vulture capitalists are making easy profits of 50 – 80% on this bank debt, and it is Irish taxpayers and other EU taxpayers who are being robbed to achieve this.

The European banks which created money out of nothing and lent it to speculators should have taken their losses and negotiated a private bailout deal with the ECB. This would have involved substantial haircuts, write offs and write downs of debt. Hedge funds and others speculators could have negotiated similar deals with the ECB. Taxpayers should not have been forced to pay for bail outs of banks, bondholders, fraudsters, and speculators. Furthermore, the EU authorities should have prosecuted and jailed those guilty of serous financial crimes in the EU. This would have enforced responsibility and moral hazard among the guilty parties. But unfortunately this was not done. One has seen robbery and theft from taxpayers, and cover ups and perversions of the course of justice which enabled bankers and fraudsters to escape justice. This is something which the German politician Mr. Wolfgang Schauble needs to process.

(iii) Under normal conditions Central Banks bail out bankrupt banks, as they are the lender of last resort and it's their historical duty to do so, but the ECB refused to do this after the 2008 crash. The ECB forced the Irish taxpayers to bail out Irish and European banks and speculators. Little Ireland was forced to pay 42% of the total cost of the whole European banking crisis, at a cost of close to €9,000 per person, according to Eurostat. In June 2012, the EU acknowledged that this was too harsh and too burdensome for the Irish and an agreement was made between the EU and the Irish government to refund the Irish government most or all of the bank bail out costs. The Irish Prime Minister Enda Kenny failed to implement this deal in Ireland or possibly forgot to do so.

The Germans and Finns opposed giving the ECB the historical power to bail out bankrupt banks and they forced national governments or taxpayers to be the lenders of last resort to the European banks. This was an extraordinary error and deficiency in Central Banking. The ECB is not a properly constituted and functioning central bank, it is behaving like a political bank expounding the failed theories of some German and Finn politicians obsessed with protecting gamblers, speculators, bondholders and fraudsters while blaming and punishing innocent taxpayers. This greatly increased the national debt in Ireland and the national debts of Spain, Portugal, Belgium, Italy, Cyprus and Greece where governments were forced into bailouts of national and mostly foreign banks, hedge funds, private equity firms, financial institutions and speculators. The ECB failed to fulfil the duties of a central bank and bail out bankrupt banks which posed systemic risks to an economy. This was a major failing of the ECB and of the EU authorities, and was highly irresponsible.

(iv) In the early 2000's, the ECB implemented this easy credit policy and low interest rates to stimulate the German economy, but failed to see that it created massive speculative bubbles, massive borrowing, and unsustainable debt in other EU countries through the euro system and common interest rate system. This over-heated periphery countries and led to a speculative frenzy and bubble which was wrongly presumed to be an investment and jobs boom. German interests were prioritised at the expense of EU countries in the periphery. This exposed wide divergences and imbalances within the EU and the Eurozone and fatal defects in the design of the euro.

(v) The ECB is tasked with maintaining low inflation in the EU and has no powers to interfere in national government policies, fiscal policies and government functions. Yet the ECB failed in this. The ECB allowed large inflationary rises in the prices of shares, assets, property and derivatives and the fuelling of this with easy credit from EU banks and low interest rates during the boom years prior to 2008. Then when the crash came in 2008, the ECB went beyond its powers when it enforced austerity fiscal policies on some national governments (Ireland, Greece, Cyrus, Italy, Spain and Portugal) to bail out banks, bond holders, speculators and fraudsters. The ECB used threats and blackmail to enforce this, including bomb threats in one case and the withdrawal of Emergency Liquidity Assistance (ELA). This interference in government policies, including the use of blackmail, was illegal and unethical under EU laws. Furthermore, the ECB failed in its own mission and its own responsibilities, it failed to control inflation of speculative assets, regulate and oversee the EU banking system, failed to establish a monetary union, failed to act as a lender of last resort to banks, and failed to maintain its independence from governments.

(vi) European parliament and commission and ECB which failed to create and enforce a proper legal and regulatory environment for banking throughout the EU. There was no EU Financial Regulator and authority to oversee the EU banking system and euro currency. Billions of euros flowed across EU borders to banks in Ireland, Spain, Portugal, Belgium, Cyprus and Italy and these massive sums of money were used for speculation in property, shares, assets and derivatives prior to 2008. Yet, there was no EU level regulation and oversight. Greece received billions in loans based on false and fraudulent accounting, assets and collateral prior to 2009, and was assisted in this fraud by certain American investment banks. German banks were exposed to fraudulent CDO's and MBS's from Wall street and there was no EU body to regulate, audit and oversee this and stop the fraud.

Also, there was no New EU Securities and Exchange Body for the EU to investigate insider trading, price rigging, laddering of shares and spinning of shares and assets and other financial crimes. The European parliament and commission and ECB have consistently failed to deal effectively with over-speculation and the development of financial bubbles which pose systemic risks to economies.

(vii) there was no EU level guarantee of deposits in the euro area. In the USA, the FDIC insures and guarantees deposits and protects deposit holders. This was a great failing of the euro currency and it's designers, especially when one considers the systemic risks posed to economies and peoples from Europe-wide speculative bubbles and crashes.

(viii) A Neo Liberal Globalisation, supported by the EU authorities, which caused a stagnation or fall in real wages for most people in North America and Europe, especially the working class and the middle class. This increased the need for debt among such classes in order for them to maintain a 'normal' standard of living. This was a highly important factor in the build up of debt in both Europe and North America, and there are graphs which show a massive increase in private debt and household debt from 1985 onwards. This debt was facilitated by banks creating and loaning new money, international flows of capital, and cynically used by developers and speculators to bid up the prices of houses and other assets far beyond their real worth. This increased the vulnerability of such debt to crashes and other shocks. All of this was supported by politicians, government at national and EU levels, and by regulators and central banks, who ignored the growing dangers of this.

(ix) The bailout loans given to Ireland, Greece, Spain and Portugal costing hundreds of billions of euros have been used to bail out big German, French, Dutch, Swiss, American, British banks, bondholders, hedge funds, brokers, developers and speculators, some of the wealthiest people and families in the world. They have not been used to bail out countries and peoples. These wealthy speculators lost their bets or speculative investments and expected taxpayers to bail them out. And the EU centre enforced this bailout on taxpayers in several countries. The taxpayers of these countries have been left with a massive debt from this bail out of wealthy speculators. In effect, taxpayers were forced to bail out the richest 10% of Europeans. This fact was exposed in the shocking documentary 'State Secrets and Bank Bailouts' in 2013 and is available on the Internet. All Germans, French, Dutch, Finns, and eurocrats in Brussels should watch this important documentary.

This raises the question - Why should Irish taxpayers or Spanish taxpayers bail out big German / French / Dutch / Swiss / American / British banks, bondholders, hedge funds, brokers, developers and speculators who are some of the wealthiest people in the world ?

(x) German, French, British, Danish, Finnish, Swiss, American and Dutch banks, hedge funds, financial institutions and investment vehicles bought large amounts of high yield government bonds in Greece, Italy, Portugal, Spain in the hope of making high returns and gains from them, but they failed to carry out due diligence on these risky investments and make adequate provision for defaults and national bankruptcies. It was assumed that European Union bodies would enforce full payment of yields and asset prices on these countries, even if this involved bankruptcy and the imposing of further debt on these countries, and this in turn caused a moral hazard. Investors were shielded from the risks and protected by EU bodies and EU taxpayers. Another example of privatisation of gains and socialisation of losses.

(xi) EU institutions and senior eurocrats did not declare their conflicts of interest during the speculative boom and during the crash. What were the effects of lobbyists and special interests in EU decisions to fuel the boom with flows of easy credit throughout Europe, low interest rates, deregulation, denial of oversight of the banks and financial system. And what were their conflicts of interest during the crash, and the enforced EU bail out of bankers, speculators and fraudsters by taxpayers in EU countries, and the EU enforced austerity policies which led to the enrichment of vulture funds, hedge funds and private equity firms. We need to establish the relationships and conflicts of interest at EU level. There are 30,000 lobbyists in Brussels lobbying the EU and billions of years are spent every year lobbying eurocrats.

(xii) In addition to the flaws mentioned above, the euro currency tied many countries together in a common currency area, the euro, but made no provision for

(a) financial system failure through over-speculation in assets and excessive speculative debt. This bankrupted the banks and then the governments which attempted to bail them out

(b) excessive capital account and current account flows out of a country, and large deficits in some countries and surpluses in other countries within the common currency.

There was no EU mechanism for resolving (a) and (b) above. This created instability and paralysis at EU level. In the USA, the Federal government acting through government bodies and the Federal Reserve Bank can bail out banks, financial institutions and states which become bankrupt (through speculation in assets or over-borrowing or de-industrialisation), and can provide stimulatory fiscal and monetary measures to improve the economies of individual states. This bailout comes from the Federal government in the form of American taxpayer funds and lower interest rates and new funds from the Federal Reserve Bank, including Quantitative Easing, and represents a transfer from the centre to the periphery. An individual state does not have to bail out the banking system, but all states working together in the form of the Federal government bails out the banks. The centre assists and helps the periphery, and this does not involve the imposition of massive debt and repayments and harsh austerity on individual states. This is how a proper, well structured monetary union is operated.

In the Eurozone, this did not happen. In the Eurozone, an individual nation state was forced to bail out the big European banks, financial institutions, bondholders and hedge funds, and the EU and European Central Bank refused to assist them and refused to carry out the duties of a central bank and central government in a common currency area. Furthermore, the ECB under Claude Trichet refused EU governments the right to 'haircuts' or write downs of bank debt and speculator debt. These measures bankrupted certain nations and put them into Troika bailout programmes. This lead to a transfer of funds from the periphery to the centre, in the form of a massive imposition of debt and debt repayments and the enforcement of austerity in nations in the periphery. It was the complete opposite of the USA, and their currency union. This led to the enforcement of austerity by governments in the middle of a recession in Europe and has worsened the recession in Europe. And contributed to deflation. This has proven to be a disaster.

(xiii) Financial Ratings agencies which failed to carry out their legal duties and provide independent and fair assessments of financial risks ; this gave bondholders and other institutional investors the wrong information and lies. These same failures by regulators were repeated for CDO's, mortgage backed securities, derivatives, shares, property, and other assets, and this played a major role in the bankruptcy of banks, financial institutions, businesses, and countries.

(xiv) the euro currency prevents nations from raising or lowering their interest rates and the currencies to adapt to changing market conditions, such as recession, depression, national bankruptcy, and inflation. National governments are also restricted in their fiscal policies under the euro currency rules, and cannot respond adequately to recessions and depressions. This has removed some very important monetary and fiscal tools from national governments. The result has been an over-valued currency in weak Euro countries and an under-valued currency in stronger Euro countries, and the development and continuation of large trade imbalances and balance of payment deficits in the weaker countries. These imbalances worsened employment, investment, spending, growth and emigration figures in the weaker countries, worsening the recession in Europe, and added to the austerity / bankruptcy arising from the transfer of private banking debt and speculator debt to the state and the taxpayers in the weaker countries. The very means for countries to grow strongly to reduce debt have been taken away from them, while more debt has been piled on to these countries, creating a desperate economic mess. This loss or surrender of national sovereignty and national economic tools has not been replaced with any stabilisation tools or recovery tools, as discussed above. This has forced some governments to become beggars, begging for bailouts from bigger EU countries in the centre. Begging has proved to be disadvantageous to the beggars. The big countries at the centre have imposed massive debt and repayments and harsh economic conditions including austerity on national governments and nations, and a worsening of economic recession and deflation.

(xv) The EU allowed Greece to enter the euro currency which has strict debt, deficit and other requirements, yet the EU refused to analyse Greece's suitability in terms of tax collection, tax fairness, levels of tax evasion and corruption, the accuracy and integrity of government accounting and reports, bribery and corruption of government, the quality of collateral offered for public loans, public sector expenditure and wages, and levels of corruption in this sector. The EU's failure to do this, led to events which collapsed the Greece economy in 2009 and subsequent years and damaged the credibility of the euro currency.

More specifically, Greek government officials and certain investment banks worked together to devise frauds and false accounts and collateral based on false accounting to access international loans. There was no oversight by the EU authorities and by the Greek regulatory authorities. No persons were punished or held accountable for criminal fraud. This was worsened by the fact that tax evasion was widespread in Greece, and the means to pay back government debt was defective.

(xvi) Irish bank executives who engaged in fraudulent accounting, and were criminally negligent and reckless in their lending and operated the banks to provide large bonuses for themselves and other executives involved in speculation and corrupt dealing. Only 2 were criminally prosecuted and jailed for these financial crimes. Many others escaped justice.

The banking whistleblower Jonathan Sugarman tried to expose this fraud and criminality in Ireland prior to 2008 but he was ignored and fobbed off by the Financial Regulator and by Irish government ministers and politicians. Readers should read the story of Jonathan Sugarman as it explains how the Irish banking system really worked prior to the crash in 2008 and still works. Irish taxpayers should not have been forced to bail out fraudsters and criminals.

(xvii) the big accountancy firms and auditors approved of false accounting and several accounting frauds in the banks in their audits and financial reports in Ireland other EU countries. There have been no massive court fines imposed on accountancy firms to cover the bank bailout costs, and no accountants have been charged by their accountancy bodies and no accountants have been prosecuted in court.

(xviii) the Irish financial regulator who did not regulate the banking system, was incompetent and corruptly accepted large payments from the government for non performance of his duties, and the Irish Central Bank which did not oversee the banking system yet ran numerous so called "stress tests" which turned out to be a tissue of lies and deception on each occasion.

(xix) a financial system where governments are prevented from printing their own currency and are forced to borrow money from central banks and private banks which print money out of nothing and charge interest on it. A system which creates massive levels of government debt and business and private debt. In Ireland's case this amounted to over 660% of GDP for government, business, banking and households in 2011.

(xx) the issues raised in Chapter 2 above in relation to excessive concentrations of power in the EU centre and the disempowering of nations and the periphery.

All of these parties bear responsibility, and all should and must play a part in rectifying the situation.

Alternative Courses of Action

There were alternatives. Irish and other national governments in Europe could have done the following:

1) Use Quantitative Easing by a national government or national central bank or ECB to purchase distressed assets from the banks, recapitalise the banks, pay off the bondholders at a discount, and fund the bank bail out activities. Taxpayer's money should not be used to do this. And increased government borrowing higher national debt should not be used to do this. And place a debt repayment upon the bankrupt banks which can be saved, where the banks would pay back the government for bailing them out.

2) Put the totally bankrupt banks into receivership and bring about an orderly bankruptcy

3) Guarantee the depositors and ensure their deposits are protected up to a value of 400,000 euros per person. Allow the ATM's to work and deposits and withdrawals to take place while the bank is in receivership and being prepared to be sold off or closed down

4) Fire the executives responsible for the bubble and crash, fire them, and replace them with honest, reliable and accountable executives who will be held accountable

5) Government apply a levy on future bank profits, shareholder dividends, and executive salaries to pay for this bail out

6) Give hair cuts to senior bondholders of 35% or more. Give junior bondholders a haircut of 50%

7) Pay off the creditors at a discount or offer them shares in a new bank

8) Write off the bad debts and sue bankers involved in fraud and criminality. And pay off some liabilities and creditors via Quantitative Easing.

9) Allow share capital to fall to 1 cent in the euro. Then the state could acquire it, repair it and prepare it for sale to the private sector.

10) Sell off the assets of the banks to other banks, including offices, ATM's and deposit accounts

11) Prosecute and jail the corrupt bankers and regulators

This solution does not involve taxpayers paying for the bail out of banks, financial institutions, speculators and bondholders, and does not involve government austerity policies.

Section 2 Solutions Based on Causality : Building Economic Democracy

Chapter 7   Ending Massive Debt Enslavement and Austerity & Learning from the New Deal, Marshall Aid Programme and London Debt Agreement (1953)

'Man is born free but is everywhere in chains'
Jean Jacques Rousseau

'And Jesus went into the temple of God, and cast out all them that sold and bought in the temple, and overthrew the tables of the money changers'
The Bible

"Banking was conceived in iniquity and was born in sin. The Bankers own the earth. Take it away from them, but leave them the power to create deposits, and with the flick of the pen they will create enough deposits to buy it back again. However, take it away from them, and all the great fortunes like mine will disappear and they ought to disappear, for this would be a happier and better world to live in. But, if you wish to remain the slaves of Bankers and pay the cost of your own slavery, let them continue to create currency."
Sir Josiah Stamp, Director of the Bank of England, Speech at the Commencement Address of the University of Texas in 1927. Ref: The Legalized Crime of Banking (1958) by Silas W. Adams

'one penny invested at the time of the birth of Jesus Christ, about 2,000 years ago, and paying a compound interest rate of 5% would produce wealth worth the weight of 3 earths in gold. Compound interest is not sustainable.'
An Economist

Relearning the Lessons of the Past - A Short and Important History Lesson

What crisis dominates your society ? the hospitals crisis, the healthcare crisis, the housing crisis, the homeless crisis, the evictions crisis, long traffic jams and lack of infrastructure investment, the pensions crisis, the insurance crisis, farming crisis, military pay crisis, the national debt crisis, budget deficit crisis, currency crisis, inflation or deflation crisis, war / conflict crisis, the policing crisis, the crime and drugs crisis, etc.. All of these emerge from a few common factors. The most important core factors are debt or money created out of nothing (when loans are made by private banks), and compound interest which is not created with the new money and must be extracted from the existing money supply. These core factors fuel speculation in the prices of assets, shares, land, property, housing, currencies, etc. and a rise in the cost of living and in the prices of goods and services. These in turn feeds into other factors such as inflation, speculative bubbles and crashes, political corruption and vast tax evasion, deflation, taxpayer bail outs of banks and speculators, increases in national debt, and government austerity combined with cutbacks in public services, wages and increases in taxation. It is the core factors – debt and compound interest and how they are created, used, abused, misused which creates the crisis in all societies.

Prior to American Independence and for a few decades after, Americans used a local currency called 'scrip' to buy goods and services locally. This scrip acted as a Promissory note between the producer / seller and the buyer and no interest was charged. A fair price was charged for works, goods and services and there was no speculation and price rigging. Banks were not involved. Some state governments printed scrip to pay for basic government administration and services. This money was spent into state economies creating jobs, sales, business growth etc.. This scrip encouraged work, enterprise, production, commerce and trade and proved to be very effective and successful at the time. It cut out commercial bankers and central bankers, and provided debt free and interest free money for people, businesses and local government, and an important line of credit and purchasing power for ordinary Americans and for the economic development of farms, small industries, localities and regions. The American founding fathers all used scrip and supported it, with Benjamin Franklin being one of its strongest supporters. There are many accounts of Benjamin Franklin's praise of scrip or colonial currency on the Internet and in historical records, and I would encourage readers to access these and read them.

However, the British government opposed this scrip at the time as British banks and the English Central Bank created money out of nothing and lent it to businesses, individuals, families and government and kept them debt enslaved. This debt enslavement had negative effects in Britain – mass poverty, destitution, homelessness, unemployment and low levels of demand and supply were common in Britain at the time. The British class system ensured that the richest 2% controlled most of the wealth and political power. The British government passed the Currency act in 1764 so as to stop the use of scrip in North America and this severely restricted scrip and caused a large reduction in the scrip currency in North America. This created an economic depression in America, many business failures and there was an increase in unemployment, homelessness, destitution and in the numbers in poor houses. The British sought to centralise currency creation via the Bank of England (the central bank) and commercial banks and eradicate American scrip. This created great anger and resentment in the American colonies.

In fact, one of the four reasons for the American War of Independence in 1776, was the British attempt to abolish scrip and deprive Americans of the right to create and use their own currency, scrip, at the time. The writings of Benjamin Franklin and others confirm this.

"We would have gladly borne the little tax on tea and other matters, had it not been that they took from us our money, which created great unemployment and dissatisfaction. Within a year, the poor houses were filled. The hungry and homeless walked the streets everywhere." Benjamin Franklin

During the American War of Independence (1776 -1784), the American soldiers were paid in Continental notes, a type of scrip. For the Founding Fathers in America, the right to print and to use their own currency was a fundamental part of American Independence and of American commerce. The right of nations to create their own currency was and still is a vital part of national sovereignty. This lesson from history has been forgotten in modern America, Europe and other countries.

The American Constitution stated that only Congress would have the power to create money. This was an important protection for America and ordinary Americans. During the early 1800's some bankers and business people tried to take this power away from the US Congress and give it to themselves, and create a private monopoly for money creation, in the form of a central bank. President Thomas Jefferson, President James Madison and President Andrew Jackson strongly opposed these bankers and opposed a private central bank, which would have the power to create money out of nothing and lend it to government (and businesses), charge interest on this debt, and reduce government down to beggars begging for their own currency, and place massive debt on American taxpayers. Attempts were made to establish a private central bank at the time, but after a short period of operation, the government refused to renew the charter for it and it closed. Powers were restored back to Congress for a while. Free of central banks, President Jefferson was able to balance the Federal budget for 8 years, while President Jackson was able to achieve balanced budgets and pay off the national debt in 1834.

During the American Civil war in the 1860's President Abraham Lincoln used this Constitutional power and Congress printed debt free and interest free money, the greenbacks, and used it to finance the war effort. He also raised taxes and sold war bonds. These measures paid for soldiers, military equipment, boats, war supplies, food, etc. and helped the Union side win the war. The money printed (greenbacks) was based on the wealth, credit worthiness and productive capacity of the USA. President Lincoln's government printed 400 million dollars 'greenbacks' (the exact amount being $449,338,902) during the American Civil War. The government did not borrow this money from a Central bank or commercial banks. This saved the American taxpayers over $850 million, when one includes interest over several decades.

In fact, President Lincoln refused to borrow money from London banks and New York banks at rates of 24 - 30% interest. Lincoln's actions enraged the powerful banking and financial interests in London, England and New York. Here is excerpt from an editorial in the London Times in 1865

"If this mischievous financial policy, which has its origin in North America, shall become endurated [sic] down to a fixture, then that Government will furnish its own money without cost. It will pay off debts and be without debt. It will have all the money necessary to carry on its commerce. It will become prosperous without precedent in the history of the world. The brains, and wealth of all countries will go to North America. That country must be destroyed or it will destroy every monarchy on the globe."
London Times, 1865

President Lincoln was assassinated before he could extend the money printing to the period of peace and reconstruction after the Civil War. After the war, it would have been possible for Lincoln to continue government printing of money within certain inflationary or deflationary limits or through links to the Gold Standard to provide enough money to grow the young American economy, as provided by for under the US Constitution. These greenbacks would have provided sufficient money to grow and enhance the industrial revolution in America in the late 19th century and early 20th century, providing the credit and liquidity and aggregate demand for industrial and agricultural expansion and for innovation and productivity and the necessary liquidity and money supply expansion to overcome crashes and downturns.

There is some suspicion that bankers may have played a role in Lincoln's assassination as shortly after his assassination, private 'national banks' took over the money printing power from government. This was against the US Constitution which gave that power solely to the US Congress. Obviously this gave national banks a new power which they fully exploited, and it drove many state banks out of business in the late 19th century and early 20th century. And the US returned to the Gold Standard and convertibility of notes to gold in the decades after the Civil War which had the effect of imposing deflationary and austerity pressures on a growing and expanding young US economy. Later studies in monetary economics showed that lack of money or scarcity of money or liquidity at a time of industrial and economic growth can bring about instabilities which are compounded by over speculation and debt based on it which bring about bubbles and crashes. And certainly after crashes, these studies show the money supply needs to be increased to counter the deflation and retrenchment caused by panics and crashes. Money is the lifeblood of an economy particularly for a young and growing economy such as America in the period after 1865. The deflationary gold standard worked against this and deepened deflation, austerity and retrenchment

The Robber Baron era coincided with a high concentration of economic power in the USA, mainly in the hands of a few national banks, the railway companies, the big wall street firms and big steel and oil companies with multiple links and cross share holdings between these. It was a period where the use of private bank created money was funnelled into speculation, bubbles and crashes, deflation and asset stripping, increased returns to creditors and savers, tariff protection, anti competitive practises and more industry concentration, all of which contributed to the accumulation of massive wealth by a tiny privileged minority.

Then in 1913 a central bank, the Federal Reserve was set up. This replaced the national banks and took over money printing from them. The Federal Reserve was given power to print the US money (currency) and lend it to the US government at an interest rate, and taxpayers had to repay this loan and compounded interest over time. This is known as the national debt. This money or debt was created out of nothing by the Federal Reserve. It could also lend money to private banks. This private entity, the Federal Reserve consists of 12 Federal Reserve banks, one for each region of the USA. Several private commercial banks in each region own shares in the Federal Reserve bank in their region. And they receive dividends from the Federal Reserve bank in their region and have a right to elect boards and carry out other shareholder activities. So the Federal Reserve is privately owned by private banks in the 12 regions of the USA ; it is a private entity and this has been affirmed in court cases. The governing board of the Federal Reserve in Washington DC is appointed by the President of the USA.

Today, these loans to the government are known as the bonds market or treasuries market where the government borrows new money from the Federal Reserve, other banks and investors, and this is added to the national debt. A bond is a promise to pay back the lender, though the lender has the advantage of being able to create money out nothing and charge interest on it. As the national debt increased since 1913, this proved to be very profitable for the small number of banks and bankers who owned the Federal Reserve. The First World War provided the first major boost to the profits of the Federal Reserve, while stock market bubbles, another world war, regional wars, colonial wars, and massive increases in government expenditure in the post war Keynesian era and Cold War era greatly inflated profits. Private banks profiteered from their shareholdings in the Federal Reserve bank and from making loans, money created out of nothing with compound interest, to the warring parties and war industries and to government social programmes an infrastructure programmes . In the case of war, these banks even funded both sides of the conflict to increase their profits, and this became a feature of wars from the early 19th century to the present day.

This creation of the Federal Reserve transferred real economic power from the aforementioned national banks to the 12 regional Federal Reserve banks which comprised the Federal Reserve system. Thus the Constitutional power of government to print money was blocked again, and given to private bankers who held shares and ownership of the Federal Reserve system, and profiteered from this change. This has continued to the present day, with trillions of dollars in US national debt and high interest payments going to a small number of banks and bankers who own and operate the Federal Reserve. This is one of the most profitable businesses in the world, especially when one considers that this money is created out of nothing.

The Federal Reserve has not been audited since it was set up in 1913, yet it has received trillions of dollars in tax monies to pay off US national debt and it has used a few trillion dollars to fund bailouts of (favoured and politically connected) bankers and private businesses after crashes. There are genuine concerns that some of this money has been misappropriated yet there have been no audits to establish the scale of this. Other similar private organisations and businesses and even private business people are subject to regular audits. Central banks in other countries and the BIS are also not subject to audits and oversight. This is a scandal when one considers the trillions of taxpayer dollars / euros used to prop up these organisations

During the first few years of World War One the British government printed debt free and interest free money to finance the war. This was known as the 'Bradbury pound'. This paid for soldiers, equipment and war supplies. This proved to be very successful. However Lloyd George was contacted privately by bankers and asked to stop this and to begin borrowing from private banks at high interest rates. Lloyd George borrowed the money from the banks and put Britain into massive debt by the end of the war. Britain's National Debt went up from £650 million in 1914 to a staggering £7,500 million in 1919. This was the subject of a notable book 'The Financiers and the Nation' by the Rt. Hon. Thomas Johnston, ex-Lord Privy Seal. It was written in 1934 and republished in 1994.

The following chart shows the explosion in Canadian national debt after it decided to stop printing money (Quantitative Easing) and borrowed it from banks in 1977. This represents a massive new debt tax burden imposed upon all Canadians. Other countries have similar charts marking the period that government stopped printing money and the period it started borrowing from private banks, including private central banks.

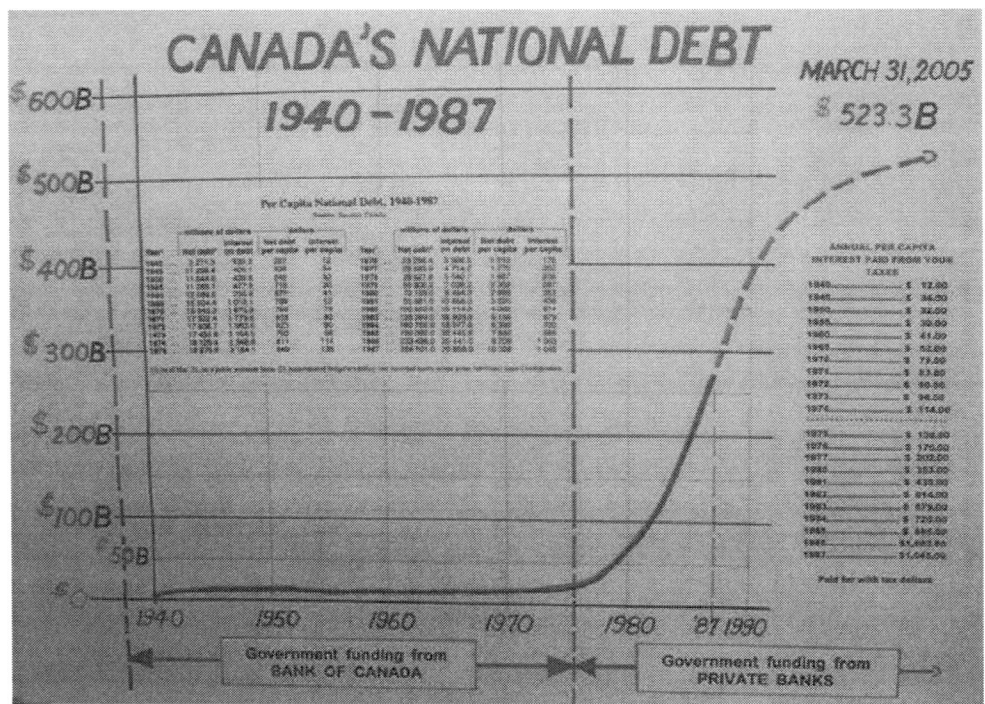

Source Jack Biddell, Canada ©

Since the Bretton Woods system broke down in 1971, currencies are no longer tied to gold. This means that private banks can create unlimited amounts of fiat money backed up by nothing. One has seen a massive increase in the money supply and accompanying debt (which is newly created money) since 1972. The chart above confirms this for Canada and this also applies to most countries worldwide. Throughout the world, private central banks, semi private central banks, state central banks, and later, commercial banks took over the printing of money and creation of money over the last 200 years and now they have the power to create as much as they want. Banks, both central banks and ordinary private banks create this money out of nothing and lend it to government, businesses and individuals and charge interest on it. Today, approximately 97% of money is created by commercial banks when they make loans to people for mortgages, businesses and governments, and 3% is created by central banks, according to a recent report issued by the Bank of England. This has deprived governments of the right, often the Constitutional and legal right, to print and create debt free money and interest free money. This Quantitative Easing by commercial banks and central banks has been in operation for many decades now. The large accumulations of debt in countries worldwide need to be seen in the context of a private banking system which has the power to create money out of nothing, loan it and charge interest on it, and make substantial profits, and use loans (or newly created money to stimulate speculation in asset prices, bubbles and make massive profits from this, and bring about financial

270

crashes, bail outs and government austerity policies and load more debt on to taxpayers backs. Its a system which creates more and more massive and unsustainable debt, all of which enslave peoples and nations. This is modern day slavery.

Governments and democracies have been disempowered and weakened by this loss of power to create money. President Abraham Lincoln had the following to say about the 'greenbacks', and the right of governments to print money.

The government should create issue and circulate all the currency and credit needed to satisfy the spending power of the government and the buying power of consumers..... The privilege of creating and issuing money is not only the supreme prerogative of Government, but it is the Government's greatest creative opportunity. By the adoption of these principles, the long-felt want for a uniform medium will be satisfied. The taxpayers will be saved immense sums of interest, discounts and exchanges. The financing of all public enterprises, the maintenance of stable government and ordered progress, and the conduct of the Treasury will become matters of practical administration. The people can and will be furnished with a currency as safe as their own government. Money will cease to be the master and become the servant of humanity. Democracy will rise superior to the money power.
President Abraham Lincoln, Senate document 23, Page 91. 1865

The Seven Great Interlinked Issues Concerning Debt Today

The issues mentioned in the previous section continue to haunt most countries worldwide. These issues play a dominant role in today's world and its myriad economic and social problems. There are seven major economic impediments or problems which must be addressed and overcome, and which are the source of much dynamic disequilibrium, economic disequilibrium and indeed social disequilibrium and hardship in the world today ; these are the 7 types of Debt Trap :

1. Debt Trap Arising from the Nature of Debt Creation and Money Creation

In earlier Chapters we saw that 97% of all money is created of nothing when banks give out loans and mortgages, and we have examined the fraud inherent in this. Massive debt and the oppressive burden of debt servicing lies at the root of the Irish and EU Financial Crisis and continuing austerity, deflation and recession. Non EU countries such as UK, USA and other countries have a similar debt problem. Central to this is the fraudulent money creation process and banking system which enables commercial banks to create money out of nothing and lend this to governments, businesses, individuals and charge interest on it, creating massive government debt and private debt. Central banks, many of them semi private banks also create money out of nothing and lend it to governments at an interest rate. Sadly, governments have been deprived of the traditional right and in some cases Constitutional and legal right to print money or create money to fund itself. So commercial banks and central banks have taken over this government activity of creating money out of nothing and have made large profits from this over time. While governments and taxpayers are left with massive debts. Taxpayers are then forced to pay taxes and other levies and charges to pay off this government debt to the banks. This is one aspect of the Debt Trap.

As banks are allowed to create money out of nothing, individuals, families, businesses and governments are forced to rely on banks for money for survival and the more money banks lend to governments and individuals and businesses, the more debt is created. And compound interest multiplies this debt over time. Furthermore, bank debt fuels speculation in house prices forcing many people to take on higher and higher debt to buy homes and other essentials of life. This is another aspect of the same Debt Trap and is the essence of debt slavery.

In the Eurozone, after the 2008 crash, the ECB refused to lend to governments via the bonds market, or bail them out via Quantitative easing (money printing), yet the Bank of England and Federal Reserve had full powers to do so. The ECB and EU authorities foolishly enforced this bail out burden on the taxpayers within certain countries and created much unnecessary economic and social hardship in Eurozone countries and deepened the recession / depression during this time. German politicians enforced this on the EU, putting German interests ahead of European interests. Eurozone governments themselves had long lost the power to print money or have their national central banks do so. This changed for the ECB in 2015 due to the scale of austerity, deflation and economic stagnation inflicted on Eurozone countries, and the rules were relaxed to enable lending to governments at low interest rates. Yet this only increased the debt burden further. This showed the level of debt dependency and debt enslavement which exists and how it undermines the real economy.

Commercial banks create money out of nothing when making loans, then they supposedly destroy money when it is repaid back. This inflates the money supply, contributing to economic bubbles, and then contracts the money supply when repayments are made or during crashes when austerity, difficult repayments, foreclosures, evictions and asset stripping are commonplace. This contraction or suction of money out of the system means there is not enough money circulating in the system for debtors to pay off debts worsening crashes, recessions and depressions. This inbuilt instability adversely affects demand and consumption and investment levels. It imposes Debt Traps and Debt Dependency on countries as a condition for economic growth. This imposes significant constrained, unrealised, unmet supply and constrained, unrealised, unmet demand or deficiencies in effective demand, making 'equilibrium' impossible. It is a strong dynamic disequilibrium factor.

Another aspect to this conundrum is that banks do not create interest money when creating new money and lending it out, and this means there can never be enough money in the system to pay off the debt. There is a chronic shortage of money in the system to pay off both debt and interest. This creates a classic Interest Trap, which is quite fatal to economies when one considers that interest compounds over time so that the borrower often pays back 150% - 400% of the original loan. This compounding of interest, sucks money out of the system and also creates money shortages, and this affects consumption and investment and negatively affects the business cycle intensifying and deepening it depending on debt levels. Compound interest adds to the cost of production, mining / extraction, farming, distribution, storing, selling and buying goods and services ; it is a parasite on society. As overall debt increases in society, interest payments impose higher costs on goods and services in the economy. Interest hurts the real economy affecting investment and supply levels, consumption levels, and aggregate demand. Studies by Margrit Kennedy and other economists show that in addition to imposing additional costs on businesses, workers and society, interest is a form of 'trickle up' economics where the wealth and income trickles up to the wealthiest 5% in society [33]

For example, the interest on Ireland's national debt is €5 - 7 billion per year and the interest on the UK national debt is £46 billion per year and the interest on total government, business and household debt in the UK is 200 billion per year ; these are massive costs. Another good example - one penny invested at the time of the birth of Jesus Christ, about 2,000 years ago, and paying a compound interest rate of 5% would produce wealth worth the weight of 3 earths in gold. Compound interest is not sustainable.

As you can see above, it is impossible for governments, businesses and individuals to totally pay off all debt or attain balanced budgets for a significant period of time as there is not enough money (created) in circulation to pay off the debt and it's interest. And there is a constant need to create more and more debt in the form of new money by banks for the system to survive and grow. The maintenance and growth of the economic system itself is dependent on money which is created through debt – it is a money system based on debt ; Money = Debt. The circulation of money is based on debt and interest, and this must be replenished with new debt and interest to replace any principal and interest which is paid down, in order to keep this circulation of debt money flowing. This system is perverse and has many perverse consequences. The only option is to remain in debt and suck increasing amounts of money out of the economic system to pay off and service this debt through high taxes, state levies and charges, mortgage payments, loan repayments, interest charges and fees, capitalizing the rents from land, natural resources and capital into interest payments, anti competitive business practices, rip offs, economic rents, and also through evictions, foreclosures and asset stripping, etc. creating imbalances and instabilities which can prevent economies reaching their true potential, which then deflate economies, create insufficient aggregate demand, and over time force business bankruptcies, asset stripping and foreclosures, personal bankruptcies, loss of jobs, unemployment, etc. And the answer is to create more debt so as to pay off existing debt and reduce the negative effects of the existing debt and it's repayment. Loading debt upon debt and loading more burdens onto ordinary people. And compound interest multiplies this unsustainable debt over time, creating greater and greater imbalances and instability. This ponzi scheme has to be funded from an insufficient amount of money in circulation which makes it physically impossible to pay off most debt. The fact that there can never be enough money in circulation to pay off all or most debt and interest means that debt slavery is engrained in the economic system. A never ending system of enslavement to debt. This is the most important aspect of economics and politics, which every person needs to know. This private creation of money and debt by banks has led to a Debt Beneficiary Class and a Debt Dependent class with one acting as a parasite on the other.

Let us consider the legal and Constitutional angle. The relationship between a borrower and producer / seller creates a position of debt between these two parties and they issue a promissory note between them. This is for the sum of the principal. People create money in the form of a promissory note. Banks intervene in this relationship, illegally take and launder the promissory note and then create money out of nothing equal to the value of the promissory note and charge interest on this money created out of nothing. The bank brings no consideration to the private contract between the borrower and the producer / seller, and thus the bank is not party to the contract.

Loans, mortgages and business contracts are based on contracts where contracting parties provide consideration (money or assets) to bind the contract. Banks create money out of nothing when they lend money to a borrower. Banks do not own the money they lend to borrowers, the money created out of nothing means nobody really owns this money created out of nothing. It is a fiction, an invention, a type of fraud where money is created out of nothing. This means the bank provides no consideration in the contract, this breaches contract law. Under contract law, one cannot lend something which one does not have. This is contract fraud, and grounds for declaring contract null and void. This is explained further on Mike Montagne's excellent web site http://www.perfecteconomy.com and in the works of Professor Richard A. Werner.

2. The Speculative Debt Trap and Bank Bail outs Trap

It was also bank debt which created the speculative bubbles and the over pricing of assets, shares, homes and derivatives and the many frauds and financial crimes and the massive conversion of company equity into debt through junk bonds and loans which is loading down many businesses with excessive debt. After the crash it was taxpayers and governments who funded the vast, wasteful government bail outs of banks, speculators, fraudsters and the rich and funded other expenditures for special political interests (military industrial complex, Deep State etc.). Speculative Debt is a very destructive debt trap as it creates asset values and derivatives which are far too high and are multiples of their true worth and far beyond the ability of persons or businesses to repay them, due to their size and the crashes they create. Yet this is tolerated by naïve and gullible persons who believe that the 'free market' is always right and who are incapable of understanding rigged markets, rigged and leveraged prices, skewed markets and dynamic disequilibrium. This is discussed in Chapter 4.

Austerity policies, to bail out banks, speculators and fraudsters, include higher taxes and charges and new taxes and charges, severe cutbacks in education, schools and Universities, hospitals and healthcare, infrastructure, pensions and social security, social housing, disability services, elderly care, policing and the justice system, etc. And all of this is accompanied by a deluded 'austerity mentality' which believes that austerity will lead to growth in the far off future, yet austerity destroys growth, destroys output, earnings and incomes and the ability to pay down debt. This is discussed later in the Chapter. Austerity ignores the fraudulent and criminal system used to create massive speculative debts. It is a fact that massive debt and austerity policies are the means by which nations and whole peoples are enslaved and robbed off their wages, their savings, their pensions, their private property, their public services and health services, their natural resources, their homes, their local businesses, etc.. And the bizarre purpose of austerity policies is to return economies to more speculative booms and more crashes. A non stop process of debt accumulation and theft from productive businesses, the working and middle classes, from the elderly and disabled.

The chart below depicts the scale of the problem facing humanity

- **Review of World Financial Instability.**
-
- **Summary: (World: US Dollars: Approx).**
- 11.   Total Value of Derivatives (Notional):   1,200 Trillion (1.2 Quadrillion).
- 10.   Total Value of All Assets (Fin. /Real Estate): 318 Trillion (8. Plus 9.)
- 9.   Total Value of Financial Assets: 198 Trillion
- 8.   Total Value of Real Estate: 120 Trillion
- 7.   All Debt. (Owned by Banks):   257 Trillion (5. Plus 6.).
- 6.   Total Priv. Debt. (Owned by Banks):   193 Trillion (Priv./Corporate).
- 5.   Total Gov. Debt. (Owned by Banks):   64   Trillion
- 4.   World GDP: 60   Trillion
- 3.   Total Value of Derivatives (Cash Val.):   20   Trillion
- 2.   Total Value of Circulating Currency: 4   Trillion
- 1.   Total Value of Gold Reserves: 1.5   Trillion
-
- Ref: World Gold Council Dec. 2013.

When this speculative bubble crashes it could crash the world economy. And the bail outs and austerity policies would rob and enslave nations, peoples and taxpayers for 30 years or more.

3. The Debt Trap arising from the stagnation or fall in real wages while prices and costs of living and debt servicing remain high and keep rising from Economic Renter activities

Globalisation's and Automation's 'race to the bottom' has been sucking jobs, income, wealth, capital, productivity related wages and growth out of developed countries and some developing countries, forcing down wages and living standards and destroying jobs, carers, livelihoods, families, individuals, communities, regions and nations, creating ghettos, industrial wastelands, crime and deep social divisions in the process. And doing the same to developing and third world countries through dumping of subsidised products, trips agreements, profit repatriation and redirection to tax havens, capital flight, pollution of land, food, water and air, speculation and crashes, the imposition of massive debt and repayments on countries, increasing concentrations of wealth, etc. which are discussed in more detail in Chapters 2, 4 and 5. This creates and increases massive unsustainable debt through the following:

(a) As real incomes stagnate or fall from increased globalisation, automation and the 'race to the bottom', and the economic rents imposed by the FIRE sector (Finance Insurance and Real Estate) private debt has increased to maintain living standards in developed countries. Several research studies show that real wages have declined in the USA since the late 1980's. In chapter 5 some statistics were provided about this, including Pikkey's recent finding that real income for the bottom 50% stagnated for 30 years while it increased by 300% for the top 1% in the USA. There are similar patterns emerging in other Anglo Saxon countries and those following Neo Liberal economic policies. There is a direct link between the stagnation in real wages and the accumulation of massive private debt. There are many graphs and charts which show a direct correlation between this. This debt accumulation was accelerated further by imposed higher prices for goods and services, an inflation which has been acceptable to governments (who claimed to oppose inflation). Higher prices from:

(i) speculation in the prices of assets such as homes which outgrew stagnant real wages

(ii) the dominance of monopolies, oligopolies, restrictive practises, and cartels (Economic Renters or Rentiers) and the FIRE sector which charge high prices and extract economic rents for many goods and services. See Chapter 4.

(iii) interest payments which impose added costs on production, extraction, warehousing, distribution, storage, selling and purchasing

(iv) the scaling back of government funding for education, healthcare, childcare, public infrastructure, which forces many people to take on new debt to fund these necessities. Government cutbacks often used to bail out bankers and speculators and provide other corporate welfare and subsidies.

(v) the selling off of government assets and infrastructure to the FIRE sector and the charging of monopoly prices by private firms.

These higher prices combined with stagnant wages have forced many middle income and lower income individuals and families into substantial debt. This includes home mortgages, student debt, credit card debt, health insurance debt, medical bills debt, term loans, car loans etc. This system of stagnant or reduced wages and higher debt provided for the simultaneous enrichment of the speculator class, the monopoly and cartel class, and the banking class, the richest 5%, and the impoverishment of the bottom 95% of a population.

(b) Major Clifford Hugh Douglas the inventor of 'social credit', in the early 20th century, also pointed out this gap between the prices of all products and services produced on one side and the wages of workers and consumers on the other side in a given country. This gap is bridged not by increasing wages or reducing prices but by increasing debt and the accumulation of more debt. There is a lack of purchasing power which is resolved by creating more and more debt to fund the purchasing power which has become depleted, creating a vicious cycle.

(c) stagnant or failing real wages reduces the ability to pay off debt for private individuals / families and for government in developed countries, and this leads to cutbacks in consumption by individuals / families and for government it leads to more austerity policies, and vicious cutbacks in basic public services accompanied by tax rises. The resulting combined effects of economic contraction (austerity) further diminishes the ability to pay off debt and this leads to more debt being created to pay off old debt, and to maintain purchasing power and basic living standards for ordinary people and funding for government services.

4. The Debt trap Arising from Globalisation and Tax Evasion by banks, large corporates and very wealthy

Globalisation's 'race to the bottom' involves:

(a) intense tax competition and government grants and subsidies competition to attract international capital to a country. This is proving expensive for countries and is leading to an erosion of the tax base and to increased debt for governments and countries

(b) lower worker wages and elimination of worker benefits. This is leading to an erosion of the wages base for workers and to increased debt and/or poverty for workers. This is discussed in point 3 above. This also affects tax revenues from labour and consumption

(c) offshore tax havens which hold wealth estimated be over $40 trillion and suck hundreds of billions of dollars out of economies annually

(d) governments subsidising speculators, bondholders, corporate raiders, and banks through tax exemption for interest payments, lower corporate taxes or zero taxes for speculators, generous depreciation allowances (even for properties which rise in price and value), debt allowances, false declarations of losses, and very low or zero capital gains taxes

All of these deplete the tax base and reduce government revenues in many countries. Large scale tax competition between countries has been accompanied by tax evasion and tax havens which are extracting vast wealth from developed countries and developing countries and diminishing the ability of the government and peoples to invest in their own countries and build up their public infrastructure, their public water systems, their hospitals and schools, their investment base, technology and productivity base and native productive capital and human capital base. This type of globalised tax evasion is also a major contributing factor to the creation of more and more debt, as governments borrow more to make up for the fall in tax revenues. Furthermore, the ability to pay off debt is reduced in developed countries, thus leading to an increased need for governments to borrow more money to pay off old debt and maintain basic government services. And this in turn creates

(a) more austerity policies, and cutbacks in education, schools and Universities, hospitals and healthcare, infrastructure, public water systems, pensions and social security, social housing, disability services, elderly care, policing and the justice system, etc.

(b) new taxes, levies and charges, and increases to existing taxes, charges and levies which rob the taxpayers

In summary, all this leads to more taxes for those people who pay taxes, more government cutbacks, more cuts to hospitals, healthcare, education, social services, disability services, pensions, police, courts, fire services, roads, etc. and the worst forms of political corruption, often termed 'pay to play politics', also called 'gombeen economics' , 'crony capitalism', 'auction politics', 'bribery and corruption of public officials', which is highly destructive of democracy and freedom in today's world. Some right wing politicians want to abolish social security, pensions, unemployment benefit, disability rights, public healthcare and destroy their own countries, but they ignore the vast tax evasion of the speculators, the bankers, the Rentiers, the big corporates and wealthy amounting to trillions of dollars. This rhetoric from right wing politicians sounds like treason and treachery and should be treated as such by the legal system and the general public. This is the debt trap emerging from globalised tax evasion and avoidance.

5. The Debt Trap and Related Asset Stripping Trap

Massive debt and accompanying economic bubbles and crashes followed by government austerity policies created an environment of reduced consumption and potential for consumption, a collapse in credit growth, a fall in new productive investment, falling sales and profits, higher unemployment and an environment of deflation. This deflation was accompanied by debt overhang (from the bubble period) and widespread deleveraging of private debt and government debt, which worsened economic conditions for individuals, families, businesses and organisations and led to increasing levels of desperation and asset stripping and debt deflation. This austerity-driven asset stripping could be seen in the increased rate of home evictions, foreclosures, the sale of repossessed homes at a discount, mass deleveraging and negative equity for many properties, the sale of large amounts of mortgages and loans to vulture funds, the acquisition of failed business assets and their sale on markets, the activities of corporate raiders, junk bonds and asset stripping viable companies, the sale of family silver and jewellery and the increasing importance of pawnbrokers, the sale of natural resources to multinational firms and banks at a big discount, the acquisition of farms and their assets and the sale of parts of them or all of them to others, the closure of some colleges and educational institutions and the sale of their properties and other assets at a discount. These homes, businesses, natural resources, and farms are usually bought quite cheaply, for 30-40 cents on the dollar by vulture funds, private equity funds and hedge funds, held for a few months or 1-3 years and 'milked' for money in the form of higher rent, interest, repayments, and then sold for inflated prices and profits for 100 cents or more on the dollar. The taxpayers maintain the value of such assets by pumping money into government sponsored bail outs and state agencies managing bail outs to prop up the prices of these distressed assets. This has enabled vulture capitalists, big private equity firms and hedge funds to make large profits, often tax free from the sale of these assets. Thus the ordinary people (including taxpayers) are robbed many times over to enrich these wealthy firms and 'investors'.

Basically, massive debt traps are created for home owners, individuals, businesses, organisations, farmers, etc. during the speculative bubble phase, with very high prices for assets and products accompanied by overly expensive mortgages and loans, and false perceptions of wealth, then once the crash comes, and aggregate demand falls and income and earnings drops or collapses for these individuals and businesses, they are left vulnerable and are asset stripped by banks, vulture funds, private equity funds etc.. The same methods are used against governments, massive loans are given to governments, often corrupt ones, and debt traps are set to entrap these governments and then asset strip their countries in the form of acquiring their natural resources cheaply or for free. This provides massive profits to multinational firms and banks and has been well documented by Perkins [10]. The treatment of Greece after the crash of 2008 by the Troika provides a classic example of how countries are asset stripped, and their workers and pensioners and taxpayers robbed to pay off banks, bondholders, speculators and fraudsters. In fact the continued imposition of new debt on Greece between 2009 – 2015 only served to reinforce this, creating a self defeating austerity process which destroyed consumption, investment, investor confidence and credit growth and the income generation to pay down debt. The same occurred in Latin America, African countries and some Asian countries for many decades prior to that. These resources often involve oil, gas, gold, silver, diamonds, indium, uranium, platinum, rhenium, rhodium, iridium, palladium, copper, water, forests, public infrastructure, islands, public assets and land, ports, and agricultural land. This is the same type of asset stripping used to deprive families of their homes, businesses of their customers and assets, farmers of their homes and land, and organisations of their assets. Asset stripping based on debts created out of nothing with interest charged inflated by speculators and Rentiers and by political corruption is a particularly nasty and malevolent activity which is destructive of nations and which the general public and more politicians need to be made aware of.

The end result of asset stripping is economies dominated by Banks, Speculators and Rentiers who extract economic rents and interest from most of the population (95%) who live in debt slavery ; a modern day feudalism. This is explored in Point 6 below.

6. The Debt Trap Arising from High Concentrations of Wealth and Income

Resources on the earth are limited, and excessive concentrations of ownership and income going to one small set of people will lead to other sets of people getting less. And the economic structures based on this will create a vicious competitive struggle where those getting less will be forced to compete against other for these lesser resources so that the wealthy can accumulate even more resources. This is basic mathematics. The vast and growing inequalities in wealth and income is creating two classes of people, and a classic parasite-host relationship. One is an impoverished and over indebted Debt Dependent Class and the other is a very wealthy Debt Beneficiary Class. The Debt Beneficiary Class lives off the Debt Dependent Class. Debt, created out of nothing by banks helps the Debt Dependent class who are deprived of adequate incomes to gain access to money at an interest rate. The banks are mainly owned by the Debt Beneficiary Class. It also provides the means for asset price speculation which mainly benefits the Debt Beneficiary class. The Debt Beneficiary class consists of the richest 1% - 5% while the Debt Dependent Class consists of the bottom 99%-95% of the population, depending on the scale of inequalities. The defective economic structures and accompanying socio-political structures both enforce and worsen this classic parasite-host relationship. Money created out of nothing in the form of new debt and interest which is not even created with money work together to extract money and value from the Debt Dependent Class (through loans based on overpriced assets, repayments, foreclosures, seizures of assets, evictions) and give it to the Debt Beneficiary Class. This is the debt trap emerging from vast, unsustainable inequalities in wealth and income. This explains the high levels of private debt which contributed to the crash of 2008 and the debt deflation which swamped economies after 2008. This parasite-host relationship is detailed further in Hudson's book 'Killing the Host' [36] There is an entirely new structure for economies and societies, this new structure means Debt and Rentier dominance of economics, politics, government, laws, and society, where the Rentier / Debt Beneficiary class act as a parasite on the Debt Dependent class, extracting interest, debt repayments and economic rents from them, which worsens concentrations of wealth and income[36] It is a return to feudalism and serfdom. This new economic structure affects aggregate demand, consumption, supply, output, investment decisions, credit allocation, credit availability, debt composition, debt vulnerabilities and economic growth.

7. The Debt Overhang Trap and Irving Fisher's Paradox

Massive accumulations of debt during the boom period and especially after the crash, known as 'debt overhang', has led to mankind being crucified on a cross of debt. In 2008, as the financial crisis erupted worldwide, Iceland had a private and public debt of 850% of GDP most of it based on speculation in shares, currencies, assets, property and derivatives. This led to the crash of the economy in Iceland and to a severe political crisis and economic crisis for some years after the crash as Iceland struggled to deal with debt overhang. In 1990, Japan had a private debt to GDP of 208% prior to its big crash, and it also struggled to deal with debt overhang leading to the 'Lost 20 years' there. Ireland had private debt to GDP of 310% in the 2008 crash and it had to deal with this through substantial private debt deleveraging, though the bail out of private banks by government added to the national debt and increased total debt overhang. Research by Steve Keen and Irving Fischer and others has shown that in America debt levels remained high after the crash of 1929 and for much of the 1930's creating a debt deflation and depression which created a self reinforcing disequilibrium during that period [1,37].

Between 2007 and 2014, global debt grew by $57 trillion (McKinsey). A substantial portion of this was government debt to bail out banks, financial institutions and bondholders and fund budget deficits caused by the loss in output, GNP, employment and taxes from government austerity programmes and economic recession. In charts below, it is shown that in 2015 -16, Japan had a total debt of 400% of GDP, Portugal had a total debt of 358% of GDP, Greece had a total debt of 317% of GDP (despite debt write downs and write offs of tens of billions of euros), Ireland had a total debt of 390% of GDP and a private debt to GDP of 293% (Irish Central Bank Quarterly Financial Accounts Ireland 2016) and Spain had a total debt of 313% of GDP (McKinsey & Company [7]). The USA with its government debt of $20 trillion has a debt of 111% of GDP while the total debt (household, federal and state governments, corporate, banking) is $67 trillion which is 372% of GDP. Total US unfunded liabilities (social security, veterans, medicare and other government debt) are $106 trillion which is 588% of GDP. The USA is a debt enslaved country with most Americans being debt slaves.

The UK had a private debt of 200% of GDP prior to the crash, the highest in its history. From 1880 to 1980 private debt in the UK was below 72%. This explosion of private debt in the decade prior to the crash of 2008 was a major factor in causing the crash there. The USA had a private debt which was 170% of GDP prior to the crash in 2008 which compares to one of 145% of GDP prior to the crash in 1929. The fact that this massive private debt was linked to speculation to assets and derivatives in the aforementioned countries is the key factor, as both the debt and the speculation were unsustainable and highly vulnerable to a crash. Today, the total debt worldwide is estimated at $195 trillion which is approximately 300% of world GDP, this too is unsustainable. In mid 2017, the ECB had acquired €4.2 trillion in distressed assets and government bonds, almost 40% of the GDP of the EU ; this is what happens when banks, speculators and markets mis-price assets and debts during a bubble period, which become distressed and worthless assets after the crash. This is dynamic disequilibrium.

These are massive figures for individual countries and indeed many countries are in bailout programmes via Quantitative Easing and zero or near zero interest rates by central banks (billions of euros per month. This system of continuously speculating, indebting, and then crashing and bankrupting economies and then bailing out banks, speculators and fraudsters and adding more national debt to existing high national debt levels is unsustainable and counter-productive. In 2015, the value of the Derivatives market, which is pure financial speculation was over $1,200 trillion ; this is over 20 times the global economy. Combined with other speculative debt the figure is $1,500 trillion. Much of this is based on debt and is interlinked between many financial institutions, posing significant systemic risks to countries and groups of countries.

Speculative manias and debt may be praised by economists, politicians and governments during the boom phase and given all kinds of names such as 'the great moderation', 'the efficiency of free markets', 'the triumph of markets', 'growth without bubbles' etc., but it imposes enormous losses on societies and economies after the crash. And causes high losses in efficiency, especially for those bankrupted by these economic policies. There is a correlation between the growth in credit and overall private debt and employment [1,35]. Figures show that rises in a rise in credit and higher private debt levels leads to economic growth and lower unemployment during the speculative boom phase, prior to a crash [1,35] .

This fuels higher consumption, aggregate demand and related investment and also speculation during the boom phase. However, after a crash, when prices fall and bankruptcies increase, the high levels of private debt and other debt remain. This is known as debt overhang. This connection between falling or collapsed prices for assets and the fact that the debt is continuous and keeps rising (via interest) for these assets is the key to understanding why economies crash and then remain in recession or depression. This is largely the consequence of debt overhang. This is characterised by :

- continuing high private debt, bank debt, business debt, and in some cases government debt (especially where private bank debt is converted into government debt)

- high repayments on loans, mortgages and government debt which suck money out of the economy

- a disconnect between the income and earnings generated to pay debt and the actual repayment of debt. Many cannot meet their debt obligations. This suction out of the economy is often ignored by some Keynesian economists and all Neo Liberals

- widespread deleveraging and panic selling of assets which destroy asset price values, investment planning, future investor expectations, and investor confidence (animal spirits)

- converting massive bank debt into government debt via bail outs and then enforcing austerity and the reduction of government deficits, which depress economic activity and growth

- very low or zero growth in credit which severely reduces or blocks economic growth

after a crash or during a recession / depression leads to serious losses in income, earnings, consumption and demand, supply and investment which is dependent on demand, employment, and GDP with only slight reductions in debt. In fact the potential losses in economic growth can be very high, especially if government austerity measures are added to this, Dr. William K Black estimated that the 2008 cost the US economy $24 trillion in lost output, gdp, productivity, income, and other costs associated with bail outs and higher unemployment. Other countries endured similar losses. Irving Fisher found in the 1930's that widespread debt deleveraging and liquidations at the same time after a crash or during recession depresses the prices of the assets and the earnings one can make from them. This undermines the ability to pay down debt and does not bring high Debt to Income / Earnings / GDP ratios down to sustainable or normal levels. This widespread insatiable urge to reduce debt and deficits at the same time actually becomes counterproductive and leads to 'Fisher's Paradox'. The important point here is that austerity polices which destroys both the income generation of assets and of people and the price level of assets through reduced consumption, investment, credit growth and output, mass deleveraging at the same time, deflation, and panic selling destroys the basis for reducing debt and leads to continuing high total debt to income / GDP ratios, and the lingering effects of debt overhang. Many years of liquidations, bankruptcies, panic deleveraging, foreclosures and evictions, deflation, high unemployment, recession or depression may bring debt down to a level where new credit can be created again. And this new credit creation may create a slow and gradual recovery. The Depression in the USA in the 1930's being the most notable example of this. Japan and its 'Lost 20 years' being a prime example of continuing debt overhang which can depress growth.

In all countries, debt overhang after crashes has acted to reduce or deflate aggregate demand and consumer purchasing power. And this fall off in demand adversely affected investment and aggregate supply especially productive businesses and small and medium sized businesses dependent on local trade, regional trade and national trade. This typically produces slow growth, recessions and depressions. This in turn reduced the profitability and investment potential of such firms when compared to the easy returns and high profits from speculation in certain assets ; thus providing new incentive for new speculative bubbles and new crashes in future.

The recent form of Quantitative Easing since 2008 has emerged as a result of great defects in the market system, many of them discussed in Chapter 4 above. Quantitative Easing is a sign of the failure of the market system. Economies and governments unable to generate sufficient economic growth, recovery, productive sector expansion, tax revenues, aggregate demand and growing levels of employment and productive investment have resorted to printing money or Quantitative Easing to bail out bankers, bondholders and speculators, and some corporations. And this Quantitative Easing has proved ineffective and disappointing. They failed to understand the structure and dynamics of debt traps, debt overhang, failed markets overly reliant on continuous speculation, and Dynamic Disequilibrium.

Crucified on a Cross of Debt

These 7 debt traps carry serious economic consequences for economies and societies. It would be true to say − 'crucified on a cross of debt'. These debt traps suck money out of economies, worsening economic crashes, downturns, recessions and depressions, and exacerbating austerity and debt deflation. In fact most economies have been restructured by Neo Liberal economics and this new structure means Debt and Rentier dominance of economics, politics, government, laws, and society, where the Rentier / Debt Beneficiary class act as a parasite on the Debt Dependent class, extracting interest, debt repayments and economic rents from them, which worsens concentrations of wealth and income[36]. It is clearly a return to feudalism and serfdom. Democracies have been debased into oligarchies. This new economic structure reduces and depletes aggregate demand, consumption, supply, output, investment decisions, credit allocation, credit availability, debt composition, debt vulnerabilities and economic growth. Whole societies are sacrificed to over price, to overcharge, to rip off, to indebt ordinary people and to bail out, to enrich, to maintain, to protect, to facilitate the Rentier or Debt Beneficiary class, and their money creation out of nothing, their speculative bubbles, their offshore tax evasion, their government tax breaks for the rich and vicious cutbacks in public spending for the rest of society, their 'socialism for the rich and their imposition of massive bank bail out debt on taxpayers, their austerity policies which grind down countries, and their economic rents which impose high costs of living. People in all countries need to wake up and realise what is going on.

 It is the scale of this debt overhang in each country and why and for what purpose this debt was accumulated which is of immediate importance and which will be examined below. The research and works of the economists Dr. Steve Keen and Dr. Richard Werner have shone a new light on this in recent years. Credit growth is absolutely essential for economic growth and employment growth. Yet credit growth, debt, and accompanying money supply growth carries both hidden dangers OR great opportunities ; it can be funnelled into the productive sector or the speculative sector or the consumption sector. During financial bubbles most credit growth is put into the speculative sector. The bubble phase may produce temporary economic growth and lower unemployment but it comes at a very high price once the crash and bail outs arrive. His findings have been confirmed by Dr. Richard Werner of the University of Southampton and others. The evidence is quite clear that excessive private debt to GDP, high credit growth funding speculative manias, and high private debt after crashes or debt overhang are recipes for economic disaster. This debt overhang creates drag on the economy, preventing the growth of new credit to stimulate consumption, demand, productive investment, employment, economic growth, etc.

These incredible levels of debt in many countries raises some vitally important questions ; should credit growth (bank loans) and accompanying money supply growth be channelled into:

(a) production and the productive sector to produce stable and strong economic growth and low inflation. And produce stable growth in incomes, earnings, tax revenues and profits to pay down debt OR

(b) speculation in assets, land and derivatives which creates bubbles and crashes, and massive debt overhang after crashes based on over priced assets, land and derivatives. And produces highly unstable incomes, earnings, tax revenues and profits to pay down debt, often leading to bankruptcies, insolvencies and debt defaults

OR

(c) consumption and the risk of higher inflation (if production is not increased by greater amounts). And produces weak incomes, earnings, tax revenues and profits to pay down debt.

This debt overhang is not harmless, as it severely impeded new credit growth and related economic growth and thus halted full recovery and growth after crashes, leading to what is now known as 'secular stagnation' or 'zombie economies' which are not growing and mired in economic stagnation. Quantitative Easing to bail out banks soley could not bring about full economic recovery and strong growth on conditions where high debt levels were impeding the economy. Critical research and studies undertaken by Dr. Steve Keen [1] and Dr. Richard Werner [35] and others show the important role of new credit growth in terms of consumption, employment levels, investment levels and economic growth and how excessive debt or debt overhang severely blocks this. This is an important new discovery in economics. All of the 7 debt traps above and the massive build up of debt and of debt overhang is ignored by Neo Liberal and Neo Classical economists, and are presumed to be irrelevant and unimportant, and are omitted from their economic indicators, their school books, University books and their models. This explains why the same mistakes and disasters keep getting repeated again and again.

McKinsey Report, 2015

Between 2007 and 2014, global debt grew by $57 trillion. Much of this was government debt to bail out banks, financial institutions and bondholders and fund budget deficits caused by the loss in output production and taxes from government austerity programmes and economic recession. The Report 'Debt and not much deleveraging' (February 2015) by McKinsey & Company provides an excellent analysis of government debt and business, banking and household debt levels and their effects on economic growth in many countries. Source: McKinsey & Company. 'Debt and not much Deleveraging', February 2015.

http://www.mckinsey.com/insights/economic_studies/debt_and_not_much_deleveraging

Specific Cases which depict the General Debt Problem Globally

On March 11th 2015, the Governor of the Irish Central Bank, Mr. Patrick Honohan, stated to an Irish Parliamentary committee investigating the banking crisis that the gross cost of bailing out the banks in Ireland so far was €64 billion and the total direct and indirect cost of the bank bailout in Ireland was **over €100 billion** – Patrick Honohan: Cost of banking crisis 'more than €100bn', Irish Times, March 11th, 2015. http://www.irishtimes.com/news/politics/oireachtas/patrick-honohan-cost-of-banking-crisis-more-than-100bn-1.2134967. This total direct and indirect cost of €100 billion included **(a)** government borrowings from the troika and international lenders AND the accumulated interest on this massive debt over time **(b)** use of higher taxes, new taxes, charges and levies to fund the banks and bondholders bailout and cutbacks to public services which depleted economic growth **(c)** lost economic output, income, productivity and taxes from imposing austerity to bail out the banks and bondholders. Ireland's GNP in 2010 the year of the bail out was 130 billion euros (CSO, Ireland). The direct cost of the bail out programme was estimated at 85 billion euros in 2010 and 67 billion of this was borrowed from the Troika (IMF, EU and ECB) to meet this. So far, by 2017, the bail out cost was 64.5 billion euros, and the indirect cost of this bailout was 100 billion euros in terms of lost output, GNP, productivity, employment and growth by 2015. This means :

- the direct cost of the bailout of banks and financial institutions so far was 49% of GNP (64.5/130)
- the indirect cost of the bail out was 76% of GNP (100/130), using the GNP at the time of the bailout in 2010. Using GNP for 2015, 193 billion euros, the cost was 52% (100/193)

This is the most costly bailout in the history of the world. Also Ireland paid 42% of the total cost of the whole European banking crisis, at a cost of close to €9,000 per person, according to Eurostat. The German people paid €491 per person and the average banking crisis debt across the EU was €192 per person. Ireland was robbed to bail out European banks, bondholders, and speculators.

According to estimates made by McKinsey, a well recognised research and consultancy organisation, in 2011, Ireland's total debt, including government, business and private debt was over 660% of GDP (see diagram below). This represented both debt overhang from the era of speculation prior to 2008 and the bail out costs and the indirect costs of austerity policies and recession. In 2016-17, Ireland had a national debt of €200 billion which is €42,000 per person, compared to an average of just €24,000 among the EU's 28 member states. This debt per head is the second highest n the world, after Japan according to numerous reports. Ireland had a total (government, business, bank and private) debt of 390% of GDP and a private debt to GDP of 293% (Irish Central Bank Quarterly Financial Accounts Ireland 2016). This is unsustainable and lies behind most of the austerity policies and severe cutbacks in public services and social goods and economic stagnation.

The evidence and facts are quite startling and need to be shown. Some studies estimate the debt per person in Ireland is as high as $60,000, second to Japan. Some charts and graphs illustrate the level of debt involved and compares it internationally.

Government debt per person 2014

Country	Debt per person
Japan	$99,725
Ireland	$60,356
US	$58,604
Singapore	$56,980
Belgium	$47,749
Italy	$46,757
Canada	$45,454
France	$42,397
UK	$38,938
Switzerland	$38,639
Austria	$38,621
Greece	$38,444
Netherlands	$37,233
Germany	$35,881
Norway	$34,910
Spain	$30,031
Finland	$29,930
Denmark	$28,778
Portugal	$26,770
Sweden	$25,155
Israel	$24,947
Australia	$18,110
New Zealand	$15,011
Hong Kong	$13,261
Hungary	$11,099

Source: Irish Times newspaper. Who owes more money - the Irish or the Greeks? June 4 2015.
https://www.irishtimes.com/business/economy/who-owes-more-money-the-irish-or-the-greeks-1.2236034

Spain, Italy, Greece, UK, Belgium, France, Cyprus and Portugal have government debts which are over 100% of GNP and total debt (government, business, banking, household debts) which are a few times GNP (see charts below). In Ireland 50% of mortgage holders in arrears are in danger of losing the family home.

Source: Half of mortgage borrowers in arrears may lose properties, Irish Times newspaper, April 3rd 2015. http://www.irishtimes.com/business/economy/half-of-mortgage-borrowers-in-arrears-may-lose-properties-1.2162581

The following chart puts the Irish taxpayer bailout of bankers, bondholders, speculators and fraudsters in the context of government finances:

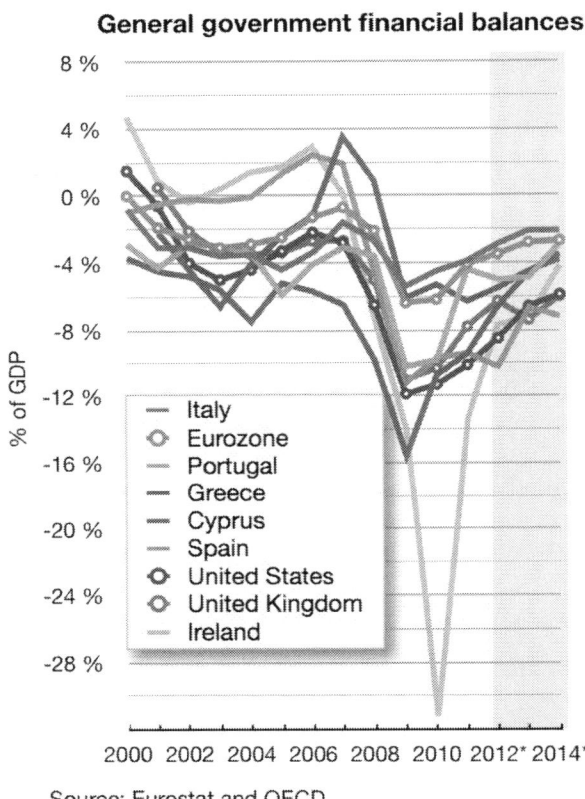

General government financial balances

Source: Eurostat and OECD
* 2012-2014 Eurostat estimates from January 2013

Between 2009 and 2013, Ireland lost more than €18,000 per capita while Spain saw its average wealth shrink by €13,000 per person – as a result not only of their respective rescue programs but also the burst of their spectacular real estate bubbles. The Greeks, meanwhile, saw their national wealth contract by €17,000 per capita.

By contrast, in the Netherlands, Belgium, and Germany, wealth grew during the same period by €33,000, €24,000, and €19,000 per capita respectively, due in large part to the massive influx of the ECB's flood of liquidity and of financial investments, mainly from the euro's loser nations. See Chart below.

As its monetary policies spread over the Eurozone, the ECB is powerless to reduce these gaping disparities that its own policies helped create, it said. Its economic stimulus plan, if you can call it that, distributed funds among Eurozone nations based purely on their relative size, without taking into account the particular economic needs of each one.

Source http://wolfstreet.com/2015/10/21/ecb-sheds-doubt-on-its-power-euro-stuck-in-limbo/

There is also a serious disconnect between the ECB interest rate of less than 1% from 2012-2014 and 0.05% in 2015 and the Irish mortgage and loan repayment interest rates of 3% - 8% during the period 2010 – 2015, which is adding thousands of euros more to mortgage repayments every year. Ireland had the highest mortgage interest rates in Europe from 2013 – 2015. This was at a time of great financial hardship, austerity and recession in Ireland.

By 2012 Ireland had paid €41 billion in bank bailout costs. This amounted to over 25% of GDP and cost every Irish person €9,000. This was accompanied by severe austerity policies, recession, high unemployment and deflation. The gross cost of bailing out the banks was estimated at €85 billion, and the actual cost was 64.5 billion euros and indirect costs were at over 100 billion euros and rising by 2017. This does not including compound interest charged on this massive debt. This massive and excessive debt represents criminal theft from Irish taxpayers, vulnerable social groups, consumers, mortgage holders and productive businesses to pay for over-inflated assets and property, and the bail out of national and foreign bankers, speculators, bondholders, hedge funds, politicians, regulators and private equity firms. The following charts show the scale of the debt problem internationally.

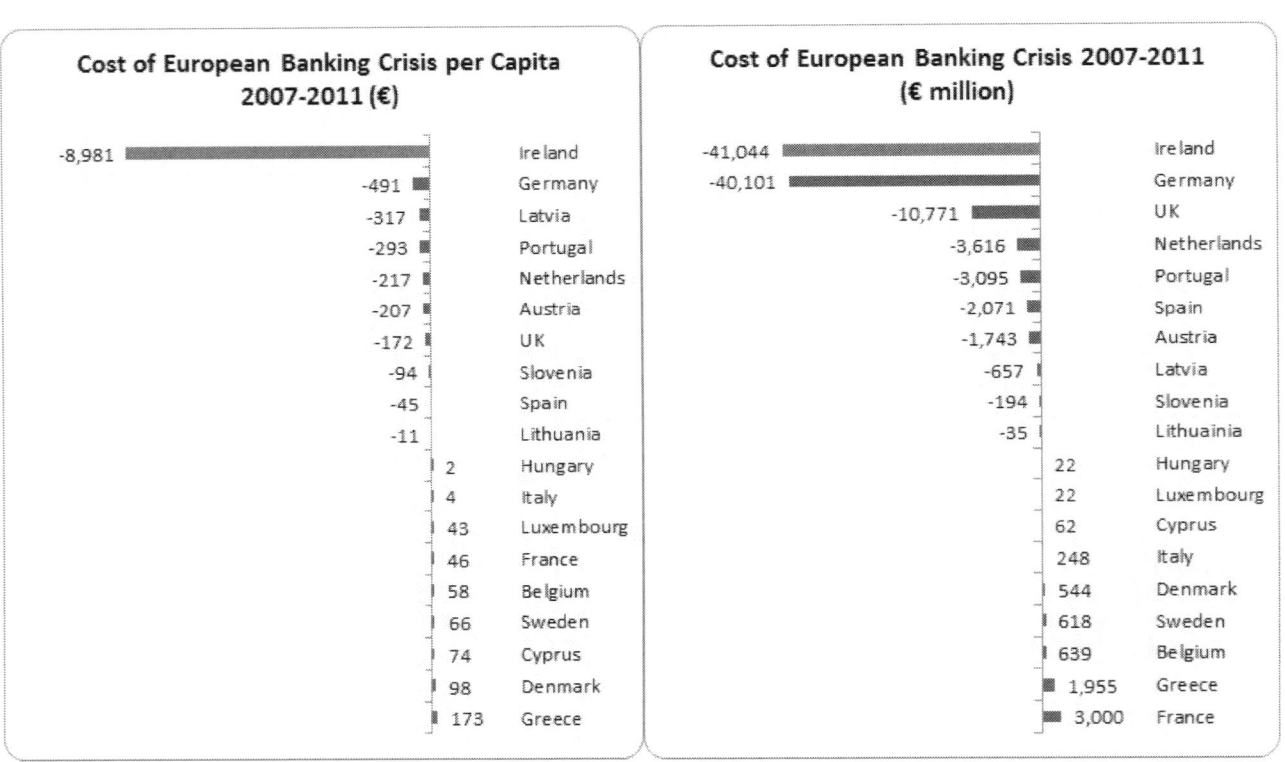

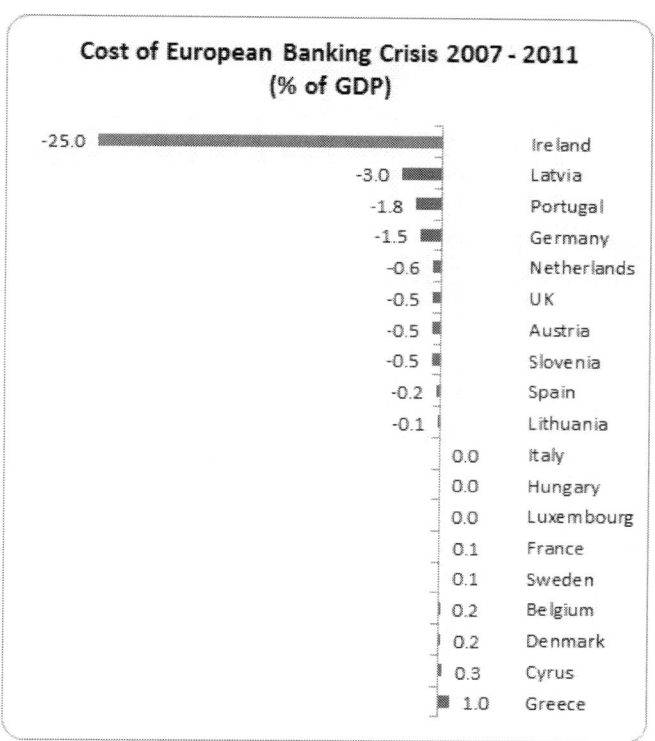

Source: http://notesonthefront.typepad.com/politicaleconomy/2013/01/with-considerable-speculation-about-an-impending-deal-on-bank-debt-with-the-taoiseach-and-the-german-chancellor-jointly-sta.html

Source: Mckinsey Report, January 2012,

https://www.mckinsey.com/~/media/McKinsey/Global%20Themes/Global%20Capital%20Markets/Uneven%20progress%20on%20the%20path%20to%20growth/MGI_Debt_and_deleveraging_Uneven_progress_to_growth_Report.ashx

and Sunday Independent, 2011

Debt-to-GDP Ratio 10 Year Trend		
Country	2004	2014
Japan	165.5	227.2
Greece	98.6	175.1
Italy	103.9	132.6
Portugal	57.6	129.0
Singapore	98.0	105.5
United States	62.7	101.5
Belgium	94.2	101.5

Source: Forbes.com http://www.forbes.com/sites/mikepatton/2014/09/29/the-seven-most-indebted-nations/

Global Financial Instability from Excessive Debt and Speculation

- Review of World Financial Instability.
-
- Summary: (World: US Dollars: Approx).
- 11. Total Value of Derivatives (Notional):   1,200 Trillion (1.2 Quadrillion).
- 10. Total Value of All Assets (Fin. /Real Estate): 318 Trillion (8. Plus 9.)
- 9.   Total Value of Financial Assets: 198 Trillion
- 8.   Total Value of Real Estate: 120 Trillion
- 7.   All Debt. (Owned by Banks):   257 Trillion (5. Plus 6.).
- 6.   Total Priv. Debt. (Owned by Banks):   193 Trillion (Priv./Corporate).
- 5.   Total Gov. Debt. (Owned by Banks):   64 Trillion
- 4.   World GDP: 60 Trillion
- 3.   Total Value of Derivatives (Cash Val.):   20 Trillion
- 2.   Total Value of Circulating Currency: 4   Trillion
- 1.   Total Value of Gold Reserves: 1.5 Trillion
-
- Ref: World Gold Council Dec. 2013.

Total GovernmentBusiness, Private Debt to GDP ratio & Changes from 2007 to 2014. (See below)

Change in debt-to-GDP ratio since 2007 by country

Ranked by real economy debt-to-GDP ratio, 2Q14[1]

■ Advanced economy   ↑ ■ Leveraging
▪ Developing economy   ↓ ■ Deleveraging

Rank	Country	Debt-to-GDP ratio[1] %	Real economy debt change, 2007–14 Percentage points				Financial sector debt change
			Total	Government	Corporate	Household	
1	Japan	400	64	63	2	-1	6
2	Ireland	390	172	93	90	-11	-25
3	Singapore	382	129	22	92	15	23
4	Portugal	358	100	83	19	-2	38
5	Belgium	327	61	34	15	11	4
6	Netherlands	325	62	38	17	7	38
7	Greece	317	103	70	13	20	1
8	Spain	313	72	92	-14	-6	-2
9	Denmark	302	37	22	7	8	37
10	Sweden	290	50	1	31	18	37
11	France	280	66	38	19	10	15
12	Italy	259	55	47	3	5	14
13	United Kingdom	252	30	50	-12	-8	2
14	Norway	244	13	-16	16	13	16
15	Finland	238	62	29	17	15	24
16	United States	233	16	35	-2	-18	-24
17	South Korea	231	45	15	19	12	2
18	Hungary	225	35	15	21	-1	10
19	Austria	225	29	23	6	0	-21
20	Malaysia	222	49	17	16	16	6
21	Canada	221	39	18	6	15	-6
22	China	217	83	13	52	18	41
23	Australia	213	33	23	-1	10	-8
24	Germany	188	8	17	-2	-6	-16
25	Thailand	187	43	11	6	26	21
26	Israel	178	-22	-4	-21	3	-2
27	Slovakia	151	51	28	8	14	-5
28	Vietnam	146	13	10	-1	5	2
29	Morocco	136	20	8	7	5	3
30	Chile	136	35	6	20	9	9
31	Poland	134	36	14	9	13	9
32	South Africa	133	19	18	2	-2	-3
33	Czech Republic	128	37	19	9	9	4
34	Brazil	128	27	3	15	9	13
35	India	120	0	-5	6	-1	5
36	Philippines	116	4	-3	9	-2	-5
37	Egypt	106	-9	9	-18	0	-8
38	Turkey	104	28	-4	22	10	11
39	Romania	104	-7	26	-35	1	-4
40	Indonesia	88	17	-5	17	6	-2
41	Colombia	76	14	1	8	5	3
42	Mexico	73	30	19	10	1	-1
43	Russia	65	19	3	9	7	-4
44	Peru	62	5	-10	11	5	2
45	Saudi Arabia	59	-14	-15	2	-1	-8
46	Nigeria	46	10	7	1	2	-1
47	Argentina	33	-11	-14	1	2	-5

1 Includes debt of households, non-financial corporations, and government; 2Q14 data for advanced economies and China; 2013 data for other developing economies.
NOTE: Numbers may not sum due to rounding.

SOURCE: World economic outlook, IMF; BIS; Haver Analytics; national central banks; McKinsey Global Institute analysis

Source: McKinsey & Company http://www.mckinsey.com/insights/economic_studies/debt_and_not_much_deleveraging

The ratio of debt to GDP has increased in all advanced economies since 2007

Change in debt-to-GDP ratio,[1] 2007–14
Percentage points

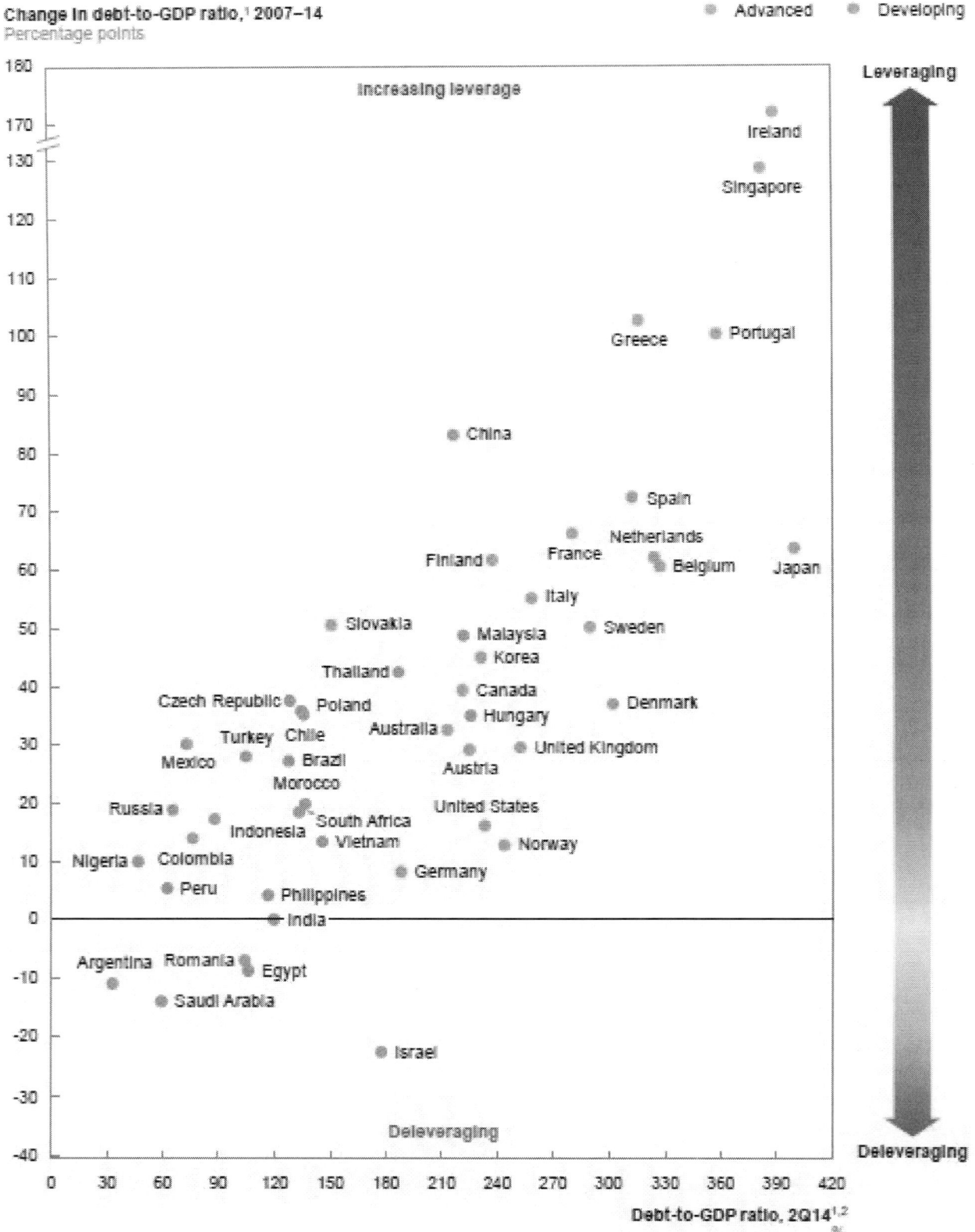

Source: McKinsey & Company http://www.mckinsey.com/insights/economic_studies/debt_and_not_much_deleveraging

Ireland paid 42% of the total cost of the whole European banking crisis after 2008 at a cost of close to €9,000 per person, according to Eurostat. The EU and IMF bailout loans given to Ireland, Greece, Spain and Portugal costing hundreds of billions of euros which have been used to bail out big German, French, British, Dutch, Swiss, American, Japanese banks, bondholders, hedge funds, brokers, developers and speculators, some of the wealthiest people and families in the world. They lost their bets or speculative investments and expected taxpayers to bail them out. And the EU centre, led by Germany, enforced this bailout, which has bankrupted Ireland, Greece, Spain, and Portugal and enforced several years of austerity, cutbacks, unemployment, recession and depression on these countries. This is a disgrace and is against the ideals of the European Union. In effect, taxpayers (many of them over indebted and underpaid) were forced to bail out the richest 5% of Europeans and North Americans. The documentary 'State Secrets and Bank Bailouts' exposed this recently. The real question is - why should Irish taxpayers or Spanish taxpayers or Greek taxpayers bail out big German, French, Dutch, Swiss, American, British banks, bondholders, hedge funds, brokers, developers and speculators who are some of the wealthiest people in the world ?

In addition to bailing out banks, speculators and fraudsters, the Irish and EU taxpayers also have to pay off high mortgage costs, household debts, and other high costs of living imposed by the (monopolistic / oligopolistic / cartel dominated) economic system. The issue of excessive household debt is particularly important in the worsening of the current recession and financial crisis in the USA and Europe, as found by Mian and Sufi, Keen and other leading economic researchers [6]. They found that excessive household debt and business debt had far reaching consequences for economies, reducing the impact and effectiveness of fiscal and monetary stimulus and Quantitative Easing in the USA. Growth remained weak or negative, unemployment high, and there was deflation and debt deflation in many sectors and very weak money growth and aggregate demand in the period 2009-2014. The United States witnessed a dramatic rise in household debt in the years before the Great Recession, the total amount of debt for American households doubled between 2000 and 2007 to $14 trillion [6]. Once the crash came in 2008, credit growth and debt growth slowed down radically, while debt overhang persisted, and these combined factors dragged the economy down. The resulting Great American Recession led to the loss of over eight million jobs between 2007 and 2009, and more than four million homes were lost to foreclosures [6] . By 2016, there were still over 30 million Americans jobless many of whom gave up looking for work, and did not appear in official statistics.

Social Consequences of Fraudulent Debt Driven Austerity

Under normal conditions Central Banks bail out bankrupt banks, as they are the lender of last resort and it's their historical duty to do so, but the ECB refused to do this after the 2008 crash. The ECB forced the Irish taxpayers to bail out Irish and European banks and speculators. In June 2012, the EU acknowledged that this was too harsh and too burdensome for the Irish and an agreement was made between the EU and the Irish government to refund the Irish government most or all of the bank bail out costs. The Irish Prime Minister Enda Kenny failed to implement this deal in Ireland or possibly forgot to do so. This deal needs to be honoured and implemented. Ireland should be given a refund of €120 billion from the ESM and ECB immediately to cover the total direct and indirect cost to Irish taxpayers of bailing out the European banking system and speculators up to 2019. Similar measures should be applied in other EU countries which suffered similarly. This failure to resolve the Irish debt problem has had disastrous economic and social consequences.

- over 40,000 Irish businesses were made bankrupt since 2009 as a result of the banking crash and austerity programmes and accompanying recession by the government. This added over 200,000 people to unemployment over that time period. Unemployment was at 14% in 2009 – 2011. And 300,000 young Irish people emigrated in the years after 2007. Also tens of thousands of foreign migrants returned to their own countries during that time.

- Unemployment peaked at 14% after 2008 and remained at that level for a few years. It has dropped in recent years due to high levels of emigration (300,000 emigrated after 2007) and a high influx of American and foreign multinational firms into the country lured in by tax concessions, grants, educational infrastructure, English language, and proximity to the EU market. Though the unemployment rates for disabled people (willing to work) and for travellers (a minority) was over 50% during that period and today

Ireland has a small population of 4.7 million people, so the following high figures need to be factored for a small population in 2019. See points below.

- In 2019 Ireland was 213 billion euros in debt (CSO Ireland statista.com). The Irish national debt is over 252 % of government income (a figure used by investors and banks). Ireland had a 38 billion euro national debt in 2007 (NTMA and Finfacts). This increase in the national debt occurred as a result of the crash in 2008 and the bank and speculator bail outs by the government and the accompanying austerity, higher unemployment, lower tax revenues, and recession. The interest on the national debt amounted to 5 - 7 billion euros per year, and over 60 billion euros was paid in interest from 2009 - 2019. This national debt in 2019 amounts to 44,000 euros for every man, woman and child in Ireland. Ireland has the highest national debt per capita in the EU and one of the highest in the world. Other countries in Europe and in North America, South America and Japan have similar high debt levels and high debt per capita ratios and many were also forced to bail out banks and speculators after crashes. In reality it is mass theft and robbery from taxpayers.This explains the high taxes, the cutbacks in hospitals, schools, social housing, affordable housing, disability services, the homeless crisis, public transport crisis, the traffic gridlock every morning and evening, the hospital waiting lists and thousands of people forced to wait days in busy corridors on trolleys in hospitals, the farming and rural crisis, the military wages crisis, the cuts to garda resources at a time when crimes including gang crime are very high etc.

- Ireland has 30,000 mortgages in 5 years arrears. Ireland had 100,000 mortgages restructured over the last ten years.

- 10,200 people homeless and 3,800 of these are children. Over 12,000 Irish children have experienced homelessness between 2014 and 2019. Pictures of small children eating meals on the cold streets of Dublin were on the press and media. Ireland has the worst homeless crisis since the 1930's.

- 120,000 people on the social housing list because of the refusal to build social housing after the 2008 crash. The government was bankrupted by the extra private debt added on to the government debt to fund bail outs of bankers, developers and speculators after the 2008 crash.

- 400,000 people on hospital waiting lists, and thousands of people forced to wait days on trolleys in busy corridors in hospitals as a result of health service cutbacks (caused by massive national debt)

- Ireland is one of the most highly taxed countries in Europe when one includes direct taxes on wages, salaries and profits and indirect taxes in the form of VAT, property tax, VRT on cars, bin charges, excise duties, road taxes, levies, and many new charges for public services. This is not being used for the benefit of Ireland and the Irish people. It is being used to pay off debt which is explained in the point below

- This fraudulent debt created out of nothing could be written off, written down, cancelled as bad debt (from excessive speculation), corrupt debt, or odious debt. Other countries have done this and it has been done for thousands of years. But the Irish government and EU authorities have refused to do this. The main political parties in Ireland have supported this debt fraud.

- This debt based system created the financial bubbles and the crashes, and allowed Vulture Funds to acquire over 80 billion euros of distressed over-indebted properties in Ireland, enforced many evictions against families, farms and businesses, made massive profits, and evaded billions of euros in tax. They were not prosecuted for tax evasion.

Elderly lady begging in Dublin, Ireland in 2016

The German Experience of Massive Debt in the Past

The facts suggest that it is Germany, by which I mean German politicians, senior civil servants, government advisors, bankers, bondholders and their lobbyists, central bankers and their representatives on the ECB who are pushing unfair, unnecessary and unsustainable private, banking debt burdens onto innocent Irish taxpayers, and taxpayers in other EU countries, and enforcing it through harsh government austerity measures. The Germans have refused debt write offs, debt write downs, debt forgiveness, debt restructurings, and Quantitative easing and all forms of fiscal and monetary stimulus in the middle of a European recession / depression. The Germans have enforced higher debt burdens on countries and accompanying austerity policies in order to bail out bankers, fraudsters and speculators from several European countries and non European countries. Germany has forgotten it's own history and how it benefitted from debt write offs and write downs and debt forgiveness in the past.

There are examples from history where massive, unsustainable and unfair debt burdens were forced onto the backs of innocent taxpayers, and countries were made to endure harsh austerity measures and very little or no economic growth for many years. The Versailles treaty (1919) which bankrupted Germany with debt and austerity in the 1920's and 1930's is one good example of this and it led to the collapse of Weimar Germany and to the rise of Hitler. The Germans were forced to pay 132bn Goldmarks in war reparations debt after World War I and severe government austerity policies were introduced in the 1920's in Germany to pay off this debt. This caused a massive contraction in production, investment and productivity. In addition to this, the loss of the steel and coal industry in the Ruhr (to France) reduced Germany's ability to pay off debt and grow the economy, and these losses in production, productivity and raw materials destroyed the production and income base of the German economy and contributed to the hyperinflation in Germany in the early 1920's. This massive debt and compounded interest combined with (a) government austerity policies (b) the losses in production and the productive base (c) the Wall street crash of 1929 and Great Depression and recall of German loans (d) collapse in exports and global trade after 1930 destroyed the German economy and the Weimar Republic by 1933 and this directly led to the rise of the Nazi party and Hitler becoming leader of Germany. The same political idiots who loaded more debt and austerity onto Germany also allowed Germany to begin a massive re-armament plan and an increase in it's military from the early 1930's onwards, which had serious consequences for the world. American and European bankers, financiers, speculators and some industrialists fully exploited Germany's massive debt and bankruptcy in the 1920's and 1930's to drain resources out of the country and profiteer from it and later they funded and formed partnerships with German industries under Hitler and the Nazis and profiteered from this also [30]. Interestingly they were the same greedy imbeciles whose ideology delivered the Wall street crash of 1929 and Great Depression. Yet these idiots were considered "experts" at the time, unfortunately this keeps repeating even in the 21st century. In the end, the Germans paid only 22.78bn Gm of this debt, while 110bn Gm was not paid and was written off, showing the stupidity and hubris of imposing massive debt and austerity on nations.

Germany has conveniently forgotten that under the London Debt Agreement of 1953, its debt was reduced by 50% and the remainder restructured over 50 years. Repayments were only due while West Germany ran a trade surplus, and repayments were limited to 3% of export earnings ; this encouraged

German industry to export. Also, The Marshall Plan aid to Germany and some European countries after world war 2 totaled $13 billion at that time and most of it did not have to be repaid. It was supplemented by technical assistance worth a few billion dollars, and by additional post-war aid totaling $12 billion, and loans by the (American backed) export-import bank to European industry totally several billion dollars. Germany got most of this aid, totalling several billion dollars in free money under the Marshall Plan and only paid 15% of this back to the USA. This generosity and other aid programmes helped Germany recover from the war, and enabled Ludwig Erhard to implement expansionary economic policies in the 50's and 60's. These expansionary economic policies built up the German economy and its infrastructure and factories, improved the competitiveness of industry and its workforce and wages, while stimulating aggregate demand. The German growth model was based on enhancing the productive sector and productivity, industrial peace with unions, developing export markets, small and medium sized banks to facilitate industry and government supporting public infrastructure and education. Some right wing idiots today would wrongly call this 'communism' or 'socialism'. The German economic model was not based on speculation in assets, property and derivatives and on inflating economic bubbles and on rentier exploitation. These expansionary economic policies and accompanying economic growth were only made possible by free financial aid, debt reductions, write offs and debt forgiveness, and restructuring of debt. <u>All of these measures were far better than imposing massive national debt and austerity policies on Germany and suffocating economic growth. There is a need for Germany to remember that it has been the recipient of generosity, massive financial aid, debt forgiveness, debt write downs, debt write-offs and debt restructurings in the past.</u> The German Minister Mr Schauble and other austerity hawks should study German history more carefully. This idea of punishing and enforcing debt and austerity on peoples and nations, particularly innocent parties, is a negative and self-defeating ethos which does not serve the interests of Germany or any other European country or the European ideal of brotherhood, unity, progress and peace.

Japan also benefitted from a similar arrangement after World War Two. The Japanese Central Bank took over all non performing loans and assets from bankrupt Japanese banks and put them onto their balance sheet from 1945 – 48. The allies wrote off some Japanese debt debts and also injected new funds into the Japanese economy. This injected new funds into the Japanese banking system and enabled banks to write down some business debts for businesses while at the same time providing fresh new loans to them, and this allowed Japanese businesses to rebuild, invest in new buildings, machinery employees and this stimulated the economy. The Japanese government also had more funds for investment and funding. This stimulated a massive building boom, industrial boom, farming boom and employment boom in Japan. By 1950, Japan had a growing and prosperous economy. In 1990 when the Japanese banks were bankrupted by speculation in Japan, the Japanese Central Bank refused to apply the same solutions which worked in the 1940's and Japan experienced a recession for over 25 years. Sadly nations and peoples refuse to learn the important lessons from the past. (They prefer listening to the ignorance and naivety of "experts", "advisors" and "consultants")

Over the course of history it was customary for different cultures to hold debt jubilees every 60 – 80 years where debt would be written off or written down considerably. This custom has been practised since money and banking was first invented, 5,000 years ago in Sumer. It has a long history of use in Jewish culture for thousands of years.

The Failure of Austerity

Austerity policies are enforced by those people who have high paid and secure jobs with many benefits, who live privileged and luxurious lives, and are smug, comfortable, self contented and self serving. They do not suffer austerity. Wolfgang Schauble and his austerity hawks in many countries have conveniently forgotten the debt forgiveness, debt write downs and Marshall Plan aid and other financial aid to Germany after the second world war. They have forgotten German history. These Neo Liberals who are enforcing austerity on countries are following a bizarre policy which has consistently failed throughout history. This is detailed by economist Mark Blyth in his seminal book Austerity: The History of a Dangerous Idea (Oxford: Oxford University Press. 2012). This austerity involves higher taxes and charges and new taxes and charges and vicious cuts to essential public services for the taxpayer bail out of their favourite banks, gamblers and speculators, and they also involve the breaking of the unions, the end of secure wages and benefits, significant reductions in real wages, many bankruptcies and business closures during the initial stages of austerity, globalisation and de-industrialisation, high levels of unemployment, etc. and a massive build up of private debt and total debt known as debt overhang. This is what austerity hawks call "reforms" or "discipline", and it is viciously imposed on the working and middle classes, the poor, the disabled and elderly. Yet the perpetrators of crashes and causes of crashes are ignored and allowed to continue committing frauds and crimes and wrecking economies. The objective of austerity is to protect and bail out the banks, speculators, the Rentier class (Debt Beneficiaries) at taxpayer expense and at the expense of asset stripping families, individuals, businesses and organisations, in the hope that new 'equilibriums' can be reached and new bubbles created to produce more speculative wealth and more crashes and bail outs by governments and taxpayers. A never ending cycle of speculation, fraud and theft from the working and middle classes, pensioners, the unemployed, the disabled and children - ordinary people.

It is important re-emphasise again that austerity polices destroy both the income generation of assets and of people and the price level of assets through reduced consumption, investment, credit growth and output, mass deleveraging at the same time, deflation, and panic selling destroys the basis for reducing debt and leads to continuing high total debt to income / GDP ratios, and the lingering effects of debt overhang. Government austerity policies from 2008 onwards have been enforced this economic madness on peoples. This increased total debt to GDP / income ratios for countries, as more debt was added onto economies and the ability to generate economic growth and income was reduced due to austerity policies in the middle of downturns, recession / depression. This in turn increased the debt as governments borrow more to make up for the shortfall in funds from austerity policies ; and this vicious cycle continued. The paper 'The Permanent Effects of Fiscal Consolidation' (Fatas et al. 2015) published in Economics journals in 2015 is a particularly good analysis of the failures and permanent damage of austerity policies in Europe, North America and other countries.

Modern Monetary Theory first proposed by Dr. Stephanie Kelton supports the above. Her studies clearly show that government deficits lead to private sector surpluses and increased consumption, investment and growth, while government balanced budgets lead to private sector deficits and to reduced consumption, investment and growth. This is especially true after financial crashes and during recessions and depressions. Austerity hawks are mentally incapable of understanding this.

The issue of permanent, long term and ongoing damage to an economy from austerity is an important one, and provides important new insights into economics and politics. The cost of financial system crashes similar to that in 2008 in terms of bailout costs, austerity policies, recession, lost output and lost GNP is estimated to be trillions of dollars for large countries like USA, Britain, France, Spain, Italy, etc. and hundreds of billions of dollars for small countries such Ireland, Belgium, Portugal, Latvia, etc. according to research by Reinhart and Rogoff and several other top economists (Reinhart and Rogoff 2010, 2014, Will Hutton 2010, Summers and Fatas 2015, Ball 2014, Blanchard, Cerutti, and Summers 2015). In fact, the financial crash cost the US economy $24 trillion, a massive loss (Dr. William Black).

This adds up to trillions of dollars of losses over several years or decades, and lost opportunities and lost economics growth which under current circumstances cannot be regained. The main point here is that austerity reduces GNP and incomes and future growth, thus increases the national debt to income ratios over time, producing a self defeating paradigm for governments. The same reasoning applies to business debts and individual and family debts.

The failure of austerity is echoed in Paul Krugman's new book 'The Return of Depression Economics' [27], where he charts the failures of austerity in the early 1930's in the USA and in Japan, Latin America and Asia in the 1990's, and provides examples of similar failures in the modern world. This provides an important historical context for modern day policy makers. Krugman focuses on the collapse in demand side factors, aggregate demand and business confidence which results from austerity policies, balanced budgets in the middle of recession or depression, excessive debt overhang and hoarding.

The failures of austerity policies have also been detailed and discussed in some depth by the economist Mark Blyth in his book Austerity: The History of a Dangerous Idea (Oxford: Oxford University Press. 2012). His book is quite thorough and he provides a deep analysis of the bubbles and crashes in the USA and Europe and accompanying austerity policies to bail out bankers, speculators and fraudsters, and supplements this with an historical analysis of austerity and its failures throughout history, going back over 200 years. He provides several reasons for the failure of austerity, which include reductions in consumption, aggregate demand, real wages, economic growth, investment, income growth, and blocking the ability to grow an economy out of an economic recession or depression. Austerity increases debt and reduces GDP and income growth, thus increasing Debt to GDP ratios. This in turn reduces the income necessary to pay down debt. This is a key factor in the failure of austerity policies. He is highly critical of austerity and provides important facts, graphs and evidence which demolishes austerity and the reasons for it. This book should be recommended reading in schools and colleges in Germany, Britain, Ireland, Italy, Greece, Spain and other countries infected by austerity and neo liberal thinking. His work is a major contribution to the field of Economics.

Michael Hudson's book Killing the Host: How Financial Parasites and Debt Bondage Destroy the Global Economy (2015)[36] provides similar criticisms of austerity as Blyth's book. Hudson provides an excellent examination of the crash of 2008 and the bail outs and how the economic system is set up to enrich banks and speculators and the 1%, while starving the productive sector and the working and middle class of adequate funds and incomes, and reduce them down to debt slavery and servitude. He provides historical context to this, going back hundreds and thousands of years, and shows how creditors manipulated governments to create oligarchies and serfdom. He analyses the ideas of Adam Smith, Ricardo, John Stuart Mill and many others how the Rentier class and economic rents have destroyed and continue to destroy the free market and whole economies [36]. He is highly critical of the loading of private bank debt onto governments and taxpayers (after crashes) and debt deflation, both of which enrich the top 1% while impoverishing and indebting the bottom 99% [36]. Yet governments and policy makers in the USA and Europe have failed and continue to fail to learn from this and the bitter experience of the 1930's.

Richard Koo, the famous Japanese based economist has written some strong criticisms of austerity and debt deflation based on the 'lost 20 years' in Japan [4]. He termed it **'Balance Sheet Recessions'** and mentioned the importance of 'fallacy of composition' or austerity in worsening this type of recession in Japan and now in Europe and the USA. Balance Sheet Recessions are unusual and are based on indebted consumers being fearful of losing their jobs or losing assets engaging in more savings and repayments of debt, while indebted businesses pay down debt instead of increasing sales and profits and investing in expansion. This combines together to severely reduce borrowings, money supply growth, aggregate demand and aggregate productive investment and creates severe recessions or depressions. He too compares the financial crisis and depression after the 2008 crash to the 1930's. Interestingly, Dr. Koo points out in his works and lectures that China faced a Balance Sheet Recession during the 2008 crash, but the Chinese government decided to implement a massive fiscal and monetary stimulus programme and this helped stabilise incomes and GDP and prevented China from entering a recession or depression. He contrasts this with the failed austerity programmes implemented in Europe and the USA after 2008. In terms of solutions, Dr. Koo is very specific and recommends fiscal stimulus, increased government borrowing to match or exceed the higher savings and repayment rates in the private and business sector, monetary stimulus, private sector debt write downs, Quantitative Easing and combining investment growth with consumption growth to prevent or stop Balance Sheet Recessions and to grow one's way out of post crash recessions and depressions. This can stabilise and increase GDP and incomes and increase the capability to reduce debt.

Looking at these works and other works, and data from countries worldwide, it is clear that austerity is a failure, and there are some parallels with the 1930's. For example:

(i) the gold standard has been replaced by the euro and excessive debt overhang which imposes fiscal, monetary and currency contraction after financial crashes and during recessions and depressions

(ii) government austerity policies which are obsessed with paying off debt and balanced budgets instead of debt write downs, write offs, removals and restructurings after massive financial crashes and during recessions / depressions. Similar to failed German government policies after Versailles Treaty of 1919.

(iii) some central banks were too scared to print money and bail out banks and buy their failed assets, and have imposed the burden on over indebted taxpayers

(iv) hoarding is encouraged by debt overhang and high debt repayments and liquidations, high concentrations of wealth and income and by austerity policies. Consumers fearful of losing their jobs save and pay down debt, while businesses pay down debt instead of increasing sales and profits and investing in expansion. While the richest 5% who benefitted the most from the boom and the austerity have a higher propensity to save and hoard.

(v) interest is not created when money is created out of nothing when banks give out loans, and this means interest acts as a vacuum sucking money out of the economic system, increasing the deflationary effects of austerity. It worsens austerity policies, intensifies them.

(vi) there are austerity hawks today similar to Mellon (in the 1930's) calling for liquidation of labour, stocks, debt, capital, real estate, farmers, etc., and this has been enforced through austerity and increased bankruptcies, liquidations and unemployment in Europe, North America and elsewhere. This has been humorously termed the 'austerity freak show' with a few German politicians and bankers playing a leading part reliving the austerity horrors of the early 1930's. Nothing has been learned from the past.

The important lessons of the 'lost 20 years' in Japan and the 1930's Depression in the USA and Europe, the post World War 2 experience in Germany and Japan, and the post crash experience in Asia and South America in the 1990's have been completely forgotten today by politicians, governments, policy makers, and economists. There is a naive, childish and immature belief that austerity will automatically lift economies out of recession, depression and deflation. This false belief has been dominant in Germany from 2008 - 2018, and through Germany this has come to dominate EU policies, yet Germany itself was the beneficiary of anti-austerity measures, free financial aid, and large debt write offs, write downs and restructurings after World War 2, in the form of the Marshall Plan aid, other aid programmes and the London Debt Agreement (1953). The evidence clearly shows that austerity worsens recessions, depressions and deflations. And austerity policies and measures have totally ignored the accumulated deflationary effects of high household, business, government and banking debt levels, and the need for debt write downs, write offs and restructurings [1,2,3,4, 6,8]

There is a naive and immature belief that the current form of Quantitative Easing will solve all the economic problems in Europe, the USA, Japan and other parts of the world. Ben Bernanke the head of the Federal Reserve was disappointed with it, as were the Japanese and the British, all of whom achieved disappointing and ineffective economic results. Quantitative Easing in its current form is based on the 'Greater Fool Theory' where some fool or sucker becomes the final buyer of worthless assets or funder of bankrupt businesses, and in this case the fool or sucker is the Central Bank. A Quantitative easing for the banks which keeps the money circulating in the banking system and asset price speculation system.

A European debt conference will be required to start this massive debt deleveraging process and fully resolve the debt crisis and financial crisis afflicting European Union countries. And provide new stimulatory policies in all EU countries to bring recovery, increase economic growth rates and provide the means to pay down debt over time. To facilitate this, the EU will need to embark on large scale Quantitative Easing for the People. This would consist of electronic credits backed up by the ECB. Quantitative Easing can and should be used to deliver debt write downs, write offs and reductions for households, government and businesses, in addition to promotion of government fiscal and monetary stimulus programmes to expand production and supply throughout Europe - A Quantitative Easing for the People

European Debt Conference and Related North American Debt Conference

There is a serious debt crisis in Europe, and this along with enforced austerity is holding back consumption, aggregate demand, money supply growth, investment confidence and growth, employment, and economic growth and recovery, and fuelling deflation and more austerity. The writings of top economists Dr. Steve Keen [1], Dr. Hyman Minsky [2] Robert Shiller [2] Charles Kindleberger [2], Galbraith [2] , Irving Fisher [3] Richard Koo [4] William Black, Bob Haugen [5] and Mian and Sufi [6] and Paul Krugman [19] , Reinhart and Rogoff,, Michael Hudson, Mark Blyth have pointed out these particular problems and their central role in the 'Great Recession' since 2008.

There is widespread agreement among economic experts that there can be no sustained economic growth, expansion and recovery until the problem of massive debt is dealt with. The McKinsey report for

February 2015 recommends large scale deleveraging or write downs of debt in the EU and North America and Japan as a means to stimulate economic growth and recovery.

Read: http://www.mckinsey.com/insights/economic_studies/debt_and_not_much_deleveraging

This deleveraging of debt could provide room for specific new policies and measures to bring about economic recovery and growth, including Quantitative Easing for the People (see below), fiscal stimulus, monetary stimulus, pro-business policies and other reforms including Economic Democracy to bring about full recovery in aggregate demand and accompanying supply. Such changes would promote sustained economic growth over time ; a transformation of economies worldwide.

Debt Solutions – A New Marshall Plan type Programme for Europe and for North America

1. Quantitative Easing for the People or People's Quantitative Easing and the removal of the private bank debt and speculator debt from the national debt of countries. The ending of taxpayer bail outs of banks and speculators.

In the past, Quantitative Easing or money printing by government was greatly feared by economists, politicians and governments. There was hysteria and panic that it would lead to high inflation and economic ruin. However since 2009, several governments in big developed countries around the world have engaged in money printing (Quantitative easing) to bail out banks, speculators, fraudsters and some corporates at a massive cost of $15 trillion. This figure of $15 trillion is an enormous amount of money and it has not led to high inflation. It was a period of low inflation and in some cases deflation from 2008 - 2018. In fact, it has led to the protection of the richest people in society, high profits for vulture funds, more speculation in assets and more bubbles, and more 'free lunches' for the rich and privileged. The printing of money for use in the bank sector only and not for the non bank sector does not lead to inflation (Dr. Richard Werner, 2016).

The following lecture by Dr. Richard Werner of De Montfort University and Southampton University (UK) in Dublin in 2016 provides an explanation of the economic reasons for these debt solutions. Its titled

'Prof. Richard Werner - Banking Industry Exposed & Solutions Presented - Dublin April 2016' and available on Youtube at: https://www.youtube.com/watch?v=MechH0ebs_c&fbclid

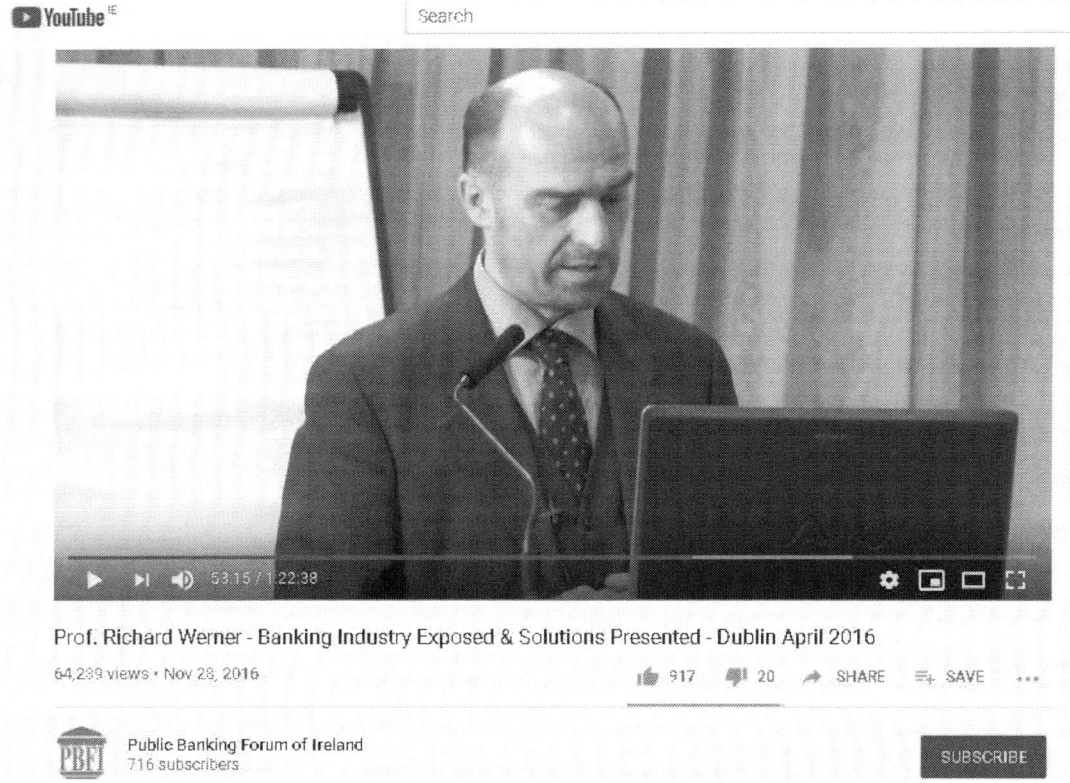

Prof. Richard Werner - Banking Industry Exposed & Solutions Presented - Dublin April 2016
64,239 views • Nov 28, 2016

There has been no Quantitative Easing for the People during this time - this is a vitally important point. There was no bail out of home owners, those who lost their jobs, hard pressed business owners, working class people, the middle class, minorities, the disabled, the elderly. Some top economists, including Dr. Steve Keen, Michael Hudson, Richard Koo, Mark Blythe, Ray Dalio, and others, including the Labour party in Britain are recommending a Quantitative Easing for the People. In general this Quantitative Easing would involve write downs and write offs of private debt, family home debt, business debt and government debt. This would bring home prices and asset prices into line with economic realities and would reduce the number of evictions from family homes. It would also provide room for greater public infrastructure spending, improvements to hospitals, healthcare, pensions and education and increased tax and grant incentives for private productive investment and innovation. These are reasonable proposals which could deliver strong economic recoveries and growth, and sustained increases in consumption and related productive investment over time, though they are strongly opposed by austerity hawks. Indeed these are the same austerity hawks who supported and want more bailouts and socialism for the rich as proposed in the paragraph above and more austerity and vicious capitalism for everybody else.

Quantitative Easing for the People would be similar to the Marshall Plan and London Debt Agreement (1953) which saved Germany and Western Europe, the Japanese Central Bank bail out of Japanese banks after world war 2 and accompanying financial aid from the allied powers, the New Deal of the 1930's in USA, the 'Bradbury pound' which saved Britain during world war 1, the greenbacks which won the civil war for the Union, the Jubilee years of past centuries, etc..

A 'Quantitative Easing for the People' delivered via the ECB OR via national central banks, owned and operated by national governments, and include the following:

• Refund Taxpayers and Governments for the bailout of private banks, hedge funds, bond holders, speculators and financial institutions in the 2008 crash and prior crashes. This would amount to over 1 trillion euros in Europe. This measure would restore justice, fairness, equity and balance to taxpayers and governments who were unjustly forced to bail out national and international banks, and now have massive national debt burdens. This refund could be delivered via the ECB or relevant national central bank in a given country. And combine this with Quantitative Easing and stimulatory fiscal and monetary policies at EU level aimed specifically at productive investment, sustainable expansion, full employment, and long term growth. Other countries around the world could follow this example.

• The Irish government and taxpayers should be refunded €120 billion to cover bank bailout costs, interest payments, and other associated costs since 2008 including losses in output, productivity, income, growth, taxes, and employment from bailing out European and American banks, hedge funds and other financial institutions and the economic costs of austerity up to 2019. This was agreed at a high level EU meeting in June 2012 where the EU agreed to refund Ireland the costs of the bail out of the banks and this deal was confirmed by the Irish Prime Minister Enda Kenny at the time. There were several press and media reports about this. This was termed 'retrospective funding'. But it was never delivered by the EU and the ECB, and unfortunately Prime Minister Enda Kenny was too weak to demand it. This refund needs to be delivered and then implemented in Ireland.

This refund in addition to other measures mentioned below would bring the Irish national Debt to GNI ratio down to sustainable levels, and help build economic expansion, recovery and growth and provide money for essential public services. (Ireland now uses Debt to GNI ratio not Debt to GDP ratio). Eliminating the cost of taxpayer bailouts of private banks, financial institutions, speculators and hedge funds would provide room for fiscal and monetary stimulus. The Spanish government and taxpayers should be refunded in the region of €150 billion to cover bank bailout costs and losses in income, economic growth, taxes, and productivity and the economic costs of austerity up to 2019. This in addition to other measures mentioned below would bring the national debt to GDP / GNP ratios down to sustainable levels, and help build economic expansion, recovery and growth.

The public spending proposals mentioned above could also be applied in Spain. The net effect in Spain would be a strong sustained increase in consumption, aggregate demand and investment, and this investment could be structured as long term productive investment, greater employee share ownership and industrial democracy, all of which would sustain demand, supply, economic growth and investment into the future.

- The Portuguese government and taxpayers should be refunded similarly to cover bank bailout costs and losses in income, economic growth, taxes and productivity. This in addition to other measures mentioned below would bring the national debt to GNP ratios down to sustainable levels, and help build economic expansion, recovery and growth.

The public spending proposals mentioned above could also be applied in Spain. The net effect in Portugal would be a strong sustained increase in consumption, aggregate demand and investment, and this investment could be structured as long term productive investment, greater employee share ownership and industrial democracy, all of which would sustain demand, supply, economic growth and investment into the future.

- Other highly indebted EU countries such as France, Cyprus and Belgium could be given similar refunds and structured write downs and reductions of national debt. This in addition to other measures mentioned below would bring the national debt to GNP ratios down to sustainable levels, and help build economic expansion, recovery and growth.

- **Strategic Uses for this Massive Reduction of National Debt and Increase in New Money and Government Revenues**

For Ireland, Greece, Spain, Portugal, Italy and other EU countries and North America, the refund and massive reduction in national debt would provide room for stimulatory fiscal policies by government, which could include:

- elimination of austerity taxes, levies, water charges, property taxes, usc charge, etc.

- reduction of taxes on labour

- massive new investment in public services, hospitals and healthcare, social housing and affordable housing, education, infrastructure, pension funds, military pay, policing and security. This would resolve the hospitals crisis, the housing crisis, the homeless crisis, the pensions crisis, the transport crisis, the terrorism crisis, the crime and drugs crisis, the military pay crisis, and the childcare crisis in many countries. See Chapter 11 for more details.

- reduction of existing taxes to increase employee share ownership, community share ownership, coops, productive investment, start ups and employment. And the creation of a foundation for sustained consumption, demand and investment over time

- encourage increased domestic and international productive investment in the country

- green energy infrastructure and energy independence spending. See below.

- cyber security infrastructure spending by government and businesses to protect power grids, utilities, public infrastructure and businesses against cyber attacks

- flood protection infrastructure spending

- scientific research infrastructure spending. Examples being DARPA and NIH in USA.

This would be a long term investment in countries and peoples, and would provide an immediate injection of purchasing power which would produce a strong sustained increase in incomes consumption, aggregate demand, credit growth, and private investment, and this investment could be structured as long term productive investment, greater employee share ownership and industrial democracy, all of which would sustain demand, supply, income, earnings and profitability, economic growth and investment into the future.

- **Resolving Private Debt Issue**

Several leading economists and researchers recommend structured write downs of private debt in countries with high or excessive private debt, as a means to stimulate these economies out of recession / depression and into recovery, growth, full employment and sustained levels of investment, profitability and consumption. This is feasible and could be distributed to both borrowers and savers via bank accounts, post office accounts, and use of electronic credits. The financial value of write downs and write offs could be correlated with payments to savers, so that borrowers and savers benefit from

Quantitative Easing for the People.

Quantitative easing would provide funds for these structured write offs, write downs, reductions, and restructurings of family home mortgages and other types of private loans for individuals, though they would have be carefully considered and applied and be fair, equitable, economically feasible, accountable and transparent. This would involve channelling funds into the banks for the purpose of writing them down, writing them off or restructuring them and this would be passed on to family home mortgage payers or loan payers in the form of a greatly reduced principal and reduced repayments. This could be accompanied by other measures such as home equity arrangements to reduce repayments further. Many of these overpriced mortgages were based on speculation, artificially leveraged prices, 'gazumping' or price manipulation, pricing fraud, Ponzi schemes, bank frauds where money was created out of nothing to artificially inflate high asset prices further, false accounting, false investment information, false investment ratings, asset price rigging, laddering of stocks and spinning of stocks, and other financial crimes. These borrowers of money were the victims of frauds and crimes.

• Structured write offs, write downs and restructurings of some business debt. This could be similar to the proposal above and carefully planned and managed. Some of this business debt was acquired through businesses being misled, lied to and deceived by false investment information, false investment ratings, frauds, asset price rigging, laddering of stocks and spinning of stocks and assets, speculation, 'gazumping' or price manipulation, pricing fraud, Ponzi schemes, bank frauds where money was created out of nothing to artificially inflate high asset prices further, false accounting, and other financial crimes. This is detailed in sections below.

• **Bank Responsibility**

Banks should take some responsibility for inflating asset bubbles through reckless lending policies. Governments could ensure this by implementing a legal mark down to market price policy for banks which engaged in reckless and irresponsible lending during the bubble period. This would make the mortgages and loans on their books correspond to the actual market price of the assets acquired by these mortgages / loans, which would be price depressed after a crash and during the recession / depression which follows. This would force a significant reduction in mortgage payments and loan repayments and some losses for banks. Also jingle mail measures could be carefully applied to banks which were proven to be reckless in their lending.

This would provide an effective deterrent against lending to inflate future asset bubbles and speculative manias.

- Eliminate all interest payments on national debts in Europe. The interest was not created when the loan of money was created (out of nothing), thus there is not enough money in the system to pay off the interest. Interest is a parasitic suction of income, wealth and assets from ordinary working people, the taxpayers to the super rich. It imposes additional inflationary costs on products and services and negatively affects economic growth, consumption and investment. It makes existing debts less sustainable. For centuries interest was illegal, we need to re-apply this ancient wisdom. Banks could charge a small administration fee for processing transactions and storing money.

- Government repayments only due to creditors when running a trade surplus, and that repayments be limited to 5% of export earnings. This would be similar to the terms offered to Germany after world war two, and would strongly encourage economic growth.

- Infrastructure for the 21st Century and Beyond

Use a combination of refunds for bail outs, Quantitative Easing and interest free loans for large scale infrastructure investment and long term strategic investment in the public sector. As the economist Dr Stephanie Kelton stated Congress / Parliament can mandate or authorise a fiscal stimulus and public infrastructure programme costing billions of trillions of dollars / euros and the funds can be acquired through refunds for bail outs, Quantitative Easing and interest free loans to fun it. The government has the power to create money.

Public or state strategic investment could have a long term focus and should be directed into public infrastructure as follows:

(i) building, expanding, repairing, upgrading of highways, national roads and secondary roads and their capacity , of bridges and their capacity, of railways and their capacity, of light rail in cities and their capacity, of shipping ports, of river transport and boat transport, of tourism facilities and capacity, of water infrastructure and repair of piping

(ii) building, expanding, repairing, upgrading of airports and their capacity

(iii) building, expanding, repairing, upgrading of primary schools, secondary schools, Universities and apprenticeships. Improving and upgrading of the educational and skills infrastructure. This is extremely important.

(iv) building, expansion of social housing and affordable community housing

(v) building, expanding, repairing, upgrading of hospitals, especially accident and emergency departments and psychiatric hospitals

(vi) building, expanding, repairing, upgrading of primary health care centres

(vii) building, expanding, repairing, upgrading of prisons

(viii) building, expanding, repairing, upgrading of various forms of public transport and their capacity

(ix) building, expanding, repairing, upgrading of broadband and its capacity, especially in rural areas.

(x) building, expanding, repairing, upgrading of back to work initiatives and social inclusion for the unemployed and disabled (who can work), of childcare facilities, effective care for the elderly and social inclusion of these people, reforms of the monetary system and credit creation system to assist production focussed firms, technological innovation and organisational innovation in the state sector and private sector to improve productivity and income diffusion.

(xi) public projects and public-private projects focused on greater investment in and deployment of green alternative energies to promote industry, commerce, trade and employment growth. This must be strategic and geared at attaining energy independence, energy security, energy sustainability and renewability, cheaper energy and energy sources which cause no damage or very little damage to the environment. This in turn would facilitate greater social stability and political stability worldwide. These green energies would include substantial new private investment and state investment in the following:

- wind energy
- solar energy
- biomass energy
- Geo thermal energy, deep earth pumps
- wave energy from the sea
- large machines which convert carbon dioxide and carbon monoxide into oxygen. Re-engineering cars and other transport vehicles to convert carbon dioxide and carbon monoxide into oxygen
- hydro-electric energy. New hydro-electric power dams in deep mountain valleys (Spirit of Ireland project, fjords in Scandinavia, etc.)
- re-chargeable batteries
- magnetohydrodynamic generators which generate energy in the same way the earth, sun and planets generate energy.
- magnetic levitation for travel and transport purposes
- Keshe free energy generators and molecule friction generators

- hydrogen batteries and devices

- fusion torches

- zero point energy devices, over-unity devices using magnets

- gravity manipulation machines

- use of exercise bicycles and running treadmills to create electricity in batteries for personal use, home use or business use

- free energy devices

- The building of smart infrastructure encompassing communications Internet of 5G and 6G, renewable energy Internet coordinating many green technologies and grids and driverless or automated mobility Internet and linking these together for a 3rd Industrial revolution. See writings of Professor Jeremy Rifkin

all of which are renewable and sustainable and provide increased energy independence for a country. The provision of Quantitative Easing and interest free loans for government infrastructure investment and private sector production and productivity would lead to savings of 50% or more, due to zero interest payments. This has been the experience in several countries which have tried it. Furthermore, the returns from these productive investments in the private sector and public or state sector would provide a long term payback, and increase domestic consumption and continuing savings and investment over time, bringing them to a new higher level, providing a sustainable basis for economic growth into the future.

- Health infrastructure spending and investment. This would include:

- new clinical centres of excellence

- new hospitals and additions to others

- new diagnostic labs using highly advanced technologies and upgrading them every 3 - 4 years

- new diagnostic technologies and new treatment technologies

- new medical and scientific research facilities

- promotion of new innovations in medicine and science

- new ways to clean up the environment and remove toxins and other poisons from it which are negatively affecting human health.

This spending and investment could be directed at the state sector and private sector. These are discussed further in Chapter 11.

- Using Quantitative Easing and interest free loans to inject liquidity directly into production businesses and long term productive investment and employment expansion. There would be no funding of speculation. This could be achieved via

(a) investment loan vouchers totalling hundreds of billions of euros for productive investment, redeemable in cash loans at banks throughout Europe. This would enable governments to use Quantitative Easing to increase productive business expansion and employment, and the growth of the economy. And not waste billions of euros on financial speculation.

(b) Special investment tax credits, tax reductions and tax incentives for productive investment and employment generation in the productive sector. This would cover monies spent and loans undertaken for this purpose.

(c) Injecting over €1 trillion into the European Investment Bank and national governments and using this to (i) provide interest free loans via commercial banks and credit unions to production businesses and new business start ups throughout Europe (ii) provide grants to existing businesses and new start ups in the production sector (iii) assistance in getting venture capital and angel investors through the provision of joint funding, tax incentives and tax credits (iv) National and regional government buying shares and equity holdings in production companies / businesses (not involved in asset price and derivatives speculation) (v) fund research and development and continuous innovation in these businesses

The objective would be to greatly increase new loans and new money via commercial banks and public savings banks, venture capital and investors and funnel this into production firms and productivity, innovation and new job creation, and eliminate or restrict funding for speculation in shares, asset prices, commodities and derivatives. The consumption and aggregate demand levels necessary to sustain this level of new investment would arise from many of the stimulatory policies recommended in this book.

- Quantitative Easing and interest free loans should be used to increase employee share ownership, profit sharing, wider capital distribution and economic democracy. This could be in the form of grants, interest free loans, and tax incentives to reconfigure capital ownership ; fund employee share ownership, share options and community share ownership of companies and businesses, and cooperatives and networks of cooperatives. This would be vital to building up and maintaining aggregate demand and associated business investment and supply and economic growth in a country over time. This is detailed in Chapter 9 of this book.

- **Fiscal Responsibility**

The notion of 'fiscal responsibility' needs to be seen in a wider context. Fiscal responsibility should be aimed at a balanced economy, full employment, economic growth, mass employee ownership, social inclusion, proper regulation of banking and a reduction of speculation and systemic risks, and low to moderate inflation for goods, services and asset prices.

- Reduce the borrowing requirement of governments ; give governments the right to print their own money and currency, debt free and interest free, within Constitutional inflationary and deflationary limits. This is discussed later in the Chapter.

- Repair the banks and system of credit for productive businesses in countries afflicted with massive debt, debt deflation, austerity and recession / depression. Reduce the cost of credit and increase credit availability for productive businesses.

- Social security programme protection and economic stabilizers protection to maintain aggregate levels of demand and social and political stability.

- Grants for balanced regional development within countries focussing on productive investment. Poorer regions receiving priority.

- Grants and tax incentives to stimulate research and development and innovation in products, services and processes in several EU countries.

- Grants, interest free loans and tax incentives to encourage people to improve their education and skills, with skill shortages being prioritised in this funding programme. This would help workers move from less productive sectors to more productive sectors, and improve overall productivity.

- Tax incentives and grants for green energy and renewable energy investment which reduces the costs of doing business and reduces consumer costs.

Other necessary reforms could include:

- New EU laws to make it compulsory to reveal for all bank bail outs and financial institution bail outs
(i) where all bank monies went prior to the crash including all payments to politicians and political parties, and payments to political projects which benefitted politicians
(ii) where all bank monies went after the crash, including all payments to big banks, hedge funds,

bondholders, politicians, speculators, etc.

There must be total transparency and accountability enforced on all EU countries, through these new EU laws.

- a well funded and resourced EU Financial Regulator body to monitor and oversee the European banking system. Disequilibrium is the reality of markets. Total independence from governments and political parties.

- discourage speculation in assets through the introduction of controls such as maximum prices being linked to average industrial earnings and average industry prices, and the consumer price index. This would allow a very limited level of speculation within certain price boundaries.

- the introduction of the Bancor. This is explained later in this book.

- The principles of the Ubuntu movement in South Africa to more widely distribute income and wealth in a reformed monetary system and free market system, and also build stronger community stability and cohesion, and use of renewable energies / energy independence.

The Energy Problem & Solutions

Energy is vital to economic growth and stability, and energy security is becoming vital to the economic security and national security of nations. Greater private investment and state investment in and deployment of green alternative energies to promote industry, commerce, trade and employment growth. This must be strategic and geared at attaining energy independence, energy security, energy sustainability and renewability, cheaper energy and energy sources which cause no damage or very little damage to the environment. This in turn would facilitate greater social stability and political stability worldwide. These green energies would include substantial new private investment and state investment in the green energies mentioned above.

2. End the creation of money out of nothing and the adding of interest on it as a form of Debt Slavery on Legal and Constitutional grounds and The Protection of Family Homes

This is detailed later in this Chapter and also in 'Chapter 8 Legal Protection of Family Homes and Communities against Fraud, Debt Enslavement, Evictions and Vulture Funds'. This deals with some complex legal and Constitutional issues and reforms and political issues and reforms.

3. The Processes of Debt Write Downs, Write Off's and Restructuring

It is possible for the national debts and business debts of certain EU countries to be carefully analysed, deconstructed and classified into categories and sub-categories which could be written down or written off or reduced or restructured.

The present system is upon deeper analysis a criminally fraudulent system which defrauds and robs many hard working individuals and families of their incomes, homes, jobs and livelihoods. During the boom phase, the prices of many properties were based on fraud, misrepresentation, asset price rigging, credit based on money created out of nothing by banks to fuel speculative and fraudulent prices, bogus bidding, and other criminal and unethical activities. The loans were fraudulent as no financial consideration was offered ; money created out of noting is not financial consideration. The interest was not created with the loan and is a fraud and extracts wealth from the system. The securitisation of mortgages without consent is also illegal. The bail outs of banks, speculators and fraudsters robbed people (taxpayers) of private income, earnings, wages which are personal property, and this too is unconstitutional and illegal. Governments have traditionally had the right to print money, often debt free and interest free, and depriving them of this power and reducing them down to beggars is illegal and unethical. And these same cash strapped, bankrupted governments were then forced to bail out banks, speculators and fraudsters at a cost trillions of euros. This system is one of grand theft from peoples and governments. This is discussed in more detail in Chapter 8.

These frauds and crimes are not harmless, between 1994 and 2007 new house prices rose by 400% in Dublin and second hand house prices rose by 500%, while wages rose between 60 – 70% in that time period. The United States witnessed a dramatic rise in household debt in the years before the Great Recession, the total amount of debt for American households doubled between 2000 and 2007 to $14 trillion, while real incomes stagnated for 30 years. The Great American Recession resulted in the loss of eight million jobs between 2007 and 2009, and more than four million homes were lost to foreclosures [6]. This speculation and debt system and accompanying bailout system is a system of theft, a criminal fraud, a Ponzi scheme.

A detailed and forensic examinations of all debts - state, government, business, bank, private and household debts is required in Ireland and other EU countries, and North America. These debts will need to be carefully analysed, deconstructed and classified into categories and sub-categories. There needs to be highly structured repudiations, write offs and write downs of excessive debts borne of (a) speculation in prices, frauds and Ponzi schemes, etc. during the boom years and (b) national debts arising from preventing governments printing their own currency within inflationary and deflationary limits . These measures will require the efforts and input of teams of forensic accountants, auditors, banking experts, fraud experts and consultants, debt management experts and agencies, and economists. This will involve the following:

(i) write downs, write offs, restructuring and repudiations of excessive national debts resulting from the prevention of government money printing within inflationary and deflationary limits and targets. This involves monies which the government should have had (through money printing), but was denied to them. This would include money and interest created out of nothing by central banks and commercial banks and then loaned to governments. (These loans are added to the national debt and have had to be paid back by taxpayers.) These specific measures will require the efforts and input of teams of forensic accountants, auditors, banking experts, fraud experts and consultants, debt management experts and agencies, and economists. This will lead to significant reduction in government debt levels. The government should have the power to issue the money of a country within certain agreed limits so as to avoid inflation and deflation. This is discussed in sections below. Many national Constitutions give the governments this special power. Governments should not have to rely on other parties or foreign parties to get their national currency or be put into massive debt just to get their own currency. The current system is criminal and fraudulent as it puts governments and taxpayers into massive debt just to access their own currency. Every euro, pound, dollar, etc. is a debt with interest. These write off's, write downs and restructurings will adversely affect the balance sheets of many banks. To protect bank balance sheets, the ECB could provide long-term (35 year or more) interest-free bridging loans to these financial institutions. This would prevent the formation of holes or losses in the balance sheets of banks. The banks would pay back these loans over an extended time period to the ECB. This would enforce fairness, honesty and responsibility in the banking system and government funding system.

(ii) write downs, write offs, restructuring and repudiations of excessive private debts resulting from money created out of nothing by banks and then lent out to fund speculation in over priced assets, over priced houses and mortgages, derivatives, financial investment packages, over priced commodities and currencies, Ponzi schemes, asset price rigging, laddering of stocks and spinning of stocks, false investment ratings, etc. with no regulatory oversight. This fraudulent, criminal over priced debt was loaded onto businesses, organisations, governments, taxpayers, and mortgage holders.

322

This could be coordinated with proposals in Chapter 8 of this book. Individual cases, groups of cases and classes of cases will need to be carefully examined to uncover the scale of fraud and criminality and how it contributed to over pricing and excessive debt levels. Debt write downs and write offs will need to be carefully administered. These measures will require the efforts and input of teams of forensic accountants, auditors, banking experts, fraud experts and consultants, debt management experts and agencies, and economists. To protect bank balance sheets, the ECB could provide long-term (40 year or more) interest-free bridging loans to banks. This would prevent the formation of holes or losses in the balance sheets of banks. The banks would pay back these loans over an extended time period to the ECB. This would enforce responsibility and accountability on the banks for their defective lending policies to asset price speculators in the past which crashed the financial system and economy.

Debt write downs, write offs and debt repudiations could be in line with earnings or average industrial earnings and historical values for the assets acquired and could be in the order of:

- 70% or more write down of government debt. Based on debt which would not have existed if the government had money creation powers.

- 50% write down of home mortgage debt which was based on over speculation in prices and fraudulent debt creation. Bring house prices into line with historical prices and average industrial earnings, typically 4 - 5 times these earnings. Turn houses and homes into consumer products not speculative products. Detailed measures are provided in Chapter 8.

- 60% write down of student debt. Most of the baby boom generation got a free University education and these people are now the heads of banks, financial institutions, hedge funds, private equity funds, vulture funds, Universities and corporates. Government has failed in its responsibilities and duties to the people and nation over time and should not punish students for this. Replace debt with a small graduate tax of 2% for several years.

- 40% write down of productive business debt.

- The elimination of compound interest on loans and replacing it with a small bank administration fee (See sections below)

- The restructuring of the remainder of a loan over an extended period of time so that it is made affordable and eliminates the risk of default

These measures would bring total debt levels down to sustainable levels and enable a new economic banking, credit and money creation system to be put in place. Less debt overhang and repayments would provide the conditions for new credit growth, consumption growth, productive investment, employment growth to take place within a sustainable economic system.

4. Greece

The excessive Greek national debt was acquired through fraud, false accounting, false government information, false ratings, criminality and corruption by certain politicians, their advisors, lobbyists, certain international bankers, hedge funds, and widespread tax evasion in Greece. The massive loans given to Greece by the Troika has not been given to the Greek people and economy, they have been given to foreign banks, bondholders, hedge funds and speculators in Germany, France, Britain, Switzerland, Belgium, Spain, USA, Netherlands, and Scandinavian countries. Yet the loans have been added on to the Greek national debt and their repayment is being enforced via harsh austerity policies which have shrunk the Greek economy and reduced its ability to pay off debt. Greek taxpayers would be given the following options:

- Greek's creditors should sue the big American investment banks and Consultancy firms who assisted the previous Greek government in providing false and fraudulent government financial information, false ratings, and false collateral to international banks and investors in order acquire large loans prior to the Greek crash in 2009. They could successfully sue for approximately €50 billion. This compensation to these victims of fraud could be used to reduce the Greek national debt considerably.

- The Greek politicians involved in fraudulent and illegal accounting related to the massive accumulation of national debt should be arrested and prosecuted and also sued for damages. Their assets in Switzerland and offshore tax havens should be frozen and seized to pay for this.

- The credit default swaps and contracts taken against Greek debt defaults should be allowed to be activated. This insurance payout amounting to billions of euros would compensate investors, banks bondholders and hedge funds who loaned money to Greece. And save the Greek taxpayer billions of euros.

- Greeks have hundreds of billions of euros in offshore tax havens. This will need to be taxed. This would bring in 40 – 50 billion euros. Whistleblowers should be generously rewarded.

- An incremental debt write off of €30 billion to cover national debts accumulated by corruption and fraud in the banking system, political corruption, criminality and tax evasion by the wealthy and politically connected, and misguided lending policies and lack of due diligence by lenders in the past.

This incremental write down of debt would be tied to a vigorous new tax collection system In Greece managed and overseen by the EU authorities. Tax evasion could be ruthlessly targeted by many teams of highly trained tax inspectors. Back taxes owed by business people, doctors and other professionals would be vigorously pursued by the tax authorities. Offshore accounts and tax havens would be targeted. Greek and EU Court and international court warrants would assist in freezing offshore bank accounts, and seizing assets. This write down would be linked to arrests and criminal prosecutions of those guilty of fraud, false accounting, fraudulent government figures and reports, theft of state assets and state monies, share rigging, assets rigging, false ratings, breaking of banking and commercial laws, the provision of wrong information to regulators and government, and other financial crimes during the boom years, through the EU Court of Justice and its branches in Europe. EU institutions should manage, monitor and oversee this anti-corruption programme and anti-tax evader programme in Greece. In some cases EU experts in tax could be drafted in to Greece to enforce tax collection and payments.

- A wealth tax similar to the one proposed below in the Taxes and Policies section needs to be introduced in Greece. Foreign bank accounts and properties owned by Greek citizens need to be identified and taxed at the standard rate. New more innovative ways of identifying assets and properties in foreign banks and countries will need to be used in order to tax them.   This would bring more fairness to the Greek tax system.

- Structured write offs, write downs and restructurings of private debts, house mortgages, and business debts which were based on fraud, Ponzi schemes, 'gazumping' or price manipulation, false accounting, false investment information, false investment ratings, asset price rigging, laddering of stocks and spinning of stocks, bank frauds where money was created out of nothing to artificially inflate high asset prices further, and other financial crimes. This is detailed in sections above.

- A debt rescheduling where 30% of remaining debt is scheduled to begin to be repaid 10 years into the future, another 30% would begin to be repaid 20 years into the future, while the other 40% continues to be repaid with interest. This would reduce the immediate debt burden and provide room for the economic growth and recovery necessary to pay off all debts. This would greatly benefit Greece. The ECB or national central bank could provide bridge financing to government to facilitate this

- The role of the euro currency in worsening Greece's speculative and debt mania and worsening its crash and austerity needs to be more closely examined and remedies put in place to protect the Greek economy.
- Apply Quantitative Easing for the People in Greece. See Quantitative Easing proposals in Section 1 above.
- The above measures would enable Greece to grow its way out of debt and recession through stronger economic growth, high employment levels, aggregate demand levels and investment levels, and high levels of tax compliance.

5. Switch from Bonds to Fixed Low Interest or Zero Interest Loans for Government

Governments could save large amounts of money, billions of euros per year, by stopping all borrowings from bond markets and getting loans from national banks in their own countries at low interest or zero interest. The bond markets are too volatile and speculators regularly work against the interests of governments and nations. Dumping bonds or threats of such and the manipulation of news to influence bond rates are often used to undermine or destroy governments. Many schemes are used to manipulate bond interest rates, debt ratings, and to bankrupt governments and to enforce unnecessary taxpayer bail outs worldwide.

6. Credit Guidance for Banks and Credit Creators applied at EU level and New Credit Creation to stimulate economic recovery and growth

The facts and evidence clearly show that credit creation by banks and financial institutions are absolutely vital to economic recovery and to economic growth [1,35]. The quantity and the uses of this credit is equally important. Dr. Richard Werner has provided proposals for credit guidance for central banks and governments based on the highly successful policies applied by East Asian countries and Germany after the second world war. These proposals call for central banks and governments to provide guidance to banks in their lending and credit policies, prioritising credit for productive enterprises, and severely restricting credit for speculation in assets, land and derivatives [35] . This would eliminate the booms and busts and bring more stability to the banking system and economic system in Europe. This could be applied at EU level so that it affects all European countries.

His proposed reforms include:

- Central banks and government provide guidance to banks in credit creation, prioritising loans and credit for productive investment and severely restricting loans for speculation in assets, land and derivatives.

- Central banks bailing out banks through Quantitative Easing, not taxpayers. This would saved governments and taxpayers trillions of euros / dollars.

- Governments replacing borrowing from the bond markets with loan contracts from banks in their own country. Borrow at prime rates, 2% or below. This would lead to new credit creation. This could be used as a fiscal stimulus by government. It would also remove bond speculators from this process.

- Basel capital adequacy (even anti-cyclical)

- Basel risk-weights adjusted for productive vs. unproductive credit creation, favouring productive credit creation

- Decentralising bank concentration in countries. Creating more public savings banks, community banks, cooperative banks, credit unions, microcredit and microfinance organisations to increase credit to the productive sector and small and medium sized firms in a country.

- Direct monitoring of bank credit creation for
  - non-GDP transactions, (speculation) and using an array of tools to restrict it
  - loan/income ceilings
  - LTVs (Germany: 60%)
  - Banking sector structural policy (Germany)
  - Quantitative Credit Guidance (QCG)

  Source: The Quantity Theory of Credit and Some of its Applications. Dr. Richard Werner. Delivered at Robinson College Cambridge, 30 October 2012.
  https://www.postkeynesian.net/downloads/Werner/RW301012PPT.pdf

7. Financial Firewall and New Bail Out Mechanisms

As mentioned earlier in this Chapter, it is the Central banks which should bail out banks and financial institutions not the taxpayers. This bail out process would involve the following:

1) Use Quantitative Easing by a national central bank or the ECB to purchase distressed assets from the banks, recapitalise the banks, pay off the bondholders at a discount, and fund the bank bail

out activities. Taxpayer's money should not be used to do this. And increased government borrowing higher national debt should not be used to do this.

2) Put the banks into receivership and bring about an orderly bankruptcy

3) Guarantee the depositors and ensure their deposits are protected up to a value of 500,000 euros per person. Allow the ATM's to work and deposits and withdrawals to take place while the bank is in receivership and being prepared to be sold off or closed down

4) Fire the executives responsible for the bubble and crash, fire them, and replace them with honest, reliable and accountable executives who will be held accountable

5) Government apply a levy on future bank profits, shareholder dividends, and executive salaries to pay for this bail out

6) Give hair cuts to senior bondholders of 35% or more

7) Give junior bondholders a haircut of 50% or more

8) Pay off the creditors at a discount or offer them shares in a new bank

9) Write off the bad debts and sue bankers involved in fraud and criminality. And pay off some liabilities and creditors via Quantitative Easing.

10) Allow share capital to fall to 1 cent in the euro. Then the state could acquire it, repair it and prepare it for sale to the private sector.

11) Sell off the assets of the banks to other banks, including offices, ATM's and deposit accounts

12) Prosecute and jail the corrupt bankers and regulators

This solution does not involve taxpayers and government paying for the bail out of banks, financial institutions, speculators and bondholders. It does not involve massive bank bail out costs being imposed on taxpayers in the form of austerity policies and higher taxes, levies and charges and cuts to essential public services.

The establishment of a permanent financial firewall would provide the financial back up for this system in Europe. This would bolster the central bank(s) involved in a bail out and protect the value of the currency. And enforce 'moral hazard' on bankers and heads of financial institutions via close liaison with the European Court as advised in section (iv) below.

Historically central banks have acted as lenders of last resort in a banking and financial crisis, and this continues to be the rule in most countries. But in the financial crisis of 2008-2015, the ECB failed to do this, and the EU authorities and IMF forced national governments and taxpayers to be the lenders of last resort, and they were forced to bail out the banks. This has bankrupted certain governments and nations. This financial firewall would be provided by national Central banks and backed up by the ECB and ESM. It would facilitate the Central bank bail out of banks and financial institutions.

These measures would break the link between government debt and bank debt, while punishing the guilty parties, enforcing 'moral hazard' and protecting taxpayers, governments and vulnerable social groups and health systems from the effects of speculative booms and crashes and expensive bail outs.

8. New Indicators for Measuring Systemic Risks, Bubbles, Crashes and Financial Crisis

Funding new national and international institutions and the use of better economic indicators to identify regional, industry, national, and systemic risks to the financial system and the economy and the level of dynamic disequilibrium. And to provide accurate and correct economic forecasts. And take pre-emptive actions to prevent massive bubbles from arising and crashes from occurring. These indicators should be made available to the general public and should contain red flag warnings based on previous crashes.

1. Total private debt to GNP / GNI and it's growth per year for the last 10 - 20 years. In Ireland and some other countries where GDP figures are unreliable and distorted by large flows of BEPS funds and tax avoidance / evasion funds into a country, the Gross National Income (GNI) and debt per capita figures are more accurate and reliable. Is private debt to GNP (or GNI) at or greater than 130% and is the growth of private debt to GNP at or greater than 10% per year for 1 year or more ? Is this debt based on speculation in rising asset prices ? Sudden slow downs in such high debt growth would suggest a crash may be imminent. This is based on the latest research findings of Dr. Steve Keen and Richard Vague [1]. Richard Vague has shown that financial crashes since the 1850's have involved private debt to GNP / GDP of 150% or more and an increase in that ratio of 17% or more over 5 years [21]

2. For Banks: total bank debt to capital / income / assets / reserve levels / share price ratio. This must include all off balance sheet vehicles and instruments. And exposure of this debt to speculative bubbles and the FIRE economy (Dr. Michael Hudson). This would measure the

sustainability and viability of the debt. Stress tests involving simulated losses should be made public to all investors and members of the public.

3. For Shadow Banking: total debt to capital / income / assets / reserve levels / share price ratio. This must include all off balance sheet vehicles and instruments. And exposure of this debt to speculative bubbles and the FIRE economy (Dr. Michael Hudson). This would measure the sustainability and viability of the debt. Stress tests involving simulated losses should be made public to all investors and members of the public.

4. Price-Earnings ratios, Price-Sales ratios, Debt to Capital ratios, Debt to Earnings ratios for assets, stocks, bonds, property, derivatives, companies, groups of companies, industries, sectors, and indexes. Including CAPE as proposed by Robert Shiller. And comparison to historical Price-Earnings ratios and the other ratios with particular emphasis on previous booms and busts. And total stock market valuation to GDP. High ratios have been linked to bubbles and excessive risk.

5. Growth in Private Debt, Household Debt and Bank Debt by themselves and in relation to Growth in Speculative Asset Prices. Sudden slow downs in this high credit growth would suggest a crash may be imminent [1]. This needs to done for speculative asset categories, such as property, shares, derivatives, commodities, bonds and other assets prone to speculation.

6. Inter bank lending volumes. Repo rates, Repo volume. Sudden declines indicate a crisis is about to begin or has already occurred. This may require central bank and government action.

7. Inverted yield curves. Fall in the velocity of money or very low number.

8. Broad Bank Credit Growth to Nominal GDP / GNI growth, Productive sector credit growth to Nominal GDP /GNI growth and Speculation sector credit growth to Nominal GDP / GNI growth and other indicators proposed by Dr. Richard Werner of Southampton University.

9. Level of Speculation and level of Crowding Out of Productive Investment
   - Speculative Credit and Debt which rises faster than income, earnings, and profits for the whole economy, the banking sector, and other sectors. Credit for speculation rising faster than Nominal GDP / GNI.
   - Total Debt for speculative FIRE economy (Financial, Insurance and Real Estate firms) and debt for non speculative economy. Rate of credit growth for both.
   - The growth of (i) non speculative GDP and GNI and (ii) speculative GDP and GNI, including the FIRE economy (Finance Insurance and Real Estate) as used by the economist Dr. Michael Hudson.

- The amount of economic output, GDP and GNI due to monopolies, oligopolies, restrictive practises, and cartels and speculative increases in land values and capital gains. And ratio of this to output, GDP, and GNI created by competitive productive firms.

- Growth in Quantitative Easing measured against growth in Speculative Asset prices. This would facilitate closer analysis of Quantitative Easing.

- Quantitative Easing for speculation in FIRE economy measured against Quantitative Easing for non FIRE economy and production. In absolute terms and in GDP and GNI terms.

    This could be on year by year basis and a quarterly basis. This would compare and contrast the real economy against the speculative economy.

10. Total debt — government, bank, business, private, and household debt as a percentage of GDP / GNI. How fast debt is growing for government, bank, business, private sectors relative to GDP and Tax Revenues.

11. Total National debt as a percentage of Government revenues. National debt per capita.

12. The exact or precise composition of all derivatives, CDO's, MBS's and other types of packaged securities and packaged assets including all tranches and subdivisions of the product. And verification of the income and earnings integrity, feasibility, capacity and potential for each product and sub product. This will require forensic and independent analysis of these types of products and what they contain and the credit worthiness and payment details of the constituent parts of the investment product / derivative.

13. New indicators for measuring increases in land values from the provision of public infrastructure and services nearby and proximity to towns and cities and measuring capital gains from financial assets. This would serve as a means of taxing these economic rents and measuring the extent of speculation.

14. House Prices

    House prices need to be compared against historical prices adjusted for inflation and adjusted for average industrial earnings. In general throughout history house prices have been stable, and have been 4 – 7 times average industrial earnings. Though in speculative bubbles they can rise much higher, reaching 10 – 20 times average industrial earnings. These new indictors and measurements would identify housing bubbles and help end them or prevent them.

15. Measuring National Overhead Costs

    New GDP and GNI measures to separate overhead costs from national output. Dr. Michael

Hudson in his works advised that it is necessary to calculate the overhead costs imposed by the interest, capital gains, land value gains, and the economic rents of the Financial, Insurance and Real Estate sector (FIRE sector)[36] And subtract these overhead costs from national output in order to get accurate GDP and GNP figures. These firms are not involved in producing goods and services, but they impose significant overhead costs on producers. This would provide net national output, or net GDP / GNI.

16. Indicators derived from some of William Black's works

- Level of coercion and pressure applied to appraisers to keep pushing up the prices of assets beyond their true worth or intrinsic worth and inflate a bubble

- Level of liar's loans, ninja loans and subprime loans for assets and level of packaging of these into other investment products and sale of them to investors, eg. CDO's, MBS's prior to 2008.

- Level of regulator failure or refusal to regulate assets and derivatives posing contagion risks and systemic risks to an economy

17. Corruption and Fraud Indicators

Special software will need to be developed to identify patterns in financial trading which would indicate price rigging, insider trading, rigging of IPO prices, laddering of stocks and spinning of stocks, ponzi schemes, frauds, sec filings, debt and bond transactions, financial flows between main players and all intermediaries, growth of private credit and debt, offshore flows of funds, false ratings, rigging property, derivatives or other assets. Information from whistleblowers and police and regulators could also be fed into this system. It would have a heuristics system, dynamic adaption and artificial intelligence system to provide precise tracking.

18. Measures or weights for assessing Contagion risk and Systemic risk in the FIRE sector. This would be based on the interconnections and inter-relationships between firms in FIRE sector and also between firms in the FIRE Sector and non FIRE sector.

19. Inter Sectoral transfers of funds outlining surpluses and deficits which may pose instability and crash risks as devised by Wynne Godley

20. Revised GNP and GNI measures. We need the following:

GNP and GNI Diffusion figures

The level of diffusion of wealth and income to the general population needs to be measured.

- Concentration of wealth and income. See table in Chapter 5.

- Employee share ownership, Cooperative ownership and Community share ownership expressed in GNI terms and GNP terms and Population terms. How much of the GNP and GNI goes to them.

- The rate of diffusion of capital and wealth to the general population via Employee share ownership and Community share ownership measured in deciles of the population.

- The Capital income (dividends, profits, interest capital gains) going to deciles of the Population.

- The Wage income going to deciles of the Population.

GNP and GNI and Social Indicators

- Measuring Child Well Being, Stress and Anxiety levels, Mental illnesses, Civic Participation, Support for Populist leaders, Child Bullying, Teen pregnancies, Crime levels, Imprisonment rates, Bullying in the workplace, Anti Social Behaviour, Homelessness, Life Expectancy, Gambling, Drug Abuse, Educational Performance, and Social Mobility against GNP and GNI diffusion figures

GNP and GNI Renewable Energy and Resources figures

- Per capita and GNP and GNI level of Renewable Energy and Resources figures. These indicate the level of economic resilience and energy independence of a country.

21. Daily / Weekly and Monthly Liquidity ratio and Cashflow ratio. How dependent is a bank / firm on outside liquidity to remain in business and how vulnerable is a business.

22. Inclusion of home prices and mortgage payments and rental payments in the Consumer Price Index and all measures of inflation

23. Indexes of dividends paid by a business or range of businesses or composite of businesses in a given year and historically. And contrasting this with the rise in prices of these investments. This would show the exact correlation between dividends and share prices. This would help identify speculation..

9. Auditing of All Central Banks

The ECB, the Federal Reserve, the Bank of England and the central banks of all countries receive trillions of euros / dollars in taxpayers money to pay off (central bank and private bank created) debt for many years, over a century in some cases and have engaged in various bailouts of banks and businesses after crashes costing trillions of dollars. It's time to audit these central banks and establish where the money went and for what purpose it was spent. The role of central banks in propping up speculative manias and in worsening crashes and austerity also needs to be investigated.

10. A New European Financial Regulator

This new office would have the power to regulate the entire EU financial services industry. It should have a headquarters in Paris or Brussels and a branch in every European capital. This would involve (i) the regulation, monitoring and overseeing of all banks, trusts (which engage in trading), hedge funds, shadow banking, financial companies, private lending companies, currency traders and (investment) derivatives trading in the European Union and (ii) protecting investors and consumers from the predatory activities of banks and financial institutions, hedge funds, and assets, property and derivatives speculators, investment firms in each EU country. .

This Regulator must be independent of all EU national governments, the EU government and commercial banks. The Regulator would have the power to monitor and intervene in any national economy, and demand conformance either through a national high court order or a European court order. National governments would not have the power to undermine or obstruct this European Financial Regulator. The national financial regulators within EU countries would be under the direct control of this European Financial Regulator. This new European Financial Regulator would be independent, well staffed, well financed, well resourced and ever vigilant. Criminal prosecutions and fines for financial crimes would be in proportion to the fraud committed and the cost to customers, investors and government, and would be calculated for every year of fraud or abuse, with interest added. If billions of euros are involved then billions of euros in fines will be imposed. This would impose order on the flows of monies between debtor nations and creditor nations and vice versa, and reduce the risk of asset bubbles and massive crashes of the financial system.

The Indicators mentioned in this book could be used to assess risks to the banking system and to economies. It would have powers to make certain financial instruments or investments illegal on an EU scale. Determining the legality or illegality of such financial instruments could be done on the following grounds :

(a) the indicators mentioned in Section 8 above.

(b) the part played by a financial instrument or investment instrument in the financial crash of 2008. The Indicators listed above in a previous section should be used. the part played by such in other crashes over the last 100 years (1929, 1967, 1970, 1973, 1982, 1987, 1992, 1997,1998, 2000)

(c) shares, assets and financial instruments with excessive price-earnings ratios for the industry it is in and in an historical context

(d) share and asset price or derivative rigging. Are front (false) companies or businesses being used ?

(e) The exact or precise composition of all derivatives, CDO's, MBS's and other types of packaged securities and packaged assets including all tranches and subdivisions of the product. And verification of the income and earnings integrity, feasibility, capacity and potential for each product and sub product. This will require forensic and independent analysis of these types of products and what they contain and the credit worthiness and payment details of the constituent parts of the investment product / derivative. A total and thorough analysis, while ignoring the presumptions of a ratings agency. And learning and applying the lessons learnt from subprime mortgages, and fraudulent mortgage backed securities and CDO's prior to the 2008 crash

(f) are off balance sheet transactions and assets and vehicles being openly or secretly used by banks, hedge funds, investment brokers, advisors and financial companies ?

(g) business risk ; do they exceed recommended risk policies

(h) industry risk ; do they exceed recommended risk policies

(i) systemic risk to the financial system and to national economies ; do they exceed recommended risk policies

A new EU Securities and Exchange Body for the EU and an Irish Securities and Exchange Body to investigate insider trading, price rigging, Ponzi schemes, laddering and spinning of shares and assets and other financial crimes

EU and Global Clearing House for Derivatives

Set up an EU and Global Clearing House for processing and transacting futures contracts and credit default swaps, derivatives, other financial instruments and all shadow banking deals which are prone to speculative activity. This would include full disclosure of the content and sources of all derivatives, all subdivisions and tranches and all sources of revenue for them to investors. There are four type of derivatives which would be governed by four types of laws and regulator and processed accordingly.

(i) derivatives with insurance aspects which would be governed by insurance laws and an Insurance Regulator. Not covered by the deposit insurance of banks.

(ii) derivatives with a gambling aspect which would be governed by gambling laws and a Gambling Regulator. Not covered by the deposit insurance of banks.

(iii) derivatives with a long term investment aspect which would be governed by securities and investment laws, the EU SEC and EU Financial Regulator.

(iv) derivatives which are frauds and governed by criminal laws.

The Global Clearing House could be established under a binding WTO agreement and would have a world headquarters and branches in many countries in the world. It would be well capitalized and the individual traders would take financial responsibility for their derivatives. Governments and government bodies would not underwrite or guarantee any derivative. The world headquarters would be staffed by the most highly qualified and most experienced economists, ex-retail bankers, ex-central bankers, ex hedge fund managers, business people and investment experts. This branch network in every country would ensure the application of the exact same standards worldwide, and create a level playing field for all financial institutions. This would favour stability and order over speculation manipulation and fraud. Those people responsible for its operation and running at branch level would also have personal financial liability for abuses of the system.

11. Democratisation of Money and Banking using New Types of Money Creation and New Types of Banking for Long term Productive Investment & Consumption

This explained in more detail later in this Chapter

12. European Court of Justice to try cases of financial frauds and corruption by politically connected people

Use the European Court of Justice and its branches in Europe to try powerful persons from the financial industry, big business and politics for financial crimes. And fund the prosecution in European level courts of those persons guilty of financial crimes in member states. Nation states and national governments cannot be trusted to run independent courts where powerful financial and political interests would be tried. Commissions of Inquiry, Tribunals, Parliamentary committees and national courts have proven to be ineffective and useless.

Use the European Court of Justice and its branches to legally seize the personal assets of corrupt politicians, advisors, regulators, bankers, speculators, tax evaders, managers and business persons responsible for the banking and financial crashes. This would include all personal assets in bank accounts in offshore tax havens and other anonymous havens. These assets would be kept by the ESM or ESM supported body.

The immunity from prosecution for bank executives of 'systemic' banks, and employees and executives of the ESM, BIS, FSB and IMF should be ended. This would make all banks accountable, subject to the law, and enforce 'moral hazard' on these institutions.

13. Offshore Banks, Tax Havens, Tax loopholes and Tax evasion schemes

Taxes are required to pay off government debts and deficits and to inject money into an economy to build and upgrade public infrastructure, education and human capital, hospitals, police and courts, stimulate private investment and the returns to private investment via higher levels of consumption and aggregate demand. The scale of this problem is exposed in the following facts

- The total cost of tax evasion has been estimated at $3.1 trillion per year. This is a large financial loss to government and taxpayers and public services (Tax Justice network report, James Henry, November 2011, http://www.tackletaxhavens.com/Cost_of_Tax_Abuse_TJN%20Research_23rd_Nov_2011.pdf)

- Total untaxed monies lodged in offshore tax havens is estimated to be $32 trillion (Tax Justice Network, James Henry, 2012, http://www.taxjustice.net/cms/upload/pdf/Price_of_Offshore_Revisited_120722.pdf)

- $12 trillion of the $32 trillion figure mentioned above was managed by 50 international banks, many of which received bailouts during the financial crisis of 2008 – 2014.

- Over the period 1970 to 2007, at least $150 – 200 billion per year was taken out of developing and third world countries and lodged into offshore tax havens. This over time accumulated 6.2 trillion in offshore tax havens (Total untaxed monies lodged in offshore tax havens is estimated to be $32 trillion (Tax Justice Network, James Henry, 2012,

http://www.taxjustice.net/cms/upload/pdf/Price_of_Offshore_Revisited_120722.pdf)

- By 2014, over $12.1 trillion has been taken out of developing and third world countries and lodged in offshore tax havens (James Henry, Tax Justice Network,

  http://www.taxjustice.net/2016/05/09/17103/)

- The December 2013 report from Global Financial Integrity, "Illicit Financial Flows from the Developing World: 2002-2011," found that the developing world lost $5.9 trillion in tax evasion and other illegal financial flows from 2002-2011, with illegal outflows increasing at an average rate of more than 10 percent per year. (http://www.gfintegrity.org/report/2013-global-report-illicit-financial-flows-from-developing-countries-2002-2011/)

- Profit shifting by multinational firms cost the global economy $660 billion in 2012 and have cost hundreds of billions per year for many years. This often involves the use of foreign tax havens. (http://www.taxjustice.net/scaleBEPS/)

- In 2015, The Wall Street Journal estimated that corporations evade paying taxes of over $200 billion per year [16] but this is a conservative estimate, the real figure is likely to be several hundred billion dollars per year when one includes big banks, hedge funds, vulture funds, speculators in assets, property and derivatives and the accounting and law firms.

These tax havens serve as places for tax evasion for big corporations, big banks, speculators in assets, property and derivatives, law firms, accounting firms, big real estate firms, vulture funds, politicians, hedge funds, insurance companies, terrorists and criminals. Sales, revenues, profits, costs, fees, charges, salaries, bonuses, capital gains, invoices, receipts, assets, structured investment vehicles, off balance sheet items, bribes, grants, subsidies, aid, etc are redirected through these tax havens to escape taxes. Tax loopholes in developed and developing countries are fully exploited. These tax havens and tax loopholes suck massive amounts of money out of developed and developing countries every year depriving governments and businesses of vital monies for essential public services and infrastructure and for private investment. Read:

http://www.businessinsider.com/afp-oecd-vows-to-change-the-game-with-new-tax-rules-2014-9

http://www.financialbuzz.com/oecd-says-worldwide-crackdown-on-mncs-from-2017-global-news-151271

http://www.independent.ie/business/irish/pressure-rises-to-close-tax-loopholes-30602181.html

Tax Havens: How Globalization Really Works (Cornell Studies in Money) by John Christensen The Tax Justice Network

https://www.youtube.com/watch?v=znYA0yIQMq0

Small countries such as Ireland lose tens of billions of euros to tax evasion and loopholes, while bigger countries such as the USA, Canada, Australia, Britain, Netherlands, France lose hundreds of billions of euros in tax revenues. This is money which governments could have invested in hospitals, healthcare, education, skills development, community development, police, crime reduction, infrastructure projects, research and development in the private and state sectors, etc. And businesses could have invested in new plant and equipment, new technology, new jobs, new products and services, marketing and advertising, innovation and research and development. This represents a massive loss to nations and to peoples.

The EU authorities working with the WTO, USA, BIS, IMF, World Bank, and other trading blocs should close down the tax loopholes, the tax evasion schemes between countries, offshore tax evasion banks and tax havens. This would also involve the following:

o Tax is paid on the product and service where it is sold. If it is sold to a customer in France the tax is payable in France, regardless if it is sold online or offline. All offshoring of the sale is closed legally.

o Tax is paid on the product and service where it is produced. If it is produced offshore then a country or the EU which is importing the product or service applies the tax applicable for production of such a product or service in their own country.

o Capital allowances are capped at 33% and have certain financial limits set by a national government or the EU. Capital allowances are only applied for capital raised within the country. All offshoring of capital for capital allowance applications in another jurisdiction are made illegal.

o Shell companies invented for avoiding tax are made subject to a minimum tax, public reporting requirements, public scrutiny, and regulations.

o Multinational businesses pay a certain minimum of tax to their home country if they are involved in substantial international offshoring and tax avoidance. This could be used strategically to attract more jobs back to the home country.

o All special purpose vehicles and quaifs and similar products are made subject to a minimum tax, public reporting requirements, public scrutiny, and regulations.

o The strategic use of national loans and international loans, intermediaries and charities to evade taxes are closed by governments and EU. The closing of "Dutch Double Dipping" type tax evasion.

- All offshoring activities between countries / big businesses and tax havens are constantly investigated and analysed to identify the loopholes used and this knowledge is used to inform governments, tax authorities, regulators, academics and the press and media with a view to changing laws and regulations.

- New Reporting laws requiring all individuals, banks, businesses and organisations to report all transactions with offshore tax havens. And criminal penalties, fines and the right to be sued for not reporting.

- Greater international powers for tax authorities to investigate tax evasion through foreign tax havens. This will involve international agreements or treaties.

- The use of new technologies including new tracking technology and artificial intelligence systems to identify sources of tax evasion

- Use of whistleblowers in businesses and banks and in offshore tax havens

- International agreements whereby governments would implement the measures stated here.

- Individual tax status should be determined from place of birth and primary and secondary school education and the location where the individual created their wealth, while for business it should be determined in the place of production and the place of sales, this may involve separate production taxes, sales taxes and capital gains taxes depending on where the activity took place.

- In cases where an offshore tax haven refuses to cooperate, a court order of tax debt enforcement could be attained and processes put in place to acquire assets or monies from this tax haven. In some cases monies could be printed against the tax haven, using its currency. This currency could be printed to the value of the tax debt.

- Charging international tax and levies on these offshore tax havens

- Rigorous auditing and investigations of tax loopholes and tax havens

- Refusing financial transactions with tax havens

14. Progressive Global Taxes to tax Economic rents and Stabilise and Improve Government Revenues Worldwide

The famous economist Thomas Piketty has called for global taxes to help reduce the extreme concentrations of wealth globally and within nations. This would help end the tax competition between countries to attract international capital, which has resulted in a race to the bottom worldwide. There needs to a level playing field globally for all businesses and governments, so that businesses can thrive and make profits and governments can stabilise and improve their tax revenues. This will require some profound changes globally. The following could be coordinated at a global level or a trading bloc level:

- A Tobin tax of 0.5% on all financial trades and transactions, introduced at EU level and at WTO level or the global level would create billions of euros / dollars in tax revenues for governments and for important public services and investment. It would help balance government budgets globally and enable strategic public investments to be made eg. schools, hospitals, clean drinking water, housing, infrastructure etc.. It would also discourage excessive speculation in financial assets and derivatives which tend to create economic bubbles and crashes and expensive bail outs.

- A new wealth tax for those who made millions of euros during the speculative booms and from predatory vulture capitalism during the crash and austerity years. This could be set at a net worth of 3 million euros or more, not including the family home. A flat tax of 0.3% of net worth up to 15 million euros and 0.6% for over 15 million euros. This would include wealth held in offshore tax havens and trusts. Eliminate all forms of tax avoidance and tax shelters for this tax. Tax status should be determined from place of birth and primary and secondary school education and where most of the wealth was originally generated or inherited.

- A conspicuous consumption tax of 35% on luxury products and services. These would be highly priced products and services used by the wealthy.

- A floor for corporate tax of 15% for productive investments and 25% for speculative investments and no lower. Encourage countries to compete on the basis of education, public infrastructure, scientific infrastructure, stable society, low crime rates, good laws, location, membership of a trading bloc, value added services.

- A capital gains tax of 20% and no lower for productive investment. A capital gains tax of 35% and no lower for speculative investments

- A global taxation of robots and Artificial Intelligence (AI), of 20-25%, applied in every country could provide the means for funding employment schemes and training, up-skilling and career advancement schemes in the private sector and state sector, and the expansion of employee share ownership and community share ownership to the masses.

- Land Value Tax set at 35% of the increased value of the land as a result of the provision of public infrastructure and public services near the land and proximity to towns and cities. This would be aimed at reducing land speculation, site speculation and property speculation. Fred Harrison in Britain has carried out a lot of research into this.

- A natural resources tax of at least 20% of the markup price and the elimination of existing loopholes which redirect sales and profits of natural resources through offshore tax havens to avoid paying any tax

- Break up monopolies, oligopolies, cartels and restrictive practises into smaller competing units. If this cannot be achieved then set a monopoly / cartel tax of 40% on profits.

- Tax interest on debt at the same standard tax rates which apply to workers and middle income families in a country

- Set the inheritance tax to 15% for all wealth under €3 million, 23% for all wealth between €3 million and €20 million, and 33% for all wealth over €20 million. This would include wealth held in offshore tax havens and trusts. Eliminate all forms of tax avoidance and tax shelters for this tax. This would tax unearned income, and prevent the formation of oligarchies, aristocracies, and plutocracies which undermine democracy and freedom.

15. Capital controls and new measures to improve trade imbalances and increase incomes, earnings, profitability and the ability to repay debt

The EU and other similar trading blocs in North America, South America, Asia, Africa, Australasia, need to strengthen their own internal market and give preference to the manufacturing of goods and services inside a trading block. For the EU, this means trade within the EU, investment within the EU, production of goods and services in the EU, and the creation of jobs and full employment within the EU. This will involve

- EU capital controls to favour production and employment inside the EU

- EU trading controls to favour production and employment inside the EU

- Preferred investment and trading status to EU based businesses.

- Use of 'Guaranteed EU employment' labels to differentiate which products and services are actually generating jobs inside the EU

- New investment tax credits and tax reductions for productive investments which increase jobs and employment in an EU country

- Tax increases on companies and businesses which create jobs outside the EU. This would provide further incentives to create jobs inside the EU.

These measures would improve the overall economic effects of the debt deleveraging and fiscal and monetary stimulus programmed mentioned in this paper. The great economist Keynes recommended these measures in times of recession and depression in order to raise aggregate demand, money growth and aggregate supply, and bring about full economic recovery and sustained growth. Quantitative Easing could be used to assist these new capital controls and trading controls through incentives for 'Preferred trading and investment status' where the EU provides new financial and other incentives and rules for all EU countries and international companies to trade with and invest in other EU countries. Ireland, Spain, Italy, and Portugal and Greece could be given special status or incentives in order to speed up economic growth and recovery in these countries, and help pay down debt. Imports from the Far East and Africa could be reduced through new taxes, levies and charges and other disincentives at EU level. These measures would involve mass relocations of European companies and businesses back into the EU, and increased inter-trade between EU nations, creating new jobs and new growth throughout the EU.

It would end the "global race to the bottom" or "global race to the sewer" which has pitted low-cost developing and third world countries against Western developed countries and delivered high and growing numbers of business closures and relocations, down-sizing and international subcontracting, higher unemployment, higher under-employment, economic instability, falling tax revenues, a diminishing taxation base, higher state spending followed by pressure for increased taxes to finance the resultant higher national debt burdens, higher costs in attracting international capital, etc..

These type of capital controls and trading controls within the EU and other trading blocs around the world would help improve worker's rights, worker's incomes, financial and banking regulations, tax revenues, pension funds and pension payments, aggregate demand and money supply growth and employment levels within countries and within the trading bloc, and improve social and political stability within countries and within trading blocs.

16. Related North American Debt Conference

The same measures mentioned above could be applied in a Debt Conference for the USA and Canada to reduce their national debts and total debts (household, government, corporate and banking). This would include a very detailed analysis of debts and interest and significant reductions of such to bring debt down to sustainable levels. Let us look again at current US debt levels:

- The USA with its government debt of $20 trillion has a debt of 111% of GDP

- the total debt (household, federal and state governments, corporate, banking) is $67 trillion which is 372% of GDP

- Total US unfunded liabilities (social security, veterans, medicare and government debt) are $106 trillion which is 588% of GDP

This debt is totally unsustainable and has turned the USA into a debt enslaved country. One must remember that debt and interest is created out of nothing when banks make loans. Thus debt is privatised fraud, which deprives government and ordinary communities of the traditional legal power to create money.

This massive debt has greatly reduced the spending and investment powers of the US Congress and US President and state governments. It has destroyed the financial health of the US federal government and state governments and of the US economy. It also has adversely affected 90% of American households who struggle to survive on stagnant or falling real wages (since 1983) and massive household debts and student debts.

The Vast Misallocation of Scare Resources

Economics is supposed to be about the allocation of scarce resources. In reality, economics is about power imbalances and exploitation and the vast misallocation of scarce resources, and the resultant implementation of poverty, want and misery in the midst of great abundance. Scale is vitally important in the present world, and differentiates the current era from previous eras - the global cost of bailing out the banks and financial institutions between 2007 and 2014 was $13 trillion and the global value of the arms trade is $2 trillion per year (Stockholm International Peace Research Institute), and the amount of untaxed monies sitting in offshore tax havens is estimated to be $32 trillion, and the value of the Derivatives market, which is pure financial speculation was over $1,200 trillion ; this is over 20 times the global economy. This amounts to $1,247 trillion wasted on speculation, banking frauds, financial frauds, corrupt special interests, tax evasions, and the promoting of wars, mass murder, and criminality. In 2015, the cost of giving all persons on the planet adequate health care and a decent wage was $86 billion per year (http://www.anielski.com/real-cost-eliminating-poverty/). This figure of $86 billion is very tiny fraction of the $1,247 trillion wasted on banking bailouts and war, and special interests. Considering the trillions of dollars wasted on speculation, bailouts of banks and speculators, and mass slaughter and war, there are plenty of financial and economic resources and money to build different types of economies such as economic democracy, social justice, peace industries, productive industries, social and political stability in all countries and peace on earth.

The money system or monetary system has proven to be totally ineffective and inefficient, resulting in the creation of artificial scarcity, mismatches between aggregate demand and optimum output and employment, and consistent massive losses in economic terms and human terms over time. In summary, a massive misallocation of resources and massive waste of 'scarce' resources.

Diagram of The Defective and Flawed Monetary System of Today (See below)

Resources

Abundant natural resources, high technology and innovation producing increased yields and high productivity, rising levels of productivity over time, abundant skilled workers and unskilled workers desiring work or seeking work, high levels of creativity and innovation in the population, plenty of work needed to be done, desire and need for investment in necessary products and services and new start ups, great potential for the development of skills and knowledge among most people, high levels of potential demand for goods and services, high investment potential, high potential for full employment

The Monetary System and the Creation of Artificial Scarcity

Suction of money away from the production sector, infrastructure sector and the human development and creation of deficiencies of effective demand and supply via :

- depriving governments of the facility to print money, Quantitative Easing, and starving them of the funds for public investment and for infrastructure and forcing them to borrow money at high interest rates (the bond market). Increasing national debts and the repayment burdens on taxpayers.

- money rationing and credit rationing via central banks and private banks which starves the productive sector of funds forcing it to borrow at high interest rates or not to invest in production. Lost productive investment.

- excessive credit or too much money for speculation in assets, financial products, and derivatives involving billions and trillions of dollars / euros.

- the high costs of speculative crashes, including bailing out banks, monetary systems, financial institutions and speculators costing trillions of dollars and imposing higher national debt levels, austerity and recession on peoples which reduces aggregate demand, investment, jobs and economic growth. Costing trillions of dollars / euros in bail outs and lost GNP, output and growth as a result of austerity, recession / depression

- creation of excessive debt levels at individual, household, corporate, banking and government levels after crashes. Interest rates multiplying debt. Debt overhang. High debt repayments burden which negatively affects consumption and productive investment and economic growth, producing deep recessions and depressions, despite reductions in interest rates to zero or near zero and monetary stimulus. [9]

- excessive government spending and debt on arms races, wars, regime changes, corporate welfare and subsidies, and the projects of special interests with political power. Costing trillions of dollars.

- too many financial restrictions on potential home owners which prevent them buying homes. Deficiencies in the building of and supply of homes. Unmet aggregate demand and lost productive investment in the building sector. Excessive rent prices, higher levels of homelessness.

- economic rents by monopolies, oligopolies and restrictive practises with political connections, which artificially inflate prices and costs and levies, and suck money out of the productive economy reducing output and employment

- global outsourcing, de-industrialisation, downsizing, capital flight and higher levels of unemployment and under-employment which destroys consumer purchasing power and present and future investment.

- insufficient aggregate demand and aggregate supply, and insufficient money creation (directed at productive investment) to produce full employment levels. Deficiencies in effective demand and effective supply.

- tax evasion costing governments trillions of dollars / euros per year and reducing government investment and necessary public services.

- excessive stress on governments and budgets from factors mentioned above, reduced taxes, excessive build up of debt, eg. Detroit

- policies which promote and worsen high concentrations of wealth

There is a relationship between the suction of money out of the productive economy through various factors mentioned above AND the failure of low interest rates or zero interest rates, Quantitative Easing or money printing and expansionary monetary policies to bring about recovery and strong, sustained economic growth.

Distortions and Defects in the Supply of Capital

Tax payers and the government

Governments intervened in markets to bail out banks, bondholders, speculators, assets, and financial institutions. Bailouts were mostly funded by taxpayers and in some cases by the printing of money, Quantitative Easing. This involved the transferring of massive banking and private debt onto government balance sheets, and the enforcement of austerity, recession and tax increases and additional taxes, levies and charges on taxpayers.

It was the taxpayers and the state which paid the cost of bailing out these assets and preserving their prices over time, while the vulture capital Funds and large equity funds and wealthy investors made the profits from this. This was not equitable and fair to the taxpayers and government which bailed out the assets and financial institutions.

For example: the taxpayer pays 100% of the original cost of bailing out the asset or its added to the national debt. The vulture capital fund buys the asset at 25% of its original value and sells at a profit for 100% or more of its original value. The profit would be millions of euros / dollars per deal. The taxpayer or government made a massive loss and had an increase in its national debt while the vulture capital fund made a massive profit.

Prices of distressed assets. Profits to be made from Enforcement of Bailouts and Austerity

This bailout and austerity had the effect of protecting the prices of assets at prices ranging from 30 – 90% below the original cost. It provided a 'floor price' for this capital. Vulture capital Funds and large equity funds and wealthy investors were able to buy these assets at prices ranging from 20% - 50% of their original value. The continuing bailout and austerity enforced on taxpayers protected the prices of these assets, and the gradual improvement in the economy, in addition to Quantitative Easing which enabled speculators to enter and bid up prices again in the market, led to price increases for these assets.

The vulture funds profit from higher interest, rent, and repayments and from selling the asset(s) at 100% more of the value. And engineering the sale and profits through tax havens to avoid paying tax. Individual deals would have involved profits ranging from tens of millions of euros to hundreds of millions of euros for individual investors. Yet, it was the taxpayers and the state which paid the cost of bailing out these assets and preserving their prices over time, while the vulture capital funds and large equity funds made the profits from this. The net result was the taxpayer or government made a massive loss and had an increase in its national debt while the vulture capital fund made a massive profit. This was not equitable and fair to the taxpayers and government which bailed out the assets and financial institutions. This gross distortion of capital supply markets represents a new paradigm in economics termed 'socialism for the rich'.

The present system of banking is not working in the best interests of productive businesses, government, households and the economy. In the period from 2012 to 2015, while ECB interest rates were less than 1%, many Irish banks were charging their customers 4% - 8% interest on mortgage payments and loans, and they refused to reduce their interest rates in line with ECB rate reductions. This was at a time of great financial hardship, austerity and recession in Ireland and other EU countries, and added thousands of euros more per year to mortgages. Ireland had the highest mortgage payments in the EU at this time. Governments, households and businesses are paying billions of euros in excessive interest rates every year. Figures are provided for this below. The massive accumulation of household debt, business debt, bank debt and government debt, which is a few times GDP and GNP, and the large repayments every year in addition to excessive interest rates, means the banking system is sucking away resources from long-term productive investment, consumption and aggregate demand, and stifling economic growth and prosperity.

Furthermore, Central bank policies in several countries are highly discriminatory and can skew markets ; they have the effect of bailing out large national and international banks and financial institutions, and supporting large salaries and bonuses for bank executives and loans for speculation in shares, assets, and derivatives, while refusing monies to smaller banks and community banks and effectively bankrupting them. This was clearly established in FOI requests concerning the Federal Reserve and it's bail out of banks programme after the 2008 crash [8]. There were conflicts of interest and bias concerning which banks would be saved and which ones would be allowed to fail. Many of these smaller banks and community banks which were forced into failure, bankruptcy or take overs provided credit to small and medium sized businesses, and this is vital to most economies, and their loss had a negative impact. [8] And it is a well established fact that big banks often reject loans for small and medium sized firms, thus limiting their growth and employment capacity, research by Professor Richard Werner in the University of Southampton confirms this. This central bank policy can in many circumstances be very destructive of viable banks and of small and medium sized businesses and of less developed or developing regions within countries.

A Democratisation of Money and Banking using New Types of Money Creation and New Types of Banking for Long term Productive Investment & Consumption

Before we proceed to examine alternative democratic forms of banking, credit and money creation I would urge readers to read Margrit Kennedy's book 'Interest and Inflation Free Money' and Michael Montagne's web site at http://www.perfecteconomy.com for an excellent analysis of the effects of interest on economies and businesses [33]. Montagne's work is notable as it provides mathematical proofs of how compound interest and accompanying debt multiplication leads to financial crashes and to inflation and deflation. Their research is backed up by many others including Dr. Richard Werner of the University of Southampton who has published many works and lectured on the subject of debt free and interest free money and reformed banking. Compound interest acts as a parasite, it sucks money out of the real economy affecting consumption levels, aggregate demand and accompanying investment levels, imposing extra costs on extraction, production, storage, distribution, selling, delivering, and purchasing. It imposes a 'trickle up' economics benefitting the richest 5%. And this interest is not created at the time when money is created (via loans) so there is not enough money in the system to pay it off ; the compound interest rate system is unsustainable. For example, the interest on Ireland's national debt is €8 billion per year and the interest on the UK national debt is £46 billion per year and the interest on total government, business and household debt in the UK is 200 billion per year ; this is both excessive and very costly, and enforces many cutbacks in public services and economic activity.

The research of Richard Vague, Dr. Steve Keen, Hyman Minsky, Galbraith, George Stiglitz, Irving Fisher, Wynne Godley, Mian and Sufi and many other top economists show that credit growth is vital to economic growth, to full employment, to business growth, to investment and increasing output, to consumption and aggregate demand. However, this credit growth needs to be sustainable and aimed at productive activity, expanding the amount of physical goods and services in the economy and on creating sustainable income returns or earnings from production and productivity over the medium term to long term. Income and earnings generation is absolutely essential and would provide the means to make debt sustainable over the short to long term. The elimination of interest in loans or usury recommended in this Chapter would greatly boost the earnings of workers, owners of capital, large pension funds and investment funds, and capital re-investment schemes. It would be a powerful incentive for productive investment, innovations and technology, and long term outlooks in investing. Not on inflating speculative bubbles, as is presently the case. This will require a major change in direction for credit creation, banking, debt and money creation processes and the politics which underlies this.

There was an interesting banking and money experiment carried out in Worgl in Austria during the Depression of the 1930's. The local government there used the economic theories proposed by Silvio Gesell and printed a local currency and used it to fund local government, state projects and infrastructure, and to stimulate private investment in the town and region. The local currency was subject to a demurrage charge of 1% per month or 12% per year, which had the effect of discouraging hoarding of this money and strongly encouraging consumption. During Depressions hoarding of money is a major factor in the worsening of economic conditions, a fact pointed by the economist John Maynard Keynes in his works. This local currency was used for wages and salaries and for buying and selling locally and became very popular. It was also used for public works and infrastructure, and for local government projects. This created new investment opportunities in the private sector and new employment and this in turn stimulated consumption, particularly local consumption. The velocity of money was 463 in one year, while the Austrian Schilling stagnated at 21 per year. This consumption improved returns to businesses and to capital, and created a virtuous circle of high and growing consumption, investment, business profitability, employment and economic growth. Unemployment fell to less than 5% in Worgl as more people became employed. Worgl went from economic depression to an economic boom within a short period of time. This was in direct contrast to the rest of the Austrian economy where unemployment was 24% - 26% during the early to mid 1930's and remained over 20% for most of the Depression of the 1930's. In fact, every one of the new local currency in Worgl created between 12 and 14 times more employment than the normal currency or schillings circulating in parallel. This showed the total ineffectiveness and failure of the old state currency, the Schilling. Other localities and towns tried to copy Worgl, and they also had some success. However the Austrian Central Bank intervened and closed down the local currency in Worgl and throughout Austria through using court cases and compliant judges in late 1933. This led to a return to the old state currency and to economic depression and high unemployment.

Similar local currency projects had the same benefits in other parts of the world, as outlined by the economist Lietaer [10]. For example the WIR currency in Switzerland serves as a second currency for the Swiss, mainly for business to business transactions and it has proven to be highly successful. It is often cited as one of the main reasons for the stability of the Swiss financial system. Others include the successful LETS schemes, Regios currency in Germany, the Terra, Time dollars and Ithaca hours and many social purpose currencies which deal with pressing social issues such as elderly care, childcare, reducing crime in communities, protection of the environment, etc.. Money and banking play a vitally important role in economics, they are the primary drivers of economics, they are not secondary issues as presumed by many mainstream economists. Local currencies with demurrage costs which (a) encourage consumption and investment locally and regionally (b) increase the velocity of money (c) serve important social needs which cannot be met by a national currency (or euro) based on excessive debt and compounded interest (d) provide resilience in response to economic crashes, downturns and recessions need to be explored further and should be implemented in those countries suffering from economic depression, austerity, deflation and high unemployment, and accompanying social ills such as crime, addiction, neglect of elderly and children. Their successes in the Great Depression in Austria during the 1930's and elsewhere at other times of history [10] prove their viability and effectiveness. The main economic effects of local currencies in the past and today appear to be anti-hoarding, higher consumption, higher velocity of money, higher state investment and private investment, greater incentives to invest by private businesses and local governments, increased returns to productive investments, higher employment generation, faster payment of taxes which in turn increased revenues for use in public investment projects, and sustained economic growth. This gives local currencies better stability and resilience than national currencies or euros which are currencies based on excessive debt, compounded interest and speculation. I have integrated this into my proposals below.

The Chicago Plan devised by economists in the 1930's and supported by Irving Fisher and many others provided much needed reforms to banking and money creation [37]. It was a response to the wall street crash of 1929 and Great Depression. Some of the proposals were implemented by the US government in the 1930's while most were rejected due to ferocious opposition by bankers and lobbyists. In recent times the Chicago Plan has been revisited by economists and the IMF, with one study claiming that it could deliver output gains of 10% and reduce inflation down to near zero, and there have been calls to implement its recommendations to resolve the economic and financial crisis in Europe and the USA [37]. I have included the recommendations of the Chicago Plan in my proposals below.

The East Asian Economic Miracle Model could serve as a guide for a new reformed system of banking. For decades central banks and private banks were instructed and encouraged to funnel the vast majority of their loans into productive companies and investments, and to build up the industrial base and agricultural base of these countries. Loans for speculation were discouraged and loans for consumption were limited. The productive base was used to build up consumption and aggregate demand. As these economies grew and matured, the limits to loans for consumption were gradually removed. These economies had very high growth rates. By the mid 1980's some of them introduced American and European forms of speculation and banking, and their economies suffered bubbles followed by severe crashes and economic downturns as a result. Also the German banking model of many community banks, credit unions and public savings banks could serve as a model for reformed banking. I have integrated these into my proposals for reform below.

The money system and banking system is capable of many combinations and permutations in order to provide optimal outcomes for businesses, consumption, employment and growth, but the present one is overly expensive, costly, parasitical, speculative, and destructive of businesses and growth. We need to look at some new and innovative ways for using money and banking to stimulate long term productive investment, production led consumption and demand which increases returns to these investments, sustainable economic growth, fair trade, and full employment. For the long term this could progress along the following fronts:

1.   National Money Creation

Restore money creation and currency creation back to national governments or government controlled bank. The government would create debt free and interest free money to finance many of its activities with an emphasis on productive investments of strategic value to a nation. This would involve the government spending debt free and interest free money into the economic system as proposed by Modern Monetary Theory (MMT). This would produce paybacks in the form of increased aggregate demand, user fees (for government), incomes growth, credit growth, infrastructure enhancement, skills and productivity growth, increased productive investment opportunities, and rising productivity and profits for the private sector. This would be Quantitative Easing for the People, not for private banks, speculators and bailouts, and has been detailed in previous sections of this Chapter. It would correspond to Richard C. Cook's proposal of 'credit as a public utility', the Chicago Plan of the 1930's, and Modern Monetary Theory (MMT). It would also include aspects of Michael Montagnes' Mathematically Perfected Economy (MPE) where interest would be abolished and debt would be made sustainable and affordable, not speculation based, and repayment based on the consumption or depreciation of assets, goods and services over long periods. Money in circulation, including debts, would be fully backed up by assets and goods. Newly created money could be diffused into the production of real goods and services, infrastructure and many of the projects mentioned earlier in this Chapter in relation to

Quantitative easing for the People.

2. Decentralised Banking, Breaking up Concentrations of Banks, New Types of Banks for promoting productive investment, innovation, start-ups, industry, human capital, and sustainable consumption and development

➢ Fractional Reserve needs to be restored to 100% so as to stabilise the banking system, the business cycles and prevent bank runs and reduce national debts. To reach this level of 100% fractional reserve, banks would have to borrow from the government treasury. This large scale borrowing from the government could be offset by the bank's holding of government bonds. This would result in a massive reduction in national debt. And restore money creation back to government. It would also separate money creation from credit creation as advised by the Chicago Plan [37].

Money would no longer be created out of nothing by private banks and interest charged on it. Banks would lend what they have. Money would change from being debt and interest based to being non debt based and interest based and being sovereign. Banks could increase their available funds for lending through (i) repayments of existing debts to the bank (ii) borrowing monies from government or central bank, as described below (iii) deposit accounts and checking or current accounts would be 100% fractional reserve and would not be lent out, while money in savings accounts could be lent out. This would stabilise banking and prevent bank runs and systemic crisis (iv) borrowing from other banks (v) through the retained earnings of the bank. The government could use money printing or Quantitative Easing to lend money to many types of banks and credit institutions, including commercial banks, public savings banks, community banks, regional banks (such as in Germany), credit unions, cooperative banks, microfinance, microcredit institutions (similar to Grameen bank), local currency systems and public banks (as envisaged by Richard C. Cook). These banks would be subject to Credit Guidance by governments, as explained below, and would provide loans for productive investment, expanding production, productivity, innovation, start ups, employment, and employee ownership and consumption. Prioritising loans for the productive sector would be a government condition. Banks would borrow money from government / central bank at zero interest rates, and loan out the money to bank customers at zero interest rates. A small administration fee could be charged annually by banks for providing credit to customers. Importantly, money would no longer be created out of nothing by private banks and interest charged on it. Loans would be backed up by assets and real reserves. Loans and mortgages could be supplied for non speculative assets. Banks and credit institutions could use credit to take equity stakes in productive businesses, thus reducing leverage ratios and associated burdens and risks. Most small and medium sized productive businesses today cannot get loans for investment from banks, and these reforms would change this, giving productive firms easier access to credit on very good terms. The Grameen banks in Asia could serve as a model of excellence for this new type of banking, and enable the growth of employee owned firms and cooperatives and small businesses, building economic democracy at all levels of society worldwide. This new form of credit would empower ordinary working class individuals, families, communities, small and medium sized businesses and new entrepreneurs.

➢ The elimination of interest and the provision of debt free money to government and the provision of interest free loans to individuals, households, businesses and organisations which is sustainable and affordable and not speculation based, and in line with consumption / depreciation would greatly reduce the costs of goods and services and the severe imbalances and instabilities in economic systems. This would greatly increase both consumption and investment levels and combined with wider economic democracy including greater employee ownership and community ownership and the elimination of monopolies, cartels and economic rents would improve the sustainability of debt and reduce the risk of default.

➢ The creation of several public savings banks, state banks (as advocated by Ellen Brown in the USA), community banks, cooperative banks, credit unions, gold banks, microfinance, microcredit institutions in and around cities and within rural regions. There should be hundreds of these type of banks and financial institutions in a country or state (such as states in USA). The purpose of these banks would be to create and lend money for productive investments and for small and medium sized firms, and also provide small loans for consumption purposes. Loans for speculation would be severely restricted or banned. This should be facilitated by government financial grants, tax incentives and national and European deregulation to assist the setting up of these banks. This would be the engine of credit growth.

➢ Integrate private banks, public savings banks (such as in Germany), credit unions, cooperative banks, community banks and regional banks, microfinance, microcredit institutions (similar to Grameen bank), local currency systems and state banks into (i) national electronic clearing houses (ii) national ATM networks so as to provide high speed clearing of payments between all financial institutions and liquidity to consumers and businesses while encouraging a fairer and more competitive banking system.

➤ Bancor Protocol, Bitcoin and Blockchain technologies have recently created a paradigm change in banking, money creation and exchange, these would be used to distribute, track and monitor this distribution of funds locally, regionally, nationally and internationally. The recent invention of Smart Blockchains and Smart Contracts under the Bancor Protocol has made this easier for small, local, community based and medium sized financial institutions. The Bancor Protocol has made it possible to convert between multiple national currencies, gold, local currencies and crypto currencies and maintain high levels of liquidity for all these currencies online. These new technologies have very low cost or zero cost for electronic transfers of money between countries, and this is a very significant innovation in the modern world.

Bitcoin in 2017 has become a speculative currency whose exact value cannot be determined but the technology it uses could have many different applications in banking, money creation and digital currencies. In the future, Bitcoin and other crypto currencies may be tied to real world variables such as gold, silver, rare metals, or baskets of such, national GDP, a multiple of average industrial earnings, or productivity growth so as to give the currency some value stability. This would eliminate speculation and make it a reliable and effective means of exchange and a trusted store of value.

➤ Promissory notes

The greater use of Promissory notes between buyer and seller / producer, which are interest free. Blockchain technologies could be used to coordinate this regionally, nationally and internationally.

➤ Conversion of vast amounts of business debt and junk bonds and corporate raider debt into equity in businesses. This would reduce the indebtedness of many businesses

➤ Some further ideas on money creation are presented on the following web sites:

▪ http://www.positivemoney.org/

▪ http://perfecteconomy.com

▪ Research 'bradbury pound' on Google and other search engines

▪ Public Savings Banks around the world - http://republicirelandbank.com/

▪ Grameen bank   http://grameen.com/

▪ www.healingcentres.org/monetary.htm

3. The German banking model and Mittelstander companies, and the East Asian banking model and the state bank model proposed by Ellen Brown

The German banking model could serve as a guide for banking reforms worldwide as it has a stable banking system with many types of banks such as commercial banks, public savings banks, credit unions or cooperative banks, community banks, regional banks, state banks, and microfinance firms. These banks are competitive and provide various funding schemes for different sectors of the German economy. There is no high concentration of banks and banking power in Germany. And loans and credit for productive investments are prioritised over speculation in assets and derivatives. Public savings banks have been very successful in Germany and have provided great assistance to German industry for several decades, and they could serve as a model for a new banking system in Europe and North America. These public savings banks supported the development and continued successes of German small and medium sized companies, the Mittelstander companies which are the backbone of the German economy. These are behind the success of German exports, in addition to larger firms such as BMW, Mercedes and Volkswagen. In other EU countries and North America, and around the world, public savings banks and the others mentioned above could meet the needs of small and medium sized businesses, start ups, small and medium farmers, ordinary working people and the unemployed. Public savings banks would remove speculation and speculative risks and provide a stable platform for banking and credit expansion based on productive investment and sustainable consumption.

In Germany and some other countries Public Savings Banks are :

1. Operated on commercial principles with the aim of maximising sustainable lending and not on maximising profits.

2. Operated on the Principle of "Local deposits into local loans" keeping capital in their own area.

3. Surpluses remain with the Bank & within the region: Profits are used to increase equity and for non-profit purposes (the public benefit principle).

4. Banned from engaging in financial speculation.

5. Only allowed to lend only to local people and businesses in its designated catchment area.

6. Controlled by stakeholders from the local community.

7. Independent of political influence and control.

8. The Joint Liability Scheme provides protection for all Savings Bank Branches.

9. A combination of new laws, tax incentives and grants and reduction in 'red tape' and regulations could encourage the growth of these new types of banks in all countries.

Dr. Richard Werner of Southampton University is an expert on this type of banking and has written and lectured extensively on it. These banks could be jointly owned by employees and communities and by big pension funds and investors so to diffuse the profits from banking more widely to the population.

The East Asian Banking model shared some of the characteristics of the German model. For several decades East Asian countries relied on Central Bank and / or Government guidance for banks, particularly in lending policies. Loans were prioritised for productive firms and for small and medium sized firms in the productive sector. Loans for consumption were restricted so as to curtail inflationary pressures. While loans for speculation were severely restricted and discouraged so to prevent bubbles and crashes.

Ellen Brown has proposed state banks in the USA and uses the Bank of North Dakota and the successful state banks in Germany, China, South Korea, Taiwan and Singapore as role models and proof that state banks are necessary for economic success [38]. These proposed state banks would process and hold the tax revenues, wages and pension funds of all state employees and also accept deposits from the general public. They would provide loans for state infrastructure, small businesses and medium sized businesses, farmers, exporters of goods and services, and innovation and new business start ups in a state or country. No loans would be provided for speculation. Several states in the USA have bills before their state parliaments to create state banks, in 2016 and 2017. Her web site is based at https://ellenbrown.com .

Combining the German model and East Asian Banking models with Ellen Brown's state banks, with the microcredit and microfinance models of the Grameen bank, credit unions and community banks would provide a diverse banking structure which would suit everyone, providing enough new credit to grow economies, while prioritising productive investment and output as a means to sustain and increase incomes and aggregate demand over time.

4.   Use of Local Currencies and Regional currencies to stimulate economic activity

Historically, currencies represented the economic strengths and weaknesses in a certain part of the world and they devalued or revalued against other countries accordingly. Indeed Keynes's Bancor proposal in 1945 was based on this. Local currencies and regional currencies would have much the same effect as found in the Worgl experiment in Austria in the 1930's. During recessions and depressions and times of deflation, and after crashes, and for the stimulation of depressed economic regions, local governments should encourage and facilitate the creation and use of local currencies which use zero interest rates and forms of demurrage to increase consumption, investment and labour activation (employment) at local level, regional level and national level. This local currency creation could be carried out by local governments and by reputable private providers. This should be assisted by central governments' Quantitative Easing and diffusion of these monies and tax credits to provide initial finance to these local currency schemes. Local currencies will involve distinctions between checking accounts which are used regularly and savings accounts which are used rarely and are focussed on saving over the medium to long term. Checking accounts would incur a small demurrage fee, while savings accounts would retain their value over time. Banks loaning out money could charge an administration fee not interest. Local currency would discourage hoarding and encourage local consumption, a higher velocity of money, and new productive investment at local and regional levels. This would reduce unemployment and regenerate regions within a country.

Bancor Protocol, Bitcoin and Blockchain technologies could be used to create local currencies and scale up local currencies and link them to regional and national currencies and international currencies and local currencies and crypto currencies worldwide. The recent invention of Smart Blockchains and Smart Contracts under the Bancor Protocol has made this easier for small, local, community based and medium sized financial institutions. As mentioned earlier, the Bancor Protocol has made it possible to convert between multiple national currencies, gold, local currencies and crypto currencies online and maintain high levels of liquidity for all these currencies. Now, local and regional currencies can be easily scaled up to national and international level on the Internet or by other electronic means. This innovation (Bancor Protocol) in 2017 has been revolutionary and will facilitate the greater development of local currencies globally. These new technologies have very low cost or zero cost for electronic transfers of money between countries, and this will greatly assist commerce within countries, within regions and trading blocs and internationally, and is a very significant innovation in the modern world.

These local currencies could also be dynamically linked to work done, production, supply, higher productivity, innovations and trade, thus reducing any inflationary concerns. This would enable economic and business development at local level which would at the same time be connected into global level local currencies and global economic development. This would empower local communities everywhere. Insights, methodologies and working models are included below:

- The Swiss dual currency system, consisting of the Swiss Franc and the Swiss business to business currency, the WIR.
- The successful LETS schemes, the Danish and Swedish JAK system, the BCI system in Germany, Time dollars, Ithaca hours, Time banks, the Sol in France, Regios currency in Germany, the Terra, the Bristol pound, and various social purpose currencies
- The Bancor Protocol and Smart Contracts and Smart Blockchains
- The money and banking reforms proposed by Silvio Gesell
- The Worgl experiment in Austria
- Others listed in 'The Future of Money: Creating New Wealth, Work and a Wiser World' by Bernard Lietaer, the global exert in this field.
- http://www.lietaer.com/
- Blockchain technology can be researched on Google and other search engines

5. Social Credit

The elimination of interest and the provision of debt free money (to government) and the provision of sustainable credit (interest free) and structured repayments in line with consumption / depreciation would greatly reduce the costs of goods and services and the severe imbalances and instabilities in economic systems. Wider economic democracy including greater employee ownership and community ownership in addition to wages and the elimination of monopolies, cartels and economic rents would help bridge the gap between incomes and prices. This would achieve most of the aims of social credit as envisaged by Major Clifford Hugh Douglas in the early 20th century. However social credit could be restructured in a way to further improve supply, productivity and output and from this improve the ability to consume and aggregate demand, thus improving this virtuous circle as many other proposals in this book attempt to do.

(i) empower all persons to access credit as part of their human rights. This would enable individuals to create their own credit and provide access to interest free credit and accompanying facilities to pay down low sustainable debt through employment, hard work, services, training and higher productivity, wider share ownership, and state policies which promote these and also facilitate health and well being (instead of the present one of neglecting serious physical illnesses and underfunding poor shoddy, health services and hospitals). This human right to access credit would come with responsibilities. Only individuals and families could apply for social credit. It could be administered via community banks, credit unions, microfinance (similar to Grameen bank), public savings banks, and local currency schemes and the use of Blockchain, Bitcoin and Bancor Protocol technologies. There would be a gradual diffusion of this credit to a person over time, and this credit would be linked to

(a) the acquisition of a long term non speculative assets (such as a family home) or a valuable skill or professional qualification

(b) access to important medical services in order to return to work

(c) to work whether full time, part time or voluntary work or community / charity work and increase the supply of goods and services in an economy

(d) increases in national productivity from use and deployment of newer and newer technologies and continuous innovation of products, services and processes, and continuous training and the deployment of higher level skills

Distributed technologies such Bancor Protocol, Bitcoin, and Blockchain technologies could be used to distribute, track and monitor social credit and ensure integrity, reliability and accountability.

6. Public Education and Awareness about Money Creation

The general public has been poorly informed about money creation and banking for many decades, even centuries. Most people do not understand money creation, credit and banking. Yet money, credit and debt have played a central role in many people's lives. This ignorance has facilitated many abuses and the debt enslavement of peoples and nations. More public debates and Parliamentary debates and TV debates are required to inform politicians and the public about banking, credit and money creation. See UK House of Commons debates on money and banking https://www.youtube.com/watch?v=EBSlSUIT-KM

A new system needs to be implemented to allow a natural expansion of the money supply through debt free and interest free money or credit created by national government and by local authorities (local government) and diffused into the many types of banks and financial institutions mentioned above. These measures have been proposed for years by Mike Montagne, Dr. Bernard Lietaer, and many other leading economists at http://perfecteconomy.com   http://www.positivemoney.org/ and http://www.lietaer.com/ . We cannot continue to have governments reduced down to the level of beggars looking for loans from (private) central banks and commercial banks. And in the modern world, many governments have become over indebted beggars, barely able to borrow the necessary funds to run the basic services of government. Also we cannot have artificial rationing of credit by a few big banks starving productive businesses and small and medium sized businesses of much needed funds. We need to restore money creation back to government and restrict this power to prevent inflation and deflation and encourage price stability. Inflation could be controlled by:

❖ legal and Constitutional limits to government money printing
❖ legal and Constitutional provisions to use this government money printing for productive investment, innovation and productivity in the productive sector, increases in total production and the supply of goods in the economy. A high focus on increasing supply. Production would be prioritised over consumption, with a ratio of 6 : 1 of new money favouring production. It would not be used for speculation in assets, commodities and derivatives. This would have a strong anti inflationary effect. The German banking model and East Asian Economic Miracle Model could serve as a guide.
❖ abolition of interest rates. This would significantly reduce the cost of producing goods and services, distributing them, storing them and selling them and the cost of purchasing them. This would greatly reduce inflation.
❖ abolition of excessive (speculative and economic rent caused) debt which would greatly reduce the cost of goods and services, improve supply and productivity, and reduce inflationary pressures
❖ wider use of employee share ownership and profit sharing and networks of cooperatives to encourage wage flexibility and price flexibility. This would discourage excessive wage demands and price increases. This is part of our proposals for economic democracy and industrial democracy. (See Chapter 9 on Format of Economic Democracy)
❖ some wages could be given in the form of deferred stock options, deferred productivity bonuses, deferred additional share ownership, deferred earnings, and savings bonds to prevent over consumption during periods of inflation and maintain costs at a competitive (non inflationary) rate
❖ break up monopolies, oligopolies, cartels, and restrictive practises and encourage freer competition and a lowering of prices. This policy is recommended in a few chapters in this book.
❖ ending the corporate welfare and corporate subsidies which keep taxes high and prices high in many countries

- special tax incentives and grants specifically to increase supply of goods and services and / or to decrease excessive demand

- special taxes levied on those firms which raise prices excessively

- use of new technologies to reduce the costs of producing goods and services and their distribution costs

- increasing loan refusals if prices are rising too fast

- reduction of import quotas or restrictions to supply. Increase total supply and reduce prices

- a fractional reserve of 100% in all banks (see Chicago Plan) would have a strong anti inflationary effect

- loans would be backed up real assets and /or productive activity in the economy

- extensive investment in alternative technologies and green technologies and use of these technologies. And the building of excess capacity and excess storage to ensure energy security into the future. This would build up economic resilience and reduce the effect of oil price and gas price shocks.

- during periods of recession / depression and deflation, use of local currency demurrage specifically to stimulate productive investment and an increase of supply locally and overall supply nationally

Stimulating both state and private productive investments and overall supply in the economy would expand total goods and services produced and this would have anti inflationary effects. The government of Guernsey provides one successful example of this.

Money printing or Quantitative Easing does not always lead to inflation as seen in the period 2009 – 2017 when $15 trillion was printed globally via Quantitative Easing. Though there was an increase in speculation and the prices of assets, but this strangely is not included in the inflation statistics of most countries. We live in an Orwellian world of 'doublespeak' where price increases in some products cause panic and hysteria about inflation, but bigger rises in the prices of speculative assets are ignored and not included in measures of inflation by mainstream economists, government statistics offices, and governments. Neo Liberals, Neo Classicals and Monetarists seem very confused about inflation.

The new system above would have the characteristics and effects of Quantitative Easing, but very different outcomes to that of the period 2009 - 2017. It would be focussed on increasing productive investment, consumption and employment, and on serving the needs of small and medium sized businesses and ordinary people. It would reach the ordinary working people of a country and transform their lives in a positive and constructive manner. These banks and credit organisations could provide interest free loans for 'productive investment' for private businesses and local governments. The 'interest free' aspect would stimulate investment incentives and undertakings. The emphasis on expanding total output, production and distribution of products and services and productivity levels, not speculation in asset prices, would be a vital foundation of this new system. Further fiscal, monetary and other anti-inflationary measures could be integrated over time to expand output and productivity while controlling or moderating costs, wages and prices.

All commercial banks should be required to have a fractional reserve of 100%. This would limit the scale of credit expansion and asset price increases. Charging interest on money created out of nothing is ethically wrong, and economically unsustainable, as the interest itself has to be created out of nothing in the form of a debt, in order to pay off existing debts. Interest leads to a multiplication of debt. Interest rates should be abolished and replaced with an administrative fee paid to banks. Banks could compete against each other on administrative fees, other services and value added services. This limits the scale of parasitical activity, while encouraging productive investment and a more stable banking system. A comparison of banking systems is provided in the table below. These are the two possibilities for banking.

New Proposed System of Banking	Old System of Banking
The provision of debt free and interest free printed money for certain government spending and services, within inflationary and deflationary limits. Mass reduction of government debt which was based on money created out of nothing and lent to it. Achieve low government debt and low debt to GNP ratios. Integration with Bancor international currency to improve trading conditions for all countries, and resolve trade imbalances over time and encourage fair trade. Fractional reserve of 100% for all deposits (see Chicago	Governments prevented from printing money. Governments begging for money from private central banks and /or commercial banks which create money out of nothing and charge interest on it. High and excessive national debt burdens and high debt to GNP ratios, bankrupt governments. Excessive private debt. Fractional reserve of 1-10% for checking accounts or current accounts. In the case of savings accounts, time deposit accounts, CD's, mutual funds, money markets, and shadow

Plan).

- New interest free and debt free money created by government and diffused into productive investments in the state sector and private sector which would fund large scale increases in the supply of goods and services and increases in productivity. Including state investments in infrastructure, vital public services, grants for start ups and small businesses and research and innovation, and into commercial banks, public savings banks, state banks, credit unions, microfinance, microcredit, (similar to Grameen bank), local currencies using forms of demurrage, and social credit schemes which would provide interest free loans and equity funding for productive businesses, cooperatives, farmers, individuals, and households. Funding prioritised for production first and then consumption not speculation.

- Funding productive capital formation for existing and new businesses. A direct investment in production equipment, new capacity, new buildings, new technologies, innovations of products, services and processes, research and development, training and human capital development. All aimed at higher productivity, increased supply of goods and services, and higher

banking a fractional reserve of zero. Several big developed countries have no reserve requirements.

- Money created out of nothing by central banks and private banks and loaned at compound interest to governments. Multiplication of debt via compound interest and constant borrowing to maintain circulation in a debt based money system. A system designed to (a) impose debt slavery and (b) to crash from excessive funding of price speculation in assets and land combined with excessive debt and interest.

- Massive bank funding for speculation in the prices of property, assets, commodities, derivatives and currencies and the creation of large economic bubbles involving trillions of dollars / euros and massive levels of speculative debt.

- Speculation, including company buybacks and corporate raiders and junk bonds which crowds out productive investment and innovation and research. Misallocate vast amounts of capital in order to fund speculation in asset prices and derivatives followed by higher debt and debt servicing costs.

- Increase the costs for productive businesses through higher speculative prices and interest driven prices for commercial property, assets, equipment, and services and higher costs of profitability.

- Interest free loans for local entrepreneurship which is production focussed and employment focussed. These loans could take the form of equity stakes in a firm.

- Investment in green energies and alternative energies by both the private sector and state sector for use in homes, businesses, transport, education, health etc.. Strategic energy self sufficiency.

- Investment in Research and Development of revolutionary new green energy technologies and alternative energy technologies.

- Investment in greater long-term employee share ownership, stock options, profit sharing and bonuses for all workers and greater community share ownership, and networks of cooperatives similar to Mondragon in Spain. This being used to

  o   more widely distribute wealth and income, and the financial benefits of economic growth, technology automation and globalisation

  o   help improve worker loyalty and productivity

  o   In addition to this improvement in productivity, it would enable businesses to achieve greater wage flexibility and wage restraint, all of which would be important

living for workers, which put upward pressure on wages.

- Less credit availability and higher interest rate costs for productive investment and output.

- Provides loans and credit which have the effect of reinforcing the use of fraud, false ratings, false investment information, false accounting, Ponzi schemes, share rigging, insider trading and other financial crimes to fuel speculation in asset prices and derivatives and increase the debt burden on many victims.

- Speculation which crashes banking systems and whole economies during busts. The 2008 crash cost over $24 trillion in bail out costs, austerity costs, and lost economic growth, GDP and productivity in the USA alone.

- Charge taxpayers for bailing out the banks and financial system through increased taxes, new taxes, levies and charges and cutbacks in essential public (state) services.

- Increase the national debt burdens on governments and taxpayers through prevention of money printing and other economic policies. High debt to GNP ratios in many countries. High debt servicing costs. Bankrupt governments.

- Major losses for pension funds in the private sector and public sector as a result of speculation in assets, property and derivatives and accompanying crashes. And the misuse of globalisation to undermine jobs, consumer in inflationary periods, stagflationary periods, and during recessions and depressions.

(See Chapter 9 on Format of Economic Democracy)

- Promoting non speculative prices and non interest driven prices for assets, goods and services. This would have strong anti inflationary effect.

- Local apprenticeship courses in businesses and organisations to train the youth or retrain unemployed people. Developing people's full potential instead of neglecting, ignoring and blaming them.

- Repayments of debts for affordable assets, goods and services based on consumption or depreciation over time.

- Help in the conversion of new ideas, new innovations and new breakthroughs into new products and services. This could be geared at Universities, Colleges, start ups, innovation centres, inventors, innovation firms, and small private enterprises.

- Encouraging research and development in the public sector and private sector. Creation of clusters of these to enhance collaboration and the commercial effects of research.

- Supporting, advising and mentoring businesses in continuous innovation of products, services and business processes

demand and productive investment within countries.

- Compound interest is not created when money is created (through a loan) and it sucks money out of circulation and also adds to the cost of production, mining / extraction, farming, distribution, storing, selling and buying goods and services ; it is a parasite on society. Interest hurts the real economy affecting investment and supply levels, consumption levels, and aggregate demand.

- Hoarding of money during economic recessions and depressions. The Paradox of thrift.

- Use of Quantitative Easing to fuel speculation in shares, assets, property and derivatives, and rises in executive bonuses and salaries and more bubbles and crashes.

- Interest rate rigging (libor rate). This imposes high costs on businesses, organisations and government bodies.

- Less credit for small and medium sized businesses. Most of the credit is created for big businesses, hedge funds and speculators in asset prices and derivatives

- Overcharging for variable interest rates (difference between central bank rate and commercial bank rate)

- Overcharging customers for credit card transactions and overcharging businesses for processing credit cards online and offline

- Overcharging bank customers, including

- Funding of national and international market penetration and growth in productive sectors of the economy
- Increase the total supply of goods and services produced and productivity levels, and support stable prices
- Support for small and medium sized businesses and regional economic development. Funding of long-term regional economic development, and prioritisation of poorer regions with focus on a combination of indigenous investment, development of local resources, skills and amenities, state and infrastructure spending, export development, and foreign direct investment.
- Use of Quantitative Easing to fund public infrastructure such as roads, bridges, airports, railroads, electricity, schools, Universities, apprenticeship courses, telecommunications etc., private productive capital formation and increased production of goods and services and improved productivity, research, and innovation and combining this with more balanced regional economic development within countries.
- Use of the Bancor Protocol, Bitcoin and Blockchain technologies to create immediate currency conversions, price discovery and liquidity between national

- businesses for currency conversions and electronic transfers of money abroad
- Pro cyclical policies which encourage boom and bust and the high costs associated with this.
- ECB bank and central bank's policy excessively focussed on inflation which has delivered financial instability, speculative booms and busts, austerity, deflation and higher unemployment.
- Quantitative Easing which encouraged companies to buy their own stock in order to make money out of share price rises and share options, instead of investing this money in new productive capital, new technologies, innovations of products, services and processes and human capital to enhance productivity and profitability.
- Provide false and misleading statistics about growth while ignoring systemic risks to the financial system, the economy public finances and employment.
- Bank savings are taken out of regions and transferred to big cities and invested there or in the hinterland or abroad. Local communities and regions do not benefit from their savings.
- Speculation which prices many individuals and families out of the housing market. The provision of over-priced and unaffordable housing and excessive mortgage debt which traps people. Entrapped families in massive mortgage debt with adverse effects on

currencies, gold, local currencies and crypto currencies. Very low cost or zero cost electronic transfers of money between countries.

- Counter cyclical policies which prevent booms and busts. Focus on long term productive capital investment.

- An economy which generates high levels of consumption and aggregate demand through wider wealth and income distribution and high levels of productive investment to meet this demand. Ends deficiencies in effective demand and effective supply.

- Low and sustainable debt to GNP ratios. Low debt servicing costs.

- More competition for credit card services. An end to predatory lending.

- Discourages hoarding of money during recessions and depressions.

- A government bank which is focussed on full employment and financial stability

- As technology and automation and globalisation delivers higher returns to capital and displaces more labour, there could be a provision of social dividends such as a national dividend as advised by the economist Richard C. Cook or universal basic income or negative income tax. This would give everyone a guaranteed income and encourage them to take up work and return to the work force. This could be

consumption.

- Increased evictions of families from their homes after the financial bubble crashes, and austerity and recession is enforced by governments, with many people and families losing their jobs and ability to pay off debt.

- Increased asset stripping of businesses, farms, homes, organisations etc. after bank and speculator created crashes

- Support for zero hour contracts and bad working conditions and low levels of worker loyalty and productivity as businesses struggle to make loan and interest repayments and cope with deflation and recession.

- Promotion of "Jobless Growth" which keeps inflation artificially too low and unemployment and poverty artificially too high.

- An economy which generates unstable levels of consumption and aggregate demand through the build up of massive debt, and unstable levels of productive investment to meet this demand. Creates deficiencies in effective demand and effective supply.

- A financial system where vast sums of money are made by banks and speculators from rises in share prices arising from the closure of factories and companies and asset stripping, the downsizing of workforces and mass lay-offs, and the re-location of businesses to third world and developing countries.

- Using globalisation to achieve a 'global race to

supplemented by wages, and wider employee and community share ownership and dividends.

Private companies, universities and state bodies could be given government incentives to hire locally in socially deprived communities and ghettos. This would give people living in these areas employment and the means to advance themselves through further training, retraining and up-skilling while working.

The above measures would help sustain aggregate demand in the economy and reduce the effects of constrained, unrealised, unmet demand or deficiencies in effective demand. Thus producing strong and sustained economic growth over time – regenerative demand.

- Provide more accurate and meaningful statistics about growth. Economic growth with job creation and low unemployment
- Bank savings are kept within regions and and invested there or in the hinterland. Local communities and regions benefit from these savings.
- Provide affordable housing and sustainable mortgage debts
- Pension funds which are stable over time, and make sustainable returns based on productive investments
- Abolish interest rates and replace with a small administration fee.

the bottom' pitting low-cost developing and third world countries against Western developed countries driving down wages, health, holidays, welfare and pension benefits, undermining worker's rights and working conditions in western developed countries.

- A parasitical economic system which sucks money and economic activity out of local communities and regions and into large cities and foreign offshore banks and tax havens. Neglects and ignores local and regional economic development.
- Lend to bankrupt governments and create greater bankruptcy for them, to prop up and bail out large international banks, bondholders, speculators and hedge funds in other countries. And enforce payment through acquiring their national assets and their national taxes, charges and levies through government austerity programmes eg. the treatment of Greece by some other EU countries.
- A money system which reinforces economic rent, and monopolistic and oligopolistic competition which over charge consumers and businesses.
- It greatly distorts international trade through manipulation of currency rates, 'beggar they neighbour policies', and a race to the bottom, - impoverishing or weakening nations.
- Funding businesses which degrade and pollute the environment, and increase the intensity of

- Using globalisation to promote decent and fair wages and salaries and wider share ownership, profit sharing and bonuses for all workers, and stable prices for goods and services.
- A non parasitical economic system which keeps money and economic activity in local communities and promotes balanced regional development. And reduces the role of foreign offshore banks and tax havens
- Social development schemes, community centres, sports facilities to improve the social development and economic opportunities of communities and regions.
- Increased government revenues for spending on essential health, schools, social services and community services
- Less stressed societies, less crime, more social solidarity and cohesion and more volunteerism.
- Support for a land value tax which is progressive and fair, and helps pay for infrastructure and public (state) services.
- Funding businesses which invest in long term sustainable and green energies which reduce costs and dependency.
- Protection of family homes. Evictions would be rare. A properly regulated derivatives and shadow banking system so as to reduce systemic risk to countries.
- A low tax burden on workers and

- environmental catastrophes for higher profit. Economic externalities and public disutility are not factored into loans, investment and profit decisions.
- High taxes for workers, production businesses, the elderly, disabled and unemployed and very low or no taxes for speculators, the very rich, and bankers. Trillions of dollars in offshore tax havens
- No proper funding of public infrastructure. Crumbling and decaying public infrastructure and accompanying loss of efficiency and competiveness.
- No support for employee share ownership, profit sharing and bonuses for all workers.
- Create systems which cause high inequalities in income and wealth. Destructive social divisions and instability.
- Continued high levels of insecurity and stress which contribute to high family and relationship breakdowns, and addictions and crime rates. Inadequate and ineffective government expenditure on essential health and social services.
- An unregulated derivatives and shadow banking system, which is worth $1,200 trillion globally, which poses contagion risks and systemic risks to several developed countries and the global economy.
- Create more social injustices and more social instability
- Perpetuate dishonesty, lack of transparency

productive businesses • Provide greater level of compliance with banking regulations • Provide greater financial system stability, economic stability and social stability • Build honesty, trust, transparency, reliability, and accountability in banking, business, politics, society and government	and accountability in banking, housing and asset price speculation. • Fund the corruption of politics, government, the legal system and the corruption of societies

Chapter 8 Affordable Housing for All. Legal Protection of Family Homes and Communities against Debt Fraud, Ponzi schemes, Debt Enslavement, Evictions and Vulture Funds

Family home evictions using battering ram and armed police in 19th century Ireland and Statues of Irish Famine victims

Do societies, peoples and governments learn from history ? or do they keep repeating the same mistakes again and again throughout history ? One of the major casualties of the financial crash of 2008 and accompanying economic downturn and austerity policies and globalisation ('race to the bottom') have been the millions of families who lost their homes in Europe, North America and around the world. The highly emotive images of family evictions, families and small children made homeless and forced to live in hostels, guesthouses and hotels, the homeless people sleeping on the streets and doorways, the tent cities, the break-up of families, the high rate of suicides, etc. have proved shocking. They have been innocent victims of a corrupted political, economic and banking system which has existed, for a long time, to serve the elites or oligarchy. This is the perverse morality and 'moral virtues' of corrupt political, economic, social and religious institutions. Banks, speculators, vulture funds and monopolists / cartels have replaced the landlords of past centuries. They use massive debt and monopoly powers to drain peoples and countries dry.

As mentioned earlier in Chapter 7, it was the massive fraudulent debt and fraudulent money creation process and fraudulent speculative processes which artificially increased the prices of property and other types of speculative assets to unsustainable levels creating a bubble which was guaranteed to burst. When it did burst in 2008 the taxpayer bailout of bankers, speculators and fraudsters through government austerity policies created recession / depression and a deflationary environment which led to business closures, bankruptcies, unemployment etc. and to asset stripping. This asset stripping included evictions from homes and the seizures of farms, and business assets. Its a system carefully designed to rob ordinary people while enriching the elites, the richest 1%. We need to look at root causes here and causality in order to devise effective and fair solutions.

The same patterns keep repeating over history. One sees high concentrations of wealth, capital and land ownership where a few people own most of the wealth / capital / land and the rest of the population are denied access to this and reduced down to the level of peasants or debt slaves. And some banks and financial institutions ruthlessly exploit this situation for their own profit. Constitutional rights and human rights are downtrodden and denied and new lawless and unconstitutional laws are devised to legitimise fraud, theft and robbery from the ordinary people. The lives of vast numbers of ordinary people and families are destroyed by this. It was the same 100 years ago, 200, 300, 500, etc. years ago.

Economic democracy and political democracy proposes radical changes and include the following measures.

Protection of Family Homes through use of Existing laws, Constitutional Provisions, and Court cases, and the Passing of New Laws, New Amendments to Constitutions and new Government Policies

There are existing Constitutional protections and legal protections in many countries for those people who are the victims of banking frauds and asset price frauds, and courts and judges need to be made more aware of them. As these measures deprive citizens of their income, their personal property, and puts citizens in danger of losing their homes which they have paid for and are paying for. Repossessions of homes which are based on fraudulent rigged high asset prices and fraudulent debt and fraudulent money creation raises very serious Constitutional issues which need to be resolved in the courts and in parliaments and congresses.

Its worth repeating some material from chapter 7 here. From a legal and Constitutional perspective and from a human rights standpoint the following legal matters will need to be adjudicated on in courts in many countries and where necessary new laws passed and new Constitutional provisions passed to protect family homes, the family, basic human rights and social stability :

- 97% of all money is created of nothing when banks give out loans and mortgages. We have already discussed this and promissory note in prior chapters. This raises important Constitutional and legal issues such as :

  - ➢ creating money out of nothing and then lending it out to others is a criminal fraud, and is a breach of contract law and other laws. Grounds for declaring contract null and void.

  - ➢ banks do not own the money provided in the mortgage or loan to a 'borrower', as the banks create this money out of nothing. No financial consideration was offered by the bank in the contract. Who can legally own fraudulent money created out of nothing ?

  - ➢ under contract law, one cannot lend something which one does not have. This is contract fraud, and grounds for declaring a contract null and void.

  - ➢ misrepresentation and non disclosure of all relevant facts about the contract by the bank in it's dealings with the borrower

  - ➢ under the banks accounting rules and money creation rules, it is the borrower who owns the newly created money through the Promissory note and the lodgement into his / her bank account. Its a deposit, which means the bank now owes the borrower this money. How can the borrower owe this money to the bank ? Can any person or bank owe money which is created out of nothing ?

  - ➢ the bank refuses to explain the role of the promissory note and creation of money out nothing to the value of the promissory note, and the lodgement of this into the customer's account before, during and after the contract. This non disclosure renders the contract null and void in law.

  - ➢ the bank illegally accessing a customer's account to issue a cheque or withdraw money from it, and then pretend that it is a loan or mortgage to the account holder. This breaches the criminal law.

  - ➢ several breaches of contract by the bank

  - ➢ the bank refuses to issue an Invoice for (a) the mortgage or loan contract (b) the repayments of the mortgage or loan, yet the bank alleges it is providing a service - the provision of loan money to the borrower. The borrower should receive an Invoice when he/she pays money to the bank in the form of repayments, but he / she does not receive this from the bank. This is illegal and suggests that the contract and repayments are fraudulent and illegal.

- when giving loans or money created out of nothing to someone, the bank deposits credits into the borrowers account. This in itself could be deemed fraud as no actual money changed hands, as the money was created out of nothing.

- use of a fraudulent contract to take personal property in the form of "repayments" or seizures of property. This infringes one's Constitutional rights.

- use of this money creation fraud to fuel speculative and fraudulent asset prices, asset price fraud or price rigging and massive mortgage debt and interest based on this fraud all of which deprives citizens of their income and their personal property, and puts citizens in danger of losing their homes. There is significant price rigging by certain parties to bid up the price of properties far beyond their real price or real worth so as to increase the profits of appraisers, real estate agents and bankers

- interest based on fraudulent loans which is not created at the time of the loan or when the money is created, and is thus not in circulation. Interest represents a new fraud based on a prior fraud.

- repossessions of homes or seizures of assets which are based on fraudulent asset prices and fraudulent debt and fraudulent money creation. Private property is protected from this illegal activity under the Constitutions of most European countries, USA, Canada and other developed nations.

- How can a bank suffer loss in the event of non payment. How can a bank lose money which was created out of nothing and is fictitious ?

- the securitisation and selling on of these fraudulent mortgages to other parties without the agreement of the mortgage payer. This is illegal.

- Under Securitisation, does the bank own the property or do investors who bought the packaged mortgages own the property ? and do they have the deeds and property registration to prove ownership ?

- These illegal loans and securitised products are then insured. This protects the banks and third parties from debt default on their illegal loans. If a borrower defaults on the illegal loan, the bank can claim an insurance payout and also claim possession of the property or asset. Yet the borrower is denied this insurance or the benefits of this insurance. This led to the evictions of thousands of families from their homes, which is destructive in economic and social terms. Grounds for declaring evictions null and void.

- The bank can receive payment several times for the same mortgage ;

  a) it securitises the loan or mortgage, meaning it sells it to a third party

  b) it receives money from the insurance company in the event of a mortgage default (non payment by borrower)

  c) it can repossess a property or asset and sell it off on the market

  d) it can enforce repayment of the mortgage or loan by the borrower via the courts after the property or asset has been repossessed and sold off on the market

  f) the tax write off on bad debts

  e) the bail out monies received by banks. This was paid for by government and taxpayers.

  The bank can be repaid back several times for the one mortgage or loan, and make profits of 200% - 400% on the one mortgage or loan. This is a fraudulent abuse of the system.

- fraudulent loans and mortgages are converted into assets and reserves by banks such that they can create 10 times more loans and mortgages and defraud many more people of their incomes and assets. This is a mass Ponzi scheme which will require legal actions and political actions.

- Illegal overcharging of thousands of borrowers by banks was revealed in 2017, and sadly many evictions and foreclosures and asset seizures resulted from this overcharging. The need for court cases to reverse these eviction orders and asset seizure orders and compensate the borrowers.

- banks act as agents not owners to collect interest on illegal loans based on illegal contracts. This is grounds for declaring contract null and void.

- did the bank bail outs by government and taxpayers clear all banking debts and mortgages ? if so, then why are people being forced to pay off mortgages and loans ?

- banks did not adhere to banking regulations, and the rules and policies laid down by their own governing articles of association, banking licences, the banking authorities and regulars, the law and the government. Were they legally able to provide loans and mortgages ?

- the European Union and other legal jurisdictions have laws which protect consumers, such as mortgage holders from unfair terms, clauses and contracts. These need to be enforced in all European countries. Other non EU jurisdictions should also follow this example. Only circuit court judges and high court judges can determine what is fair or unfair in these contracts in terms of EU law, it is illegal and unethical to have County Registrars determine it. This was highlighted by the Master of the High Court in Ireland in 2016.

> failure of government bodies to regulate the banks and companies involved in fraudulent asset price speculation. Many politicians and political parties are bought off by lobbyists and big developers, banks and businesses during the bubble period and in the crash period also. Politicians were complicit in this fraud and criminality.

Government bailout of private European banks, bondholders, developers, hedge funds, and speculators being funded by taxpayers and leading directly to increased business closures and loss of jobs through government austerity programmes and accompanying recession. Many Irish families forced into unemployment or poverty could not pay for their homes, and the banks threatened to repossess them. A terrible injustice to ordinary working families, comparable to the crimes of landlords during the 19th century in Ireland.

The onus is on politicians to rectify this and provide compensation mechanisms to their many victims, in the form of new laws, Constitutional provisions, write downs, write offs and restructurings of debt, and new mechanisms to offer financial restitution.

- In court it will be necessary for a borrower and bank to produce the following:
  - The signed mortgage or loan contract
  - The signed promissory note
  - The documents showing the financial consideration offered by the bank as part of the contract
  - The invoice showing repayments of alleged mortgage or loan, and the goods or services acquired with this mortgage or loan money. This suggests a contract is in place between the bank and borrower.
  - The documents showing where exactly the bank got the money to fund the mortgage or loan
  - The bank's accounting entries for the mortgage or loan. And the accounting entries for the Promissory note and the source of the money allegedly lent. Proof that the money was created out of nothing.
  - Proof of bank loss in the event of non payment. How can a bank lose money which was created out of nothing and is fictitious ?
  - Documents validating the alleged 'debt'
  - Documents proving non disclosure of relevant facts by the bank prior to, during and after the contract

- ➤ The documents showing the securitisation of the mortgage

- ➤ Deeds and property registration showing who owns the property. Under Securitisation, does the bank own the property or do investors who bought the packaged mortgages own the property ? and do they have the deeds and property registration to prove ownership ?

- ➤ Sworn affidavits attesting to and verifying the points above

- ➤ The Laws, Constitutional provisions and EU Directives which apply in the case

- The relationship between a borrower and producer / seller creates a position of debt between these two parties and they issue a promissory note between them. This is for the sum of the principal. People create money in the form of a promissory note. Banks intervene in this relationship, illegally take and launder the promissory note and then create money out of nothing equal to the value of the promissory note and charge interest on this money created out of nothing. The bank brings no consideration to the private contract between the borrower and the producer / seller, and thus the bank is not party to the contract. This is explained further on http://www.perfecteconomy.com

- Mortgages for homes and properties are based on contracts where contracting parties provide consideration (money or assets) to bind the contract. Banks create money out of nothing when they lend money to a borrower. Banks do not own the money they allegedly "lend" to borrowers, the money created out of nothing means nobody really owns this money created out of nothing. It is a fiction, an invention, a type of fraud where money is created out of nothing. This means the bank provides no consideration in the contract, this breaches

Further Points for Consideration

- Legal Research and Academic Research

  - ➤ Professor Richard Werner of the University of Southampton has carried out important academic and legal research in this area in recent decades. His work and other's work can be found on the Internet, academic journals, and books, and can be cited in future legal cases, court cases and future research.

- The Book 'How the Banks are screwing you & What you can do about it' by Marcus McKeown, the Foundation for Transpersonal Consciousness (2012). This details the legal issues and recommends some legal actions. This can be cited in future legal cases, court cases and future research.

- These illegal loans with signatures are then illegally securitised which means they are sold on to third parties. This securitisation of an illegal loan is carried on without the permission of the borrower, and this is also illegal. The third party has illegal possession. The massive crash in mortgage backed securities and CDO's in the USA in 2008 was based on this and significant fraud using ninja loans. In the USA many mortgages were declared null and void as a result of this illegal activity by the banks. Nobody was jailed for these massive frauds and criminal actions. Grounds for declaring contract null and void.

- From an economics and business perspective, interest is not created with the new money at the time of the loan and represents an additional charge on money created out of nothing. Interest is an extra cost burden on a fraudulent loan, which means interest itself may be fraudulent. The repayment of this illegal interest requires that new money be created out of nothing to pay this interest, but this is not done. Interest is instead extracted from the existing economic system. The problem here is that interest is not created when money is created, and thus there is not enough (created) money in the system to facilitate the payment of interest. Interest has to be extracted from the existing money supply thus depleting the money supply and the available money to pay interest over time. Furthermore, interest leads to a multiplication of debt which sucks even more money out of circulation. They have created an impossible position for borrowers where the money in circulation keeps depleting as more interest is paid, more debt created and more money sucked out of the system, creating the conditions for debt unsustainability, defaults and crashes. This criminal extraction is grounds for declaring a contract null and void.

- Lenders (banks and mortgage firms) and real estate firms pressurising appraisers to keep inflating the prices of property beyond their real worth. New debt and money creation by lenders facilitated this price rigging upwards and fraud, drawing in many desperate people looking for homes and property. These parties made commissions, extra fees, higher mortgage loan profits, and higher profits from speculation from pumping up the prices of properties. Ordinary people and families were forced to buy over priced houses and take out massive over priced mortgages, which were far greater than the real price and worth of properties. This amounted to theft and robbery from ordinary people and families. Theft of private property is unconstitutional and thus illegal.

- Private banks own very little real money, they own promissory notes, bills of exchange and negotiable instruments and electronic credits which are not real money. These illegal activities by private banks has created a master class which illegally creates money, debt and interest out of nothing and a slave class which is entrapped in illegal contracts and forced to repay these illegal loans.

- Massive and unsustainable mortgage debt based on the above fraud. This massive fraudulent debt remains even after prices collapse during the crash and leave many people in negative equity. If prices are flexible downwards, then mortgage debt should be flexible downwards. This must include write downs, write offs, and restructurings of debt.

- There should be reversal of all court orders for evictions from family homes on legal and Constitutional grounds, until such time as the true scale of fraud, price rigging, criminality, illegality, counterfeiting of currency by banks to fund fraudulent speculation, Ponzi schemes and other financial crimes are fully investigated, uncovered, detailed and prosecuted. During the boom the prices of many properties were based on fraud, misrepresentation, asset price rigging, credit based on money created out of nothing by banks to fuel speculative and fraudulent prices, bogus bidding, and other criminal and unethical activities. For home mortgage holders, the consequences of this are very serious, as they become entrapped in a fraudulent system which over-prices properties including their property, and then crashes the system, leaving them with an under-priced property, an over-priced mortgage debt, increased taxes, levies and charges (for bank and business bailouts) and a higher probability of them losing their jobs and the means to pay back the mortgage debt. The present system is upon deeper analysis a criminally fraudulent system which defrauds and robs many hard working individuals and families of their incomes, homes, and livelihoods. For example, between 1994 and 2007 new house prices rose by 400% in Dublin and second hand house prices rose by 500%, while incomes rose between 60 – 70% in that time period. The United States witnessed a dramatic rise in household debt in the years before the Great Recession, the total amount of debt for American households doubled between 2000 and 2007 to $14 trillion. The Great American Recession resulted in the loss of eight million jobs between 2007 and 2009, and more than four million homes were lost to foreclosures [6]. This speculation and debt system, and accompanying bailout system is a system of theft, a criminal fraud, a Ponzi scheme, which robs people of private income, personal property, and is illegal and unconstitutional.

- Vulture fund capitalism

Vulture fund capitalism which relies on economic crashes followed by government bail outs and austerity policies and Quantitative Easing to stabilise and improve the prices of distressed assets and stablise speculative markets, so vulture funds can acquire these assets cheaply at 20 - 40 cents or less on the dollar and sell them at 100 cents or more on the dollar. For example, vulture funds acquired hundreds / thousands of mortgages at 20 - 40% of their value, held them for a short period, charged higher interest or higher rents or higher repayments, and then sold them at 100% or more of their value. The sales and profits were engineered to pass through foreign tax havens so as to avoid paying tax. The owners of these individual mortgages (for homes and properties) were prevented from bidding for their own mortgages at 20 – 40% of their value by laws and government policies. It was a system designed for the benefit of vulture funds. This imposed large unnecessary costs on ordinary people and societies while depriving governments of important tax revenues. This distorts capital markets, returns, supply and pricing mechanisms.

The same applies to government debt for countries in distress (Ireland and other EU countries after the 2008 crash and Latin American, Asian and African countries in the past) where debt can be bought cheap for 20 – 40 cents on the dollar and then sold for 100 cents or more on the dollar once the government enforces bail outs and austerity on the taxpayers and people of a nation to maintain the value of the debt.

In 2009 -2011, vulture funds, hedge funds, speculators and private equity firms made a double win from Ireland or the Irish government, they profiteered from (a) buying Irish debt cheap in secondary markets and then selling it at 100 cents or more on the dollar after the Troika bail out (b) buying distressed Irish properties cheap and then selling them at 100 cents or more on the dollar and charging excessive rents. Governments and Troikas now provide the floor for asset prices and the means for them to increase which enables vulture capitalism to thrive and make massive profits. Profits for vulture capitalism are typically in the millions or billions of dollars worldwide.

There are Constitutional and legal issues here in relation to depriving home owners or mortgage holders of the right to bid for their mortgage on the open market, the charging of excessive interest or rents or repayments which amount to theft, and evictions based on this theft. This will need to be tested in many courts.

- **iCare Solution**

  The creation of an organisation known as iCare in 2017 in Ireland marks a new and welcome development in this area. It was set up with the assistance of David Hall, the Irish Mortgage Holders' Organisation and AIB bank. The system works as follows – a person or family with an unsustainable mortgage surrenders their home to the bank. The person or family are allowed to stay in their own home until the sale of the home to another party is completed by the bank. The bank closes the mortgage and prepares the property for sale at a discount. iCare buys the home from the bank at a discount. Once iCare buys the home it signs a 30 - 40 year lease with the previous owner – a person or family. This lease involves the payment of rent which is considerably lower than the previous mortgage payment, typically 40 - 80% lower. The local city council or county council pays some of this rent, and the person / family pays the remainder of the rent. The person or family has the option to buy back the house at the discounted price some time in the future if their financial circumstances improve. The benefit of this is that families are allowed to stay in their own homes and pay an affordable rent with some assistance from a local authority. This prevents the evictions of families from their homes. This system provides a national and international model of excellence for preventing evictions of families from their homes. It should be copied nationally and internationally. It's web site is at https://www.icarehousing.ie/

- The Quantitative Easing for the people mentioned in Chapter 7 could be applied here. This would include mortgage write downs, write offs and reductions combined with debt restructurings as proposed in Chapter 7. The central bank could reimburse banks for any losses incurred by this. This would restore prices to the actual value of properties, which historically are 4-7 times average industrial earnings. And measures could be put in place to ensure house prices are kept within this range over the long term, see proposals for this below. These historical prices for homes are detailed in the Property and Housing sections below - Dealing with Housing Shortages While Preventing Speculation in Housing Prices and the Accumulation of Massive Banking Debts.

- The proposal put forward by Michael Montagne at www.perfecteconomy.com could be applied here in amended form as following:

  1) interest should be abolished for the mortgage

  2) the principal is only payable, and all prior interest payments should be used to reduce the remaining mortgage principal balance

3) restructure the time period from payment to 50 years − 100 years

4) Protections in place to prevent price speculation and price rigging of assets, property, land, goods.

5) replace interest with a small bank administration fee in the region of 200 − 400 euros per year

This would make the mortgage sustainable and affordable and prevent many defaults.

- Establishing the ownership of a property and the contract and the contracting parties where the mortgage is sold off in packages of mortgages to investors and private equity funds.

- Constitutional and legal protections for family homes. Existing provisions should be utilised to protect family homes. If these are not enough then Constitutional changes, including referendums and changes to laws should be introduced to safeguard and protect family homes. And to protect family homes and other types of assets from the frauds and crimes of bankers and asset price speculators.

- A debt rescheduling where 20% - 35% of remaining debt is scheduled to begin to be repaid 10 years into the future, another 30% would begin to be repaid 20 years into the future, while the other 35% - 50% continues to be repaid with interest. This would reduce the immediate debt burden and enable many families and couples to continue staying in their own home. It would also provide room for the new consumption, investment, and economic growth and recovery which would enable all persons to pay off debts. The ECB could provide bridge financing to the banks to facilitate this.

- Debt for Equity Deals

  Debt for equity deals for a certain period, where the bank or city council / county council takes partial ownership of the property − 25% or 33% or 50% of the property. The mortgage owner / family would pay 50% or 66% of their mortgage, while the local council or bank would pay the rest of the mortgage. Or the mortgage holder could sell their property to a bank leasing body, and then rent it back from them at a low rent to reflect the reduced value of properties. The Irish Mortgage Holders Organisation (IMHO) has proposed some innovative solutions similar to this, see http://www.irishtimes.com/business/financial-services/state-run-split-mortgages-urged-by-home-loan-body-1.2168015

- Create debt for equity laws which would allow banks to convert home loans to equity in the home, and facilitate lower repayment or repayment holidays or rescheduling of repayments during crashes or severe recessions / depressions.

- Include a hedging contract into all home mortgages, where home owners are provided with an investment instrument which goes up in value if the price of the home falls in price during a crash and an insurance policy to protect a home owner against home loss through unemployment or disability. These two hedging products would save many people and families from evictions and loss of homes.

- Allow a 'Chapter 11 type bankruptcy' clause where the home owner and bank accept a write down in the mortgage debt and mortgage payment, of 15 or 20% or 25%, in return for the bank getting a share of the capital gain in the property price when it is sold.

- Constitutional protections and promotion of the services of organisations such as Get out of Debt Free (www.getoutofdebtfree.org) in Britain and the New Land League in Ireland (http://www.thelandleague.net/). These have helped many families and individuals deal with fraudulent debts and illegal evictions in Britain and Ireland.

- Encouraging banks to re-finance and re-schedule mortgages at a lower interest rate and/or extend for a longer time period such as 60 – 90 year mortgages. This would reduce the financial burden on families

- Allow courts to re-write the terms of all mortgages for family / personal homes which are in danger of foreclosure. This may involve a judge ordering some of the options proposed above.

- Utilise the provision for write downs and restructurings of mortgage debt in certain EU countries mentioned in Chapter 7 of this book.

The New Land League

The New Land League (http://www.thelandleague.net/) was set up to protect Irish families from forced evictions from their homes, and could serve as model for other countries around the world. It has much the same policies as the Land League in the 19th century where it stopped Irish farmers and their families from being evicted by the landlords. Today, we have a similar situation with many Irish families being threatened with eviction by banks which have the power to create money out of nothing and lend it out at interest and profiteer from asset price speculation. This criminally fraudulent system of speculation and asset pricing and debt creation now endangers many Irish families. Some of this is outlined in a previous chapter. In 2015, 31,000 families have been officially threatened with evictions by the banks and 120,000 families are in serious danger of being evicted. Over 50% of mortgage holders in arrears are in danger of losing of the family home. This New Land league has many new and innovative ideas for protecting the family home from predatory banks and vulture funds. The provisions mentioned in the list above could be used together to help families stay in their homes and protect the vulnerable in society. Obviously this will require substantial legal actions and political actions from the New Land Leaguers and other organisations devoted to protecting basic human rights and dignity.

Dealing with Housing Shortages While Preventing Speculation in Housing Prices and the Accumulation of Massive Debts

The solution to the housing crisis in Ireland and other countries will need to encompass new policies, new thinking, new mindsets, new measures and new incentives. In strategic terms this will involve the following actions :

(i) Empty Properties and Sites

 in most countries with a housing crisis and homelessness there are many thousands of empty properties and empty building sites in prime locations. This is one of the great contradictions of free market economics, or more accurately skewed market economics. This market system exists to exploit the situation and suck more funds out of people via higher prices and higher rents, and worsening housing crisis and homelessness, not provide solutions. In Ireland there were 150,000 empty houses in Ireland in 2014 – 2016, at a time of a severe housing crisis and homelessness. Most of these properties were owned by NAMA or by speculators waiting for a rise in house prices in the future. This is scandalous when one sees tens of thousands of people homeless and the 100,000 people on social housing waiting lists.

There are three combined options available to remedy this.

Firstly the government should impose a high tax on all empty properties and empty land banks ready for development. This tax should encourage owners to rapidly convert these properties or land banks into rented accommodation or sell them to persons who will rapidly use them for housing.

Secondly there should be compulsory government purchases of empty private houses, housing estates and empty buildings from NAMA and speculators and conversion of these into housing.

Thirdly, compulsory state purchases of derelict properties and abandoned properties in cities and towns and empty land banks from private property owners and conversion of these into housing.

All of these compulsory purchased empty properties and land banks and estates could be transferred from the state to private developers who would be contractually forced to rapidly convert the properties and land into combined social housing and private housing subject to the conditions below. Times for starting and completion should also be set, so as to better control the supply, resource allocations, credit priming, and predictability.

(ii) Kenny Report

 implement the Kenny Report of 1974 (Ireland) allowing councils to purchase zoned land and unzoned agricultural land, unused properties, derelict sites, and potential development land at its existing agricultural value plus 25% or derelict price plus 25%. Compulsory purchase orders by government and councils should be used if necessary. This land could be rapidly provided with zoning, public services and planning permission and then sold off to the private sector subject to the conditions below. This would prevent excessive speculation in land, political and legal corruption and the formation of excessive debt levels. Combining social housing with private housing would prevent the development of ghettos and crime hotspots.

(iii) Building Social Housing and Affordable Private Housing

The objective of most housing policies worldwide is to increase the supply of housing not increase the prices of them to overly high levels where they become unaffordable, cause excessive debt and speculation and present serious threats to the banking and financial system. The emphasis must be on increasing supply not on increasing prices and debt. A diagram of this is provided below. Housing supply can be greatly increased and expanded without price rises. This can be achieved via expanding the supply of state subsidised social housing and affordable private housing simultaneously. This massive increase in supply would cause prices to fall and increase overall affordability. This will involve a three flank attack

(a) large scale building of government social housing for rent or for sale and options for future sale to renters. This could be built by the private sector under contract to the government. In Ireland for example, conversion / building of 40,000 units in Dublin city and county and 40,000 units in other counties nationwide. This would help reduce the housing deficit and burden. Social housing should integrate with private housing so as to avoid ghettos. And should include social and community amenities, sporting facilities and family and community supports to provide community stability and cohesion. Rents would be kept affordable and within the means of individuals and families, on a sliding scale. Sales of social housing would follow much the same guidelines as for private housing below.

(b) massive expansion of affordable private housing. Prices historically over 130 years have been a low multiple of average industrial earnings. Bring the prices of all homes and rents into accord with a low multiple of average industrial earnings, this will involve some control of prices and rents. This would be built by the private sector and sold to the private sector. The emphasis would be on expanding supply and maintaining affordability not on increasing prices or use of speculation and debt creation to increase prices and create property bubbles. This will involve the state introducing price caps so that prices remain controlled within certain ranges or parameters, in this case based on a multiple of average industrial earnings. This would mean keeping house prices at :

- 3.5 times annual average industrial earnings for houses with 2 or less bedrooms which is in line with long term or historical prices
- 4.5 times annual average industrial earnings for houses with 3-4 bedrooms which is in line with long term or historical prices
- 5.2 times average industrial earnings for houses with 5 bedrooms which is in line with long term or historical prices
- 6.2 times average industrial earnings for houses with 6 bedroom
- 7.2 times average industrial earnings for houses with 7 bedrooms
- 8 bedrooms or more would be exempt from price controls.

(In 2016, average industrial earnings was €36,900 per year)

Tax incentives and grants could be used to achieve this. This will involve price controls, as the old system has proved to be a disaster economically, financially and socially. This would stop the rise in homelessness and provide a means for ordinary working people and the unemployed to save money, buy property, improve their position in life and become owners of property in the future. It would give young people and ambitious people a fair chance in life. Houses and homes would be seen legally and economically as consumer products not speculative products.

(d) Georgism and Cooperatives

Land redistribution, Georgism, may be necessary. This would involve communities or home buyer's cooperatives or the state acquiring the use of private land, with users paying a fee. This would provide strong incentives for people to acquire land for private use, build an affordable house and then pay a user's fee to the community or to cooperative or the state for use of the land (the site the house). House prices could be fixed and slightly adjusted once every few years to account for changes in average industrial earnings, as recommended above. This would provide a structured and controlled means of price increases or decreases, free of speculation and speculative manias. Alternatively communities and cooperatives could buy this land and build affordable, price controlled housing on it. Governments could undertake compulsory purchases or rents of private land to facilitate these measures, and also provide tax incentives and grants, including buyer grants to communities and cooperatives to encourage them to buy or lease land to produce affordable, price controlled housing.

Georgism is not communism or socialism, as it involves private operators making profit out of working and developing the land owned by private individuals, communities (many families and neighbourhoods) or cooperatives or the state.

(iv) Addressing the inflated and fraudulent house prices which emerge from fraudulent money creation

The over inflated (and unaffordable) house prices and mortgages are based on money created out of nothing by banks, a clear fraud. Excessive growth in the money supply (created by banks) has historically pushed up prices of products and services, in this case house prices. And there are fraudulent mortgages based on these fraudulent, over inflated house prices. As stated above house prices should be reduced to some multiple of average industrial earnings, this would make housing affordable to all people. The would have to include the following changes:

a) immediate reduction of house prices to some multiple of average industrial earnings

b) immediate reduction of mortgages to align with these new house prices

c) compensation of those house buyers who fully paid off the over inflated house prices

d) adjustments to the accounts of banks to implement these new house prices and mortgages. As the bank created this money out of nothing (in the form of mortgages) it would involve no major losses to the banks.

(v) Lower house prices would facilitate lower rents.

Monthly private sector rents could to be capped at

- 1.3% of (annual) average industrial earnings for flats or houses with 2 bedrooms or less
- 1.6% of (annual) average industrial earnings for flats or houses with 3 bedrooms
- 1.9% of (annual) average industrial earnings for flats or houses with 4 bedrooms
- 2.1% of (annual) average industrial earnings for flats or houses with 5-6 bedrooms
- 2.4% of (annual) average industrial earnings for flats or houses with 7 bedrooms

(In 2016, average industrial earnings in Ireland was €36,900 per year).

The tax system could be used to achieve this objective. This would stop the rise in homelessness and provide a means for ordinary working people and the unemployed to save money, improve their position in life and become owners of property in the future. It would give young people and ambitious people a fair chance in life.

(vi) Land Value Tax

A land value tax was supported by leading economists in the past including John Stuart Mill, David Ricardo, Henry George, Herbert Spencer, Patrick Dove, Alfred Wallace. Introduce a land value tax to tax land owners and property owners who financially benefit from the provision of public services near their land / property. This would be a tax on economic rent. Research below by Fred Harrison in the UK below shows the rise in land prices measured against the rise in wages, house prices, and building costs over the period 1983 – 2007 in the UK. As you can see, land prices have risen much higher than wages, house prices, and building costs. The rise in land prices also inflicted costs on the wider economy, yet was not taxed and rarely commented upon by economists and those concerned with inflation and rising costs. This massive increase in land prices would have yielded large tax revenues, but the UK government failed to collect them. Other economies in Europe, the Americas and elsewhere could benefit from taxing this.

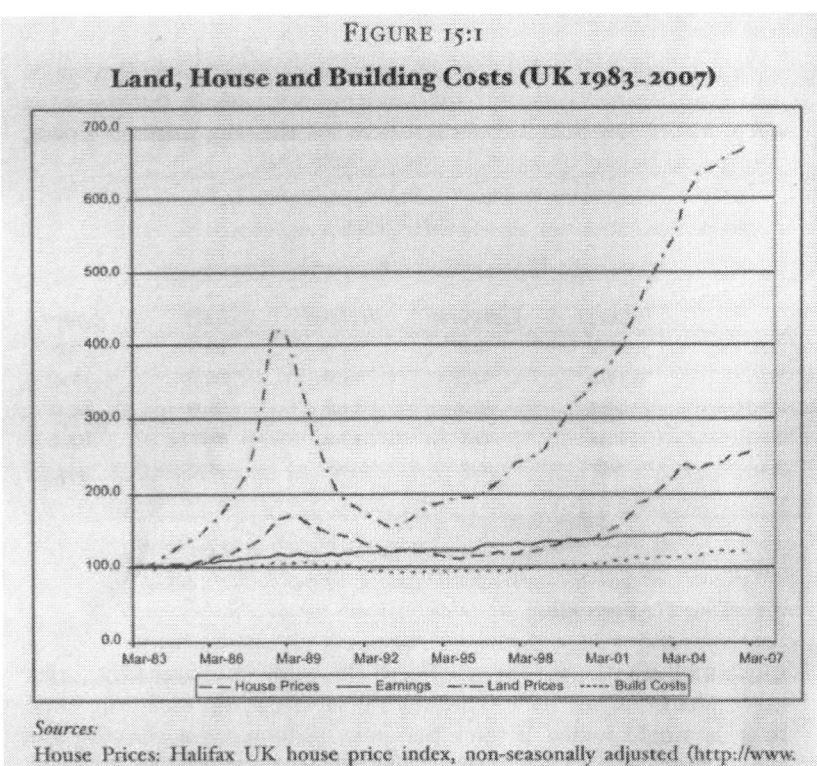

FIGURE 15:1

Land, House and Building Costs (UK 1983-2007)

Sources:
House Prices: Halifax UK house price index, non-seasonally adjusted (http://www.hbosplc.com/economy/NationalPressRelease.asp).
Average Earnings: Office of National Statistics, Average Earnings Index 196301-200704 (whole economy, seasonally adjusted, including bonuses).
Land Prices: Valuation Office Agency, Residential Building Land Index (England and Wales excluding London) (http://www.voa.gov.uk/publications/property_market_report/pmr-jan-07/residential.htm).
Build Costs: BCIS (Building Cost Information Service) House Rebuilding Cost Index.
All series rebased to March 1983 = 100 and adjusted for inflation using the Office of National Statistics Retail Price Index.

Source: Boom Bust ; House prices, Banking and The Depression of 2010, Fred Harrison, Second Edition 2007, Shepheard Walwyn.

(vii) Interim Measures to increase housing supply

While governments struggle with housing crisis and the delays involved in planning processes, re-zoning, public services provision, and the time it takes to build housing, certain interim provisions could be put in place such as

- making public land or compulsory acquired private land available for 3D printed houses, PODS, log cabins, and mobile homes which can be deployed immediately or within a few weeks or months. This would take the pressure off families and individuals, providing them with suitable accommodation while houses are being built elsewhere, and the total housing stock gradually increases.

(viii) Reformed Banking

The new reformed banking system, proposed n Chapter 7 could provide loans for the purchase of housing. The combination of home price controls, increased supply and lower house prices, lower priced mortgages, the abolition of interest, and the extension of mortgages beyond 30 years would increase the affordability of homes and reduce the risk of default by borrowers, while reducing the scope for speculation in such assets. For example, a (price controlled) house costing 200,000 euros could be paid over 50 years at a cost of 4,000 euros per year plus annual bank administration fees of 300 euros. The cost could be 4,300 euros per year which is 358 euros per month. This is very affordable when one considers that the average industrial wage is 36,000 euros (2016).

(ix) The Benefits of Wider Wealth and Income Distribution in an Economic Democracy

The economic democracy measures proposed in this book would disperse the wealth of a country to the ordinary people, give them a stake in the capitalist system and would improve the incomes and credit worthiness of all persons, thus improving the ability to pay for homes and further reducing default risk.

(x) The iCare Solution

This is mentioned in a section above and would bring significant relief to families and individuals facing eviction.

Overall Benefits of Proposed Changes

As wages and salaries rise from increased jobs in house building and conversions of existing properties and land and the accompanying economic boom, average industrial earnings would rise, and this would cause a structured and highly predictable rise in the price of houses. The rise in house prices would be intimately linked to average industrial earnings and thus would be affordable and in alignment with the status and growth of the Irish economy. The Irish state pays over €1.4 billion each year to private landlords in the form of rent allowance, hostels and hotels to accommodate homeless families, and tax reliefs for landlords. It is far cheaper and sustainable to build or buy social housing than pay rent supplement for families, provide emergency accommodation, hospital care, residential care or prison for them. For private housing, the above measures would prevent housing price speculation and the accumulation of excessive debt, and boom bust cycles and systemic risks to financial systems and economies. They would impose order on chaos. House prices would rise naturally in line with rises in average industrial earnings and rises in productivity. This would encourage economies to raise their productivity levels and work rate, and invest in education, skills, new technologies and innovations in order to raise productivity and raise house prices. The diagram below provides an analytical framework for this.

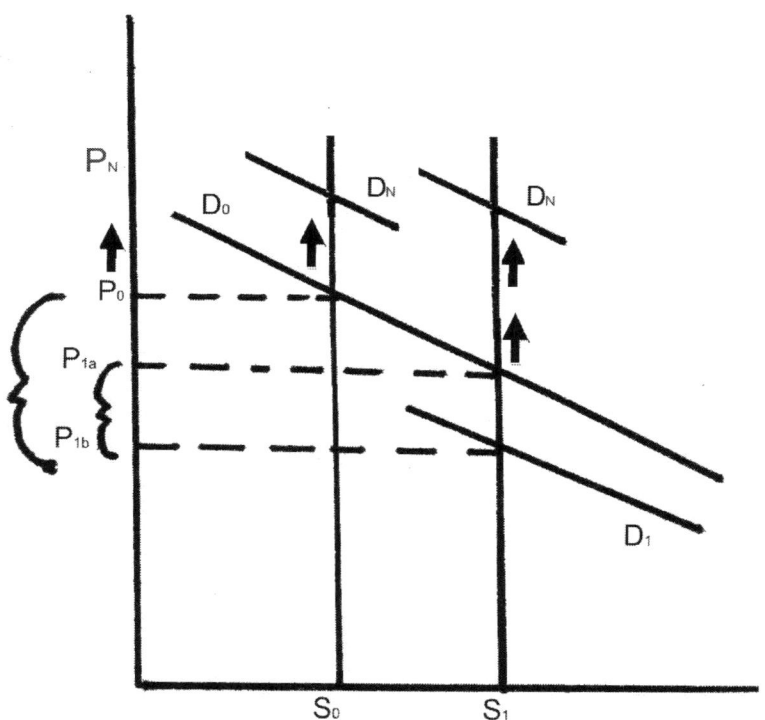

In the diagram above, the initial position is (supply) S_0 intersecting (demand) D_0 to give (price) P_0. This price P_0 is not static and there is upward pressure on prices caused by hoarding of empty properties, zoned sites and land banks by developers, population growth and migration into a country, banks creating money out of nothing to create new mortgages and loans and fuel speculation in prices and rents, and price manipulation by real estate agents, all of which drive prices higher and higher. This is also assisted by a government refusal to build social housing, and their strong belief in skewed markets (wrongly assumed to be free markets). Credit availability for speculation also assists these price rises. This move to higher speculative prices is represented by P_N and D_N. In reality, the market settles at price P_N, which encompasses the price of properties and rental price of properties. This proves unaffordable for many people, and some are forced to rent or to move elsewhere or into homelessness. A government which is supportive of skewed markets will accept this position and this is accompanied by a housing crisis and a homelessness crisis.

Under the new proposals above, the housing supply increases from S_0 to S_1 through a combination of government building more social housing and providing strong incentives to the private sector to increase affordable private housing and the achievement of higher levels of aggregate demand, employment, wider share ownership, and credit to fund these purchases. This massive expansion of housing supply is the key factor. Price falls from P_0 to P_{1a}. The price P_{1a} is the price control (introduced by government) based on a low multiple of average industrial earnings, which is linked to worker productivity and the productivity of the economy and to affordability. This price P_{1a} is based on real, sound, strong variables linked to the real economy which adjust slowly over time, instead of the unregulated market speculative price, P_N, which fluctuates wildly and causes bubbles and crashes. The price P_N represents the unregulated speculative market price which would occur if there was no price control. The difference between price P_N and P_{1a} would be the difference between the speculative price and the actual price, this is of central importance. This speculative price P_N would not remain static as there would be strong upward price pressures driven by speculation, and would increase upwards towards prices higher than P_N. Demand D_N represents speculators entering the market and banks providing more credit for speculation and profiteering from this. Sensation and hype in the news and media would drive this speculation and price increases. Demand D_N would move up along the supply curve S_1 and price would move up to P_N, and beyond it.

As housing needs are met and made affordable to most people, possibly all people who require it, the demand for housing will fall. Most people require only a home and have no desperate need for multiple homes and properties. Demand for housing would become sated. This is represented by D_1 and a fall to Price P_{1b}. This would provide a cushion for a sudden rise in demand in the future, by changes to population, while improving the affordability of housing and preventing a sudden housing crisis. Over time the measures mentioned above would expand supply naturally in response to an increased demand. Thus the longer term difference between the real price and the speculative price would be P_N – P_{1b} for housing stock S_1. This is a very large difference and shows the level of exploitation and profiteering existent in the present speculative system of housing. This difference is the 'speculative price gap' and also represents the amount of extra money house owners have to borrow in order to buy a speculative over priced property. This could be 3, 4, 5 or even 10 times more expensive than the controlled price of P_{1b}. This massive increase in prices, credit, debt, and financial instability to fund speculation in house prices also represents the scale of a credit and speculative bubble in housing. This always drives it towards the 'Minsky Moment' and a crash.

Over time, as demand grows the price would fluctuate between P_{1b} and $P_{1a,}$ and this would signal to the government and private sector that a new round of expansion in public and private housing is required, thus pushing the supply of housing out to S_2 (not shown on the chart), indicating an increased supply of housing and lower prices or stable prices.

The same reasoning can be applied to rental of housing where landlords push up the prices of rents and this is also facilitated by credit, hoarding of properties and land, false scarcity of housing speculation and market manipulation. Even increases in supply can be subject to speculation and upward price pressures.

Affordable housing and affordable rents is something which is vital to all workers, their families, communities, and to the economy and society as a whole. The stabilisation of house prices would help moderate wages and claims for wage rises, encourage increases in productivity, and keep a nation competitive internationally, while increasing the disposable income of workers and encourage sustainable levels of consumption and investment over time, thus ensuring economic and national stability. When combined with the wider share ownership and profit sharing proposed for all workers and communities in Chapter 9, the effects on demand would be even stronger and more sustained over time, than is presently the case. A Land League organisation would work with Government policy makers, advisors and civil servants and politicians the public savings banks, credit unions, and the EU institutions to achieve these objectives above.

Chapter 9 The Format of Economic Democracy and Its Wider Diffusion through Taxes, Detailed Policies, Reformed Banking and Investment, and New Types of Trade Deals

that all men are created equal

US Declaration of Independence

We the People of the United States, in order to form a more perfect Union, establish justice, insure

domestic tranquility, provide for the common defence, promote the general welfare...

US Constitution

I have a dream that one day this nation will rise up and live out the true meaning of its creed: "We hold

these truths to be self-evident, that all men are created equal."

Martin Luther King, famous 'I have a Dream' speech, Washington DC, 1963

The founders of the American Republic, including Washington, Jefferson, Adams, Hamilton, Madison and Lincoln all supported wider property ownership, profit sharing, wider share ownership, wider land ownership, and giving workers a financial stake in land, property and businesses ; a stake in the capitalist system [11]. This belief was deeply engrained in the American mindset in the early decades of the American Republic. They felt that this was important for political democracy and the success of republicanism, freedom and capitalism. This has been researched and documented by the distinguished professor and author Dr. Joseph Blasi in the USA [11]. They rejected the oligarchy and the landed aristocracy of Europe with its class divisions, monarchy, feudalism, prejudices, hatreds and political and legal system corruption. The New World of America rejected and hoped to replace the Old World of Europe.

Unfortunately, the achievements of Washington, Jefferson, Adams, Madison, Lincoln, Roosevelt and other similar people in other countries has been undermined and is being destroyed in recent decades, and a new Iron Curtain has descended upon many countries in the developed world and the developing world. This great social divide is characterised by massive concentrations of wealth and income and great social injustices and a new feudalism and oligarchy similar to the aristocracy of the past. This has been discussed and analysed in Chapter 5 of this book.

There is an opportunity to reverse this and to restore power, wealth, land, property, decision making, governing powers, sovereignty, and democracy back to the people in these countries. This will involve restructuring, re-engineering, rethinking, re-applying the key factors which govern the direction of societies - taxes, incentives, disincentives, government grants, government contracts, government policies, state strategic investments, government money printing or electronic credit creation, banking, Quantitative Easing, laws, Constitutional amendments, strategic policies. Schools and Universities, and social and political institutions. They could and should be coordinated to build economic democracy and industrial democracy as a means to

- growing the economy and achieving sustainable economic growth
- widely spreading out the financial benefits of high technology, automation, high productivity levels, increased trade, and economic growth to the entire population of a country
- ending high concentrations of wealth and income. Attainment of full employment levels.
- the full development of the human being in terms of higher education, skills, trades, employment, realising human potential, mental and spiritual development, social responsibility and the building of social capital. This would be a big improvement over the present system which relegates many people to the ghettos, the barrios, violent housing estates, industrial wastelands and to addictions and crime.
- embracing new technologies and innovations and using them for the economic and social advancement of all. Building more stable, honest, accountable and sustainable banks and financial systems. Reducing the impact of dynamic disequilibrium
- protecting and strengthening political democracy and freedom and social capital

Ending Excessive Concentrations of Wealth and Income via Economic Democracy, Industrial Democracy and Political Democracy

In previous chapters, the concentrations of wealth and income were detailed. This involved looking at the facts and statistics provided by Piketty, Saez, Zucman, Smith, Harvard University, Reich, Stiglitz, Hickel, the World Bank, etc.. All show a very high concentration of wealth and income in the USA and other developed countries. The causative factors (a) – (m) were outlined in Chapter 5. And it is these causative factors we will address throughout Section 2 of this book and specifically in this chapter. While the aforementioned changes, detailed in previous chapters, to the debt burden, to the banking and money systems, to international trade, and to fiscal and monetary policies would help reduce wealth and income inequalities and would be vitally important aspects of economic democracy, and generate more economic activity and more wealth, it would be important to provide much deeper mechanisms of economic democracy to more widely distribute the wealth and income to the people. This could be achieved via many forms of employee ownership and cooperatives, each adapted to the circumstances in different environments and countries. This would disperse greater economic, social and political power to the people and facilitate the responsibilities attached to freedom and political democracy. And it would also resolve the problem of constrained, unrealised, unmet demand or deficiencies in effective demand and accompanying deficiencies in effective supply, and act to both increase and then sustain aggregate demand, consumption, purchasing power, supply, investment, output and economic growth over time, through various economic multiplier effects. It would provide a sustained multiplier effect over time.

It would include the following:

1. Grants of long term shares to all workers in a firm, OR chunks of profit sharing or revenue sharing to all workers. This would be funded and paid for by the methods detailed in Points 16 - 32 below. Worker income would consist of different formulations depending on the business environment

    (i) wages income and the income from owning shares in the firm. Dividends could be paid weekly, fortnightly or monthly or quarterly.

    (ii) wages combined with profit sharing or revenue sharing payable weekly, fortnightly or monthly (Professor Weitzman's proposal)

    (iii) wages combined with end of year income in the form of dividends or profit sharing / revenue sharing, and/or new shares, share options

    (iv) income exclusively from a pure profit sharing / revenue sharing system payable weekly (Professor Weitzman's proposal)

    (v) wages and dividend income from cross share holdings between all employee owned firms including cooperatives. This is discussed below in terms of creating collaborative networks and synergies between employee owned firms.

(vi) adding on productivity bonuses for individual workers or groups to the incomes mentioned above so as to increase productivity levels and innovation. This could be based on a composite of measurable productivity rates, sales and profits, and rises in share value. It should be available to all workers in a firm and be fair and transparent.

This total pay would have sliding scale aspects tying pay to the revenues and profits of a firm. This would be achieved via implementation of the new structures listed below.

2. These must involve long term employee share ownership of companies and businesses. Long term in order to prevent shares being traded into fewer and fewer hands and concentrating capital ownership and wealth.

3. Revenue or Profit Sharing by all workers as proposed by Professor Martin Weitzman of Harvard University [22] . This would involve a profit sharing or revenue sharing system by workers, and dividing total revenue into that delegated for worker owners and managers and that delegated for running costs and overheads. Workers would receive (i) a certain proportion of revenues or profits or (ii) alternatively a fixed wage and proportion of revenues or profits per week or fortnight or month. It would be a system where the marginal costs of labour are below the average costs of labour. Total worker income consisting of wages and profit sharing / revenue sharing, productivity bonuses, and dividends from shares, and dynamic adjustments to these to maintain employee levels and increase them over time, maintain output, full employment, price stability and improved competitiveness. [22]

4. Weitzman's share economy could be further extended to make the total factors of production, namely combined labour and technology costs, variable or linked to business performance. This would involve making technology costs partially or fully dependent on business performance. New forms of business contracts could be put in place where the marginal costs of technology are below the average costs of technology. A new more flexible technological costs structure to encourage the use of new technologies and a constant state of innovation and continuous improvement. This would provide incentives to increase both workers and technology, thus promoting higher levels of productivity and higher probabilities of survival and success.

5. Long term community & neighbourhood share ownership of companies and businesses. Long term in order to prevent shares being traded into fewer and fewer hands and concentrating capital ownership and wealth.

6. Voting rights for workers who own shares. This could be one vote one share or one vote one shareholder depending on the rules of each business. The main issue is the introduction of workplace democracy.

7. Productivity linked share options and productivity bonuses for all employees and for communities to encourage higher productivity, sales, profitability or better performance. This would be in addition to the share ownership plans mentioned above. This should include most workers in a business not just a few executives. Tax incentives could help ensure that most workers are included in this.

8. Long term employee share ownership should include cooperatives. Encourage the building of networks of employee owned firms and cooperatives similar to Mondragon in Spain. Long term in order to prevent shares being traded into fewer and fewer hands and concentrating capital ownership and wealth.

9. Consumer cooperatives, tenant cooperatives, property development cooperatives, farmer cooperatives, retail cooperatives, community cooperatives, banking cooperatives need to be established to widen the wealth and income distribution from economic growth and empower the ordinary people.

10. Government and banking support for farm worker buy outs of large farms and agricultural businesses where they work in or do business with. This is working in South Africa where native African farmers are been given assistance to buy out the large farms and wine growing businesses they work in. These large farms and businesses were established centuries ago during the period of foreign colonial domination. This gives poor farmers and their families a long term financial stake in farming and agricultural capital.

11. Break up large private monopolies, oligopolies, and cartels and state monopolies into smaller employee owned and community owned businesses and cooperatives, including social coops. Employee ownership and community ownership should be long term. This would have the effect of ending economic rent, redistributing vast wealth to ordinary people, stimulating investment and innovation, and producing lower more competitive prices. And tax economic rent in order to discourage abuse of monopoly, cartel or restrictive practise powers. This is discussed below.

12. Reform social security by implementing the recommendations in the book 'Capital Homesteading for Every Citizen: A Just Free Market Solution for Saving Social Security' by Norman Kurland (2000)

[superscript]30[/superscript]. This would give every person a right to social security (government pension) AND to capital ownership and to own capital accounts or long term productive investment accounts which would generate incomes from several sources and complement their income and retirement savings to provide greater security in old age and during sickness or disability. A combination of social security which is government backed and of capital ownership encompassing a broad diversified portfolio would provide security for those who retire and those who develop severe illness or disability and cannot work. This combination could be in the order of 70% social security and 30% capital ownership. This process would start in early childhood and build up over time. It would in addition to other changes mentioned here regenerate the social security systems and investment systems in many countries and return them to solvency, and enable them to meet their obligations in future. The ending of mass speculation and fraud in the financial markets, as advocated in this book would provide a means for capital investments and savings to grow steadily over the years, and provide substantial retirement benefits to people when they retire. While more stable governments and increased economic growth and less tax evasion and more tax revenues would improve the status of social security.

13. Using privatisation of state or public bodies and resources and the civil service to create new employee owned firms. These would supply services to the state. This would enable privatisation to benefit more people in terms of wider share ownership and sharing in the profits of these new firms, while providing governments with more efficient, productive and motivated labour and better cost structures. The highly successful Social Co-ops in Italy should serve as a model for this.

14. Georgism or land redistribution in developing and third world countries would be necessary to achieve these objectives. This would involve (i) community land ownership (ii) farmer's cooperatives (iii) limited state ownership of land and the private use of this land, with users paying a fee. This would provide strong incentives for people to work the land and sell the produce locally or nationally for private profits. This would encourage free enterprise and private profit from working the land while ensuring the ownership of the land is widely owned whether through communities, farmer cooperatives or privately. This would end the high concentration of land ownership in these counties where the richest 5% own between 80 – 100% of the land, and most of the population live in dire poverty as landless labourers. Margrit Kennedy has provided some insights into how this could be done in third world countries and developed countries [33]

15. Globalisation. Those international companies which wish to locate in other countries and compete against local businesses should be allowed to do so on certain conditions (a) set up a subsidiary of the foreign company in the developing country (b) be required to devote a certain percentage of their subsidiary company share capital, say 33%, to local employee ownership and community share ownership. And gradually increase this shareholding by local workers to 100% over 30 years. This would give local workers and communities a share in these international companies and spread out the wealth from globalisation. The WTO could be used to draw up and enforce such schemes.

16. The provision of hedged risk derivatives on a yearly basis to employee share owners and community share owners which would enable them to hedge against their share prices falling below a certain price level. This would be similar to automated short selling options once price falls to a certain level. This would prevent employees and communities suffering massive financial losses from speculators speculating in their company's shares on stock exchanges. It would also help protect employee pension funds.

17. Funding of Economic and Industrial Democracy

- leveraged buy outs by employees. This would involve Quantitative Easing by the central bank and the provision of this money to banks, credit unions, public savings banks, innovation banks, state banks, microfinance (similar to Grameen bank), and financial institutions to provide interest free loans to employees to buy long term shares in their businesses, and to provide community share ownership where communities get similar loans to invest in local businesses. These loans should be structured to be interest free and long term with very low payments per month. Government tax incentives should be used to provide further incentives and reduce the costs to employees, firms, former owners, and banks. Repayments could be made from future revenues and profits. This was first proposed by Louis Kelso in the 1960's and has been developed by others since, and has become known as 'Binary Economics'.
- ordinary workers and communities could provide their own monies in return for ordinary shares and other types of shares and investment instruments in these new type of businesses and cooperatives. This could form a part of a wider pension plan or savings plan with diversified portfolios
- tax incentives and government grants itemised in this Chapter
- use of the capital accounts mentioned in this Chapter

- the revenue sharing and profit sharing aspect could be supplied as part of human labour or work

- use of new local currencies to fund these new type of businesses and cooperatives and for productive capital formation.

- set up public savings banks to specifically invest in these new type of businesses and cooperatives. The German example of this is in Chapter 7.

- the creation of banking cooperatives and extension of others to fund these new type of businesses and cooperatives and for productive capital formation.

- tax incentives for venture capitalists and commercial banks to invest in these firms

- loan guarantees from the state to employees or employee ownership schemes in these firms

- the government and private sector could jointly set up new Innovation Banks which would be regional based and specifically fund innovative start ups, and continuous innovation in existing employee owned firms

- a government supported Innovation Fund consisting of hundreds of millions of euros to provide grant support to innovative start ups, and continuous innovation in existing employee owned firms use of big pension funds, ethical investment funds, private equity funds to fund these new type of businesses and cooperatives. The government could assist by providing generous tax incentives for this.

18. Tax incentives

new government tax incentives and grants to spread economic democracy and industrial democracy. Tax incentives could be progressive starting with incentives aimed at businesses having 40% or more of the workforce owning shares, proceeding to 50%, 70% and 100% of the workforce owning shares. In order for businesses to get tax incentives they must have a minimum of 40% of the workforce involved in employee ownership or profit sharing. This would set a floor or basic minimum and encourage businesses to widen employee ownership. These separate incentives would provide for a gradual transition towards full economy democracy. This could include:

- providing tax breaks for businesses to grant shares or profit sharing or revenue sharing to workers. This taxation could be progressive with ranges of 40% - 50%, 51% - 70%, 71% - 89%, 90% - 100% employee ownership plans qualifying for different tax concessions and government grants and contracts.

- making a certain portion of income, say making 33% or 40% of all employee income from profit sharing, revenue sharing, dividends and productivity bonuses tax free.
- tax incentives for banks which provide the loans or leverage for such deals.
- providing tax breaks to workers who buy shares in their business
- lower corporation taxes for these firms
- government grants to these firms
- government contracts for these firms
- tax incentives for venture capitalists and banks to invest in these firms
- loan guarantees from the state to these firms for transition to employee ownership
- tax credits for productive investment or grants for such investment
- generous pension contribution tax breaks for employees and employers
- lower taxes on dividends
- low or zero capital gains taxes for these types of shares
- tax incentives for cooperation between networks of employee owned firms
- giving tax incentives for big pension funds, ethical investment funds, private equity funds to invest in these new type of businesses and cooperatives.

  This would guarantee a broad diffusion of economic democracy to the working population, and overcome some of the mistakes made in North America and Europe in the past.

19. Government funding for clusters of employee owned firms collaborating with each other and with employee owned banks and financial institutions and with Universities and Institutes of Technology and research and innovation bodies. This would provide the basis for business growth and expansion and sustainability into the future.

20. Strategic Use of Natural Resources to Fund This

    All nation states should have a shareholding of at least 45% in the mining, extraction and sales of their natural resources. This would ensure that the ordinary citizens of a country benefit from the natural resources of their country. Renegotiate the oil and gas drilling deals so that the Irish state is given a 50% stake in all mining and extraction companies, and entitled to 50% of revenues and profits, similar to that in Norway. As of 2014, The Government Pension Fund Global of Norway has assets of $889 billion. It is estimated to reach $1.3 trillion within a decade. These are oil and gas revenues and their invested returns. This money is being used to invest in Norway and improve health, education, training, infrastructure, employment, agriculture, reduce taxes and the tax burden, and improve research and development and national business investment.

In Ireland and other countries these oil and gas tax revenues ranging from an estimated €2 - 5 billion per year would amount to almost €80 billion over 20 years, and these could be used to fund employee share ownership, community share ownership, industrial clusters, business research and innovation, public savings banks (similar to Germany), new domestic and international investment and public infrastructure and telecommunications, and to eliminate water charges, property tax, Universal Social charge, reduce VAT and eradicate all the other planned charges under the austerity program.

21. Use wider employee ownership and community ownership to build human capital and vice versa. This human capital would include skills, apprenticeships, crafts, University level qualifications, high tech skills, continuous professional development. This would increase the return on investment and the ability to raise funds for investment in employee share ownership and community ownership.

22. Training, mentoring and educational programmes to convert to employee ownership plans or cooperatives and how to access finance, use tax incentives, and implement management strategies and plans to actively use these employee share ownership schemes to drive (i) productivity (ii) wage and price flexibility (iii) worker loyalty (iv) new innovations in products, services, processes and technologies (v) better business performance. This could be coordinated through Universities, technical colleges, schools, centres of excellence, and training institutes

23. Provision should be made in laws to enable employees to diversify their pension plans and use both employee share ownership plans and other private pension funds (IRA's in the USA) and state sponsored pension plans, which would have diversified investment portfolios. This diversification would reduce the risk to employees.

24. Using the new type of Quantitative Easing, local currencies, social credit schemes, and microfinance (similar to Grameen bank) to fund the capital, machinery and expertise required for extraction of natural resources via employee owned firms and cooperatives. This would diffuse out the wealth of nation's natural resources to the whole people, benefitting most families and communities throughout the nation.

25. Promotion of social enterprises which are for profit and non profit, so as to fulfil important social needs which the market does not provide or provides inadequately. The provisions in point 15 and 16 could apply in relation to funding.

26. Co-ownership of many types of assets which would be used by communities. Examples being co-ownership of cars, community buildings, crèches and kindergartens, sports fields, homes, dishwashers, washing machines, tools, water wells, holiday homes, etc.. This could be promoted via government tax incentives and grants. This would enable private ownership to exist alongside co-ownership and community ownership.

27. Government / state protection of the rights, redundancy entitlements, health entitlements, and benefits of workers involved in employee share ownership and cooperatives

28. Use of economic democracy to protect workers' rights in all countries through structured fair trade agreements between countries and trading blocs. This is discussed in more detail later.

29. Shorter working hours so as to draw more workers into the workforce, and provide them with important economic opportunities

30. Greater state investment in training and skills development for workers in the private sector and public sector. This investment in intellectual / skills capital would increase the value of workers and the total value of their shares and businesses. State contracts could be given to employee owned firms.

31. A government supported Innovation Fund consisting of hundreds of millions of euros / dollars to provide grant support to innovative start ups and for continuous innovation in employee owned firms. And tie this to industrial clusters and research clusters to further drive innovation and competitive advantage.

32. Greater state investment in public infrastructure which would support these new type of businesses and cooperatives and for productive capital formation. State contracts could be given to employee owned firms.

33. Credit and money creation which favours economic democracy and productive investment instead of speculation in assets, property and derivatives

The Advantages and the Success Factors

Economic democracy has been tried and tested and proven to be a success in several parts of the world, many examples are provided below. The principal advantages of economic democracy and industrial democracy would be dynamic adaption for businesses and wider wealth and income distribution for societies and political democracy. This dynamic adaption is vital in an environment and world governed by dynamic disequilibrium. Yet, this is missing in today's world and in modern economics. Professor Martin Weitzman of Harvard provided some examples of economic democracy in his book, 'Share Economy', and recommends it as a solution for inflation, stagflation , deflation, recession, and depression [21] . His thesis hinges on a share owning economy which would result in the marginal cost of labour being less than the average cost of labour and this would give firms an incentive to hire more labour and to dynamically adjust worker income (wages and shares, dividends, profit sharing, revenue sharing, productivity bonuses, and dividends), prices and quantities to optimise output and employment. He provides mathematical examples and practical tax measures of how this could be achieved and to prove his point. Importantly, it's dynamic adaption features would prove very resilient to shocks and changes, and would optimise employment levels and output over the short to long term. This would if implemented nationally maintain high levels of demand and purchasing power in an economy, thus providing the grounds for sustained aggregate demand, output and accompanying employment, which would insulate an economy from the regular occurrence of shocks, unexpected events and other dynamic disequilibrium factors. In doing this it would greatly reduce unemployment levels, reduce product and service prices, increase output, maintain high demand levels to mop up excess products and services, and provide a good standard of living for all. In the current failed system the average cost of labour equals the marginal cost of labour under the old wage system. This disconnects the worker and wage from the actual business and its economic viability, activities and ability to pay. It actually encourages high unemployment, reduced output, high prices, reduced aggregate demand and supply, and disequilibrium.

Specifically, during inflationary periods, dynamic adaption in the form of changes to total worker income (share income, dividends, profit sharing, revenue sharing, and wages), to prices by businesses, and to state policies and bank anti-inflation policies would work together to reduce inflation and inflationary pressures, and protect job numbers, output, demand levels, and the solvency of firms. While during deflationary periods, this same process would work with other measures including fiscal and monetary stimulus and debt deleveraging or write downs to protect job numbers, output, demand levels and the solvency of firms. The share owning economy provides many advantages and superior benefits over the old wage system. Professor Weitzman and others are correct in their analysis and their support for a share economy or full economic democracy [11, 13, 14, 22] . Extending Weitzman's share economy proposal to include technology, and making total factors of production costs (labour and technology) variable and linked to business performance as proposed above would reduce both the marginal costs of labour and technology below the average costs of labour and technology, and provide a means to increase both and achieve high productivity levels. This would have many further advantages in terms of employment, output, sustained purchasing power and economic growth.

In assessing the need for a move to a worker share owning economy or nation, one must weigh up the costs and benefits of the present failed system and the costs and benefits of the new proposed share economy and economic democracy. Massive differences would be seen in unemployment rates, output, GNP, business solvencies, home repossessions, social welfare, home purchases, health expenditures, and crime levels. The economic benefits of economic democracy are substantial and there is now a need for governments to undertake this analysis and assessment in their own countries, and implement economic democracy and industrial democracy.

There many successful business examples of economic democracy. The following successful employee owned enterprises should serve as role models or models of excellence for economic democracy and industrial democracy:

➢ Mondragon cooperative and network of cooperatives in Spain and other countries

➢ Scott Bader Commonwealth in Britain

➢ John Lewis Partnership in Britain

➢ Suma Wholefoods in Britain

➢ Winco Foods in USA

➢ COOPECAN in Peru

➢ Eileen Fisher in USA

➢ Google, Microsoft, Cisco, Exxon Mobil, Chevron, Proctor and Gamble, Southwest Airlines, Coca-Cola, UPS, ConocPhillips in USA

➢ The Plywood Cooperatives and Haedads Coop in the USA

- The cooperatives in Canada and in Bologna and the Emilia Romagna region of Italy provide successful models
- Lincoln Electric Company in USA
- WL Gore & Associates (makers of Goretex) in USA
- Seymour Speciality Steel in USA
- Fletcher Jones company in Australia
- JZD of the Czech Republic
- Semco in Brazil is an excellent example
- Many successful Japanese companies
- The many business examples listed by Professor Joseph Blasi in his book The Citizen's Share: Reducing Inequality in the 21st Century (2014) and his book Employee Ownership (1988) [11]

These have been very successful and show that economic democracy can work and succeed in the marketplace. The National Centre for Employee Ownership estimates that 32 million Americans own some form of stock in the companies they work in, this includes ESOP and non ESOP ownership plans. It is estimated that there are 9,300 employee stock ownership plans (ESOP) involving approximately 10,000 firms and 15 million employees and the market value is worth $1 trillion in the USA in 2015 [28]. Some of these are in the Fortune 500 and 100 companies. Approximately 50% of all firms in America have some form of employee share ownership, profit sharing, revenue sharing or cooperative style ownership. They are growing in many countries as the political and social benefits of economic democracy in terms of wider and fairer wealth and income distribution and the business and employment benefits are being acknowledged in parliaments around the world. This in turn is stimulating the creation of new laws, new tax incentives and grants and new funding resources to drive this progression forward.

The top author and researcher in this area is Dr. Joseph Blasi in the USA, who has written several books and research papers on the subject [11]. He has made some very important contributions to this field for over 30 years, providing deep insights into the business reasons, economic reasons, political reasons and social reasons for wider share ownership and economic democracy. He also provides some critical success factors for these new type of enterprises. Some of these reasons and factors will be analysed and discussed in sections below.

The literature and research citing the benefits of economic democracy and industrial democracy is extensive [11, 12, 13, 14, 15, 22] The many research studies conducted show that it has the following benefits for business:

(a) increase in worker loyalty, motivation and performance. Reductions in worker turnover and absenteeism.

(b) higher worker productivity levels than other firms

(c) elimination of 'free rider' problem as all workers have a stake in improving the performance, profitability and viability of the firm

(d) better wage flexibility and cost control during inflationary periods and deflationary periods

(e) improved industrial relations and better cooperation and respect between workers and management

(f) better worker cooperation in the innovation of products, services, processes and human capital and in the use of new technologies

(g) better linking of high productivity levels to wages and share income, and thus a fair living wage for workers

(h) better business performance in terms of sales, profits, return on investment, costs, market share, and competiveness

These are important strategic competitive advantages for a business. Research in the area strongly recommends that share capital ownership by employees would have to be long-term, as there is a risk that shares would be sold and pass into fewer and fewer hands, thus depriving workers of capital in the future. Other complementary factors in relation to these benefits are itemized below in the following paragraphs.

Mondragon is one of the most successful employee owned businesses globally, it employs 74,300 people in 257 companies and organizations in four areas of activity: finance, industry, retail and knowledge, and has annual revenues of €12 billion and total assets of €24 billion. Mondragon comprises a large cooperative and a network of many types of cooperatives and employee owned firms, including worker cooperatives, supplier cooperatives, industrial producer cooperatives, supply chain cooperatives, educational cooperatives, financial and banking cooperatives, natural resources cooperatives, retail cooperatives which network and work together to improve purchasing power, sources of savings and investment, new market opportunities, new technologies and innovation, consumer sources, etc. to build market share and to optimise and improve business performance over time. It copies the way corporate conglomerates use their business units, subsidiaries, partner networks and strategic alliances to achieve market dominance.

Networking and Synergies and Higher Levels of Productivity

Semco in Brazil also provides an excellent organisational and management structure for these type of democratic enterprises. Like Mondragon it also uses networks of cooperatives and employee owned firms and synergies. The experience of successful employee owned firms and cooperatives and of research cites networking and synergies as being vitally important, particularly during the early stages of a firm when it faces unique difficulties. The Japanese system of 'Keretsu' involving extensive networking of firms and employee share ownership, cross shareholdings and cooperation and the similar Korean system of networking of firms also provide another successful model of this. Synergies is the key point here. This type of networking of employee owned firms and many types of cooperatives would have advantages in terms of :

I. access to loans and funding channels provided by banking cooperatives, credit unions, microfinance (similar to Grameen bank), public savings banks, tax incentives for leverage or bank loans, use of Quantitative Easing by government, contacts within the banking industry, etc. These financial firms and other employee owned businesses and cooperatives could also provide cross shareholdings, angel capital, venture capital, transitional capital.

II. access to new markets, new contacts, new leads, the acquiring of new contracts. Cooperation in achieving highly effective marketing plans

III. linking producer cooperatives to other producer cooperatives and linking producer cooperatives to consumer cooperatives in order to create networks and network synergies. In some cases producers would be consumers in the same firm, with share ownership by both being a unifying principle.

IV. government funding for clusters of employee owned firms collaborating with each other and with employee owned banks and financial institutions and with Universities and Institutes of Technology and research and innovation bodies. This would provide the basis for business growth and expansion and sustainability into the future.

V. greater coordination in bulk purchasing and supply chain integration and synergies

VI.   getting consumers who are workers to see the value of (a) employee share ownership and community share ownership and (b) shopping for products and services produced by firms with employee share ownership and community share ownership. And that this ultimately benefits everybody including the consumer.

VII.   integration of new technologies across these cooperative networks for competitive advantage. Examples of such technology synergies include the ATM's of banks, Intranets and Extranets, VPN's, Credit Card Payment gateways for the Internet and non Internet, the new Bancor Protocol for blockchain technologies, etc.

VIII.   strategic use of data analytics, A.I. technologies and methods, BPM and business analytics to improve customer numbers, sales and business growth across the network of cooperatives, employee owned firms, banks and supply chains.

IX.   access to worker training and management training and upgrading of skills

X.   access to specialist consultancy services for change management, BPR, technology matters, gaining more market share, market positioning, mergers, acquisitions, research, etc.

XI.   setting up / funding centres of excellence for employee owned firms and economic democracy. This would serve as a knowledge bank and promoter of economic democracy. This would provide information to the general public, and specialist information to firms or employees or persons wishing to start employee ownership businesses, or grow these type of firms, or expand into new markets, merge, form alliances, acquire, etc. These centres would have outreach programmes and extensive coordination with Universities, institutes of technology, training institutes, and think tanks.

XII.   customer relationship management and synergies in this area

XIII.   subcontractor synergies

XIV.   social Co-ops such as those in Italy for providing state services and community services, and some voluntary services

XV.   assistance in achieving affordable employee benefits and loyalty in terms of health insurance, pensions, housing, loans, crèches and childcare, family services, holidays, etc. through tapping into the wide variety of cooperatives and employee owned firms

XVI. strategic alliances, partner networks and enterprise groups consisting of vertical cooperation and horizontal cooperation for cost savings, innovation, and access to new markets. Japan has some good examples.

XVII. how to engage and make the best use of automation, TQM, JIT systems, lean production

XVIII. access to industrial clusters and research clusters and the synergies from this

XIX. assistance in achieving best international practises and standards

XX. assistance in achieving better cost efficiencies

XXI. synergies directed at continuous innovation and improvement of products, services, processes and human capital over time

This would apply to firms with employee share ownership and cooperatives. Many diverse employee owned firms and cooperatives working together through networks, alliances and collaboration and realising synergies would provide the resilience necessary to succeed in competitive marketplaces. Recent research findings at MIT in Boston supports this, and shows that cooperatives tend to thrive when they network together for mutual advantages and synergies [34]

Networks and synergies exist not just between firms themselves and between industries but also between workers, management and boards of directors. These benefits and increased productivity and business performance do not automatically occur in employee owned firms. They require strategic guidance and direction and total commitment and close cooperation between workers, management and directors and outside forces. The research shows that the key factors are :

➤ Workplace democracy. This can take varying forms depending on firm, industry, market environment and national culture. Greater worker participation in the appointment of management and boards of directors of the firm, and greater worker representation on such boards and management teams. This workplace democracy would also include worker involvement in strategies and planning, in feedback mechanisms, in the running of the firm, in financial reporting and cost reporting, in recommendations for improving processes, structures, products and services, and the creation of workplaces where trust, solidarity, mutual respect, open communications, creativity and initiative, cooperation and collaboration exist between workers themselves and between workers and management. Workplace democracy and worker self management structures will take some time to diffuse into the larger economy as most countries and peoples still believe in dictatorship and oligarchy and the master-servant model in the workplace.

➤ checklists for strategic business targets, time schedules, sales and market share, costs, and time and cost savings. Checklists for Business Performance Methods (BPM), service and quality standards, BPR, continuous improvement and innovation methods, and Value Chain analysis. Checklists to continuously implement, monitor, and improve all aspects of the business, and it's products, services and processes.

➤ combining this with strong motivation in the form of worker ownership and sharing of revenues or profits on a weekly / fortnight / monthly basis, and a cost structure which is flexible and directly related to business performance. Giving the workers a stake in the business, making them owners of the business is a powerful motivating factor and can result in workers feeling valued and respected, and this can help achieve higher productivity levels. The goal being total commitment from workers and management to improving business performance, sales, profitability and productivity

➤ linking both individual performance to pay and group performance to pay, so that there are enough incentives to motivate all persons. This could be through productivity bonuses or higher revenue bonuses or higher profitability bonuses. Elimination of 'free rider' externalities.

➤ a total commitment to hard work and to achieving business objectives by workers and management which is based on the fact that the proceeds or surplus value of their labours are shared out to all workers and management in the form of wages, share ownership, profit sharing, productivity bonuses, stock options, and end of year bonuses. And artificial class divisions are abolished and ended as all persons are given the respect and dignity they deserve (as human beings) and every person is given the chance to develop their potential and skills to the highest level.

➤ strong leadership from management, workers and boards to introduce economic democracy and to make it work every day and every week.

➤ work environments which encourage integration of workers with leading technologies and a commitment to continuous innovation of processes, technologies, products, services and human skills for the attainment of competitive advantages. This would include extending Weitzman's share economy thesis to include both labour and technology, as suggested above in previous paragraphs to improve productivity and profitability.

➤ regular use of specialist consultancy services for change management, BPR, technology matters, up skilling, gaining more market share, market positioning, mergers, acquisitions, research, etc.

- use of proper funding channels and availability of finance as advised above. Finance is extremely important.

- use of supportive tax structures and grant structures and Quantitative Easing which favour employee share ownership, revenue sharing or profit sharing in 50% or more of the workforce in a business, as advised above

- education, mentoring and advising in the formation of such enterprises and the growth of these enterprises using various higher educational institutes and training bodies.

- use of networks of employee owned firms, cooperatives and specialist services, and the creation of synergies as advised in a previous paragraph above.

- the support of government, unions, chambers of commerce, trade organisations, business associations and employer organisations

These are the vital ingredients of successful economic democracy and industrial democracy projects [11, 12, 13, 14, 15, 22]

Many writers and thinkers have criticised the alienation of workers in the Industrial Age, and also in our Information Age. This is an ongoing issue of some importance. Workplace democracy would help end the era of worker alienation, bad industrial relations, and low productivity levels which have plagued the world and economics for over 150 years. Mondragon uses a highly successful business model, which combines extensive worker ownership with worker representation on boards of directors and management structures, and aligns worker owners, management, suppliers, partners, investors, consumers with business strategies to achieve excellent results in several markets. Worker representation on boards of directors and management boards would be essential to this economic democracy, and provide for full democratic participation by workers in their place of work and in the larger economy. The economist David Schweickart is a strong believer in this and has lectured and written extensively on the subject, and proposed that economic democracy should consist of these 4 elements:

- Workplace self-management, including election of supervisors
- Management of capital investment by a form of public banking
- A market for goods, raw materials, instruments of production, etc.
- Protectionism to enforce trade equality between nations

These elements are of strategic importance to economic democracy and are proposed in this book. Essentially, worker ownership and participation and representation at company board level and management levels and in strategy formation and business plans, and in greater localised decision making, and in the feedback mechanisms of vital strategic and competitive significance would give workers a stake in their work and firms, align the interests of workers with management and directors, and improve worker loyalty and productivity [11] . An international study of more than 50 different democratically owned and controlled companies supports this and has found that a minimum of six specific organisational components including political, economic, psychological and juridical processes were all equally necessary for the effective running of these businesses over the long term [13] All firms with degrees of employee share ownership could quite easily integrate these lessons into their business cultures, policies, codes of conduct and organisational structures, and reap their benefits. There are several leading businesses and cooperatives which serve as models of excellence in this area and their system could be copied in part or in full by those businesses wishing to become more democratic. These type of firms would by their nature, structure and long term focus support long term productive investment and growth instead of the short term quarterly returns and share price movements, and speculation, which dominates too many industries at present.

Worker participation should include giving employee shareholders a greater legal say in the pay packages of top executives and managers. It will be necessary to replace executive share options with bonuses based on increases in production and sales of products and services. This would remove the incentive for executives to engage in company buybacks and insider trading to inflate share prices and the capital gains for executives. In this book we recommend capping executive pay at 25 times average industrial earnings in a country in order to create enough financial space for re-investment of profits in new capital, productivity enhancement, new technologies, innovations in products, services and processes, human capital or skills, market share growth, and incentives for ordinary workers. It would also help reduce the massive disparities between executive pay and the pay of ordinary workers, and help build greater mutual respect, trust and loyalty among all employees and directors.

Workers and their representatives on boards of directors and management structures could be given a greater say in corporate governance matters, oversight and accountability matters, including whistleblowing on wrong doing. This would ensure that frauds, Ponzi schemes, insider trading, share rigging, tax evasion, illegal activities, pollution which is harmful to human health, and other wrong doing is exposed and dealt with before it threatens the business or whole industry. This could also include a commitment to environmental protection, and cleaning up and renewing polluted environments, which is becoming increasingly relevant and important in our modern world. In fact, cooperatives and employee owned firms have an excellent track record in environmental protection and the protection of worker's rights around the world, far better than large businesses and banks. This commitment to environmental protection, environmental clean ups and the protection of worker's rights could be enhanced further in countries which commit themselves to economic democracy and industrial democracy.

Employee owned firms and community owned firms would also be more inclined to pay taxes in their home countries and in those other countries they operate in. This would have major financial benefits for governments and countries, and would also reduce the total tax burden on existing taxpayers. This would be encouraged by more physical localisation and a more ethical type of business ownership and commitment to honesty and integrity. This has become vitally important in current times, due to the trillions of dollars lost to tax evasion and the need for governments to pay off debt, reduce deficits while providing essential public services. In summation, all of these positive, social goods, are more likely to be achieved under employee and community owned firms operating in an economic democracy than under the current dictatorial form of business ownership and political oligarchy which is responsible for most banking frauds, speculation and massive debt accumulation, economic crashes, environmental destruction, climate damage and mass tax evasion costing many trillions of dollars per year to the global economy.

There are precedents for this, share incentives and share options have been used to increase executive salaries in the past with some good business results, and they could be used to improve ordinary worker incentives and improve business performance and more widely disperse wealth to the workers and to communities and neighbourhoods. This wider share ownership and profit sharing among workers would spread out the wealth from increased economic activity, fair trade and globalisation, high technology, robotics and automation and stimulate and empower local communities and regions. It would reduce the large income and wealth inequalities in many countries, which have been the subject of some recent books by Stiglitz, Piketty, and Smith. By reducing these large inequalities and high concentrations of wealth and income, it would act to build social cohesion, solidarity, and social capital, protecting democracy and freedom in the process.

The building of smart infrastructure encompassing communications Internet of 5G and 6G, renewable energy Internet coordinating many green technologies and grids and driverless or automated mobility Internet and linking these together for a 3rd Industrial revolution could be facilitated by greater employee share ownership and community share ownership. The famous Professor Jeremy Rifkin has stated that this will greatly improve productivity and create zero marginal costs for many industries.

Moving up the Value Chain

It will be necessary for many farmers, primary producers, extractors to join cooperatives or employee owned companies in order to increase their bargaining power and the prices they receive for their labour. And benefit from owning shares in such enterprises. It is much easier for large multinationals or other large firms to exploit individual producers, divided producers, than unified ones. There is strategic value in all producers coming together, uniting together, and working together for the benefit of all. However, these cooperatives and employee owned firms need to be able to add value to their products. This will involve building or leasing production facilities, which can process the product, convert the product into new products which can be sold in shops, integrate the product with other products to create synergies and new high value added products. And use innovation and research to find new ways to process the product(s) to create new ranges of commercial products for which there is a strong and growing demand. Specialist IT and engineering staff could be employed or hired for a period, or the government could offer special apprenticeship courses and part fund the employment of these people. This could be complemented by adding design facilities to the firm or subcontracting such out to other employee owned firms, where innovative new designs for the product(s) would provide a marketing advantage and strategic competitive advantage. Image, design and perception have become vitally important in the modern world. There would need to be a structured programme of continuous innovation and improvement of products, services and processes in such firms in order to survive and thrive in a competitive world. As they grow, they could move further up the value chain into distribution and sales nationally and internationally. The Internet, e-commerce and new digital or crypto currencies are making this much easier. They could also network with other employee owned firms and cooperatives and create synergies as mentioned in the section above. This growth could be organic over time, and would be ably assisted by a new type of banking system based on financing productive investment. One successful example of this type of firm is COOPECAN in Peru.

Models and Adaptation over Time

Scandinavian economies have proven that it is possible to have high growth economies which are more equal. They have less crime rates, less people in jail, high quality education and healthcare systems available to all, good infrastructure, and have a higher standard of living for the bottom 50% than Neo Liberal countries. There is also more social stability. It should be possible for Scandinavian countries to adopt this economic democracy model to enhance its egalitarian system and political and social democracy. Other countries may encounter varying degrees of difficulty depending on the opposition by special interests and oligarchies.

There are several employee ownership models and structures and all should be encouraged. This would enable them to meet the needs of different sectors of an economy, different industries, different regions of a nation, and different cultural environments. Economic democracy can integrate the very best from successful models and strive to achieve excellence and to improve upon it by continuously innovating and improving over time. Over years and decades, through adaption to changing market conditions, environmental challenges, and human expectations, different forms of democratic ownership and representation of workers in the workplace and boardrooms would inevitably develop, producing variants of economic democracy, which would help sustain and deepen democratic structures while achieving optimal business performance and outcomes. As new challenges occur in the form of global resource restraints and environmental damage, employee owned firms would have the flexibility and democratic accountability necessary to adapt to such changes and provide optimal solutions which are socially acceptable. This economic democracy would display aspects of emergence theory, systems theory and complex adaptive systems in a new more innovative and socially beneficial manner, optimising outcomes for most persons in society in all countries. This flexibility and adaptability to change would make economic democracy and industrial democracy more resilient over time.

Cultural and national characteristics will also play a role in this diffusion of economic democracy and industrial democracy worldwide and influence the type of models used. The Japanese model is quite advanced in terms of economic democracy and industrial democracy. Many firms in Japan have worker share ownership, profit sharing, revenue sharing, share options and productivity bonuses for workers. It is widespread in Japan. Workers are also involved in corporate planning and decision making, and there is harmonious and respectful relations between workers and management and boards of directors. Corporate executive pay is controlled and is a few times higher than the lowest paid worker. This pay is not as large or as extravagant as corporate executive pay levels in the USA. Symbols of class divisions are avoided in Japanese workplaces and trust, solidarity, cooperation and collaboration are strongly encouraged between workers themselves and between workers and management. The Japanese system is more egalitarian than in other developed countries and this has many economic and social benefits. It does not have the same level of industrial strife and strikes seen in other developed countries and developing countries.

This Japanese model easily integrates flexible manufacturing systems (FMS), high levels of automation, TQM, JIT systems, lean production, highly trained workers, green technologies, continuous innovation, and strategic alliances with economic democracy to deliver high levels of productivity and business performance. In this system, long term investment and returns are favoured over short term returns, eg. quarterly returns and capital gains and this gives Japanese firms the ability to grow and develop. This is in direct contrast to the short term financial speculation and national bankruptcies one finds in other developed and developing countries. These aspects of economic democracy in Japan are analysed and discussed in some depth in the book 'Human Capitalism' by Robert Ozaki. Yet Japan could do more in terms of economic democracy and industrial democracy, including converting the whole economy to full economic democracy and industrial democracy. The only big defect in the Japanese economy was its recent implementation and use of the Anglo-American model of speculation and it's flawed banking and money creation system in the 1980's and 1990's. This destroyed the Japanese economy in the early 1990's and led to the 'lost decade'. Japan needs to reject this Anglo-American model and continue moving towards a new model of full economic democracy and industrial democracy, including the deleveraging of fraudulent debt and money creation mentioned in previous chapters.

The Nordic economic model in Scandinavian countries provides a similar approach, where workers, unions, employers and government all work together through collective agreements and social partnership to enhance economic growth, free trade, wealth generation, wider wealth distribution and social solidarity through adequate social safety nets. It also includes strong support for cooperatives and employee share ownership. The Nordic Model has been a highly successful economic model and could be integrated with economic democracy and industrial democracy to achieve even better outcomes. However, the Nordic model is coming under increasing pressure as it's tax structure and over reliance on state provided services places a huge strain on it in a new globalised world intent on achieving international production targets via a 'race to the bottom', increasing automation, Taylorist or dictator style management methods, and mass evasion of taxes via tax havens. It is becoming impossible to compete against big firms involved in these practises. The international trade reforms, Bancor currency proposal, banking, money and debt reforms and economic democracy reforms proposed here could be used to protect Nordic models, further improve social cohesion and solidarity, lower taxes, while providing new avenues for the private employee owned sector to provide goods and services under contract to the state. This economic democracy form would enable the Nordic model to adapt more rapidly to changing conditions, and to realise new efficiencies while realising their business, social and political objectives. Nordic countries have great potential in the area of economic democracy owing to their strong industrial base, abundant natural resources and their belief in fairness, honest dealing, productivity and social equality.

The German model is similar in some respects to the Nordic model, but is more formalised. In Germany, the German Codetermination Act 1976 requires 50% worker representation on the supervisory boards of companies and a worker representative on the management board. And many big companies are required to have worker representation on the board of directors, and workers directly elect works councils which send committee members to boards of directors. This has empowered German workers and played a major part in achieving industrial peace, worker loyalty and cooperation, and high productivity levels in Germany. This German model has some useful aspects which need to be greatly expanded in terms of employee ownership and revenue sharing or profit sharing plans to achieve far better outcomes for workers, management, businesses, government and society in Germany. Germany has great potential in this area due to its strong industrial base and its belief in productivity and social equality in the post war years.

The Northern Italian model is quite advanced and integrates traditional Italian values around family and community and regional loyalty, and includes many types of cooperatives, both business cooperatives which provide many types of products and services and social co-ops which are contracted to provide some state services and community services. One also sees networks of these and resultant synergies. They employ persons with disabilities and illnesses and indeed prioritise this, giving them jobs and careers and provide a form of social inclusion. This could be a model for other countries. They have in general proved to be viable, well run, very competitive and successful, with the most successful being concentrated in the Emila Romagna region and around Bologna. These have played a significant role in improving the competitiveness of industry in Northern Italy, making it one of the most competitive in Europe.

The Progressive Utilisation Theory (Prout) first formulated in India by Sarkar has several aspects of economic democracy and industrial democracy. It has three levels of organisation, integrating (i) private ownership of very small firms with (ii) employee ownership and cooperatives with (iii) community ownership and state ownership. In addition to promoting employee ownership and cooperatives, it also includes state ownership and community ownership of strategic resources to ensure that important public goods are distributed free or at very low cost to poorer sections of society, eg, food, water, shelter, electricity. Prout believes in using this to maintain high levels of demand and purchasing power in an economy, thus providing the grounds for sustained aggregate demand, output and accompanying employment. It facilitates co ownership or community ownership of products and services of strategic benefit to communities. It insulates against the market failures consistently found in dynamic disequilibrium. It also promotes technology and innovation in products, services and processes, as a means to improving competitiveness and quality of life. Interestingly it also supports greater work sharing and reductions in working hours in light of high and growing productivity levels. This theory also includes important ecological aspects which are becoming important in light of climate damage and continuing food and water pollution and the accompanying rising costs of healthcare. It certainly adds to the body of knowledge concerning economic democracy, and some aspects would be value to countries worldwide.

The share owning by all workers as proposed by Professor Martin Weitzman of Harvard provides yet another model or structure. This system would involve dynamic changes to total worker income (wages and shares, revenue sharing, profit sharing, and dividends) and to prices to maintain employee levels and increase them over time, increase output and economic growth improving competitiveness. [22] His book provides an added dimension to the issue of employee ownership.

And there are consumer cooperatives, tenant cooperatives, property development cooperatives, housing cooperatives, retail cooperatives, farmer cooperatives, community cooperatives, banking cooperatives which would enhance the overall economic effects of employee share ownership and the wider diffusion of wealth. They could differentiate themselves from competitors by offering ordinary people shares, bonus points, safer and healthier products, lower prices, better quality products, discounts, fair trade products, and special deals on related items. These cooperatives would act as a continuous economic feedback loop, creating and circulating wealth within communities and regions, and within a nation. This would facilitate greater and more sustainable economic growth. It would also instigate deeper societal changes, providing new opportunities for personal, family and community development which would create new synergies, which would over time benefit all persons in society.

The Bigger Picture

The economist Louis Kelso provided the philosophical reasons and the practical legal and business case for economic democracy back in the 1950's in the USA [14] . His company assisted the formation of employee owned firms in the USA and also lobbied for legal recognition and tax incentives for these type of firms. Kelso provided important new insights into this area which are still relevant today. He termed it 'binary economics' to describe income streams for workers which would come from both capital ownership (dividends, profit sharing, new share issues, retained profits) and from wages. He went beyond employee ownership to advocate for interest free loans from central banks to fund employee share ownership in companies and businesses and productive capital formation in the private sector and infrastructure development in the state sector. He correctly reasoned that by increasing productive capacity and worker productivity it would reduce inflationary pressures while stimulating economic growth via new investment and expansion of consumption. And that it would sustain the economic multiplier effect over time providing high levels of consumption, investment and full or near full employment. Kelso also believed that economic democracy and industrial democracy were vital to the development and protection of political democracy and freedom. In this, he was also correct. Kelso's contributions to the field of economic democracy have been very significant and have had a lasting impact. Today his company Kelso & Company is one of the biggest private equity firms in the world, it specialises in employee share ownership plans, and handles several billion dollars in assets. Binary Economics as proposed by Kelso has a strong following today. Its main proponent is Professor Rodney Shakespeare. He has written books [29] delivered many lectures and has a web site and blog on the subject at http://www.binaryeconomics.net . He provides strong economic arguments for Binary Economics which build upon and greatly expand the work of Louis Kelso. He has also contrasted Binary Economics with the failures of neo liberal economics and the bubbles and crashes which consistently emerge from it.

Eliminating Waste and Fraud

Wider employee share ownership and community share ownership would help encourage honest investment, the payment of taxes, and integrity and ethics in business and more accountability in politics and reduce the large scale waste and fraud at government level and corporate level in several countries including :

- o over speculation and related frauds and crashes involving speculation in trillions of dollars and losses of trillions of dollars globally
- o derivatives which are speculation based and worth over $1,200 trillion
- o bank and speculator bail outs by government and taxpayers involving trillions of dollars
- o manipulated wars and regime changes which cost trillions of dollars per year and mostly benefit large banks, the military industrial complex, and the Deep State
- o corporate welfare and subsidies, and tax evasion schemes, costing tens / hundreds of billions of dollars each year in many countries.
- o a Deep State and Shadow Government (in big countries) which commands hundreds of billions of dollars per year and where trillions of dollars have gone missing, been misappropriated, and are unaccounted for. In 2001, Donald Rumsfled the defence minister of the USA claimed that over $2 trillion was missing and unaccounted for. In 2018, the US government has stated that 21 trillion is missing and unaccounted for. The CAFR scandal is just one example of this.
- o the robbing of natural resources such as oil, gas, minerals and depriving governments and taxpayers of many billions of euros / dollars per year

IMF Support

The IMF supports a wider distribution of wealth and income as a superior means to grow GDP and grow an economy. In a report in 2015 titled 'Causes and Consequences of Income Inequality: A Global Perspective' it cited

'Our analysis suggests that the income distribution itself matters for growth as well. Specifically, if the income share of the top 20 percent (the rich) increases, then GDP growth actually declines over the medium term, suggesting that the benefits do not trickle down. In contrast, an increase in the income share of the bottom 20 percent (the poor) is associated with higher GDP growth. The poor and the middle class matter the most for growth via a number of interrelated economic, social, and political channels.'

The economic democracy proposals here in this Chapter and Book would help achieve and maintain this over time, providing a sustainable path for economic growth over the long term.

Democratisation of Credit and Money in an Economic Democracy

This was discussed and detailed in Chapter 7 of this book in the section - 'A Democratisation of Money and Banking using New Types of Money Creation and New Types of Banking for Long term Productive Investment & Consumption'

Economic Democracy in order to fully succeed in financial and business terms, must support new types of money creation, banks, credit and local currencies to stimulate and maintain economic growth at local and regional level so as to (i) maintain high and sustained credit growth at all levels of society so as to bring consumption, demand, employment, production and investment to optimal levels (ii) diffuse credit access and financial competence and capacity out to neglected and marginalised local communities, inner cities, deprived regions, and ordinary working class families and individuals while simultaneously improving their credit worthiness via economic democracy and social inclusion initiatives (iii) widely diffuse the vast wealth created in the economy to the general population and resolve the issue of the 1% gaining at the expense of the 99% and the deficiencies in effective demand and effective supply which have plagued economies for centuries. The following image provides some insight into the uses of local currencies, credit unions and microfinance (similar to Grameen bank) in the context of Economic Democracy and much wider employee share ownership and community share ownership.

TYPES OF MICROFINANCE USED BY POOR PEOPLE

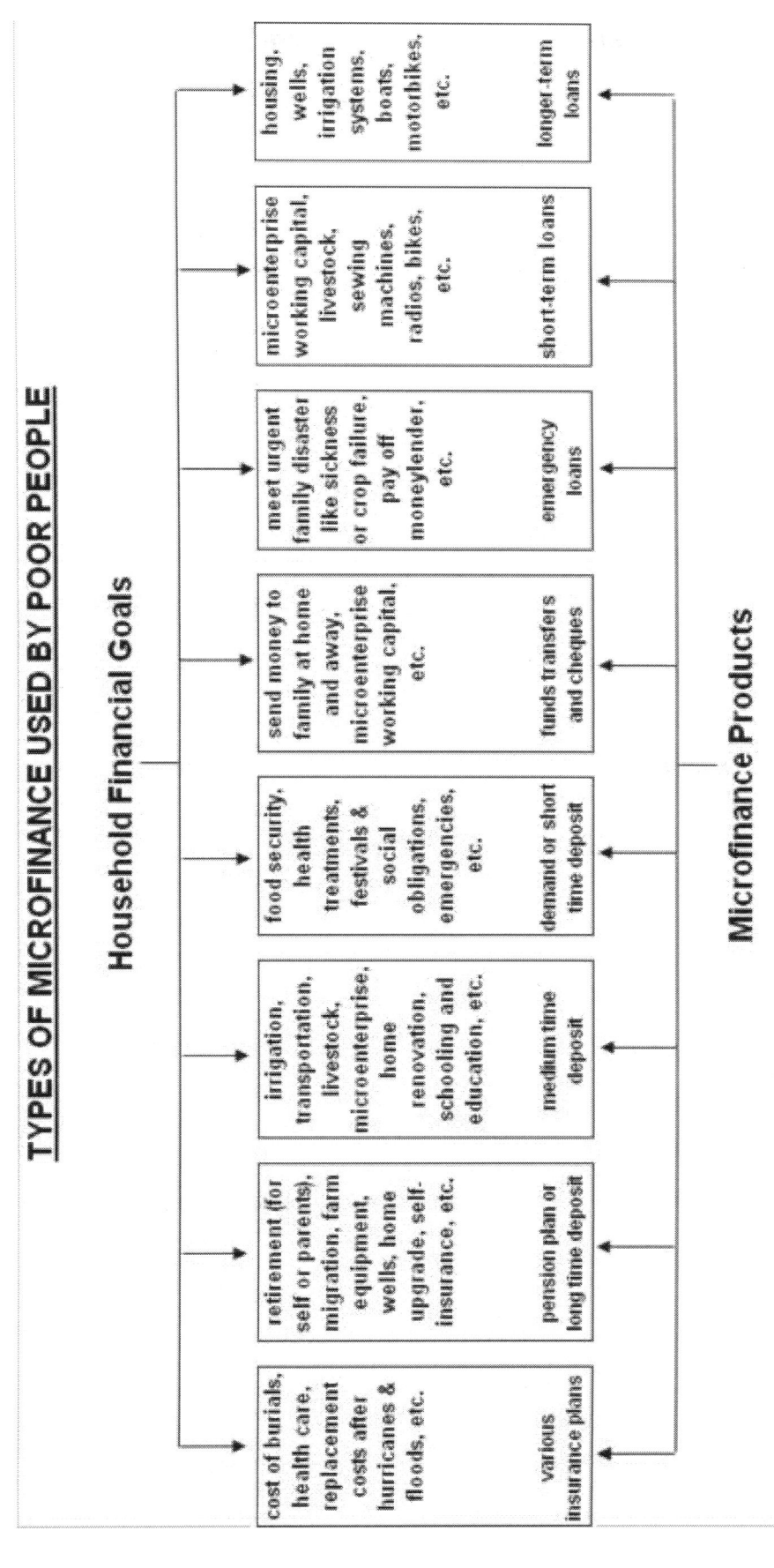

Source: Brett Matthews, Mathwood Consulting Company.

Government Assistance to the Private Sector

In the USA government bodies such as DARPA, RAND, the National Science Foundation, the NIH, and other government research organizations many of them tied to Universities created the most important inventions of the Digital Age and Modern Age, including the Internet, computers (in cooperation with the British government), microchips, computer networks, computer programmes and software, Google, GPS systems, computer screens, encryption, touch screens for computers, mobile phones and smartphones, the Bar Code, the accelerometer (used in Wii), satellite communications, supercomputers, optical digital recording, funding for Universities and research centres, seismic imaging, RSA cipher, infant formula, fire resistant clothing, goodyear tyres, vaccines, civilian aviation, wind turbines, cleaning bacteria, the Human Genome project, led lighting, fluorescent lights, modern water purification techniques, memory foam, anti corrosion coating, cochlear implants, insulin pump, charge coupled device, water filters, MRI imaging, research funding for new treatments for Cancer, advanced prosthetics, and Doppler radar. In Britain government sponsored research led to the deciphering of DNA, invention of jet engines, computers, enigma and cipher technologies, carbon fibre, DNA profiling, the atomic clock, iris recognition, graphene. Many inventions came about inside government funded Universities. These inventions changed the world. This is often forgotten by Neo Liberal and Neo Classical economists, Monetarists, Hayekians, and Libertarians. Indeed, depriving governments of funding for research and innovation while focusing solely on increasing share holder value and speculative gains every quarter as advised by these economists tends to reduce the amount spent on research and development, innovation and long term growth.

The Government research agency in a country (Forfas in Ireland, RAND and DARPA in USA) should supply to every business a set of international best practices for stimulating and achieving innovation in their industry and engage with and help out small and medium sized businesses and help them commercialize these innovations to achieve international competitive advantages. This would encompass continuous improvement and innovation in people (skills), product, services, and processes. This could be customized to the innovation needs of small, medium and large sized businesses in an industry. Extensive use would be made of successful case studies from around the world. This set of innovation best practices would become a metric which Irish businesses would measure themselves against. This set could be updated by Forfas on a yearly basis, so that businesses are given the newest and most relevant material in this area. Distribution could be carried out via email to every Irish business, this would save on costs. Forfas could for a fee provide professional assistance to individual Irish businesses for the purposes of innovation and continuous improvement.

Forfas should also supply a set of best international practices for growing a national business into an international business to every Irish business. Again this could be customized to the innovation needs of small, medium and large sized businesses in an industry. Extensive use would be made of successful case studies from around the world. This would enable Irish businesses to benefit from globalization and further enhance Ireland's export-led growth. This set would also be updated yearly by Forfas. Distribution could be carried out via email to every Irish business, this would save on costs.

This could be accompanied by an expansion of the government's policy rewarding research and innovation. The process of continuous improvement and innovation in people (skills), product, services, and processes should be given additional tax incentives and grants similar to those given to property developers and private investors during the property boom years. The resources in FAS and Universities and Institutes of Technology should be deployed into courses which upskill workers in line with the existing and future needs of industry. A mixture of tax incentives, grants and EU monies should be used to encourage this upskilling. The onus must be on businesses to quantify continuous improvement and innovation in people (skills), product, services and processes so as to qualify for tax credits, tax allowances, and special investment schemes which private investors could invest in. This scheme would be carried out in conjunction with Forfas, Enterprise Ireland, the IDA, Universities, Institutes of Technology, business innovation centres, research centres, training institutes and agencies and foreign collaborations with third level colleges. Direct grants could also be used for these purposes and categorised as an "Economic Stimulus package" for the economy. The EU has relaxed the rules on this in order to give member countries enough room to stimulate their respective economies during this recession.

Government should encourage and facilitate continued development of clusters of industries and centres of excellence, as focal points for new foreign and domestic investment. This would involve coordination between Enterprise Ireland, the IDA, Forfas, the third level colleges, the innovation and research initiative mentioned above, and national and foreign investors / businesses. The tax system could be altered to encourage clusters of industries. This could be used in conjunction with regional development to provide hubs of industry and excellence. The government could add further assistance by increasing levels of government funds into key scientific and technology educational programmes, particularly state of the art equipment, lecturers, professors and tutors, lab. assistants and research doctorate students in Universities and Institutes of Technology directly involved in these clusters. The proposal to give double points to higher level maths and applied maths subjects in the Senior Cert should be immediately introduced in the CAO system.

The same incentives used to inflate the property bubble could be used to increase productive investments, research, innovation, renewable energy, industrial clusters, up-skilling and infrastructure improvement in Ireland

In addition to foreign direct investment, Ireland should also encourage stronger indigenous investment by Irish firms and entrepreneurs. Israel managed to transform its economy into a world leader in high technology and science during the 1990's. This was achieved through the Yozma Fund. This is a state sponsored venture capital fund which encourages the formation of indigenous private companies and start-ups. It prioritises investment in technology and science areas, and the deployment of leading-edge research from around the world into new products and services. This venture capital fund is actually building an international-class 'Knowledge Economy' in Israel. This in turn is also attracting in foreign direct investment. In 1993 the Yozma Fund was set up with $200 million, today it holds investments worth $10 billion. Israel has the highest rate of business start-ups in the world and has 120 companies on the US NASDAQ exchange. The Irish Government should study closely the workings of the Yozma Fund in Israel and try and replicate it here in Ireland.

Retirement and Social Security Aspects

There is a pension crisis in most developed countries in the world today. Many developed countries cannot afford to pay out pensions, and this is afflicting both public sector pensions and private sector pensions. This pensions disaster is a natural outcome of the bubbles and crashes and globalisation 'race to the bottom' being promoted by neo liberal and classical economists and politicians. Pensions have been wiped out or greatly reduced by the fraud, criminality and incompetence of banks, big corporations, executives, speculators, and hedge funds and excessive government corruption. This is explained in Chapter 4. The economic democracy ideas proposed in this book provide a viable solution to this pensions crisis. Firstly it would provide more stable economic growth, based on productive investment and steady growth, not speculative manias, and it would produce no economic bubbles and crashes. This would greatly increase the returns to most pension funds for ordinary working class people. Secondly it would encourage honesty, accountability and transparency in the corporate sector and the banking sector, reduce or eliminate fraud and corruption, and would act to protect investors, savings and pensions.

Thirdly it would provide a sustainable means for pensions and savings to grow and accumulate over time for most and possibly all persons. Sustainability is vitally important. Fourthly it would combine social security with increased capital ownership as explained in Point 11 above. It would also provide the financial and credit infrastructure for pensions and incomes to grow and for the elderly to access credit and affordable localised support services via local currencies. This has been expanded upon by Norman Kurland in his book 'Capital Homesteading' where capital accounts are proposed for every citizen encompassing employee ownership, community share ownership and diversified investments in utilities, bonds, shares, property and non speculative stocks and assets [30]. The objective being to provide steady income over one's whole life from birth to working years to retirement. This capital income and savings would be further supplemented by social security in this overall package so that there are adequate safeguards to ensure security and dignity for those who retire and those who become ill / disabled. The new type of economic democracy proposed in this book would greatly boost growth rates in developed countries and in developing countries, providing greater returns to capital and to labour, and these returns would be stable and sustainable over time, and this in turn would build up and strengthen pension funds.

Lastly, as Alan Greenspan (Fed chairman) stated before the US Congress, the government has the power to fund pension payments by money printing (or Quantitative Easing) if necessary. Though this relates to the desperate measures governments may be forced to take in today's failed economic and political world with it's speculative bubbles, frauds, crashes and bail outs and austerity which have robbed and bankrupted pension funds, taxpayers, and nations.

Entrepreneurs and New Ecosystems based on Economic Democracy

Entrepreneurs and business opportunities exist in an ecosystem. These ecosystems differ in their structure and format, and exhibit various degrees of demand insufficiency and supply insufficiency. Entrepreneurs depend on a customer's spending money, and customers rely on wages / salaries and income from investments and assets. The entrepreneur is not some wizard or magician with special knowledge of how to make money, the entrepreneur is at the mercy of the spending power of consumers, and this is dependent on the ecosystem. Naive and gullible neo liberal, Hayekian and classical economists presume that the ecosystem is unimportant and irrelevant and that markets will magically appear for entrepreneurs and that everybody will live happily in some imagined utopia, but this fairytale has been disproven many times, especially after the financial and economic crashes initiated by the ideas of these economists. Consumers reduced down to penury, poverty, excessive debt and negative wealth (to enrich global corporations and banks) cannot spend enough to create proper markets for entrepreneurs to thrive and succeed.

The economic democracy proposed in this book would end the deficiencies in effective demand and effective supply which have plagued the world for centuries. It provide more than sufficient levels of demand and consumption and accompanying levels of supply and investment opportunities to enable most entrepreneurs to thrive and succeed. It would convert many ordinary workers into entrepreneurs via wider employee share ownership, profit sharing and community share ownership. It would free up more capital and credit to be invested in productive activities and converting derelict and underused assets to economic uses, while reducing the scope for speculative capital. This expansion of entrepreneurship to all areas of society would encourage greater work and effort and would in combination with new technologies and new innovations lead to very high increases in productivity. This in turn would create greater levels of aggregate demand in the economy, including higher levels of regenerative demand which would sustain economic activity and growth over the long term. This would provide a new type of industrial revolution – The Digital and Economic Democracy Revolution.

A new virtuous circle would be created over time. This is illustrated in the flowchart on the following page, which shows the Circular Flow of Income for Economic Democracy

Income of Workers

- Wage income & Profit Sharing or Revenue Sharing income for all workers as proposed by Professor Martin Weitzman of Harvard
- And long term employee ownership by all in one's workplace and Dividend income from shares weekly / monthly / yearly
- Productivity bonuses and widespread share options aimed at increasing production, sales, innovations in products, services & processes
- Income from community share ownership in businesses. This would benefit ordinary families and communities.
- Income from community based businesses using local currencies – LETS schemes, WIR system, JAK system (Nordic), BCI system (Germany), Time dollars, Ithaca Hours
- Income from wider land distribution to more small and medium sized private owners. Georgism and private incentives.
- Income from community based banks, credit unions, public savings banks and microfinance organisations
- Some worker pension funds invested into share ownership plans and also into other diversified portfolios including stocks, real estate, art, bonds, etc. This will provide income on retirement.
- Basic Income / Negative Income Tax for all persons and higher for those displaced by technological or economic changes
- Real incomes and living standards protected by severe restrictions on speculation in all types of assets.
- Bancor currency and fairer global trade which creates high economic growth and better distribution of incomes and wealth which fuel continued consumption, investment and wealth creation.

Spent on Products and Services produced by

- National businesses with long term employee ownership and profit sharing plans. And cooperatives.
- International businesses with long term employee ownership and profit sharing plans. And cooperatives.
- Local and Regional based businesses and organisations using local currencies – LETS schemes, WIR system, Time Dollars, Ithaca hours
- Community based banks, cooperative banks, credit unions, public savings banks, microfinance organisations

Funding Capital Formation, Businesses, Wealth Generation and Technological Progress

- Capital in the form of employee share ownership, many types of cooperatives, community share ownership, community banks, credit unions, banking cooperatives
- Long term outlook encouraged in businesses. Less frenzied capital markets, less focus on the short term and quarterly returns. Restrictions on speculation. This would encourage stability and discourage booms and busts.
- Debt and money creation aimed at productive investments not speculation in assets, commodities and derivatives
- Good industrial relations between workers and management as all have a financial stake in the business and the success of the business
- Technological innovation and accompanying innovation of processes, goods, services and people's skills would be strongly encouraged and used to constantly improve business and productivity
- Capital raised through the capital markets, banks, employees and communities. A merging of many interests, working together to improve the living standards of all.
- Bancor currency and fairer global trade to encourage full employment and economic growth in countries
- Energy sustainability and independence achieved through strategic investments in green, sustainable energies. This would be vital to business.
- Payment of taxes to support the education systems, training systems and infrastructure necessary for technical innovation and business innovation, and business growth & success

Human Capital, Education and Sociological and Psychological Impacts

Socially or in sociological terms, it would give more and more people and their families, who are currently excluded from the economy and society, a stake in the capitalist system and more self confidence and opportunities for economic advancement. It would provide entirely new and better forms of Social Inclusion, some market driven and some state driven, which would combine to provide more social capital and increased opportunities for adding to this social capital over time. It would be a system which encourages people to come together, to work together, to unify together, to transcend divisions, and to cooperate together for the benefit and upliftment of all, in an environment of mutual respect and dignity. Robert Putnam's famous book 'Bowling Alone' shows the destructive effects on individuals, families, communities and societies of the current system of economics and politics which promotes social exclusion, greed and excessive individualism. The continuous bad news on the television, and in the national and local press and media gives one an idea of how destructive this has become. Economic Democracy would help reverse this trend.

Empirical evidence from more socially equal societies show that they have relatively high economic growth rates, less crime, less poverty, less alcohol and drug addictions, less mental illnesses, less jail incarceration rates, less domestic abuse and family breakdown rates, less political corruption, less diseases, less ghettos, and more civic engagement, more family stability, greater community cohesion, better healthcare and hospital care for most of the population, and higher third level education rates among lower and middle income groups than countries which are highly unequal in wealth and income terms. Extreme inequalities create externalities and excessive costs which affect both economic growth and social stability and progress. Neo Liberal and Neo Classical economists, Hayekians and Monetarists may praise high levels of inequality and social injustices but none of them or their families would like to endure it. ; they may love globalisation's race to the bottom but they refuse to live in the sewer. The 'ivory tower' and it's nonsense is far too comfortable for them.

Under Economic Democracy, greater economic equality would provide a more positive and virtuous dynamic between economics and society and civic engagement, creating new forms of social capital. The increased employment and career opportunities, and improved wealth and income for all persons, would facilitate and encourage individual stability, family stability and community stability, and supportive networks, and the social capital inherent in this would help foster higher educational attainment by parents and their children, and the formation of new human capital in the form of skills, qualifications, knowledge, expertise, self confidence, self belief, etc.. This would involve ordinary people in both the physical capital and human capital accumulation processes, with both working to advance the socio-economic status of all workers and their families. Economic democracy would provide many more working class people, farm workers and the present underclass with the capital and funds to educate themselves and to improve their skills. This would play a vital part in bringing about greater equality in societies.

The extra wealth created within economies and kept within economies would provide the funding for new schools, colleges, Universities, technical institutes, research and development, and training companies and extensions to existing ones, and improvements to public infrastructure, roads, hospitals, healthcare, which would improve existing human capital and build up even more human capital over time. This along with other changes mentioned above would create virtuous circles, simulating and maintaining technological innovation and continuous innovation of products, services, processes and human capital over time.

This would have a self reinforcing effect over time, leading to higher worker participation rates, more highly skilled workforces, higher levels of productivity, more advanced innovations, high economic growth, and better returns to workers via shareholdings, productivity bonuses, higher wages, etc. which would fuel further increases in human capital, more innovation, and so on. Greater progress in human capital would facilitate progress in social capital and vice versa, creating a reciprocal dynamic. It would also have a strong social inclusionary dimension, in the sense that it would draw in presently excluded sections of society. The overall effect would be transformative, it would transform present day ghettos, industrial wastelands, homeless shelters, boarded up towns, and underprivileged sections of society into a new economy, providing them with jobs, careers, skills, money, hope, self belief, many new opportunities, options, capital investments, homes, dignity and respect. It would empower whole populations to progress, to move forward, to reach their potential in life.

This would help end the divisions based on social class, race, religion, gender, national identity, age, ethnic group, disability, and colour, providing all persons with the opportunities for economic and social advancement and also provide new opportunities for a raising of one's consciousness and deepening of one's spiritual depth. The latter two are discussed in some detail in Chapter 12 of this book. It would be a new powerful and enduring form of social inclusion. And provide new opportunities for coming together, uniting together to work in common cause for high ideals and better societies. This would totally transform individuals and societies in positive and constructive ways, providing innumerable new benefits to all. It would cure many of the psychological and psychiatric conditions and illnesses caused by today's failed economic ideologies and political systems.

The social capital aspects of this are expanded upon in Chapter 12 of this book. They build upon developments and research in consciousness, psychology and inter-personal relations and how to avoid negative social capital. Economically, it would lead to more stable economies and an end to boom and bust cycles. Stable economics would translate into stable societies, stable people, stable families and stable communities. The vast amounts of money used for speculation in assets, property and derivatives, over 1,200 trillion at present and rising, and for conflicts and wars, could be re-directed into employee share ownership, cooperatives, community share ownership, and into specific government programmes to improve health, education, infrastructure, training, human capital, and innovation and building more civilized, more respectful, more orderly, more stable, and more contented peoples and societies.

Financial Responsibility

These changes would encourage greater financial education and financial responsibility among working class people and among the currently poor, the ill, the disabled, minorities and excluded sections of society. It would lift them up, give them new hope, provide them with a firm foundation upon which to build new and better lives, giving them jobs, career opportunities, (long term) shares, dividends, profit sharing, social credit, access to loans and credit, access to affordable housing, new skills and further training, higher education, new confidence, greater promotion and career advancement opportunities, entrepreneurial opportunities, new investment prospects, etc. and enable them to participate more fully in society. Involving these people in the economy would enable them to learn about finance and how to analyse and to assess investments, and to invest wisely, and to take financial responsibility. This investment and accounting knowledge would also include a deep knowledge of money creation, the Bancor Protocol, Bitcoin and Blockchain technologies, local currencies, alternative types of banking and investment. These important skills could be passed on their children within families and supplemented by changes to the curriculums of schools and the structure of the educational system.

It would build greater self confidence and self reliance within people and this would stimulate new virtuous circles of prosperity and so on. This would totally transform societies and would be a win-win situation for everybody and resolve many, many social ills. It could over time replace some aspects of the social welfare state which has led to vast misallocations of resources, to waste and to lost lives. It would also provide the means to mass fund health insurance plans, pension plans, home insurance plans, car insurance, educational plans and enable more people to make contributions, thus spreading out the burden and reducing the costs for everybody. It would regenerate people's lives, inner cities, neighborhoods, ghettos, and lead to more positive and constructive engagements between people. This in turn would build greater social cohesion and social stability in societies.

Inflation and Deflation Worries

Let us examine inflation and deflation in the context of this new proposed economic democracy and industrial democracy. Inflation and deflation has confounded and distressed monetarists, neo liberals, Hayek free marketers, Keynesians and others for many decades. This proposed economic democracy and industrial democracy would control the aforementioned causes of inflation in the following manner:

(i) ending the dominance and power of monopolies, oligopolies, restrictive practises, land owners, economic renters, patent holders, political patronage of industries, state protected sectors, etc. This would greatly reduce prices for goods and services in an economy and have an anti inflationary effect. Even in difficult economic periods, it would reduce inflationary pressures in the economy.

(ii) legal and constitutional constraints on the printing of money by governments. This is explained in Chapter 7. This would have anti inflationary effects.

(iii) use of this government money printing (Quantitative Easing) for productive investment, innovation and productivity in the productive sector, increases in total production and supply of goods and services in the economy, conversion of company shares into employee owned shares geared at increasing productivity and rewarding it. Not for speculation in assets, commodities and derivatives and massive accumulations of debt to speculate. In summary, in the private sector, money printing which is focussed on improving public infrastructure, productive investment and wider share employee ownership would lead to the expansion of productive investments, production of goods and services, aggregate supply, technological innovations, continuous process, product, service and quality innovations, continuous training, skills enhancement and upgrading, long term employee share ownership and community share ownership, greater wage flexibility, and investment in newer forms of cost control. And this would have anti inflationary effects, and keep inflation low.

(iv) abolition of interest rates. This would significantly reduce the cost of producing, extracting / farming, distributing, storing, selling and purchasing goods and services, and reduce prices and reduce inflationary pressures. It would have a strong and sustained anti inflationary effect.

(v) abolition of excessive (speculative and economic rent caused) debt which would greatly reduce the cost of goods and services, improve supply and productivity, reduce inflationary pressures. It would have a strong anti inflationary effect over time.

(vi) fractional reserve of 100% (see Chicago Plan). This would stop the excessive creation of money by commercial banks which imposes higher costs through fractional reserve lending, debasement of the currency, and the funding of speculation which drives up costs.

(vii) a focus on full employment, high levels of employee ownership and long term productive investment would help sustain consumption and low to moderate debt levels which would be sustainable over time. This would scale down the money printing processes and allow economies to derive consumption from improvements in production and productivity.

(viii) investment in energy sustainability, renewability and independence to reduce the probability of energy price shocks. Laws and regulations against speculation in energy prices, commodity prices and currencies. Investment in the natural regenerative capacity of land, agriculture and other natural resources.

(ix) ending the corporate welfare and corporate subsidies which keep taxes high and prices high in many countries

(x) total worker income flexibility through employee ownership, profit sharing, revenue sharing, dividends, share options, productivity plans, community share ownership etc. and more harmonious industrial relations. This flexibility is discussed in sections above and would enable dynamic adaption which is necessary in markets which are subject to dynamic disequilibrium.

(xi) special taxes levied on those firms which raise prices excessively during inflationary times.

(xii) Special tax incentives and grants specifically to increase supply of goods and services and / or to decrease excessive demand during inflationary times

(xiii) increasing loan refusals if prices are rising too fast

(xiv) reduction of import quotas or restrictions to supply. Increase total supply and reduce prices

(xv) replace executive share options with bonuses based on increases in production and sales of products and services. This would remove the incentive for executives to engage in company buybacks and insider trading to inflate share prices and the capital gains for executives

(xvi) use of new technologies to reduce the costs of producing goods and services and their distribution costs. Economic democracy would facilitate the use of newer technologies and innovations.

(xvii) anti inflation fiscal policies and monetary policies which work with underlying factors in the economy mentioned here to control inflation and reduce it.

(xviii) Policies to counter deflation and depression have been mentioned in previous chapters of this book.

An end to sharp divisions between Capital and Labour which encouraged industrial strife in the past. Labour would own stakes in Capital and Capital would have an interest in protecting the interests of Labour. There would be a new alignment of interests between Capital and Labour. This would encourage greater flexibility in wages, costs and prices and dynamic adaption to changing marketplace conditions. And an end to Capital enforcing higher prices, higher debt, higher rents and lower wages to control or destroy Labour. In effect, a win-win situation for everybody.

Inbuilt Flexibility in Costs and Prices

All economies are subject to unexpected shocks which worsen the effects of dynamic disequilibrium, and create new levels of disequilibrium. The 1970's being one of many examples of this. The new system proposed here would introduce new levels of flexibility in wages, salaries, share dividends, share options and profit sharing, costs and prices, debt and costs of debt, national currencies and local currencies and counter cyclical government policies enabling economies to dynamically adapt to shocks and adverse circumstances. The break up of monopolies, oligopolies, cartels and restrictive practices which keep prices high and maintain 'price rigidity' would also play a major role in this flexibility and adaption process. This adaption would end the 'Insider-Outsider' dilemma in economics, and enable full or near full employment levels to be maintained and high levels of aggregate demand to be preserved to help an economy adjust to changed circumstances and to grow and overcome these challenges. The key factor would aggregate demand while the other factors would play a supporting role. The encouragement and expansion of new technologies, new inventions, and new innovations would greatly assist this adaption process. These new measures would create more resilient economies and more resilient peoples, ending the stagnation and sclerosis which has accompanied economics shocks for many decades.

Government Action

Governments in Europe, North America and around the world should use new tax incentives and grants to implement these new forms of economic democracy and industrial democracy in their own countries. Tax incentives could be progressive starting with incentives aimed at businesses having 40% or more of the workforce owning shares, proceeding to 50% or more, 70% and 100% of the workforce owning shares. These separate incentives would provide for a gradual transition towards full economy democracy. These proposals are itemised above.

These tax incentives would be of vital importance in the transition to economic democracy and industrial democracy. It could also use Quantitative Easing or money printing and new local currencies to fund this switch to economic democracy. Provision should be made in laws to enable employees to diversify their pension plans and use a combination of employee share ownership plans and other private pension funds (IRA's in the USA) and state sponsored pension plans which would have diversified investment portfolios. This diversification would reduce the risk to employees, and help guarantee the safety of pensions. All employees and workers should be legally entitled to be advised to diversify their share holdings and pension plans so as to reduce risk. In addition, employee pension funds could be diversified into many types of employee share ownership businesses and cooperatives, which would encourage employee ownership in firms across many sectors while providing enough diversification to reduce risk. the government will need to provide disincentives for current dictatorial forms of company ownership and concentrations of wealth in the form of taxes and tax increases. This would be of vital importance in the attainment of full economic democracy and industrial democracy.

In today's Internet Age or Digital Age, new technologies and automation have greatly improved productivity and profitability and the potential to increase them even more, while globalisation has complemented these new technologies and further increased revenue and income growth potential, and this new proposal would widely distribute this massive new wealth to the working classes and whole populations so as to build sustainable consumer spending patterns which will fuel business and investment growth and associated employment, which will in turn fuel pension contributions, tax returns and total tax revenues and ultimately government stability and national stability.

Amending the Factors of Production

Conventional economics claims that there are 4 factors of production, these being land, labour, capital, and technology. However, the long experience of economics shows that there may be an additional factor. This being 'Organisation'. There may be 5 factors of production. Organisation is a factor as it does the following:

(a) organises the individual factors of production and the relationships between these factors

(b) ties all the other factors together into a coherent structure or whole to create value, add value and conduct economic activity.

(c) provides government laws, regulations, courts, contract enforcement and public infrastructure for businesses to exist

(d) the opposite is also true in the sense that lack of organisation, disorganisation, chaos, and disorder (often misconstrued as freedom) such as one finds in politically unstable countries and during the libertarian 'Dark Ages' several hundred years ago and in countries undergoing a financial crash similar to 2008, shows that organisation is a vital factor.

It is the unifying factor. For Capital, the Organisation factor provides plans, strategies, management structures, feedback mechanisms, financial and management accounts, adjustment or correcting mechanisms, strategic competitiveness whether short term or long term, entrepreneurship skills, taxes, contracts with financing sources and shareholders, courts and police to enforce contracts and maintain social order. It also provides regulations and regulators which provide proper regulation of the banking and financial system to maintain order and stability. Organisation links into the Labour factor via recruitment, employment contracts, and terms and conditions for labour, and into Technology factor via the sourcing and use of technical expertise, technological equipment and innovation methodologies, and into Land via rent and mortgage contracts.

For Labour it provides employee plans including wages, pension plans and employee benefits, time schedules, production schedules and targets, productivity bonuses, employee ownership, taxes, and career development, and various links to Capital, Land and Technology. For Land, it provides contracts for paying commercial rents and mortgages by Capital (businesses and organisations) and residential rents and mortgages by Labour, and a contracted area or location for technological innovation, research and development by Technology. This factor is the organising principle of all societies and economies and of economics itself. Organisation pulls all of the other factors together. Organisation also includes government and regulation, which provide a structured and coherent environment for businesses and organisations to thrive. Defects in government and regulation undermines the Organisation factor, and can in certain circumstances have a devastating effect on Organisation, and this in turn affects the other factors of production. The crash of 2008 being one of many such examples from history. Other examples of failure to recognise Organisation as a factor include the economic and social breakdown one sees in African countries, in South American countries and some Asian countries and the growing social instability in some developed countries where gun crime is prominent. The chaos of unregulated so called 'free markets' negatively impacts the Organisation factor and the other factors of production, and intensifies the adverse effects of dynamic disequilibrium.

The proposal for economic democracy and industrial democracy seeks to use the Organisation factor in new more constructive ways to enhance Organisation itself and all the other factors of production. And bring about a new alignment of land, labour, capital, technology and organisation to achieve the best social, political and economic outcome for all, including a wider diffusion of wealth and income, and a freedom which fully integrates its responsibilities.

Other Taxes and Policies to Build and Enhance Economic Democracy

Economic Democracy has it's own government policies, tax structures and institutional structures. These would have the effect of expanding the democratic rights, freedom, and democratic participation of all members of society. A democratisation of wealth, of power, of national resources, of social relations, and of political representation. It will require the following:

1. For Ireland the €120 billion refund and debt write down of odious debt mentioned above. For other countries this would mean a write down of write off of debts used for bailing out bankers, speculators and fraudsters, and debt attained by corrupt means, money creation fraud, misrepresentation, threats or extortion, theft of funds or deals negotiated by corrupt dictators.
2. Funds from new land value taxes
3. Taxing economic renters in the FIRE sector

4. The closing of tax avoidance, tax loopholes, tax evasion and tax havens would release trillions of euros for productive investment and consumption around the world, detailed in Chapter 7.

5. New revenues from taxing oil and gas fields and other natural resources, and making provision for gradual employee ownership and community ownership in this field

6. National government money printing or Quantitative Easing for the people and for funding the transition to economic democracy and industrial democracy

7. Extra tax revenues from economic democracy and the reduction in constrained, unrealised, unmet demand and constrained, unrealised, unmet supply which would fuel higher economic growth

8. Government spending tax revenues on projects which would benefit all sections of society, instead of the very wealthy and politically connected. An equalisation of tax money spending to promote high quality education and health for all, and economic democracy and industrial democracy to widely spread out the wealth and increase socio-economic opportunities for all persons in society.

This would enable governments to do the following:

Land Value Tax & The Ending of Economic Renter activity and Deadweight losses

A land value tax was supported by leading economists in the past including John Stuart Mill, David Ricardo, Henry George, Herbert Spencer, Patrick Dove, Alfred Wallace. In order to fully resolve the crisis in the government finances, we will require some new, more innovative and effective tax revenue-generating measures. Measures which are fair and equitable and encourage productive investment, innovation, work, etc. but discourage speculation, economic rents, and rising costs. The best option is a Land Value Tax [32]. Land prices are dependent on the public services such as roads, rail, bridges, water supply, sewerage supply, public parks, public amenities, public urban and rural planning, public schools, public hospitals, public bus transportation, airports, etc. which are paid for by the taxpayer. It is a well established fact that land which is close to these public services experienced a massive growth in price over the period 1995 – 2008. Yet landowners and landlords got all the benefits of this rise in prices and kept the benefits for themselves while the taxpayer got no benefit from the rise in such land prices. Furthermore, landowners and landlords benefitted from a reduction in capital gains taxes during this period. The taxpayer paid all of the costs of these public services which led to a big rise in land prices, yet the taxpayer got very little or nothing in return ; not even enough to cover the costs of building and maintaining these public services. This represents very bad value for money for the taxpayer.

The rising land prices also fuelled a property bubble built on easy bank credit and now the taxpayer is required to bail out the bankrupt banks and bankrupt economy ! This is very bad value for money for the taxpayer. I have included a page below from a famous book written by Oxford University economist Fred Harrison detailing the relationship between government infrastructure spending, including the provision of public services and the rise in the price of land which is close to this infrastructure / public services. It was developed by economist Fred Harrison who has studied the relationship between public services provision and the rise in land prices and the accompanying loss in tax revenues, for over 20 years [32].

Note: The term 'Deadweight losses to national income' pertains to the loss of output and loss of national income due to current over-taxation of worker income, over-taxation of goods and services, and over-taxation of productive investments, and the failure to tax land and land speculation and the failure to charge taxpayers on a "user pays' principle or "public rent" principle. I have included the results of research by Fred Harrison below showing the increases to national income if these 'Deadweight losses to national income' had been eliminated by his proposed reformed taxation in a number of developed countries.

§2 The Pay-Off

ECONOMISTS USE the term 'excess burden' to describe the distortions inflicted by conventional taxes. This burden delivers *deadweight losses*. Finance ministers never disclose the scale of those losses.

Concealed in the specialist academic literature, wrapped in jargon, are a few numbers that offer hints on the losses. Two American economists decided to remedy this constraint on the democratic discourse by offering estimates for the G7 countries that people could understand. Professors Nic Tideman and Florenz Plassmann asked: if a government scrapped the taxes that damage the economy and invited people to pay rents that were proportionate to the value of the services that they used, how would the economy be affected? The answer, using 1993 national income data, appears in Table 14:1. Nearly $7 trillion ($7,000bn) in goods and services was lost to those seven countries alone because of the negative impact of conventional taxes. This is a measure of the gain, if the governments were to switch to rent-as-public-revenue.

TABLE 14:1

G7: Gain in Output and *Per Capita* Income under the Public Rent Policy (1993)

	Net domestic product $ bn	NDP per capita $
USA	1,602	6,902
Canada	275	9,142
France	879	15,166
Germany	1,018	12,406
Italy	815	14,128
Japan	1,535	12,284
UK	716	12,133
Total	6,840	

Source: Nicolaus Tideman and Florenz Plassmann, Ch. 6, *The Losses of Nations* (ed.: Fred Harrison), London: Othila Press, 1998.

Sources: Boom Bust ; House prices, Banking and The Depression of 2010, Fred Harrison, Second Edition 2007, Shepheard Walwyn.

In 2000, the British economy could have generated an additional 880 billion pounds in income from a reformed taxation system which eliminated Deadweight losses, according to Fred Harrison.

Further research by Harrison in the UK below shows the rise in land prices measured against the rise in wages, house prices, and building costs over the period 1983 – 2007 in the UK. As you can see, land prices have risen much higher than wages, house prices, and building costs. The rise in land prices also inflicted costs on the wider economy, yet was not taxed and rarely commented upon by economists and those concerned with inflation and rising costs. This massive increase in land prices would have yielded large tax revenues, but the UK government failed to collect them. Other economies in Europe, the Americas and elsewhere could benefit from taxing this.

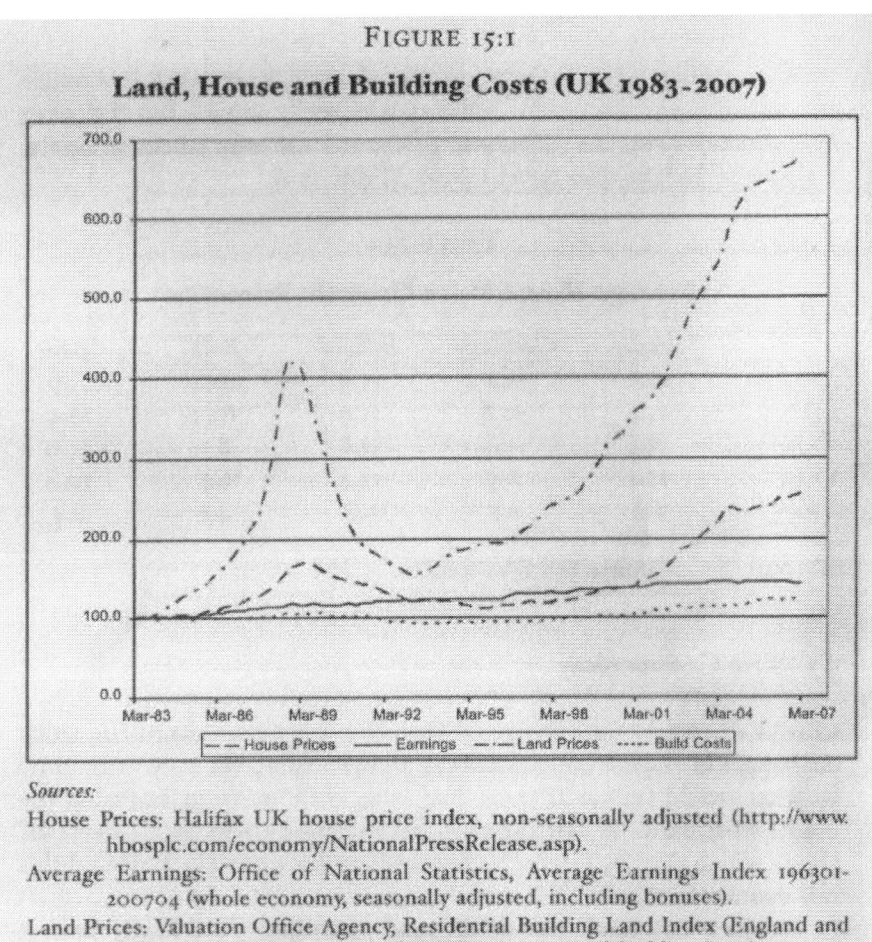

FIGURE 15:1

Land, House and Building Costs (UK 1983-2007)

Sources:

House Prices: Halifax UK house price index, non-seasonally adjusted (http://www. hbosplc.com/economy/NationalPressRelease.asp).

Average Earnings: Office of National Statistics, Average Earnings Index 196301- 200704 (whole economy, seasonally adjusted, including bonuses).

Land Prices: Valuation Office Agency, Residential Building Land Index (England and Wales excluding London) (http://www.voa.gov.uk/publications/property_ market_report/pmr-jan-07/residential.htm).

Build Costs: BCIS (Building Cost Information Service) House Rebuilding Cost Index.

All series rebased to March 1983 = 100 and adjusted for inflation using the Office of National Statistics Retail Price Index.

Source: Boom Bust ; House prices, Banking and The Depression of 2010, Fred Harrison, Second Edition 2007, Shepheard Walwyn.

So there are massive losses to the government and to the economy from not having a land value tax, not having a tax system based on "user pays" principle, and then there are Deadweight losses to national income and output. These figures are for the UK. The loss in tax revenues and loss in output and national income for Ireland would be very similar to that of the UK.

The following graph shows the effects of a land value tax

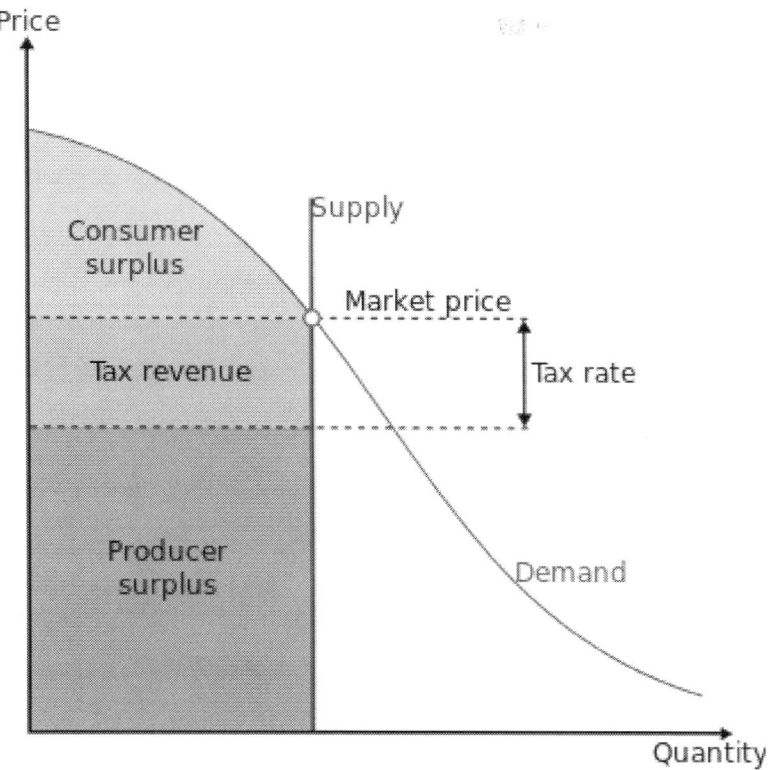

Source: Wikipedia. https://en.wikipedia.org/wiki/Land_value_tax

This tax has no effect on production, investment and consumption, and solely affects land owners who benefit from land holdings, particularly in areas of high strategic economic value. It taxes monopolies or oligopolies, some of the richest people in any given country, and would reduce the tax burden on workers, production based businesses, small and medium sized firms and organisations.

Governments should introduce a land value tax. The amount of land value tax payable should correlate to (i) proximity to public services and its effect on the land price (ii) proximity to cities and large towns which benefit from public services and it's effect on the land price (iii) current land prices. Different tax rates would apply in different areas of the country. This would be fair and equitable both to the landowner / landlord and to the taxpayer. If a landowner / landlord wishes to sell land or acquire loans based on the value of his land, he would have to pay a land tax which would directly relate to the benefits his land and it's price enjoys from the provision of public services. Taxation laws should establish precise metrics for assessing land at its original nominal value and the increase in land price due to the provision of public services or public decisions to rezone land. Thus different landowners would pay different rates of tax dependent on how their land prices benefitted from public services. This would ensure fairness and equity in land taxation. It is much fairer than capital gains tax on land. Abolish capital gains tax on land and replace it with this new land tax.

Higher land value taxes could be charged on land banks held by speculators and on unused plots of land and dilapidated buildings in or close to cities and towns where there is a shortage of housing. This would encourage development and house building programmes, and the resolution of housing crisis's. Price controls using multiples of average industrial earnings as proposed below would prevent speculation.

This land value tax could be set at 35%. This tax would prevent yet another property bubble from arising, raise tax revenues for public services, enable the government to reduce many other taxes including taxes on wages, production, research and innovation. This would stimulate consumption, investment and economic growth, while raising more tax revenues for productive (public and private) investments which would deliver long-term competitiveness, growth and stability.

Further Tax and Policy measures

- Progressive Global Taxes to tax Economic rents and Stabilise and Improve Government Revenues Worldwide' in Chapter 7.

- A flat rate income tax of 23% for all workers. This would reduce the tax burden on the working and middle classes and reward their efforts. It will encourage people to work and to take up employment and progress in their careers and businesses. Taxes on speculation, Rentiers, economic rents, land values, monopolies / cartels, the FIRE sector and inherited wealth would help pay for this reduction in income tax on labour.

- VAT reduction down to 15% for Irish, British and EU produced goods and services and 20% for non Irish, British and EU produced goods and services. And make VAT payments easier for business.

- A global taxation of robots and Artificial Intelligence (AI), of 20-25%, applied in every country could provide the means for funding employment schemes and training, up-skilling and career advancement schemes in the private sector and state sector, and the expansion of employee share ownership and community share ownership to the masses.

- A natural resources tax of at least 20% of the markup price and the elimination of existing loopholes which redirect sales and profits of natural resources through offshore tax havens to avoid paying any tax

- Break up monopolies, oligopolies, cartels and restrictive practises into smaller competing units. If this cannot be achieved then set a monopoly / cartel tax of 40% on profits.

- Special tax credits, tax reductions and tax incentives for production companies and businesses (not involved in asset price speculation and derivatives speculation) which increases jobs and employment in Ireland. This could also include new tax incentives to encourage businesses to expand their plant and buildings and offices and take on extra employees. Employment and job creation would be the key factors. Delivered via ECB/ESM and government.

- Special tax measures on corporate raiders and takeovers to strongly discourage takeovers which increase debt to earnings ratios by a factor of 5:1 or more. This would prevent a massive accumulation of debt and junk bonds to take over businesses and then bleed them dry through high debt repayments and increased pressure to provide high quarterly returns.

- Increase taxes on companies and businesses which create jobs outside an EU nation and outside the EU, while decrease them for those creating jobs within Ireland and the EU. See proposals below. This would provide further incentives to create jobs inside Ireland and the EU.

- **End the Monopolies, Oligopolies, Cartels and Restrictive Practises which are enforcing higher costs on societies, consumers and businesses**
  New laws to break up the cartels, restrictive practices, economic renters, oligopolies and monopolies in Ireland (and other countries). Several government, statistical, consumer and business bodies could quantify and assess the high costs of doing business in Ireland, and take relevant actions via the High court or European court to curb abuses of the consumer and Irish businesses. Penalties should include breaking up the economic renters, opening them up to more competition and highly taxing economic renters. This would include investigation of and rectifying the economic rents and restrictive practices of:
  - lawyers, barristers, accountants
  - doctors, hospital consultants and dentists
  - insurance for cars, taxis, homes, offices, etc.
  - pharmacies and chemists
  - banks overcharging customers and abusing their market position

- the very high prices for drugs charged by pharmaceutical companies, through government agreement. Ireland is the most expensive country in Europe for medical drugs.
- state contracts where private firms overcharge government for products and services.
- selling of state assets at very low cost or below cost to (politically connected) private firms who then have monopoly, oligopoly or cartel power. This includes natural resources, infrastructure, tv, radio, mobile phone and telecommunications bandwidths, state lands and properties.
- private property owners, land owners and landlords who financially benefit from the provision of free public services and infrastructure near to their property or lands.
- land owners. In many countries, including Ireland, 10% of land owners own most of the land ; typically 53 – 90% of the land.
- excessive pricing and profits from patents
- car dealerships
- undertakers
- commercial property landlords. Upwards only rent.
- cosy relationships between some businesses and professional services firms and local government and central government which has led to very high costs
- the pricing by semi-state bodies
- building materials
- oil companies, gas companies and electricity companies, and other energy and resource companies with a monopoly or oligopoly or engaged in restrictive practises
- telecommunications companies and cable companies with a monopoly or oligopoly or engaged in restrictive practises

These impose significant extra costs on businesses and workers, and have driven up the costs of doing business in Ireland. They have also driven up the cost of living in a country, putting pressure on wages and livelihoods. These costs need to be reduced drastically through abolishing anti-competitive practises, monopolies, cartels and restrictive practises, breaking up economic renters, and increasing the number of competitors in these sectors and greater competition in pricing, offers, deals and advertising. In the USA, the Sherman act could be used to break up monopolies and monopolistic practises and price collusion and cartels in many industries there. Laws similar to the Sherman act should be enacted and enforced in other countries.

The computer, the mouse, computer networks, the Internet and many other electronic products and services were developed from research undertaken by DARPA and the US government in the past. And governments provide funding for schools, Universities and many other forms of public infrastructure which benefit researchers, innovators and patent developers. Patents derive from both the private effort of individuals and public infrastructure and services, and patent prices should include a social price or dividend and social access, payable in the form of a fee and / or tax to the government where the patent was developed and access provided to many businesses so no one business can monopolise it. Excessive patent fees could be taxed at 90 – 100% to discourage abuses of the system. This competition would greatly reduce the prices of many products. Highly taxing economic renters, monopolies, oligopolies and cartels could also be undertaken to discourage this activity. Reducing the high costs and prices imposed by these type of firms would help improve a country's international competitiveness.

In addition to this, a new Constitutional amendment is required (in Ireland and several other countries) to eliminate upward only rent reviews and leases for commercial properties. The ridiculous upward only rent / lease law in Ireland has ruined and bankrupted many profitable businesses in Ireland, and was introduced by the corrupt politician Charles Haughey many years ago to facilitate a business friend of his who made financial contributions to Haughey himself and to his political party.

- Abolition of water charges in Ireland and other countries
  In Ireland this has been paid for from VRT tax, VAT and motor tax under laws passed between 1998 and 2013. People are being double taxed through these new water charges, and this is very unfair. This is an oppressive new tax, in addition to other taxes, levies and charges, and high mortgage debt payments in the middle of an economic recession. This is pushing too many Irish families into financial difficulties, poverty and threat of evictions. Water charges were included as part of the agreement between the Irish government and the Troika to bail out the national and foreign banks, speculators and fraudsters. The massive cost of the bank bailout and the economic austerity has reduced central government revenues, and forced the government to raise money through water charges and property taxes, and other taxes, levies and charges. It is robbery of the Irish people to bay for the bail out of national and foreign private firms. Furthermore, approximately 100,000 Irish residences have leaking pipes and people will be forced to pay for this wasted water. The refund of €100 billion from the EU mentioned above and the new types of wealth taxes and speculation taxes

above would help pay for the cost of water and upgrading the nation's water infrastructure and eliminate the need for water charges, property taxes and other taxes and levies.

- Abolition of the property tax on family homes (in Ireland)

  People have already paid stamp duty for their property and should not be double taxed for the same property with this new property tax. The property tax is double taxation for the same property and is very unfair. This is an oppressive new tax, in addition to other taxes, levies and charges, and high mortgage debt payments in the middle of an economic recession. This is pushing too many Irish families into financial difficulties, poverty and threat of evictions. The massive cost of the bank bailout and the economic austerity has reduced central government revenues, and forced the government to raise money through water charges and property taxes, and other taxes, levies and charges. It is robbery of the Irish people. The refund of €100 billion from the EU mentioned above and the new types of wealth taxes and speculation taxes above would help pay for the cost of water and upgrading the nation's water infrastructure and eliminate the need for water charges, property taxes and other taxes and levies.

  After abolition of the property tax, a reduced rate of stamp duty could be implemented along with other measures to stimulate the building of affordable and sustainable new housing, and meet the housing shortage. Some of this funded from the €100 billion refund mentioned below.

- Cut and then abolish the Universal Social Charge (in Ireland)

  Cut the Universal Social Charge on wages and salaries by 50% for all workers and employers in the first year, and eliminate it in the second year, once the €100 billion refund from the EU has been paid to Irish taxpayer and the government. This charge was brought to help bail out the national and international banks and hedge funds. Ordinary working people and their families should not have had to pay additional tax on their wages to bail out multi-millionaires. The €100 billion refund from Europe mentioned below would take several months to acquire, and the Universal Social Charge would provide an interim source of funding for government activities while awaiting the refund. Once the refund is acquired from the EU, the government could eliminate this Universal Social Charge which is punishing workers and investment in the country.

- Variable interest rates on mortgages

  There is also a serious disconnect between the ECB interest rate of less than 1% from 2012-2014 and 0.05% in 2015 on one side and the Irish mortgage and loan repayment interest rates of 4% - 8%

during the period 2012 – 2015 on the other side, which is adding thousands of euros more to each mortgage repayment every year. Ireland had the highest mortgage interest rates in Europe from 2013 – 2015. Many mortgage holders have been overcharged by the banks and this overcharging is estimated to run into millions of euros. Cap variable mortgage interest rates at 1.5% above the ECB rate while the economy is in recession, or until economic growth produces unemployment of less than 4%. This would reduce the financial burden on families in the current recession while putting more money into people's pockets for consumption. And it would reduce the interest costs to existing businesses and new start ups. Stimulating both aggregate demand and aggregate supply. Over time, as advised above interest rates or usury could be abolished and replaced with a small administration fee which is not compounded over the years.

- Pension Levy

Most private sector and public sector pensions are in deficit and bankrupt, and will not be able to pay out basic pensions in the future. Abolish the pension levy on public sector wages and introduce a new pensions system for all workers and non workers and radical new economic changes to improve the profitability and returns of (productive) investments in the economy. Central to this will be the economic changes proposed in this book, including joint cooperation and ventures between Ireland and the EU to improve the returns to private investments and pension funds throughout the EU.

- Zero hour wage contracts

Abolish all zero hour wage contracts in Ireland and the EU. Workers have families to support and mortgages and household bills to pay, and they should not have to endure zero hour contracts which provide wage and livelihood insecurity and job insecurity and a return to Victorian age hiring fairs. The 'global race to the bottom' or 'global race to the sewer' needs to be stopped, and the rights and dignity of workers and their families protected, and the determinants of aggregate demand and (commercial bank) money supply growth kept secure within countries. Ordinary working people and their families are largely powerless in the face of the high prices charged by monopolistic, oligopolistic, cartel, state protected sector, government subsidized (private firms), economic renter and restrictive practices organisations and their 'sticky' prices for products and services, professional fees, and (professional and executive) salaries and bonuses. (Economic rents meaning monopolistic, oligopolistic, anti-competitive, cartel and restrictive practises behaviour and pricing by private firms.)

- **The Reinstatement of some Natural Public Monopolies for strategic economic areas and national interests**

  Natural monopolies have been built up by the state and taxpayers over time, and required large financial outlays over decades. Examples include water, public transport, electricity and waste collection. There is a choice between private ownership of these natural monopolies which overcharge customers, and extract economic rents, are inefficient, reduce services and reduce quality in order to maximise profits, are in many cases customer unfriendly, politically corrupt, and unaccountable, and enrich a few people and concentrate wealth and income more OR state owned natural monopolies owned by the state which charge reasonable and affordable prices, are customer friendly, maintain quality and services, serve the public good, and are made accountable. This has been borne out by some bitter experience over the years. Even within state owned natural monopolies many functions can be privatised for efficiency reasons while retaining state ownership. These natural monopolies are very strategic to an economy and society, and require large financial outlays to build, maintain and upgrade properly over time. Their strategic significance lies in their importance to the consumers, businesses, and organisations which rely on dependable, well funded and well resourced natural monopolies

- New tax incentives and reduction of 'red tape' to encourage business start ups. No corporation tax for first 2 years, reduced income tax for employer, PRSI incentives to employ more people, 50% reduction rates for first 2 years, 50% VAT reduction for first 2 years, and faster and easier granting of planning permission for first 2 years, subject to the employment of 3 or more people. These incentives should be graded according to the numbers of people employed ; those who employ more people get slightly better incentives. This in addition to other reductions and eliminations of certain taxes mentioned above and the use of start up grants and improved consumer spending in the economy would strongly encourage entrepreneurs to start up new businesses.

- Replace government bonds with standard loan contracts between a bank and the government. Borrow at prime rates, 2% or below. This would reduce the costs of such borrowing. This would lead to new credit creation. This could be used as a fiscal stimulus by government. Speculators cannot manipulate loan contracts but they can manipulate government bonds and actively attack governments and countries.

- Changes to the tax and PRSI system should allow entrepreneurs and business owners who become bankrupt or go out of business to access social welfare payments. This is an important social safety net for these people. Government austerity programmes to bail out the banks and the accompanying recession it caused, bankrupted over 40,000 Irish businesses in the period 2008 – 2014.

- The economist Dr Stephanie Kelton stated that Congress / Parliament can mandate or authorise a fiscal stimulus and public infrastructure programme costing billions of trillions of dollars / euros and the funds can be acquired through refunds for bail outs, Quantitative Easing and interest free loans. The government has the power to create money and can use this power in addition to other powers. In Europe this will involve restoring this power back to national governments. The reasons for this are outlined in Chapter 2 and Chapter 6.

- New system for reducing the time, costs, paperwork, bureaucracy, challenges, taxes, charges, rates and levies involved in setting up a new business
Meetings every 4 months between government, state bodies, new entrepreneurs, established and successful entrepreneurs, and representatives of national businesses to discuss new ways to reduce the time, costs, paperwork, bureaucracy, challenges, taxes, charges, rates and levies involved in setting up a new business and running it for the first 2-3 years. Agreed recommendations would be acted upon and implemented within 6 months.

- Gradually shift the tax burden – reducing income taxes and increasing taxes on products, land and property especially unused land and property, capital gains and wealth. Reduce the costs of labour, and make it more profitable for businesses to hire workers and to maintain high employment levels.

- Grants, interest free loans and tax incentives to encourage people to improve their education and skills, with skill shortages being prioritised in this funding programme. This would help workers move from less productive sectors to more productive sectors, and improve overall productivity. Delivered via ECB/ESM, government, commercial banks and European Investment bank.

- New tax incentives to encourage research and development and the acquisition of specific high tech skills by the employed and the unemployed. Tax credit or rebates up to 20% for research and development and post-graduate and 4th level research qualifications and skills which leads to new products and services and jobs should be given to businesses.

- Those people making over €200,000 per year would pay a minimum of 30% tax regardless of all tax loopholes, tax deductions and tax avoidance schemes.

- There are 5.6 million mobile phone users. In Ireland, over 15 billion text messages were sent in 2014. This represents a large amount of economic and social activity which is untaxed. Importantly, this economic and social activity is price inelastic (not price sensitive), particularly in relation to young people, those under 35, who are obsessed with texting. Small price increases are unlikely to cause a significant fall-off in demand, particularly in such a high growth market. A tax of 2 cents on every text message would yield €300 million in tax revenue. It is estimated that 12 billion mobile phone calls were made in 2014. A tax of 2 cents on each mobile phone call would yield €240 million in tax revenue.

  These two new taxes would bring €540 million in tax revenue per year.

  This would serve as a useful source of tax revenue as the economy grows over time

- New tax incentives to encourage or facilitate expansion of the housing stock while introducing house price limits and new bank loan limits and reserve requirements so as to prevent a bubble and another financial crash. See new provisions in law for this below.

- As technology and automation and globalisation delivers higher returns to capital and displaces more labour, there could be a provision of social dividends such as a national dividend as advised by the economist Richard C. Cook and Douglas and others advocating for social credit or basic income / negative income tax. This would give everyone a guaranteed income and encourage people to take up work and return to the work force. This Basic Income / Negative Income Tax could be higher for those displaced by technological or economic changes. This national dividend / basic income / negative income tax could be supplemented by wages, and wider employee and community ownership and dividends from such.

  The Alaska Permanent Fund could be used as an example of how this could be funded. This would help sustain aggregate demand in the economy and reduce the effects of constrained, unrealised, unmet demand or deficiencies in aggregate demand. It would also reduce the propensity to borrow excessively in the private sector.

- Abolish mortgage / interest rate tax relief on the rental properties of landlords. The government should not be subsidising private landlords. According to research by the ESRI and some Trade Unions this would bring in approximately €850 million in tax revenue per year.

- There should be a time limit for holding shares before selling of 5 years in order to avail of the lower capital gains tax of 20%.

- The closing of all tax shelters for property, racehorse breeding and artists. Artists would include rock stars, musicians, wealthy book authors, sports men and women, many of these people are multi-millionaires and do not pay any tax. These wealthy artists and horse breeders could be taxed at the normal rates.

- The notion of tax exiles or non-resident status needs to be analysed and changed. Those persons with Irish citizenship and resident in Ireland for any period of 10 years (including childhood) and whose specific business or financial dealings were based in Ireland for any period of 6 months prior to the massive financial windfall from the stock-market, property or some other business would be liable for Irish taxes and not be able to suddenly claim non-resident status. The specific business or financial dealings must be related to the financial windfall. Those people who claim tax exile status would be targeted under this legislation. This would prevent people from suddenly claiming to be non-residents in order to avoid paying Irish taxes. Under this new regime, if an Irish citizen makes his / her money in Ireland they will pay their taxes in Ireland. We've had Irish men and women who died for Irish freedom, self-determination and self-government, and they lost their wealth, their homes, their loved ones, they lost everything in the process and today we have sly and devious men and women who refuse to pay their fair share of tax like everybody else. Under the new regime, all Irish people would be encouraged to see it as their patriotic duty to pay their taxes so as to build up and strengthen Ireland in these hard economic times.

- The government should employ teams of tax accountants, forensic accountants, auditors and tax lawyers to closely study and analyse all tax avoidance schemes and all tax shelters. Close all tax avoidance schemes through targeted legislation. Close tax shelters used for property speculation and create new tax reliefs for productive investments, research, innovation, renewable energy, industrial clusters, up-skilling and infrastructure improvement in Ireland.

- Social security or the state pension schemes should remain in state ownership in all countries. This ensures protection against corporate and banking fraud, criminality and mismanagement, ensures lower transaction costs, insurance against inflation, insurance against loss. The free market cannot do these things.

- Increase the state pension (social security) to 47% of average industrial earnings to ensure a minimum decent standard of living for the elderly. The more stable economic environment and continued economic growth would provide for this.

- Abolish the pension levy. The public pension funds and most private pension funds are in deficit and bankrupt. Reform the entire pension system to make it fairer, clearer and more consistent. New state supported retirement and pensions fund paid for by the employee, employer and state, and which would provide a defined benefit scheme of 53% of one's old income on retirement up to certain limit. It would be payable by all private and public workers and the self employed. Set the tax reliefs on all pension funds at 20%.

- Move away from a blanket taxation for all taxpayers to a new system – a "user pays" principle. Under this new system, those who use a public resource or benefit from the provision of a public resource / service(s) would pay for it. They should not expect other taxpayers to pay for it. The government should analyse all public resources and public services and identify ways in which only those users who use a given public resource / service(s) pay for it. While those taxpayers who do not use it will not be forced to pay for it. Obviously the government will have to differentiate between those public resources and services used or (privately) benefitted from by (a) most if not all taxpayers (b) some taxpayers and (c) very few taxpayers. This would provide greater fairness in taxation, and give taxpayers more freedom to make choices. The net effect of this would be to reduce government expenditure and tax burdens.

- Why is the government paying such high prices for acquiring land under the National Development Plan (NDP) ? The government is still being charged the high land prices of 2007. Can the government achieve downward adjustment in prices for land of 35% or more below 2007 prices. Re-negotiate all prices for land acquired under the National Development Plan, and demand downward adjustments in land prices. The government should be able to get a land price reduction of between 35% - 40% below 2007 prices. It may be necessary to bring cases to the Supreme court in order to establish a legal precedent for this. We are now in a recession and a public finances crisis, and the government should take advantage of lower prices in its spending. Estimated savings for the government: €300 million per year.

- Renegotiate all prices for labour, materials, services and buildings under the National Development Plan and demand price reductions ranging from 15 – 25 % for the first two years and 5-10% per year after this. We are now in a recession and a public finances crisis, and the government should take advantage of lower prices in its spending. Estimated savings for the government: €150 million per year.

- EU level tax refunds to businesses to stimulate job creation in manufacturing and services firms throughout the EU. The mass transfer of EU jobs to China, India, North Africa and other places must be discouraged through targeted taxation measures and other measures designed to protect EU jobs. EU workers pay the taxes which sustain governments and pensions and infrastructure and consumer spending in the EU, and this needs to be protected.

- **Infrastructure Spending via Quantitative Easing and Interest Free Loans**
  (i) expansion of social housing. Build or redevelop existing properties
  (ii) building, expansion, upgrading of national roads and secondary roads and their capacity, of bridges and their capacity, of railways and their capacity, of light rail in cities and their capacity, of river transport and boat transport, of airports and their capacity, of shipping ports and their capacity, of public transport and their capacity, of tourism facilities and their capacity, of water infrastructure and repair of piping
  (iii) building, expanding, repairing, upgrading of primary schools, secondary schools, Universities and apprenticeships. Improving and upgrading of the educational and skills infrastructure. This is extremely important.
  (iv) improvement / upgrading of hospitals, especially accident and emergency departments and psychiatric hospitals
  (v) building of more primary care centres
  (vi) improvement / upgrading of national schools and secondary schools
  (vii) 2 new super prisons (in Ireland)
  (viii) improve and upgrade broadband and its capacity, especially in rural areas.
  (ix) public projects and public-private projects focused on greater investment in and deployment of

green alternative energies to promote industry, commerce, trade and employment growth. This must be strategic and geared at attaining energy independence, energy security, energy sustainability and renewability, cheaper energy and energy sources which cause no damage or very little damage to the environment. This in turn would facilitate greater social stability and political stability worldwide. These green energies would include substantial new private investment and state investment in the following:

1. wind energy

2. solar energy

3. biomass energy

4. Geo thermal energy, deep earth pumps

5. wave energy from the sea

6. large machines which convert carbon dioxide and carbon monoxide into oxygen. Re-engineering cars and other transport vehicles to convert carbon dioxide and carbon monoxide into oxygen

7. hydro-electric energy. New hydro-electric power dams in deep mountain valleys (Spirit of Ireland project, fjords in Scandinavia, etc.)

8. re-chargeable batteries

9. magnetohydrodynamic generators which generate energy in the same way the earth, sun and planets generate energy.

10. magnetic levitation for travel and transport purposes

11. Keshe free energy generators and molecule friction generators

12. hydrogen batteries and devices

13. fusion torches

14. zero point energy devices, over-unity devices using magnets

15. gravity manipulation machines

16. use of exercise bicycles and running treadmills to create electricity in batteries for personal use, home use or business use

17. free energy devices

18. The building of smart infrastructure encompassing communications Internet of 5G and 6G, renewable energy Internet coordinating many green technologies and grids and driverless or automated mobility Internet and linking these together for a 3rd Industrial revolution. See writings of Professor Jeremy Rifkin

all of which are renewable and sustainable.

The economic reason for these new policies centres on the Keynesian multiplier effect which lifts economies out of recession and depression. The multiplier effect is well known. A better quality infrastructure will also attract in new international investment and encourage indigenous investment, creating even more jobs and economic activity.

- The passing of a Glass-Steagal and Dodd-Frank type law by the EU Parliament to cover all of the EU. This would stabilise the banking system across Europe and reduce the systemic risks to the banking system, financial system and nations. It would prevent a boom and bust on the scale of that prior to and after 2008.

- Increase margin requirements for loans to buy stocks and speculative assets to 50% to stop bubbles.

- The creation of new classes of investment such as dividend pricing products. These products would be based on the actual dividends paid by a business, not on share prices.

- Classes of new shares could have an investment focus, and a time limit set on them of 40 - 50 years. These could be classed 'investment shares' as opposed to speculative shares which are common today. This would encourage long-term investment planning and decision making and encourage medium to long term investors to buy them and see them as a long-term investment with annual returns. This would discourage speculators only interested in speculative price movements and capital gains.

- Invest in free energy research and continuous renewable energy research. In the future, if successful, this would reduce energy costs and make communities sustainable and independent enabling them to grow and prosper and would help make the world more sustainable. Some interesting scientific research into free energy, based on molecular and quantum level energy manipulation has been undertaken by the Keshe Foundation http://www.keshefoundation.org/ . These and other scientific initiatives should be prioritised for national and EU level funding.

- Green Energy Investment
  The government through its representatives in state research bodies and Universities and Institutes of Technology should draw up a detailed plan for encouraging investment in renewable energy

technology in every county of a country eg. Ireland. The implementation of this plan should be left to private sector businesses, private investors, entrepreneurs, semi-state companies, international investors and community-based investors. The focus should be on developing renewable energy technologies which have application in Ireland such as wind energy, solar energy, biomass energy, wave energy, hydro-electric energy, re-chargeable batteries, combined wind and hydro-electric power dams in deep mountain valleys (Spirit of Ireland), Keshe free energy generators, hydrogen batteries and devices, fusion torches, over-unity devices using magnets, gravity manipulation machines, deep earth pumps, free energy devices, all of which are renewable and sustainable. The building of smart infrastructure encompassing communications Internet of 5G and 6G, renewable energy Internet coordinating many green technologies and grids and driverless or automated mobility Internet and linking these together for a 3rd Industrial revolution. See writings of Professor Jeremy Rifkin

The state development, educational and research bodies should engage more closely with businesses and investors who are interested or already involved in developing green energy technologies. This will involve assisting these businesses develop these technologies, assistance in sourcing and using innovations from around the world, use of successful case studies and visits to countries such as Denmark and Norway which are world leaders in renewable energy. If required, human expertise should be sourced by government bodies and assistance provided to businesses in bringing this expertise into the country to facilitate development of these technologies. The government should facilitate this renewable energy development through targeted tax allowances and shelters, grants and other incentives to invest in green energy technology. This would be aimed at both national and international investors. The continuous innovation mentioned in Section 4 above would also apply here, ensuring a continuously competitive business model over time.

In Denmark ownership of wind farms has been widely distributed to farmers and rural communities and some urban communities, and this serves as a second income for these people. This is distributing out the profits and financial benefits of wind farms and other renewable energy businesses. This has encouraged widespread public support for wind farms and renewable energy businesses in Denmark. The same system could be applied in Ireland.

- The government should prioritise the opening up of gates on the power grid throughout the country and fast-track work to reduce queues for entry to the power grid. This will enable businesses to get on the power grid faster and this in turn will speed up investment and deployment of these green technologies. The government should get the European Central Bank to issue interest-free loans for renewable energy development in all Eurozone countries. The money would be created out of nothing, like most Central Bank money. These interest-free loans totaling €70 billion could be packaged into an EU Renewable Energy Fund, which could be administered through the main banks in each Eurozone country. The Irish government should fast-track planning permission for developing these technologies around Ireland.

- Deployment of green energy in businesses, farms, communities and homes
The government through its representatives in state research bodies and Universities and Institutes of Technology should draw up a detailed plan for encouraging businesses, farms, communities and homes to invest in their places of work and residence. It is possible to deploy green technologies on a small scale, a medium scale and a large scale. The government should facilitate all scales with similar incentives. These green energy technologies include : wind energy, solar energy, biomass energy, wave energy, hydro-electric energy, re-chargeable batteries, combined wind and hydro-electric power dams in deep mountain valleys (Spirit of Ireland), Keshe free energy generators, hydrogen batteries and devices, fusion torches, over-unity devices using magnets, gravity manipulation machines, deep earth pumps, free energy devices, all of which are renewable and sustainable. Businesses should be given tax incentives and small grants to invest in green technologies for their own use and to export it into the national power grid. The tax incentives should include a complete VAT write-down which is absent at present. Investment decisions will factor in the following – interest on borrowed money / capital, tax, depreciation, payback in the form of reduced electricity costs, and revenues from exports into the national grid ; the government should adjust the tax and grants system over time to make it viable for businesses to invest in green technologies. Once the green technology becomes profitable for a business (loans / capital paid back, and revenues greater than outlays) the tax scheme could be automatically adjusted for a given business, such that the tax incentives and grants gradually end and the business pays tax in the normal manner. At that stage a small tax on energy exports could be used to earn tax revenues from the use of green energies. Farmers should also avail of this system in a similar way to businesses. As for homes, the tax incentives should be similar but less generous. Tax incentives for homes should include a complete VAT write-down which is absent at present. A home wind generator is only likely to generate 6KW or less of energy per day, and cost outlays vary from

€20,000 to €30,000 which is considerable, and would require a long time frame to recoup. An alternative would be to tailor a new set of tax incentives and grants for encouraging homes in a community to invest in community green energy generator(s). The green energy generator or generators could be paid for by several homes and they all would benefit from the electricity produced. Costs could be less than that for stand-alone generators for individual homes, and could conceivably range from €10,000 to €15,000 per home in the community. In addition to a reduction in electricity costs, they would all share equally in the revenues gained from exporting excess energy into the national power grid. If community green energy generators were used nationwide in conjunction with business use of green energy, and large-scale wind farms and combined wind and hydro-electric power dams in deep mountain valleys, we would see the elimination of dependence on fossil fuels within a generation. In time, Ireland could become a net exporter of electricity into the European power grid.

- Balancing business with environmental issues so as to protect public health. International agreements around climate change and environmental destruction, pollution and degradation need to be re-negotiated and new firm rules put in place internationally accompanied by taxes, levies and excise charges and nation level insurance premiums and payouts to enforce compliance. New international agreements to get all other countries, including developing countries, third world countries, and big polluters, to implement full cost accounting standards which include the environmental, health and legal costs of pollution, and meet their environmental obligations so as to level the international business and investment field. This will a global strategic plan and strategic plans and operational plans and targets for individual countries for every year, and the costs of not meeting these targets in terms of the increased economic costs of flooding, fire damage, storm damage, drought and famines, food shortages, earthquakes, water shortages, and armed conflicts over diminishing resources. There should be the same environmental laws and targets for all countries worldwide. This needs to be fully integrated into all WTO trade agreements. Too many past environmental conferences and agreements were mere 'talking shops' with nothing achieved and nothing implemented, and these past failures have worsened environmental destruction, pollution and storms and flooding, and have imposed enormous costs on individuals, families, communities, businesses and nations. Those countries and businesses who continue to be big polluters should be subject to new charges, levies, and taxes on their goods and services at the international level and higher national insurance costs and payouts to cover the damage caused by global warming and environmental destruction and pollution.

International Trade & International Aid Programmes and International Cooperation and Security Obligations

I refer readers to the analysis of TTIP in Chapter 2 of this book. It itemises many of the defects and flaws in TTIP and in current and previous WTO treaties. Economic democracy and industrial democracy, international trade, investment and growth and employment all rely on a stable international order and this in turn relies on stability within nations and between nations. Stability and its maintenance requires strategic guidance and direction and the application of money, resources, manpower, strategic treaties, and international cooperation. The present international trading system is a disaster and offers accumulation of massive national debt, financial and economic failures and crashes, bail outs of the rich, austerity policies and deflation, vast trade imbalances, capital flight, de-industrialisation and unemployment, sweat shops and exploitation of women and children, environmental destruction and accompanying diseases, funding of dictators and tyrants, human rights abuses, mass tax evasion, vast political and legal corruption, social injustices and mass poverty, incitement of extremism, and conflicts and wars.

In addition to this, big developed countries and trading blocs continue to use subsidies for agriculture and some industries to block trade between it and developing nations, while demanding that developing nations open up their markets to developed countries. This is particularly damaging to developing countries which opened their markets to mass speculation in financial assets and derivatives. Economic development in developing countries has mainly benefitted small corrupt elites and multinational companies, while pushing these countries into massive debt [12]. This has created major imbalances in world trade and global wealth distribution. Importantly, this is holding back economic and social development and the spread of democracy in developing countries. It is contributing to mass poverty in developing and third countries, and rising unemployment and poverty in western developed countries, and a lose-lose situation for most people worldwide.

The WTO needs to be radically reformed. The emergence of new power centres in economics such as BRICS could play a role here. Trading blocs such as the EU, EFTA, North America (USA and Canada) , ASEAN, APEC, CARICOM, MERCUSOR could work with A UN body, Transparency International, Amnesty International and international bodies such as the IMF, World Bank, G8, G20, etc. to coordinate trade agreements and international activities in achieving a more stable international order. This would include the following :

(i) There should be free trade within trading blocs such as EU, EFTA, North America (USA and Canada) , ASEAN, APEC, CARICOM, MERCUSOR and the imposition of tariffs on goods and services produced outside these trading blocs, this would facilitate re-industrialisation, the return of jobs to developed countries and developing countries, full employment, optimum output levels, sustained aggregate demand and economic growth within these trading blocs, and a more balanced and fairer economic growth worldwide and a greater diffusion of wealth and income to ordinary people and communities. This in turn would provide an excellent breeding ground for democracy, freedom and democratic values.

For example trading blocs such as the EU, EFTA, North America (USA and Canada) , ASEAN, APEC, CARICOM, MERCUSOR could impose new capital controls and new measures to improve trade imbalances. The EU and other trading blocs mentioned above need to strengthen their own internal markets and give preference to the manufacturing of goods and services inside their trading bloc. This will involve:
- Trading bloc **capital controls** to favour production and employment inside the Trading bloc
- Trading bloc **trading controls** to favour production and employment inside the Trading bloc
- preferred investment and trading status to Trading bloc based businesses.
- use of 'Guaranteed EU employment' or ' Guaranteed North American employment' or other trading bloc labels to differentiate which products and services are actually generating jobs inside the Trading bloc
- new investment tax credits and tax reductions for productive investments which increase jobs and employment in a Trading bloc
- tax increases on companies and businesses which create jobs outside the Trading bloc

This would provide strong incentives to create jobs inside the trading bloc. These measures would:
a) improve employment, output, purchasing power, credit and money growth, economic growth and tax revenues in countries within trading blocs
b) reduce government debt and government deficits in countries within trading blocs
c) improve the overall economic effects of the debt deleveraging processes at government, business, banks, family and individual levels in countries
d) increase the economic benefits and multiplier effects of fiscal and monetary stimulus in countries within trading blocs. This resulting from reductions in leakages out of countries and trading blocs.

The great economist Keynes recommended some of these measures in times of recession and depression in order to raise aggregate demand, money growth and aggregate supply, and bring about full economic recovery and sustained growth. Quantitative Easing could be used to assist these new capital controls and trading controls through incentives for 'Preferred trading and investment status' where the EU provides new financial and other incentives and rules for all EU countries and international companies to trade with and invest in other EU countries. Ireland, Spain, Italy, and Portugal and Greece could be given special status or incentives in order to speed up economic growth and recovery in these countries, and help pay down debt. Imports from the Far East and Africa could be reduced through new taxes, levies and charges and other disincentives at EU level. These measures would involve mass relocations of European companies and businesses back into the EU, and increased inter-trade between EU nations, creating new jobs and new growth throughout the EU.

It would end the "global race to the bottom" or "global race to the sewer" which has pitted low-cost developing and third world countries against Western developed countries and delivered many economic and social ills and economic crashes, etc..

These type of capital controls and trading controls within the EU and other trading blocs around the world would help improve worker's rights, worker's incomes, financial and banking regulations, tax revenues, pension funds and pension payments, aggregate demand and money supply growth and employment levels within countries and within the trading bloc, and improve social and political stability within countries and within trading blocs.

We all want jobs and full employment, and it is jobs within countries / trading blocs which will help finance the tax revenues, finance the state spending, fund the hospitals and healthcare, reduce the debts, the deficits, finance the welfare and disability payments, finance the government, finance the pension funds and payment of pensions, and stimulate consumption, investment and economic growth in Europe and other trading blocs.

(ii) the introduction of the Bancor as a unit of account for each country for international trade, first proposed by the economist John Maynard Keynes in 1945. This would be accompanied by an International Clearing Union to process this. Each nation would have a country Bancor rate determined by their trading status, their balance of payments, their current and capital account. Country Bancors would differ between countries. This would allow country Bancors to depreciate or appreciate according to how much Bancor they receive or pay out for international goods, services and capital and their balance of payments. Bancor would be an objective and independent means of measuring global trade and trade imbalances. It would be free of speculation and government manipulation. The Bancor could be backed up by gold, silver and a basket of currencies or precious metals. Those countries in deficit would have depreciated country Bancors while those in surplus would have inflated country Bancors. This would encourage nations to trade with each other and help manage the trade differences and imbalances between nations, so that all benefit from trade and investment. It would enable weaker nations to build up their industries and export markets. The purpose of Bancor and managed international trade would be the attainment of full employment in all countries or as many countries as possible worldwide. It would have the opposite effect to the euro in Europe which ties all countries into a German dominated euro which mostly serves German interests. The scope of the Bancor would facilitate national sovereignty and economic development, trade, investment, growth and full employment within trading blocs such as the EU, EFTA, NAFTA , ASEAN, APEC, CARICOM, MERCUSOR. Free trade within these trading blocs and the imposition of small tariffs on goods and services produced outside these blocs would assist this overall objective.

(iii) Full integration of some basic fundamentals :

(a) the UN Declaration of Human Rights and the ECHR into the laws and Constitutions of all countries worldwide

(b) worker rights and benefits

(c) environmental protection and food safety

(d) a commitment to international security and cooperation, so that all nations feel secure

(e) implementation of industrial democracy and economic democracy

into all trade treaties and all WTO trade treaties, and as the main condition for all trade and investment. And providing the means for international organisations such as the UN, Amnesty International and Transparency International to monitor them. This would provide a basic foundation for all international trade, and could be the central plank of WTO policy and its trade treaties, and all international aid programmes. This would enable international trade to build a more humane and just world. This could be reinforced further by new educational requirements in all countries, compulsorily educating all peoples about their human rights, democratic freedoms and responsibilities, and the need for environmental protection and food safety through school programmes and adult education programmes worldwide.

(iv) Africa, Poor Asian countries and South American countries

Use the UN, World Bank, IMF and international cooperation between trading blocs and nations to invest $700 billion per year to eliminate poverty and the causes of poverty and to encourage very low or sustainable population growth worldwide. Population control is vital as excessive population growth in an environment of limited resources is a major cause of poverty, malnutrition and conflict. Most of this could be distributed via NGO's and community banks, public savings banks, crypto currencies, and the social credit schemes mentioned in this book. This could be invested in:

a. Provision of food and shelter for people in those countries worst affected by poverty, wars or 'regime changes', famines, climate damage, and globalisation. And complementing this with employment programmes and training programmes in the state, private and voluntary sectors to build independence and self sufficiency for these people.

b. Georgism or land redistribution in developing and third world countries would be necessary to achieve these objectives. This would involve (i) community land ownership (ii) farmer's cooperatives (iii) limited state ownership of land and the private use of this land, with users paying a fee. This would provide strong incentives for people to work the land and sell the produce locally or nationally for private profits. This would encourage free enterprise and private profit from working the land while ensuring the ownership of the land is widely owned whether through communities, farmer cooperatives or privately. This would end the high concentration of land ownership in these counties where the richest 5% own between 80 – 100% of the land, and most of the population live in dire poverty as landless labourers. Margrit Kennedy has provided some insights into how this could be done in third world countries and developed countries [33]

c. Fund effective and affordable healthcare, hospitals and primary care. And giving contracts to local suppliers and businesses with employee share ownership, promoting economic democracy and industrial democracy.

d. Fund clean drinking water projects. And giving contracts to local suppliers and businesses with employee share ownership, promoting economic democracy and industrial democracy.

e. Fund adequate sanitation to protect public health. And giving contracts to local suppliers and businesses with employee share ownership, promoting economic democracy and industrial democracy.

f. Fund high quality education and skills development And giving contracts to local suppliers and businesses with employee share ownership, promoting economic democracy and industrial democracy.

g. The schemes such as 'Zero Hunger' and the Family Grant' system in Brazil and the Aadhaar system in India could serve as models for relieving extreme poverty and lifting people up. While the digital currency and mobile phone banking in Kenya could be serve as funds distribution models, cutting out middle men and bureaucracies.

h. Fund proper public infrastructure (roads, rail, bridges, stations, shipping ports, airports, telecommunications, etc.) to encourage local and regional business development. And giving contracts to local suppliers and businesses with employee share ownership, promoting economic democracy and industrial democracy.

i. Fund the deployment of Open Source technologies for use in businesses and homes and the state sector in African countries and poor Asian countries and South American countries

j. Fund Fair trade and businesses and start ups involved in Fair Trade

k. Fund and oversee more fair and just legal systems

l. Fund cheap, affordable and good quality housing for workers and small business people, and social housing schemes. And giving contracts to local suppliers and businesses with employee share ownership, promoting economic democracy and industrial democracy.

m. Fund new types of Quantitative Easing, local currencies, public savings banks, microfinance (similar to Grameen bank) and social credit. This is outlined in detail in Chapter 7.

n. Encouraging, financially assisting and mentoring local business start ups, and their growth and continued success. These would supply goods and services at competitive prices and provide local employment.

o. Funding economic democracy and industrial democracy in the form of greater employee share ownership, profit sharing, bonuses, and community share ownership, and networks of cooperatives. (See Chapter 9 on Format of Economic Democracy)

p. Funding the development of farmer cooperatives, cooperative banks, credit unions and microfinance bodies (similar to Grameen bank) for farmers. New government policies and laws to achieve this, and to prioritise local food supply for native peoples over 'cash crops' for export.

q. Fund effective birth control in all these countries and link birth control to economic aid. Also provide well funded education and schools, especially for the education of women.

r. Local government, regional government and national government prioritising local producers, suppliers and businesses with employee share ownership when awarding state contracts.

s. Co-ownership of many types of assets which would be used by communities. Examples being co-ownership of cars, community buildings, crèches and kindergartens, sports fields, dishwashers, homes, washing machines, tools, water wells, holiday homes, etc.. This could be promoted via government tax incentives and grants. This would enable private ownership to exist alongside co-ownership and community ownership.

t. Funding measures to increase worker productivity, capital productivity and land productivity.

u. The social and economic inclusion of the disabled, the unemployed, women and minorities

v. Help developing countries meet human rights objectives and their international obligations and duties

w. Funding Cross-community cooperation, integration and peace initiatives and projects. Ways to live together and work together in harmony, tolerance and peace.

x. Building social justice and economic justice for all persons in terms of employment, housing, education, training, wealth distribution, community groups, civil rights, political representation, laws, legal processes, etc.

y. Ubuntu Movement

The principles of the Ubuntu movement in South Africa to more widely distribute income and wealth in a reformed monetary system and free market system, and also build stronger community stability and cohesion, and use of renewable energies / energy independence. This system is proving to be very successful and a blueprint for sustainable economic growth over time, and more stable economic and social systems worldwide

These measures would build greater stability within countries and stop and discourage extremism, terrorism and crime, and encourage greater business activity, trade, investment and cooperation between nations.

In the widely acclaimed book 'Africa's Odious Debts: How Foreign Loans and Capital Flight Bled a Continent by Leonce Ndikumana, James Boyce, they state that in the period 1970 – 2008 over $944 billion was taken out of Africa in capital flight and tax evasion much of it to tax havens abroad. And it is estimated by the Tax Justice network that $12.1 trillion from developing and third world countries lies in offshore tax havens. According to world bank studies, 60 of the world's poorest nations owe $520 billion in loans.

Africa and other third world countries need the following solutions:

a) There needs to be national debt write downs and write offs for developing and third world nations, similar to those proposed above in Chapter 7 of this book. This should be in region of write offs of 50% - 70% of national debt and should be gradual and subject to certain conditions below:

b) **Condition 1:** corrupt debt contracted by dictators and corrupt leaders and elites needs to classified as criminal debt, and should not be paid for by taxpayers in these countries. Link these debt reductions to the prosecution and jailing of corrupt dictators, political leaders, business people and bankers, the return of monies hidden away in offshore tax havens and the implementation of economic democracy and industrial democracy in these countries.

c) **Condition 2:** the wider diffusion of wealth and income to the ordinary African people through economic democracy measures mentioned in Chapters 7-11

d) **Condition 3:** the ending of corruption in African countries through the measures advised in Chapter 10 and by Transparency International, Amnesty International and the UN.

e) **Condition 4:** the building of peace and cooperation within and between all African countries as advised in Chapter 12 and by Amnesty International and the UN.

f) Future loans could be linked to the full implementation of these conditions above and the introduction of the reforms and changes proposed in this book. This would inject trillions of dollars into developing and third world countries, these monies and savings in debt repayments and the new loans could be used to improve health systems, education systems, housing, safe water systems, roads and infrastructure, honesty and integrity in politics, environmental protection, effective birth control, full employment, wealth distribution via economic democracy and local business development in developing countries.

g) those international companies which wish to locate in developing countries and compete against local businesses should be allowed to do so on certain conditions (1) set up a subsidiary of the foreign company in the developing country (2) be required to devote a certain percentage of their subsidiary company share capital, say 33%, to local employee ownership and community share ownership. This would give local workers and communities a share in these international companies and spread out the wealth from globalisation. The WTO could be used to draw up and enforce such a scheme.

(v) Use of methods for identifying and taxing monies hidden away in offshore tax havens mentioned in previous chapters in this book so as to stablise government revenues and socio-political systems. And linking this to international trade treaties.

(vi) Use of international legal tools and treaties to stop the plundering and raping of the natural resources of developing nations by large international businesses working with corrupt political leaders. Spread out the financial benefits of a developing nation's natural resources to stimulate economic growth, tax revenues, export revenues, greater employee share ownership and community share ownership, and implement 'Quantitative Easing for the People' to benefit the native peoples in these countries.

(vii) Implement full cost accounting standards which include the environmental, health and legal costs of pollution in all countries in all trade treaties

(viii) Fund the use of new Green technologies and alternative technologies in third world and developing countries. These are listed in a section above.

(ix) Regulating population growth in line with available resources. This will involve promotion of birth control by governments and the provision of economic incentives for this.

(x) eliminate subsidies for agriculture in developed countries which causes dumping of these products in developing countries and punishes poor farmers in these countries. Encourage local farmers in developing countries to develop their own markets regionally and nationally and feed their own peoples.

(xi) end the TRIPS agreement and other similar agreements at WTO level.

(xii) Put into operation a new economic order globally, where the financial benefits of business activity and natural resources are more widely distributed to the people in developing countries and third countries. Implement economic democracy and industrial democracy, encompassing extensive use of long term employee share ownership, profit sharing, networks of cooperatives, and community / neighbourhoods share ownership of businesses and all natural resources, including oil, gas, minerals, diamonds, land. This would be supported by community banking, micro banking, local currencies, and social credit schemes. And the implementation of fair trade policies mentioned above. This would replace the unregulated free market and colonial economics which has caused deep divisions, injustices and conflicts worldwide.

(xiii) monitor and resolve corruption, injustices and human rights abuses in all countries. And bring cases to the international court in the Hague.

(xiv) encourage the development of religious tolerance, pluralism and liberal democracy, and new institutions and laws to support this in all countries

(xv) work for the sovereignty and self determination of distinct peoples and protection of indigenous peoples and their lands, and encourage fair trade, fair investment, cooperation, mutual understanding, goodwill, peace and harmony between groups, races and all nations. And many international projects to build this and strengthen this.

China

China has become a major player in international trade and investment. It is a major exporter, yet it imports comparatively little from countries outside China. This has created trade imbalances, balance of payment imbalances and capital account imbalances and placed the EU, North America and other countries at a major disadvantage. The EU is importing 10 times more from China than China is importing from the EU. This is destroying jobs and investment in the EU. Economic blocs such as the EU, NAFTA , ASEAN, APEC, CARICOM, MERCUSOR need to address this issue through some new policies

- encourage China to spend more on consumption of foreign imports and reduce its saving rate from 30% down to 10% . A spending, consumption and credit boom in China with higher imports from other countries would benefit all countries, including the Chinese.

- increased Chinese government spending and private individual spending on EU goods and services, which would benefit both the Chinese population as a whole and EU producers. This will need to increase by over 500% (over 2015 levels) and keep increasing over time. Targets for imports into China from the EU, could be agreed between the EU and China. This could be tied to markets in Europe and North America opening up to more Chinese goods and services.

- increased trade missions by all EU countries to China, every year, to encourage trade.

- the Chinese government could increase taxes on savings while reducing VAT and consumption taxes to encourage more consumption of Chinese goods and foreign goods

- the introduction of the Bancor as a unit of account for each country for international trade, first proposed by the economist John Maynard Keynes in 1945. This would be accompanied by an International Clearing Union to process this. Each nation would have a country Bancor rate determined by their trading status, their balance of payments, their current and capital account. Country Bancors would differ between countries. This would allow country Bancors to depreciate or appreciate according to how much Bancor they receive or pay out for international goods, services and capital and their balance of payments.

- the Chinese government could provide incentives in the form of tax rebates and grants for the purchase of consumer products and services for a limited period of time, say 4 months. And repeat this special offer a year later. Chinese people like getting special deals.

- the Chinese government could introduce Economic Democracy into China and spread out the wealth and income from economic growth to the whole Chinese population. This would reduce concentrations of wealth and income and help them achieve important social objectives.

- the Chinese should focus more on productive investment and less on speculative investments in property, assets and derivatives, so as to avoid crashes and expensive bail outs.

- the Chinese government could be encouraged to improve the social safety net and pensions, and also impose tighter controls on property prices. This would encourage Chinese to spend their savings and more of their disposable income.

Chapter 10   Social Justice, Accountability and Ending Corruption : Implementation of the Checks and Balances and Individual Responsibilities and State Responsibilities essential for Democracy

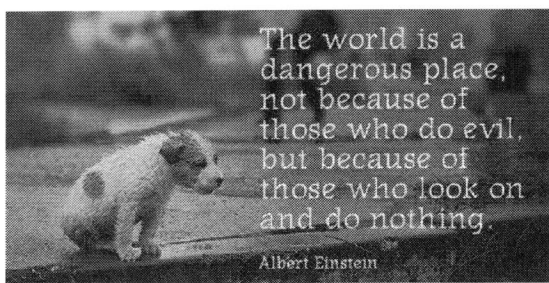

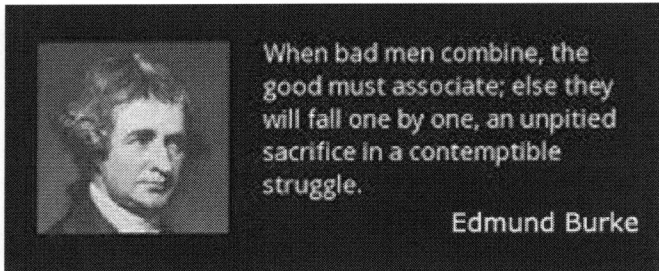

The only thing necessary for the triumph of evil is for good men to do nothing.

attributed to Edmund Burke

Bad men need nothing more to compass their ends, than that good men should look on and do nothing

John Stuart Mill

When people fear their government, there is tyranny. When the government fear their people there is liberty.

President Thomas Jefferson, US President and author of Declaration of Independence

Now I will tell you the answer to my question. It is this. The Party seeks power entirely for its own sake. We are not interested in the good of others; we are interested solely in power, pure power. What pure power means you will understand presently. We are different from the oligarchies of the past in that we know what we are doing. All the others, even those who resembled ourselves, were cowards and hypocrites. The German Nazis and the Russian Communists came very close to us in their methods, but they never had the courage to recognize their own motives.......................We know that no one ever seizes power with the intention of relinquishing it. Power is not a means; it is an end. One does not establish a dictatorship in order to safeguard a revolution; one makes the revolution in order to establish the dictatorship. The object of persecution is persecution. The object of torture is torture. The object of power is power. Now you begin to understand me...........................Big Brother is watching you

1984 by George Orwell

In previous chapters in this book we examined how freedom, responsibilities, human rights and Constitutional rights are undermined and destroyed by defects, flaws and corruptions in different political systems and ideologies. This has included an analysis of how an unaccountable and out of control Big Brother and a '1984' type environment now exists in our modern world, primarily due to failures and defects in Democracies, the National Security State, Liberalism, Hayekism, Monetarism, Neo Liberalism, Globalism, Libertarianism, Marxism and Socialism, Militarism, Fascism, Religious Fundamentalism and State Capitalism. These failures and defects are systemic not isolated or minor. All of these ideologies and systems do not have adequate checks and balances to protect freedom, rights, responsibilities and democracy, and many of them oppose and act against such measures.

It was the famous Christian Minister, Desmond Tutu who once declared
"If you are neutral in situations of injustice, you have chosen the side of the oppressor."
and he was 100% correct in his statement. This quotation along with the others above provide the most important lesson for mankind. Their truths convey exactly why the world has been in turmoil, discord, disharmony and conflict for a long time.

The Individual VS The Corrupt State

The writings and works of Locke, Rousseau, Diderot, Voltaire, Jefferson, Madison, Paine, De Tocqueville, and Mill spoke of the conflict between the individual and the state and the need for laws, rights and checks and balances to moderate, reduce and resolve this conflict and ensure justice and fairness for both the individual and the state. And the means for the individual to redress imbalances and injustices. The creation and maintenance of an equal playing field for the individual and the state. This today is an essential component of democracy and freedom. Today, we see Commissions of Investigation, Tribunals of Inquiry and various other forms of state inquiries in developed and developing countries to establish the nature of this conflict between the individual and the state and the role of rights, enforcement of laws and duties in this. Yet these inquiry structures have serious defects, flaws and weaknesses which render them ineffective and useless, and in many cases they serve to cover up crimes and injustices facilitate further crimes. Deep imbalances have creeped in. In many cases, the individual is denied justice by the corrupt state and he / she is fobbed off, ignored, denigrated, slandered, mocked, lied about, and undermined by the corrupt state. This conflict between the corrupt state and the individual is one of the most serious threats to freedom and democracy in our modern world. It often involves aspects of the Deep State or 'Shadow Government' and its national security state which has become over powerful and has no safeguards to defend democracy and rights. This attack against democracy and freedom is coming from internal enemies, corrupt elements of the state, and it is the duty of all state and government employees, all legal system employees, and all citizens to oppose this attack, to expose it and to stop it.

Let us examine the seriousness and the scale of this attack on the individual by the corrupt state. Most of these cases were called "Conspiracy Theories" for many years, but today they are Conspiracy Facts backed up by evidence and proofs.

- MK-Ultra program run by CIA
- COINTELPRO programme by FBI
- Tuskagee experiments on African Americans for many years by US government agencies
- The denial of child sex abuse and child murders by the catholic church for many decades. The cover up by governments and by police forces and public prosecutors for over a century.
- The information released by Edward Snowden and Julian Assange and Wikileaks
- The findings of the Church Committee of the US Congress in 1978
- Operation Whitecoat
- Project Bluebird
- Operation Midnight Climax,
- Project QKHILLTOP
- The Bayer scandal where people were infected with the AIDS virus in medical products
  https://www.youtube.com/results?search_query=bayer+aids
- The police shootings of unarmed civilians in the USA over the period 2002 - 2017
- The police corruption cases in Europe and North America and South America in the period 2000 – 2019. In Ireland, the McBrearty case, Maurice McCabe case, penalty points scandal, Fr. Niall Molly case, Mary Boyle case, Ian Bailey case, non prosecution of thousands of minors, the Abbeylara case, Kieran Boylan case, the non prosecution of thousands of paedophiles for decades, etc. etc.
- The political corruption cases in most developed countries (including "democracies") in the period 2000 – 2019.
- The political and legal corruption exposed in the film 'All the Plenary's Men' by John Titus in 2017

- Nazi concentration camps and also the experiments on innocent civilians. Some of these criminals were punished at the Nuremburg trials. Some others were given protection and a new life in the USA under Operation Paperclip

- Unit 731 experiments by the Japanese on innocent civilians during the 1940's.

- North Korean human experimentation programmes

- Soviet experiments using chemical, biological and radioactive agents on people in Gulags, prisons, hospitals, psychiatric hospitals and orphanages.

- TB experiments at the St. Vincent's House orphanage in Philadelphia in the early 1900's.

- The cholera experiments with Filipino prisoners by the US military and some academics

- The malaria experiments on hundreds of prisoners in Stateville Penitentiary and psychiatric patients in Illinois State Hospital

- The University of Pennsylvania experiments on 200 female prisoners using viral hepatitis

- The 1946 to 1948 study in Guatemala, where U.S. researchers infected hundreds of people including children using syphilis and other sexually transmitted diseases

- The Willowbrook State School in Staten Island, New York where hundreds of disabled children were deliberately infected with deadly viruses and bacteria for over 2 decades.

- The Sloan-Kettering Institute Cancer experiments on prisoners at Ohio State Prison and 300 healthy women in the 1950's.

- In 1956 and 1957, several U.S. Army biological warfare experiments were conducted on the cities of Savannah, Georgia and Avon Park, Florida. It involved insects carrying Yellow fever and dengue. Hundreds of people became very ill, and some died.

- The Cancer experiments on patients in the Jewish Chronic Disease Hospital in Brooklyn, New York by Chester M. Southam.

- From 1963 to 1969 as part of Project Shipboard Hazard and Defense (SHAD), the US military sprayed biological and chemical warfare agents onto US military ships to test their effects on US military personnel. The US military personnel were not informed about this.

- In 1986 the United States House Committee on Energy and Commerce released a report entitled American Nuclear Guinea Pigs : Three Decades of Radiation Experiments on U.S. Citizens. This details how US citizens were used in nuclear experiments without their knowledge

- In 1953, the U.S. Atomic Energy Commission (AEC) ran several studies at the University of Iowa on the health effects of radioactive iodine in newborns and pregnant women.

- Between 1946 and 1947, researchers at the University of Rochester carried out experiments using uranium-234 and uranium-235 on six people

- Three patients at Billings Hospital at the University of Chicago were injected with plutonium In 1946, six employees of a Chicago metallurgical lab were given water that was contaminated with plutonium-239.

- The experiments from 1946 to 1953, at the Walter E. Fernald State School in Massachusetts where disabled children were fed radioactive material to determine the adverse health effects.

- From 1955 to 1960, Sonoma State Hospital in northern California carried out radioactive and chemical experiments on disabled children. It is estimated that 1,400 children died as a result of these experiments.

- The Atomic Energy Commission funded the Massachusetts Institute of Technology to administer radium-224 and thorium-234 to 20 people between 1961 and 1965

  The book Plutonium Files : Americas Secret Medical Experiments in the Cold War details many of these radioactive and radiation experiments on people. These findings were confirmed by the US President's Advisory Committee on Human Radiation Experiments.

- In the 1950s, researchers at the Medical College of Virginia performed experiments on severe burn victims using additional burns and radioactive material.

  Between 1960 and 1971, the Department of Defense funded non-consensual whole body radiation experiments on poor, black cancer patients, who were not told what was being done to them

- Nasal radium irradiation was carried out on children and adults in several American hospitals for many years despite the fact that it leads to increased risk of Cancers.

  In 1963, University of Washington researchers irradiated the testes of 232 prisoners. This led to birth defects and other health problems.

- In 1956, Walter E. Fernald State School, researchers gave mentally disabled children radioactive material in order to assess its damaging effects on humans.

- Harvard University experiments on pregnant women using diethylstilbestrol, a synthetic estrogen, in the late 1940s.

- From 1950 through 1953, the U.S. Army sprayed chemicals over six cities in the United States and Canada, in order to test dispersal patterns of chemical weapons

- MYCOPLASMA The Linking Pathogen in Neurosystemic Diseases. Donald W. Scott

  The linking pathogen in CFS, Parkinsons, MS, Alzheimers disease. Donald W. Scott

Gulf War Syndrome and other illnesses have been researched by Dr. Garth Nicolson and other scientists. Dr. Nicolson has publications, reports and made sworn testimonies to Presidential Commissions and committees of the U. S. Congress. He exposed illegal experiments on US military personnel, exposures to dangerous toxins and tests on people in American nursing homes, prisons and hospitals.

http://www.projectdaylily.com

- The Vanderbilt University experiments where 829 pregnant mothers in Tennessee were given radioactive material to determine the adverse health effects.

  During the atomic bomb tests in the 1940's and 1950's , the US Public Health Services were instructed to tell citizens downwind from bomb tests that the increases in cancers were due to neurosis, and that women with radiation sickness, hair loss, and burned skin were suffering from "housewife syndrome". (Goliszek, 2003: pp. 132–134). This shows how psychiatry is used to cover up physical and biological illnesses.

- Scientific experiments on children

  Unethical, illegal and dangerous scientific experiments were carried out on children in orphanages and state run institutions in the USA for several decades. This involved dangerous chemicals, radioactive material, experimental vaccines, LSD and other illegal drugs, electric shocks, biological toxins, and deadly viruses. Children were also starved while given these poisons. Children died or were left disabled and traumatised by this.

  From 1951 to 1974, the Holmesburg Prison in Pennsylvania was the site of extensive biological and chemical experiments on prisoners on behalf of on behalf of Dow Chemical Company, the U.S. Army, and Johnson & Johnson. Many prisoners developed serious illnesses and disabilities.

- Paedophile rings involving (i) very wealthy, influential and politically connected people and (ii) powerful religious organisations. And whose crimes have been covered up.

- Banking frauds which have indebted, enslaved and bankrupted nations, and continue to do so. And are fully supported by the state. Banking frauds which have indebted, enslaved and bankrupted businesses, individuals and families, and continue to do so. And are fully supported by the state.

- Mafias within the legal system, involving corrupt police, prosecutors, judges, lawyers and court staff who obstruct justice and pervert the course of justice

- Many other cases are listed on www.healingcentres.org/law.htm

Solutions

There is a need for democracy to defend itself and to defend the people against corrupt elements of the state. In many oaths of allegiance this involves challenging domestic enemies, often embedded within the state. In the first chapter I stated the importance of effective checks and balances and of decentralising power and ensuring multiple oversight systems to enforce honesty, integrity and accountability. New structures, new processes, new systems, new laws, new rights, new bodies need to be put in place in many countries to defend the people against corrupt elements of the state. The following sections provide a means for governments and peoples to do this

1. Checks and Balances And Anti Corruption Policies and Structures

There is a high level of political corruption, legal system corruption and policing corruption in most countries around the world today. This includes most EU countries, North America and South America, all African countries and most Asian countries. This is destroying democratic rights and freedoms, Constitutional rights and human rights. It is a form of terrorism directed at the most vulnerable people in society. This corruption is attacking hard won freedoms and disgracing and denigrating those brave men and women who sacrificed and died for national freedom, democracy, and rights. Popular perceptions need to be changed radically, those "suits and ties" engaged in corruption should be viewed as vermin, parasites, gombeens, filth, destroyers of people and freedom. The processes of dealing with corruption are outlined in more detail in this chapter but they would encompass the following:

a . Enforcement of Checks and Balances

In democracies we have the executive, the legislative, the judiciary, protected whistleblowers, a free press and media and international oversight bodies eg. UN, AI, the ICC, European court. These act as checks against the others so that all parties are held accountable. The executive should be subject to investigation, oversight and actions by the legislative, the judiciary, protected whistleblowers, a free press and media and international oversight bodies. The legislative, the judiciary, protected whistleblowers, a free press and media and international oversight bodies should be subject to similar investigation, oversight and actions by the other parties. This is highly important and acts as a vital safeguard against corruption, injustices and tyranny.

b. **Independent Anti Corruption Agency** which would investigate allegations of political corruption, judge corruption, police corruption, military and secret service corruption, prosecutor corruption and state employee corruption. It would be well resourced and staffed and would conduct covert investigations of corruption. There would be rigorous and covert processes for identifying the many forms of corruption. And exposure lies, perjuries, deceptions, misdirections, political favours, collusion, cover ups, bribes, fraud, etc. which aim to conceal crimes and corruption.

c. This agency would liaise with the new types of Circuit Court Inquiries mentioned below. It could also be delegated investigative powers in coordination with other independent agencies and other parties mentioned in point a. above by the Circuit Court Inquiries system.

d. Structures of Accountability in the state sector, the government sector and the non state subcontractors sector (which supply goods and services to the state / government) to prevent and also to identify and expose (i) abuses of power (ii) cover ups (iii) corruption of state employees and government (iv) fraud, overpricing, embezzlement and misappropriation of funds (v) malpractise and bad practises (vi) incompetence which endangers lives and imposes excessive costs. This would include policies, rules, work practises, contracts, audit rules and oversight systems. The aim would be implementation of full accountability, honesty, fairness, and transparency at all levels, especially at the highest level of the state and government.

e. Fast and efficient means for removing corrupt persons from power and authority

f. Replacing corrupt persons with persons of high integrity, honesty, good character, and dedicated to serving the public good

g. Laws, rules and codes of conduct which enforce honesty, integrity, fair dealings, transparency and accountability for all state and government employees and all persons and businesses having dealings with such authorities, including non state subcontractors

Measures should be constantly put in place to ensure a stronger separation of powers between the parties mentioned in point a. above including separate election processes, separate appointment processes, strict enforcement of anti conflict of interest, new counter-balancing systems, and independent and vigilant oversight systems. This would prevent dictatorship by one person and abuses by one person or a small group of persons. <u>The price of freedom is eternal vigilance.</u>

The separation of powers between the executive and the legislative on one side and between these and the judiciary on the other is extremely important, and has become undermined in recent years in many countries. For example, in many countries

(i) politicians appoint judges who are often members or strong supporters of their political party. This is done for political reasons and can influence court decisions.

(ii) the executive using threats to enforce its views on the legislative which often involve use of the party whip or expulsion

(iii) the legislative becoming disempowered and controlled by a dictatorial leader or executive

(iv) judges and / or prosecutors being members or ex members of political parties which can lead to prosecution decisions or court decisions which have political bias

(iv) judges and / or prosecutors being members of secret societies which can lead to prosecution decisions or court decisions which have are biased and prejudiced

(v) the non prosecution of certain politicians or politically connected business people. This can involve politically connected police and public prosecutors.

(vi) the non arrest and non prosecution of royalty, heads of state and their family members and members of the aristocracy for serious crimes

(vii) the framing of and bringing false charges against innocent people, including activists, for political reasons. And politically connected judges making politically biased decisions in court

(viii) judges interpreting the law or Constitution wrongly or in such a way that it benefits a favoured political party which they are associated with while sacrificing the public good, the Constitution, the laws, and justice under law.

These are very serious threats to democracy and freedom today which need to be reversed, stopped, ended.

2. All judges should be subject to the following checks and balances to ensure justice under law and fairness, equity and impartiality:

   a) The Irish and other European governments need to implement a Judicial Council to oversee all judges and ensure that high standards of practise are used in all courts and that all judges comply with the law and the Constitution and codes of practise including conflicts of interest provisions.

   b) Judges shall be appointed by a panel of independent assessors with Constitutional expertise and cross party politicians from all parties and senior representatives of human rights bodies, charities and voluntary bodies involved in social justice and ending poverty and corruption in open hearings in parliament, where all relevant factors are raised, probed and discussed. This would ensure a broad section of society is involved in the process and would ensure fairness and impartiality in the judge selection process

c) Judges shall be independent of party politics and swear an oath in the High court to this effect and express this independence in court and in public. Judges are there to serve all the people and the nation. This is a Constitutional requirement in most democracies where there is a separation of powers between the legislative, the executive and the judiciary.

d) Judges will be independent and strictly lawful and fair in their judgments and not be influenced by any other forces

e) Judges shall not be a member of any secret society

f) Judges shall ensure that due process is followed in courts and that persons are given a fair hearing. And that all laws, all precedents and rulings from superior courts and provisions of the Constitution and Common law are taken into consideration in court hearings and obeyed at all times in court. And that lay litigants, McKenzie friends and members of the public can stand up in court and affirm these laws and legal requirements in court and ask for adherence to them without fear of being threatened, harassed and assaulted.

g) Courts are in place to serve the general public and ensure that justice under law is delivered not to serve judges or police. Members of the public must be given full legal right to raise reasonable objections in court where they feel that laws are being broken in court, and to cite the relevant laws or precedents from the superior courts, and request adherence to them.

h) Judges shall allow all court proceedings to be video recorded and audio recorded to ensure that due process and fair procedures are followed at all times in courts. And that such evidence can be provided in subsequent court cases or tribunals of inquiry. And that measures are put in place to prevent tampering with such evidence.

i) All judges shall be removed from court cases where their family or extended family are involved as a defendant, plaintiff, lawyer in the case.

j) If a judge breaks the law or his/her oath of office while in court, then the court hearing and its ruling is to be declared null and void and a rehearing in a different jurisdiction with a different judge scheduled.

k) Judges shall acknowledge that members of the public are not bound to obey unlawful or illegal directions from a judge or police in court. Any controversial directions must be accompanied by citation of the relevant laws.

l) Judges shall be subject to the laws and Constitution of the land and subject to arrest and prosecution if they disobey laws while performing their duties in court. This affirms the supremacy of the Constitution and laws and that no person is above the law

m) Judges shall acknowledge that a member of the public is entitled to prosecute a judge in court for breaking the law via public prosecution or private prosecution

n) Judges can be impeached for breaking the law in court, denying a person due process or justice in court, or engaging in corruption.

o) Citizens be given the right to carry out citizen's arrests in court in accordance with law

p) Judges shall be subject to independent oversight regularly and to impeachment by a panel consisting of the Judicial Council, a representative of the Bar Council and Law Society, some experts in Constitutional law, and representatives of human rights bodies and voluntary bodies involved in social justice and cross party politicians in parliament in open hearings

q) Judges shall respect the democratic rights, Constitutional rights and human rights of all persons before the court, and give a firm commitment to truth and the exposure of lies, perjuries, corruptions, crimes and injustices without fear, favour or prejudice. And no special favours be granted to prosecutors, lawyers, court personnel or police in this. This affirmation should be read out at all court hearings and copy given to all litigants.

r) The judges or judiciary should be subject to the oversight systems mentioned in Point 1 (a) above.

s) All public prosecutors and the DPP should be subject to the same selection processes and rules and oversight as that for judges. They should also provide reasons for a non prosecution decision including passages from laws to support their decision to victims of crime and their families. It should be made possible in law for victims of crime (and their family) to seek a judicial review through the Supreme court to overturn a DPP or prosecutor decision not to prosecute. This protects the democratic right to appeal

3. Oversight systems and Checks and Balances in all democratic countries need to be reviewed every 4 years and changes, reforms, abolitions, new laws, new amendments to laws, new Constitutional provisions or amendments, and new bodies and agencies implemented to ensure that there is (a) proper and effective oversight and (b) effective checks and balances. This Review (every 4 years) could be done in collaboration with legal and Constitutional experts, politicians, representatives of many voluntary bodies and charities involved in social justice, senior members of Amnesty

International, Transparency International, the UN, and international human rights bodies. This process should be open to the public and be transparent and accountable. This would ensure involvement, engagement and input by many sections of society.

Terms of Reference for State Inquiry into Matters where an Innocent Individual(s) is being attacked or has been attacked by Corrupt Elements of the State

Since 1970, many Commissions of Investigation and Tribunals of Inquiry have taken place in Europe and North America and other countries, and in the majority of cases they have failed to bring criminal prosecutions in court against the guilty parties. Serious crimes have gone unpunished. Outrageous crimes have been committed including perversions of the course of justice, false imprisonment, lies and perjuries (in Commissions of Investigation and Tribunals and Courts), bribery and corruption of public officials, politicians and government, murders, child sex abuse, child trafficking, child murders, illegal experiments on vulnerable children, non investigation of hundreds of crimes and attempts to cover this up, tax evasion, state leaks of information and breaches of the Official Secrets act and Data Protection laws, vile and malicious slanders and gossip designed to undermine justice and harass and destroy the lives of innocent people and incite further crimes have been brought before Commissions of Investigation and Tribunals and nobody has been properly investigated for this, nobody has been prosecuted in court for this, and nobody has been held accountable.

The evidence and facts clearly show that Commissions of Investigation and Tribunals are a means to :

(i) cover up the crimes committed by state employees and by powerful people and wealthy people and by certain institutions with political connections. They have served as a smokescreen, and have been deliberately deprived of powers to investigate and establish the facts and truth, while accepting lies, perjuries and deception as facts, truths and 'evidence'. They have derived false 'balance of probability' results or judgments based on these lies and perjuries, which call into the question the integrity of such structures and the real reason for their existence. They have acted to mislead the public and to prevent due process under law and justice under law. Commissions of Investigation and Tribunals are obstructions to justice and facilitators of perversions of justice.

485

(ii) aid and abet continuing criminality by employees of the state or government and by powerful business people. The non prosecution of guilty parties carries with it other high social costs and threats as they aid, abet and facilitate the committing of crimes in the present and in the future.

(iii) undermine the Constitution and the Constitutional rights, legal rights and human rights of victims of crime.

(iv) to corruptly and illegally elevate some people to being above the law, and prevent them from being prosecuted for crimes. And bring the whole legal system into serious disrepute. Prior to the 1990's, most developed countries and developing countries had a system where privileged members of society were allowed to commit crimes and get away with them for centuries, and this created great resentment and anger in these countries. This feudal system needs to be finally eradicated.

This criminal activity by representatives of the state typically has the following elements:

a. Corrupt state employees, including corrupt police, prosecutors, politicians, senior civil servants, secret services, and military committing crimes, including many of the serious crimes mentioned above and not being investigated, prosecuted, jailed and fired for these serious offences

b. Corrupt state employees, including corrupt police, prosecutors, secret services, and military lying under oath and committing perjury and providing false evidence against an innocent party. And harassing and threatening this innocent party, including assaults, injuries and deaths in some cases.

c. Corrupt employees and ex employees of the Deep State and Shadow Government breaking the Constitution, undermining Constitutional rights, human rights and legal rights. Misuse of laws to break laws and Constitutional protections and to cover up serious crimes.

d. Corrupt employees of the state leaking confidential state information to private individuals or groups. This often done when they off duty and in public places. And the use of this information to undermine others, harass them, discriminate against them or harm them.

e. Corrupt state employees subcontracting out criminal activities to criminals and thugs to undermine, harass or attack an innocent party. And covering up the crimes of these individuals through perverting the course of justice in police investigations, interference with evidence, prosecutor manipulation and perverting court evidence and activities.

f.   Corrupt judges accepting lies and perjuries and allowing convictions to take place based on this. And allowing certain criminals with powerful political, legal or businesses connections to evade prosecution, conviction or jail. This may also involve giving them overly lenient sentences which are out of all proportion to the crime committed.

g.   Politicians illegally interfering in legal cases and court cases to prevent a prosecution or conviction of another party or alternatively attain the wrongful conviction of an innocent party

h.   Political use of the press and media to pervert the course of justice, and prevent a prosecution from taking place or encourage the prosecution and harassment of an innocent party

i.   Secret deals between police, prosecutors and judges to pervert the course of justice, block justice and undermine justice in court cases and legal cases

This type of corruption is very difficult to investigate and prosecute, as it involves powerful people, the abuse of state authority and the strategic misuse of state powers, lies, perjuries, cover ups, hidden evidence, false evidence, and deception to undermine justice under law.

Commissions of Investigation and Tribunals have been totally discredited and are now seen as a means to cover up crimes and injustices and prevent due process under law. They need to be disbanded, eradicated and replaced by new more effective structures. I propose a two tier state Inquiry system which is comprised of:

a. Circuit Criminal Court Inquiry (in US, a Federal Criminal Court Inquiry)

This Inquiry would investigate, gather and establish the facts, truth and evidence and assess these. It would be politically independent in its structure and functions. It would be chaired by judges from the criminal circuit court, high court and supreme court who would manage the Inquiry. It would be subject to four forms of independent oversight.

(i) 4 – 5 independent parties from outside the country – representatives from the UN, the EU, the ICC, Amnesty International, Transparency International, civil rights bodies based in other countries. No conflicts of interest.

(ii) a grouping of upstanding law abiding citizens from many sections of society with no criminal records, no political connections and no conflicts of interest

(iii) a grouping of top legal experts, including highly experienced lawyers, judges, ex prosecutors, law professors with no political connections and no conflicts of interest

(iv) cross party politicians from the parliament / congress with no conflicts of interest

(v) representatives of the free press and media, including social media. The freedom of whistleblowers to expose any wrong doing or corruption in the Inquiry to the press and media

These multiple systems of oversight would act as vigilant watch dogs and help ensure honesty, due process, fairness, and integrity. Once the Inquiry is concluded, then the Circuit Criminal court case(s) begins immediately.

b. Circuit Criminal Court Criminal case(s) (in US, a Federal Criminal Court case)

This would be the court case which would use the facts, truth and evidence established in the Inquiry above to bring a criminal prosecution against the guilty party. The court case would carefully examine and cross examine all facts, evidence, testimonies, witnesses, experts, reports and proofs to establish the truth. This would have the same oversight as above.

Operation of Circuit Criminal Court Inquiry

The Circuit Criminal Court Inquiry would be delegated powers of the Circuit Court and the High Court to:

A. Establish the Facts, Truths and Evidence and Expose Lies, Perjuries and Deception. This would involve the Inquiry directing:

   I. Covert investigations and undercover investigations involving electronic surveillance, recording equipment and the use of agents and private investigators or military intelligence personnel

   II. Seizures of computers, mobile phones, ipads, smart phones, electronic equipment and telecommunications equipment, bugging devices, files, letters, and emails from offices, homes and other public places to use as evidence

   III. Seizures of bank accounts and credit card accounts and freezing of such within the country and other jurisdictions

   IV. Seizures of safes and safe deposit boxes

   V. Seizures of court documents and other government documents, including classified and secret government documents

   VI. Acquisition of private and public CCTV evidence

VII.   Identification of and use of whistleblowers, informants, witnesses and witness protection schemes to gather information

VIII.   Subpoena victims, witnesses, whistleblowers, police, prosecutors, state employees and other relevant parties to the Inquiry and demand that they provide testimony and evidence under oath

IX.   Get sworn affidavits from witnesses, whistleblowers and informants

X.   Interviews of eye witnesses and covert methods to verify the accounts of eye witnesses. Multiple forms of corroboration to establish the truth and facts.

XI.   Use of forensic experts in different fields to examine and forensically analyse evidence, establish the precise facts and proofs, and the sequence of events

XII.   Use of forensic computer experts, data recovery experts, GPS signal experts, IP address experts

XIII.   Use of forensic accountants

XIV.   Use of GPS signals and Mobile phone signals for mobile phones and computers

XV.   Acquire data and audio / video footage from the smart phones of third parties and bystanders

XVI.   The use of DNA samples, blood samples and finger prints for letters, files, computers, mobile phones, electronic equipment, clothing and furniture.

XVII.   The preservation of all samples and all evidence for a period of 30 years so that important cases can be revisited in future for further analysis and investigation

B.   Demand criminal investigations of a whole case or portions of a case or related cases to establish facts, truths and evidence by the police or military or ombudsman or other state agencies or a private detective agency given jurisdiction to conduct such investigations by the Inquiry. This may also involve re-investigations and re-analysis of previous evidence and alleged facts and the re-opening of previous cases.

C.   Compel attendance of persons at the Inquiry. Non compliance would carry a prison sentence for contempt of court.

D.   Gather sworn affidavits, sworn in the presence of an investigator, a lawyer, a witness and police officer, from defendants and plaintiffs. These will be presented in the Inquiry and the court case. Compel the telling of the truth at the Inquiry and court case, and remind all participants of the crime of perjury and that perjury will be prosecuted. Seperate investigations and court proceedings for perjury should begin once a perjury is discovered in the Inquiry or court case. All perjuries must be prosecuted.

E. The delegated High Court powers would include the power to issue Orders of Discovery, Orders of Mandamus and Orders of Certiorari and a specified time period for completion. Non compliance would carry a prison sentence for contempt of court.

F. Powers to over-ride High Court decisions. Only the Supreme Court would have a higher jurisdiction and would only consider matters of Constitutional importance. The Supreme court would not be used for the purpose of supporting or assisting the committing of perjuries, provision of false evidence, long delays and hindering of justice, hiding of evidence or tampering of evidence in the Circuit Criminal Court Inquiry. The Constitutional right to protect the facts and truth, victim's rights and their right to due process under law would over-ride any attempts by powerful persons or wealthy persons to use legal processes or loopholes to undermine this.

G. Investigate all persons regardless of social status, rank, and social importance. There would be an end to the feudal system of some persons being above the law.

H. Cross examine witnesses, suspects, whistleblowers, informants, victims, police, military, state investigators, and private investigators, and use evidence obtained by covert means and non covert means in these cross examinations.

I. All witnesses, suspects, whistleblowers, informants, victims, police, military, state investigators, and private investigators would be entitled to a solicitor to represent them at the Inquiry. The state would cover partial costs (50%) for this. In the case of persons lying to the Inquiry the state would not cover legal costs for the liar and would compel the liar to pay the state's costs in investigating him/her.

J. Prepare the facts, truth and evidence for the Circuit Criminal court case(s). This would involve close liaison with the DPP to proceed to the court case stage. Once the Inquiry is concluded the Circuit Court case(s) should begin immediately.

Proceeding to Circuit Criminal Court case

The Circuit Criminal Court Inquiry would establish 'Lines of Causality' based on evidence and facts. This is a relatively new term for the legal profession and politics. For example, the exact details of what happened, the chain of events, how each event affected other events in this chain of events, the people involved, the motivations of the people involved, the instigators of events, the secret deals and agreements, the attempts to cover up and conceal, etc. and the use of covert means and non covert means to establish these facts and the relationship of the facts to each other.

(i) All evidence and findings of fact and truth from the Inquiry would be admissible in the Circuit Criminal Court case(s) and would form part of the criminal prosecution in court.

(ii) The crimes associated with the allegations being made in the Inquiry would be listed by law and Constitutional provision and jail sentences based on previous cases in the past also listed. This would be made public and open for all to view.

(iii) The purpose of this two tier structure of Circuit Criminal Court Inquiry and Circuit Court case would be to (1) establish a fact finding body which would be completely independent and be given extensive legal powers to investigate and cross examine (2) establish the facts, truth and evidence and effective use of this (3) exposure of lies, perjuries, deceptions and slander by guilty parties and punishment of this (4) provide justice under law for all persons, encompassing a time efficient and effective means for doing this, including criminal prosecution of guilty parties and the accompanying opportunity to pursue civil cases and compensation in the High Court.

(iv) The Inquiry structure would help restore the reputation and integrity of the legal system in countries worldwide. Specifically, it would ensure that all victims of crime and serious injustices by state employees, police, politicians, solicitors, barristers or judges, and politically connected business people and bankers would be entitled to (a) justice under the criminal law and (b) financial compensation in the High Court for losses, injuries and damage to character suffered under the civil law. The Inquiry's ability to establish the facts, truth and evidence would play a major role in this, facilitating justice in Irish society. State employees who abuse their position to target innocent members of the public need to be made personally financially liable for their actions, and made to pay from their bank accounts, salaries and assets. They should not be allowed to hide behind the state and use the state to pay out compensation payments to victims.

Further Practical Measures and Policies

The following will be necessary to achieve and to protect the people, political democracy, freedom and economic democracy :

1. The checks and balances mentioned in this Chapter should be included in the Constitutions and in Constitutional rights of nations so as to protect ordinary citizens against corrupt elements of the state and powerful private individuals with links to corrupted elements of the state. And to uncover lies, manipulations, deceptions, cover ups, frauds, perversions of justice, hidden evidence and other means of depriving people of justice under law.

2. **Political Reforms which implement Fuller Accountability, Transparency, Honesty and Integrity**

- New Constitutional provisions in the USA and other countries worldwide to:

   (a) end corporations defined as 'persons'. Corporations should be defined as non human entities. These 'entities' would not have the rights of persons or individuals. These 'entities' would have the clearly defined rights and responsibilities of an organisation, complete with social responsibilities. One of the responsibilities would be full accountability including full disclosure of any payments to politicians and political parties, any political favours asked, and full disclosure of any corrupt practises. It would be a criminal offence not to disclose this.

   (b) provisions and ideas expressed in the following proposed laws in the USA

   - proposed American Anti Corruption Act

   - proposed Citizen Equality Act

   - proposed Voting Rights Advancement Act (2015)

   to provide representative democracy and rid "democracies" of bribery, corruption, fraud, gerrymandering, injustices and oligarchy.

- Get all politicians to swear an oath in court, in the presence of a judge and independent witnesses, that they will not engage in any form of corruption and that if they do, they will resign and face criminal penalties for corruption. This will also include all situations where conflicts of interest may occur.

- Prior to the passing of any legislation in parliament, all politicians would be legally required to state and publically disclose which lobbyists contacted them in relation to the proposed legislation. Failure to disclose this should be a criminal offence and also carry civil penalties allowing the politician to be sued.

- A register of all Lobbyists for a Parliament / Congress and all city councils and town councils. Criminal prosecution and fines for non compliance.

- A register of all financial and business interests and all sources of funding for all local politicians and councillors, national politicians and EU politicians. This will include all situations where conflicts of interest may occur or have occurred. Criminal prosecution and fines for non compliance

- Ethics in Public Office Act should state that a 'connected person' is a person with any material stake in a decision made by public servants.

- Ban politicians and civil servants from acting as lobbyists for 5 years after leaving office.

- Abolish the guillotine mechanism in parliament (or congress), and make it possible to debate and amend all legislation proposals. Extend parliament (or congress) opening hours and video-conference services to facilitate this.

- Make senior civil servants and advisors responsible for the advice and information they provide to Ministers and for the tasks they undertake as civil servants. Ministers should not be punished for the mistakes and errors of senior civil servants and advisors.

- New laws compelling all political parties and individual politicians to publish fully audited annual accounts. This would incomes and expenditures and balance sheet items.

- Implement a gender quota for woman of 33% for all political parties and for the parliament (or congress) and all city councils and town councils. Women need to be included more in politics in order to balance it properly.

- New independent private body for mid level and high level appointments of all public servants. This would be subject by oversight by a special parliamentary (or congressional) committee.

3. **Necessary Reforms in Policing and Legal System to Ensure Honesty, Integrity, and Accountability and Adherence to Best International Practises**

The following link is to a Questionnaire which should be filled out by all victims of crime and corruption. These questions and their answers will provide the data which can be used to devise, design and implement reforms for any Police force, and for the Courts and Legal system. http://www.healingcentres.org/victim.doc (Can be found on Internet and the Internet Archive)

4. One permanent Parliamentary committee with legal powers to compel attendance by individuals. These committees would have powers to demand attendance, overturn corrupt decisions, intervene where there is active or ongoing corruption, overturn active cases where corruption is present, rectify wrongs and send cases to the DPP for prosecution.

(i) Committee to investigate or expose corruption, abuses, incompetence and misconduct in the police, Ombudsman body, DPP office, the executive, the judiciary and the legal system and the press and media.

(ii) This committee could liaise and coordinate with the Anti Corruption Agency and Special Inquiries mentioned above and be part of the Checks and Balances system.

5. In Ireland and other countries, Constitutional amendment to make the Senate a democratic institution which represents all the people of Ireland. One candidate per county, with Dublin entitled to 4 candidates due to its population size. To ensure a vigorous, insightful and intellectual debating environment in the Senate, especially with regard to important legislation regarding the people's rights, all candidates for the Senate would have to have a degree from a University or Institute of Technology.

6. Campaign Finance

The major political parties and independents should be given media credits, which would entitle them to free equal air time on commercial television stations, the radio, the press and media and major Internet stations during election time, which could range from 7 months prior to the election to 1 month prior to it, depending on the country. Furthermore the government could give a grant to major political parties and independents to assist with the costs of campaigning during elections. The government could raise this money by levying high taxes on campaign funding by corporations, banks and individuals, lobbying, lobbyists, and campaign adds on television, radio and the newspapers and on posters and billboards. The more lobbyists and advertisers spend, the more tax there would be for government to deploy to level the playing field for all candidates. This would bring more fairness and equity into politics and reduce the amount of money required for election.

7. Government by Decree or Government by Consensus : Dictatorship or Democracy

There is a choice between a narrow government dominated by a prime minister and his advisors and lobbyists which impose their own narrow views on the cabinet and everybody else in parliament (or Congress) through the party whip system OR a government dominated by democratic participation by elected representatives and the will of the ordinary voters and the reaching of a consensus on issues. The former is dictatorial in nature and often leads to rash, unpopular, poorly considered, and ineffective solutions which serve the narrow interests of a prime minister, special interests and lobbyists. This dictatorship posing as democracy common in Ireland, Britain and other European countries and North America has led to disastrous political decisions including the enrichment of crooks and fraudsters during speculative bubbles, political corruption costing billions of euros / dollars, financial crashes costing trillions of euros, and destructive bailouts of gamblers and fraudsters and accompanying austerity policies and cutbacks. While the latter, government by consensus, could produce well thought out solutions which integrate many different aspects and important points, and express the will of the people and would generally prove quite effective. The dictatorial party whip system needs to be abolished and replaced by government by consensus or government by the will of the people which would directly engage and have the support of the vast majority of the parliament (85% or more) and of ordinary voters, the people, on new laws, amendments, policies and budgets, especially controversial laws. This would involve and empower both the entire parliament and ordinary voters in law making. This would act as a safeguard against the dictatorship and tyranny of special interests and protect the freedoms and democratic rights of all citizens. This may involve changes to party policies, parliamentary rules and laws and constitutions.

8. **Direct Democracy**

    Put Direct Democracy provisions into the Constitution and laws of all countries. Switzerland, California and some US states could service as role models for direct democracy. This direct democracy will encompass the following

a. Make all national politicians and local politicians accountable to their constituents and provide for recall of politicians if they break their pledges, promises and agreements with their constituents or the people. This recall would include the politician being legally recalled, losing office and a fresh new election being held in his / her constituency. The politician would have the option to stand again in this election. Politicians must serve the people and the nation, and the people must no longer serve the politicians and beg for favours off them. Similar systems exist in Switzerland and California and 18 other US states. Promises by politicians to their constituents and to all voters is a Social Contract, not a means to lie to and deceive voters, and to serve wealthy, privileged interests and lobbyists.

b. Referendums for Constitutional amendments proposed by parliament and for laws and treaties passed by trading bloc laws

c. Referendums where a certain percentage of the population signs a petition calling for the changing of a certain law or abolition of a law. In small countries this could be set at 250,000 signatures and for large countries a multiple of this number. This would apply to national government, regional government and local government.

d. Referendums based on power of initiative, where ordinary members of the public could make proposals for (i) a new law (ii) new constitutional provision or amendment and on gaining a certain number of signatures, the government would be forced to hold a referendum. In small countries this could be set at 250,000 signatures and for large countries a multiple of this number. This would apply to national government, regional government and local government.

e. For cases of serious state corruption where the government refuses to remove a corrupt person from office ; this could be a judge, a policeman, a politician, a prosecutor, a registrar, a state lawyer, a civil servant, then the people should have the power to force a referendum on this matter after gaining so many signatures demanding it. The referendum would decide whether to fire or continue employing this corrupt official. In small countries this could be set at 250,000 signatures and for large countries a multiple of this number. This would really empower the ordinary people in their struggle against certain corrupt elements of the state.

f. Provisions made for citizens assemblies, comprised of ordinary people, voters, to inform and guide local government, regional government and national government, and have an input into law making, policies, budgets and constitutional changes. This ties into the proposals in point 6 above. This would give ordinary people, voters, a direct input into local, regional and national government decision making and law making.

g. Special provisions should be made in referendums and laws governing them to protect the rights of minorities and disadvantaged social groups so that the 'tyranny of the majority' is not imposed upon minorities, a nation, a region or locality. Fundamental democratic freedoms and rights must be protected and be matched with their responsibilities.

h. New technologies should be used to allow greater participation and greater deliberation by all the ordinary people, the voters, in a direct democracy environment. Advanced, modern technologies could more fully inform the voters and provide forums for reasoned, intelligent, rational and logical debate on issues, a deeper analysis of causality or causes and effects, and respect for different viewpoints. Extremist viewpoints should be carefully analysed and the defects and flaws of the extremist position presented to all persons. This would act against the extremists. Technology should be used to inform and for the highest good of all persons, and enable all persons to see that their rights come with responsibilities.

i. All referendums and elections should have a paper trail and a comprehensive auditing system. Voters should vote on paper and keep a record of that vote via photographing it (via smart phone) or photocopying it, as electronic voting is susceptible to fraud and rigging, as proved by the testimonies of software experts in the recent past. Political corruption is a serious problem in western developed countries and developing countries and one needs to have a paper based system which can be properly audited, with paper trails and accompanying monitoring and oversight systems.

j. Over time this direct democracy would change and evolve and empower the ordinary people of a nation, the voters, giving them a greater say in the formation and passing of laws, policies, budgets, constitutions and constitutional amendments. This would be pure democracy, the will of the people expressed, the great ideal of the Enlightenment, the people empowered and respected as sovereign.

9. End the super delegate system and electoral colleges system in the USA and replace it with the popular vote of the people. This will require Constitutional changes. Party leaders and potential parliamentary candidates and local government candidates should be elected by the ordinary people of the party not by super delegates (as in USA) or appointed by senior party officials or party leaders. Appointments, privileged delegates, elitist control and secret deals always lead to corruption and this corruption infects a political party and sets it against the interests of the people, the country, and against democracy.

10. Impose term limits on politicians so that they do not become career politicians who can be bought and corrupted.

11. Representative democracy needs to be balanced by greater direct democracy at all levels of society, and in organisations, parties, structures and mechanisms. Over time representative democracy has become corrupted and this corruption is at its worst in federalist government structures where powerful special interests and lobbyists control the centre and its many states and other countries. Representative democracy in this context means representing the interests of powerful lobbyists and special interests and the big banks, and engaging in the 'pay to play' system of corruption. This corruption and corrupt laws and policies are undemocratically enforced on peoples thorough a

hierarchal system. At the bottom of this hierarchy (or pyramid) are the police and courts holding a gun to the heads of ordinary people, the voters, and enforcing corrupt laws, procedures, policies, activities, and system upon them. This is dictatorship and tyranny posing as democracy. The power must be restored to the people through direct democracy and the many checks and balances proposed in this book. Over time, greater and wider direct democracy and more accountability for representative democracy would reduce or eliminate the corruption and defects in representative democracy and provide a new system of constant vigilance for the protection and safeguarding of democracy, rights and freedoms.

12. All mid level and senior police officers should be subject to the same selection processes and rules and oversight as that for judges. Appointments should be fully independent of fellow police officers and politicians, and be fair, transparent and accountable. Procedures for removal of police officers should also follow this process. Political interference in policing and in criminal cases is a very serious threat to democracy, freedoms and due process in several countries, and needs to be ended.

13. The Police Commissioner or Head of a Police force in a country or state should be a civilian who is not a member of the police or judiciary. He or she should have some legal qualifications. And should be subject to the same selection processes and rules and oversight as that for judges. He / she would be independent fair, impartial and have no conflicts of interest. He / she would know the duties and responsibilities of the police and not be influenced by police officers. He / she would be accountable to the people as a whole and to Parliament / Congress, and this would be enforced through several checks and balances, the press and media, and the use of whistleblowers.

14. All lawyers should be held to a high standard of practise and behaviour. All attempts to deny justice or pervert justice or support lies and tampered evidence in court should be fully investigated by an oversight body. To ensure high standards, accountability, transparency, fairness and equity, lawyers involved in wrong doing should face removal of licence by a panel consisting of 25% representatives of the Law Society, and the other 75% being a supreme court judge, University experts in Constitutional law, and cross party politicians from parliament and representatives of human rights bodies in open hearings

15. All attempts to microchip people should be opposed and be banned by laws and Constitutional amendments. The microchipping of people would lead to abuses of rights, further abuses of power, more corruption, the destruction of freedoms, and the development of a totalitarian state.

16. All Admiralty laws, rules and customs should be immediately banned and removed from courts on the land. No person should be subject to Admiralty law in courts on the land. The sovereignty of the individual as affirmed in national Constitutions must be given recognition in courts, and courts must give precedence to Constitutional rights and human rights first and then to parliamentary laws, statutes and common law.

17. All Persons requiring state assistance or a lawyer in court cases should have their assets and income assessed before being given assistance by the state. If assets are illegally seized by another party then that party must give full account of this and provide funding for legal assistance of the defendant in court. If the defendant has no assets and income, then lawyers should be contracted from the private sector and payment by the state made in the form of a fee and tax credits. The public defender system in the USA and other countries is a disaster and has been under funded, under staffed, under resourced, and underperforming for decades resulting in the undermining of the Constitutional and legal rights of many people and the denial of due process under law.

18. The immunity from prosecution for bank executives of 'systemic' banks, and employees and executives of the ESM, BIS, FSB and IMF should be ended in all countries. This would make all banks accountable and subject to the law, and enforce 'moral hazard' on these institutions and employees. Rights come with responsibilities.

19. There are many excellent grassroots organisations working for justice in countries around the world. Parliament / Congress, legal systems and state bodies and community bodies need to work with organisations such as **Integrity Ireland, and Justice4All, the Innocence Project** and other grassroots organisations to identify abuses of laws, the legal system and policing, and the denial of human rights and legal and Constitutional rights to ordinary people. And remedy them via enforcement of laws, enactment of new laws, amendment of existing laws, overturning of corrupt convictions, re-investigation of corrupt cases, the firing of Police, judges, and corrupt and negligent state workers, prosecuting and disbarring corrupt solicitors, and use of legal and Constitutional provisions to protect citizen's rights.

20. We live in democracies where the police should serve the people, the nation, and this should be overseen by independent authorities and state authorities to ensure accountability, justice and integrity. This is an important part of checks and balances and systems of oversight within democracies. We are seeing increasing evidence of police misconduct and abuse of members of the public in many countries. A minority wrongly believe that a uniform gives them the right to dominate, oppress, mock, slander and intimidate their fellow citizens. The police shootings in the USA, police brutality in several countries, the police corruption and abuses in several EU countries, the misuse of police information, police data protection and resources in social environments such as bars, pubs, nightclubs, restaurants, sports clubs, insurance businesses, private investigator businesses, etc., and the disrespect of victims of crime and members of the public points to very serious problems which need to be addressed and rectified. Some cases have come to prominence in Ireland in recent times. They include the Maurice McCabe case and Wilson case and McBrearty case in Ireland and many other cases show that some police like to abuse their position and authority while working and while out socialising. In addition to police misconduct at work, some like to mock, belittle, laugh at, gossip about, slander and intimidate other persons while they are out socialising in bars, pubs, restaurants, nightclubs, sporting venues, live concerts, theatres, etc. Even victims of crime have suffered from this abuse by some Police. This is unacceptable behaviour and has created a lot of distrust between Police and the general public.

Give the Police Ombudsman full legal powers to conduct many types of undercover operations, using human intelligence and technical intelligence, and use whistleblowers to uncover hidden corruption, incompetence, abuses, misconduct, cover ups, and lies by Police, and use evidence from Commissions and Tribunals, and use exposure of lies by criminals and other parties which impact on police investigations. The Police Ombudsman should be given high court powers or delegated such by the high court. Police Ombudsman investigators must not be Police, they must have experience in policing duties in other countries or in military or intelligence work or in high level investigations abroad. Use of checklists to ensure all personnel comply with best international practises and regulations. New laws to make this Police Ombudsman evidence admissible in court.

21. National policing should be separated from intelligence services. National security should not be used as a smokescreen to prevent investigation of police wrong doing and corruption

22. Too many victims of crime have been denied justice as a result of the lies and perjuries of criminals. Most criminals lie to police, to lawyers and to courts and are never punished for this lying. Their lying is not exposed through undercover work, use of spies and informers, breaking of false alibis, and detailed forensics. In most cases these lies are accepted as facts and truths in court or ignored by police and the legal system, and victims are deprived of justice. A Police Intelligence unit should exist in all police regions or divisions. This would consist of full time police undercover teams and agents who would use undercover methods, human intelligence and electronic intelligence to uncover truths, facts, evidence and combat the use of lies, perjury and dishonesty by criminals. New laws and policies to give these police teams powers to use whistleblowers, informants and make extensive use of electronic surveillance, computer and mobile phone surveillance and human surveillance. Use of checklists to ensure all police comply with best international practises in covert investigations. Accompanied by new laws to make this evidence admissible in courts and punish lying to police and courts, and oversight of this by the Department of Justice, the Parliament, the judiciary, and a free press and media.

23. Gather sworn affidavits, sworn in the presence of a lawyer, a witness, and police officer, from defendants and plaintiffs. These will be presented in the Inquiry and the court case. Compel the telling of the truth at the Inquiry and court case, and remind all participants of the crime of perjury and that perjury will be prosecuted. Seperate investigations and court proceedings for perjury should begin once a perjury is discovered in the Inquiry or court case. All perjuries must be prosecuted.

24. Police who lie to courts should also be made subject to perjury charges and prosecution in court and jail. The law needs to be applied equally to everyone. This may involve the Police Ombudsman and Anti Corruption Agency to uncover hidden facts and evidence.

25. All legal and criminal cases where the police refused to investigate properly or were negligent in their duty or accepted lies and perjury as facts, and cases which were allowed to fester over time with damage to victims of crime should be stopped, overturned, declared null and void, dismissed and later re-opened by other police in other jurisdictions in another province and overseen by the Police Ombudsman, a Barrister and a senior officer from the Department of Justice. The Anti Corruption agency mentioned above should also be allowed to liaise in these type of investigations to uncover corruption. If required, the Circuit Court Criminal Inquiry should be utilised. New laws

need to be enacted to ensure that innocent victims of crime should not be hounded or punished by police and / or criminals.

26. For controversial cases, use of an independent 'People's Advocate' when giving statements to the police. This 'People's Advocate' would act as an independent witness to protect against abuses of the policing system and legal system. This 'People's Advocate' would receive a thorough education in the legal, Constitutional and human rights of citizens, and swear an oath of duty before a High Court judge, and be legally and financially accountable for this oath, and he / she would sign the Official Secrets Act and be bound by it. Integrity, honesty, transparency and accountability would be essential to this new system of 'People's Advocate'.

27. **Mandatory Sentences, Repeat Offenders and New Panels for Assessing Mitigating Factors**

In 2012 in Ireland a man with 438 criminal convictions, 50 for burglary and some for road traffic offences killed a man while drunk driving. In 2017 he was given another soft sentence by the court. In most developed countries one sees criminals with 30, 40, 50, 100, 200 or more criminal convictions often for serious crimes free to roam the streets and continue committing crimes. Most judges are far too liberal, smug and tolerant and their soft sentencing aids and abets these criminals in their crimes. This corrupted legal system is the root cause of most crimes in developed countries especially liberal countries. New laws and Constitutional provisions need to be introduced to deal with this problem. Mandatory sentences need to be introduced for all serious crimes so as ensure consistency in court decisions and bring accountability and order to all courts. Mitigating factors would be weighed up and determined by an expert panel of judges and professors of law, and mandatory sentences reduced or not reduced by them, prior to being served.

Those criminals with 4 or more convictions for serious crimes would receive an increase of 33% sentencing time, in addition to the mandatory time, for every crime committed thereafter and given no parole and no early release. They would also be denied community service orders and suspended sentences. Those criminals with 6 or more convictions for petty crimes (or misdemeanours) would receive an increase of 25% sentencing time, in addition to the mandatory time, for every crime committed thereafter and given no parole or early release. They would also be denied community service orders and suspended sentences. This would impose an increasing burden on repeat criminals as they commit more crimes and strongly discourage them from committing crime over time. It would strongly discourage repeat offences, reduce the workload of the police and the courts, and facilitate lower crime rates. The beneficial effects for societies worldwide would be enormous and would create more civilised, peaceful, productive and orderly societies. This would be fairer than the "3 strikes and you are out" law in the USA, where persons can get life imprisonment for petty crime or minor crime or a misdemeanour.

28. For road traffic offences the state should have the power to seize and take permanent ownership of the vehicle after so many serious traffic offences, this could be a realistic figure of 10 or more serious offences. And to jail persons for a mandatory 7 years in the case of causing the deaths of others in road accidents, through drink driving or speeding or reckless driving. This would help end the nonsense of judges applying unfair and inequitable sentences and bringing themselves and the legal system into disrepute.

29. All soft sentences and lenient sentences by judges should be challenged by the DPP or Public Prosecutor. Victims and victim families should also be given legal powers to challenge soft sentences and lenient sentences and be given the right to appeal them to a higher court or court of appeal. Provision should be made for courts to consider legal precedents in the country and other countries and case studies concerning sentencing for certain crimes. These could be used to overturn soft sentences or lenient sentences and ensure justice under law.

30. **Fines**

    Most offenders don't bother paying their fines, as it is rare for court officials and police to check up on unpaid fines. Fines worth billions of euros have not been paid in European countries and North America. Many fines have been unpaid for several years. This provides an incentive for some criminals to keep breaking the law. There is a need to computerise the Fine system in every jurisdiction and coordinate it via secure communications and a centralized national database . Provide a financial incentive for police to collect fines, such as setting up a special police team every week to go hunting for fines. Police would receive bonuses for every 10 fines collected.

31. End laws such as the Probation act and the Court Poor Box which enable wealthy and powerful people to escape prosecution and jail for serious offences in courts.

32. **Bail Laws**

    A high and growing percentage of crimes are committed while an offender is out on bail. This defeats the whole purpose of the bail laws, and places law abiding citizens at unnecessary and unjustifiable risk. There is a need for reform of the bail laws. Bail should be automatically denied to those criminals who are any one of the following (a) a flight risk (b) accused of a violent crime, including harassment, stalking and threats against another person, and have 4 or more serious criminal convictions or 6 or more petty criminal convictions. This specific mandatory bail law needs to be passed which would be binding on all courts.

33. **Gun Rights & Gun Responsibilities**

Gun rights come with responsibilities. In fact, all rights have certain responsibilities attached to them in order for society to function in a civilized manner. Every person who desires to own a gun should undergo the following:

a) get an independent psychiatric and psychological evaluation by a psychiatrist and psychologist appointed by the state before getting the licence. If the person is mentally ill, the gun licence application should be revoked and blocked. If there is any question raised about the mental health of the person, the state should carry out their own independent evaluation of the person after the licence is granted.

b) a gun owner with a licence should be required a get an independent psychiatric and psychological evaluation every year. The state would choose the psychiatrist and psychologist. If the person is mentally ill, the gun licence should be revoked and the gun seized. Healthy people can become mentally ill over time due to adverse life events and its important for law enforcement agencies to monitor this.

c) the state should regularly monitor gun owners to see if they have got serious criminal convictions or developed a psychiatric illness. This would disqualify him / her.

d) guns should be locked in cabinets and the keys kept secure at all times so as to prevent children getting them. Regular checks by state inspectors would help enforce this.

e) any person convicted in the past of a serious crime would be automatically blocked from having a gun and gun licence.

f) illegal possession of a gun should carry the same sentence as one for manslaughter.

g) illegal arms sales should carry the same sentence as one for manslaughter. Murders or injuries resulting from such illegal arms sales should result in criminal cases and civil cases ; the civil cases involving the suing of the owner, the seller and the manufacturer of the gun.

h) mandatory courses on gun responsibilities in schools and colleges and for all gun owners. Personal Responsibility courses could be integrated into these courses. All gun owners should be required by law to take these courses.

34. Police acting as Public Prosecutor in court

A Police Inspector is not sufficiently qualified and experienced enough and not independent or impartial enough to represent the Public Prosecutor (DPP) in District court cases. Only a qualified and experienced lawyer or barrister trained specially for the Public Prosecutor (DPP) job should be appointed to represent the Public Prosecutor (DPP) in District court cases. This person should not be known to the victim or alleged criminal. This would ensure impartiality.

35. Magistrates system

The magistrates system in Britain and the Commonwealth needs to be abolished as they lack the legal qualifications and legal experience to hear court cases. They should be replaced by judges and subject to the rigorous selection processes and oversight above. See the book 'The Hidden Barrister'.

36. When the police come upon a crime scene they must immediately photograph it, including all injuries suffered and all damage witnessed and all witnesses and bystanders. This would be in addition to the personal video camera carried by all police. This evidence must be preserved in a secure area in a police station or state facility. If evidence is lost or tampered with this must be prosecuted as a serious crime in court.

37. Witness tampering and witness intimidation by the police or other parties must be classified as a serious crime and prosecuted in court.

38. Manslaughter pleas in cases of murder, often first degree murder, need to be made illegal in all courts. Too many murder cases have been misrepresented as manslaughter in court, often through the use of lies, perjuries, manipulation and deceptions. This needs to end and the grounds for rejecting false pleas of manslaughter should be more clearly defined in new laws and Constitutional provisions.

39. Contract murders should carry a mandatory 30 year jail sentence with no sentence remission and no early release.

40. All victims of crime and their families should be informed of the date and location of any appeals by the convicted criminal so that they can attend the appeals court case. The victim's family should be given the legal power to appeal a criminal court decision to the Supreme Court. This would ensure

that justice is done and is seen to be done, and it would end the current system where appeals are held without the knowledge of the victims and their families and lies and perjuries presented to the appeals court and wrongful and unjust decisions made by the appeals court.

41. ASBO's should be abolished as they have failed to deter young criminals. Young offenders should be subject to the same laws regarding anti social behavior, and instances of violence as adult offenders. Soft sentences should be abolished for anti social behavior and mandatory jail sentences enforced for 4 or more cases of anti social behaviour.

42. Property related crime involving tenants and landlords should be dealt with in Rental Property Courts. These would replace organizations such as the PRTB in Ireland which has been brought into serious disrepute. Crimes and breaches of regulations have gone unpunished for years and lies and perjuries accepted as 'facts' for too long in PRTB Tribunals. Rental Property Courts would have the same powers and jurisdiction as a district court and would make court orders to compel a landlord or tenant to do something within a specified period of time. Roaring at a judge and behaving in a threatening, abusive and intimidating manner in such courts would carry a mandatory 21 day jail sentence for contempt on the first offence and this would increase to 42 days for further such offences.

43. Community police should receive special training in people management skills, communication skills, group and community dynamics, advanced problem solving, psychology, and conflict resolution, and also martial arts training up to black belt level. This training would enable them to establish friendly and cordial relations with people living in the community, gain the trust and respect of people living in the community, and handle problems as they arise.
They would attend community meetings and community forums and work with community leaders and groups to (i) identify problems and areas where crime and anti social behaviour are rife (ii) devise solutions including effective evidence gathering and prosecutions in court (iii) provide intelligence to other police units and assist them (iv) resolve problems at family and community level (v) provide feedback to the community (vi) improve service over time (vii) assess police performance in liaison with the community and improve it over time (viii) help out in the community.

44. All persons given the following by courts or legal systems should be electronically tagged. These tags would have GPS tracking facilities and could be picked up at airports, sea ports, train stations and bus stations and border crossings.

- those persons given bail

- those persons bound to the peace for a specified time period. Tagging for that time period

- those persons banned from driving for a certain period of time

- those persons given suspended sentences. Tagging for a specified duration

- those persons given community service

This would enable the police to identify the locations of these individuals and establish if they were at a crime scene or in a moving vehicle or in the presence of criminals.

45. Remand institutions should be built to house persons refused bail by courts. These persons should be considered innocent until proven guilty, and should be kept in separate institutions to convicted prisoners who are jailed. The presumption of innocence lies at the heart of justice and this needs to be affirmed through the building of remand institutions which would be completely different to prisons.

46. **Court Procedure**

- Changes are required to court procedure in many countries. Under the current system, the criminal's legal team can attack the victim in court and present irrelevant and slanderous material to undermine and destroy the victim. But, the prosecution cannot mention the criminal's prior convictions, criminal past and bad character in court. This works to protect the criminal and to undermine the victim, and to pervert the course of justice in court. New laws and court procedures should prevent the criminal's legal team from attacking, slandering, defaming and undermining the victim in court.

- In countries with long waiting times for court cases, the government should immediately implement a 24 hour court system, 6 days a week. This would include night courts and day courts, and would involve hiring extra judges and court personnel. This would end the scenario of "justice delayed is justice denied".

47. Police forces in most countries need to be increased and also supplemented by more civilians working within police stations and use of the army and special forces for preventing gang crime and

gun crime. Increase police force numbers in countries where crime rates are high and/or rising quickly, and try to exceed international averages for police numbers per capita. Employ more civilians within police stations, up to 30% of the Police force numbers, to carry out administrative duties and paperwork for Police. This would enable thousands more Police to be put on the beat and patrolling the streets, neighbourhoods, communities, rural areas, and known trouble spots. Allow soldiers from the army and special forces up to 33% of the Police Force numbers to accompany and assist the police on the beat, patrolling neighbourhoods, late night road blocks, tracking criminals and other police activities. This would provide the necessary armed force to meet threats and other problems.

48. Increase police funding in all developed countries up to optimum levels, prioritising expansion of resources such as cars, police equipment, computers, electronic and technology products, personal or wearable police cameras, cctv cameras and other cameras, secure communications, better forensic labs, new facilities, training and upgrading of skills at home and abroad, stab proof vests, tear gas, riot gear, dogs, etc.
International best practises in policing could be attained via links to top police force agencies worldwide eg. FBI, Scotland Yard, French Gendarmes etc. and the taking of online courses and offline courses with these institutions, and rigorous project work and examinations.

49. Use of statistics and data analytics at regional level and national level to determine areas of high criminal activity and the deployment of additional police and military resources to reduce this. Monitoring of this to assess effectiveness.

50. Use of data analytics and whistleblowers to determine points of failure and points of ineffectiveness in the police, crime detection rates, police methods, the courts, the legal system and laws. This would form the basis for reforms of the police, the judiciary, the courts, the legal system and the laws.

51. Thorough and continuous reforms of the legal system, the judiciary and courts, the policing system and Police Ombudsman to eradicate corruption, incompetence, misconduct, abuses and cover ups. Use of best international practises by all police, judges and legal system personnel and the enforcement of compulsory ethics for these parties and the regular use of dismissal for breaches of these ethics.

52. Harassment and Cease and Desist Orders

All countries should make it possible for district courts and circuit courts to issue 'Cease and Desist Orders' in cases where there is clear evidence of harassment of an innocent person. This should be for non family members, strangers and former friends. Breaking of such court orders would carry an automatic jail sentence. This sentence could increase in proportion to the amount of times the court order is broken. This offence would be separate to the criminal offence of harassment which would carry it's own set of legal penalties.

53. Hate crimes against disabled people

The Department of Justice (in all countries) should include a special section in the crime statistics detailing crimes against disabled people. Special forms should be distributed to every police station to collect this data. Hate crimes against disabled people should be a separate category from ordinary crime and anti-social behaviour where a disabled person is a victim, and should be classified as 'serious crime' where violence against disabled people has taken place or is threatened and this is accompanied by harassment. Court 'cease and desist orders' should be applied in such cases of harassment, so as to provide a basic level of protection for these vulnerable people.

54. Youth Diversion Programmes were originally set up to deal with young offenders, but have proved mostly ineffective. Youth Diversion Programmes should be abolished and replaced with **Youth Responsibility Programmes** involving the police, young offenders and their parents, psychologists and psychiatrists, religious leaders in the community, community leaders, victims of the young offenders, and representatives from employers and training organisations – the emphasis for young people would be on personal responsibilities, social responsibilities, the importance of parental responsibilities, the value of hard work and contributing positively to society, developing one's talents to the highest level, personal and family relationships based on respect and trust, spiritual values, civic responsibilities and the ideals put forward by leading psychologists such as Dr. Jordan Peterson in Canada. This focus on responsibilities would help redirect many young people away from crime and into other positive, uplifting, law abiding, productive and socially useful activities.

55. Early intervention Programmes in many countries have helped family development. These need to be converted into Family Responsibility Programmes where both parents and children are taught responsibility, extending from ages 1 - 7. They encourage the parents to discharge their parental responsibilities such as feeding and clothing their children, getting them ready for school in the

mornings, helping with homework, teaching children respect for themselves and others, encouraging love, respect and tolerance in the family home and in the child's development, positive male and female role models, teaching them basic civic duties, getting them involved in positive activities in the community, encouraging involvement in sports, hobbies, dancing, music, the arts, charity work, and positive living, etc.. Social workers, family resource centres, marriage guidance counsellors, psychologists and psychiatrists, community leaders, religious leaders, community police, sports stars, sports organisations, and community centres can all play a role in this. This can break the cycle of anti-social behaviour running in families across generations.

56. Marriage guidance counsellors and money and budgeting advice experts should be used by the state and/or religious organisations in deprived economic areas to assist the Programmes mentioned above, and provide greater family stability. The state could fully subsidise it or partially subsidise it. This in turn would help reduce young offender crime rates and later adult crime rates.

57. Crèches could be provided in special rooms in community centres and community owned buildings in working class areas and deprived economic areas. These could be operated privately with crèche owners paying a low rent to the community centre management committee. The provision of crèches at low cost to users would enable many women to re-join the work force and earn extra money for their family. This would greatly benefit single mothers who by re-joining the workforce would be able to improve their standard of living, their social connections, their dignity and their sense of being a participating partner in the development of the economy and society. They would also be strong role models for their children. This would be an example of communities working together for the betterment of all. This would pay back social dividends in the form of greater social cohesion and lower crime rates in the future.

58. The great success of the regeneration of Fatima Mansions and Ballymun in Dublin in Ireland should be used as examples for community building and regeneration in deprived inner cities and towns in countries worldwide. Communities everywhere can learn much from the recent changes in Fatima Mansions and Ballymun.

59. All police must be required to wear small video cameras with microphones to record all contacts with the general public and with each other. This would provide accurate accounts of what exactly happens when Police interact with the public. Too many lies have been told by police and non police and criminals, and too many innocent people have been destroyed by this. Video storage could be provided in police stations or online through the state purchasing mass storage online.

These cameras and microphones would enforce honesty, integrity, the truth and fairness and encourage Police and non Police to behave well.

60. All police interviews and taking of statements must be video recorded and audio recorded, with the defendant also given the right to record the interview. And photocopies of statements given to the person interviewed by the police and video recordings and audio recordings provided on request.

61. All court cases need to be video recorded and audio recorded so as to ensure that proper procedures are followed and people are treated with fairness, respect and dignity. These videos could be used as evidence in appeals, judicial reviews, criminal cases, civil cases, and circuit court inquiries. Any interference with these recordings by state employees should be classified as perjury and perversion of justice and prosecuted as such.

62. All crime cases should be given a unique number, the police numbers of those police involved, an estimated date of completion, a progress report schedule for regularly updating victims of crime (this could be once every 3 weeks), actions taken, video recording references of police interaction with victims, witnesses, criminals and members of the public, intelligence or covert channels and the information obtained to counteract lies and perjuries, the reference numbers for evidence storage, and the results achieved including successful or non successful prosecutions, and lessons to be learned for future cases, and the application of these lessons in future cases. This will help protect innocent members of the public from criminality, corruption and abuses of power.

63. Extensive use of Ethics and Codes of Behaviour for Police and the Police Ombudsman built into Checklists and a military style of discipline and integrity will be need to be implemented as soon as possible.

64. Get all Police and all Police Ombudsman personnel, all DPP personnel and all judges to swear an oath in court, in the presence of a judge and independent witnesses, that they will not engage in any form of corruption and abuses of power, and that if they do, they will resign or be fired. Breaches of sworn oaths constitute perjury under the law.

65. The illegal leaking of police information should be viewed as treason under the law and carry a mandatory 4 year jail sentence. There is a long history of confidential police information being sold to insurance companies, private investigators journalists, criminals, business people and members of the public. In some cases the information is provided free via gossip in bars and nightclubs. Leakers should also be liable for slander and defamation under the law.

66. Build more prisons in European countries. This would take a lot of criminals off the streets and help reduce crime levels and the pressures and stresses on Police, DPP officials, courts, and judges. These new prison spaces would facilitate tougher sentences and mandatory sentences by the courts, and provide more effective deterrents against crime. These prisons need to be places of incarceration, rehabilitation and reform of character. Prisoners should be given plenty of medical and psychological support and programmes to help them change their thinking, mindsets, behaviour and relationships with other people. The importance of respect for oneself and for others, one's responsibilities, self discipline, tolerance of others, ethics and morality, rights with responsibilities, hope, encouragement of spiritual practises and values, and ambition to become a productive member of society would be constantly reinforced through these educational programmes and the prison environment. These would be the core of rehabilitation and reform of character. And they would be supplemented with training and education programmes to improve skills and qualifications, and exercise and nutritional programmes to improve general health and help them get back into the workforce when released. If necessary, extensive use of medication should be used to sedate violent aggressive and disruptive prisoners and provide a means for them to reform their character. Post prison support should include these aforementioned psychological and educational programmes, and help prisoners find housing, health support, training and education, employment and re-integrate with society and the workforce.

67. The drugs gang warfare is out of control in most countries. A war, involving guns, bombs and various weapons, is being carried out against innocent civilians. This type of war against ordinary people is new in developed countries and developing countries. It is a war against the people of the nation and most of the people are not armed and defenceless. Wars are fought by the military not by the police. Governments will need to deploy the military to take over the investigation, arrests and prosecution of these criminals and crimes. This will involve the use of court martials and military prisons. This will need to involve special forces units of the military and also regular army and naval units to constantly combat this war. Ordinary army and naval units, including marines, will need to receive additional training to prepare them for this type of warfare. The police could play a minor supporting role and assist the military in this and work alongside elite military units. Powers of arrest and detention need to be given to the military, under the supervision of top military officers and senior police officers. This will involve the deployment of thousands of troops in their own countries, and a 24/7 operation, non-stop for several years if necessary to end this war. All

avenues of corruption of public officials, government bodies, and politicians will need to be investigated by the combined efforts of military intelligence, national intelligence services and police intelligence. Any top government officials involved in corruption with these criminal gangs must be given long jail sentences, be made subject to charges of treason, and sued for compensation by the victims of crime in courts.

68. Freedom of the Press and Responsibility of the Press

The increasing concentration of press and media ownership by fewer and fewer people presents a serious threat to democracy. This needs to be halted and reversed. Reforms are detailed in Chapter 3 of this book.

69. All immigrants into countries should be compelled to read and sign a social contract detailing their responsibilities and rights. Responsibilities should take precedence over rights, and those who engage in serious crime, terrorism, plots or planning of such, promoting religious extremism or racism should be prosecuted by the courts and sentenced and then deported after their sentence.

70. Make voting in national elections and local elections a legal requirement with fines for not voting. This would encourage all citizens to take a more active interest and part in politics. This applies in countries such as Australia, Belgium and Luxemburg.

71. A reformed International Criminal Court with new powers to bring charges and prosecutions against all criminals, including powerful politically connected people in western countries. This should ensure that no individual, politician, ex government minister, ex leader is above the law. It would have the power to hand down multiple life sentences to be served consecutively, which may involve serving a full 100 year or 200 year jail sentences with no parole.

72. Countries burdened by unelected royalty and aristocracy should remove the powers and privileges of these institutions, abolish them, and establish democratic institutions to replace them. All national institutions should be freely elected and representative of the people, and be accountable to the people. The era of monarchy, imperialism and class distinctions is over and finished, and this needs to be more widely acknowledged.

73. Limit the number of directorships of public and private companies a person can hold to 5. This would break up the 'golden circle' of a small number of persons holding directorships in many companies, and using this to acquire excessive salaries and bonuses, and other corrupt or unethical activities.

74. New legally binding standards for planning to prevent corruption. Planners and Planning departments should be subject to the Public Sector Reforms mentioned in sections above. They should be held legally and financially accountable for corrupt planning decisions and corruption. Give the National Spatial Strategy a Constitutional status.

75. Ban all city councillors and town councillors from working as auctioneers, property developers, property consultants or planning consultants while they are councillors. This would prevent conflicts of interest and corruption from arising.

76. New criminal laws and amendments to increase the criminal penalties for white collar crime, including new custodial sentences and increases of existing ones, to strongly discourage such crimes.

77. **Establish a Democratic Republic with a Separation of Church and State**

    The Ryan Report and the Murphy Report in Ireland outlined the dangers of religious control of educational institutions funded by the state and religious control of politicians and governments. And the dangers of lack of accountability, responsibility transparency, regulation and oversight. Laws and regulations will need to be amended and introduced to bring about a clear separation of church and state in Ireland, and end religious discrimination in education and in the healthcare sector. Freedom of religion means that no one religion should dominate the state and government, and state funded public bodies, and dominate other religions. This is important in the multi-cultural Ireland of today. There should be non sectarian (non religious) ownership and management of all public (state) schools and public hospitals in Ireland. And changes to laws and regulations to make teacher training colleges non sectarian, ending discrimination against non catholics. These primary and secondary schools, teacher colleges and hospitals all receive public (state) funding and should be open to all members of the public. Private hospitals should be prevented, under law, from discriminating against people on the grounds of religion, race and political beliefs. Religious classes should be conducted outside school hours and supervised by priests or pastors or rabbis or gurus or mullahs, etc. depending on one's religion. This is a basic requirement of republican democracy.

78. End religious discrimination in employment and bring these laws into line with the Constitutions in countries

79. Make those people and religious organisations and non religious organisations responsible for child abuse financially liable for compensation payments to victims and their families. International

organisations should be liable through their international headquarters, where their leaders or CEO's reside and work. The taxpayers should be not be held financially liable for this abuse. The taxpayers are being unjustly punished for the crimes and sins of very wealthy organisations and corrupt politicians and civil servants.

80. Amend the party whip system to make it possible for TD's (MP's) to vote against their own party or government on the grounds of conscience on certain limited issues. This is common in some other democracies and would encourage some freedom of expression within the party system. There are serious concerns that democracy itself can be undermined by dictatorial party leaders or a tiny group within a party, which can impose their own will on others and the majority through threats and intimidation, and that this may conflict with conscience, integrity, democratic rights, and the public interest.

81. **Corporate Governance**

Corporate governance laws should require all companies, businesses and charities and foundations to be independently audited and provide full financial reporting to investors and the public at regular intervals. Shareholders should be given more power over executive salaries and bonuses. During the boom prior to 2008, many bank executives and business executives paid themselves combined salaries, bonuses and share options of over €1 million per year. Average chief executive pay was over €1 million per year. Many executives had pensions worth millions of euros. In the USA many executives made 50 to 400 times more than ordinary workers in their business, which meant 50, 80, 100, 200 million dollars per year. Investment bankers made hundreds of millions of dollars per year. Were these people highly talented or scarce or worth it ? Many of them worked in banks and businesses which were bankrupt or going bankrupt. In the case of the banks, it was the taxpayers who had to bail them out. These highly paid executives were paid very well for failure. Use the tax system to make the maximum total salary a multiple of average industrial earnings. For example the maximum total salary (including bonuses) could be pegged at 20 times average industrial earnings. In 2015, this would be €750,000 per year. A tax rate of 100% could apply for salary amounts over this amount. This total salary would provide adequate incentives and would rise in line with rises in average industrial earnings and rises in national productivity.

Chapter 11   Social Inclusion : The Provision of Affordable Healthcare and Education, State Reforms, and Regeneration of Inner Cities & Regions

'We cannot solve our problems with the same thinking we used when we created them.'
Albert Einstein

The civil service and public service consists of hard working, decent and honourable people who work hard and provide good, useful and effective services for the general public. Most populations benefit directly and indirectly from this, and these services continue to be of strategic importance to nations. Yet the systems of government fail them and fail the people who use them, including members of the general public. There is a need for deep and far reaching reforms which address the chronic under funding of the civil service, the chronic under staffing in certain areas, the chronic under investment in key assets, in skilled staff and technologies, and the inefficiencies, waste, fraud, mismanagement and abuses which blight the civil service and state sector in many countries. There is also a vicious Neo Liberal economic policy in several countries which has aimed to starve the public services of basic and necessary investment so as to undermine them, close down or severely reduce public services, and turn public opinion against them. Though these same Neo Liberals are the strongest and most vocal supporters of spending trillions of taxpayer dollars on the military industrial complex, wars, regime changes, corporate subsidies and corporate welfare, the use of tax loopholes and havens, and the bail outs of banks, speculators and fraudsters ; all of which have robbed the taxpayers and led to vicious cutbacks in public services.

The Public Service and State Sector should be subject to the following reforms:

- **Strategic Funding of Public Services and the State sector**
  In most countries the government does not have the funding or "resources" to invest in modern, effective and efficient public services. They are starved of funding and this has produced disastrous

results. The massive national debt and high interest payments are responsible for this "lack of funding" for public services. There needs to be:

1. large scale write downs and write offs of national debt and the removal of bank, bondholders and speculators bailout debt from the national debt as proposed in Chapter 7. Monetisation of debt by central banks and compensation to governments for funding prior bail outs could provide the latter.

2. restore the money printing powers to governments and placing limitations of the scale of this as proposed in Chapter 7 and by MMT economists.

3. economic democracy as proposed in Chapters 7-11 to provide the high economic growth and the growth in tax revenues and incomes to fund a public services infrastructure

This would provide governments with new funds to invest in public services and ensure that they are adequately funded. A significant part of this new money or new funding could be deployed into new more efficient technologies, new skills, new personnel, new work practises, new processes, and new innovations to improve the efficiency and productivity of all public services.

- The abuse of many severely disabled people and frail and vulnerable elderly people in a residential facility for disabled persons in Mayo in Ireland caused shock and outrage to the Irish nation in 2014 and 2015. There are reports of similar abuse in other places where disabled people stay or attend. Other investigations revealed a lot of excessive costs and over-charging for expenses and corruption in some areas of the public service and civil service ; this was exposed in two books at the time – 'Wasters' by Shane Ross and Nick Webb (2010), 'The Untouchables' by Shane Ross and Nick Webb (2012), http://www.shaneross.ie/books/ . There is a need for whistleblowers in the civil service and public service, and laws which protect whistleblowers.

- Use whistleblowers and undercover investigation methods and covert methods by independent bodies to identify all forms of abuse, corruption, fraud, waste, and inefficiencies in the public sector, and punish the guilty parties, regardless of status and rank. Use of checklists to uncover and identify all forms of abuses, corruption, waste, over-staffing, inefficient practises, bullying, lack of compliance with regulations and standards, duplication, low throughput, poor motivation, large cost-inefficiencies, dubious sick leave, unexplained leaves of absence, un-needed holidays in expensive hotels, lack of coordination, lack of effectiveness, and fraud in the health system, education system, welfare system, environment and planning systems, agriculture system and justice system and punishing the guilty parties. These checklists would be updated regularly to include best international practises, new discoveries and new innovations in exposing abuses and corruption.

- New laws to tackle these abuses and make whistleblower and covert evidence admissible in court. Widespread use of anti-fraud and anti-abuse software which monitors computers, databases and phones, and uses pattern recognition technologies.

- Carefully analyse all aspects of the civil service, public services, semi-state bodies and privatise some of them. This could take the form of tendering out and selling off to employee owned firms, cooperatives and Social Co-ops in the private sector. The highly successful Social Co-ops in Italy should serve as a model for the provision of state services. In Italy these have replaced many state services and civil service jobs and delivered very high levels of efficiency, cost savings quality and customer service. This would disperse the wealth to the general population via the employee ownership mechanisms. Businesses and individuals would compete for these government tenders on the basis of costs, adherence to certain standards, productivity, throughput, quality, overall customer satisfaction and overall effectiveness. Through contractual agreements, make private businesses accountable for meeting high standards of service and delivery and subject to the same Business Performance Methods, Service and Quality standards, Continuous Improvement and Innovation methods and Checklists for achieving these as state bodies. This could include Six Sigma and Balanced Scorecard and Value Chain analysis. Recommendations would be included in new Checklists to continuously implement, monitor improve all products, services and processes.

- Use of customer feedback from the general public who use state funded services whether publicly or privately provided, and anonymous feedback from members of staff in the civil service and public service to identify deficiencies, bottlenecks, methods of cost cutting and time improvements, long delays, inefficiencies and cost over-runs in services, products and processes. Feedback results would be included in new Checklists to continuously improve all products, services and processes.

- Independent external auditing of all processes and uses of Business Performance Management methods and achievements and non achievements and under achievements of objectives. Recommendations would be included in new Checklists to continuously improve all products, services and processes.

- Use of e-procurement and e-procurement specialist firms to improve the supply chain and costs for all products and services in the civil service and public service.

- Bring the pay of mid level and senior civil servants into line with that of other EU countries. This would involve some pay cuts.

- The government should access more private competitors and demand cuts in the professional fees of PR consultants, management consultants, barristers, solicitors, accountants, IT consultants, medical personnel, etc. who carry out contracts for the government. These cuts and savings should range from 15 - 25% in the first 2 years and 5 - 10% in subsequent years. This would save €200 - 300 million per year.

- Use of Intranets, Extranets, the Internet, social media, skyping, and smart phones and ipads to improve communications, coordination, conferencing, time and costs of services and processes within the civil and public services and links with other bodies and the general public. Strategic plans and operational plans to achieve better coordination, efficiencies, and reduced time and costs.

- Continuous Improvement and innovation of products, services and processes across and between all sections of the civil service. Continuous improvement should involve all personnel, all workers. There would be independent external auditing of this continuous improvement programme. Recommendations would be included in new Checklists to continuously improve all products, services and processes.

- End the monopolies, oligopolies, cartels, economic renters and restrictive practises which are keeping costs artificially high. This includes:
  - overcharging the civil service and government in the provision of goods and services
  - selling state assets at very low cost or below cost to private firms. This involves issues of 'regulatory capture'. These economic renters need to be broken up or highly taxed.
  - break up the monopolies, oligopolies, cartels, economic renters and restrictive practises which are overcharging government, businesses and consumers in Ireland. This is detailed in the 'Taxes and Policies' section above.

- It is now well accepted that the Financial Regulator up to 2008 (in Ireland) did not do his job properly, was negligent and careless. Yet he was paid a salary for this and then got a "golden handshake" of €630,000 and a pension of €140,000 per year. This is an outrageous situation. Taxpayers money was wasted, and poor, shoddy work has been generously rewarded. The government should subpoena this man before a parliamentary committee and establish why he did what he did and exposed the banking system to such systemic risks and the country to national bankruptcy. This parliamentary committee should pass and implement a law for a clawback where this man pay back a certain percentage of his salary as Financial Regulator over the years and 50% of his "golden handshake" and pension to the government. He should be made pay a price for his negligence. This would set a legal precedent for future Financial Regulators and other senior civil servants and encourage them to be responsible and vigilant.

Deep Reforms to National Healthcare Systems

Healthcare systems worldwide are under financial attack from globalisation and it's 'race to the bottom' and the continued dominance of monopolies, oligopolies and special interests and the high costs of speculative booms, crashes and austerity. For state health care this has resulted in reduced tax revenues, and reduced investment, resources and personnel, and higher pressure on existing personnel and resources. Less tax revenues mean less funding for the Health systems and massive cutbacks in hospital beds, wards, medical care, diagnostic equipment, health services etc. For private health systems this has resulted in the elimination of health benefits for many workers, less people contributing to the insurance fund pool, higher insurance costs, less health care services for insured people, insured people forced to sell homes or other assets to pay for health care, and excessive pricing and profiteering by insurance companies. Yet health bodies worldwide also suffer from inefficiencies and large misallocations of resources. There are three choices available

(i) universal private health care for all

(ii) state control and provision of health care

(iii) a system of apartheid where underfunded and under resourced state systems provide poor quality health care and reduced services while private systems provide excellent quality health care and services.

The third choice, the apartheid system, has failed miserably in several countries.

The Options for Healthcare

Option 1   Government Universal Health Care For All

Option 2   Private Universal Health Care For All

Option 1 Government Universal Health Care For All

State provision of all healthcare. Universal state health care. This would be similar to Medicare in the USA, the Scandinavian healthcare systems, the French healthcare system, the UK health system, the Canadian health system, and the German health system, which are reasonably successful. This would involve a health tax on wages, capital income and other forms of income and in some cases sales taxes on products. The German, French and Scandinavian healthcare models serve as models of excellence in this area. They can deliver significant cost, production and time efficiencies, high quality services, bulk purchasing of drugs, generics, medical supplies and equipment by government, cost ceilings imposed by government, privatisation of some services which are provided by the state, high levels of productivity and innovation, total customer focus where the money follows the patient (customer), and high levels of customer choice and satisfaction. While most state health systems stagnate and refuse to innovate and produce outdated, ineffective and inefficient services, these German, French and Scandinavian systems are constantly innovating their products, services, processes, technologies and their personnel to deliver better customer (patient) value, in a similar manner to globally competitive businesses. This type of healthcare system will require :

- **Strategic Funding of Hospitals and the Healthcare sector**

  In most countries the government does not have the funding or "resources" to invest in modern, effective and efficient hospitals and health services. They are starved of funding and this has produced disastrous results. The massive national debt and high interest payments are responsible for this "lack of funding" for health services. There needs to be:

  1. large scale write downs and write offs of national debt and the removal of bank, bondholders and speculators bailout debt from the national debt as proposed in Chapter 7. Monetisation of debt by central banks and compensation to governments for funding prior bail outs could provide the latter.

  2. restore the money printing powers to governments and placing limitations of the scale of this as proposed in Chapter 7 and by MMT economists.

  3. economic democracy as proposed in Chapters 7-11 to provide the high economic growth and the growth in tax revenues and incomes to fund a national healthcare infrastructure

  This would provide governments with new funds to invest in hospitals and health services and ensure that they are adequately funded. A significant part of this new money or new funding could be deployed into new more efficient technologies, new skills, new personnel, new work practises, new processes, and new innovations to improve the efficiency and productivity of all healthcare services.

- Use of data analytics and whistleblowers to determine points of failure and points of ineffectiveness and cost over-runs in the health system, hospitals, diagnostic programmes, treatment programmes, healthcare outcomes, etc. This would form the basis for reforms of the health system. A special health committee in the national parliament, consisting of cross party politicians, the Minister for Health, and senior civil servants of the Department of Health should oversee this and make quarterly reports to the parliament and to the press and media. This would form the basis for continuous reforms over time.

- Significant investment by governments in planning, design, restructuring and extending the capacity of healthcare systems to meet the high standards of the Scandinavian, French and German models, and other models of international excellence

- The most important factor here is the ability of patients (customers) to pay state health insurance contributions and of the state and private organisations having adequate funding to invest in an effective healthcare system. The Economic democracy proposed in this book will help economies achieve (a) higher economic growth (b) wider diffusion of wealth and income to ordinary people through employee share ownership and community share ownership which would give them more resources to pay state health insurance (c) large scale reduction in personal and family debt, see Chapter 7 (d) sufficient funds for state insurance bodies through the closure of tax havens and vast tax evasion involving trillions of dollars. This would create vast amounts of new funds for payment of health insurance and necessary investments in healthcare systems, hospitals and health infrastructure.

- It's important to emphasise again that governments must end tax loopholes and the use of offshore tax havens in order to get the tax revenues necessary to invest in these new healthcare systems. Over $32 trillion is known to be in offshore tax havens, though the real figure could be as high $60 trillion. Returning these trillions of dollars to countries and to national governments would enable them to properly fund their healthcare systems, hospitals, staff and new technologies.

- **Strategic Analysis of Healthcare Costs and Chronic Illnesses**

  According to Dr. Richard Horowitz, a world famous American medical doctor, 86% of the health care costs, and 70% of the deaths in the United States are due to chronic disease, yet the medical authorities and hospitals don't even have a model for effectively diagnosing and treating chronic disease. Every government in every country is trying to figure out how to lower healthcare costs and yet they are not looking at the underlying causes of what is causing chronic disease, which costs over 50% of their total health care costs. In most cases, patients are neglected and left to suffer, rot and die slowly over many years, often with misdiagnosis and the wrong medications (and their side effects) while doctors are left frustrated and powerless by lack of effective guidelines, diagnostic protocols, and treatment protocols and a lack of joined up thinking, and basic strategic planning in healthcare systems. This is leading to unnecessary high health care costs and a massive wastage of time, energy, money and resources in health care systems worldwide. This needs to change radically in North America, all European countries, Asia and throughout the world. The following measures need to be applied.

- The 16 point MSIDS model proposed by Dr. Richard Horowitz needs to implemented for all chronic diseases. This has proven to be effective in thousands of cases of chronic disease in the USA. It greatly reduces the risk of misdiagnosis and helps doctors get to the root causes of chronic disease.

- Many recommendations for diagnosing and treating chronic disease are made in Dr. Richard Horowitz's book How Can I Get Better?: An Action Plan for Treating Resistant Lyme & Chronic Disease. It is available on https://www.amazon.com/How-Can-Get-Better-Resistant/dp/1250070546/ref=cm_cr_arp_d_product_top?ie=UTF8 This could serve as a model for most chronic diseases.

- The building of national clinics or state clinics for chronic illnesses such as neurological illnesses, immune system illnesses, Chronic Lyme Disease and Co-infections, Chronic viral and bacterial illnesses, cardiac and vascular illnesses, mitochondria illnesses, illnesses caused by environmental toxins and pollutants, and endocrine illnesses so as to treat them earlier and help people recover or continue working and living normal lives. This could be one the projects funded by Quantitative Easing for the People mentioned in Chapter 7 above.

- The use of world class private laboratories for diagnosing chronic diseases. This may involve sending patient samples for foreign countries. Many government and state laboratories use old outdated diagnostic technologies which provide false negatives and other forms of misdiagnosis, which have destroyed the lives of millions of patients worldwide. Over time, government or state labs could upgrade to integrate these new diagnostic technologies into them. This could be one the projects funded by Quantitative Easing for the People mentioned in Chapter 7 above.

- Build new national or state research centres to research the causal factors in chronic illness and develop diagnostics and treatments to address causal factors. Collaborate with private industry in this. This could be one the projects funded by Quantitative Easing for the People mentioned in Chapter 7 above.

- The use of Big Data and Analytics to identify and analyse the costs and effectiveness of medical treatment, and how to reduce these costs via innovation, more competition among suppliers of medical treatments and services at home and abroad, price transparency, new investment in facilities and equipment, better work practises, new services and products, and healthier diets and lifestyle choices.

- The poisoning of land, rivers, air, food and water has played a major role in the development of many diseases and illnesses in the developed world and developing world. This has placed massive and unsustainable burdens on national healthcare systems both public and private, and most are over-crowded, cannot accommodate patients, have long waiting lists, and are at breaking point and provide low quality, substandard diagnostics and treatments. Reforms and changes have consistently failed. Governments in all countries will need to abandon their neo liberal deregulation policies and ensure that there are proper laws, Constitutional protections to protect human health from this poisoning of land, rivers, air, food and water for profit. There should be vigorous enforcement of the law by government and by police and if necessary by people and communities. And this may in certain situations require force by use of arms. Ordinary people and communities have a legal and Constitutional right not to be poisoned. This should not be denied or blocked by corrupted politicians and judicial processes. The big corporates and banks need to forced to clean up and remove their poisons through the courts and court judgments, whether from national courts or international courts, free of corruption and political interference.
This removal of poisons from food, water, land, and air would significantly reduce diseases and illnesses and the heavy burden on healthcare systems in many countries.

- End the monopolistic, oligopolistic, cartels and economic rents which are keeping costs artificially high in hospitals and healthcare. In the USA, the Sherman act could be used to break up monopolies and monopolistic practises and price collusion and cartels in the pharmaceutical industry and healthcare industry there. Similar methods could be used by other governments in Europe and countries around the world. This includes excessive prices for

- medical drugs. Including price discrimination between countries involving price differentials of 100% - 5,000%.
- health insurance which is excessively expensive due to monopolies, price collusion and cartels
- patent holders' excessive prices
- consultants fees
- doctors fees
- stays in hospital beds
- overcharging the health service and hospitals in the provision of goods and services
- selling health service assets at very low cost

This will require very deep analysis of cost structures, over pricing, monopoly power and oligopoly power, abuses of power, conflicts of interest, corruption and other factors.

The computer, the mouse, computer networks, the Internet and many other products and services were developed from research undertaken by DARPA and the US government in the past. And governments provide funding for schools, Universities and many other forms of public infrastructure which benefit researchers, innovators and patent developers. Patents derive from both private individual effort and public infrastructure and services, and patent prices should include a social price or dividend and wide social access, payable in the form of a fee and / or tax to the government where the patent was developed and access provided to many businesses so no one business can monopolise it. For example, patent holders would be entitled to hold the patent for their own drugs, but many other manufacturers could pay royalties to the patent holder to manufacture the patented drug. Excessive patent fees could be taxed at 90 – 100% to discourage abuses of the system. This competition would greatly reduce drug prices. Similarly, consultants in hospitals in a region or state / country / adjoining countries could compete against each other on price and quality for operations and other medical procedures. The patient would make the choice based on price, quality and his / her preferences. Reforms and changes could include breaking up monopolies, oligopolies and restrictive practises, opening them up to more competition, outsourcing to cheaper places, locations and countries, more competition between highly skilled suppliers of medical services, better use of communications technologies to drive down health costs, bulk buying and massive discounts, and highly taxing economic renters. This would help drive down health costs.

- A fair health insurance tax on wages and profits. This tax should not be excessive and there should be highly effective and efficient cost controls used in healthcare systems to rigorously control costs.

- Build in spare capacity or subcontract in spare capacity into areas of the health service which suffer from excessive demand at certain periods of the day or week or month or year. Examples being the following:

  o Build special 'Accident and Emergency Wards' which would be special wards in close proximity to an Accident and Emergency department. These special wards would provide sleeping quarters for patients seeking diagnosis and further tests in Accident and Emergency departments. They would serve as an overflow facility. Once beds become available in the normal hospital wards, these patients would immediately transfer from the Accident and Emergency ward to the normal hospital wards which have full facilities and dedicated staff. These Accident and Emergency wards would be temporary holding areas for patients and would relieve the pressure on Accident and Emergency staff. These special wards could be a mixture of state provided facilities or subcontracted private facilities. These special wards could be doubled in size every 10 years for the first 20 years. And thereafter doubled in size every 15 years. Provision should be made for continuing demand and growth in demand over time, 5, 10, 20, 30, 50 years.

  o Spare capacity staff. These would be part time and full time staff on call to deal with peak periods in hospital activity, especially Accident and Emergency activity. This would also relieve the pressure on Accident and Emergency staff.

  o All Accident and Emergency departments should be doubled in size immediately. And then doubled again in size after 10 years for the first 20 years. And thereafter, doubled in size every 15 years. This will involve significant investment by the state in building projects in and around hospitals. This would build spare capacity into hospitals and the health system.

  o Private and state nursing homes should be utilised to house elderly patients and transfer them from hospitals, once they are well. This could be achieved via government grants, tax incentives and government cost-sharing arrangements.

- New hospitals should be built to cater for growing populations in and around big cities and population centres. Once demographics reach a certain level in a city, town or region, construction of a new hospital should begin.

- Hospitals in a region, state or country should coordinate their spare capacity between them. Patients in hospitals which are over-crowded and in crisis should be moved to hospitals which have spare capacity. This would distribute out health resources to achieve the maximum benefit for patients, doctors, nurses and hospitals and save many lives and improve many outcomes.

- Primary care centres should be used by GP's (doctors) and hospitals to re-direct patients from overcrowded hospitals to primary care centres. This could be done a number of less serious conditions.

- Coverage for treatment in all hospitals and all medical practises so that patients are not discriminated against and over charged for treatment in other parts of the country

- Regularly screen all persons in the state for chronic infections, including latent infections, and chronic infections of the nervous system and brain . And use the top labs in the world to carry out these tests. Some top private German labs and American labs should be used. This would help identify the root causes of many illnesses and enable doctors to effectively treat them. This would save the state and the insurance system many millions of euros per year. The current system of leaving chronically ill persons to suffer for many years and decades at great expense to the state and insurance systems is a financial disaster and a disgrace.

- There should be a national price list for all doctors, medical procedures, hospital stays, medical drugs and insurance plans. This would establish a clear and transparent system for all patients, insurance holders, insurance companies and doctors.

- there is a shortage of Irish doctors in the Health Service, as most newly qualified doctors are driven out by poor pay and conditions in the Health Service. The Health Service should employ newly qualified Irish doctors instead of searching in far off countries for new doctors. Entry level salaries for doctors will need to be increased in order to bring them up the standard of pay in similar developed EU countries and provide incentives for Irish doctors to remain in Ireland. Make 4 years mandatory service to the HSE or the provision of medical services within Ireland a requirement for all new doctors after graduation in return for free University education. Otherwise they will be billed by the government for the cost of educating them.

- End the scandal of junior doctors and trainee doctors in hospitals working over 45 hours per week and not getting over-time. The maximum hours should be 45 hours per week.

- Bring the pay of hospital consultants and doctors into line with the pay in Britain, Germany, France and Netherlands.

- Increase the number of GP's to levels in Norway, Sweden, Britain, Germany, France and Netherlands. Increase University places and reduce points for direct entry into medicine from secondary school and advertise abroad for doctors.

- Focus on lean production in healthcare where administrators and overheads are reduced to a bare minimum and new technologies and innovations are deployed to attain and maintain high productivity.

- Continuous computerised feedback to monitor inefficiencies, mistakes, bottlenecks, overcrowding, etc. throughout the healthcare and use of staff and technologies to rectify them as soon as possible. This would involve using up resources which are under used, below capacity and available to resolve the above issues. Resources within the health system and outside the health system could be utilised.

- Providing full employment levels in an environment of full economic and industrial democracy would provide the means for people to pay for state health insurance. More people paying would reduce premiums for everybody.

- The state using many of the methods and cost efficiencies used by the private healthcare sector mentioned in **Option 2** below.

Option 2   Private Universal Health Care For All

Universal private health care for all is the other option as it ends the discrimination one finds in other types of health systems. The Dutch and Swiss healthcare models provide models of excellence. It enables health systems to implement cost efficiencies in drugs and services, production efficiencies, productivity plans and targets, customer targets, waste elimination, duplication reduction, greater employee input into continuous improvement of services, costs, and processes, total quality management (TQM), wider sources of investment both public and private, and continuous innovation in technologies, services, products, and processes. The government could assist the private sector here by bulk purchasing of drugs, generics, medical supplies and equipment by government for all hospitals, ending monopoly and oligopoly control of health products and healthcare, imposing cost ceilings and holding public auctions for insurance in all states to drive down costs and prices. The private insurance companies could pass on these cost savings to customers (patients) in the form of lower premiums and lower prices for medical services. Economic Democracy and Industrial Democracy would play an important role in the implementation and success of a Universal health care system as it would keep more wealth within countries and distribute this wealth more widely and fairly to the whole population, providing them with the financial means to pay for health insurance.

The following options could be implemented for Private Universal Health care or the State Universal Health care:

- **Strategic Funding of Hospitals and the Healthcare sector for Government and for Private Sector**
  In most countries the government does not have the funding or "resources" to invest in modern, effective and efficient hospitals and health services. They are starved of funding and this has produced disastrous results. The massive national debt and high interest payments are responsible for this "lack of funding" for health services. There needs to be:
  1. large scale write downs and write offs of national debt and the removal of bank, bondholders and speculators bailout debt from the national debt as proposed in Chapter 7. Monetisation of debt by central banks and compensation to governments for funding prior bail outs could provide the latter.
  2. restore the money printing powers to governments and placing limitations of the scale of this as proposed in Chapter 7 and by MMT economists.
  3. economic democracy as proposed in Chapters 7-11 to provide the high economic growth and the growth in tax revenues and incomes to fund a national healthcare infrastructure
  This would provide governments with new funds to invest in hospitals and health services and provide incentives for the private sector to invest in hospitals and health services. A significant part of this new money or new funding could be deployed into new more efficient technologies, new skills, new personnel, new work practises, new processes, and new innovations to improve the efficiency and productivity of all healthcare services.
- The most important factor here is the ability of patients (customers) to pay health insurance contributions (to the private insurance firms) and of the state and private organisations having

adequate funding to invest in an effective healthcare system. The Economic democracy proposed in this book will help economies achieve (a) higher economic growth (b) wider diffusion of wealth and income to ordinary people through employee share ownership and community share ownership which would give them more resources to pay health insurance (c) large scale reduction in personal and family debt, see Chapter 7 (d) sufficient funds for private insurance firms through the closure of tax havens and vast tax evasion involving trillions of dollars and the pumping of these funds into the national economy to expand investment, consumption and output. This would create vast amounts of new funds for payment of health insurance and necessary investments in healthcare systems, hospitals and health infrastructure.

- Use of data analytics and whistleblowers to determine points of failure and points of ineffectiveness and cost over-runs in the health system, hospitals, diagnostic programmes, treatment programmes, healthcare outcomes, etc. This would form the basis for reforms of the health system. A special health committee in the national parliament, consisting of cross party politicians, the Minister for Health, and senior civil servants of the Department of Health should oversee this and make quarterly reports to the parliament and to the press and media. This would form the basis for continuous reforms over time.

- It's important to emphasise again that governments must end tax loopholes and the use of offshore tax havens in order to get the tax revenues necessary to invest in these new healthcare systems. Over $32 trillion is known to be in offshore tax havens, though the real figure could be as high $60 trillion. Returning these trillions of dollars to countries and to national governments would enable them to properly fund their healthcare systems, hospitals, staff and new technologies and allow private health providers to provide affordable healthcare and private insurance firms to provide affordable health care. The additional funds circulating in a national economy would ultimately boost the profits and revenues of all private firms operating in the health sector.

- **Strategic Analysis of Healthcare Costs and Chronic Illnesses**
  According to Dr. Richard Horowitz, a world famous American medical doctor, 86% of the health care costs, and 70% of the deaths in the United States are due to chronic disease, yet the medical authorities and hospitals don't even have a model for effectively diagnosing and treating chronic disease. Every government and most insurance firms in every country are trying to figure out how to lower healthcare costs and yet they are not looking at the underlying causes of what is causing chronic disease, which costs over 50% of their total health care costs. In most cases, patients are

neglected and left to suffer, rot and die slowly over many years, often with misdiagnosis and the wrong medications (and their side effects) while doctors are left frustrated and powerless by lack of effective guidelines, diagnostic protocols, and treatment protocols and a lack of joined up thinking, and basic strategic planning in healthcare systems. This is leading to unnecessary high health care costs and a massive wastage of time, energy, money and resources in health care systems worldwide. This needs to change radically in North America, all European countries, Asia and throughout the world. The following measures need to be applied.

- The 16 point MSIDS model proposed by Dr. Richard Horowitz needs to implemented for all chronic diseases. This has proven to be effective in thousands of cases of chronic disease in the USA. It greatly reduces the risk of misdiagnosis and helps doctors get to the root causes of chronic disease.

- Many recommendations for diagnosing and treating chronic disease are made in Dr. Richard Horowitz's book How Can I Get Better?: An Action Plan for Treating Resistant Lyme & Chronic Disease. It is available on https://www.amazon.com/How-Can-Get-Better-Resistant/dp/1250070546/ref=cm_cr_arp_d_product_top?ie=UTF8 This could serve as a model for most chronic diseases.

- The building of private clinics or state clinics for chronic illnesses such as neurological illnesses, immune system illnesses, Chronic Lyme Disease and Co-infections, Chronic viral and bacterial illnesses, cardiac and vascular illnesses, mitochondria illnesses, illnesses caused by environmental toxins and pollutants, and endocrine illnesses so as to treat them earlier and help people recover or continue working and living normal lives. This could be one the projects funded by Quantitative Easing for the People mentioned in Chapter 7 above.

- The use of world class private laboratories for diagnosing chronic diseases. This may involve sending patient samples for foreign countries. Many government and state laboratories use old outdated diagnostic technologies which provide false negatives and other forms of misdiagnosis, which have destroyed the lives of millions of patients worldwide. Over time, government or state labs could upgrade to integrate these new diagnostic technologies into them. This could be one the projects funded by Quantitative Easing for the People mentioned in Chapter 7 above.

- Build new national or state research centres to research the causal factors in chronic illness and develop diagnostics and treatments to address causal factors. Collaborate with private industry in this. This could be one the projects funded by Quantitative Easing for the People mentioned in Chapter 7 above.

- The use of Big Data and Analytics to identify and analyse the costs and effectiveness of medical treatment, and how to reduce these costs via innovation, more competition among suppliers of medical treatments and services at home and abroad, price transparency, new investment in facilities and equipment, better work practises, new services and products, and healthier diets and lifestyle choices.

- End the system of apartheid and implement Universal Health Care
Ireland spends almost 10% of GNP on health, which is similar to Norway Sweden, Britain, the Netherlands and France, yet these health systems provide universal health cover and better quality hospitals and medical services. Fund and fully implement Universal Health Care for all citizens and stop the system of apartheid in the Health system. Both public and private patients would buy private health insurance, with illness, disability and age factors integrated into the premiums, and the government would pay or part pay this private insurance for those on social welfare, disability payments or very low income. All citizens would be covered by private health insurance. Gradually introduce a fully private hospitals system and healthcare system where there is no distinction between public and private patients, and all are treated equally. All persons would be privately insured and entitled to the same medical treatments and hospital care and clinic care. Money would follow the patient, and doctors and hospitals would be paid for every patient they diagnose and treat by insurance companies. There would be no discretionary state funding, arbitrary withdrawals of funding by politicians, political favouritism and political games played with the health service and hospitals. Privatisation would put patients, not politicians, at the centre of the health service. The HSE could coordinate this new system with private health insurance providers, hospitals, senior civil servants, medical professionals, accountants, banks, management accountants, economists and IT specialists and give preference to employee owned firms, cooperatives and Social Co-ops.
At present hospital consultants are double paid - they can use designated public patient treatment hours to treat private patients, and receive payment from the private patient or his/her insurer and payment from the government (though they did not treat a public patient). This double payment is a national scandal and is imposing extra costs on the health service, and needs to be ended.
At present, public patients on long waiting lists for public hospital care are put on the National Treatment Purchase Fund which uses national and foreign private hospitals, private clinics, private

care, private Consultants and surgeons – privatisation - to treat public patients who have been waiting many years for treatment in public, state-supported hospitals. This is a shameful indictment of the public hospitals and public health services which have failed these public patients. The public system has become a gravy train to be milked by some people in privileged and protected occupations. This needs to reformed and changed radically.

- The poisoning of land, rivers, air, food and water has played a major role in the development of many diseases and illnesses in the developed world and developing world. This has placed massive and unsustainable burdens on national healthcare systems both public and private, and most are over-crowded, cannot accommodate patients, have long waiting lists, and are at breaking point and provide low quality, substandard diagnostics and treatments. Reforms and changes have consistently failed. Governments in all countries will need to abandon their neo liberal deregulation policies and ensure that there are proper laws, Constitutional protections to protect human health from this poisoning of land, rivers, air, food and water for profit. There should be vigorous enforcement of the law by government and by police and if necessary by people and communities. And this may in certain situations require force by use of arms. Ordinary people and communities have a legal and Constitutional right not to be poisoned. This should not be denied or blocked by corrupted politicians and judicial processes. The big corporates and banks need to forced to clean up and remove their poisons through the courts and court judgments, whether from national courts or international courts, free of corruption and political interference.

This removal of poisons from food, water, land, and air would significantly reduce diseases and illnesses and the heavy burden on healthcare systems in many countries.

- The reforms mentioned in **Option 1** above

- End the monopolistic, oligopolistic, cartels and economic rents which are keeping costs artificially high in hospitals and healthcare. In the USA the Sherman act could be used to break up monopolies and monopolistic practises and price collusion and cartels in the pharmaceutical industry and healthcare industry there. Similar methods could be used by other governments in Europe and countries around the world. This includes excessive prices for
- medical drugs. Including price discrimination between countries involving price differentials of 100% - 5,000%.
- health insurance which is excessively expensive due to monopolies, price collusion and cartels

- patent holders' excessive prices

- consultants fees

- doctors fees

- stays in hospital beds

- overcharging the health service and hospitals in the provision of goods and services

- selling health service assets at very low cost

This will require very deep analysis of cost structures, over pricing, monopoly power and oligopoly power, abuses of power, conflicts of interest, corruption and other factors.

The computer, the mouse, computer networks, the Internet and many other products and services were developed from research undertaken by DARPA and the US government in the past. And governments provide funding for schools, Universities and many other forms of public infrastructure which benefit researchers, innovators and patent developers. Patents derive from both private individual effort and public infrastructure and services, and patent prices should include a social price or dividend and wide social access, payable in the form of a fee and / or tax to the government where the patent was developed and access provided to many businesses so no one business can monopolise it. For example, patent holders would be entitled to hold the patent for their own drugs, but many other manufacturers could pay royalties to the patent holder to manufacture the patented drug. Excessive patent fees could be taxed at 90 – 100% to discourage abuses of the system. This competition would greatly reduce drug prices.

Similarly, consultants in hospitals in a state / country / adjoining countries could compete against each other on price and quality for operations and other medical procedures. The patient would make the choice based on price, quality and his / her preferences. Reforms and changes could include breaking up monopolies, oligopolies and restrictive practises, opening them up to more competition, outsourcing to cheaper places, locations and countries, more competition between highly skilled suppliers of medical services, better use of communications technologies to drive down health costs, bulk buying and massive discounts, and highly taxing economic renters. This would help drive down health costs.

- For people burdened by excessive health insurance costs in their own country, the option is open to get cheaper health insurance in a nearby country, where health insurance is 8 – 12 times cheaper. This insurance could cover hospital diagnostics and treatments in this other country, and some add ons could cover visits to the doctor in one's home country up to a certain amount per year. This would greatly reduce healthcare costs and bring more international competition into the health insurance market.

- The highly successful Social Co-ops in Italy should serve as a model for the provision of health services and products. These involve employee share ownership and community share ownership. In Italy, these Social Co-ops have replaced many state services and civil service jobs and delivered very high levels of efficiency, cost savings quality and customer service.

- All private insurance plans providing coverage for treatment in all hospitals and all medical practises so that patients are not discriminated against and over charged for treatment in other parts of the country

- Build in spare capacity or subcontract in spare capacity into areas of the health service which suffer from excessive demand at certain periods of the day or week or month or year. Examples being the following:

  o Build special 'Accident and Emergency Wards' which would be special wards in close proximity to an Accident and Emergency department. These special wards would provide sleeping quarters for patients seeking diagnosis and further tests in Accident and Emergency departments. They would serve as an overflow facility. Once beds become available in the normal hospital wards, these patients would immediately transfer from the Accident and Emergency ward to the normal hospital wards which have full facilities and dedicated staff. These Accident and Emergency wards would be temporary holding areas for patients and would relieve the pressure on Accident and Emergency staff. These special wards could be a mixture of state provided facilities or subcontracted private facilities. These special wards could be doubled in size every 10 years for the first 20 years. And thereafter doubled in size every 15 years. Provision should be made for continuing demand and growth in demand over time, 5, 10, 20, 30, 50 years.

  o Spare capacity staff. These would be part time and full time staff on call to deal with peak periods in hospital activity, especially Accident and Emergency activity. This would also relieve the pressure on Accident and Emergency staff.

  o All Accident and Emergency departments should be doubled in size immediately. And then doubled again in size after 10 years for the first 20 years. And thereafter, doubled in size every 15 years. This will involve significant investment by private investors and the state in building projects in and around hospitals. This would build spare capacity into hospitals and the health system.

- o Private and state nursing homes should be utilised to house elderly patients and transfer them from hospitals, once they are well. This could be achieved via government grants, tax incentives and government cost-sharing arrangements.

- o New hospitals should be built to cater for growing populations in and around big cities and population centres. Once demographics reach a certain level in a city, town or region, construction of a new hospital should begin.

- o Hospitals in a region, state or country should coordinate their spare capacity between them. Patients in hospitals which are over-crowded and in crisis should be moved to hospitals which have spare capacity. This would distribute out health resources to achieve the maximum benefit for patients, doctors, nurses and hospitals and save many lives and improve many outcomes.

- o Primary care centres should be used by GP's (doctors) and hospitals to re-direct patients from overcrowded hospitals to primary care centres. This could be done a number of less serious conditions.

- Regularly screen all persons in the state for chronic infections, including latent infections, and chronic infections of the nervous system and brain . And use the top labs in the world to carry out these tests. Some top private German labs and American labs should be used. This would help identify the root causes of many illnesses and enable doctors to effectively treat them. This would save the state and the insurance system many millions of euros per year. The current system of leaving chronically ill persons to suffer for many years and decades at great expense to the state and insurance systems is a financial disaster and a disgrace.

- There should be a national price list for all doctors, medical procedures, hospital stays, medical drugs and insurance plans. This would establish a clear and transparent system for all patients, insurance holders, insurance companies and doctors.

- Patients and insurance companies should be give the freedom to identify the lowest prices or best value prices for medical care and use them, regardless of geography or location

- Use of e-commerce and e-business technologies, such as Alibaba, to drive down medical prices, healthcare prices, hospital prices and insurance prices. E-bidding should be extensively used to drive down prices and costs.

- Focus on lean production in healthcare where administrators and overheads are reduced to a bare minimum and new technologies and innovations are deployed to attain and maintain high productivity.

- The proposals in this book would help achieve fair and affordable health insurance prices for customers. Greater competition in the insurance price and in the provision of medical services and hospital care, the break-up of monopolies and restrictive practises, and greater price transparency along with e-commerce and e-bidding technologies would help drive down costs and price. This should involve some controls on excessive profiteering by insurance companies and excessive insurance executive pay levels, hospital fees and consultant fees.

- Greater use of alternative medicines and dietary changes to treat the chronically ill. This would have a sound scientific basis in all cases and would utilise the knowledge and findings of organisations such as Commission E, top scientific researchers in this field and top complementary medical doctors and top herbalists. This would reduce treatment costs, improve health outcomes, and also reduce the side effects of medical drugs and their threat to health and life. Germany and some Asian countries lead the way in this.

- Disease Prevention

  This will involve the health care system or insurance companies applying customised diets and vitamin supplements and exercise regimes for people over 30 so as to prevent diseases. Encourage greater individual responsibility for health and provide financial incentives for this. HSE and insurance company support for health clubs for the general public, and healthy living, and sponsoring participation in sports and gyms and outdoor activities and the use of equipment to monitor one's fitness activities daily. Use of grants, tax rebates, private health insurance reductions, part payment of health club attendance, social welfare rebates for gym membership and use and purchasing of vitamins, workplace support for membership of gyms, health food sections in work canteens, etc. to encourage healthier living by all persons.

- Directly address and resolve the causes of 400,000 people waiting for outpatient treatment (in Ireland). Use new and innovative methods including new work regimes, employment of additional doctors and consultants, new investment in personnel, new technologies and buildings, new pay regimes and bonuses, outsourcing to cheaper places, privatisation and national treatment purchase fund programme to reduce this number and waiting period.

- Introduce new high technology diagnostic equipment to quickly and accurately diagnose diseases, illnesses and syndromes in Irish hospitals and state labs. Most diagnostic equipment is old and outdated in Irish public hospitals and state labs, and there exists problems with wrong diagnosis, misdiagnosis, late diagnosis, mistakes, missed diagnosis and long waiting periods for an accurate diagnosis. Patients often have to wait many months or years for an accurate diagnosis. Some people have to go to private labs or clinics in Ireland or abroad for an accurate diagnosis.

- New compulsory cancer screening, diabetes screening, heart disease screening and neurological disease screening for all men and women over 45, so as to detect cancer, diabetes, neurological disease and heart disease earlier. These four particular illnesses impose enormous costs on the health service in Ireland and other countries, and need to be detected earlier and treated earlier through medical drugs, diet, lifestyle, stress management and fitness changes so as to prevent higher costs later on when degeneration is more advanced.

- Tackle the suicide problem in a new more effective manner and more coordinated manner which will deliver results. The present system of inadequate funding for psychiatric hospitals and support services and small voluntary organisations achieving very little or nothing is a national disgrace. The government needs to increase funding for psychiatric units in hospitals and bring funding into line with EU and OECD averages, and build holistic healing centres to integrate and coordinate mental health services and support services and community services, and anti-suicide strategies. Some ideas on this are presented on www.healingcentres.org

- Bring the number of neurologists, cardiologists, immunologists, infectious disease specialists, stem cell transplant specialists, and cancer specialists up to the levels found in countries such as Norway, Sweden, Netherlands, Germany, Canada and France

- End expensive agency hiring which is imposing excessive costs on the health system. Employ people on medium to long term contracts with fair terms and conditions.

- End the scandal of people retiring and getting pensions or lump sum payments, and then being rehired privately or publically for the same position and paid the same salary in addition to their pension and lump sum payments.

- The building of 80 more Primary care centres (in Ireland) to meet the agreed targets set some years ago. This would take the pressure off the hospitals.

- Use of Intranets, Extranets, the Internet, social media, skyping, and smart phones and ipads to improve communications, coordination, conferencing, time and costs of services and processes within the civil and public services and links with other bodies and the general public. Strategic plans and operational plans to achieve better coordination, efficiencies, and reduced time and costs.

- Implement a system of continuous improvement and innovation in healthcare services, including new technologies and innovative drugs and alternative health treatments and programmes. Benchmark innovation against private hospitals in other developed countries such as USA, Germany, France, Norway, Sweden, Canada, etc.

- Get ordinary workers in the Health Service to drive changes and innovations. They have an expert knowledge of conditions inside the Health Service and how they can be improved.

- Checklists for hygiene for all members of staff and for all equipment in hospitals and for visiting members of the public

- The legalisation of and wider use of herbs which have hundreds of anti bacteria and anti viral compounds and anti inflammatory and anti Cancer compounds within hospitals and community health care

- Health insurance coverage and state insurance coverage of the costs of acupuncture, chakras healing and other forms of energy healing with proven effectiveness.

- The expansion of care in the community programmes and support services for the elderly, those people with mental illness and those people with chronic illnesses, and the use of private firms to achieve this. This would encourage independent living and many forms of support in the community. These should be subject to regular monitoring to ensure high quality standards and effectiveness.

- Strategic positioning of ambulances in counties so that they are near to where accidents occur and health emergencies arise. This would involve identifying accident hotspots and medical emergency hotspots.

Regeneration of Inner Cities & Deprived Regions

It would be possible to economically and socially regenerate many ghettos, deprived areas of cities, deprived regions, rural areas and rural towns through the measures outlined in this book. The implementation of economic democracy with its wider employee share ownership, community share ownership, profit sharing, cooperatives and social coops detailed in Chapter 9 would be a start. And this needs to be combined with the following:

- the massive reduction in national debt, household debt and business debt mentioned in Chapters 7 and 8
- new trade deals to prioritise investment and employment within developed countries and within trading blocs listed in Chapter 9
- new forms of local banking and local currencies to stimulate economic activity, employment and access to credit in deprived regions and inner cities
- wider availability of affordable and good quality healthcare
- higher education as a civil right and as a means to economic advancement
- the social inclusion measures listed below

These would greatly increase consumption, investment and economic activity within developed countries and increase the demand for labour. This in turn would create increased employment opportunities for persons in inner cities, ghettos, industrial wastelands and deprived rural regions. The return of tax monies from tax havens to developed countries would also assist local and central governments and provide them with abundant resources to plan strategically and invest strategically in public infrastructure, apprenticeship and training programmes, College / University access courses, Social Inclusion programmes for the disabled, unemployed and elderly, playgrounds and sports facilities, and other types of urban regeneration in inner cities and deprived regions.

This new wealth generation would create increased businesses opportunities for local entrepreneurs to set up businesses providing goods and services locally, including in inner cities and deprived regions. And this in turn would create further employment opportunities in these areas. The synergies created by all the factors above would drastically reduce poverty in these areas of the economy. As people in inner cities and deprived rural regions become employed and become owners of shares and capital, their wealth will increase, and they will gain greater self confidence, respect and self belief and they will invest more in their health, their families, homes and communities and become more responsible citizens. This will have multiple beneficial effects on society, producing lower crime rates, lower drop out rates from high school, lower rates of addiction to alcohol and drugs, lower mental illness rates, lower domestic violence, lower divorce and separation rates, etc..

This could be accompanied by other reforms to empower people to participate in this economic democracy and engage positively with society :

Educational Reforms

- Higher education in University or Institutes of Technology or Trade Apprenticeships needs to be viewed legally as a civil right in the same way as other civil rights. It should be a legal civil right. This would build on the great work of Martin Luther King in the 1960's and provide the means for full social inclusion regardless of race, class, gender, religion, disability, etc.. This type of social inclusion would encourage self reliance, responsibility and the means for economic advancement and the realisation of one's potential in life.

  Education up to the end of secondary school (high school) and Higher education (University or Institutes of Technology or Trade Apprenticeships) should be free and paid for and provided for by the government. For higher education a graduate tax could be applied to the salaries of graduates and qualified tradesmen for 10 years to cover the costs of educating them. The system of apartheid between government schools and private high schools should be ended, as it has many of the disadvantages and evils of apartheid. All persons should be encouraged to be educated together in preparation for working together in an environment of economic democracy and industrial democracy and voting together in a political democracy. This new education system would help build mutual respect, trust, teamwork skills and cooperation between different income classes and this would yield benefits in the workplace and in larger society. Respect would help build and enhance individual responsibility and group responsibility.

- The books 'Debunking Economics' by Professor Steve Keen and 'Killing the Host: How Financial Parasites and Debt Bondage Destroy the Global Economy' by Michael Hudson, should be made compulsory reading in all business studies courses, accountancy courses, and economics courses in all secondary schools / high schools, Universities, Institutes of Technology and professional accountancy courses. These books explain what causes booms and busts, contagion, systemic risks and financial crashes, and why economies fail, and how governments, regulators, organisations and businesses can work together to prevent them. This knowledge would save governments, taxpayers and businesses trillions of euros / dollars in bailout costs and losses in GDP, output and productivity.

- The book 'The People's History of the United States' by Howard Zinn should be made required reading in all secondary schools / high Schools and all Colleges and Universities. This would give students a more in-depth knowledge of history, current affairs and how to do critical thinking and analysis.

- Reintroduce University fees and IT college fees for those students from very high income families and those possessing wealth, property or land over a certain value. This would include wealthy business people, bankers, speculators, and big farmers. Taxpayers should not be forced to pay for the University education of the children of the wealthy. The children of the wealthy could if they wish take out student loans. This would increase the available funds for Universities and Institutes of Technology, and improve their educational facilities and research programmes. All students found guilty of anti social behavior or crimes should have their fees exemption removed and / or grants reduced or loans revoked. This would enable many students to learn responsibility and to take their studies seriously, and help reduce the rowdy, childish, anti-social behavior we have seen among students in recent decades.

- Educational systems in Europe, the Americas and around the world should introduce many of the aspects of the Finnish educational system which is considered to be one of the best in the world. This would include many changes and reforms to strike a better balance between project work, research, continuous assignments, team work, oral assessments, PowerPoint and graphical presentations and exams in national schools and secondary schools.

- Using Education to combat Ignorance

  Make 'Civics, Constitutional rights and Social Responsibility' compulsory and necessary for secondary school (high school) graduation and acceptance into University, Institutes of Technology, state training schemes and apprenticeship courses. This subject would fully educate students about their Constitutional rights, civil rights, legal rights, common law rights, natural law, and human rights, and their legal responsibilities. And also the responsibilities attached to rights, civic responsibilities, the importance of "social capital" in one's own life and in society in general. The social responsibility section would emphasise involvement in democracy and democratic processes, paying taxes for the provision of public services and infrastructure, being respectful, taking responsibility in their own lives, the dangers of alcohol abuse and drug abuse, the benefits of work and healthy living and good relationships, and the importance of voluntary work in charities, foundations and voluntary bodies to improve society and the wider world.

- Upgrade the educational system to improve the education of those children from lower income classes. Many of them receive substandard education, lack of encouragement, and are excluded from Universities and Institutes of Technology. Most middle income and upper income families buy 'grinds' or private tuition for their children or send their children to 'grinds schools', and most go to University and Institutes of Technology. The state could provide remedial classes after the normal school hours to help and assist children from lower income groups and disadvantaged communities to learn difficult topics, gain deeper understanding, build better self confidence, and practise answering questions and solving problems. This could be undertaken by trainee teachers, trainee lecturers, unemployed teachers, and part time teachers after normal school hours.

There are savings in terms of reduced social welfare bills, reduced healthcare, reduced crime and prison costs, and increased employment, increased GDP growth, increased foreign and domestic investment, and increased tax revenues, as these children become adults.

Social Welfare Reforms

- End the scandal of unemployed people and people falsely claiming disability payments spending their social welfare on abusing alcoholic drinks, illegal drugs, and engaging in criminal activities, gossip and slander, inter-personal conflicts and domestic abuse. Many states are wasting billions of euros per year on these anti-social activities which are ruining lives, communities and national economies. These people need to be encouraged to participate in the economy and society and be constructive and positive.

- A careful and highly detailed study of all poverty traps should be undertaken by government bodies and advisors and expert economists twice a year to identify ways to remove them and encourage people to get back working. This could include reforms such as national dividend / basic income or negative income taxes as proposed in this book. This would encourage people to take up work and return to the workforce. The cap on housing prices mentioned above would help remove the high costs of mortgages and renting which have played a role in poverty traps in the past.

- Employers should be encouraged through tax incentives, grants, quotas, laws and other incentives to employ persons who are long term unemployed and the disabled who are able to work. The most disadvantaged should be prioritised in getting people back to work again. This should be targeted at socially deprived communities, ghettos and low income areas, giving people living in these areas employment and the means to advance themselves further through further training, retraining and up-skilling while working.

- All social welfare recipients and those on disability who wish to work should put their CV's and Resumes up on a national employment database. Employers could advertise vacant positions on this employment database. The names of the unemployed would be protected via codes so as to comply with privacy and data protection laws. Employers could choose workers and workers could choose employers. Social media and the Internet should be used to advertise this employment database and Jobs Clubs.

- A One Stop Shop for Employment or Training
  the Jobs Clubs could serve as a coordination and collaboration point between social welfare officers, specialist mentors and coaches, psychologists, other jobs clubs in other counties and countries, private recruitment firms, training and educational institutions, national employment databases, social media and the Internet and employers so that all of these parties work together to improve the employment prospects of all unemployed individuals and disabled individuals who can work. These would involve new innovative 'joined-up' proactive measures designed to encourage, empower and uplift all unemployed persons and disabled persons who can work. Win-win scenarios should be encouraged for all persons involved.

- State and private training schemes involving apprenticeships, trades and crafts, and third level education should be tied in to this national employment database and Jobs Clubs to facilitate (i) the acquisition of skills, trade or qualifications by unemployed persons which are in demand by employers (ii) the upgrading of one's skills (iii) linking employers to those in these people in training courses or educational courses. This would encourage a close link-up between employers and potential employees, and be highly proactive in relation to employment.
  The unemployed and disabled who can work would have the choice of acquiring an apprenticeship, trade / craft or third level education which is in high demand by employers OR getting a job.

- A global taxation of robots and Artificial Intelligence (AI), of 20-25%, applied in every country could provide the means for funding these employment schemes and training, up-skilling and career advancement schemes in the private sector and state sector, and the expansion of employee share ownership and community share ownership to the masses.

- There is a grouping of people in Irish society, (and other countries) numbering 400,000 people, who are mostly excluded from Irish economic life and social life. They are disabled people. There still exists a stigma attached to disability and most employers still discriminate against disabled people in the hiring of workers. This is unacceptable and unnecessary. Several studies show that disabled people are just as capable of doing work as able-bodied people. The government should introduce an official quota requiring that 5% of state and semi-state employees should have a disability. The same should be applied for all businesses involved in working on outsourced state contracts. This would be a helpful start and would draw more disabled into the workforce. As regards the private sector the government should negotiate with the EU and with all trading partners in the WTO on getting a binding international agreement requiring that 5% of total employees in private businesses have a disability. This would help end discrimination against disabled people in employment. This new measure would bring tens of thousands of disabled people in Ireland and millions of disabled people in the EU into the workforce. This would uplift many millions of people and their families and enable them to participate more fully in their respective societies. It would provide new hope and new dignity to existing and future generations of disabled people.

- Social welfare payments should be cut for those healthy able bodied people refusing to take up work

- Some people are falsely claiming disability payments but are not disabled. They have enough energy to engage in drinking, illegal drugging, gossip, fighting and anti-social behaviour, but claim to have no energy for working. This is depriving genuine disabled people of their payments and support services. There needs to be a crackdown on these fraudsters by social welfare inspectors, police and private investigators.

- Social welfare inspectors should have the power to enter pubs, bars, parks, river banks, playgrounds, public places, and homes between 10am and 7pm in the company of a police officer and check up on people who prefer to go drinking and drugging than working. They should be given powers to ask people for identification. Defrauding taxpayers of money by refusing to work and engaging in drinking and drugging and anti-social behaviour is a criminal offence and a terrible waste of public (state) funds which is costing the Irish state billions of euros per year and destroying many lives in the process.

- Speed up the process and time involved in acquiring trades qualifications so as to address skill shortages in this area. Apply grants, free tuition, tax incentives and other incentive to fast track this

Social Inclusion I

Over 400,000 people suffer from disability in Ireland and are excluded from economic life and social life. Many suffer from discrimination, prejudices, stigma and persecution and injustices in job seeking, housing, the legal system and courts, education, health care, dating, relationships, sports, and social life. The same is true in many other countries. The following measures would help resolve these problems

a) The return to full employment via economic democracy and the policies mentioned in this book would create more job opportunities and employment for disabled people, and give them more financial independence, choices and options, dignity, freedom and responsibilities, and social inclusion.

b) Reverse the cutbacks to disability payments and services and supports since 2008. Invest more in improving the health, the education and skills, the job prospects, the self confidence and well being of disabled people as a means to enabling greater social inclusion. This would be facilitated by the higher economic growth from economic democracy measures

c) Fund existing and new and innovative social inclusion programmes for the disabled.

d) Greater involvement of disabled people and advocates in decision making at state local, regional and national levels.

e) Support the rights of the disabled and other disadvantaged groups in society and work to end discrimination and stigma in society.

f) Use the proposals in the Checks and Balances section of this book to empower disabled people to get justice under law in the legal system and the courts

g) Use and fund many methods to build social inclusion and economic inclusion for all disabled people. This could be facilitated by new organisations and new structures at local and community levels, city and county council and town borough levels, regional levels, and national levels.

h) The government should introduce an official quota requiring that 4% of state and semi-state employees should have a disability. The same should be applied for all private businesses and companies involved in working on outsourced state contracts. This would be a helpful start and would draw more disabled into the workforce. As regards the private sector the government should negotiate with the EU and with all trading partners in the WTO on getting a binding international agreement requiring that 3% of total employees in private businesses have a disability. This along with other economic stimulatory measures mentioned in this book would help provide more job opportunities and end discrimination against disabled people in employment. This new measure would bring tens of thousands of disabled people in Ireland and millions of disabled people in the EU and other trading blocs into the workforce. This would uplift many millions of people and their families and enable them to participate more fully in their respective societies. It would provide new hope and new dignity to existing and future generations of disabled people.

Social Inclusion II

Uplift, encourage and provide hope for socially disadvantaged communities and communities suffering from discrimination, prejudices, racism and stigma. This could include:

- Increased funding for early intervention in education and training, community regeneration, sports and social facilities, teaching them social responsibility, spirituality and love for others, involvement in charity and community work, and support for anti-crime measures in the community.

- The use of strong role models, big brother systems and mentoring of troubled youths, and new social tools to help them integrate into society and make positive and constructive contributions to society and the economy.

- Involving older people in the community and the provision of new services and supports for older people in the community and region. This could be facilitated by new organisations and new structures at local and community levels, city and county council and town borough levels, regional levels, and national levels.

- Use the proposals in the Checks and Balances section of this book to empower disabled people to get justice under law in the legal system and the courts

Build Active Citizenship and Local Democracy. Strengthen Democracy and Freedom at all levels

- Economic Democracy and it's positive effects on the economy and the distribution of wealth and income and government finances would provide the financial resources for building up communities, repairing communities, healing communities, and regenerating communities. This could be guided by city and town councils, rural councils, regional councils and by local community groups and partnerships aimed at improving the lives of all persons, especially disadvantaged persons in cities, towns and rural regions and building strong social inclusion programmes.

- Give more revenue raising power and spending power to local councils around the country, while ensuring equity in terms of services and quality delivered nationwide. This would involve a combination of local tax/ charge/ levy revenue collection and central government funding. The land tax proposed above would be a valuable source of local revenue in addition to local rates, charges and other levies

- Set up community forums, social inclusion forums, disability organisations forums, joint policing forums, planning forums, road, rail and infrastructure forums, and citizen's voice forums in city councils and town councils to engage with ordinary citizens, and give them some input into local government decision-making and the provision of local services and use of state resources.

- Increase local and central government funding for volunteer centres around Ireland, with at least one in each county. Market and advertise these centres in the press and media and on social media and the Internet.

Paying for it all

The proposals in Chapters 7 encompassing Debt write downs and write offs and Quantitative Easing for the People and the proposals for Economic Democracy in Chapter 9 would provide a means for paying for this new system of healthcare and for the social inclusion programmes listed above. Ending the robbing and bankruptcy of social security plans, private pension plans, state pension plans, life savings in banks and other financial institutions, medical care plans for the elderly, disabled and unemployed, and government healthcare systems through the following:

o over speculation and related frauds and crashes involving speculation in trillions of dollars and losses of trillions of dollars globally

o derivatives which are speculation based and worth over $1,200 trillion

o bank and speculator bail outs by government and taxpayers involving trillions of dollars

o manipulated wars and regime changes which cost trillions of dollars per year and mostly benefit large banks, the military industrial complex, and the Deep State

- corporate welfare and subsidies, and tax evasion schemes, costing tens / hundreds of billions of dollars each year in many countries.

- a Deep State and Shadow Government (in big countries) which commands hundreds of billions of dollars per year and where trillions of dollars have gone missing, been misappropriated, and are unaccounted for. In 2001, Donald Rumsfled the defence minister of the USA claimed that over $2 trillion was missing and unaccounted for. In 2018, the US government has stated that $21 trillion is missing and unaccounted for. The CAFR scandal is just one example of this.

- the robbing of natural resources such as oil, gas, minerals and depriving governments and taxpayers of many billions of euros / dollars per year

would provide a massive injection of funds for healthcare, hospitals, public services, education, training, and infrastructure. These vast amount of monies could be refunded and clawed back from the bloated sectors of the Deep State, big banks, oil and gas companies, and speculators.

Measuring Progress - New more Accurate Economic and Social Indicators

How do we measure progress ? measure economic progress and social progress in this new world ? As we saw in Chapter 1, the GDP and GNP measures are inaccurate, overly narrow, contradictory and ambiguous. Many countries have had GNP growth but suffered a fall in key social indicators. Research studies have concluded that the following new economic and social indicators should be used alongside GDP and GNP.

- Oxfam Humankind Index
- Genuine Progress Indicator
- OECD Better Life Index

- The Social Progress Index
- Unicef Index of Child Well Being
- Index of Health and Social Problems (Wilkinson, 2009)

Chapter 12 A New Global Peace Architecture Based on Political, Social and Economic Democracy and a Raising of Consciousness

'Every gun that is made, every warship launched, every rocket fired, signifies in the final sense a theft from those who hunger and are not fed, those who are cold and not clothed. This world in arms is not spending money alone. It is spending the sweat of its labourers, the genius of its scientists, the hopes of its children. This is not a way of life in any true sense. Under the clouds of war, it is humanity hanging on a cross of iron'
President Dwight D. Eisenhower, 1953

'Since Auschwitz we know what man is capable of. And since Hiroshima we know what is at stake.'
Viktor Frankl, Man's Search for Meaning

War is a racket. It is the only one international in scope. It is the only one in which the profits are reckoned in dollars and the losses in lives.
General Smedley Butler, most highly decorated marine corps officer

"War is peace. Freedom is slavery. Ignorance is strength."
1984 by George Orwell

'War would exist without countries. War emerges from consciousness immersed in division / separation and accompanying injustices'
Anonymous

War is very wasteful of scarce economic resources and in our modern age with its nuclear, chemical and biological weapons it threatens the annihilation of these economic resources. War destroys economies, peoples, infrastructure, investment, technologies and new innovations, GDP, skills, careers and the means to create wealth and distribute it. Regional wars typically cost hundreds of billions of dollars while world wars have cost trillions of dollars. While war is destructive to ordinary people, especially working class people and farmers, war and preparation for war is highly profitable for certain businesses and banks. Every year over $2 trillion is spent on the arms industry with some of this used to conduct regional wars and civil wars worldwide. The arms industry or military industrial complex now relies on a continuous state of war, terrorism, social injustices, tribalistic hatreds, and international tension in order to exist and keep growing, and this incentivises some parties to instigate a worsening of tensions and incitement of hatreds in order to justify increased military spending by domestic and foreign governments and private entities. There are powerful politically connected banks and corporations which make massive profits from preparation for war, actual wars and regime changes and regional conflicts and reconstruction after wars, and they have a strong incentive to promote wars and regime changes. These banking and corporate interests are closely allied to the Deep State, and 'Shadow Government', and many belong to both. The Deep State or 'Shadow Government' exercises considerable control over governments in western countries and politicians some of whom regularly appear on television calling for military action, sanctions, embargos, intervention, attacks, regime changes, and various other forms of scare mongering. None of them publicly declare their conflicts of interest and their financial interest in war.

These business, banking and Deep State interests have cross shareholdings in the press and media, which is highly concentrated in most developed countries, thus narrowing and restricting real freedom of the press and the public's access to verifiable facts, truths and evidence. There is also the power of the State and of State forces to directly influence, manipulate and legally censor and coerce the private press and media, adding further to this synchronistic relationship. These political incentives and business incentives are very powerful, and lie behind policy making and policy decisions and how the general public perceives events. As we saw in Chapter 3, public perception is everything.

General Smedley Butler, the most highly decorated marine corps soldier of all time, wrote a book called 'War is a Racket' where he provided evidence and proofs that war is a criminal racket, designed to enrich a few businesses and banks, while killing thousands of young soldiers and innocent civilians and destroying countries. He had a unique insight into the workings of political systems and the influence and power of large corporations and banks which thrive on war and actively use war for business purposes. He also exposed a plot to overthrow President Franklin Roosevelt in the 1930's organised by wealthy businessmen and bankers. This caused a legal and political scandal at the time. There was a lot of evidence provided by a Dr. Anthony Sutton in the USA that powerful American banking and corporate interests funded, supplied and invested in Hitler and Fascism in nazi Germany and also funded Communism in the USSR, Korea, Vietnam and other places. This was used as a means to profit from funding their industrial development and war machines, and also to fund the war machines of communism, fascism, and capitalism during wars and during the cold war. His three books 'Western Technology and Soviet Economic Development' provide evidence of this profiteering by some big corporate and banks, and his other books and writings corroborate this [39]. Most people today are ignorant of these facts, in particular the deeper criminal reasons for war which serve to enrich the war racketeers and the corrupt.

One of the best examples of the power and reach of this Deep State and it's corporate and banking interests was the **Project for the New American Century**, a foundation run by neo cons in the USA from 1997 to 2007. (Later renamed 'Foreign Policy Initiative'). This Foundation published many papers and publications calling for wars, regime changes, and increased military spending (including lucrative contracts for big defence companies and banks) during the Clinton Presidency and throughout the presidency of George W Bush. This included calls for US intervention to bring about regime change in Iraq, Syria, Libya, Afghanistan, Egypt, North Korea, Iran, China and Lebanon. One year prior to the 9/11 attack on America they published the following:

"Further, the process of transformation, even if it brings revolutionary change, is likely to be a long one, absent some catastrophic and catalyzing event – like a new Pearl Harbor."

On September 11, 2001 they got their Pearl Harbor wish. This provided the means to implement the aims and objectives of this Foundation. In fact, many of the neo cons in this Foundation got top jobs in the Bush administration which came to power in January 2001, including Cheney, Rumsfeld, Wolfowitz, Perle, Abrams, Bolton, Edelman and Zoellick. They quickly put the aims and objectives of the Project for the New American Century into official US policies. Wars, regime changes and massive military spending followed. President Obama also implemented these policies after he came to power in 2008, creating more mayhem and chaos throughout the Middle East and North Africa. Both Democrats and Republicans are ultimately controlled by the same Deep State and it's corporate and banking allies. Vast sums of money were involved in this and massive fortunes were made by a few people, much of it tax free.

This $2 trillion per year for war is a massive waste of economic resources, which could have been used for peaceful purposes and for long term productive investment, for schools, education, infrastructure, affordable healthcare, for GDP growth, and employment if the necessary peace infrastructure was in place globally. It crowds out resources which could be deployed to more constructive and positive economic outcomes, regenerating economies, growth and peoples. This $2 trillion per year would enable humanity to reach all of its development goals globally and provide a safe, economically and socially sustainable, healthy and happy life for all of the earth's inhabitants.

Do you as a reader value your children, your spouse, your parents, your grandchildren and your loved ones ? what kind of world are you giving them ? what kind of world do we have today, and what kind of world is possible ? Images below show the type of world we have today

We live in a world bristling with nuclear weapons and chemical and biological weapons and many countries and groups are willing to use them, for offensive, defensive and deterrent reasons, and this is

often backed by misguided, self righteous and flawed 'moral', political and religious beliefs. All presuming to have a monopoly on what is right and 'moral' but none declaring their hidden agendas, their conflicts of interest, their financial incentives and their own wrongs, mistakes, and misguided policies. Many so called 'deterrents' are in reality offensive in nature and designed for attack not defence. During the 1930's, Hitler convinced many countries and their leaders that his arms build up was for defensive purposes, to defend Germany. Hitler also claimed that his invasion of the Soviet Union was to defend Germany. War mongers, profit seekers, and tyrants have always used the lie of defence to build weapons and armies for offensive purposes. It is an ancient lie, over used and still being used. Manipulated and artificially induced tensions and wars between major world powers and also between regional powers provides a means for all manner of unscrupulous profit, hypocrisy and corruption to thrive.

War, Conflicts, Terrorism and Human Misery as Profit Centres, a Business Model and Business Strategy

Revelations concerning scandals in big banks from the 1980's to the present have revealed that certain big banks were involved in many types of crime, arms dealing, wars, regime changes, funding terrorism, drug running, political corruption and money laundering. This has been confirmed by court cases, whistleblowers, witnesses, film documentaries and books. It is well known that wars, conflicts, regime changes, terrorism, etc. are highly profitable for big banks, big corporates and speculators. And these events and problems tend to exist for the purpose of large scale profit and as a Business Model to extract more revenues and profits over time. Whole industries and military industrial complexes have been built for the purpose of war and to exploit human weaknesses, frailties, divisions and low consciousnesses. Their profits are the highest of all industries. This business involves networks of big banks, exchange dealers and financial institutions who act as the intermediaries, big corporates, the Deep State and 'Shadow Government' and their vassals such as the secret services, the police, high level military officers, bought and corrupted politicians and manipulated sections of the press and media. The latter shamelessly act as cheerleaders for war and conflicts. Vast sums of money are moved through tax havens, foreign exchanges and money dealers, and banking systems to create, manipulate and profit from conflicts and wars, and many forms of criminality, and most of this is largely unknown to the general public. One sees an endless cycle of :

- wars and regional conflicts and 'regime changes'

- manipulation of the divisions between people, the incitement of hatred and violence between religious groups, racial groups, social classes and political groups for "regime change". This is done for (i) geo-political domination (ii) resources such as oil, gas, gold, precious minerals or cheap labour (iii) war profits for war industries and contractors (iv) new market acquisition and domination. Or a combination of these. These are the real reasons for wars. This is not reported in the press and media in western countries or taught in schools and Universities.

- tit for tat terrorism between groups and between groups and states for geo-political purposes or for resources or for war profits or new market domination. Or a combination of these.

- terrorism and accompanying wars which are created and manipulated by states for geo-political purposes or for resources or for war profits or new market domination. Or a combination of these.

- support for corrupt, tyrants and their regimes and their injustices and human rights abuses especially where access to oil and other natural resources are at stake

- the encirclement of other major powers for the purpose of war or fear of war, coercion and manipulation, control of natural resources and geo-political dominance

- many of the criminal activities and 'experiments' listed in Chapter 10

- drugs trafficking, child trafficking and arms trafficking across international borders for profits which are recycled back into these activities and into arms, wars, regime changes, political corruption and the activities mentioned above and below.

- the cover up of banking frauds, money laundering for criminals, drug cartels, terrorists, child traffickers, arms dealers and other crimes. A cover up supported by politicians and governments. This was the subject of a great film 'All the Plenary's Men" by John Titus in 2017.

This fuels more and more injustices, resentments, hatreds, and terrorism which ultimately feed back into more wars, terror, crime, and so on. Vast profits and sums of money of money are made out of this misery by businesses, banks, and politicians, new weapons, war supplies, large loans, and funding and arming both sides, and this money is recycled back into more conflict, more 'regime changes', more terrorism, more crime, including child trafficking, drug trafficking, more money laundering, more bribery of politicians and state officials, and more profits. An endless cycle of greed and misery, which destroys nations and peoples and makes them powerless. This has been verified by banker whistleblowers. And some of this is detailed in the film 'All the Plenary's Men' by John Titus in 2017. All of these wars and crimes feed off the ignorance, passiveness and low consciousness of ordinary people and voters in developed western nations who are brainwashed and deceived by the war mongers, by a compliant and bribed political elite, and by a submissive press and media which spouts lies and manipulations.

This criminality, war and corruption is also supported by religious leaders, spiritual leaders and moral leaders and spiritual institutions who have lost all sense of right and wrong and of morality. The facts and evidence clearly show that many religions exist to support the political, financial and economic structures which promote this war, crime and injustices, and most importantly, many religions and spiritual organisations make the people subservient, submissive and obedient to these structures. A Pharisee system based on hypocrisy which refuses to challenge the real evils in the world, the corrupted political, financial and economic structures which create havoc, chaos and injustices and grind down the ordinary people in most nations. One sees well dressed (religious / spiritual) self righteous preachers screaming at people and judging people, but never mentioning or opposing these particular evils in the world. Religious / Spiritual / Moral leaders and their lieutenants have always opposed change, reform, transformation, restructuring, protests, grassroot movements, protest marches, activist movements, rebellion, etc. They prefer to have people on their knees to corrupted, evil and unjust political and economic masters. The ordinary people need to wake up and question their religious leaders and moral leaders, make them more accountable, and even remove the corrupted and the cowardly.

This is not minor, as war feeds increasingly desperate actions and reactions, and endless cycles which worsen over time, and the danger of terrorists acquiring weapons of mass destruction remains very real, as is the danger of a major conflict between the big nuclear powers. Flashpoints continue to arise around the world, and these can easily escalate, giving cause for concern. Various competing interests, both internal and external, feed this escalation, which has in the past led to major wars, and in the future this dynamic may push humanity towards nuclear, biological and chemical war. The political and economic forces of instability are strongly incentivised to keep destabilising and profiting from conflict. People should worry about their children, grandchildren and loved ones.

Solutions Arising from Causality

Complex problems require complex, multi faceted solutions. There is no one solution to fit all. Multiple lines of causality and overlaps must be analysed, understood, addressed and resolved. It starts with deconstructing root causes and attempting to understand and analyse them, to model them and to model probable solutions and options. And to involve all affected and relevant parties in this process, including representatives from all strata of society. And to acquire new, unique and deep insights from these parties. This may be a long process. And from this, build consensus, agreements and compromises around proposed solutions to facilitate their implementation and probability of success. One must also evaluate and analyse the effectiveness of such options or solutions and establish their effectiveness or non effectiveness. And amend, change, renegotiate, or replace these solutions. This may require multiple iterations.

In the context of this Chapter, we could progress along the following path

1. The Important Role of Consciousness

2. War, Conflicts, Terrorism and Human Misery as Profit Centres, a Business Model and Business Strategy mentioned above

3. The Lessons of History - 1914 and the Colonial Era

4. The Core Issues

5. Intensification of the Pain Body and Pain Field

6. Strategising for Peace Locally, Nationally and Internationally

7. Money and Resources for Peace and Stability or Money for Wars and Conflicts

1. The Important Role of Consciousness

All problems emerge from a certain level of consciousness and all solutions emerge from a certain level of consciousness. It is consciousness which ultimately determines the motivations, the inner desires, the needs, the wants, the preferences which underlie choices and actions, and the effects and results of all changes, reforms, revolutions, rebellions, etc.. History consistently proves that consciousness is the key factor. Consciousness determines everything.

Is it possible to build lasting peace in the world where a majority of political leaders and followers live in a state of low consciousness ? Can selfish, neurotic, greedy, spiritually and mentally ill politicians and their followers ever build peace and justice ? Can screaming, self righteous, egotistical, neurotic, hypocritical (religious / spiritual) preachers who ignore serious injustices and evils in the world achieve peace ? Can peace ever be attained by those trapped in low consciousness ? can reformers, new revolutionary leaders and rebel leaders trapped in low consciousness build a better world for all ? The answer is 'no' and this is true today and has been true throughout history. And it always will be true. All attempts to build lasting peace and better more just societies in the world have failed while humanity remains trapped in low consciousness. The forces of low consciousness ultimately find expression, creating the necessary tensions, divisions, injustices, paranoia, distrust, and conflicts to undermine harmony, justice, order and peace in the world. The road to higher consciousness is ultimately the road to peace. Healing is a substantial part of this journey to higher consciousness.

Looking at the world today and its myriad problems, most of which have 3 or 4 common denominators, it is obvious that healing on a massive scale is required. The healing of humanity has substantial economic effects and benefits. It could in itself create entirely new economies, and further enhance the productivity and innovation of the existing economies. To understand where we are today, we must find out where we came from, and what is the prevailing social and economic order and how did it emerge ? We must observe our world today from a comprehensive historical context, which would impart greater meaning to our situation today. Below we will look at the build up to World War One prior to August 1914 which has many of the characteristics of the modern world. The level of consciousness is identical.

2. War, Conflicts, Terrorism and Human Misery as Profit Centres, a Business Model and Business Strategy

This is detailed in a section above

3. The Lessons of History - 1914 and the Colonial Era

History is full of repeating patterns, which keep emerging from low consciousness, and this distinguishing feature describes most of the problems in our world today. The big economic / military powers have repeated the same mistakes of their forefathers prior to World War One, just observe the evidence of low consciousness or unconsciousness in the world today :

- economic colonialism between the major powers, a vicious competition for resources around the world in the name of an unlimited and unregulated free market. Though this 'free market' is not free, it is skewed and manipulated to serve the interests of the very wealthy and powerful.

- exploitation of native peoples and theft of their natural resources, oppression of the native people through corrupt laws and brute force, and corruption of their leaders or elites [11]

- it is imperialism and colonialism not nationalism which has caused so many wars in the past. From the time of kings and emperors to the times of colonial governors and their gombeen supporters to the times of dictators and fascists to the times of corporate controlled governments, it is imperialism which is the desire to take over control and exploit other countries and peoples which has fuelled wars and conflicts. It was and still is the imperialist presumption of superiority and the imperialist suppression of national identity, national culture and national sovereignty and national expression which created reactionary often violent nationalist movements for freedom ; that is freedom from imperialism. Imperialism centralises power and takes power away from nation states. The imperialist desire to dominate, control, manipulate, denigrate and belittle, and exploit others, whether it is other individuals or nations or peoples is the cause of much evil, hatreds, and wars in the world. Imperialism is the opposite of nationalism. Nationalism when understood as respect and love for one's own people is a positive thing, and encourages self respect, dignity, respect for others, tolerance and generosity. These are virtues within nationalism which can be developed further to encompass a respect for other peoples and other cultures, and an environment of tolerance, mutual support, cooperation and peace between nations. This positive nationalism can be used to build peace worldwide, a peace based on respect for human rights and human dignity, freedom, equality, wider distributions of wealth, fairness and social justice, and an international trading system which integrates these values fully, which is for the benefit of all nations and all peoples, not a privileged few rich individuals and families.

- imperialism has several forms, as already mentioned above, in the 20th and 21st century, it involves geo-political games between countries to surround or isolate other major countries who are economic competitors. This includes putting countries into massive debt and dependency to fund public projects or speculation or political projects or waste / corruption and then using this debt to over tax, over price, and enslave whole nations [11] (see works of the economist John Perkins [11]). Other forms involve covertly funding extremist political groups and movements, and covertly arming extremist groups, rebels and assassins, to destabilise other powers and using their reaction to attack them in the international press and media, putting in new dictators or removing old ones. The objective being to gain military supremacy and use this to expand corporate and banking supremacy and the economic exploitation and political (and mental) control of peoples and nations worldwide.

- covert support of religious extremists, nationalist extremists, senior military officers, right wing or left wing dictators to undermine and overthrow governments for geo-political objectives and profit objectives. These engage in widespread human rights abuses. This has domino effects in the form of reactionary movements against the new regime / dictatorship and their imperialist backers, in some cases this is called 'terrorism'. Though the terrorism of governments against their own people is ignored in the international press and media and academia.

- these covert actions may also allow operations to take place against one's own people to induce fear and panic, and an increased need for military spending and security spending which benefit some politically connected businesses.

- misuse of old outdated and ineffective borders established by previous colonial powers many decades ago.

- use of political corruption to undermine other companies and countries in contracts and negotiations

- covert manipulation of religious, racial and ethnic divisions and tensions by the big powers for geo-political objectives and profit objectives

- Using the press and media to promote fear and panic in a population so as to increase spending on arms and security, and fuel arms races.

- the financial profiteering from war by politically influential business people and bankers involved in the military-industrial complexes and big central and commercial banks.

Instead of building peace, cooperation, understanding, tolerance and harmony between nations, and respecting the sovereignty and independence of nations and peoples, they work (every day) on dividing people against each other, and building envy, greed, social injustices, social divisions, prejudices and hatreds, military occupations, group conflicts, nation conflicts and wars between nations. And it is the working classes of the developed countries and developing countries who will be forced to fight and die in these wars, where nuclear, biological and chemical weapons may be used. And ironically it is the corrupt laws, legal systems and political processes and perverted moralities which support this criminality and mass murder.

4. The Core issues

The core issues afflicting humanity can be categorised as follows :

1) Excessive selfishness, self-centredness, greed, acquisitiveness, avarice, corruption, corrupt deals, materialism, ego, claiming to be correct all of the time in one's views, dogma or beliefs, self aggrandisement, self importance. Modern factors such as the widespread prevalence of Neo Liberal economics and a selfish, materialistic "me, me, me" culture creates a harsh uncaring climate, promotes greed, selfishness, misunderstandings, mockery, judgmental attitudes, a 'blame the victim' mentality, fuelling excessive divisions and conflict between people. This is accompanied by factors below:

2) Not caring for others, neglecting others, dismissing others, fobbing off others, being too busy all the time, being irresponsible and not giving a damn about oneself and others and one's community and society, excessive self centredness and meanness accompanied by:

3) Judging others, condemning others, belittling and mocking others, denigrating others, gossiping about others, slandering others, prejudice and discrimination, bullying others, religious hypocrisy, irresponsibility and a failure to understand personal responsibility, undermining others, inciting hatred against others, abusive and destructive family environments and community environments which leads to

4) Tensions, misunderstandings, distrust, suspicion, anger, resentment, hateful divisions, violence, hatred, crime, conflicts, wars, genocides, holocausts, acrimony, break ups, bitterness, etc

5) Irresponsibility as people behave like docile, fearful and submissive sheep, and 'go along' with all manner of corruption, injustices and abuses, and refuse to take responsibility for their own lives, the lives of their families, and their communities and societies. The greatest of abuses, corruption and injustices are committed and allowed to be committed, by those individuals who refuse to accept personal responsibility, and refuse to act in a responsible and conscientious manner, and refuse to say stop to the tyrants, the dictators, the corruptors, the criminals, the abusers, etc..

6) The effects of physical abuse, sexual abuse, psychological abuse and emotional abuse in childhood and also in adulthood in the form of broken relationships and marriages and friendships are an important environmental factor. This tends to be worsened by the above factors.

7) Traumatic loss, traumatic stress including the loss of parents, a partner, a wife / husband, a child, a close friend, a job, a career which can intensify and worsen the above factors

8) The effects of political manipulation and religious manipulation which set people against each other, and intensify the above factors, and led to more injustices, abuses, crimes and atrocities. This has been cynically done for power, money, property, land, wealth, by deranged and immoral political leaders and religious leaders, using God as a criminal weapon of convenience.

9) Endocrine illnesses and neurological illnesses which affect the nervous system, viral or other pathogen infections of the nervous system, and heavy metal or toxin contamination of the brain and nervous system in adulthood can increase the risk of mental illness, emotional illness, anti-social and criminal behaviour

10) An inability or unwillingness to properly fund and resource the healing of humanity and healing centres for this purpose. And in addition to this lack of healing, there is an accompanying inability or unwillingness to strategise for peace and harmony and achieve it at individual levels and groups levels and at national and international levels. This involves failures at political level and government level and inter-governmental level. Thus, sick and deranged political and authority figures - politicians, governments, advisors, diplomats, political lobbyists, etc. condemn others and themselves and their societies and world to more illness, more misery, more crime, more conflicts and more war while creating continuous conflict at all levels of their societies and world. Chronic lack of leadership, responsibility, and integrity in the modern world.

5. Intensification of the Pain Body and Pain Field

The core issues mentioned above show us the actions which emerge from a certain level of consciousness. The root causes emerge from low consciousness or no consciousness in the case of many politicians. One must analyse the Hitler's, the Stalin's, The Mao's, the Pol Pot's, the Czars, the Emperor's, the Saddam's, the Idi Amin's, the George W's, the Lyndon Johnson's, the Torquemada's, the Oliver Cromwell's, the Charles Manson's, the Ted Bundy's, etc. of this world from the childhood and young adult experiences which formed their consciousness and mindset. These people were not some strange oddities from outer space, they were ordinary people with pain bodies who existed with other people with pain bodies, in an environment consisting of pain bodies intensifying each other's pain bodies – the pain field. They derived their pain bodies and their low level of consciousnesses from this environment, the pain field. The dominant characteristics or qualities of this pain field are itemised above in the section titled The Core Issues.

The emergent actions resulting from this low consciousness include exploitation of peoples, the oppression of peoples, the enforcement of corrupt laws and legal systems, injustices and great inequalities on peoples, and the debt enslavement of peoples which intensifies the pain body at all levels of society in all countries. And this feeds back into more injustice, more revenge, more violence, more conflict, more wars, more pain, etc. This pain body finds expression in many acts of terror, crime, subversion, conflicts, wars, and all types of abuse. It also finds expression in (i) a lack of empathy for others, (ii) a psychosis which seeks false consensus and false justification from masses of ignorant and uneducated people (iii) a smug detachment from the consequences of one's actions which self entitles one to keep doing wrong. This dynamic creates dictators, tyrants, haters, psychopathic leaders, war mongers, war machines, all types of abusers etc. and lies at the root of all problems in the world today. The works and books of Eckhart Tolle provide deep insights into this subject.

6. Strategising for Peace Locally, Nationally and Internationally
New Strategic Peace Plans via International agreements between all sovereign and free nations, the UN, WTO, IMF, World Bank, G20

All lasting change begins with a change in consciousness, mass consciousness. Our being and our world is dependent on consciousness, the level of consciousness. What is required is a revolution in consciousness. This will involve radical changes in mindsets, in thinking, in communicating, in the way humanity perceives themselves and the world. This will involve an expansion of consciousness, a move to higher consciousness, a new transformative consciousness within all individuals and all of humanity, both leaders and followers. This move to a higher consciousness will require change at the individual level for all individuals, in all countries. All change begins first within individuals and diffuses out to other individuals and so on affecting groups, families, communities, regions and nations. This will require greater individual responsibility, inter-personal responsibility and collective responsibility within all individuals, and peoples in nations. A higher consciousness which integrates the heart and the mind to formulate totally new human relations, new social constructs, new ways of communicating, new ways of perceiving, new politics, new political and legal structures, and new agreements between persons, between groups, and between nations.

A Peace Plan, a Peace Strategy, a Path to Peace for Humanity would have the following core elements at the individual levels, groups levels and collective levels :

I.   Changes in the consciousness of individuals are more important than social changes, economic changes, political changes and ideology changes. The consciousness of individuals plays a major role in their decisions, their wants, their needs and preferences and their actions, and this ultimately affects family and community structures, social structures, political structures and socio-economic structures. Consciousness is the starting point, the underlying foundation, the governing principle behind all social, economic and political structures and policies.

II. Individual persons changing from within, transforming from within is the most important step globally. Deep changes in consciousness and spiritual changes which would have the effect of changing the thinking, mindsets and motivations of individuals and building peace within individuals. The attainment of peace within individuals would facilitate the building of peace between individuals, and this would extend to groups and to nations in the outer world. The raising of consciousness would involve meditation every day, a deep meditative consciousness and empathy in one's dealings with others and the world, and other spiritual practises in line with one's personal beliefs. This needs to be combined with constructive and positive actions and deeds which raise the consciousness of the individual and all persons and uplift the lives of all. These changes must firstly occur inside individuals and spread out to a majority of individuals, reaching a critical mass of people in countries worldwide.

III. Deep Healing. Emotional healing, Mental Healing, Spiritual Healing, Relationships healing, Inter-personal healing, Inter-group healing and Physical Healing. This would address the issue of pain body and facilitate the raising of consciousness and a higher level of spirituality within individuals. This will involve the building of thousands of healing centres worldwide, some examples are provided here at www.healingcentres.org .

IV. Promoting meditation and the meditative mindset and consciousnesses and lifestyle, and spiritual practises in line with one's personal beliefs at all levels of society, in a tolerant and harmonious manner. A light in the darkness. Only individuals who have changed themselves, attained healing and reached a high level of consciousness should enter politics and help their societies and the world. This would bring deep, lasting, changes to the world.

V. Using higher consciousness for the attainment of transcendence, transcending artificial human divisions which are at the root of all conflict and ego driven clashes between people

VI. Providing new structures within nations and globally for raising consciousness. This type of consciousness expansion and peace building within all persons could be taught and practised in Meditation and Consciousness Centres, and in schools, Universities, training centres, community centres, healing centres, and professional development courses in all countries. This would enable all peoples, especially leaders to approach political, economic, social and spiritual problems from different angles and much deeper perspectives. This would facilitate deeper understandings and more effective, long term solutions. Building peace and higher consciousness within all people. This is vitally important, as lasting peace emerges from within people and from their mindsets, thoughts, words, deeds and actions. The peace building within can be achieved through the expansion of consciousness and the development of unity consciousness within all persons through various methods and techniques. Expanding consciousnesses and awareness to this level would facilitate a broader and deeper perspective to analysing problems, discussing divergent viewpoints, and devising and implementing solutions. And improving these solutions over time.

VII. Once a high level of consciousness is attained by individuals they would be in a fit state to actively work for justice, conflict resolution, harmony and peace in the world. And get more involved in social reforms, political reforms, economic reforms, activism, environmental protection, political changes, equality, social justice groups and initiatives, etc. to improve communities, societies and the world. Ending structural violence, and accompanying prejudices discrimination and stigma and tribalistic divisions and hatreds in the process. Many of these are detailed on the web site www.healingcentres.org

VIII. For spiritual people this would involve applying deeply spiritual teachings in their daily lives, in their thoughts, words and deeds, and fully engaging with social issues and political issues. For non spiritual people this would involve applying humanitarian, social justice and secular humanistic values in their daily lives. Ultimately it is about engagement with other people, with society, to uplift all persons, to promote respect, tolerance and dignity for all, and help all persons reach their potential.

IX.   Building new types of societies based on the above principles and a wider distribution of wealth and income and new values such as cooperation, trust, honesty and integrity, goodwill, solidarity and fraternity, compassion, responsibility, hard work, ethical values, fair play and justice.

X.   Different religions and spiritualities accepting each other's differences and regularly praying together and meditating together for peace, justice, harmony, tolerance and understanding. Using the principles of spirituality and oneness teachings to build unity worldwide

XI.   Changes within the spirit and consciousness of many individuals which would keep driving new political changes and economic and social changes and innovations over time, improving all of humanity and its prospects.

In terms of practical political, economic, social and diplomatic actions it would include and integrate the following actions:

1. **New Peace Processes and Peace Treaties based on :**

a.   Learning the lessons and applying the lessons from successful peace processes around the world, eg. South Africa , Northern Ireland, Sri Lanka, Burma, Indonesia, Bosnia, India, South American countries, Rwanda, etc.. These can be used and adapted to suit the circumstances in each case.

b.   Learning the lessons of failures in the past, including the disastrous Versailles Treaty of 1919, the international tensions, distrust and descent into world war in 1914, the failed colonial treaties and failures of colonialism, and the failed Middle East treaties and failed African treaties. Avoidance of these mistakes and errors would be vitally important.

c.   Peace between the major powers - NATO, USA, Europe, Russia, and China
Building a peace which is based on universal security for all countries and a respect for the sovereignty of all peoples and nations, and the human rights of all peoples. New collective agreements need to be drawn up, agreed and based on understanding the security concerns of nations, and building greater collective understanding of this. Following from this:
(i) the formation of peace treaties between the large nuclear powers, such as NATO, USA, Russia and China where the sovereignty of nations would be respected and security concerns addressed. The ending of military encirclements, threatening moves, geo-political manoeuvres, isolation, sanctions, and aggressive gestures and replacing them with dialogue, diplomacy and peace building.

(ii) the formation of Security Zones encompassing several countries within or bordering the spheres of influence of the major powers. The countries in the Security Zone would be neutral and their borders protected via international agreements and UN mandates. Democracy, freedom, national sovereignty and human rights would be encouraged and strongly protected within these countries. The ultimate objective of this would be to stop and reverse the military encirclement of major powers, reduce international tensions, dissolve all contrived and artificial tensions and divisions between the big powers and build peace, trust, mutual cooperation, harmony, increased trade and investment, and the upliftment of all nations, peoples and humanity.

(iii) strategising for Peace. We need to end the strategising for war and replace it with strategising for peace. This will need to be applied to relations between all countries, especially NATO, USA, Russia and China. And also those countries which have had bitter experiences with each other in the past. This strategising for peace will need to reach into many diverse areas including diplomacy, treaties, trade, investment, migration, environmental protection, sports, human rights etc.

(iv) replacing NATO with a new international organisation devoted to building peace, cooperation, human rights protection, and mutual security between all nations. We need to replace military and war alliances with peace alliances.

(v) the rejection and ending of 'new world order' agendas which have the effect of recreating the same mistakes of the old order of the past. And an end to all forms of imperialism, federalism, and centralised control structures which oppress, control and restrict nations.

(vi) use of effective and proven conflict resolution processes used to remedy any problems or issues

(vi) terrorist threats against countries or regions dealt with through coordinated and collective actions by the large military powers in alliance with each other, and a firm commitment given to protect human rights within all countries as laid down by the UN.

(vii) use of trade, commerce, productive investment, economic growth, economic democracy, wider wealth distribution and political democracy in combination with dialogue and diplomacy to build understanding, cooperation and peace between all nations.

2. Carefully analyse and deconstruct the many factors which are the root causes of wars and terrorism within countries. This would be a highly detailed process. This would provide the basis for new solutions which are focussed on root causes, causality. This would be complex and multi

layered, and would involve conflict resolution processes and applying lessons from previous peace treaties and processes in the past, and new formulations for peace encompassing many areas of life. Conflict resolution processes are multi dimensional, and depend on implementing and integrating the following into all areas of social, political and business life and into all education systems:

- resolve the problems of over population and climate and environmental damage. The former increases the number of people to a limited set of resources which in many cases is beyond what these resources can support. This causes extreme poverty and malnutrition. The latter destroys the environment and further diminishes these limited resources, worsening this poverty, deprivation and hunger. This leads to wars over resources along tribalistic lines, to genocides and much destruction and in many cases the takeover of countries by dictators, warlords or religious fundamentalists.

  Solutions will require a combined approach of population control via legal birth control measures, better education, new peace initiatives and peace treaties, new types of economic aid and assistance, new green renewable energies, and the implementation of economic democracy as proposed in this book.

- the ending of brutal dictatorships and the oppression of peoples and replacing them with democracies and respect for human rights

- the ending of economic colonialism and geo-political colonialism in all of its forms. Education in all countries about the dangers of economic colonialism, imperialism and geopolitical games in the past and in the present. Including knowledge of the conflicts, wars, terrorisms and injustices caused by these factors.

- peace building peace from the bottom up and from the top down. This will involve peace treaties at grassroots levels, family levels, community levels, regional levels and at government level and inter-governmental levels. And far reaching changes to foreign policies, foreign aid, national debt, military assistance programmes, political corruption, laws, constitutions, legal processes, policing, political institutions, schooling, separation of church and state, wealth and income distribution within countries, discrimination and stigma, culture, spirituality, outdated social norms, etc. And the expansion of consciousness and a new higher consciousness and the formation of peace within would play a major role in this, providing the basis for building peace from the bottom of society to the top and vice versa.

- peaceful means for resolving international borders artificially created by the big colonial powers in the past. Two state, three state or four state solutions in some cases and the formation of peaceful and respectful relations between these new countries or entities.

- respects and protects the sovereignty and self-determination of peoples. Respects the cultures and traditions of peoples. Stops and reverses moves to undermine the sovereignty of peoples and nations, and stops the formation of international dictatorships, federalism, and international centralisations of power.

- the implementation of UN sponsored human rights in a tolerant and pluralistic democratic environment in all countries

- mutual respect and respect for differences into all areas social and political life.

- new institutions which respect difference and diversity. And work to promote tolerance, respect, cooperation, collaboration, and working together for the common good.

- the ending of stigma, prejudices and discrimination in social life and economic life. New laws, Constitutions, human rights, institutions, and educational processes and social norms to achieve this in every country.

- transcending all human divisions and separation to embrace a unity consciousness, an all in one and one in all perspective. And implementing this unity consciousness into all areas of social and political life and into national and international treaties.

- mutual understandings of each other. Empathy and compassion for the other

- the creation of healing processes to heal the wounds of the past. Seeing the need to end suffering and being totally committed to this

- reconciliation commissions or truth commissions to deliver justice and healing

- the importance of consent, compromises borne of mutual respect

- understanding the role of the pain body and pain field in divisions, tensions, misunderstandings and conflicts.

- acknowledging our common humanity and the interconnectedness of life and the unity underlying existence

- focussing on points of agreement and unity and building on this through consensus and agreements

- workable relationships which integrate and implement the aforementioned principles mentioned above

- full support of Constitutional amendments, laws and government policies which end stigma, prejudices, discrimination and ghettos in all countries. The ending of ghettos and social exclusion would play a huge role in achieving peace within nations and between nations. The ending of stigma, prejudices and discrimination at all levels of society.

   See www.healingcentres.org/stigma.htm

3. Peace must be defended and justice, human rights, human dignity and freedom must be defended. A global military force from 10 of the most powerful countries in the world, including NATO countries, Russia and China, comprising a total force of 1,000,000 men and women, with high-tech land, air, sea weapons, and space weapons, to combat extremism and extremist takeovers of countries, and to stop genocide. This will involve closer international cooperation between this military force and adjoining countries to work together to isolate, cut off, encircle, outflank and re-take areas controlled by terrorists and extremists.

4. Ending corruption in politics, the legal system, the economics system and the social system and building new systems based on integrity, honesty, accountability, transparency, justice and fairness for all in all countries. See Chapter 10 in this book for more details.

5. Legal Justice and Social Justice

   There can be no peace without justice. Analyse and resolve the injustices within the police, prosecutor offices, courts and legal system and political system within all countries. This is detailed in Chapter 10 of this book.

6. The use of Marshall Plan type programmes to maintain, protect and preserve peace treaties through enhanced economic growth, investment, job creation, public (state) investment, consumer spending, and trade. See Chapter 7 for insights on this topic.

   New economic structures to more widely distribute wealth and income, and ensure social stability, and political and economic stability. This will include wider employee share ownership, community share ownership, networks of cooperatives, basic income schemes, negative income taxes and social credit. See Chapter 9 on Format of Economic Democracy.

7. International Trade and International Aid Programmes

   The proposals for international trade and international aid for the attainment and preservation of stability, order, economic growth, peace and justice globally are mentioned in **International Trade & International Aid Programmes and International Cooperation and Security Obligations** section in Chapter 9 above

8. In the widely acclaimed book 'Africa's Odious Debts: How Foreign Loans and Capital Flight Bled a Continent by Leonce Ndikumana, James Boyce, they state that in the period 1970 – 2008 over $944 billion was taken out of Africa in capital flight and tax evasion much of it to tax havens abroad. And it is estimated by the Tax Justice network that $12.1 trillion from developing and third world countries lies in offshore tax havens. According to world bank studies, 60 of the world's poorest nations owe $520 billion in loans.

   Detailed solutions for Africa and developing countries are provided in page 473 of this book.

9. Combat Ignorance in all countries

   Make 'Civics, Constitutional rights and Social Responsibility' compulsory and necessary for secondary school (high school) graduation and acceptance into University, Institutes of Technology, state training schemes and apprenticeship courses. This subject would fully educate students about their Constitutional rights, civil rights, legal rights, common law rights, natural law, and human rights, and their legal responsibilities. And also the responsibilities attached to rights, civic responsibilities, the importance of "social capital" in one's own life and in society in general. The social responsibility section would emphasise involvement in democracy and democratic processes, paying taxes for the provision of public services and infrastructure, being respectful, taking responsibility in their own lives, the dangers of alcohol abuse and drug abuse, the benefits of work and healthy living and good relationships, and the importance of voluntary work in charities, foundations and voluntary bodies to improve society and the wider world.

10. The building of many Holistic Healing centres in each country worldwide to encourage the healing of all peoples in all countries. In particular the healing of the 'Wounded Child' complex. Understanding the 'pain body' of nations and peoples, and using collective efforts to heal this pain body.

11. Education about the dangers of artificial social class divisions and how they cause divisions, hatreds and conflict in societies. The promotion of tolerance and pluralism within all persons, and the brotherhood of all humanity

12. Respect for other religions and spiritualities which provides for freedom of religion, freedom of speech and freedom of expression in all countries. Separation of church and state.

13. Looking for areas of common agreement, and getting agreement on this, and building upon these agreements to foster tolerance, understanding and harmony in all countries

14. Integrating and upholding human rights within all religions and organisations, especially the rights of women, the disabled, minorities, children, the unemployed and other social groups who have suffered discrimination and abuse by religious and political authorities in the past and present.

Money for War or Money for Peace ? No Money or Plenty of Money ? Which is it ?

The global cost of bailing out the banks and financial institutions between 2007 and 2014 was $13 trillion and the global value of the arms trade is $2 trillion per year (Stockholm International Peace Research Institute), and the amount of untaxed monies sitting in offshore tax havens is estimated to be $32 trillion, and the value of the Derivatives market, which is pure financial speculation was over $1,200 trillion ; this is over 20 times the global economy. The amount of money missing or unaccounted for by the Deep state in the USA is $21 trillion. This amounts to $1,268 trillion wasted on speculation, banking frauds, financial frauds, bail outs, corrupt special interests, tax evasions, and the promoting of wars, mass murder, and criminality. In 2015, the cost of giving all persons on the planet adequate health care and a decent wage was $86 billion per year (http://www.anielski.com/real-cost-eliminating-poverty/). This figure of $86 billion is very tiny fraction of the $1,268 trillion wasted on fraud, corruption, war and special interests. Considering the trillions of dollars wasted on speculation, bailouts of banks and speculators, and mass slaughter and war, there are plenty of financial resources and money to fund peace industries, productive industries, economic democracy, social justice, political stability, order and peace on earth. 97% of money is created out of nothing when banks lend money, and billions and trillions of euros can be created within minutes in electronic credits ; should we continue lending this money for speculation, bubbles and crashes, fraud, tax evasion, massive national debt and private debt, social injustices, criminality and wars or use this money for building peace, economic democracy and sustainable growth, social justice, human capital, full employment, better hospitals and healthcare systems, disease eradication in poorer countries, new innovations, a more peaceful and prosperous humanity ?

The Road Ahead — A Coming Together to Work Together for the Progress of All

What is being proposed in this book is quite revolutionary. It supports a coming together of people to work together in common cause for the benefit and upliftment of all persons, for the common good, and for practical every day objectives and ideals. A coming together which enables societies to overcome and transcend divisions based on social class, race, religion, gender, national identity, ethnic group, age, disability, and colour. And to unite people together in the creation of new freer and fairer societies and world. This is in direct opposition to the present system which supports and encourages vicious competition between people where the nastiest aspects of human nature flourish and succeed, skewed markets misinterpreted as being 'free markets' which enrich the already rich (who own nearly all the shares), higher concentrations of wealth and income, imposes the costs of massive bail outs of bankers, speculators and fraudsters on taxpayers and ordinary people, causes greater social injustices, crimes and social instability and an intensification of tribalistic divisions and conflicts. This is the world today. And this is mistakenly called "freedom" though it is the exact opposite of freedom ; it is slavery and oppression. Every person has a duty and a responsibility to himself / herself and to one's family, community and country to inform yourselves, educate yourselves, enlighten yourselves about this, and take a principled stand and join with others and stand together with others to change this outdated, corrupted and failed economic system and accompanying corrupted political systems. People joining together, groups joining together, communities joining together to bring about economic democracy and industrial democracy through the following:

- ordinary people need to recognise their own power, their own self worth and their own importance to the political process and to society. Every person, including you the readers need to forcefully assert your own power. You have power in terms of your vote, your shopping preferences, your product preferences, your business policies, your organisation's policies, your friends, your social networks, your family, your work colleagues, your sporting friends, and acquaintances you meet in public or on social media. All of these can be used to achieve a critical mass of change, and bring about economic democracy and deep reforms to political democracy.

- voting for candidates who deliver on economic democracy and industrial democracy and the checks and balances and other democratic changes proposed in this book during elections and at the ballot box. Delivery of results is important. Failure to do so should result in mass withdrawal of support for deceitful politicians. Ordinary people should deliberately target deceitful and corrupt politicians prior to and during elections and do everything in their power to stop them being re-elected.

- calling politicians to account over the issue of economic democracy and industrial democracy and the checks and balances and other democratic changes proposed in this book while they are in power and also when they are seeking office

- public meetings between diverse people and groups to discuss and work for economic democracy and other democratic changes at local level, regional level and national level

- informing friends, family, work colleagues, sporting partners, and acquaintances about economic democracy and industrial democracy and the wider issues of fairness and justice for all and getting them involved in groups, projects and initiatives.

- using family networks, friends networks, work networks, neighbour's networks, sports networks, communities, social media to expose corrupt politicians and directly work against them prior to elections and during elections. Use of block voting by families, neighbourhoods, clubs, communities, social media to stop corrupt politicians from being elected

- set up new political parties and independents which will work for economic democracy and industrial democracy in parliaments and local government bodies. Potential names cold include 'Peoples Democracy', 'Economic Democracy', 'Social Democracy', 'Industrial Democracy', 'Democratic Capitalism'

- building strong political awareness and support for economic democracy and political democracy and emphasising its compatibility with political democracy and freedom

- political action groups to work for economic democracy and to stop or overturn corrupt politicians. Protests and strikes against injustices and corruption. Use the Internet, social media and blogs to promote economic democracy and industrial democracy

- joining or setting up blogs and web sites on the Internet to force businesses to become accountable for abuses of worker's rights, corruption, support of dictators or tyrants, exploitation of children, social injustices and environmental destruction.

- Fund political lobbyists for economic democracy and industrial democracy

- do shopping at businesses and cooperatives using economic democracy and industrial democracy. Buy products from businesses and cooperatives using economic democracy and industrial democracy. Boycott goods from corrupt companies and those involved in unethical activities

- inclusion of economic democracy and industrial democracy courses in all schools and University courses

- inclusion in the mainstream press and media and alternative press and media. Use your share holdings to call for ethical investment and economic democracy. Invest in ethical investment funds which are leading the way in environmental protection, food safety, workers rights and economic democracy

- gaining the support of all police and all military personnel. Getting the police and military to swear oaths of allegiance to the people and to economic, industrial and political democracy. Support from civil servants, support from unions and labour organisations, support from the national and international cooperative movement, support from all religious and spiritual organisations, support from community groups, support from sporting bodies, support from celebrities.

This will involve total commitment and daily, weekly, monthly and yearly activities and gradually moving towards a critical mass of change, a new system, a new consciousness, a new Enlightenment for the Digital Age, and a new democracy based on freedom with responsibilities.

The End

Bibliography

Section 1

1. Debunking Economics – Revised and Expanded edition : the Naked Emperor Dethroned?. Steve Keen, (2011), Zed Books.

   Can we avoid another financial crisis ? Steve Keen (2017), Polity Press.

2. The Financial Instability Hypothesis: An Interpretation of Keynes and an Alternative to "Standard" Theory HYMAN P. MINSKY. *Challenge.* Vol. 20, No. 1 (MARCH/APRIL 1977), pp. 20-27

   The Financial Instability Hypothesis (May 1992). The Jerome Levy Economics Institute Working Paper No. 74.

   Available at SSRN: http://ssrn.com/abstract=161024 or http://dx.doi.org/10.2139/ssrn.161024

   Minsky, Hyman P.

   Can "It" Happen Again? Essays on Instability and Finance. Hyman Minsky (1982), Routledge.

   Irrational Exuberance, 3rd Edition. Robert J. Shiller. Princeton University Press; Revised and Expanded Third edition (2016)

   Manias, Panic and Crashes. Charles Kindleberger. (1978)

   John Maynard Keynes. Hyman Minsky (2008). McGraw-Hill.

   Stabilising an instable economy. Hyman Minsky (2008). McGraw-Hill.

   "A Theory of Systemic Fragility," in E. Altman and A. Sametz, eds., *Financial Crises*, 1977;

   "Debt and Business Cycles" (with M. D. Vaughan), *Business Economics*, July 1990; and

   "The Financial Instability Hypothesis," in P. Arestis and M. Sawyer, eds., *Handbook of Radical Political Economy*, 1993.

   The Great Crash 1929. John Kenneth Galbraith. Penguin; Reprint edition (29 Oct. 2009)

   A Short History of Financial Euphoria. John Kenneth Galbraith. Penguin Books Ltd; Reprint edition (1 July 1994)

   Killing the Host: How Financial Parasites and Debt Bondage Destroy the Global Economy. Michael Hudson, ISLET (2015)

3. Fisher, I. (1933) "The Debt-Deflation Theory of Great Depressions," Econometrica 1 (4): 337-57

4. The Holy Grail of Macroeconomics-Lessons from Japan's Great Recession. Richard Koo, (2009). John Wiley & Sons (Asia) Pte. Ltd

   "The world in balance sheet recession: causes, cure, and politics", Richard Koo, Real-World Economics Review, issue no. 58, 12 December 2011, pp.19-37, http://www.paecon.net/PAEReview/issue58/Koo58.pdf

5. *The New Finance: The Case Against Efficient Markets*, 1995 (1st Edition), 1999 (2nd Edition), Prentice Hall, Upper Saddle River, NJ.

   The New Finance: Overreaction, Complexity and Uniqueness, 2003 (3rd Edition), 2009 (4th Edition), Prentice Hall,

Upper Saddle River, NJ.

Beast on Wall Street,1998, Prentice Hall, Upper Saddle River, NJ.

The Inefficient Stock Market—What Pays Off and Why,1999, Prentice Hall, Upper Saddle River, NJ.

6. Atif Mian and Amir Sufi. *House of Debt*. (2014). University of Chicago. http://www.amazon.com/House-Debt-Recession-Prevent-Happening/dp/022608194X/

   and House of Debt Blog http://houseofdebt.org

7. Graphs and Statistics

   U.S. household debt rose from approximately 65% GDP in Q1 2000 to 95% by Q1 2008. (FRED Database-Household Debt-Retrieved July 2014)

   Mortgage debt rose from $4.9 trillion in Q1 2000 to a peak of $10.7 trillion by Q2 2008. However, it has fallen since as households deleverage, to $9.3 trillion by Q1 2014. (FRED Database-Home Mortgage Liability Levels-Retrieved July 2014)

   U.S. savings rose during the 2007–2009 recession, both residential and non-residential investment fell significantly, approximately $560 billion between Q1 2008 and Q4 2009. (FRED Database-Residential and Non-Residential Investment-Retrieved July 2014)

   Private sector financial balance (gross private savings minus gross private domestic investment) rose from an approximately $200 billion deficit in Q4 2007 to a surplus of $1.4 trillion by Q3 2009. This surplus remained at $720 billion in Q1 2014. An enormous amount of savings was tied up in the banking system, rather than being invested. (FRED Database-Private Sector Financial Surplus-Retrieved July 2014)

   The fall in housing prices also caused U.S. household equity to plummet, from a peak of $13.4 trillion in Q1 2006 to $6.1 trillion by Q1 2009, a 54% decline. Household equity began to rise after Q4 2011 and was back to $10.8 trillion by Q1 2014, approximately 80% of its pre-crisis peak level. This shows the effects of deleveraging. (FRED Database-Household Owner's Equity-Retrieved July 2014)

   A Literature Summary on Balance Sheet Recession Research - **http://www.nextnewdeal.net/rortybomb/new-report-literature-summary-new-balance-sheet-recession-research**

   McKinsey Report, 2015

   Between 2007 and 2014, global debt grew by $57 trillion. Much of this was government debt to bail out banks, financial institutions and bondholders and fund budget deficits caused by the loss in output production and taxes from government austerity programmes and economic recession. The Report 'Debt and not much deleveraging' (February 2015) by McKinsey & Company provides an excellent analysis of government debt and business, banking and household debt levels and their effects on economic growth in many countries. Source: McKinsey & Company. 'Debt and not much Deleveraging', February 2015.

   http://www.mckinsey.com/insights/economic_studies/debt_and_not_much_deleveraging

8. The Price of Inequality. Joseph Stiglitz, W. W. Norton & Company (2012) http://www.amazon.com/Price-Inequality-Divided-Society-Endangers/dp/0393345068/

   The Great Divide: unequal societies and what we can do about them. Joseph E. Stiglitz, W.W. Norton & Company (2015)

   Capital in the Twenty First Century. Thomas Piketty (2014). Belknap Press. http://www.amazon.com/Capital-Twenty-First-Century-Thomas-Piketty/dp/067443000X/ref=pd_bxgy_b_img_y

   For most workers, real wages have barely budged for decades. Pew Research centre. http://www.pewresearch.org/fact-tank/2014/10/09/for-most-workers-real-wages-have-barely-budged-for-decades/

   Wage Stagnation in Nine Charts. The Economic Policy Institute. http://www.epi.org/publication/charting-wage-stagnation/

   The Conscience of a Liberal. Paul Krugman. W. W. Norton & Company (2012)

   Recent History in One Chart. The Conscience of a Liberal, New York Times. Paul Krugman. January 1 2015. http://krugman.blogs.nytimes.com/2015/01/01/recent-history-in-one-chart/?module=BlogPost-Title&version=Blog%20Main&contentCollection=Opinion&action=Click&pgtype=Blogs&region=Body&_r=0

   Harvard University Study

   https://www.youtube.com/watch?v=QPKKQnijnsM&feature=youtu.be

   Building a Better America—One Wealth Quintile at a Time, Norton et al. 2011, Perspectives on Psychological Science, http://www.people.hbs.edu/mnorton/norton%20ariely%20in%20press.pdf

   Economic Democracy: The Political Struggle for the 21st century. Smith, J. W. (2005). Radford, VA: Institute for Economic Democracy Press.

9. Weak eurozone is on the brink, warns IMF...as Nobel winner says euro could be scrapped, Daily Mail, 8 July 2016 http://www.dailymail.co.uk/news/article-3681077/Eurozone-course-economic-slowdown-Brexit-rising-uncertainty-EU-s-future-says-IMF.html

10. Confessions of an Economic Hitman. John Perkins. Plume (2005)

    The New Confessions of an Economic Hitman. John Perkins. Berrett-Koehler Publishers; 2 edition (February 9, 2016)

11. 'Poverty Overview'. World Bank, April 2015. www.worldbank.org/en/topic/poverty/overview

12. An Economy for the 99%. Deborah Hardoon, Oxfam Report, 16 January 2017. http://policy-practice.oxfam.org.uk/publications/an-economy-for-the-99-its-time-to-build-a-human-economy-that-benefits-everyone-620170

13. The Death of International Development. Thought Leader, Jason Hickel, London School of Economics. http://www.thoughtleader.co.za/jasonhickel/2014/11/24/the-death-of-international-development

14. Inequality: You Don't Know the Half of It (Or why inequality is worse than we thought) By Nicholas Shaxson, John Christensen and Nick Mathiason, Tax Justice Network, 2012 http://www.taxjustice.net/cms/upload/pdf/Inequality_120722_You_dont_know_the_half_of_it.pdf

15. Of the 1% By the 1% and for the 1%. Joseph Stiglitz. Vanity Fair, May 2011. http://www.vanityfair.com/news/2011/05/top-one-percent-201105

16. Kristof, Nicholas (July 22, 2014). "An Idiot's Guide to Inequality". New York Times. Retrieved July 22, 2014.Occupy Wall Street And The Rhetoric of Equality Forbes November 1, 2011 by Deborah L. Jacobs

17. Svaldi, Aldo (January 11, 2014). "Robert Reich: Income inequality the defining issue for U.S.". The Denver Post. Retrieved January 26, 2014.

18. The Return of Depression Economics. Paul Krugman. W.W. Norton and Company Ltd., 2009.

19. A People's History of the United States: 1492-present. Howard Zinn, (2005). Harper Perennial Modern Classics. ISBN 0-06-083865-5.

20. The next economic disaster : why its coming and how to avoid it. Richard Vague (2014) University of Pennsylvania Press

21. Boom Bust ; House prices, Banking and The Depression of 2010, Fred Harrison, Second Edition 2007, Shepheard Walwyn.

22. An excellent analysis of the effects of interest is provided by Margrit Kennedy in her book 'Interest and Inflation Free Money' (1995), Seva International; ISBN 0-9643025-0-0

23. The Best Way to Rob a Bank is to Own One: How Corporate Executives and Politicians Looted the S&L Industry, 2nd Edition. William Black, University of Texas Press; 2 edition (January 15, 2014)

24. DISTRIBUTIONAL NATIONAL ACCOUNTS: METHODS AND ESTIMATES FOR THE UNITED STATES. Thomas Piketty Emmanuel Saez Gabriel Zucman. NATIONAL BUREAU OF ECONOMIC RESEARCH. December 2016. http://gabriel-zucman.eu/files/PSZ2016.pdf

A Bigger Economic Pie, but a Smaller Slice for Half of the U.S., Patricia Cohen. New York Times, December 6, 2016.

25. Svaldi, Aldo (January 11, 2014). "Robert Reich: Income inequality the defining issue for U.S.". The Denver Post. Retrieved January 26, 2014.

26. D. Hardoon, S. Ayele and R. Fuentes-Nieva (2016) „An Economy for the 1%", op. cit.

27. The Quantity Theory of Credit and Some of its Applications. Dr. Richard Werner. Delivered at Robinson College Cambridge, 30 October 2012. https://www.postkeynesian.net/downloads/Werner/RW301012PPT.pdf

28. Killing the Host: How Financial Parasites and Debt Bondage Destroy the Global Economy. Michael Hudson. ISLET (2015)

J is for Junk Economics : A Guide to Reality in an Age of Deception. Michael Hudson. Islet (2017)

29. Writings of Professor Lawrence Lessig

Republic, Lost: How Money Corrupts Congress—and a Plan to Stop It (2011) ISBN 978-0-446-57643-7

One Way Forward: The Outsider's Guide to Fixing the Republic (2012) ISBN 978-1-61452-023-8

Lesterland: The Corruption of Congress and How to End It (2013, CC-BY-NC) ISBN 978-1-937382-34-6

Republic, Lost: The Corruption of Equality and the Steps to End It (2015) ISBN 978-1-4555-3701-3

America, Compromised (University of Chicago Press, 2018) ISBN 978-0-226-31653-6

30. Books by Professor Anthony C. Sutton, USA

Western Technology and Soviet Economic Development: 1917–1930. Stanford, California: Hoover Institution, 1968. ISBN 978-0817917913

Western Technology and Soviet Economic Development: 1930–1945. Stanford, California: Hoover Institution, 1971.

Western Technology and Soviet Economic Development: 1945–1965. Stanford, California: Hoover Institution, 1973. ISBN 978-0817911317.

National Suicide: Military Aid to the Soviet Union. New Rochelle, New York: Arlington House, 1973.

Wars and Revolutions, Part One: 1820 to 1900. 1973.

Wars and Revolutions, Part Two: 1900 to 1972. 1973.

Wall Street and the Bolshevik Revolution. New Rochelle, New York: Arlington House, 1974. ISBN 978-0870002762

Wall Street and FDR. New Rochelle, New York: Arlington House, 1975. ISBN 978-0870003288.

Wall Street and the Rise of Hitler. Seal Beach, California: '76 Press, 1976. ISBN 0-89245-004-5. LCCN 76-14011. 220 pages. Hardcover.

How the Order Creates War and Revolution. 1985

The Best Enemy Money Can Buy. 2000.

Section 2

1. Debunking Economics: the Naked Emperor Dethroned?. Steve Keen (2011), Zed Books.

   Can we avoid another financial crisis ? Steve Keen (2017), Polity Press.

2. The Financial Instability Hypothesis: An Interpretation of Keynes and an Alternative to "Standard" Theory HYMAN P. MINSKY. *Challenge*. Vol. 20, No. 1 (MARCH/APRIL 1977), pp. 20-27

   Minsky, Hyman P., The Financial Instability Hypothesis (May 1992). The Jerome Levy Economics Institute Working Paper No. 74. Available at SSRN: http://ssrn.com/abstract=161024 or http://dx.doi.org/10.2139/ssrn.161024

   Can "It" Happen Again? Essays on Instability and Finance. Hyman Minsky (1982), Routledge.

   Irrational Exuberance, 3rd Edition. Robert J. Shiller. Princeton University Press; Revised and Expanded Third edition (2016)

   Manias, Panic and Crashes. Charles Kindleberger. (1978)

   John Maynard Keynes. Hyman Minsky (2008). McGraw-Hill.

   Stabilising an instable economy. Hyman Minsky (2008). McGraw-Hill.

   "A Theory of Systemic Fragility," in E. Altman and A. Sametz, eds., *Financial Crises*, 1977;

"Debt and Business Cycles" (with M. D. Vaughan), *Business Economics*, July 1990; and

"The Financial Instability Hypothesis," in P. Arestis and M. Sawyer, eds., *Handbook of Radical Political Economy*, 1993.

The Great Crash 1929. John Kenneth Galbraith. Penguin; Reprint edition (29 Oct. 2009)

A Short History of Financial Euphoria. John Kenneth Galbraith. Penguin Books Ltd; Reprint edition (1 July 1994)

Killing the Host: How Financial Parasites and Debt Bondage Destroy the Global Economy. Michael Hudson, ISLET (2015)

3. Fisher, I. (1933) "The Debt-Deflation Theory of Great Depressions," Econometrica 1 (4): 337-57

4. The Holy Grail of Macroeconomics-Lessons from Japan's Great Recession. Richard Koo, (2009). John Wiley & Sons (Asia) Pte. Ltd

    "The world in balance sheet recession: causes, cure, and politics", Richard Koo, Real-World Economics Review, issue no. 58, 12 December 2011, pp.19-37, http://www.paecon.net/PAEReview/issue58/Koo58.pdf

5. *The New Finance: The Case Against Efficient Markets*, 1995 (1st Edition), 1999 (2nd Edition), Prentice Hall, Upper Saddle River, NJ.

    The New Finance: Overreaction, Complexity and Uniqueness, 2003 (3rd Edition), 2009 (4th Edition), Prentice Hall, Upper Saddle River, NJ.

    Beast on Wall Street,1998, Prentice Hall, Upper Saddle River, NJ.

    The Inefficient Stock Market—What Pays Off and Why,1999, Prentice Hall, Upper Saddle River, NJ.

6. Atif Mian and Amir Sufi. *House of Debt*. (2014). University of Chicago. http://www.amazon.com/House-Debt-Recession-Prevent-Happening/dp/022608194X/

    and House of Debt Blog http://houseofdebt.org

    The Next Economic Disaster. Richard Vague. University of Pennsylvania Press (July 15, 2014)

    and http://debt-economics.org/index.php

7. Graphs and Statistics

    U.S. household debt rose from approximately 65% GDP in Q1 2000 to 95% by Q1 2008. (FRED Database-Household Debt-Retrieved July 2014)

    Mortgage debt rose from $4.9 trillion in Q1 2000 to a peak of $10.7 trillion by Q2 2008. However, it has fallen since as households deleverage, to $9.3 trillion by Q1 2014. (FRED Database-Home Mortgage Liability Levels-Retrieved July 2014)

    U.S. savings rose during the 2007–2009 recession, both residential and non-residential investment fell significantly, approximately $560 billion between Q1 2008 and Q4 2009. (FRED Database-Residential and Non-Residential Investment-Retrieved July 2014)

    Private sector financial balance (gross private savings minus gross private domestic investment) rose from an approximately $200 billion deficit in Q4 2007 to a surplus of $1.4 trillion by Q3 2009. This surplus remained at

$720 billion in Q1 2014. An enormous amount of savings was tied up in the banking system, rather than being invested. (FRED Database-Private Sector Financial Surplus-Retrieved July 2014)

The fall in housing prices also caused U.S. household equity to plummet, from a peak of $13.4 trillion in Q1 2006 to $6.1 trillion by Q1 2009, a 54% decline. Household equity began to rise after Q4 2011 and was back to $10.8 trillion by Q1 2014, approximately 80% of its pre-crisis peak level. This shows the effects of deleveraging. (FRED Database-Household Owner's Equity-Retrieved July 2014)

A Literature Summary on Balance Sheet Recession Research - http://www.nextnewdeal.net/rortybomb/new-report-literature-summary-new-balance-sheet-recession-research

McKinsey Report, 2015

Between 2007 and 2014, global debt grew by $57 trillion. Much of this was government debt to bail out banks, financial institutions and bondholders and fund budget deficits caused by the loss in output production and taxes from government austerity programmes and economic recession. The Report 'Debt and not much deleveraging' (February 2015) by McKinsey & Company provides an excellent analysis of government debt and business, banking and household debt levels and their effects on economic growth in many countries. Source: McKinsey & Company. 'Debt and not much Deleveraging', February 2015.

http://www.mckinsey.com/insights/economic_studies/debt_and_not_much_deleveraging

8. The Price of Inequality. Joseph Stiglitz, W. W. Norton & Company (2012). http://www.amazon.com/Price-Inequality-Divided-Society-Endangers/dp/0393345068/

The Great Divide: unequal societies and what we can do about them. Joseph E. Stiglitz, W.W. Norton & Company (2015)

Capital in Twenty First Century. Thomas Piketty (2014). Belknap Press. http://www.amazon.com/Capital-Twenty-First-Century-Thomas-Piketty/dp/067443000X/ref=pd_bxgy_b_img_y

For most workers, real wages have barely budged for decades. Pew Research Centre.
http://www.pewresearch.org/fact-tank/2014/10/09/for-most-workers-real-wages-have-barely-budged-for-decades/

Wage Stagnation in Nine Charts. The Economic Policy Institute. http://www.epi.org/publication/charting-wage-stagnation/

The Conscience of a Liberal. Paul Krugman. W. W. Norton & Company (2012)

Recent History in One Chart. The Conscience of a Liberal, New York Times. Paul Krugman. January 1 2015.

9. http://krugman.blogs.nytimes.com/2015/01/01/recent-history-in-one-chart/?module=BlogPost Title&version=Blog%20Main&contentCollection=Opinion&action=Click&pgtype=Blogs&region=Body&_r=0

Harvard University Study

https://www.youtube.com/watch?v=QPKKQnijnsM&feature=youtu.be (Building a Better America—One Wealth Quintile at a Time, Norton et al. 2011, Perspectives on Psychological Science, http://www.people.hbs.edu/mnorton/norton%20ariely%20in%20press.pdf)

9. THE PERMANENT EFFECTS OF FISCAL CONSOLIDATIONS (2015)

   Antonio Fatás and Lawrence H. Summers. Centre for Economic Policy Research

10. 'The Future of Money: Creating New Wealth, Work and a Wiser World' by Bernard Lietaer

11. Economic Democracy and Industrial Democracy research and titles

   The Citizen's Share: Reducing Inequality in the 21st Century. Joseph R. Blasi , Richard B. Freeman , Douglas L. Kruse. Yale University Press (2014)

   Employee Ownership. Joseph Blasi. Ballinger Publishing Company (1988)

   Kruse, Blasi and Freeman, NBER (2012)

   Research on Employee Ownership, Corporate Performance, and Employee Compensation.

   National Center for Employee Ownership (2016) http://www.nceo.org/articles/research- employee-ownership-corporate-performance

   Small is Beautiful. EF Schumacher. Harper Perennial (1973)

   Small Is Beautiful: Economics As If People Mattered : 25 Years Later...With Commentaries. **EF** Schumacher, Hartley & Marks Publishers (1999).

   Employee ownership and participation effects on outcomes in firms majority employee-owned   through employee stock ownership plans in the US. Brent Kramer. Economic and Industrial Democracy. November 2010 vol. 31 no. 4 449-476

   Economic Democracy: The Political Struggle for the 21st century. Smith, J. W. (2005). Radford, VA: Institute for Economic Democracy Press.

   The Share Economy. Martin L. Weitzman. Harvard University Press (1986)

   After Capitalism. David Schweickart. Rowman and Littlefield, (2002)

   Closing The Iron Cage: The Scientific Management of Work and Leisure. Ed Andrew. Black Rose Books (1998)

   The Man Who Gave His Company Away: A Biography of Ernest Bader, Founder of the Scott Bader Commonwealth. Susanna Hoe, London, William Heinemann (1978)

   Capital and the Debt Trap. Claudia Sanchez Bajo, Bruno Roelants. Palgrave Macmillan (2011)

   - The Seven-day Weekend: A Better Way to Work in the 21st Century. Ricardo Semler. Century; New Ed edition (2004)

   Incentive Management. James F. Lincoln, Lincoln Electric Company, Cleveland, Ohio, 1951

   Human Capitalism. Robert Ozaki. Kodansha International ltd. 1991

12. Confessions of an Economic Hitman. John Perkins, Plume (2005)

    The New Confessions of an Economic Hitman. John Perkins. Berrett-Koehler Publishers; 2 edition (February 9, 2016)

13. Workplace Democratization: Its Internal Dynamics. Bernstein, Paul (2012). Chelsea, MA: Educational Services Publishing

14. The Capitalist Manifesto, by Louis O. Kelso and Mortimer J. Adler, Random House, New York: 1958; reprinted Greenwood Press, Westport, Connecticut: 1975. Also published in French, Spanish, Greek and Japanese. ISBN 0-8371-8210-7 Available in PDF format from The Kelso Institute.

    The New Capitalists: A Proposal to Free Economic Growth from the Slavery of Savings, by Louis O. Kelso and Mortimer J. Adler, Random House, New York: 1961; reprinted Greenwood Press, Westport, Connecticut: 1975. Also published in Japanese.

    Two-Factor Theory: The Economics of Reality, by Louis O. Kelso and Patricia Hetter, Random House, New York: 1967; paperback edition, Vintage Books: 1968. (Originally published under the title How to Turn 80 Million Workers into Capitalists on Borrowed Money.)

    Democracy and Economic Power: Extending the ESOP Revolution Through Binary Economics, by Louis O. Kelso and Patricia Hetter Kelso, Ballinger Publishing Co., Cambridge, Massachusetts: 1986; reprinted by University Press of America, Lanham, Maryland: 1991.

15. Resilience and Retirement Security: Performance of S ESOP Firms in the Recession. Swagel, Phillip and Robert Carroll. Georgetown University. 10 March 2010

    - Employee ownership and participation effects on outcomes in firms majority employee-owned through employee stock ownership plans in the US. Brent Kramer. Economic and Industrial Democracy. November 2010 vol. 31 no. 4 449-476

16. 'Poverty Overview'. World Bank, April 2015. www.worldbank.org/en/topic/poverty/overview

17. Companies avoid paying 200 billion in tax, Wall Street Journal, 2015, http://www.wsj.com/articles/companies-avoid-paying-200-billion-in-tax-1435161106

18. 'Poverty Overview'. World Bank, April 2015. www.worldbank.org/en/topic/poverty/overview

19. Forbes, January 23, 2014. Laura Shin. http://www.forbes.com/sites/laurashin/2014/01/23/the-85-richest-people-in-the-world-have-as-much-wealth-as-the-3-5-billion-poorest

20. The Death of International Development. Thought Leader, Jason Hickel, London School of Economics. http://www.thoughtleader.co.za/jasonhickel/2014/11/24/the-death-of-international-development

21. Inequality: You Don't Know the Half of It (Or why inequality is worse than we thought) By Nicholas Shaxson, John Christensen and Nick Mathiason, Tax Justice Network, 2012 http://www.taxjustice.net/cms/upload/pdf/Inequality_120722_You_dont_know_the_half_of_it.pdf

22. The Share Economy. Martin L. Weitzman. Harvard University Press (1986)

23. Of the 1% By the 1% and for the 1%. Joseph Stiglitz. Vanity Fair, May 2011.

http://www.vanityfair.com/news/2011/05/top-one-percent-201105

24. Kristof, Nicholas (July 22, 2014). "An Idiot's Guide to Inequality". New York Times. Retrieved July 22, 2014.

25. Occupy Wall Street And The Rhetoric of Equality Forbes November 1, 2011 by Deborah L. Jacobs

27. The Return of Depression Economics. Paul Krugman. W.W. Norton and Company Ltd., 2009.

28. Statistics from National Center for Employee Ownership, California, USA

The Citizen's Share: Reducing Inequality in the 21st Century. Joseph R. Blasi , Richard B. Freeman , Douglas L. Kruse. Yale University Press (2014)

29. *Binary Economics – the new paradigm.* Robert Ashford & Rodney Shakespeare (1999)

Seven Steps to Justice . Shakespeare & Peter Challen (2002)

Capital Homesteading for Every Citizen: A Just Free Market Solution for Saving Social Security. Norman Kurland, Dawn Brohawn & Michael Greaney (2004)

The Modern Universal Paradigm. Rodney Shakespeare (2007)

30. Capital Homesteading for Every Citizen: A Just Free Market Solution for Saving Social Security Paperback –by Norman G. Kurland, Michael D. Greaney, Dawn K. Brohawn. Center for Economic and Social Justice (5 Sept. 2000)

31. The next economic disaster : why its coming and how to avoid it. Richard Vague (2014) University of Pennsylvania Press

32. Boom Bust ; House prices, Banking and The Depression of 2010, Fred Harrison, Second Edition 2007, Shepheard Walwyn.

33. An excellent analysis of the effects of interest is provided by Margrit Kennedy in her book 'Interest and Inflation Free Money' (1995), Seva International; ISBN 0-9643025-0-0

34. Hoyt, Lorlene; Luviene, Nicholas; Stitely, Amy. "Sustainable Economic Democracy: Worker Cooperatives for the 21st Century" (PDF). *colab.mit.edu*. MIT Community Innovators Lab with support from the Barr Foundation.

35. The Quantity Theory of Credit and Some of its Applications. Dr. Richard Werner. Delivered at Robinson College Cambridge, 30 October 2012. https://www.postkeynesian.net/downloads/Werner/RW301012PPT.pdf

36. Killing the Host: How Financial Parasites and Debt Bondage Destroy the Global Economy. Michael Hudson. ISLET (2015)

J is for Junk Economics : A Guide to Reality in an Age of Deception. Michael Hudson. Islet (2017)

37. The Chicago Plan Revisited by Jaromir Benes and Michael Kumhof. IMF Working Paper, 2012. http://www.imf.org/external/pubs/ft/wp/2012/wp12202.pdf

38. The Public Bank Solution. Ellen Brown, Third Millennium Press (June 11, 2013)

The Web of Debt. Ellen Brown, Third Millennium Press; 5th Revised ed. edition (January 1, 2012)

39. See references for 30 in Section 1 of Bibliography above

Index

587

Printed in Poland
by Amazon Fulfillment
Poland Sp. z o.o., Wrocław

54913183R00331